The Financial Times Guide to the Financial Markets

Glen Arnold

Harlow, England • London • New York • Boston • San Francisco • Toronto • Sydney • Auckland • Singapore • Hong Kong
Tokyo • Seoul • Taipei • New Delhi • Cape Town • São Paulo • Mexico City • Madrid • Amsterdam • Munich • Paris • Milan

PEARSON EDUCATION LIMITED

Edinburgh Gate
Harlow CM20 2JE
Tel: +44 (0)1279 623623
Fax: +44 (0)1279 431059
Website: www.pearsoned.com/uk

First published in Great Britain 2012

© Glen Arnold 2012

ISBN 978-0-273-73000-2

British Library Cataloguing-in-Publication Data
A catalogue record for this book is available from the British Library

Library of Congress Cataloging-in-Publication Data
A catalog record for this book is available from the Library of Congress

ARP Impression 98

Typeset in Stone serif 9/13 by 30
Printed in Great Britain by Clays Ltd, St Ives plc

Contents

Preface

This book is designed to be an easy-to-read introduction to the financial markets, describing the main financial instruments, markets and institutions. It is written for those who need an authoritative, comprehensive, but not too burdensome, run-down of the workings of modern financial systems.

The target readers include many people working in finance and banking who require a guide to the wide range of markets and instruments. It will also assist business students attempting to gain a good grounding in the activities undertaken by the financial services sector. Then there are investors who wish to understand better the array of financial securities available to them and the way in which these securities are issued and traded.

The way I see it, these readers are looking for a good, up-to-date, jargon-busting book that does not over-load them with academic finance theory and calculations, but does describe how the markets work, what securities are traded and how they impact on all our lives.

I have attempted to make the book international in its outlook, with frequent comparisons of the workings of the major financial centres. However, given that London is the leading international financial centre in the world and that the majority of the expected readership needs to understand the European context, there will be a special focus on the City.

There is a reinvigorated interest in finance following the recent crisis, which originated in the banking world and spread to engulf the wider financial markets and then devastated people's lives through unemployment and lost investments. There is now a recognition like never before of the importance of financial markets, and that has produced a hunger to understand how they function. This book should make a contribution to satisfying that hunger.

I hope you enjoy it.

Glen Arnold

An extensive glossary appears on the free website linked to this book. You can access it at www.pearson-books.com/financialmarkets

Author's acknowledgements

Any work of this kind is a team effort and I would like to thank a number of people who helped to bring this project to fruition over a period of two years. Susan Henton, my personal assistant, contributed enormously to the content of the book. She searched for data, grappled with complex material and helped to write key sections of the text. The cheerful and willing way she gets on with tasks is a real blessing. They say that you should always hire people smarter than yourself. I have certainly done that with Susan. Her English is much better than mine. She is also getting very good at investment and finance – I'll soon be out of a job!

The team at Pearson Education have been highly professional and very supportive (and patient with me, despite missed deadlines). I would particularly like to thank Christopher Cudmore, Rachel Hayter, Laura Blake, Linda Dhondy and Viv Church.

Publisher's acknowledgements

We are grateful to the following for permission to reproduce copyright material:

Figures

Figure 2.2 after The Global Financial Centres Report, www.zyen.com, The Z/ Yen Group of Companies; Figure 2.4 from www.thecityuk.com, TheCityUK; Figures 7.1, 8.4, 17.3, 17.4, 17.5, 17.11 from www.thecityUK.com; Figure 7.3 from UBS Pension Fund Indicators (TheCityUK Pensions Report 2011), www. thecityuk.com; Figure 7.4 from BTPS Annual Report, www.btpensions.net; Figure 7.5 from BTPS Annual Reports, www.btpensions.net; Figure 7.7 from www.ici. org, Investment Company Institute, Washington, DC [2011]; Figure 7.8 from www.incademy.com; Figures 8.1, 8.2 from www.swissre.com, Swiss Re, *sigma* No 2/2011; Figure 8.3 from Association of British Insurers (ABI), www.abi.org.uk; Figure 8.5 © A. M. Best Company, Best's Special Report, September 6 2010, www. ambest.com, used with permission; Figure 8.6 from www.abi.org.uk; Figures 9.4, 9.5, 9.6, Crown Copyright Source, UK Debt Management Office (DMO); Figure 9.7 from U.S. Department of the Treasury, Bureau of the Public Debt; Figure 9.15 from www.bankofengland.co.uk (see Bank of England Revisions Policy (http:// www.bankofengland.co.uk/mfsd/iadb/notesiadb/Revisions.htm)) (Figures 10.1a from Bank for International Settlements, www.bis.org; Figures 10.1b from Bank for International Settlements, www.bis.org; Figures 10.1c from Bank for International Settlements, www.bis.org; Figure 10.3 from Barclays Capital, Equity Gilt Study 2010, www.barcap.com; Figure 10.5 from The Guardian, http:// image.guardian.co.uk/sys-files/Guardian/documents/2009/05/22/Credit-rating. pdf; Figures 11.7a from Bank for International Settlements Quarterly Review, March 2010, http://www.bis.org; Figures 11.7b from Bank for International Settlements Quarterly Review, March 2010, http://www.bis.org; Figure 12.2 from Credit Suisse Global Investment Returns Yearbook 2011, www.credit-suisse.com/researchinstitute, Credit Suisse Research Institute. Copyright © 2011 Elroy Dimson, Paul Marsh and Mike Staunton. Elroy Dimson, Paul Marsh, Mike Staunton are authors of *Triumph of the Optimists: 101 Years of Global Investment Returns*, Princeton University Press, 2002.; Figures 12.4, 12.5, 12.6 from World

Federation of Exchanges, www.worldexchanges.org; Figures 12.9, 12.12 from London Stock Exchange, www.londonstockexchange.com; Figures 12.10, 12.11 from London Stock Exchange factsheets, www.londonstockexchange.com; Figure 13.2 from www.londonstockexchange.com; Figure 13.6 reproduced with permission of Yahoo! Inc. ©2011 Yahoo! Inc. YAHOO! and the YAHOO! logo are registered trademarks of Yahoo! Inc.; Figures 16.1, 16.2, 16.3, 16.5 from Triennial Central Bank Survey: Report on global foreign exchange market activity in 2010, www.bis.org; Figure 16.7 from www.oanda.com, OANDA Corporation; Figure 16.9 from CME Group website, with permission; Figure 17.6 from Hedgefund Intelligence, www.thecityuk.com.

Screenshots

Screenshots 14.7, 15.8 from www.euronext.com.

Tables

Table 10.11 from Fitch Global Corporate Finance Average Cumulative Default Rates 1990-2010, www.fitchratings.com; Table 13.7 from www.londonstock exchange.com; Table 14.6 from www.futuresindustry.org.

The Financial Times

Article 2.3 adapted from HK eclipses rivals as the place to list, *Financial Times*, 07/10/2010, p.34 (Cookson, R.); Article 3.5 adapted from Afghan savers lay siege to Kabul Bank, *Financial Times*, 03/09/2010, p.7 (Fontanella-Khan, J.); Figure 4.1 from Bonuses for performers to rise, *Financial Times*, 05/12/2009 (Murphy, M. and Saigol, L.); Article 4.2 adapted from Pressure rises for formal bank fees inquiry, *Financial Times*, 26/03/2010, p.6 (Burgess, K.); Article 4.3 from Outsized risk and regulation inhibit entrants, *Financial Times*, 24/03/2010, p.22 (Jenkins, P.); Article 4.4 adapted from Conflicts of interest bubble beneath the surface, *Financial Times*, 14/12/2009, p.21 (Saigol, L.); Article 4.5 adapted from Investors angered as costs soar over $750m, *Financial Times*, 02/06/2010, p.21 (Saigol, L.); Article 4.7 from Goldman looking at an own goal, *Financial Times*, 05/03/2010, p.21 (Saigol, L.); Article 4.7 adapted from Goldman stung by backlash in China, *Financial Times*, 07/06/2010, p.19 (Anderlini, J.); Figure 7.9 from Schroders table – unit trust prices, *Financial Times*, 04/03/2011; Figure 7.10 from Exchange Traded Funds, *Financial Times*, 15/07/2010; Article 7.11 from ETFs 'risk causing confusion', *Financial Times*, 12/04/2010, p.2 (Flood, C.); Figure 7.12 from Investment trust prices in the Financial Times, *Financial Times*, 04/03/2011; Article 8.11 adapted from High-net-worth investors keen to sign up as Names, *Financial Times*, 19/01/2009, p.18 (Kelleher, E.); Article 8.13 from Lloyd's considers riskier investments, *Financial Times*, 05/04/2010, p.3 (Johnson, S.); Article 9.1 adapted from New rules for money funds, *Financial Times*, 14/12/2009, p.2 (Johnson, S.); Article 9.3 adapted from Little room for Libor to fall further, *Financial Times*, 14/10/2009, p.38 (Oakley, D. and Atkins, R.); Article 9.8 adapted from Life returns to short-term lending market, *Financial Times*, 10/01/2009, p.25 (Davies, P.J.); Article 9.11 adapted from Run on banks left repo sector highly exposed, *Financial Times*, 11/09/2009, p.55 (Mackenzie, M.); Figure 9.14 from Interest rates – market, *Financial Times*, 16/03/2011; Article 10.2 from Britain draws strong demand for 50-year gilt, *Financial Times*, 24/02/2010, p.32 (Oakley, D.); Figure 10.4 from Gilts – UK Cash Market, *Financial Times*, 26/03/2011; Article 10.6 from Bonds – Benchmark Government, *Financial Times*, 29/03/2011; Article 10.7 from Bonds – Global Investment Grade, *Financial Times*, 29/03/2011; Article 10.8 from Bonds – High Yield & Emerging Market, *Financial Times*, 29/03/2011; Article 10.9 adapted from Corporate bond issues go local to deliver capital lift, *Financial Times*, 24/03/2010, p.17 (Oakley, D.); Article 10.10 from Ratings agency model left largely intact, *Financial Times*, 22/07/2009 (van Duyn, A. and Chung, J.); Article 11.1 adapted from Junk bonds new appeal shows little sign of fading, *Financial Times*, 15/12/2010, p.33 (van Duyn, A., Bullock, N. and Sakoui, A.); Article 11.2 from Brakes applied to convertible bond market FT, *Financial Times*, 06/04/2001, p.35 (Bream, R.); Article 11.4 adapted from Recent deals signal market's reopening in the same old style, *Financial Times*, 29/10/2009, p.37 (Hughes, J.); Article 11.5 adapted from US bill raises fears for covered bonds, *Financial Times*, 28/03/2011, p.19 (Hughes, J.); Article 11.6 adapted from FT article – Philippines set to price $1bn of samurai bonds, *Financial Times*, 16/02/2010, p.32 (Whipp, L. and Landing, R.); Figure 11.9 from www.markets.ft.com/markets/bonds.asp, Copyright (c) The Financial Times Ltd.; Article 12.3 adapted from Shenzhen takes over as China's listing hub, *Financial Times*, 19/10/2010, p34 (Cookson, R.); Article 12.8 adapted from Emerging market bourses hunt western blue chips, *Financial Times*, 09/08/2010, p.1 (Johnson, S.); Article 13.3 from Photo-Me fined £500, 000 by FSA for late disclosure, *Financial Times*, 22/06/2010, p.19 (Masters, B.); Article 13.4 from Tighter rules forcing nomads to run from smaller companies, *The Financial Times*, 18/06/2008, p.21 (Masters, B.), Copyright (c) The Financial Times Ltd.; Figure 13.5 from London Share Service extracts: Aerospace and Defence, *The Financial Times*, 07/03/2011, Copyright (c) The Financial Times Ltd.; Figure 13.8 from FTSE actuaries share indices, *The Financial Times*, 09/03/2011, Copyright (c) The Financial Times Ltd.; Article 14.1 from Northern Foods passes price rises to customers, *The Financial Times*, 10/07/2007, p.25 (Warwick-Ching, L. and Crooks, E.), Copyright (c) The Financial Times Ltd.; Article 14.3 from Farmers left short-changed by a margin call squeeze, *The Financial Times*, 23/11/2010, p.35 (Meyer, G. and Farchy, J.), Copyright (c) The Financial Times Ltd.; Figure 14.4 from Equity Index Futures, *The Financial Times*, 27/10/2010, Copyright (c)

The Financial Times Ltd.; Figure 14.8 from Interest rates – futures, *The Financial Times*, Copyright (c) The Financial Times Ltd.; Figure 15.1 from Call options on AstraZeneca shares, 17 December 2010, *Financial Times*, 18/12/2010; Figure 15.6 from Equity Options, *The Financial Times*, 18/12/2010, Copyright (c) The Financial Times Ltd.; Article 15.7 from Mexico buys $1bn insurance policy against falling oil prices, *The Financial Times*, 09/12/2009, p.19 (Meyer, G. and Blas, J.), Copyright (c) The Financial Times Ltd.; Figure 15.9 from Interest rates – swaps, *The Financial Times*, 17/12/2010, Copyright (c) The Financial Times Ltd.; Figure 16.6 from Currency rate, *The Financial Times*, 13/11/2010, Copyright (c) The Financial Times Ltd.; Figure 16.10 from www.ft.com, Copyright (c) The Financial Times Ltd.; Article 17.1 adapted from Investing stars lead bumper year for hedge funds, *Financial Times*, 02/03/2011, p.32 (Mackintosh, J.); Article 17.2 adapted from Hedge funds struggle to justify their star rating, *The Financial Times*, 29/08/2010, p.22 (Mackintosh, J.), Copyright (c) The Financial Times Ltd.; Article 18.1 from Oversight of banks costs US far more than EU, *The Financial Times*, 24/01/2011, p.8 (Masters, B.), Copyright (c) The Financial Times Ltd.; Article 18.2 from FSA fines two City brokers for not ringfencing clients' money, *The Financial Times*, 08/06/2010, p.22 (Gray, A.), Copyright (c) The Financial Times Ltd.; Article 18.4 adapted from Broker fined for 'market abuse' in FSA commodities crackdown, *Financial Times*, 03/06/2010, p.17 (Blas, J.).

In some instances we have been unable to trace the owners of copyright material, and we would appreciate any information that would enable us to do so.

1

The purpose of financial markets

The financial markets are incredibly exciting places. Every day there is a financial event that deserves reporting to the wider community in TV news broadcasts or newspapers. While not always as dramatic as the collapse of Lehman Brothers or the slashing of interest rates to less than 1 per cent, nevertheless the daily reporting of billions raised for a company to invest in mines in South America, or of one company taking over another, builds up to a picture that tells us that the sector is vital to us all. When the markets fail to work properly we all notice how important they are. For example, take the excessive lending to home buyers in the US in 2004–07 based on poorly thought-through models of the likelihood of default. This was banking at its worst, caused by bad leadership and perverse incentives in the system, which were compounded by idiotic ideas on the distribution of risk through the financial system using complex derivatives deals.

The extent of the power of the financial markets can be amply illustrated by the fear of a bad market reaction expressed in the faces of our political leaders when they announce their economic strategies. If the markets come to believe that there is a risk that a government is pursuing a policy that will result in rising inflation or an inability of the state to finance itself many years from now, they will refuse to buy the bonds that the government is selling to cover the gap between what it raises in taxes and what it spends. To start with they might merely shun the bonds until the interest rate offered has been raised by the government, for example Spain in 2011 had to pay over 3 per cent more to borrow than Germany, despite borrowing in the same currency, the euro. If things get worse the markets will refuse to lend to the country at almost any interest rate (e.g. Greece in 2011).

So you do not need me to tell you of the power and the excitement of the financial markets, from the ups and downs of the bond markets to the mood swings of the share markets, from the frenetic pace of the hedge funds and investment bank traders to the thrills and disasters of private equity investments. What you might need me to explain is how it is that movements in financial markets flow through the system to impact on you and others. What are the mechanisms at play? What are the different types of financial instruments that people put their money into? What do all the bankers and other financial service workers do with their time?

This book is designed to answer questions such as these. This chapter starts that process by explaining in everyday terms why we need financial markets and institutions, and begins to unravel the complexity present in modern markets by looking at their roots.

Why create financial markets and institutions?

To appreciate the importance of finance and financial markets in our lives, try this mental exercise: envisage a world without them. In such a world there are numerous problems that cannot be overcome. So, if we imagine that we are transported back in time to the dawn of history, perhaps we arrive at a small trading settlement at the heart of an agricultural society. Once a week, farmers from the surrounding villages gather to trade by barter. Also, travelling hawkers bring exotic items from hundreds of miles away. Barter trading makes sense because one farmer might produce beef and needs to exchange some of that for grain, cloth and wood. Such trades make each party better off – both sides enjoy a higher standard of living.

Money

But they could have an even higher standard of living if they could solve a problem. How can a beef farmer exchange his 50 bullocks in the much bigger market 120 miles away, where he could obtain a much better price, and then manage to organise the home journey of five cart loads of grain, two of cloth and four of wood received in return? While it can be done, barter is obviously not the best way of going about things. Wouldn't it be far better if the cattle could be exchanged for something that was generally accepted by traders up and down the country as being of value, and that something was small, portable and maintained its value over long periods? Then he could drive his cattle to the market and come home with the value received in his pocket, and not have to deal with 11 carts. Of course, I'm referring to money as a useful **means of exchange**.

Over the years, many varied items have been used as a means of exchange, ranging from cowry shells to cigarettes (in prisons particularly), but gold or silver became the norm. In present times, of course, money is generally represented by paper (bank notes, cheques, etc.), plastic (debit and credit cards) or electronic means. The barter system is inefficient in that it requires the buyer and seller to have mutual and simultaneous wants, a *double coincidence of wants*. The invention of tokens or coins and later paper[1] and electronic transfers as a means of exchange has revolutionised the world. It has enabled people and companies from diverse parts of the globe to conduct business with each other safe in the knowledge that each party will receive what they are due. Individuals and corporations are able to trade their goods and services for a universally accepted means of exchange – money.

In addition to being a convenient means of exchange, money is useful as a **store of value**. Thus our farmer may not want to obtain grain, cloth and wood this month. He might need these items in six months, and so he saves the money until then. This money must be capable of being stored, and keep its value until retrieved – it must not rot, tarnish or depreciate in value through inflation. Money may also be saved as a precaution to get the farmer through a bad patch, or for when he reaches old age.

A third useful thing money does for us is to act as a **unit of account**. It is important that each unit of coinage represents a particular asset value, is identical to units of the same denomination, and that units representing large amounts can be divided into smaller units. In the UK, for example, the **unit of account** is the pound sterling (£) with 100 sub-units. To have a standard unit of account is very important for business and personal decisions. Take a business with two subsidiaries, operating in different markets; it is very useful to observe their relative performances in terms of a common measuring stick.

Banking

Having money introduced to the system leads on to all sorts of wonderful opportunities for enhancing people's lives. What if our farmer has a plan to establish a second farm further up the valley. For this he will need considerable investment: the land has to be purchased, trees removed and oxen bought. If he achieves all of this then a great deal of additional food will be grown, three more families employed, there will be fewer deaths and raised living standards. He has 100 pieces of gold, but he needs 280 to complete the task. From our modern perspective some of the possible answers seem obvious:

- borrow the money

- invite neighbours into a partnership

- set up a company and sell shares in it, thereby offering capital providers a share of the profits.

---

[1] The Chinese were the first to issue paper banks notes, about 650 AD; the earliest in Europe were issued in Sweden in the seventeenth century.

This book will examine these solutions, as well as many more, in the modern financial era, but to the farmer it is not at all obvious that these are solutions. This is because society has not yet developed rules and systems to allow them to happen. People are afraid to enter into lending or profit-sharing contracts. Imagine you were one of the people the farmer comes to for a loan. What would stop you from lending your family's modest savings of gold pieces, despite the promise of an annual 10 per cent interest and the return of the principal amount at the end of five years? What is worrying you?

Trust, lack of specialised knowledge and poor diversification lie at the heart of the issue. Will the farmer simply run off with the money? Will he prove to be incompetent and incapable of repaying? Is his business plan flawed? You are just a simple farmer yourself, untrained in estimating these risks. Wouldn't it make sense if there was a specialist organisation that has staff dealing with loan applications on a daily basis? They could gather information on the failure rates of different types of business. Over time they gain experience in assessing the character and capability of potential borrowers. They also develop processes for taking other assets as security to protect themselves in the event of default. Very importantly, they can diversify away a large part of the risk because over the course of a year the organisation might lend to hundreds of such ventures. It might have to accept that a handful will fail to repay loans, but, so long as the interest rate charged to all borrowers is high enough to more than cover this, it will not be a problem.

Widespread knowledge of the existence of such an organisation would solve another difficulty for the entrepreneur/farmer. That is, finding people/organisations with capital and willing to place it in a business. He does not have to search far and wide to encounter dozens of people willing to contribute gold pieces to make up the full 180 needed. **Search costs** are reduced because there is an organisation letting the whole community know it is open for business lending.

Of course, what I am describing is banking. Banks (and other complex financial institutions) can only arise in pretty special circumstances. Society has to be sufficiently stable and well-ordered for there to be enforceable property and business rights. There must be a sophisticated legal environment that protects people from rogues and incompetents, by establishing contracts where both sides understand the terms and conditions, and the courts will enforce them. There also needs to be a high-quality social infrastructure. In particular, there needs to be a culture of decency, honesty and integrity. Even today, there are parts of the world that have not made the transition from primitive finance to the more sophisticated. There the law is frequently not obeyed, either in the letter (the rich and powerful can get around the legal system) or in its spirit, because the cultural norms are such that there is little social penalty for bad behaviour.

The terms of business deals are not enforced fairly by the organs of State or the judiciary. Property rights are not upheld and the unscrupulous can oppress the honest businessman or woman.

Depositors

So, bankers with expertise in lending combined with diversification benefits create a valuable component of a society looking to grow its output. But, where is the bank going to get its money from? Initially this might come from a few wealthy owners who each put in, say, 200 pieces of gold. This will allow some lending, but after a while, the bank will run short of cash and so lending stops. However, the bankers will be aware of a need among the savers in society for a safe place to keep their hard-earned money. If they keep it at home there is the danger of theft. Also the savers would like to obtain a rate of return on that money. It makes sense for them to deposit the money in a bank that could offer complete reassurance that it will be returned to them whenever they demand it, and that could earn some interest. Banks are able to offer such a deal by lending out only a proportion of the deposited money. Even as late as the 1840s banks would generally keep one-half of all deposits in the vaults so that (some) customers could withdraw money at any time. In order to be able to offer interest, the other half was lent out to households and businesses at a rate of interest considerably higher than that offered to the depositors. Today the proportion of deposits held back as cash is much less than 50 per cent, with the banks relying on the assumption that the pattern will continue of only a very small fraction of customers withdrawing cash each day; and, anyway, most withdrawals are offset by new deposits or borrowing from other banks.

A payments system

A further advantage of a bank is that money can be transferred between accounts. This saves the hassle of a bank customer withdrawing large sums of cash to hand over to another person in payment for goods received. Instead one account is credited while one is debited, even if the accounts are held at different banks.

Business partnerships and limited liability companies

We are running ahead of the story, so let us go back to our cattle farmer, who has already seen the introduction of money and banking in his lifetime (in reality this took thousands of years). These are important breakthroughs in the development of civilisation, but they are clearly not sufficient to solve a number of other problems. For example, banks might be unwilling to provide more than one-half of the funds needed for a project, because of the possibility that the business venture will lose money and assets used as collateral will fall in value to below the amount of loans outstanding.

The rest of the funds will have to come from the owners. The farmer does not have 140 gold pieces (one-half of the capital required) and so has to think of alternative sources of money. We have already mentioned the possibility of financing a venture by a group of investors each being willing to take a profit share. If it does not perform well then they will not be entitled to any annual return or capital sum at the end of a number of years. This is a different deal to that of lenders who can still claim interest and principal payments as set out in the lending agreement, even when the business is making losses.

One option is to form a partnership. Say there are 10 investors (other than the farmer) each willing to supply gold pieces. In return the profits are to be split in proportion to the finance supplied. If one of the partners also takes on a full-time managerial role he would be entitled to an extra income. There are two difficulties with partnerships. First, each partner is liable for the debts of the business. Thus each of 11 partners has to accept that if the business incurs liabilities it cannot satisfy then the creditors can come after their personal assets, houses, farms, etc. Second, if one of the partners wishes to leave (or dies) then they are generally entitled to a fair share of the value of the partnership. This can be very disruptive to the business, as assets have to be sold to pay the partner. Indeed, partnerships tend to be dissolved if one member leaves, and then a new partnership is created to carry on the business thereafter.

To solve these two problems society developed the idea of a company or corporation established as a 'separate person' under the law. It is the company that enters legal agreements such as bank loan contracts, not the owners of the company shares. The company can have a *perpetual life*. So, if investors wish to cash in their chips they do not have the right to insist that the company liquidate its assets and pay them their share. The company continues but the investors sell their share in the company to another investor. This is great – it gives managers the opportunity to plan ahead, knowing the resources of the business will not be withdrawn; it gives other shareholders the reassurance that the company can achieve its goals without disruption.

One of the most important breakthroughs in the development of capitalism and economic progress was the introduction of **limited liability** (1855 in the UK). There were strong voices heard against the change in the law. It was argued that it was only fair that **creditors** to a business could call on the shareholders in that business to bear the responsibility of failure. However, a stronger argument triumphed. This is that it is better for society as a whole if we encourage individuals to place their savings at the disposal of entrepreneurial managers for use in a business enterprise. Thus factories, ships, shops, houses and railways will be built and society will have more goods and services.

Insisting on *un*limited liability for investors made them hesitant to invest and thus reduced overall wealth. Limited liability companies are what (for the most part) we have today, and we should be very grateful for it. Creditors quickly adjusted to the new reality of lending without a guarantee other than from the company. They became more expert and thorough in assessing the risk of the loan going bad (**credit risk**) and they called for more information; legislators helped by insisting that companies publish key information.

Share (equity) markets

Having got to this point, it became obvious that to go any further and mobilise even more savings for investment, more problems had to be solved. For example, if you own shares (also called **equity** and **stock**) in a company for a long while you might be content receiving regular dividends as a distribution of the profits made. But, there might come a time when you would like to sell your shares. Perhaps you are retired and need to sell to finance consumption, or you would like to invest in other business opportunities. The problem is that with **ordinary shares** (**common stock** in the US) the company is under no obligation to purchase shares from you. When you bought the shares you signed up to a deal whereby you would receive a return if the managers were smart enough to produce one, but understood that the deal is a perpetual one – no promise of a fixed receipt of money in the future.

One option is for the shareholders to get together and agree to liquidate the company. That is, sell all the assets, pay off the liabilities, gather a pile of cash and distribute the proceeds to shareholders in proportion to their percentage holding. As you can imagine, this is not a very efficient way of running an economy. Thus, we clearly need a forum in which investors can buy and sell shares between themselves. This is where the share (equity) markets come in. They provide a regulated environment to minimise the risk of fraud, incompetence, etc., where shares can be traded in a market with numerous buyers and sellers every day allowing an investor to sell quickly and at low cost.

Corporate advisers – investment banks, etc.

For a company to undertake a once-in-a-lifetime event, like obtaining a quotation on a stock market for its shares, the managers usually need the help of people who specialise in bringing a company to market. A number of specialists might be involved, from brokers to accountants, but the key people often work for investment banks. They are skilled at organising fund raising for companies, both at the initial launch on the market and later in the company's development. They can also help in a host of other ways, including advising on a takeover of another firm, assisting with managing risk and helping invest short-term money held by the company (for a few days or weeks).

Bond markets

Banks often pay little or no interest on money deposited with them, while, at the same time, charging high interest rates to borrowers. Wouldn't it be better for both depositors and borrowers if the bank was bypassed and there was a market that directly connected savers to borrowers? Such markets have existed for hundreds of years. They are called bond markets, in which a contract to lend is accepted by each side, with the borrower agreeing to pay sums of money in the future.

This is only the beginning

Money, banking, shares, share markets and bond markets are just the start of it. There are many other institutions and markets that provide a vast number of social benefits connecting savers with investment opportunities and reducing risk. People need help saving for old age (pension funds) and to protect themselves against adverse events (insurance). They often decide to club together to invest money in shares, bonds, property, etc. through collective investment funds such as unit trusts, private equity or hedge funds. Then there is the need to obtain foreign exchange or to hedge against adverse movements in currency, in interest rates or in commodities.

The remainder of this chapter and much of Chapter 2 provide a brief outline of the role and importance of the main types of financial instruments, markets and institutions. The rest of the book looks at them in much more depth.

The impact of the modern financial markets on our lives

Here we jump forward to the modern era by looking at a number of financial markets and illustrate the impact they have on ordinary people's lives. The markets are:

- the share markets;
- the money markets;
- the bond markets;

▨ the foreign exchange markets;

▨ the derivative and commodity markets.

We will also look at the impact of banking.

Share (equity) markets

As a result of limited liability, millions of us now own shares in companies and are thereby entitled to receive dividends that might flow from the profits that the firm generates. We are owners of the company and can vote directors on or off the Board to try to appoint a team that will act in our best interests. These days most of these shares are not actually held directly by individuals, but through various savings schemes, such as pension funds and insurance savings schemes (e.g. endowments linked to mortgages).

Exhibit 1.1 shows that the market value of UK and US shares has been on something of a roller-coaster ride over the past 20 years (UK shares are represented by the FTSE 100 index comprising the largest 100 companies on the market; US shares by the S&P 500 index, representing the largest 500). Market prices shot up in the late 1990s as investors became excited by the new economy shares of the

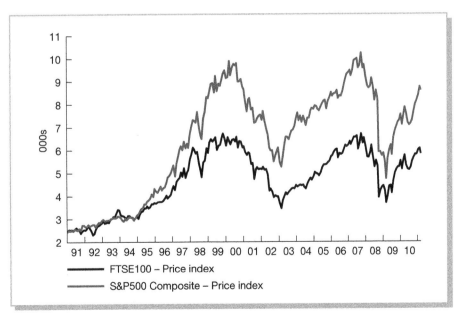

Exhibit 1.1   UK and US share market price movements, 1990–2011 (with the US S&P 500 index rebased to the UK FTSE 100 in 1991)

Source: Datastream

dot.com revolution. When equity markets are booming it can have an effect on people's confidence: they go out and spend more; they invest more in factories, machinery, etc. Thus the economy can get a lift. Conversely, when people feel poorer because their investments are down and they are told that their pensions will not have enough value left in them to support them in their old age they become more cautious spenders and investors, resulting in declining demand – as was the case in 2011. While stock market movements are not the only cause of economic fluctuations they are contributors.

Money markets

You and I might, from time to time, have the need to borrow money for a short while, say on a credit card or via an overdraft. Similarly, large organisations such as companies, governments and banks often need to borrow money for a period of a few days or weeks. They tend not to borrow on credit cards and may find overdrafts inconvenient or relatively expensive. This is where the **money markets** come in; they allow companies, etc. to issue instruments that promise to pay a sum of money after, say, 30 days if the buyer pays an amount now for owning that right. Obviously the amount the lender puts down at the beginning of the 30 days is less than what they collect at the end; thus an effective interest rate is charged. We say that the money markets are **wholesale markets** because they involve large transactions each time – £500,000/€1,000,000 or more. They enable borrowing for less than one year. Banks are particularly active in this market – both as lenders and as borrowers. Large corporations, local government bodies and non-banking financial institutions also lend when they have surplus cash and borrow when short of money.

The largest borrowers in these markets are usually governments. They issue **Treasury bills**, which do not carry an explicit interest but merely promise to pay a sum of money after a period. The most popular length to maturity is three months. The UK government is the biggest issuer in Europe, with billions of pounds worth of these sold almost every week of the year. The US government also sells a tremendous volume of these instruments, much of which has been bought by the Chinese government as it invests its savings around the world – it is poorly diversified because it has put such a high proportion of its portfolio in US Treasuries.

Exhibit 1.2 shows the interest rates that the UK government had to offer investors to induce them to buy a 91-day (three-month) promise. That is a promise that in 91 days a fixed amount of money will be paid to the holder of the security. These are rates the government paid for fresh issues in each of the weeks going back 20 years. Note that even though the bills last for a mere three months the interest rates shown are annualised up (given as an annual rate). So, if an investor

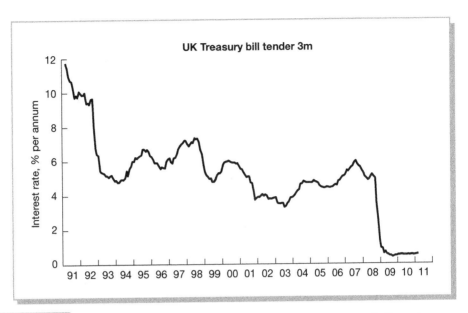

Exhibit 1.2   The interest rate the UK government offered investors in its various three-month Treasury bills issued each week 1991–2011

Source: Datastream

receives 0.2 per cent for lending for 91 days the chart will show a figure of 0.8 per cent. You can see that normally the government pays around 4–6 per cent per year to borrow using three-month loans. In an economy where inflation is around 1.5–3 per cent this allows the lender to the UK government to obtain a real return (above inflation) of around 1–3 per cent. (In the early 1990s the UK had much higher inflation rates.) However, in the wake of the financial crisis the Bank of England significantly reduced interest rates for short-term borrowing for all sorts of instruments, and this had a knock-on effect on the interest rate the government had to pay to borrow for three months – it has come all the way down to around 0.5 per cent (around 0.125 per cent for three months). This lowered the borrowing cost for the government, which is just as well given that it borrowed so much.

On the other hand, the extremely low interest rates throughout the financial system, including bank account savings rates, produced howls of complaint from savers, who received interest significantly less than inflation. Much of this saving is done through pension funds and so people's pension pots also became smaller.

Bond markets

Companies often need to borrow money so that they can build useful things such as factories and research establishments (e.g. stem cell or cancer drug laboratories).

One way for them to borrow is to produce a legally binding document, a bond, that states that the company will pay interest for, say 10 years, and a capital sum at the end to whoever buys the bond. This is an attractive way for people, pension funds and others to obtain a return on their savings. It is made even more attractive by the fact that the lender does not have to keep their money tied up in the bond for the full 10 years, but can sell it to other investors in an active market for bonds. The buyer of the bond may be willing to pay the same as the sum paid by the original owner to obtain the promise of future interest, or they may be willing to pay more or less – much depends on the current going rates of return for that type of bond given its risk and anticipated inflation.

Thus a **bond** is merely a document that sets out the borrower's promise to pay sums of money in the future – usually regular interest plus a capital amount upon the maturity of the bond. Many European bond markets are over three centuries old and during that time they have developed very large and sophisticated sub-markets encompassing government bonds (UK government bonds are called **gilts**), **corporate bonds** (issued by companies), local authority bonds and international bonds, amongst others.

Exhibit 1.3 shows the rates of interest typical, but relatively safe, corporate bond issuers had to pay over the period 2001–11. It shows the interest rates payable

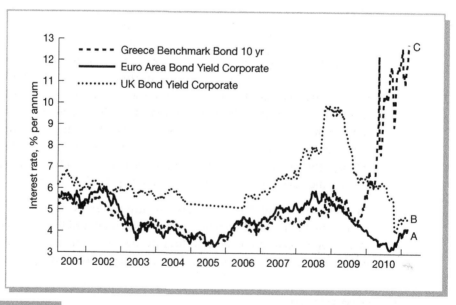

Exhibit 1.3   Yields on corporate bonds issued in pounds and euros, and yields on Greek government debt, 2001–11

Source: Datastream

if the promises to pay regular interest and the capital sum were in euros: the black line (A). The dotted line (B) shows the rate of return if the borrowing (and payments of interest and capital) was done in pounds. Notably, the sterling borrowers paid higher interest rates than the eurozone borrowers – this is mostly because of higher UK inflation expectations at the time of issue than for eurozone countries. The chart also shows the interest rates payable by the Greek government when it sold bonds denominated in euros – the dashed line (C). In most years it paid lower interest rates than the typical low-risk euro corporate borrower, but in 2011 we see a dramatic spike in interest rates demanded by lenders to induce them to place their hard-earned savings into Greek government debt. Many Greek companies had to pay more than the government to borrow because they were seen as even more of a risk. This meant that they could not afford to borrow to finance many of the investment projects that they would normally undertake, which contributed to a deep recession and rioting on the streets.

In the UK case, bond investors were very worried in 2008 and 2009 that a high proportion of borrowing companies were going to go bust, and as a result demanded interest rates as high as 10 per cent. Note that these are the rates for the most highly-respected (relatively-safe) companies; more risky borrowers had to pay much more. As a result of this high cost of finance many plans to build factories, offices, shops, etc. were shelved and thousands of people were made redundant.

Foreign exchange markets

Individuals and businesses often have the need to exchange foreign currency, sometimes purely for pleasure, a holiday say, but mostly for business. For example, a French company building a manufacturing plant in the US exchanges euros for dollars. Today the foreign exchange markets are enormous, with transactions worth $4,000 billion taking place every day. The movements of exchange rates can make a big difference to ordinary people and businesses alike. Consider Maria, who borrowed €300,000 to buy an apartment in London early in 2006. At that time she could get £1 for every €1.50 – see Exhibit 1.4 – and so she could buy a £200,000 apartment. Unfortunately, in 2009 she needed to sell her apartment to raise cash to support her Spanish business. Not only is Maria hit by the UK recession, but she is doubly unfortunate, because at 2009 exchange rates (€1.10 to £1) she can obtain only €220,000 even if she sells the apartment for £200,000. Maria has made an €80,000 loss simply because currency rates shifted. As you can see from the chart they do this quite a lot. The markets and institutions have devised various tools to help individuals like Maria as well as large organisations like Unilever reduce the impact of foreign exchange shifts.

Exhibit 1.4   The exchange rate between euros and UK pounds, 2001–11

Source: Datastream

Foreign exchange (forex, FX) markets are simply markets in which one currency is exchanged for another. They include the **spot market** where currencies are bought and sold for 'immediate' delivery (in reality, one or two days later) and the **forward markets**, where the deal is agreed now to exchange currencies at some fixed point in the future. Also currency futures and options and other forex derivatives are employed to hedge (manage) risk and to speculate.

Derivative and commodity markets

Imagine you are a cocoa farmer in Ghana. You would like to have certainty on the price you will receive for your cocoa when you harvest it six months from now. On the other hand, an organisation such as Cadbury would like to know the cost of its cocoa six months from now so that it, like the farmer, can plan ahead and avoid the risk of the spot price at that time being dramatically different to what it is now.

Fortunately financial markets have evolved to help both the farmer and the chocolate maker. Perhaps the farmer could sell a **future** in cocoa at, say, $3,800 per tonne. A future is a contract to undertake a transaction (e.g. sell cocoa) at a point – days, weeks or years from now – at a price agreed now.

If the farmer sells a future this guarantees that if he delivers the cocoa in six months he will get the price agreed. Perhaps the chocolate maker could also enter the futures markets on one of the organised exchanges to give it certainty over the price that it will pay. Each side is legally obliged to go through with the deals they signed up to – and just to make sure the exchange requires that each of them leaves money at the exchange so that if the futures price should move against them they will not be tempted to walk away from the deal: if they did they would lose this 'margin' they have at the exchange.

You can see from Exhibit 1.5 that the futures price of cocoa fluctuates over time and therefore you can understand why buyers and sellers might be concerned about the price moving to an unprofitable level for them, and so why they lock in a futures price in one of the futures markets.

A **derivative** is a financial instrument whose value is derived from the value of other financial securities or some other underlying asset because it grants a

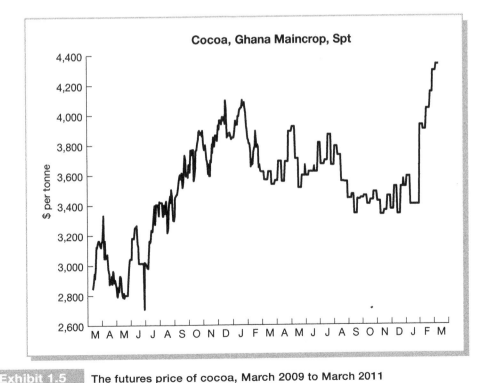

Exhibit 1.5 The futures price of cocoa, March 2009 to March 2011

Source: Datastream

right to undertake a transaction. This right becomes a saleable derived financial instrument. Futures have been illustrated but there are other derivatives. For example, an option gives the purchaser the right, but not the obligation, to buy or sell something at some point in the future, at a price agreed now. The performance of the derivative depends on the behaviour of the underlying asset. Companies can use these markets for the management and transfer of risk. They can be used to reduce risk (hedging) or to speculate. We will look at these possibilities in Chapters 14 and 15.

Banking

The interest rates banks charge can have a profound effect on people's lives. The rate that the borrower pays is often linked to the bank base rate. Some borrowers may pose a low risk to the bank and so may be charged, say, 2 per cent over the base rate. More risky borrowers pay base rate plus, say, 7 per cent. Exhibit 1.6 shows that the average base rate set by UK banks over the 10 years to 2011 has been subject to significant fluctuations. In 2009 the base rate fell to an all-time low of 0.5 per cent and so we had remarkably low interest rates charged by the banks. The actions by central banks around the world to lower interest rates

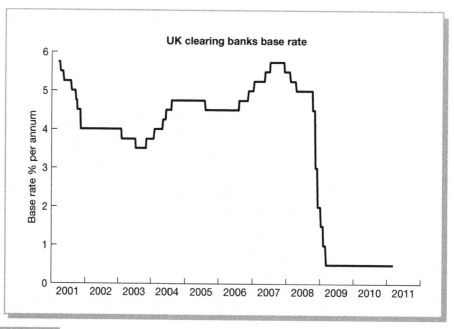

Exhibit 1.6   UK bank base rates, 2001–11

Source: Datastream

had the desired effect, as many families with mortgages or businesses with loans were saved when base rates were pushed down. If base rates had remained at 5 per cent we would have seen much higher house repossession rates, widespread business failure and mass unemployment.

2

An overview of the markets and institutions

This chapter describes the main financial centres, which have become increasingly important in every continent. It also provides a quick run-through of the different types of financial institution, and some ideas on how financial institutions and markets improve the flow of funds in a modern society. In a well-functioning financial system funds can flow easily and at low cost from savers to those with a productive use for the money. The increases in wealth we have seen over the past 100 years in most parts of the globe are in no small part due to the development of highly effective financial markets and institutions. Indeed, we can go so far as to say that one of the major reasons that some countries failed to grow out of poverty is that they have not yet created a properly functioning mechanism for mobilising the savings of their citizens so that they can be used for investment in productive assets, such as factories, within their country.

Importance of different financial centres

People and institutions involved in financial market activity tend to be concentrated in a few major centres around the world. Every six months the largest 75 financial centres are rated and ranked by drawing on both statistical data and assessments by finance service professionals in an online survey. The results are published in the *Global Financial Centres Report*, sponsored by Qatar Financial Centre Authority, and produced by the think-tank Z/Yen Group.

The five groups of factors considered are shown in Exhibit 2.1. As you can see, the centres are rated not simply by volume of business (such as share turnover) and other quantitative data, but for a number of other factors. So, for example, evidence about a fair and just business environment is drawn from a corruption perception index and an opacity index (e.g. is trading open and are the prices of deals published?). In all, over 70 indicators have been used including office rental rates, airport satisfaction and transport. Around 33,000 financial services professionals (e.g. bankers, asset managers, insurers, lawyers) respond to the online questionnaire in which they are asked to rate those centres with

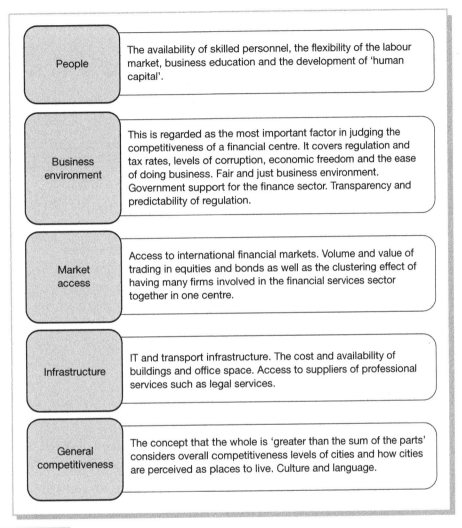

| People | The availability of skilled personnel, the flexibility of the labour market, business education and the development of 'human capital'. |

| Business environment | This is regarded as the most important factor in judging the competitiveness of a financial centre. It covers regulation and tax rates, levels of corruption, economic freedom and the ease of doing business. Fair and just business environment. Government support for the finance sector. Transparency and predictability of regulation. |

| Market access | Access to international financial markets. Volume and value of trading in equities and bonds as well as the clustering effect of having many firms involved in the financial services sector together in one centre. |

| Infrastructure | IT and transport infrastructure. The cost and availability of buildings and office space. Access to suppliers of professional services such as legal services. |

| General competitiveness | The concept that the whole is 'greater than the sum of the parts' considers overall competitiveness levels of cities and how cities are perceived as places to live. Culture and language. |

Exhibit 2.1 **The five groups of instrumental factors for judging the quality of a financial centre**

which they are most familiar on a number of factors. To ensure that there is no bias towards their home base, the assessments given on their own centre are excluded from the calculations.

The map in Exhibit 2.2 shows the ranking of the top 20 financial centres. There is very little difference in the ratings for London and New York. The respondents to the survey believe that these two centres work together for mutual benefit; a gain for one not meaning a loss for the other. The position of Hong Kong has improved immensely in recent years so that it is now a mere 10 points (out of 1,000) behind London. It is one of only a handful of genuine global financial

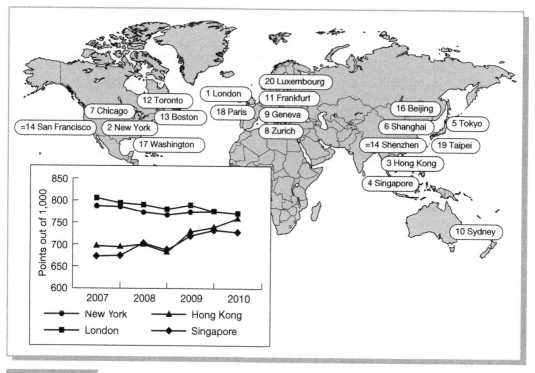

Exhibit 2.2   The top 20 global financial centres

Source: Global Financial Centres Report, sponsored by Qatar Financial Centre Authority and produced by Z/Yen Group

centres. Singapore is expected to join this trio soon. Between them the top four centres account for 70 per cent of all equity trading, for example.

Remarkably, Shanghai has now entered the top 10; and when financial professionals were questioned about which financial centres are likely to become more significant in the next few years, the top five centres mentioned were all Asian – Shenzhen, Shanghai, Singapore, Seoul and Beijing.

Exhibit 2.3 describes the relative importance of Hong Kong and Shanghai as places for companies to raise money from shareholders by issuing shares on the Hong Kong or Shanghai stock markets for the first time. This is called an **initial public offering (IPO)**. The article illustrates how international the raising of finance is these days, with Mongolian, French and Italian companies listing alongside a great number of mainland Chinese firms.

If we focus on Europe we find that while London dominates, Zurich and Frankfurt are also regarded as global leaders, with rich environments for different types of financial services. Geneva is a specialist in asset management (running funds

HK eclipses rivals as the place to list

Robert Cookson

The up-to-$20.5bn initial public offering of AIG's prized Asian business is the talk of the town in Hong Kong, but alongside that juggernaut there are dozens of other companies flocking to list in the city.

So great is the wave of listings that Hong Kong is on track for the second year in a row to eclipse its rivals Shanghai, London, and New York as the world's biggest centre for IPOs.

So far this year some 53 companies have raised a combined $23.9bn from IPOs in Hong Kong, according to data from Dealogic. That figure dwarfs the $10.7bn raised in New York and $7bn in London.

With AIG alone set to raise at least $13.9bn from the listing of AIA, its Asian business, Hong Kong is now on track to trump its rivals Shanghai and Shenzhen in terms of deal volume in 2010.

"Hong Kong is now firmly established as a major global listing venue – it's the place any issuer has to seriously look at," Mr Lam says [Ed Lam, Citigroup's co-head of global banking for Hong Kong].

International companies are being attracted by the prospect of selling shares at higher prices than could be achieved in either their home markets or the traditional capital-raising centres of London or New York.

Prada, the Italian luxury goods company, is considering a possible

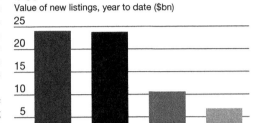

IPOs
Value of new listings, year to date ($bn)

Source: Thomson Reuters Datastream; Dealogic

listing in Hong Kong next year, following hard on the heels of French perfume house L'Occitane, which raised more than $700m there in April.

On Tuesday, the first Mongolian company to sell shares in Hong Kong completed a $650m offering.

Yet Mongolian Mining Corp and other foreign issuers still make up only a fraction of the deals on the HK stock exchange. Mainland Chinese companies remain the dominant force and are attracting strong – and at times frenzied – demand from both international fund managers and Hong Kong retail investors.

Companies that would benefit from the rise of the Chinese consumer were selling like hotcakes.

Boshiwa, a children's clothing retailer likened to Mothercare of the UK, is a good example. The Chinese company, which raised $320m in Hong Kong in September, saw its shares rocket 41 per cent on their trading debut

last week. On Wednesday, shares in Boshiwa were trading at a price of 72 times last year's earnings.

"China is clearly rebalancing the economy away from one that is predominantly export and manufacturing-driven towards a more domestic consumption-driven one," said Kester Ng, JPMorgan's co-head of equity capital and derivatives markets for Asia.

"Companies that are linked to the Chinese consumption theme have done really well." This point has not been lost on Chinese companies themselves.

Last week, China Medical System, which makes pharmaceutical products, listed in Hong Kong having raised $129m in an IPO that priced at the top of the target range. On the same day as its Hong Kong debut, it de-listed its shares from London's junior Aim market.

The company is not alone. West China Cement, a cement producer that has long complained that its shares were undervalued in London, made the same jump to Hong Kong from Aim in August. And in yet another case, Sihuan Pharmaceutical Holdings, a Chinese drugmaker that de-listed from the Singapore stock exchange last year, is seeking to raise up to $700m in a Hong Kong IPO.

Source: *Financial Times*, 7 October 2010, p. 34.

Exhibit 2.3   HK eclipses rivals as the place to list

invested in shares, etc. for individuals and institutions) but is not a fully diversified centre, lacking a number of financial services. Amsterdam, Dublin and Paris have strong international connections but lack the depth to be global leaders.

If we break down the overall results to specific aspects of financial services then the following are the top financial centres in order of size:

■ Asset management (e.g. mutual funds, unit trusts, pension funds):

    1 London

    2 New York

    3 Hong Kong

    4 Singapore.

■ Banking:

    1 New York

    2 Hong Kong

    3 London

    4 Singapore.

■ Professional services (e.g. legal, accounting):

    1 London

    2 New York

    3 Hong Kong

    4 Singapore.

■ Wealth management (advice and investing for wealthy people):

    1 London

    2 Geneva

    3 New York

    4 Toronto.

Following the financial crisis caused by the financial sector (especially the banks) the UK Chancellor of the Exchequer imposed a 50 per cent super-tax on bank bonuses. Some feared that this might cause mass relocation of financial services providers to other centres, such as New York, Zurich or Hong Kong. But many of the governments in these other centres also plan to crack down on bankers and so we have not, to date, seen an exodus. Besides which, choosing a place to work, live and raise a family is about much more than tax rates.

In the US, financial market activity is split between a number of centres. New York is dominant in equity and bond trading as well as investment banking, Chicago is big in derivatives and commodities, with Boston and San Francisco enjoying high reputations for asset management. While the US centres are particularly strong on domestic security issuance – for example the largest corporate and government bond markets in the world – the US is often outshone by London on international financial services. London, being the dominant centre in the European time-zone, has kept its position as a principal centre in international financial markets, as can be seen from Exhibit 2.4.

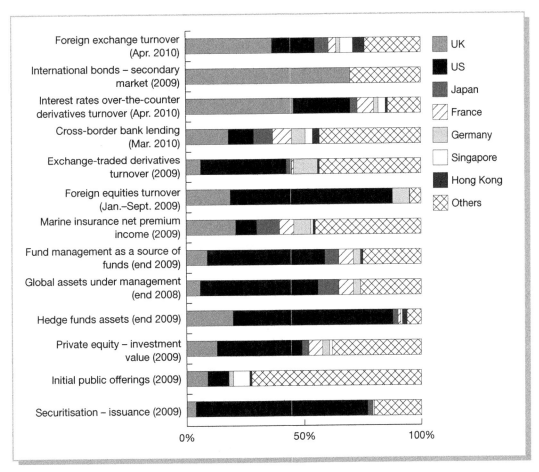

Exhibit 2.4   **Share of world financial market activity**

Source: TheCityUK estimates

Note that while Hong Kong and Singapore are highly ranked in terms of having the right infrastructure and attractiveness for financial services to grow (as we saw in the Z/Yen survey) they still have a relatively small share of world activity in most categories. France and Germany have more activity than the Asian centres in a number of segments. However, the potential of Hong Kong and Singapore, as China and other Asian countries grow, is enormous.

Growth in the financial services sector

The financial services sector has grown rapidly in the post-war period. It now represents a significant proportion of total economic activity, not just in the UK, but across the world. Firms operating in this sector have, arguably, been the most dynamic, innovative and adaptable companies in the world over the past 40 years.

Some reasons for the growth of financial services in the UK

London has historically been the most important financial centre, ideally positioned at the heart of the British Empire and the industrialised world. London is open for business when the rest of Europe is active and when the Asian markets are still operating at the end of their trading day and America is starting its working day. There are a number of reasons for the growth of the financial services sector in the UK. These include:

- *High income elasticity*. As consumers have become increasingly wealthy the demand for financial services has grown by a disproportionate amount. Thus a larger share of national income is devoted to paying this sector fees, etc. to provide services because people desire the benefits offered. Firms have also bought an ever-widening range of financial services from the institutions, which have been able to respond quickly to the needs of corporations.

- *International comparative advantage*. One of the reasons that London maintains dominance in a number of areas is that it possesses a comparative advantage in providing global financial services. This advantage stems, not least, from the critical mass of collective expertise which it is difficult for rivals to emulate. In some industries once a cluster of firms and personnel is established, their proximity allows them to be more efficient and learn from each other to improve their skills, deepen knowledge and specialise in tasks. This has happened in Silicon Valley with hi-tech and in the City with financial services. And, of course, London also has the prerequisites of a stable political and trustworthy legal system, no barriers to the flow of money and the English language.

Forty years of innovation

Since the 1970s there has been a remarkably proactive response by the financial sector to changes in the market environment. New financial instruments, techniques of intermediation and markets have been developed with impressive speed. Instruments, which even in the 1990s did not exist, have sprung to prominence to create multi-billion-pound markets, with thousands of employees serving these markets.

There has been a general trend towards deregulation and liberalisation for institutional investors, while recognising that individual investors need protection. Until the mid-1970s there were clearly delineated roles for different types of financial institutions. Banks did banking, insurance firms provided insurance, building societies granted mortgages and so on. There was little competition between the different sectors, and cartel-like arrangements meant that there was only limited competition within each sector. Some effort was made in the 1970s to increase the competitive pressures, particularly for banks. The arrival of large numbers of foreign banks in London helped the process of reform in the UK but the system remained firmly bound by restrictions, particularly in defining the activities firms could undertake.

The real breakthrough came in the 1980s. The guiding political philosophy of achieving efficiency through competition led to large-scale deregulation of activities and pricing. There was widespread competitive invasion of market segments. Banks became much more active in the mortgage market and set up insurance operations, stockbroking arms, unit trusts and many other services. Building societies, on the other hand, started to invade the territory of the banks and offered personal loans, credit cards and cheque accounts. They even went into estate agency, stockbroking and insurance underwriting.

The London Stock Exchange was deregulated in 1986 (in what is known as the **Big bang**) and this move enabled it to compete more effectively on a global scale and reduce the costs of dealing in shares, particularly for the large institutional investors. The City had become insular and comfortable in its ways, much like a gentlemen's club. Then in 1986 in the face of serious competition from abroad, it became necessary to make the City more competitive and transparent if it was to continue to service the world's economy as it had done for many years. The introduction of electronic trading, along with the end of fixed commission trading (an 'accepted rate' to charge rather than one competitively arrived at) and face-to-face dealing, and the sanctioning of foreign ownership of UK brokers successfully pushed the City into the modern era.

The 1970s and early 1980s were periods of volatile interest rates and exchange rates. This resulted in greater uncertainty for businesses. New financial instruments were developed to help manage risk, e.g. new derivatives. Many derivatives are traded on LIFFE (the London International Financial Futures and Options Exchange) which has seen volumes rocket since it was opened in 1982. LIFFE, now called NYSE.Liffe, handles around €2 trillion worth of derivatives business every day. Likewise the volume of swaps, options, futures, etc. traded in the informal 'over-the-counter' market (i.e. not on a regulated exchange) – discussed later in the chapter – has grown exponentially.

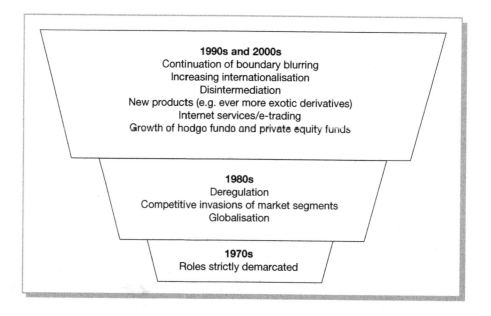

Through the 1980s the trend towards globalisation in financial product trading and services continued apace. Increasingly, a worldwide market was established. It became unexceptional for a company to have its shares quoted in New York, London, Frankfurt and Tokyo as well as on its home exchange in Africa. Bond selling and trading became global and currencies were traded 24 hours a day. International banking took on an increasingly high profile, not least because the multinational corporations demanded that their banks provide multifaceted services across the globe, ranging from borrowing in a foreign currency to helping manage cash.

Vast investments have been made in computing and telecommunications systems to cut costs and provide improved services. Automated teller machines

(ATMs), banking by telephone and internet, and payment by EFTPOS (electronic funds transfer at point of sale) are now commonplace. A more advanced use of technological innovation is in the global trading of the ever-expanding range of financial instruments. It became possible to sit on a beach in the Caribbean and trade pork belly futures in Chicago, interest rate futures in London and shares in Singapore. In the 1990s there was a continuation of the blurring of the boundaries between different types of financial institutions to the point where organisations such as JPMorgan Chase and Barclays are referred to as **financial supermarkets** (or universal banks or financial services companies) offering a wide range of services. The irony is that just as this title was being bandied about, the food supermarket giants such as Sainsbury's and Tesco set up banking services, following a path trodden by a number of other non-banking corporations. Marks and Spencer provides credit cards, personal loans and even pensions. Virgin Money sells life insurance, pensions and Individual Savings Accounts (ISAs) over the telephone. The internet has provided a new means of supplying financial services and lowered the barrier to entry into the industry. New banking, stockbroking and insurance services have sprung up. The internet allows people to trade millions of shares at the touch of a button from the comfort of their homes, to transfer the proceeds between bank accounts and to search websites for data, company reports, newspaper reports, insurance quotations and so on – all much more cheaply than ever before.

The globalisation of business and investment decisions has continued, making national economies increasingly interdependent. Borrowers use the international financial markets to seek the cheapest funds, and investors look in all parts of the globe for the highest returns. Some idea of the extent of global financial flows can be gained by contrasting the *daily* turnover of foreign exchange (approximately $4 trillion) with the *annual* output of all the goods and services produced by people in the UK of $2.15 trillion (Exhibit 2.5). Another effect of technological change is the increased mobility of activities within firms. For example, banks have transferred a high proportion of their operations to India, as have insurance companies and other financial firms.

Another feature of recent years has been the development of **disintermediation** – in other words, cutting out the middleman. So, for instance, firms wishing to borrow can bypass the banks and obtain debt finance directly by selling debt securities in the market. The purchasers can be individuals, but are more usually the large savings institutions such as pension funds, insurance funds and hedge funds. Banks, having lost some interest income from lending to these large firms, have been raising the proportion of their income derived from fees gained by arranging the sale and distribution of these securities as well as **underwriting** their issue (guaranteeing to buy if no one else will). Hedge funds (free

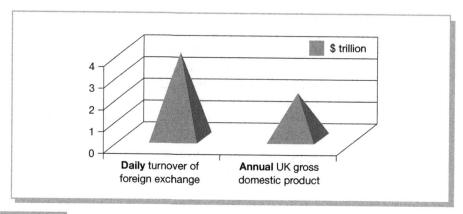

Exhibit 2.5   Daily turnover of foreign exchange v UK GDP

Source: BIS and CIA World Factbook

from most regulatory control) now account for a high proportion of financial market trading whereas they were barely heard of 15 years ago. Private equity funds too, which invest in shares and other securities of companies outside a stock exchange, have grown tremendously over the past 20 years.

The flow of money

A simple way to look at the way money flows between investors and companies is shown in Exhibit 2.6. Households generally place the largest proportion of their savings with financial institutions. These organisations then put that money to work. Some of it is lent back to members of the household sector in the form of, say, a mortgage to purchase a house, or as a personal loan. Some of the money is used to buy securities (e.g. bonds, shares) issued by the business sector. The institutions will expect a return on these loans and shares, which flows back in the form of interest and dividends. However, they are often prepared for businesses to retain profit within the firm for further investment in the hope of greater returns in the future. The government sector enters into the financial system in a number of ways. For example, taxes are taken from individuals and businesses, and secondly governments usually fail to match their revenues with their expenditure and therefore borrow significant sums from the financial institutions, with a need to return that money with interest. The diagram in Exhibit 2.6 remains a gross simplification; it has not allowed for overseas financial transactions, for example, but it does demonstrate a crucial role for financial institutions in an advanced market economy.

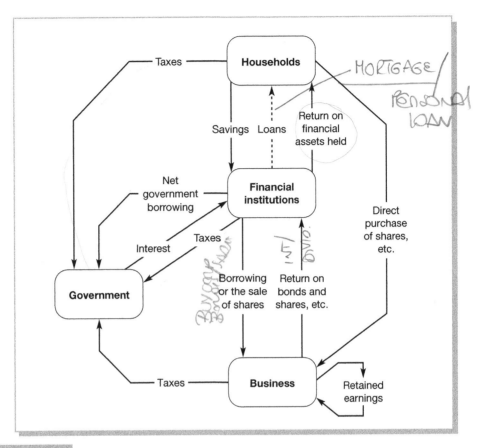

The flow of funds and financial intermediation

Primary investors HIGH LIQUIDITY & LOW RISK

Typically the household sector is in financial surplus. This sector contains the savers of society. It is these individuals who become the main providers of funds used for investment in the business sector. **Primary investors** tend to prefer to exchange their cash for financial assets which (a) allow them to get their money back quickly should they need to with low transaction costs and (b) have a high degree of certainty over the amount they will receive back. In other words, primary investors like high liquidity and low risk. Lending directly to a firm with a project proposal to build a North Sea oil platform which will not be sold until five years have passed is not a high-liquidity and low-risk investment. However, putting money into a sock under the bed is (if we exclude the possibility of the risk of sock theft).

Ultimate borrowers

In our simplified model the **ultimate borrowers** are in the business sector. These firms are trying to maximise the wealth generated by their activities. To do this companies need to invest in capital equipment, in real plant and other assets, often for long periods of time. The firms, in order to serve their social function, need to attract funds for use over many years. Also these funds will be at risk, sometimes very high risk. (Here we are using the term 'borrower' broadly to include all forms of finance, even 'borrowing' by selling shares.)

Conflict of preferences

We have a **conflict of preferences** between the primary investors wanting low-cost liquidity and certainty, and the ultimate borrowers wanting long-term risk-bearing capital. A further complicating factor is that savers usually save on a small scale, £100 here or €200 there, whereas businesses are likely to need large sums of money. Imagine some of the problems that would occur in a society which did not have any financial intermediaries. Here lending and share buying will occur only as a result of direct contact and negotiation between two parties. If there were no organised market where financial securities could be sold on to other investors then the fund provider, once committed, would be trapped in an illiquid investment. Also the costs that the two parties might incur in searching to find each other in the first place might be considerable. Following contact a thorough agreement would need to be drawn up to safeguard the investor, and additional expense would be incurred obtaining information to monitor the firm and its progress. In sum, the obstacles to putting saved funds to productive use would lead many to give up and to retain their cash. Those that do persevere will demand exceptionally high rates of return from the borrowers to compensate them for poor liquidity, risk, search costs, agreement costs and monitoring costs. This will mean that few firms will be able to justify investments because they cannot obtain those high levels of return when the funds are invested in real assets. As a result, few investments take place and the wealth of society fails to grow. Exhibit 2.7 shows (by the top arrow) little money flowing from saving into investment.

The introduction of financial intermediaries

The problem of under-investment can be alleviated greatly by the introduction of financial institutions (e.g. banks) and financial markets (e.g. a stock exchange). Their role is to facilitate the flow of funds from primary investors to ultimate borrowers at a low cost. They do this by solving the conflict of preferences.

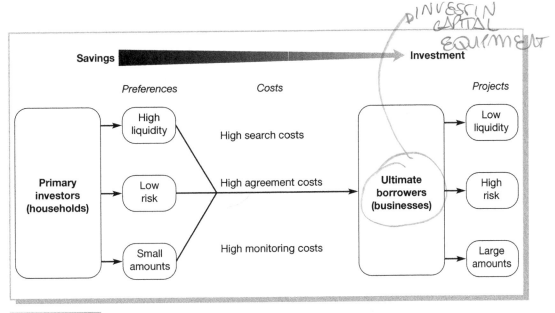

Savings → *Investment*

Preferences · Costs · Projects

∂INVESTIN CAPITAL EQUIPMENT

Primary investors (households) → High liquidity · Low risk · Small amounts

High search costs · High agreement costs · High monitoring costs

Ultimate borrowers (businesses) → Low liquidity · High risk · Large amounts

Exhibit 2.7   Savings into investment in an economy without financial intermediaries

There are two types of financial intermediation; the first is an agency or brokerage type operation which brings together lenders and firms, the second is an asset-transforming type of intermediation, in which the conflict is resolved by the creation of intermediate securities that have the risk, liquidity and volume characteristics which investors prefer. The financial institution raises money by offering these securities for sale, and then uses the acquired funds to purchase primary securities issued by firms.

Brokers

At its simplest an intermediary is a 'go-between', someone who matches up a provider of finance with a user of funds. This type of intermediary is particularly useful for reducing the search costs for both parties. Stockbrokers, for example, make it easy for investors wanting to buy shares in a newly floated company. Brokers may also have some skill at collecting information on a firm and monitoring its activities, saving the investor time. They also act as middlemen when an investor wishes to sell to another, thus enhancing the liquidity of the fund providers. Another example is the Post Office, which enables individuals to lend to the UK government in a convenient and cheap manner by buying National Savings certificates or Premium Bonds.

Asset transformers

In **asset transformation**, intermediaries, by creating a completely new security, the **intermediate security**, increase the opportunities available to savers, encouraging them to invest and thus reducing the cost of finance for the productive sector. The transformation function can act in a number of different ways:

- *Risk transformation.* For example, instead of an individual lending directly to a business with a great idea, such as exploring for oil in the South Atlantic, a bank creates a deposit or current account with relatively low risk for the investor's savings. Lending directly to the firm the saver would demand compensation for the probability of default on the loan and therefore the business would have to pay a very high rate of interest which would inhibit investment. The bank acting as an intermediary creates a special kind of security called a bank account agreement. The bank intermediary then uses the funds attracted by the new financial asset to buy a security issued by the oil company (the **primary security**), allowing the oil company to obtain long-term debt capital. Because of the extra security that a lender has by holding a bank account as a financial asset rather than by making a loan direct to a firm, the lender is prepared to accept a lower rate of interest and the ultimate borrower obtains funds at a relatively low cost. The bank reduces its risk exposure to any one project by diversifying its loan portfolio amongst a number of firms. It can also reduce risk by building up expertise in assessing and monitoring firms and their associated risk. Another example of risk transformation is when unit or investment companies (see later in this chapter) take savers' funds and spread these over a wide range of company shares.

- *Maturity (liquidity) transformation.* The fact that a bank lends long term for a risky venture does not mean that the primary lender is subjected to illiquidity. Liquidity is not a problem because banks maintain sufficient liquid funds to meet their liabilities when they arise. You can walk into a bank and take the money from your account at short notice because the bank, given its size, exploits economies of scale and anticipates that only a small fraction of its customers will withdraw their money on any one day. Banks and building societies play an important role in borrowing 'short' and lending 'long'.

- *Volume transformation.* Many institutions gather small amounts of money from numerous savers and re-package these sums into larger bundles for investment in the business sector. Apart from the banks and building societies, unit trusts are important here. It is uneconomic for an investor with, say,

£50 per month, who wants to invest in shares, to buy small quantities periodically, due to the charges and commissions levied. Unit trusts gather together hundreds of individuals' monthly savings and invest them in a broad range of shares, thereby exploiting economies in transaction costs.

Intermediaries' economies of scale

An intermediary, such as a bank, is able to accept lending to (and investing in shares of) companies at a relatively low rate of return because of the economies of scale enjoyed compared with the primary investor. These economies of scale include:

▪ *Efficiencies in gathering information on the riskiness of lending to a particular firm.* Individuals do not have access to the same data sources or expert analysis.

▪ *Risk spreading.* Intermediaries are able to spread funds across a large number of borrowers and thereby reduce overall risk. Individual investors may be unable to do this.

▪ *Transaction costs.* They are able to reduce the search, agreement and monitoring costs that would be incurred by savers and borrowers in a direct transaction. Banks, for example, are convenient, safe locations with standardised types of securities. Savers do not have to spend time examining the contract they are entering upon when, say, they open a bank account. How many of us read the small print when we opened a bank account?

The reduced information costs, convenience and passed-on benefits from the economies of operating on a large scale mean that primary investors are motivated to place their savings with intermediaries. The effects of the financial intermediaries and markets are shown in Exhibit 2.8 where the flow of funds from savings to investment is increased.

Financial markets

Financial markets exert enormous influence over modern life; every country has some sort of financial market, from Afghanistan to Zimbabwe. A financial market, such as a stock exchange, has two aspects; there is the primary market where funds are raised from investors by the firm, and there is the secondary market in which investors buy and sell securities, such as shares and bonds, between each other. In addition a well-regulated exchange encourages investment by reducing search, agreement and monitoring costs – see Exhibit 2.8.

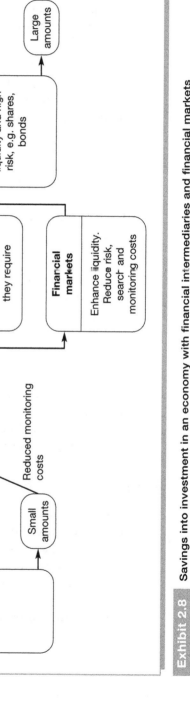

Exhibit 2.8   Savings into investment in an economy with financial intermediaries and financial markets

Primary market

When shares, bonds or other financial instruments are issued for the first time and sold directly to investors (the primary market) the sales are managed by financial institutions such as investment banks that help decide the initial price and oversee its sale to the public. When a company sells its shares on a regulated exchange for the first time, this is known as the **new issue market (NIM)**. The most common issue in the primary market is the **initial public offering (IPO)**. When it is shares that are sold this is known as a **flotation**, where they are offered for sale to the public in new, young companies or well-established private companies, wishing to obtain funding for their company in the form of equity capital. Companies already listed on a stock exchange can also raise capital in this way by issuing, say, a **rights issue** – issuing further shares in their company to their current shareholders. The world's largest IPO was the 2010 floating on the Shanghai and Hong Kong stock markets of the Agricultural Bank of China, which raised $22.1 billion, and generated fees of nearly $250 million for the coordinating group of banks, including Goldman Sachs, Morgan Stanley and Deutsche Bank.

Secondary market

Secondary trading enables the shareholder, bondholder, etc. to liquidate their shares (exchange them for cash) quickly taking a profit (or loss), while the company's holdings of assets are not diminished because it is not forced to pay the security owners for their shares or bonds. The existence of the secondary market is clearly a positive factor for potential investors in a company raising money in the primary market, and so funds are supplied at a lower cost than if there was no secondary market.

Exchange-traded and OTC markets

Exchange trading takes place on the myriad regulated share markets and other security exchanges round the world. There are regulated exchanges in bonds, derivatives, commodities, currencies and other securities. The exchanges create an environment that allows the pricing of securities through the actions of numerous buyers and sellers. The exchanges publish the transacted prices and make them available for wide dissemination. The exchanges are funded by a mixture of commission on trades (maybe 10p per share), admission fees and annual charges for listings, and selling their information to interested parties. All companies listed on share exchanges have to fulfil a number of statutory requirements and make public their financial reports. These rules are enforced by the exchange and other regulators to reassure investors about the quality of the issuer and the financial instrument.

The **over-the-counter (OTC) markets**, also known as the **off-exchange markets**, trade in securities between two parties on a private basis, not on the recognised formal exchanges such as the London Stock Exchange, New York Stock Exchange, etc. The trades can be in shares, bonds, commodities or any other security. A major part of the derivatives market is traded off-exchange, where the flexibility of the OTC market allows the creation of tailor-made derivatives to suit a client's risk situation. Some shares, called unlisted stock, are traded OTC because the company is small and unable to meet stock exchange requirements. OTC trading can be a more risky activity than exchange trading, and there is little transparency in traded prices. For example, bond dealers, who stand ready to buy or to sell company bonds in the secondary market, have the benefit of good knowledge about the trades taking place, but their customers (investors) usually do not know what deals were arranged with other customers, and so do not know if the prices they are paying or receiving are fair.

The financial institutions

To help orientate the reader within the financial system and to carry out more jargon busting, a brief outline of the main financial services sectors and markets is given here. Entire chapters are devoted to them later in the book.

The banking sector

Retail and wholesale banking

Put at its simplest, the **retail banks** take (small) deposits from the public which are re-packaged and lent to businesses and households. They also provide payment services. They are generally engaged in high-volume and low-value business which contrasts with **wholesale** banking which is low volume but each transaction is for a high value. For example, wholesale banks obtain a great deal of the money they use from the sale of financial instruments in values of tens or hundreds of millions of pounds, euros, etc. The distinction between retail and wholesale banks has become blurred over recent years as the large institutions have diversified their operations. The retail banks operate nationwide branch networks and a subset of banks provides a cheque and electronic clearance system – transferring money from one account to another – these are the **clearing banks**. Loans, overdrafts and mortgages are the main forms of retail bank lending. The trend up until 2009 was for retail banks to reduce their reliance on retail deposits and raise more wholesale funds from the financial markets. But this has since been reversed as banks found wholesale funding less reliable than obtaining funds to lend from deposits in current or deposit accounts. Northern Rock is an example of a bank that became over-reliant on wholesale funding. When those short-term loans became due for payment in 2008 it found it could not obtain replacement funding. This caused its collapse.

Investment banks

Investment banks concentrate on dealing with other large organisations, corporations, institutional investors and governments. While they undertake some lending their main focus is on generating fee and commission income by providing advice and facilitating deals. This sphere is dominated by US, Swiss, UK and German banks, see Exhibit 2.9.

Investment bank	Revenue (in $bn)	Net earnings (in $bn)	Assets under management (in $bn)
Goldman Sachs	45.2	13.4	871
JPMorgan Chase	100.4	11.8	1219
Morgan Stanley	24.7	1.7	779
Citigroup	80.3	−1.6	556
Bank of America	121.0	6.3	523
Barclays	31.8	10.3	1379
Credit Suisse	31.0	7.9	384
Deutsche Bank	25.3	4.96	181
UBS	24.0	−1.9	159

Source: Balance sheets of respective banks (2009)

Exhibit 2.9   **List of top investment banks worldwide**

There are five main areas of activity:

1 *Raising external finance for companies.* Providing advice and arranging finance for corporate clients. Sometimes they provide loans themselves, but more often they assist the setting up of a bank syndicate to make a joint loan or make arrangements with other institutions. They will advise and assist a firm issuing a bond; they have expertise in helping firms float their shares on stock exchanges and make rights issues; they may 'underwrite' a bond or share issue (this means that they will buy any part of the issue not taken up by other investors), thus assuring the corporation that it will receive the funds it needs for its investment programme.

2 *Broking and dealing.* Acting as agents for the buying and selling of securities on the financial markets, including shares and bonds. Some also have market-making arms that quote prices they are willing to buy from or sell to, say, a shareholder or a bondholder, thereby assisting the operation of secondary markets. They also trade in the markets on their own account and assist companies with export finance.

3 *Fund (asset) management.* Offering services to rich individuals who lack the time or expertise to deal with their own investment strategies. They also manage unit and investment trusts (see below and Chapter 7) as well as the portfolios of some pension funds and insurance companies. In addition corporations often have short-term cash flows which need managing efficiently (treasury management).

4 *Assistance in corporate restructuring.* Investment banks earn large fees from advising acquirers on mergers and assisting with the merger process. They also gain by helping target firms avoid being taken over too cheaply. Corporate disposal programmes, such as selling off a division, may also need the services of an investment bank.

5 *Assisting risk management using derivatives.* Risk can be reduced through hedging strategies using futures, options, swaps and the like. However, this is a complex area with large room for error and draconian penalties if a mistake is made. The banks may have specialist knowledge to offer in this area.

International banks

There are two main types of international banking:

1 *Foreign banking.* Concerns transactions (lending/borrowing, etc.) carried out in the domestic currency (e.g. euros in France) with non-residents (e.g. a Japanese company raising money in France).

2 *Eurocurrency banking.* Concerns transactions in a currency outside the jurisdiction of the country of that currency, e.g. Japanese yen transactions in Canada are outside of the control of the Japanese authorities. For UK banks and overseas banks operating out of London this involves transactions in a variety of currencies with both residents and non-residents.

There are about 250 non-UK banks operating in London, the most prominent of which are American, German and Japanese. Their initial function was mainly to provide services for their own nationals, for example for export and import trans-actions, but nowadays their main emphasis is in the Eurocurrency market and international securities (shares, bonds, etc.) trading. Often funds are held in the UK for the purpose of trading and speculation on the foreign exchange market.

The mutuals

Building societies are mutual organisations owned by their members. They collect funds from millions of savers by enticing them to put their money in interest-bearing accounts. The vast majority of that deposited money is then lent to people wishing to buy a home – in the form of a mortgage. Thus, they take in short-term deposits (although they also borrow on the wholesale financial markets) and they lend money for long periods, usually for 25 years. The number of building societies has declined with a trend by the biggest societies to move away from mutual status and convert to companies with shareholders, offering general banking services.

Many countries have **savings banks** that, like building societies, do not have outside shareholders, but are 'mutually' owned by their members (which generally means customers). There are also **savings and loans** and **cooperative banks** constituted along similar lines. Some of these have grown very large and now offer a very wide range of services beyond mortgages and the acceptance of deposits.

Finance houses[1]

Finance houses are responsible for the financing of hire-purchase agreements and other instalment credit, for example, leasing. If you buy a large durable good such as a car or a washing machine, you often find that the sales assist-ant also tries to get you interested in taking the item on credit, so you pay for it over a period of, say, three years. It is not (usually) the retailer that provides the finance for the credit. The retailer usually works with a finance house which pays the retailer the full purchase price of the good and therefore becomes the owner. You, the customer, get to use the good, but in return you have to make regular payments to the finance house, including interest. Under a **hire-purchase** agreement, when you have made enough payments you will become

---

[1] The term 'finance house' is also used for broadly-based financial service companies carrying out a wide variety of financial activities from share dealing to corporate broking. However, we will confine the term to instalment credit and related services.

the owner. Under **leasing** the finance house retains ownership. Finance houses also provide **factoring** services – providing cash to firms in return for the right to receive income from the firms' debtors when they pay up. Most of the large finance houses are subsidiaries of the major conglomerate banks.

Long-term savings institutions

Pension funds

Pension funds are set up to provide pensions for members. They usually take a portion (say 6 per cent) of working members' salaries each month and put it into the fund. In addition the employing organisation pays money into the scheme. When a member retires they will receive a pension. Between the time of making a contribution and receiving payments in retirement, which may be decades, the pension trustees oversee the management of the fund. They may place some or all of the fund with specialist investment managers. This is a particularly attractive form of saving because of the generous tax reliefs provided. The long time horizon of the pension business means that large sums are built up and available for investment – currently around £800 billion in the UK funds, for example. Roughly one-half of this money is invested in UK and overseas shares, with some going to buy bonds and other assets such as money market instruments and property.

Insurance funds

Insurance companies engage in two types of activities:

1 *General insurance.* This is insurance against specific contingencies such as fire, theft, accident, generally for a one-year period. The money collected in premiums is mostly held in financial assets that are relatively short term and liquid so that short-term commitments can be met.

2 *Life assurance.* With life insurance your life is insured. If you die your beneficiaries get a payout. **Endowment policies** are more interesting from a financial systems perspective because they act as a savings vehicle as well as cover against death. The monthly premium will be larger but after a number of years have passed the insurance company pays a substantial sum of money even if you are still alive – if premiums have been invested wisely.

   Life assurance companies also provide **annuities**. Here a policyholder pays an initial lump sum and in return receives regular payments in subsequent years. They have also moved into personal pensions in the UK. Life assurance companies have over £900 billion under management.

The risk spreaders

These institutions allow small savers a stake in a large diversified portfolio. Thus investors can contribute a small amount each month to an investment fund alongside thousands of other investors, and then the pooled fund is professionally managed.

Unit trusts

Unit trusts are 'open-ended' funds, which means that the size of the fund and the number of units depends on the amount of money investors put into the fund. If a fund of one million units suddenly doubled in size because of an inflow of investor funds it would become a fund of two million units through the creation and selling of more units. The buying and selling prices of the units are determined by the value of the fund. So if a two-million unit fund is invested in £2 million worth of shares in the UK stock market the value of each unit will be £1. If over a period the value of the shares rises to £3 million, the units will be worth £1.50 each. Unitholders sell units back to the managers of the unit trust if they want to liquidate their holding. The manager would then either sell the units to another investor or sell some of the underlying investments to raise cash to pay the unitholder. The units are usually quoted at two prices depending on whether you are buying (higher) or selling (lower). There is also an ongoing management charge for running the fund.

There is a wide choice of unit trusts specialising in different types of investments ranging from Japanese equities to privatised European companies. Of the £220 billion invested in unit trusts, 50–60 per cent is devoted to UK company securities, with the remainder mostly devoted to overseas company securities. Instruments similar to unit trusts are often called mutual funds in other countries.

Mutual funds

Mutual funds comprise a major portion of the US and Canadian investment market, where the greater part of the population own some mutual fund shares. They are attractive to individual investors because they offer investment diversification and professional fund management. Not many people have the time or expertise to devote to poring over financial statistics in an attempt to pick a good (i.e. profitable) investment. For these people mutual funds provide a satisfactory solution, but they will have to pay charges for investing in a fund.

Investment trusts (investment companies)

Investment trusts differ from unit trusts; they are companies able to issue shares and other securities rather than units. Investors can purchase these securities when the investment company is first launched or purchase shares in the secondary market from other investors. These are known as **closed-end funds** because the company itself is closed to new investors – if you wished to invest your money you would go to an existing investor to buy shares and not buy from the company. Investment companies usually spread their funds across a range of other companies' shares. They are also more inclined to invest in a broader range of assets than unit trusts – even property, or shares not listed on a stock market. Approximately one-half of the money devoted to the 400 or so UK investment companies (£100 billion) is put into UK securities, with the remainder placed in overseas securities. The managers of these funds are able to borrow in order to invest. This has the effect of increasing returns to shareholders when things go well. Correspondingly, if the value of the underlying investments falls, the return to shareholders falls even more, because of the obligation to meet interest charges.

Open-ended investment companies (OEICs)

Open-ended investment companies are hybrid risk-spreading instruments that allow an investment in an open-ended fund. Designed to be more flexible and transparent than either investment trusts or unit trusts, OEICs have just one price and a lower commission and charges. However, as with unit trusts, OEICs can issue more shares, in line with demand from investors, and they can borrow. Investors may invest in one particular OEIC, or in a variety of separate sub-funds under the same management structure.

The risk takers

Private equity funds

These are funds that invest in companies that do not have a stock market trading quote for their shares. The firms are often young and on a rapid growth trajectory, but private equity funds also supply finance to well-established companies. The funds usually buy shares in these companies and occasionally supply debt finance. Frequently the private equity funds are themselves funded by other financial institutions, such as a group of pension funds. Private equity has grown tremendously over the past 20 years to the point where now over one-fifth of non-government UK workers are employed by a firm financed by private equity.

Hedge funds

Hedge funds gather together investors' money and invest it in a wide variety of financial strategies largely outside the control of the regulators, being created either outside the major financial centres or as private investment partnerships. The investors include wealthy individuals as well as institutions, such as pension funds, insurance funds and banks. Being outside normal regulatory control hedge funds are not confined to investing in particular types of security, or to using particular investment methods. For example, they have far more freedom than unit trusts in **going short**, i.e. selling a security first and then buying it later, hopefully at a lower price. They can also borrow many times the size of the fund to punt on a small movement of currency rates, or share movements, orange juice futures or whatever they judge will go up (or go down). If the punt (or rather, a series of punts over the year) goes well the fund managers earn million-pound bonuses (often on the basis of 2 per cent of funds under management fee plus 20 per cent of the profit made for client investors).

Originally, the term 'hedge' made some sense when applied to these funds. They would, through a combination of investments, including derivatives, try to **hedge** (lower or eliminate) risk while seeking a high absolute return (rather than a return relative to an index). Today the word 'hedge' is misapplied to most of these funds because they generally take aggressive bets on the movements of currencies, equities, interest rates, bonds, etc. around the world. For example, one fund, Amaranth, bet on the movement of the price of natural gas, and lost $6 billion in a matter of days. Hedge funds' activities would not be a concern if they had remained a relatively small part of the investment scene. However, today they command enormous power and billions more are being placed in these funds every week. Already over £1,300 billion is invested in these funds. Add to that the borrowed money – sometimes 10 times the fund's base capital – and you can see why they are to be taken very seriously. Up to 50 per cent of the share trades on a typical day in London or New York is said to be due to hedge funds, for example.

Websites

Websites for statistics

www.afme.eu	Association for Financial Markets in Europe
www.abi.org.uk	Association of British Insurers
www.theaic.co.uk	Association of Investment Companies
www.bis.org	Bank for International Settlements
www.bsa.org.uk	Building Societies Association

www.cia.gov	CIA World Factbook
www.cityoflondon.gov.uk	Financial and business information on City of London
www.cmegroup.com	Chicago Mercantile Exchange
www.imf.org	International Monetary Fund
www.londonstockexchange.com	London Stock Exchange
www.oecd.org	Organisation for Economic Co-operation and Development
www.world-exchanges.org	World Federation of Exchanges
www.wto.org	World Trade Organisation

Websites for information

www.aima.org	Alternative Investment Management Association: the hedge fund industry's not-for-profit trade association
www.bvca.co.uk	British Private Equity & Venture Capital Association (BVCA)
www.fla.org.uk	The Finance & Leasing Association
www.ft.com	Financial Times
www.frc.org.uk	Financial Reporting Council: UK accounting regulator
www.ifslearning.ac.uk	Institute of Financial Services
www.investmentfunds.org.uk	Investment Management Association
www.napf.co.uk	National Association of Pension Funds
www.sifma.org	Securities Industry and Financial Markets Association
www.thebanker.com	*The Banker*: provides global financial information

3

Banking: retail and corporate

Banks provide very important services for us. We open bank accounts to deposit money to keep it somewhere safe, perhaps earning interest. That money, once deposited, does not sit in a bank vault – at least not most of it – it is lent out to people wanting to, say, buy a house or set up a business. Thus the money is put to good use and economic benefits flow from that. We also appreciate being able to make payments to others through the banking system.

While deposit facilities, lending and payments are the three core functions of banks they have branched out into a wide range of activities, from assisting with overseas trade to advising companies on interest risk management. When we look at the modern investment bank we see a fantastic array of services that our forebears would not have dreamed of, from acting as prime brokers for hedge funds to trading in commodity derivatives in dozens of currencies.

The term 'bank' has been stretched so we need to be flexible in what we regard as a banking service. In addition to those institutions that have 'bank' in their name such as Bank of Santander or Barclays Bank, this chapter and the next two discuss many other institutions that conduct banking activity, such as building societies and savings and loan associations, collectively known as **depository institutions** or **deposit-taking institutions (DTIs)**.

What is banking?

Banks started out as fairly straightforward businesses, taking in deposits, making loans and providing a payments mechanism. But they grew. They now conduct a much wider range of activities, and it can be difficult to define banking activity in the modern world. Exhibit 3.1 groups the activities into four different types of banking. Some organisations concentrate on providing services in just one, or perhaps two, of the segments, others are **universal banks** offering a full range of banking. This classification is not perfect – there are many banks that do not neatly fit into these groups, and there are other 'banking' activities not listed here

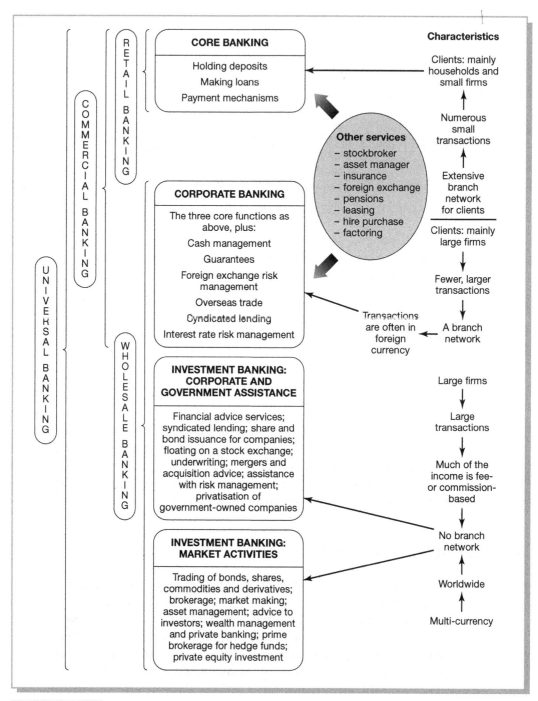

An overview of the different aspects of banking

– but it does allow us some tractability in understanding ˅
This classification will be used to structure this chapter ar

German, French and Japanese banks tend to be univeɪ
wide range of services. The UK has universal banks sι
banks such as Lloyds are not heavily committed to
there remain many smaller banks that concentrate oɪ ˵
US has thousands of small commercial banks often restricted to opⅽ˵
in particular States, and a handful of universal banks, although currently the
breadth of their activities is being curtailed by angry politicians and regulators in
the wake of the financial crisis, which is largely blamed on investment bankers.
We frequently find that banks focus on both retail and wholesale commercial
banking back home in their domestic markets while focusing on wholesale
markets in their international operations. We also find organisations that concentrate exclusively on investment banking (e.g. Goldman Sachs).

Core banking

At the heart of banking is the acceptance of deposits, the making of loans and
enabling customers to make payments. The main source of funds for banks is
deposits as shown in Exhibit 3.2 which provides a very crude breakdown of the
source of funds for banks. The proportions vary from bank to bank depending

	Proportion of assets (%)
Current accounts, also called sight deposits	10–40
Time deposits, also called savings accounts	10–40
Money market borrowing (repos, interbank, certificates of deposit[1])	10–40
Bank capital	8–12

Exhibit 3.2 The typical liabilities of banks – a rough breakdown

[1] Money market instruments are described in Chapter 9.

on whether the bank is purely retail banking-focused or has moved into corporate or investment banking (indeed many investment banks would have no deposits at all). Also some banks deliberately choose to obtain most of their money from deposits whereas others obtain a high proportion from issuing securities on the financial markets in tens or hundreds of millions of pounds, euros, etc., or borrow from other banks in the interbank market.

Banks have to recognise that any money deposited (or lent to them via the issue of a financial market security) will have to be repaid one day; thus deposits and other borrowings are classified as liabilities. If you deposit money in a bank it is an asset for you and part of your wealth because you can withdraw it, but it is an obligation for the bank (when the bank says that you are in credit, it means that you are a creditor – it owes you the money!). We will discuss money market borrowing and bank capital later. For now we will concentrate on deposits.

Current account (cheque (check) account or sight account)

An individual can walk into a bank branch and withdraw the money held in their **current account** at very short notice. Alternatively, they can transfer the money to someone else's account, either using a paper-based method or electronically. These accounts usually pay very low (or no) rates of interest and so are a low-cost source of funds for the bank from that point of view, but the bank will need to spend a considerable amount in processing transfers, monthly statements, providing conveniently located branches, etc. Banks often run current accounts at a loss in order to build up a relationship with a customer so that other services can be sold.

Time or savings deposit accounts

Depositors agree to place money with a bank on the understanding that a set period of notice is required to withdraw cash, ranging from a few days to several months. Alternatively, the customer may place the money in the account for a fixed period. There are usually substantial penalties for early withdrawal and the accounts rarely provide a cheque facility. In return for losing the flexibility to withdraw cash at short notice they offer higher interest rates than current accounts.

Lending

Some bank lending is short-term, such as an overdraft, but most of it is long-term lending – certainly longer than the notice periods on most deposit accounts. Banks have developed techniques to screen and monitor borrowers to reduce risk. They also diversify across a range of borrowers. Loans to individuals and to corporations typically account for 50–70 per cent of a commercial bank's assets. Another 10–35 per cent might be lent out to other banks and institutions in the financial markets on a short-term basis, i.e. money market instruments, loans such as interbank lending or repos (see Chapter 9). Some is likely to be invested in long-term government bonds, company preference shares or other long-term investments, but this is usually below 20 per cent. Somewhere between 1 per cent and 10 per cent of the bank's assets may be in the form of buildings, equipment, software or other assets such as gold.

It is possible for banks to lend out most of the money deposited despite a high proportion of deposits being repayable on demand because depositors usually do not all ask for their money back at the same time. However, just in case they need to meet unexpected large outflows banks hold a fraction of their capital in the form of **liquid reserves**. This is cash (the same as in your wallet or purse) in the vault, at the tills and in ATMs as well as cash deposited at the central bank (banks need bank accounts too) such as the Bank of England, the Federal Reserve in the US or the Bundesbank in Germany. These cash holdings usually account for under 1 per cent of a bank's assets. Funds kept in a highly liquid form (but not cash) may also include assets that can quickly be turned into cash, such as lending to another bank for 24 hours or seven days (interbank lending) or government Treasury bills (lending to a government for, say, three or six months), that can be sold to other investors within minutes in a very active secondary market if money is needed.

Household lending

Consumer loans (personal loans) are often **unsecured**, meaning that nothing is being specially assigned as collateral to be seized by the bank should the borrower fail to pay.[2] In the UK these loans can be up to £25,000 and are usually repayable within five years. The interest rate is usually fixed at a constant percentage of the outstanding amount throughout the period. Loans secured on property, such as a house mortgage, are typically repaid over 20–25 years and carry a lower rate of interest than a consumer loan because of the lower risk for the bank. Banks also lend via credit cards – discussed later.

Lending to businesses

For most companies banks remain the main source of externally (i.e. not retained earnings) raised finance. Total bank lending outstanding to the business sector in the UK is over £500 billion. Spanish companies owe their banks a

---

[2] In the event of default on the loan the bank will still be able to sue the borrower, who might then have to sell assets to repay a loan.

whopping €900 billion – no wonder they ran into serious trouble in 2010 (they had binge borrowed, much of it to build apartments). While the amounts outstanding are similar to those of Germany, France and Italy (see Exhibit 3.3) the Spaniards have a much smaller economy to support their loans.

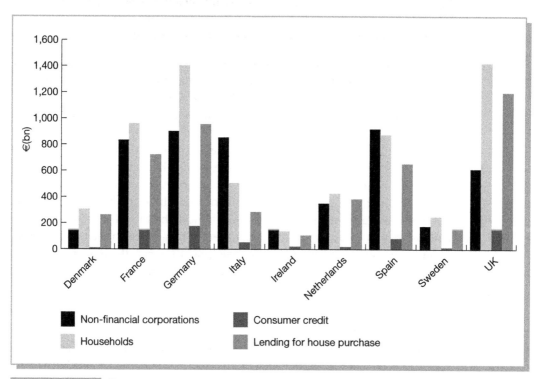

Exhibit 3.3   Lending by financial institutions (mostly banks) in selected European countries to businesses and to households – amounts outstanding 2010 (household lending is further broken down into consumer credit and house mortgages)

Source: European Commission

Banks make it attractive for companies to borrow from them compared with other forms of borrowing:

- *Administrative and legal costs are low.* Because the loan arises from direct negotiation between borrower and lender there is an avoidance of the marketing, arrangement and regulatory expenses involved in, say, a bond issue.

- *Quick.* The key provisions of a bank loan can be worked out speedily and the funding facility can be in place within a matter of hours.

▪ *Flexible.* If the economic circumstances facing the firm should change during the life of the loan banks are generally better equipped – and are more willing – to alter the terms of the lending agreement than bondholders. Negotiating with a single lender in a crisis has distinct advantages. Bank loans are also more flexible in the sense that if the firm does better than originally expected a bank loan can often be repaid without penalty. Contrast this with many bonds with fixed redemption dates, or hire purchase/leasing arrangements with fixed terms.

▪ *Available to small firms.* Bank loans are available to firms of almost any size whereas the bond market is for the big players only.

An **arrangement fee** may be payable by the borrower to the bank at the time of the initial lending, say 1 per cent of the loan, but this is subject to negotiation and may be bargained down. The interest rate can be either fixed (same for the whole borrowing period) or floating (variable). If it is floating then the rate will generally be a certain percentage above the banks' **base rate** or **LIBOR**. LIBOR is the London interbank offered rate, that is, the rate of interest charged when a bank lends to a highly reputable and safe bank in London – see Chapter 9 for more on this. Because the typical borrowing corporation is not as safe as a high-quality bank it will pay, say, 1 per cent (also referred to as 100 **basis points, bps**) more than LIBOR if it is in a good bargaining position. In the case of base rate-related lending the interest payable changes immediately the bank announces a change in its base rate. This moves irregularly in response to financial market conditions, which are heavily influenced by the central bank, say the **Bank of England**, in its attempt to control the economy – see Chapter 6. For customers in a poorer bargaining position offering a higher-risk proposal the rate could be 5 per cent or more over the base rate or LIBOR. The interest rate will be determined not only by the riskiness of the undertaking and the bargaining strength of the customer but also by the degree of security for the loan and the size of loan – economies of scale in lending mean that large borrowers pay a lower interest rate.

A generation ago it would have been more normal to negotiate fixed-rate loans but most loans today are variable rate. If a fixed rate of interest is charged this is generally at a higher rate of interest than the floating rate at the time of arrangement because of the additional risk to the lender of being unable to modify rates as an uncertain future unfolds.

Overdraft

Usually the amount that a depositor can withdraw from a bank account is limited to the amount they put in. However, business and other financial activity often requires some flexibility in this principle, and it is often useful to make an arrangement to take more money out of a bank account than it contains. This is an **overdraft**, a permit to overdraw on an account up to a stated limit.

Overdraft facilities are usually arranged for a period of a few months or a year and interest is charged on the excess drawings. They are popular in Germany and the UK and are frequently used by people and businesses whether by prior arrangement or accidentally (if unauthorised then fees/penalties are charged). In other countries (e.g. France) banks take a very tough line if you try to remove more than what you have deposited in an account, unless you have prior authorisation.

Overdrafts have the following two advantages:

1   *Flexibility*. The borrowing firm (individual) is not asked to forecast the precise amount and duration of its borrowing at the outset but has the flexibility to borrow up to a stated limit. Also the borrower is assured that the moment the funds are no longer required they can be quickly and easily repaid without suffering a penalty.

2   *Cheapness*. Banks usually charge 2–5 percentage points over base rate (or LIBOR) depending on the creditworthiness, security offered and bargaining position of the borrower. There may also be an **arrangement fee** of, say, 1 per cent of the facility, but many banks have dropped arrangement fees completely to attract borrowers. These charges may seem high but it must be borne in mind that overdrafts are often loans to smaller and riskier firms which would otherwise have to pay much more for their funds. Large and well-established borrowers with low financial gearing (low borrowing relative to the amount put in by the business owners) and plenty of collateral can borrow on overdraft at much more advantageous rates. A major saving comes from the fact that the banks charge interest on only the daily outstanding balance. So, if a firm has a large cash inflow one week it can use this to reduce its overdraft, temporarily lowering the interest payable, while retaining the ability to borrow more another week.

A major drawback to an overdraft for the borrower is that the bank retains the right to withdraw the facility at short notice. Thus a heavily indebted firm may receive a letter from the bank insisting that its account be brought to balance within a matter of days. This right lowers the risk to the lender because it can quickly get its money out of a troubled company; this allows it to lower the cost of lending. However, it can be devastating for the borrower and so firms are well advised to think through the use to which finance provided by way of an overdraft is put. It is not usually wise to use the money for an asset which cannot be easily liquidated; for example, it could be problematic if an overdraft is used for a bridge-building project which will take three years to come to fruition.

Term loans

A **term loan** is a business loan with an original maturity of more than one year and a specified schedule of principal and interest payments. These loans are normally for a period of between 3 and 7 years, but the period can range from 1 to 20 years. It may or may not be secured with collateral and has the advantage over the overdraft of not being repayable at the demand of the bank at short notice (if the borrower sticks to the agreement).

The specified terms will include provisions regarding the repayment schedule. In setting up a term loan the bank can be very flexible with regard to the conditions it sets for the borrower. For example, a proportion of the interest and the principal can be repaid monthly, or annually, and can be varied to correspond with the borrower's cash flows. It is rare for there to be no repayment of the principal during the life of the loan but it is possible to request that the bulk of the principal is paid in the later years. It could be disastrous, for instance, for a firm engaging in a project that involved large outlays for the next five years followed by cash inflows thereafter to have a bank loan that required significant interest and principal payments in the near term. If the borrower is to apply the funds to a project that will not generate income for perhaps the first three years it may be possible to arrange a **grace period** or **repayment holiday** during which only the interest is paid, with the capital being paid off once the project has a sufficiently positive cash flow. Other arrangements can be made to reflect the pattern of cash flow of the firm or project: for example a 'balloon' **payment structure** is one when only a small part of the capital is repaid during the main part of the loan period, with the majority repayable as the maturity date approaches. A '**bullet**' repayment arrangement takes this one stage further and provides for all the capital to be repaid at the end of the loan term. Banks generally prefer **self-amortising term loans** with a high proportion of the principal paid off each year. This has the advantage of reducing risk by imposing a programme of debt reduction on the borrowing firm.

Not all term loans are drawn down in a single lump sum at the time of the agreement. In the case of a construction project which needs to keep adding to its borrowing to pay for the different stages of development, an **instalment arrangement** might be required with, say, 25 per cent of the money being made available immediately, 25 per cent at foundation stage and so on. This has the added attraction to the lender of not committing large sums secured against an asset not yet created. From the borrower's point of view a **drawdown arrangement** has an advantage over an overdraft in that the lender is committed to providing the finance if the borrower meets prearranged conditions, whereas with an overdraft the lender can withdraw the arrangement at short notice.

Security for banks on business lending

When banks are considering the provision of debt finance for a firm they will be concerned about the borrower's competence and honesty. They need to evaluate the proposed project and assess the degree of managerial commitment to its success. The firm will have to explain why the funds are needed and provide detailed cash forecasts covering the period of the loan. Between the bank and the firm stands the classic gulf called '**asymmetric information**' in which one party in the negotiation is ignorant of, or cannot observe, some of the information which is essential to the contracting and decision-making process. The bank is unable to assess accurately the ability and determination of the managerial team and will not have a complete understanding of the market environment in which they propose to operate. Companies may overcome bank uncertainty to some degree by providing as much information as possible at the outset and keeping the bank informed of the firm's position as the project progresses.

Bankers encourage the finance director and managing director to consider carefully both the quantity and quality of information flows to the bank. An improved flow of information can lead to a better and more supportive relationship. Firms with significant bank financing requirements to fund growth will be well advised to cultivate and strengthen understanding and rapport with their bank(s). The time to lay the foundations for subsequent borrowing is when the business does not need the money, so that when loans are required there is a reasonable chance of being able to borrow the amount needed on acceptable terms.

There are two types of interaction a company might have with a bank. The first is **relationship banking** in which there is an understanding on both sides that there will be a long-term relationship in which the company provides information regularly to the bank and the bank can reduce its screening and monitoring costs compared with those for new customers. Over time, the bank develops special knowledge of the firm and its needs and as a result is more supportive when borrowing or forbearance in hard times is needed. The other type is **transactional banking** in which the company shops around for services looking for the lowest cost for individual tasks. This has the advantage of obtaining individual services cheap but the absence of a long-term relationship can make the firm vulnerable in tough times.

Another way for a bank to reduce its risk is for the firm to offer sufficient **collateral** for the loan. Collateral provides a means of recovering all or the majority of the bank's investment should the firm fail to repay as promised. If the firm is unable to meet its loan obligations then holders of **fixed-charge** collateral can seize the specific asset used to back the loan. With a **floating charge** the legal right to seize assets 'floats' over the general assets of the firm so they can be bought and sold or rented without specific permission from the lender. The charge only crystallises at the point of default on the loan – the assets are frozen within the firm and made available to repay lenders. On liquidation, the proceeds from selling assets will go first to the secured loan holders, including floating-charge bank lenders. Bankers may look at a firm on two levels. First, they might consider a **liquidation analysis** in which they think about their position in a scenario of business failure. Second, they will look at a firm on the assumption that it is a **going concern**, where cash flows rather than assets become more important.

Collateral can include stocks (inventories) of unsold goods, debtors and equipment as well as land, buildings and marketable investments such as shares in other companies. In theory banks often have this strong right to seize assets or begin proceedings to liquidate. In practice they are reluctant to use these powers because such draconian action can bring adverse publicity. They are careful to create a margin for error in the assignment of sufficient collateral to cover the loan because, in the event of default, assigned assets usually command a much lower price than their value to the company as a going concern. A quick sale at auction produces bargains for the buyers of liquidated assets and usually little for the creditors. Instead of rushing to force a firm to liquidate banks will often try to **reschedule** or **restructure** the finance of the business (e.g. grant a longer period to pay).

Another safety feature applied by banks is the requirement that the borrowing firm abides by a number of **loan covenants** which place restrictions on managerial action until the debt has been repaid in full. Some examples are:

■ *Limits on further debt issuance*. If lenders provide finance to a firm they do so on certain assumptions concerning the riskiness of the capital structure. They will want to ensure that the loan does not become more risky due to the firm taking on a much greater debt burden relative to its equity base, so they limit the amount and type of further debt issues – particularly debt which is higher ranking (**senior debt**) for interest payments and for a liquidation payment. **Subordinated debt** – with low ranking on liquidation – is more likely to be acceptable.

■ *Dividend level*. Lenders are opposed to money being brought into the firm by borrowing at one end, while being taken away by shareholders at the other. An excessive withdrawal of shareholder funds may unbalance the financial structure and weaken future cash flows.

■ *Limits on the disposal of assets*. The retention of certain assets, for example property and land, may be essential to reduce the lender's risk.

■ *Financial ratios.* A typical covenant here concerns the **interest cover**, for example: 'The annual pre-interest pre-tax profit will remain four times as great as the overall annual interest charge.' Other restrictions might be placed on working capital ratio levels, and the debt to net assets ratio. If these financial ratio limits are breached or interest and capital are not paid on the due date the bank has a right of termination, in which case it could decide not to make any more funds available, or, in extreme cases, insist on the repayment of funds already lent.

While covenants cannot provide completely risk-free lending they can influence the behaviour of the management team so as to reduce the risk of default. The lender's risk can be further reduced by obtaining guarantees from third parties that the loan will be repaid. The guarantor is typically the parent company of the issuer.

Finally, lenders can turn to the directors of the firm to provide additional security. They might be asked to sign **personal guarantees** that the firm will not default. Personal assets (such as homes) may be used as collateral. This erodes the principle of limited liability status and is likely to inhibit risk-taking productive activity. However, for many smaller firms it may be the only way of securing a loan and at least it demonstrates the commitment of the director to the success of the enterprise.[3]

There are two other factors on the minds of lending officers at banks:

1 *Creditworthiness.* This goes beyond examining projected future cash flows and asset backing and considers important factors such as the character and talents of the individuals leading the organisation.

2 *The amount that the borrower is prepared to put into the project or activity,* relative to that asked from the bank. If the borrower does not show commitment by putting their own money into a scheme then banks can get nervous and stand-offish.

Payment mechanisms

Banks facilitate payments between people and organisations using either paper or electronic means:

---

[3] Indeed, when the author recently contacted a number of banks to negotiate a loan for a company he controls, the corporate loan officers were all amazed at his cheek in not accepting a personal guarantee clause: 'but we normally get a personal guarantee, it is just standard practice,' they declared. Don't accept this line if you have a strong business plan and strong financial structure.

▪ *Cheque*. While still a popular means of settling indebtedness the cheque is increasingly giving way to direct debits, credit and debit cards. Already card transactions outnumber cheques by a large margin in many countries (e.g. by four to one in the UK). A number of banks are hoping to phase out this relatively expensive means of transferring money; but there is resistance from many small businesses and consumers who do not have access to a viable alternative to cheques.

▪ *Giro*. Even before the electronic age people without chequebooks could still transfer money to others by using a giro slip that instructs their bank to pay, say, the electricity company. This remains a popular means of payment to this day in Germany, The Netherlands, Austria and Japan. Giro banks were set up in many European countries using their post offices to allow those without a bank account, let alone a chequebook, to make payments. The bill could be paid at the post office counter and the money transferred to the payee. Post offices can be surprisingly big players in the financial system. Indeed, the largest deposit-taking institution in the world is not a bank but the Japanese post office. It holds around £2,000 billion in savings accounts (one-quarter of all Japanese household assets) and has bought one-fifth of all the Japanese government bonds in issue, and that is a lot of bonds given that the Japanese government has outstanding borrowings of 200 per cent of annual gross domestic product (GDP).

▪ *Standing orders and direct debits*. These are used for recurring payments. With standing orders the account holder instructs their bank to pay a fixed regular amount to a beneficiary's account. It is only the account holder who can change the order instructions. Direct debits are similar to standing orders except that the supplier of a good or service which is due to be paid (e.g. a gas or water company) gets the customer to sign the direct debit that allows the supplier to vary the amount and time of payment.

▪ *Plastic cards*. We have got so used to transferring money using plastic that it no longer seems remarkable. A bank card allows us to use ubiquitous ATMs providing a quick way of obtaining cash, checking balances or other services. The **debit card** (usually the same card as the ATM-enabled card) allows us to make payments by providing the information the retailer needs to set up what is in effect an electronic cheque to credit the retailer's account while debiting our account. Retailers use an **EFTPOS (Electronic Funds Transfer at Point of Sale)** terminal to initiate the debiting of our accounts. EFTPOS are even more numerous than ATMs. **Credit cards** allow users to pay for goods, wait for a statement of indebtedness to the credit card company, and then decide whether to pay off the whole amount outstanding that month or pay only, say, 5 per cent of the debt owed and borrow the rest until they are in a better position to pay back. They are allowed a fixed maximum borrowing.

The credit card company gains income from charging the retailers (usually 1–3 per cent of the transaction value) as well as charging the user interest if they fail to pay off the full amount outstanding each month. The rates on money borrowed this way can be very high. For example, while secured mortgages can be obtained for around 6 per cent per year, credit cards typically charge over 18 per cent. Much of this extra interest is to cover bad debts and fraud. Visa and Mastercard process transactions for the retailer and card issuer. Thousands of commercial organisations, such as high-street retailers, issue their own versions of credit cards, known as **store cards**. The retailer usually lacks the infrastructure to process credit cards and so works with a bank or a specialist organisation. American Express and Diners Club cards are different – they are **charge cards**. Here, the user is expected to pay off the balance every month. **Smart cards (electronic purses, chip cards)** store information on a microchip. This might be an amount of cash (**e-money**) loaded onto it using an ATM, personal computer or telephone download. The retailer is able to take money from the customer's card and load it onto their own, ready for paying into their bank account. To purchase goods on the internet **e-cash** is often used, which is created by setting up an account with a bank that then transfers credits to the user's PC. When the user wants to buy something, cash is taken electronically from the user's PC and transferred to the merchant's computer.

- *Land lines and mobile phones*. Telephone banking has been with us for a long time now. Many banks are principally telephone (with internet) based, e.g. First Direct in the UK, but mostly telephone banking is an extra service available for standard branch-based accounts. Not only is telephone banking available 24 hours per day but transactions such as bill paying can be conducted quickly and loans can be arranged. Banks encourage customers to use telephone banking because the cost of undertaking a transaction can be one-quarter to one-half that of using the branch. In many parts of Africa (e.g. Kenya) people, many of whom do not have bank accounts, are transferring money to each other using mobile phones – for a report on this see http://news.bbc.co.uk/1/hi/8194241.stm. Mobile phone banking, including sophisticated smartphone banking apps, is expected to become very big business over the next decade.

- *Internet*. Millions of people now use internet-based accounts, either as accounts separate from their normal branch-based account (e.g. Security First Network Bank in the US and Egg in the UK) or as an extra facility attached to their usual account. Transaction costs for banks can be a tenth of those for branch-based activity, so expect to see banks promoting greater use of the internet.

Clearing systems

After a cheque (or electronic payment) has been written and handed over to the payee there needs to be a system for transferring the money from one bank account to another. This is **clearing**. Banks within countries came together long ago to work out a way of ensuring accurate and timely settlement of payments. Usually central banks led the process. Those banks linked into the system are referred to as **clearing banks**. These are usually only the large banks with extensive retail banking operations. Smaller banks may make a deal with one of the clearing banks for it to handle its cheque (electronic) clearance. If a cheque or debit card draws money from one account for it to be credited to another person's account at the same bank then the bank will deal with clearing itself. If, however, money needs to be transferred to an account at another bank the cheque will be put through the central clearing system. This is mostly electronic because the cheque has computer readable information such as the branch sort code, account number and cheque number displayed – the amount of money is the missing element that needs to be input. Of course, direct debits, standing orders and other regular payments are already inputted into computer systems to permit electronic clearance.

Corporate banking

There are two categories of bank lending to corporates – uncommitted facilities and committed facilities.

Uncommitted facilities

With an **uncommitted facility** the bank does not enter an agreement that makes it obliged to provide funds at the borrower's request and the facility can be cancelled without notification, and so the borrower may have to repay at short notice. These are usually short-term borrowing arrangements – less than one year. The simplest type is the overdraft which may be a six-month (or annual) arrangement. There may be an expectation on both sides that the overdraft facility will be renewed – **rolled over** or **revolved** – after the six months are up, but the bank has not guaranteed that this will be possible. Indeed, the bank can insist on repayment within the six months.

An **uncommitted line of credit** is an alternative to an overdraft. The borrower can borrow up to a maximum sum for a period of, say, a month or six months, and can repay and borrow again as needed within that time period. The bank is uncommitted because it merely has to make its best efforts to make the sum available and it has the discretion to remove the facility at short notice. The interest rate is often set as a number of basis points over the interbank lending rate, say one month LIBOR.

Banks also lend by signing a document that states that the bank will pay a sum of money at a date some time in future, say in 90 days. The company (the borrower) that requested that the bank draw up the document, called a **banker's accept-ance**, holds it until it needs to borrow. They can do this by selling it at a discount price to the face value (the amount stated to be paid in the future). So, say, the acceptance states that €1 million will be paid to the holder on 1 August. It could be sold to an investor (perhaps another bank) in the discount market for €980,000 on 15 June by the borrower. The borrowing company is obliged to reimburse the bank €1 million (and pay fees) on 1 August; on that date the purchaser of the acceptance credit collects €1 million from the bank that signed the acceptance, making a €20,000 return over six weeks. Chapter 9 discusses banker's acceptances.

Committed facilities

A committed facility is one where the lender enters into an obligation to pro-vide funds upon request by the borrower, provided any agreed conditions and covenants in the loan agreement have been and are being met. With many of these forms of borrowing the borrower pays a commitment fee on the undrawn portion of the committed facility. A term loan is one example of a committed facility; here are some others.

Revolving credit

Revolving credit (revolving credit facility, RCF) allows the borrower to both draw down the loan in tranches and to re-borrow sums repaid within the term of the facility so long as the committed total limit is not breached, usually for between one and five years. The facility does not require the borrower to make a number of fixed payments to the bank (unlike instalment credit, such as hire purchase). This is usually unsecured lending. The borrower makes payments based only on the amount they've actually used or withdrawn, plus interest. The bank is committing some of its assets to providing the facility to the corporation whether or not, in the end, the borrowing is actually needed (it may be termed 'a committed line of credit'). This uses up some of the bank's loan capacity and therefore it demands fees. **Front-end** or **facility fees** are for setting it up and **commitment fees** (say 50 basis points or 0.5 per cent) on the undrawn amount are for providing the option to the borrower while the commitment remains in place. Of course, the borrower will also be charged interest on the amounts drawn under the facility, usually a number of basis points over an interbank rate.

Project finance

A typical project finance deal is created by an industrial corporation providing some equity capital for a separate legal entity (a special purpose vehicle, SPV) to be formed to build and operate a project, for example an oil pipeline or an electricity power plant. The **project finance loans** are then provided as bank loans or through bond issues direct to the separate entity. The significant feature is that the loan returns are tied to the cash flows and fortunes of a particular project rather than being secured against the parent firm's assets. For most ordinary loans the bank looks at the credit standing of the borrower when deciding terms and conditions. For project finance, while the parent company's (or companies') credit standing is a factor, the main focus is on the financial prospects of the project itself.

To make use of project finance the project needs to be easily identifiable and separable from the rest of the company's activities so that its cash flows and assets can offer the lenders some separate security. Project finance has been used across the globe to finance power plants, roads, ports, sewage facilities, telecommunications networks and much more.

Project finance is a form of finance that has grown rapidly over the past 25 years; globally, about £50 billion is lent in this form every year. A major stimulus has been the development of oil prospects. For the UK, the North Sea provided a number of project finance opportunities. Many of the small companies that developed fields and pipelines would not have been able to participate on the strength of their existing cash flows and balance sheets, but they were able to obtain project finance secured on the oil or fees they would later generate.

Syndicate lending

For large loans a single bank may not be able or willing to lend the whole amount. To do so would be to expose the bank to an unacceptable risk of failure on the part of one of its borrowers. Bankers like to spread their lending to gain the risk-reducing benefits of diversification. They prefer to participate in a number of syndicated loans in which a few banks each contribute a portion of the overall loan. So, for a large multinational company loan of, say, £500 million, a single bank may provide £30 million, with perhaps 100 other banks contributing the remainder. The bank originating the loan will usually manage the syndicate and is called the **lead manager** (there might be one or more lead banks or 'arranging' banks). This bank (or these banks) may invite a handful of other banks to co-manage the loan; they then persuade other banks to supply much of the funding. That is, they help the process of forming the syndicate group of banks in the general syndication. The managing bank also underwrites much of the loan while inviting other banks to underwrite the rest – that is, guaranteeing to provide the funds if other banks do not step forward.[4]

Revolving underwriting facility (RUF) and note issuance facility (NIF)

Revolving underwriting facilities (RUF) and note issuance facilities (NIF) were developed as services to large corporations wanting to borrow by selling commercial paper or medium-term notes into the financial markets. The paper and notes are merely legal documents stating that the borrower agrees to pay a sum(s) of money in the future, say three month from now. Thus a company could sell for £1.9 million commercial paper that gave the investor the right to receive £2 million in six months and so the investor gains £100,000 over six months (there is more on commercial paper in Chapter 9 and medium-term notes in Chapter 11).

The largest corporations often expect to be selling a series of different commercial paper issues over the next five years. Instead of handling each individual issue themselves as the need arises they can go to an **arranging bank**, that will, over the five years, approach a panel of other banks to ask them to purchase the debt. The loan obligation can be in a currency that suits the borrower at the time. The borrower can also select the length of life of the paper (say, 14 days or 105 days) and whether it pays fixed or floating interest rates. If there is a time when it is difficult to sell the paper then the borrower can turn to those banks that have signed up to be underwriters of the RUF or NIF to buy the issue. Underwriters take a fee for guaranteeing that someone will buy the issue. Most of the time they do not have to do anything, but occasionally, often when the market is troubled, they have to step in.

Cash management

Corporations with large day-to-day cash flows soon realise that they need to employ efficient systems to ensure that the potential to earn interest on the cash is not lost while also keeping back enough cash in an easily accessible form to support the business. Banks can help with this. They provide daily information on the firm's cheques that have been paid and account balances so that money can be moved out of no-interest accounts if the balance starts to build up. They

---

[4] The term 'mandated lead arranger' or MLA is often used for the managing bank(s). Also 'bookrunner' or 'bookrunner group' indicates those who solicit interest in the loan from lenders and gather offers of support. They gradually 'build a book' – a list of confirmed buyers. They do the syndication.

can be given the task of automatically redirecting money held in a number of accounts at different banks and branches to a few centralised accounts at one branch. They can also provide software to assist firms in handling money in a variety of currencies and investing it short-term.

Guarantees

Banks are sometimes prepared, for a fee, to guarantee that a transaction by a third party will take place or that compensation will be paid if the transaction does not take place. For example, a bank may grant a guarantee to an exporter that an importer will pay for goods supplied. If the importer becomes unable to pay, i.e. does not fulfil its legal obligation, the exporter is protected against that non-compliance as the bank will cover those responsibilities and will pay the exporter in a timely manner, as per the agreement.

Overseas trade

Banks provide various services to assist companies when buying and selling across borders. A **letter of credit** is a promise from a bank that an exporter will be paid after shipping goods to an importer. This reassures the exporter and allows an importer to buy even though they might not be well-known to the exporter. While a letter of credit is similar to a bank guarantee, it differs in that the bank pays out if the transaction proceeds as planned, while a bank guarantee is to make payment if the transaction does *not* go as planned. With a guarantee the issuing bank waits for the buyer to default before paying out. With a letter of credit the obligation to pay is transferred to the bank, which it will do at the contracted time; even if the importer's finances are perfectly healthy and it could pay from its own resources the bank will make the payment. Thus the exporter has much greater reassurance of getting paid because a safe bank has taken on the obligation to pay – the risk of the bank defaulting (credit risk) is much less than an unknown importer in a distant land. Naturally, the bank will expect its client (the importer) to pay it the amount concerned plus some fees and interest to provide this service.

With **forfaiting** a bank will supply cash to an exporter in return for a right to claim the payments for goods or services supplied to an importer, thus the exporter does not have to wait three months or so to receive cash for the export. The bank advances money and gets that back with interest and fees when the importer eventually pays.

Foreign exchange risk management and interest risk management

Companies usually learn through bitter experience that shifts in the exchange rate or in market interest rates can lower profits significantly, sometimes to the point of endangering the firm. There are various risk management tools that a bank can offer a client to mitigate these problems. These usually involve the use of derivatives such as forwards, futures and options. They are considered in Chapters 14, 15 and 16.

Other commercial banking services

Although some banks are State-owned, as in China, or are owned by their customers (e.g. cooperative banks), the majority are run as commercial operations with the profit motive driving them forward. They are keen on finding new sources of revenue and over the past 30 or so years have done remarkably well in using the competitive advantages they possess, such as knowledge of long-standing customers, trust and presence on the high street, to sell an ever widening range of products and services to individuals and businesses. Customers often find when walking into a branch that the original activities of the bank (e.g. paying in money) are demoted to a corner while staff are encouraged to sell other services to customers. A phrase has been coined to describe the shift to a wide ranging operation: **financial supermarkets**.

Stockbroking

In many countries (e.g. the UK) most buying and selling of shares and bonds by retail (individuals) investors takes place using independent stockbrokers as agents, rather than the banks. Having said this, the banks have established impressive stockbroking business since they were permitted to enter the industry following the Big Bang of financial reforms in 1986 (see Chapter 12). In other countries, for example many continental European countries, such as Germany and Switzerland, banks have long dominated the buying and selling of financial securities on behalf of investors.

Asset management

Banks often establish their own range of mutual funds, unit trusts or investment trusts (see Chapter 7) to offer to investors, allowing them to place their money in a wide range of shares or other securities in a portfolio under professional management. The fees on these funds are usually over 1.5 per cent per year and they can generate a lot of money for the bank. Alternatively banks may act as agents for outside fund management groups receiving a commission for sales made. In Spain the banks sell Super Fondos, in France they provide SICAVs, and most of these mutual funds can now be marketed across European borders.

Many commercial banks also have private banking arms to assist wealthy people to manage their money – this is discussed under investment banking (in Chapter 4) – but much private banking is conducted by commercial banks without an investment banking subsidiary.

Custody and safety deposits

Share- and bondowners often do not want to receive and look after certificates of ownership. The banks provide a service of safekeeping and ensure interest or dividends are claimed. They will also notify the owner of annual general meetings of companies, rights issues and other events. The bank is paid a fee for acting as **custodian**. As well as the local retail custodianship there is the big league of **global custodians** (mostly owned by banks) who safeguard the investments of enormous investments funds run by institutional investors – the amounts are measured in billions. In addition to dealing with the technicalities of transfer of ownership of shares and other securities, in a number of countries they collect income, reclaim tax and assist with other aspects of fund administration (see Chapter 7 for more on custodianship).

Banks may also provide safety deposit boxes for people to keep items such as jewellery in a vault.

Insurance and pensions

Most banks in continental Europe also own insurance operations or have a close relationship with an insurance company. The French have coined the term **bancassurance** for the selling of insurance and banking services alongside each other; the Germans have the term **allfinanz**. Banks often know their customers well and can tailor insurance offerings to their needs. For example, if a couple with children take out a mortgage with a bank it is an easy sell to point out the need for life insurance to pay off the mortgage should one of the parents die, and for buildings and contents insurance. Banks are also increasingly selling pension savings schemes to their customers.

Foreign exchange

There is a thriving business in exchanging currency for people going on holiday or for business transactions. Traveller's cheques are also available. See Chapter 16 for a discussion of the foreign exchange markets with banks at their core.

Asset-based lending

Banks also provide finance for individuals or companies obtaining the use of, say, a car, by leasing it or buying it on hire purchase. Factoring involves the lending of money using a company's trade debtors (what its customers still owe) as security. Asset-based lending is discussed under 'Finance houses' in Chapter 5.

How a bank operates

The objective of this section is to show how core banking works. The fundamentals are that a bank starts out with some money put in by its owners to pay for buildings, equipment, etc., and to provide a buffer of resources should the bank run into difficulties. Shareholders' funds, obtained by the selling of shares in the firm, have the advantage that the shareholders do not have the right to withdraw their money from the company – it is **permanent capital** (although they might sell the shares to other investors). As well as paying for the initial set-up with premises, etc., shareholders' capital provides a buffer of capital, acting as a safety margin against the event of a significant number of the loans granted to borrowers going wrong. The buffer is referred to as **capital** and loans made are **assets** of the bank. Deposits (and other loans to the bank) are **liabilities**.

> Total assets = Total liabilities + Capital

In addition to capital being raised at the foundation of the business it can be augmented over the years through the bank making profits for its shareholders and deciding to keep those profits within the business rather than distributing them as dividends. It can also be increased by selling more shares. Exactly how much the buffer of capital should be as a percentage of the assets or liabilities of the bank to provide sufficient safety without being too much of a drag on the bank's profits is a subject of much debate in the financial world. This is especially so in the aftermath of the financial crisis of 2008–10 when many banks were found to have hardly any buffer at all following the writing off of many loans (see Chapter 6 for a discussion of bank safety rules, and Chapter 19 for an outline of the crisis).

A bank is also likely to be concerned about the possibility of a high proportion of the depositors or other lenders to the bank withdrawing their money on a single day; it thus keeps a proportion of the money it raises in the form of cash (or near cash) rather than lending it all, because it does not want to run out if many depositors insist on transferring their money out of the bank (i.e. the bank faces **liquidity risk**, running out of liquid assets).

Let us assume for now that a bank, BarcSan, is required by the central bank (its regulator) to hold 8 per cent of the value of its current account deposits in reserves. These are the regulatory **required reserves**. However, the bank may judge that 8 per cent is not enough and decide to add another 4 per cent of the value of its current account liabilities as **excess reserves**. Reserves consist of both the cash (notes, etc.) that the bank is required to hold in its account with the central bank plus cash (notes, etc.) that it has on its own premises, referred to as **vault cash**. Note that we are referring here to cash reserves and not the capital reserves (the difference between assets and liabilities).

Cash reserves of 12 per cent are unusually high, but useful for illustration. A more normal figure is 1–3 per cent of overall liabilities (not just current account liabilities) held in cash, but another 10 per cent or so might be held in assets that can quickly be converted to cash, such as very short-term loans to other banks, certificates of deposit (see Chapter 9) and government Treasury bills; these are termed near-cash. The term for reserves that include near-cash is 'liquid reserves'.

To understand the working of a bank we will start with a very simple example of a change in the cash held by a bank. Imagine that Mrs Rich deposits £1,000 of cash into her current account at the BarcSan Bank. This has affected the bank's balance sheet. It has an increase of cash (and therefore reserves) of £1,000 and this is an asset of the bank. At the same time it has increased its liabilities because the bank owes Mrs Rich £1,000, which she can withdraw any time. We can illustrate the changes by looking at that part of the balance sheet which deals with this transaction. In the T-account below, the asset (cash) is shown on the left and the increased liability is shown on the right.

BarcSan partial balance sheet

Assets		Liabilities	
Value cash (part of reserves)	£1,000	Current account	£1,000

Thus BarcSan has increased its reserves because it received a deposit. This increase in reserves could also have come about through Mrs Rich paying in a £1,000 cheque drawn on an account at, say, HSBC. When BarcSan receives the cheque it deposits it at the central bank which then collects £1,000 from HSBC's account with the central bank and transfers it to BarcSan's account at the central bank, increasing its reserves. Remember: cash reserves include those held at the central bank and in the bank vault, tills, ATMs, etc.

Given that BarcSan has required reserves at 8 per cent of current account deposits, following the receipt of £1,000 it has increased assets of £80 in required reserves and £920 in excess reserves.

BarcSan partial balance sheet

Assets		Liabilities	
Required reserves	£80	Current account	£1,000
Excess reserves	£920		

These reserves are not paying any interest to BarcSan. What is even more troubling is that the bank is providing an expensive service to Mrs Rich with bank branch convenience, cheque books, statements, etc. This money has to be put to use – at least as much of it as is prudent. One way of making a profit is to lend most of the money. It does this by lending to a business for five years. Thus the bank borrows on a short-term basis (instant access for Mrs Rich) and lends long (five-year term loan). The bank decides to lend £880 because this would allow it to maintain its required reserve ratio of 8 per cent and its target excess reserve of 4 per cent.

BarcSan partial balance sheet

Assets		Liabilities	
Required reserves	£80	Current account	£1,000
Excess reserves	£40		
Loan	£880		

A bank has to keep enough cash on hand to satisfy current account holders and other customers withdrawing money from their accounts. There may be times when a large volume of cash is withdrawn and the bank has to be ready for that – this is what we refer to as **liquidity management**. A bank also needs to lend its money (acquire assets) with the expectation of a low risk of default and in a diversified manner – that is, it must have good **asset management** skills. Third, it must be capable of finding funds at low cost and risk – good **liability management**. Finally, it must keep its capital at a high enough level to reduce the chance of **insolvency** problems (assets worth less than liabilities) while balancing the need to make profits by lending – this is **capital adequacy management**. We will now explore these four tasks for bank managers.

Liquidity management and reserves

Let us look at the (simplified) balance sheet for BarcSan as a whole, all its assets and all its liabilities. We will assume that all deposits are current account deposits and so it keeps 8 per cent of those as required reserves and aims to have a further 4 per cent as excess reserves (either at the central bank or as vault cash). As well as £10 billion in deposits the bank has £900 million in capital accumulated mostly through retaining past profits. It has lent £5.7 billion and bought £3.1 billion of marketable securities such as government bonds and bills.

BarcSan's balance sheet			
Assets		*Liabilities*	
Required reserves	£800m	Deposits	£10,000m
Excess reserves	£1,300m	Bank capital	£900m
Loan	£5,700m		
Securities	£3,100m		

To satisfy its own rule of 12 per cent of current account deposits held as reserves it needs only £1.2 billion but it currently has £2.1 billion (£800 million + £1,300 million). It has a 'spare' £900 million. If there is a sudden rise in withdrawals from bank accounts as people worry about the bank system collapsing and banks not being able to repay their deposit liabilities (as with Northern Rock in 2007) this will have an impact on BarcSan. If £900 million of cash is withdrawn from BarcSan its balance sheet changes to:

BarcSan's balance sheet after a sudden withdrawal of £900 million

Assets		Liabilities	
Required reserves	£728m	Deposits	£9,100m
Excess reserves	£472m	Bank capital	£900m
Loan	£5,700m		
Securities	£3,100m		

The bank still has cash reserves above its target because 12 per cent of £9,100 million is £1,092 million,[5] whereas the bank has £1,200 million. Because it started with plentiful reserves the public panic to withdraw funds has not affected the other elements in BarcSan's balance sheet.

Now take a different case, where BarcSan has already lent out any reserves above its prudential level of 12 per cent of deposits.

BarcSan's balance sheet if actual reserves equal target reserves

Assets		Liabilities	
Required reserves	£800m	Deposits	£10,000m
Excess reserves	£400m	Bank capital	£900m
Loan	£6,600m		
Securities	£3,100m		

Now imagine a financial panic: many depositors rush to the bank's branches to take out their money. In one day £900 million is withdrawn. At the end of the day the balance sheet is looking far from healthy.

[5] Made up of 8 per cent of £9,100 million = £728 million, and 4 per cent of £9,100 million = £364 million.

BarcSan's balance sheet after £900 million is withdrawn (after the bank just met its reserve target)			
Assets		*Liabilities*	
Required reserves	£300m	Deposits	£9,100m
Excess reserves	£0m	Bank capital	£900m
Loan	£6,600m		
Securities	£3,100m		

Another day like that and it might be wiped out. It is required to hold 8 per cent of £9,100 million, £728 million as reserves, but now has only £300 million. Where is it going to get the shortfall from? There are four possibilities.

1 *Borrowing from the central bank.* One of the major duties of a central bank is to act as lender of last resort. It stands ready to lend to banks that lack cash reserves (there is more on this in Chapter 6). However, it will do this at a high price only (high interest rate) to deter banks from calling on it in trivial circumstances. If BarcSan borrows the £428 million shortfall from the central bank it can return to the regulator's minimum of 8 per cent.

2 *Securities could be sold.* Of the securities bought by a bank most are traded in very active markets where it is possible to sell a large quantity without moving the price. Let us assume that the bank sells £428 million of government Treasury bills and bonds to move its reserves back to 8 per cent of deposits. Of course, there are a few more moves that need to be made if the bank wants to reach its target of 12 per cent reserves, but after such a crisis in the financial markets this may take a few years to achieve.

3 *Borrow from other banks and other organisations.* There is an active market in interbank loans as well as banks borrowing by selling commercial paper to corporations and other institutions. Perhaps BarcSan could borrow the £428 million it needs here. Indeed, interbank borrowing is usually the first port of call for banks needing short-term cash. However, given that the cause of the crisis was a system-wide loss of confidence BarcSan may have difficulty raising money in these markets at this time. This was a problem that beset many banks in 2008. They had grown used to quickly obtaining cash to cover shortfalls from other banks. But in the calamitous loss of confidence following the sub-prime debacle, banks simply stopped lending to each other – those that were caught with insufficient reserves failed or were bailed out by

governments. A freeze in the interbank loan market was experienced by many European banks in 2011 as potential lenders feared they might not be repaid.

4 *Reducing its loans*. Banks receive principal repayments on loans every day as the periods of various loan agreements come to an end, or as portions of loans are repaid during the term of the loan. To raise some money the bank could simply refuse any more loans for a period. I was on the sharp end of this in February 2007 when trying to complete a business property deal. Suddenly Halifax Bank of Scotland refused to lend on what was a pretty safe deal for them. I was nonplussed. What were they playing at? Didn't they know they would lose my company as a customer? Of course, with hindsight we all know that this was the start of the crisis when HBOS was desperately short of cash (it only avoided complete annihilation by allowing itself to be bought by Lloyds). Another possibility is to sell off some of its loan book to another bank – but the purchasers are unlikely to pay full value, especially in uncertain times. An even more drastic solution is to insist that borrowers repay their loans immediately. This is possible with some types of loans such as overdrafts but it results in much resentment and damage to long-term relationships.

A bank has a trade-off to manage. If it ties up a very high proportion of its money in reserves it loses the opportunity to lend that money to gain a return, but the managers can feel very safe, as they are unlikely to run out of cash. On the other hand, if it goes for maximum interest by lending the vast majority of the money deposited it could run out of cash. Thus it has to have enough reserves to avoid one or more of the following costly actions to raising money quickly: (a) borrowing from the central bank; (b) selling securities; (c) borrowing from other banks; or (d) reducing its loans. Excess reserves provide insurance against incurring liquidity problems due to deposit outflows, but like all insurance it comes at a high price.

Asset and liability management

In managing the bank's assets the senior team must balance out the three factors shown in Exhibit 3.4 to try to maximise shareholder returns in the long run. The highest returns usually come from tying up bank money in long-term loans and securities where it is difficult and/or costly to release the money quickly. Also, higher returns are usually associated with higher risk taking by the bank. However, within those generalisations it makes sense for bank loan officers to search for potential borrowers who are least likely to default and most likely to accept a high interest charge. The skill in asset management comes from assessing who is a good credit risk and who isn't. Banks generally like to take a very low-risk approach and anticipate that only around 1 per cent of their loans

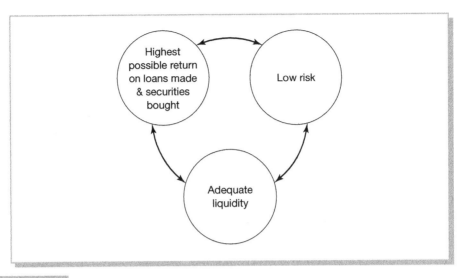

Exhibit 3.4   **The three objectives to be traded off in asset management**

will go bad. However, they occasionally engage in riskier prospects. When they do, they charge a higher interest rate to compensate for the expectation that a higher proportion of these loans will default.

A crucial aspect of asset management is to be diversified so that no one loan or no one category of loans (say, property-related, or retail-related) or securities dominates the portfolio.

Liability management is focused on the judgements made about the composition of liabilities as well as the adjusting of interest rates offered to lenders to the bank to obtain the target mix of borrowing. Banks are generally advised to be diversified in terms of where they obtain money from. Many banks (e.g. Northern Rock) found in 2007 and 2008 that they had become over-reliant on obtaining funding from the wholesale markets (selling bonds, commercial paper or borrowing from other banks, for example) and not enough of their money came from ordinary depositors with current or time deposits. A balance needs to be struck. Retail depositors tend to be more reliable in leaving their money with a bank, whereas lenders in the wholesale markets move money from place to place quickly if there is any sign of trouble or slightly lower rates of return are offered. On the other hand, wholesale money can allow a bank to grow its balance sheet rapidly, whereas it takes time to attract deposits – all those advertisements, high street branches, teaser interest rates, etc.

Capital adequacy management

How much capital should the bank hold? In deciding this managers need to trade off the risk of bank failure by not being able to satisfy its creditors (depositors, wholesale market lenders, etc.) against the attraction of increasing the return to the bank's owners by having as little capital as possible relative to the asset base. The fear here is of insolvency – an inability to repay obligations over the longer course of events – rather than illiquidity, which is insufficient liquid assets to repay obligations falling due if there is a sudden outflow of cash (e.g. large depositor withdrawals on a particular day, borrowers defaulting, unexpectedly high levels of drawing down on lines of credit, or large payments under derivative deals). Another consideration is the minimum capital rules imposed by the regulators to prevent peril to the financial system (discussed in Chapter 6). To understand the difficulty with this trade-off we can compare BarcSan's situation with a less well-capitalised bank, Mercurial.

BarcSan's opening balance sheet

Assets		Liabilities	
Required reserves	£800m	Deposits	£10,000m
Excess reserves	£1,300m	Bank capital	£900m
Loans	£5,700m		
Securities	£3,100m		

BancSan's capital to assets ratio is £900 million/£10,900 million = 8.3 per cent. Mercurial has exactly the same assets as BarcSan, but it has only £400 million in capital. It has raised an extra £500 million from deposits. Its ratio of capital to assets is 3.7 per cent (£400 million/£10,900 million).

Mercurial's balance sheet

Assets		Liabilities	
Required reserves	£800m	Deposits	£10,500m
Excess reserves	£1,300m	Bank capital	£400m
Loans	£5,700m		
Securities	£3,100m		

Now consider what happens if we assume a situation similar to that in 2008. Both banks have invested £500 million in bonds which are backed by US sub-prime mortgages. These now become worthless as house owners stop paying their mortgages. BarcSan can withstand the loss in assets because it maintained a conservative stance on its capital ratio.

BarcSan's balance sheet after £500 million losses on sub-prime mortgages

Assets		Liabilities	
Required reserves	£800m	Deposits	£10,000m
Excess reserves	£1,300m	Bank capital	£400m
Loans	£5,700m		
Securities	£2,600m		

It's capital-to-assets ratio has fallen to a less conservative 3.8 per cent (£400 million/£10,400 million), but this is a level that still affords some sense of safety for its providers of funds. Mercurial on the other hand is insolvent. Its assets of £10,400 million are less than the amount owed to depositors.

Mercurial's balance sheet after £500 million losses on sub-prime mortgages

Assets		Liabilities	
Required reserves	£800m	Deposits	£10,500m
Excess reserves	£1,300m	Bank capital	–£100m
Loans	£5,700m		
Securities	£2,600m		

One possible course of action is to write to all its depositors to tell them that it cannot repay the full amount that was deposited with the bank. They might panic, rushing to the branch to obtain what they are owed in full. More likely the regulator will step in to close or rescue the bank. Occasionally the central bank organises a rescue by a group of other banks – they, too, have an interest in maintaining confidence in the banking system.

In 2009 Royal Bank of Scotland and Lloyds Banking Group, following the sudden destruction of balance sheet reserves when the value of their loans and many securities turned out to be much less than what was shown on the balance sheet, were rescued by the UK government which injected money into them by buying billions of new shares. This was enough new capital to save them from destruction but the banks are still clawing their way back to health by holding on to any profits they make to rebuild capital reserves. In 2010 there were liquidity and solvency fears for the Kabul Bank – see Exhibit 3.5.

Afghan savers lay siege to Kabul Bank

By James Fontanella-Khan

Crowds of people queued outside Kabul Bank's main branch yesterday seeking to withdraw their deposits as fears grew that the bank was heading for insolvency, **writes James Fontanella-Khan and agencies.**

Two of the bank's executives resigned on Wednesday amid corruption allegations, and media reports claimed the bank was on the verge of a meltdown because of the mismanagement of funds, including giving unrecorded loans to allies of Hamid Karzai, the Afghan president.

"I have $15,000 deposited and now they are telling me they are out of money, and I was able to take only $1,000," Haji Tamim Sohraby, 24, said.

A run on the bank, which is partly owned by Mr Karzai's brother, would have wide political repercussions because it handles the salaries of civil servants, including teachers and soldiers.

Omar Zakhilwal, the finance minister said. "The government of Afghanistan guarantees every penny... deposited will be paid back if [people] request it."

Source: Financial Times, 3 September 2010, p. 7

Exhibit 3.5   Afghan savers lay siege to Kabul Bank

Why might banks sail close to the wind in aiming at a very low capital-to-assets ratio?

The motivation to lower the capital-to-assets ratio is to boost the returns to shareholders. To illustrate: imagine both banks make profits after deduction of tax of £150 million per year and we can ignore extraordinary losses such as the sub-prime fiasco. A key measure of profitability is **return on assets (ROA).**

$$ROA = \frac{\text{Net profit after tax}}{\text{Total assets}}$$

Given that both firms (in normal conditions) have the same profits and the same assets we have a ROA of £150 million/£10,900 = 1.38%.[6] This is a useful measure of bank efficiency in terms of how much profit is generated per pound of assets.

However, what shareholders are really interested in is the return for each pound that *they* place in the business. Assuming that the capital figures in the balance sheet are all provided by ordinary shareholders then the **return on equity (ROE)** is:

$$ROE = \frac{\text{Net profit after tax}}{\text{Equity capital}}$$

$$\text{For BarcSan: ROE} = \frac{£150m}{£900m} = 16.7\%$$

$$\text{For Mercurial: ROE} = \frac{£150m}{£400m} = 37.5\%$$

Mercurial appears to be super-profitable, simply because it obtained such a small proportion of its funds from shareholders. Many conservatively-run banks were quizzed by their shareholders in the mid-noughties on why their returns to equity were low compared with other banks, and 'couldn't they just push up returns with a little less caution on the capital ratio?' Many were tempted to follow the crowd in the good times only to suffer very badly when bank capital levels were exposed as far too daring. You can understand the temptation, and that is why regulation is needed to insist on minimum levels of capital – this is discussed in Chapter 6.

Central banks can use the level of reserves held by banks to control the amount of lending going on in an economy. If the central bank insists that banks hold more in reserves then there is less cash available to offer potential borrowers. China's central bank used this tool in 2011 to try to reduce economic activity and the threat of rising inflation – see Exhibit 3.6.

---

[6] This is at the top end of the usual range of ROAs for commercial banks.

China tightens liquidity to tackle inflation

By Leslie Hook in Beijing, and Chris Giles and Robin Harding in Washington

China raised banks' reserve ratio requirements on Sunday, the fourth time this year that Beijing has used this tool to tighten liquidity.

The move underscores Beijing's commitment to monetary tightening at a time when other economies, including the European Central Bank, are also beginning monetary tightening.

China's central bank said it was raising the reserves that commercial banks must deposit with the central bank to 20.5 per cent, an increase of 50 basis points.

Source: Financial Times, 8 April 2011, p. 5

Exhibit 3.6   China tightens liquidity to tackle inflation

Websites

www.ukpayments.org.uk	Association for Payment Clearing (APACS)
www.bacs.co.uk	Bacs
www.bankofengland.co.uk	Bank of England
www.bba.org.uk	British Bankers' Association
www.chapsco.co.uk	Clearing House Automated Payment System (CHAPS)
www.chequeandcredit.co.uk	Cheque and Credit Clearing Company (CCCL)
www.chips.org	Clearing House Interbank Payments (CHIPS)
www.ecb.int	European Central Bank
www.frbservices.org/fedwire	Fedwire
www.fsa.gov.uk	Financial Services Authority
www.ft.com	Financial Times
www.swift.com	Society for Worldwide Interbank Financial Telecommunication (SWIFT)
www.paymentscouncil.org.uk	UK Payments Council

Investment banking

Investment banks have become very powerful. The extent of their importance was harshly brought home with the financial crisis of 2008. Even those of us who work in the field of finance had hardly heard of US sub-prime mortgages or the repackaging of these mortgages into bonds issued by investment bankers, let alone the repackaging of the repackaged bonds. And yet all this financial engineering led to a calamity with enormous implications for all of us. The greedy repackaging of financial claims is to look on the dark side of the role of investment banks; their bread and butter jobs are far more down to earth and far more useful. For example, executives go to investment bankers when contemplating a once-in-a-career corporate move, such as buying another company. They lack the knowledge and skill set themselves to be able to cope with the regulations, the raising of finance or the tactics to be employed, so they turn to the specialists at the bank who regularly undertake these tasks for client companies. Another area where executives need specialist help is in raising money by selling bonds or shares. The sums raised can be in the tens or hundreds of millions, and all the details have to be right if investors are to be enticed and the regulators satisfied. Investment bankers also assist companies in managing their risks. For example, they may advise a mining company on the use of derivatives to reduce the risk of commodity prices moving adversely, or interest rates, or currency rates. Then there are their roles in assisting the workings of the financial markets, acting as brokers, market makers and fund managers. The list of people they help is long, despite most of us being unaware of their activities.

The exceptional rewards from investment banking

Investment banks are complex organisations selling a wide range of services as well as trading securities for their own profit. Not all of them are active in the full range discussed below; many are content to specialise in certain services or trading areas. It is also important to note that of the services they offer companies and governments many are regarded as loss-leaders (e.g. analysis of company shares, or even lending by the bank to companies) so that they can engage with potential clients over a long period of time, gain their trust and then offer highly lucrative services when the company makes a major move, such as the takeover of another company. Thus for investment banks to maximise profits they need to be very good at coordinating their various activities so that they can sell a number of different services to a client company or government.

It is people who form relationships rather than organisations, so investment banks have to employ talented employees who can form strong bonds with clients. Such talent is expensive, especially once they have some leverage with their employers because the client executives trust them as individuals, rather than the bank, to help them with, say, a rights issue – there is always the possibility of an investment banker taking their client contact list with them to another employer. This partly explains the high bonus culture at investment banks. And then, on the trading side, the talented individuals who make good bets on the movements of securities, commodities, exchange rates, etc. can also command high bonuses. Investment banks typically put aside around 50 per cent of income for employee compensation (salary plus bonuses, etc.). Just to give you some idea, the average compensation and benefits for each Goldman Sachs employee in 2010 was $430,000, at the investment bank arm of JPMorgan Chase it was $369,651. See Exhibit 4.1 to gain some idea of more general pay in the sector – these are the rates *after* they made a major contribution to the financial crisis! (VP = vice president of a section, MD = managing director of a section – they tend to have a lot of VPs and MDs.) There are now new rules imposed in the major economies limiting the amount that can be taken as cash to less than 30 per cent of the bonus with the rest payable over five years or so in

$'000	Base	Bonus	Total	Change on 2008	Total compensation	
					Global head	Head of Americas
Analyst*	80 to 90	40 to 60	120 to 150	▲ 25%	$7m–$11m	$5m–$7m
Associate*	110 to 120	120 to 140	230 to 260	▲ 25%	▲ 40%	▲ 35%
VP	150 to 200	350 to 500	500 to 700	▲ 35%	Head of Europe	Head of Asia
Director	200 to 250	500 to 700	700 to 950	▲ 30%	$4m–$6m	$3.5m–$4.5m
MD	300 to 400	$1.2m to $1.6m	$1.5m to $2.0m	▲ 35%	▲ 30%	▲ 25%

*1st year

Exhibit 4.1   **Average global investment bank pay, 2009**

Source: Options Group, *Financial Times*, 5 December 2009, p. 3

shares. This is an attempt to align the interests of the bankers with the long-term interests of their shareholders and wider society. It was felt that they had been focusing on short-term gains and taking high risks to do it so that they could get a large bonus – if it all went wrong then the government would bail them out, they reasoned. And anyway, after a year or two of high bonuses they already had the house in Mayfair and a bulging Swiss bank account.

But then there is the question of why investment banks generate such high profits to be able to pay bonuses in the first place. One place to look would be the small number of players in the field with high reputations for handling complex financing and deals – corporate executives are often willing to pay a great deal for what they perceive as the 'best'. On the investing side, when contemplating whether to invest money institutions often look for a big-name investment bank's stamp of approval of a firm issuing new securities (e.g. shares) or committing to a merger deal – the big names will refuse to handle an issue of shares or bonds for a company if there is a real risk of the issue upsetting investors by subsequent underperformance. The industry looks very much like an oligopoly for many areas of activity – for some services there might be only three banks in the world able to offer it. Lord Myners, who had decades of experience in the City before becoming a government minister, is certainly suspicious – see Exhibit 4.2.

Pressure rises for formal bank fees inquiry

By Kate Burgess

Political pressure for a formal inquiry into investment banking fees mounted yesterday as Lord Myners, City minister, said there was clear evidence of restricted competition in the market.

"Certain aspects of investment banking in equity underwriting exhibit features of a semi-oligopolistic market," Lord Myners told the Financial Times.

His comments come less than a week after the Office of Fair Trading revealed it was looking at the fees charged by investment banks to decide whether to launch a formal probe.

Lord Myners told an international audience of shareholders at the International Corporate Governance Network yesterday that he welcomed the OFT's focus on this area.

He criticised institutional investors for complaining about the rising fees but doing "little or nothing about it themselves – they have, for the most part, acquiesced".

He told the FT: "Here is a real opportunity for investment managers to show they are acting on behalf of their clients and launch an inquiry."

The "enormous" fees paid to investment banks for advising companies on deals might be skewing the outcome of takeovers, an ABI letter warned, and acted as a "deadweight cost" on shareholders that could swallow part of savings derived from mergers and acquisitions.

Lord Myners said yesterday it was clear investment banks had profited from raising margins

Exhibit 4.2   Pressure rises for formal bank fees inquiry

on trading and intermediating between companies and investors in capital markets.

"The rents attracted for intermediation appear on the face of it to be high for the value added of the risk taken," he said.

He noted that while banks were charging higher fees for assuring companies that a share issue went well, they have reduced their own risks by advising companies to issue shares at a discount.

Lord Myners said that if shareholders launched their own inquiry into equity underwriting, institutional investors would "head off the charge that some investment managers are unwilling to challenge existing practices or pricing because their relationship with investment banks is too cosy".

Lindsay Tomlinson, chairman of the National Association of Pension Funds, said: "Shareholders are extremely vexed about fees charged by banks for equity issues and mergers and acquisitions, but whether they would set up their own probe is another matter."

Source: Financial Times, 26 March 2010, p. 6

Exhibit 4.2   Continued

Exhibit 4.3 discusses the difficulties of introducing more competition into investment banking. Any new entrant that tried to challenge the current leaders would need large amounts of capital to be able to do the deals that clients expect. They would also need to attract the best employees, those capable of inspiring confidence and maintaining a long-term relationship of trust with corporate executives, offering exceptional expertise. They would need to offer the broad range of services that multinational corporate clients now expect. These barriers to entry are considered so strong that they rarely allow a newcomer to seriously attack the market shares of the leaders.

Outsized risk and regulation inhibit entrants

By Patrick Jenkins, Banking Editor

In all the furore over bankers' bonuses and bulging bank profits in recent months, one big question seems to have been forgotten: why is it that banks make so much money in the first place? Why does a Goldman Sachs rack up a return on equity of 22 per cent, when a BP makes 17 per cent, or a Pfizer makes 12 per cent – especially when so many of the now booming banks were at least partly responsible for the financial crisis? Is there a cartel in investment banking, as the UK's Office of Fair Trading last week implied?

The titans of Wall Street and the City of London have long seemed unassailable, that is for sure. The need for vast amounts of capital, a strong enough brand to attract staff and a compelling enough suite of products and services to draw customers has proved too big an obstacle for all but a tiny clutch of challengers. If Barclays Capital and Deutsche Bank have been winners, their number is dwarfed by the losers. The still-trying category stretches from France (Crédit Agricole, Natixis) to Japan (Nomura, Mizuho).

Rob Shafir, who heads Credit Suisse in the Americas, says: "The barriers to entry have always been

Exhibit 4.3   Outsized risk and regulation inhibit entrants

pretty high. "It takes years to build the technology, the human capital, and make the client investment."

But as politicians and regulators have grown increasingly uneasy with the size and scale of established banks – urging for balance sheets to be shrunk and universal banks to be broken up – surely now is the perfect time for new entrants to triumph.

There is certainly space for more players, bankers admit. Colm Kelleher, co-head of Morgan Stanley's investment banking operations, says: "In the old days, before the financial crisis, there were 14 or 15 firms. Now there are seven or eight. So perversely you've ended up with less competition." The investment banking chief of one European bank agrees. "Our industry is too consolidated, it is frightening," he confesses, before adding gleefully: "[Profit] margins in this business are fantastic."

Sure enough, 2009 was a bumper one for the earnings of investment banks that were not still swamped by the financial crisis. A combination of low interest rates, vanished giants (Lehman and Bear Stearns) and others weakened by toxic asset problems (Citigroup, UBS, Royal Bank of Scotland) left the likes of JPMorgan, Goldman Sachs and BarCap to profit exponentially from inflated margins and booming demand from return-hungry investors.

Yet, according to the consensus views of lawyers, bankers and regulators, no matter how desirable or logical it might be to see stiffer competition, and the break-up of what many see as a global oli-

gopoly, the odds of that happening have ironically widened. It is one of the unintended consequences of the post-crisis world that as regulators seek to make the financial sector safer, they are also insulating it from fresh competition.

One Wall Street chief says: "We'd love to have smarter competitors. But every time they ratchet up the regulations, it gets tougher."

Already regulatory authorities around the world have told banks they need to beef up their holdings of liquid funds, and the international architects of bank supervision, the Basel committee, are drawing up tougher rules governing how much capital must underpin riskier activities.

If analysts are right, the ramp-up in regulation will have an effect on banks' return on equity – cutting it from a range of 15–25 per cent to perhaps 5–15 per cent. But it will make breaking into the industry more demanding.

"The structural barriers are certainly higher than they were," says David Weaver, president of Jefferies International. "But it's not only regulatory capital that has got more demanding. If you're a lender, in these markets, you have to step up and provide capital on your balance sheet – the syndication market just isn't there."

That means life has become harder for smaller operators without the appetite to take outsized risks.

Even HSBC, which boasts one of the most powerful brands internationally, threw in the towel in 2006 and backed away from John Studzinski's aggressive three-year

expansion plan. Executives say it was impossible to compete with rivals that had a greater appetite for risk, particularly when it came to backing transactions with balance-sheet lending, or to break down their historic relationships with clients.

There is plenty of evidence of fresh competition in merger and acquisition advisory work, where virtually the only requirement for starting up in business is a contact book and a decent reputation – hence the profusion of advisory boutiques that spring up every year.

But if a typical company uses three or four advisers on a deal, only one of them would ever be a boutique, mainly because the company is often desperate for the lending capacity that only bulge-bracket banks can provide.

"It's a very, very competitive world out there," says one Wall Street M&A boss. "But there's a finite slice of the pie going to boutiques."

The big hope for those banks outside the bulge bracket is to find profitable niches. HSBC, for example, has retrenched to focus on servicing its core corporate clients, with a bent towards emerging markets.

Sergio Ermotti, head of investment banking at Italy's UniCredit, agrees.

"If you want to be everywhere in Europe, Asia, the US, it's true that the barriers are very high. But our focus is on Europe and there we have big opportunities."

Source: *Financial Times*, 24 March 2010, p. 22

Exhibit 4.3 Continued

Another place to look for an explanation for the exceptional profits is the extent of the variety of tasks undertaken by the banks – perhaps they gain some special advantage in doing so many different things for other traders, for investors or for companies. So, while helping a company issue bonds they might also act as a market maker in the bond market and provide research to clients. They might also be dealing in that company's shares and acting as a broker for its derivatives trades, while selling its commercial paper, managing its foreign exchange deals and buying commodities for it. They might also be running large investment funds for pension funds and other investors. Like spiders at the centre of information webs they can detect movements long before others and are in a position to benefit themselves from that superior knowledge. How much of this 'special knowledge' tips over into conflict of interest territory (or even insider dealing) is difficult for us to know – but some people suspect that quite a lot of it does, see Exhibit 4.4.

Conflicts of interest bubble beneath the surface

Lina Saigol

The vexed question of potential conflicts of interest between investment banks and their corporate clients has been laid bare by Citigroup's role in Terra Firma's £4bn acquisition of EMI.

Citigroup not only served as adviser, lender and broker to EMI, but it was also the sole financier to Terra Firma.

"Citi's increasing involvement with EMI in many areas led to inherent conflicts, set Citi up to broker the private equity deal that is at the heart of this action," Terra Firma's lawsuit claims.

However, by their very nature, integrated investment banks are inherently conflicted.

Their aim is to sell companies as many products and services as possible and package them together to maximise a greater "share of wallet".

By providing companies with multiple products and services – from advising on deals and financing them to hedging the related interest rate and currency exposure, and refinancing the debt when the deal closes – a bank can squeeze substantial fees from just one company.

Terra Firma claims, in its lawsuit, that its relationship with Citi was "highly lucrative" for the bank. Citi not only received £92.5m in fees for its multiple capacities on the EMI deal, but also raked in more than £135m between 2000 and 2007 for providing Terra Firma with advice and/or financing in connection with almost 20 transactions worth $57bn (£35bn).

According to the lawsuit, it seems that some EMI executives were worried that Citi was using the same bankers that had previ-

ously worked on the renegotiation of EMI's credit facilities and as a result had access to confidential EMI information, to also arrange the debt financing package for Terra Firma's acquisition.

This, Terra Firma argues, suggests that Citigroup had more knowledge about EMI than it did, and would have therefore known what the business was valued at. Citi denies this.

Usually, such arrangements do not cause a problem unless a client complains.

In 2006, for example, during Linde's €12bn (£10.8bn) takeover of BOC Group, the UK gases company asked Deutsche to step aside as its broker because of the German bank's multiple roles in the transaction.

Deutsche owned 10 per cent of Linde, was providing it with

▶

Exhibit 4.4   Conflicts of interest bubble beneath the surface

financing and the bank's chief executive, Josef Ackermann, was also a member of Linde's supervisory board. But when a client is not worried about the thorny issues of potential conflicts, the banks can put all their services into play.

That can even involve a bank co-investing alongside their client in a deal – a strategy Terra Firma should be familiar with.

Four years ago, Citigroup not only provided Terra Firma with the equity, mezzanine debt and advisory service to back the £7bn buy-out of Viterra, the real estate arm of Eon, but the US bank invested alongside its client in the deal.

This approach – known as the "triple play" in the industry – works until the banks start competing with their clients for an asset.

The more principal money the banks have to invest, the greater the chances of a conflict, which is what happened at the height of the debt boom.

One of the most controversial examples took place in 2006 when Goldman Sachs, having offered to advise airports operator BAA against a hostile bid from Ferrovial, put together its own bidding consortium for the UK airports operator.

Source: Financial Times, 14 December 2009, p. 21

Exhibit 4.4   Continued

A generation ago we had **merchant banks** operating in the UK and a few other countries, now they have been relabelled as investment banks following the US nomenclature. In modern usage (i.e. US influenced) merchant banking is sometimes used for the subset of investment banking activities concerned with using the bank's capital to facilitate a transaction such as engaging in mergers and acquisitions.

Assets and liabilities

The balance sheet of an investment bank is somewhat different to that of a commercial bank. Investment banks do not (generally) hold retail deposits – unless they are part of a universal bank, of course. Their liabilities come in the form of promises to pay on securities such as bonds or short-term wholesale money market instruments – they would also be using money placed in the company by shareholders (or by partners in a partnership – some investment banks are still partnerships rather than companies). Most of the money lent to investment banks is for repayment at a fixed date in the future and so they are less vulnerable to the risk of unforeseen withdrawals than retail banks: thus they hold little money in a truly liquid form. However, their reliance on wholesale market funding makes them vulnerable to a loss of confidence in the money and bond markets leading to a lenders' strike – the bank may have to pay off old loans as per the original agreement but not be able to replace the money by borrowing again. This happened to a lot of banks in 2008 and 2009. Instead of holding deposits with the central bank, investment banks tend to place cash at the retail banks or buy money market instruments if they have a temporary surplus of cash.

Global investment banks

Bulge bracket investment banks are those that are regarded as the leaders. They are dominant in key activities such as assisting corporations with bond and equity issuance, underwriting and mergers and acquisition, particularly for larger companies. Goldman Sachs and Morgan Stanley Capital are examples of bulge bracket firms. **Global banks** are those active in a number of countries. The US investment banks became very large in the US between the 1930s and 1990s because after the Great Depression US banks could either become commercial banks or investment banks, they could not do both.[1] Investment banks were not allowed to take deposits but they were allowed to assist with the issuance of securities, underwriting, securities dealing and other market-related activities. Commercial banks could take deposits and lend but were restricted in their business activities, in particular they were not to engage in underwriting and trading of securities.[2]

Thus, as corporations grew and realised they needed investment banking-type services they went to the few Wall Street investment banks that dominated the scene. In addition, the US is an economy that is very much oriented to financial markets when it comes to raising finance – much more so than, say, Europe where bank loans and equity investments by banks into companies are much more normal. Thus, the US developed enormous bond markets (corporate, local authority, government) and enormous equity markets; and at the heart of these markets grew a handful of investment banks. As countries around the world reduced the restrictions inhibiting cross-border banking in the past three decades the US investment banks became dominant in many other countries too. They bought up many of the local operators and integrated them into a global operation, leading to more economies of scale and even greater dominance. Having said that, the Americans do not have it all their own way – there are some other large investment banks around: e.g. Barclays ('Bar Cap') of the UK; Credit Suisse of Switzerland; Deutsche Bank of Germany; Nomura and Daiwa Securities of Japan.

There are two main types of investment bank today. Firstly, there are the huge, global banks that perform the wide variety of functions described in this chapter. Secondly, there are much smaller outfits that specialise in particular areas. Thus

---

[1] The Glass-Steagall Act 1933, named after the Congressmen who steered it into US law, was repealed in 1999, but following the 2008 crisis new restrictions are coming into place because the commercial banking arms that provide vital services to society were dragged down to near-bankruptcy due to the 'casino-type' activities of the investment banking wing of the universal banks.

[2] Similar restrictions were placed on Italian and Japanese banks.

you might have a **boutique investment bank** that simply advises companies on financing issues and mergers, but does not raise finance for the firm, or underwrite, or engage in securities trading. Rothschild and Lazard are two of the more established names, which, while not exactly boutique, do have fewer potential conflicts of interest as they concentrate on advice and do not undertake secondary-market trading or many other aspects of the securities business conducted by the global investment banks.

Corporate and government assistance

Advice on financing and raising finance

A corporation reaching the point when it needs to raise capital from outside the firm (i.e. not rely on retained profits) faces a dizzying array of alternative types of finance and ways of raising that finance, from a syndicated bank loan to a bond to selling new shares. Investment banks can advise on the advantages and disadvantages of each and suggest paths to take.

Furthermore the bank often has the knowledge, contacts and reputation to bring a company needing finance to potential investors. They can help price a new issue of bonds or shares, having awareness of market conditions. They can assist in selling those securities, often roping in a number of other financial institutions to have a greater impact in attracting investors. They know the legal and regulatory hurdles that have to be stepped over or manoeuvred around. They will also **underwrite** new security issues – guaranteeing to buy any not purchased by other investors. Just to confuse everybody the Americans commonly refer to the entire process of organising an equity or bond issue on behalf of a firm as 'underwriting' even though true underwriting (the guarantee of a sale) is only a part of it. To confuse even more: the US's (and some other countries') investment bankers describe the process of 'underwriting' shares or bonds as meaning that the investment bank purchases the entire issue at an agreed price and then resells it in the market. In the UK and elsewhere the bank does not usually buy and then sell, but merely insures that it will be sold (if no one else buys then the underwriters will).

Investment banks help with initial public offerings, IPOs (new issues), when a company issues shares on the stock market for the first time. The investment bank will coordinate the whole process, advise on price and try to find buyers for the shares. When underwriting it usually gets other institutions to take most of the underwriting risk for a fee. Total underwriting fees are typically 6–7 per cent in the US and 3–4 per cent in Europe. There is more on IPOs in Chapter 13.

Investment banks also assist with **seasoned equity offerings (SEOs)** – the issue of new shares for a company already listed or publicly traded on the exchange, also called **follow-on offerings**. This may be through a **rights issue** in which the existing shareholders are offered the new shares in proportion to the percentage of the shares issued that each investor already holds, thus an investor that has 4 per cent of the ordinary shares will be offered 4 per cent of the new shares. Again, the investment bank(s) will charge fees for many services, including advice, finding buyers and underwriting. There is a lot more on rights issues and other types of SEOs in Chapter 13.

Corporations are frequently attracted to the idea of raising money by selling a bond; they can often be sold with a lower rate of interest than that charged on a bank loan, and the restrictions placed on managerial action and demand for collateral can be less. Bond issuance, like share issuance, is an infrequent event for the typical firm (or local authority, or some governments) and so the directors are unfamiliar with the rules and regulations, with the process and with the methods of attracting buyers. Investment banks, for a fee, can help in these areas. Also, investment banks have high reputations amongst the investing institutions which buy bonds, thus they have more credibility when it comes to selling securities than would a company doing this on its own. Bond sales are usually underwritten by the bank (and sub-underwriters who work with the bank). Chapters 10 and 11 are devoted to bond markets.

Companies often need to raise short- and medium-term finance through the issue of financial instruments such as commercial paper and medium-term notes: investment banks stand ready to help them – for a fee, of course. There are also many other types of finance investment banks advise on and assist companies with, including project finance, sale and leaseback (in which the firm sells an asset, say a building, and then rents it back so it can continue to use it), preference shares and convertible bonds (see Chapter 11).

The origin of many investment (merchant) banks was as providers of a service to assist overseas trade in the eighteenth and nineteenth centuries. Importers and exporters have always been nervous about trading with each other; goods are sent to a foreign country with a different legal system and payment is made months later. This exposes the exporter to all kinds of risk, from the importer simply not paying to the risk of running out of money before being paid and the risk of currencies moving adversely. One way of reducing risk is for the exporter to get the importer to sign a document guaranteeing that in, say, 90 days it will pay, say, $1 million to the holder of the document. In most cases the exporter does not even have to wait 90 days; it can sell the right to receive $1 million in a discount market (run by investment banks) and then the purchaser of the bill can collect the $1 million – this is the **bill of exchange market**, discussed in Chapter 9. The risk for the importer and for the potential purchaser in the discount market can be lessened even more if the guarantor for the payment is a respected bank; thus a bank '**accepts**' the bill (for a fee) from the importer – bank acceptances are also discussed in Chapter 9.

A number of investment banks were given a big boost hundreds of years ago when governments in Europe were keen to borrow money outside their home territory. The banks organised the borrowing. Still today there are dozens of governments faced with poorly developed domestic capital markets which need to raise funds by selling bonds on the international markets, and they often turn to the investment banks to assist with this – thus they issue **emerging market bonds.**

Here is a point of confusion: in order to distinguish the central activities of financial advice, raising funds for companies and governments and underwriting issues of shares and bonds are sometimes collectively referred to as 'investment banking' within investment banks – they are also referred to as **corporate finance** (in some banks these terms may also encompass mergers, acquisitions and corporate restructuring). But as you can see below there are many other activities within investment banks other than 'investment banking'. I suppose at least it separates some of the core elements focused on helping companies (and governments) from the rest.

Mergers, acquisitions, corporate restructuring

Investment banks often have large departments ready to advise companies contemplating the merger or takeover of another firm. This sort of help can be very lucrative for the bank – it would seem that for once-in-a-blue-moon corporate actions like this directors do not look too carefully at the amount they have to pay for what is supposedly the best advice available. Indeed, the M&A departments of the banks do attract some very able people, but the fees do seem on the high side for hand-holding and guidance. But then, they do offer, besides expertise on, say, takeover regulation and tactics, a recognised 'name' respected by investors should the acquiring company need to raise additional finance through a bond issue or a rights issue. The fees for a bundle of services like this can run into tens of millions – see Exhibit 4.5. For pure advice (without fund raising) the fees for smaller company deals are around 3–4 per cent of the total sale value; for larger deals (billions) they are generally in the range of 0.125 per cent and 0.5 per cent. When you consider that Goldman Sachs and Morgan Stanley each assist over $600 billion of M&A each year even 0.125 per cent in fees amounts to a large income for advice. And they make a lot more on top by raising finance for the deal makers. Other players in this market, usually near the top of the rankings in terms of value

Investors angered as costs soar over $750m

By Lina Saigol, M&A Editor

Prudential risks further enraging its sharholders after incurring costs estimated by bankers of more than $750m (£511m) on its seemingly doomed $35.5bn takeover of AIA.

The British insurer will have to pay AIG a break fee of £153m if it abandons the deal. Bankers said it could also incur costs of about $500m in currency hedging and other financing expenses.

A collapsed deal would also deprive 30 banks of one of the biggest fee-generating opportunities in the City over the past decade at a time when their traditional revenue streams from M&A advisory have dried up.

Estimates from Thomson Reuters and Freeman Consulting suggest the

M&A advisory fees and underwriting fees on the planned £14.5bn ($21.2bn) rights issue would generate about $850m.

That compares with Vodafone's £101bn hostile takeover of Mannesmann in 1999, which produced fees of $283m for the advisers.

More recently, the 16 banks that worked on Royal Bank of Scotland's takeover of ABN Amro took home an estimated $275m in fees.

If Pru's deal succeeds, on the AIA side Citi, Morgan Stanley, Goldman Sachs, Blackstone Group and Deutsche Bank will split about $53m. On the Prudential side, JPMorgan, Credit Suisse, Lazard and Nomura will split about $59m.

The proposed $21.7bn rights offer would generate

about $740m in underwriting fees to lead bookrunners HSBC, Credit Suisse and JPMorgan Cazenove, to be divided among the 30-bank syndicate.

Banks traditionally pay sub-underwriting fees to institutional investors for their help in guaranteeing to take up all new shares issued, ensuring companies receive their money.

Historically, companies paid 2 per cent in underwriting fees, of which banks kept about a quarter.

The Pru was paying banks between 3.5 and 3.75 per cent for underwriting the rights issue, of which 1.75 to 2 per cent would go to the sub-underwriters.

Source: Financial Times, 2 June 2010, p. 21

Exhibit 4.5   Investors angered as costs soar over $750m

---

of mergers advised on, include Credit Suisse, Citigroup, Deutsche Bank, JPMorgan, Lazard, UBS, Barclays and Bank of America Merrill Lynch.

Corporate restructuring comes in many forms, from selling off a subsidiary (a **divestiture**) to assisting a company that has borrowed too much, found itself in difficulties and needs to 'restructure its debt'. This kind of **balance sheet restructuring** usually means the lenders accepting a reduction in their claim on the firm (e.g. a £100 million loan is reduced to £70 million or the interest that is in arrears is written off), an extension of the time period to pay, the acceptance of shares in the company in return for writing off debt or the replacement of one bunch of debt agreements with others more suited to the company's reduced circumstances.

Investment banks can assist with valuation and procedural matters for bolt-on acquisitions, for example, the purchase of a subsidiary from another firm. They might also help with organising an alliance or joint venture of firms or represent the interests of one of the firms in an alliance or joint venture.

Sometimes the chief executive of a corporation announces that they are undertaking 'a strategic review' of the company. This is usually code for 'at the right price we might be in favour of someone buying the company, in the meantime we will try to improve matters'. The review is often assisted/conducted by an investment bank that is likely to receive telephone calls from prospective buyers. Of course, the bankers will have to work out the value of the firm as a revitalised creature and its value to other companies, and will have to polish up their negotiating skills. A confidential memorandum presenting detailed financial information is likely to be prepared for prospective buyers and the bankers may screen enquiries to narrow them down to serious potential owners only.

The corporate finance bankers within investment banks are generally sophisticated, suave communicators who nurture long-term relationships with key executives in the large corporations. These **relationship managers** tend to spend their time visiting chief executives and chief financial officers of companies, either those who already work with the investment bank or prospective clients. They are not trying to push one particular product onto clients, but give advice on the most suitable from across the bank's full range for the client at that stage of its development – offering the right solution at the right time. The very best relationship managers (often the corporate broker in the UK) put the needs of the client first at all times. Over a period of years they develop a good understanding of the client's business strategy and financing needs. They are then in a position to draw on the various product specialists within the bank to put together a suitable package of services. They are focused on a very distant horizon, often providing financial advice without a fee for many years in the hope that when the time is right for the corporation to launch an IPO, an SEO or a merger bid it will pay large fees to the bankers it has trusted for so many years.

The following is a crude stereotyping but contains enough truth to be interesting: the traders within the banks – see below for trading activities – tend to have a different personality and culture and there can be a degree of suspicion and mutual misunderstanding between them and the corporate bankers. Traders are focused on making money over short time periods. Corporate bankers sometimes characterise the traders as pushy and uncouth. On the other hand, the traders often fail to understand the corporate bankers' lack of impatience at making money.

Risk management

The treasury departments of large companies have to deal with significant amounts of temporary cash, and to try to earn a return on this cash for a short period. They also need to manage various risk exposures that the firm has, e.g. the problems that can be caused by shifts in interest rates, commodity prices or foreign exchange rates. Investment banks are able to assist with the investment of temporary cash surpluses and discuss with corporate treasurers the outlook for risk exposures, advising them on how to mitigate risk.

Lending

With a syndicated loan the investment bank may do more than simply advise and arrange the deal; it might participate as a lender. Investment banks may make other loans available to firms. The fact that most investment banks are part of universal banks is used as a competitive weapon – they can use the big bank's enormous balance sheet to offer low-cost loans to help win investment banking business.

Privatisation

The Thatcher government in the 1980s hit upon the idea of selling off state-owned assets such as Rolls-Royce, British Airways and British Gas. The investment banks assisted in this process, advising and organising the sell-offs, and thus built up a specialised knowledge of **privatisation** which they were then able to take to other countries as the idea caught on around the globe. The banks have also helped set up **public-private partnerships (PPPs)** in which governments persuade private firms to build and operate, say, a school or a prison, in return for an income flow in subsequent years.

Market activities

Alongside great skill in assisting companies with primary market issuance of bonds and shares, investment banks have developed experience and superior capability in secondary market dealing for equities, bonds, money market instruments, derivatives, commodities, currencies, etc. They perform one, two or all three of the following roles in market trading:

1 **Brokers**. Act on behalf of clients to try to secure the best buy or sell deal in the market place.

2 Market maker. Quote two prices for a security, the price at which they are willing to buy and a (slightly higher) price at which they are willing to sell the same security. They 'make a market' in an instrument and expect to make numerous purchases and sales during a day, taking an income from the gap between the two prices.

3 Proprietary trading. The bank takes positions in securities in order to try to make a profit for itself (rather than for its customers) from subsequent favourable movements of prices.

As **brokers** investment banks earn commissions on purchases and sales of a wide range of securities. Brokers do not own the securities but merely act as middlemen helping buyers and sellers to match up and do a deal. They mainly serve wholesale institutional (e.g. pension funds) and corporate clients rather than individuals, although they may own retail brokerage organisations that serve private investors.

An investment bank may also have a **corporate broker** arm, which acts on behalf of companies, for example, providing advice on market conditions, representing the company to the market to generate interest, advising on the rules and regulations applying to stock market-quoted companies. They can also gauge likely demand should a company be interested in selling bonds or shares to investors. And then, during the process of a new issue, they can gauge a suitable price and organise underwriting. They work with the company to maintain a liquid and properly informed market in a client company's shares. They often stand ready to buy and sell the company's shares when market makers and others are refusing to deal. Companies are charged a regular fee by the corporate broker for regular services but the broker keeps this to a minimum. The idea is to build up a long-term relationship so that the bank might earn a substantial amount should the client need advice and services during a major move such as a rights issue. The corporate broker can also be a bridge linking the client executives to other product providers within the bank.

Market makers, also known as **dealers**, fulfil a crucial role in the markets: in those securities in which market makers agree to make a market there will always be someone available who will quote a price at which they will buy or sell – as a purchaser or seller you may not like the price but at least someone is making a trade possible. To take share trading as an example: imagine if you wanted to invest in a small company's shares and there were no market makers, then you might hesitate because the shares would fail to have the important quality of **liquidity**, that is the ability to sell the shares quickly at a low transaction cost without moving the price against you. Investors in companies lacking an active secondary market will demand higher rates of return (lower share prices) to compensate for the inability to quickly find a counterparty willing to trade.

We refer to a trading system with market makers at the centre as **a quote-driven system** because client-investing firms can obtain firm **bid** and **offer (ask)** prices on a security and the dealers stand ready to trade. A bid price is one that the market maker will buy at (what the client firm could get from selling). An ask or offer price is what the market maker is willing to sell at (what the client firm would have to pay should they want to trade). Naturally because the market maker is trying to make a profit, the bid price is always lower than the offer price. If the gap gets too wide then clients will be lured away by better prices being offered by competing market makers in that security. The difference between the prices is known as the **trader's spread** or **bid–offer spread**. Many of these prices are displayed on electronic systems so that clients can see them displayed on their computer screens throughout the day. Other security bid–offer prices are only given to you if you telephone the market maker and ask for a quote.

Market makers take a considerable risk: they have to hold inventories of shares and other securities to supply those who want to buy. Tying up a lot of money in inventories of shares, bonds, etc. can be very expensive, and there is always the possibility of a downward movement in price while they hold millions of pounds or euros in inventory. The degree of risk varies from one security to another and this helps explain the differences in the size of the bid–offer spread. For some securities it is significantly less than 0.3 per cent of the value, in others it can be 20 per cent or more. The other major factor influencing the spread is the volume of trade that takes place relative to the amount that has to be held in inventory – high volume gives access to a liquid market for the market maker. Thus Marks and Spencer has millions of shares traded every day and so the market maker is not likely to have M&S shares on its hands for long, because they are going out of the door as fast as they are coming in – spreads here can be around a tenth of 1 per cent. Shares of a small engineering company on the other hand might trade in lots of only a few hundred at two- or three-day intervals. Thus the market maker has money tied up for days before selling and is fearful of a price fall between trading days.

We can see how the quote-driven system works through Exhibit 4.6. This could apply to markets in a wide variety of securities and instruments, from bonds to commodities, but we will assume that it is company shares. The demand curve shows that as the price declines the amount demanded to buy from the market maker rises. The supply curve shows rising volume offered by investors with higher prices. The **clearing price** is 199p; this is where the demand from clients wanting to buy and the supply of the securities from those wanting to sell is evenly matched. Naturally, the market makers in this security will be taking a spread around this clearing price so the true price to the buying client might be 199.5p, whereas the price that a seller to the market makers can obtain is only 198.5p.

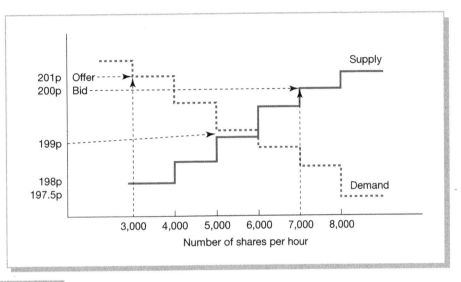

Exhibit 4.6   **Supply and demand in a quote-driven market**

If one of the market makers is currently quoting prices of 200p–201p (offering to buy at 200p and sell at 201p) then he will experience a flood of orders from sellers because investors are willing to sell 7,000 shares per hour if offered 200p. On the other hand demand at 201p is a mere 3,000 shares. The market maker will thus end up buying a net 4,000 shares per hour if he takes all the trade. In fact it is even worse than this for our market maker because the potential buyers can pick up their shares for only 199.5p from other market makers and so he ends up buying 7,000 per hour and not selling any.

Even if our market maker is exceptionally optimistic about the market equilibrium price rising significantly above 201p in the next few hours he is not doing himself any favours by quoting such high prices because he could buy a large number of the shares he wants at a price a lot less than this – there are 5,000 per hour going through other market makers at 199.5p for example. Thus there is a strong incentive for our market maker to move his prices down towards the intersection of the supply and demand curves.

Now consider a market maker who quotes 198p–197.5p. She will experience a flood of buy orders from clients given the prices offered by other market makers in this competitive market. Under the rules governing market makers she is obliged to deal at the prices quoted up to a maximum number of shares (decided by the exchange that controls this particular market). Perhaps this obligation to sell 8,000 shares per hour to clients when she is attracting few (no) clients to sell to her may lead to problems in satisfying demand. She will thus be tempted (unless she has a lot of shares to shift) to move her bid and offer prices to around the market equilibrium price.

A market maker that tries to maintain a large bid–offer spread will fail when there are many market makers for a security. For example, consider the five market makers offering the following prices:

Market maker	Bid price	Offer price
1	198.5p	199.5p
2	197.3p	199.5p
3	197.0p	200.0p
4	198.5p	199.7p
5	198.3p	202.0p

Any potential seller (or broker for the buyer) would look at the various market makers' prices and conclude that they would like to trade with either market maker 1 or 4 at 198.5p. Any buyer of shares would want to trade with 1 or 2. Market maker 4 may be temporarily under-stocked with these shares and is content to see inventory build up – he is not going to get many to buy from him at 199.7p when buyers can get away with paying only 199.5p. On the other hand, market maker 2 will see more sales than purchases – perhaps she has excessive inventory and wishes to allow an outflow for a while.

Of course, for most securities the intersection of the supply and demand 'curves' moves over time. Perhaps the company announces that it has won a large export order at 2 p.m. Immediately the investors see this news on their computer screens and the demand curve shifts upwards while the supply curve shifts downwards. Market makers also read the news and anticipate the shifts and quickly move their price quotes to where they think they can trade with a reasonable balance between bid deals and offer deals, aiming for a large number of each making a profit on the spread.

Proprietary trading ('**prop trading**') uses the bank's capital in order to try to make capital gains called **trading income** which consists of both **realised gains** where the trade is completed (there has been both a buy and sell) and **unrealised gains** – say a buy has taken place and there is a paper gain but it has not yet been turned into cash by selling, thus all the accountant has to go on is the **marking to market** of the value at the current price. Proprietary trading grew in volume significantly in the 20 years to 2010, but now governments and regulators around the world are clamping down on what can be risky high-geared (lots of borrowing or using derivatives) bets; there is a fear that if a number of large bets go wrong in one bank it can lead to a domino-like collapse of other banks as one after the other reneges on its obligations, i.e. **systemic risk**.

You may think there might be some conflict of interest between advising a firm on its finances or acting as a broker to a pension fund, thus gaining advance and special knowledge of client actions on the one hand, and trying to make profits by trading the same or similar securities on their own account on the other. You may think that, but I could not possibly comment. The banks themselves protest that they have strong and high '**Chinese Walls**' that separate the individuals who act as advisers or brokers (and others) from the proprietary traders within the banks – see Exhibit 4.7 for some people's views on conflicts of interest.

Goldman looking at an own goal

Lina Saigol

Sir Alex Ferguson, Manchester United's manager, is not slow to react when a player incurs his wrath. It seems that the club's owners take the same approach with investment banks.

The Glazer family are considering severing ties with Goldman Sachs after Jim O'Neill, the bank's chief economist, was revealed as a member of a consortium looking to buy the football club.

Goldman insists that Mr O'Neill is working in a personal capacity, but his role brings back uncomfortable memories of a clash United had with JPMorgan four years ago when Malcolm Glazer first bid for the club.

At the time, JPMorgan Cazenove was acting as United's stockbroker while its parent company, JPMorgan, had been arranging £265m ($398m) of debt for Mr Glazer's bid.

The dual role infuriated Sir Roy Gardner, then chairman of United, who claimed it represented a clear conflict of interest

and was hostile in nature.

The row also had wider repercussions. Two months later, Centrica dropped JPMorgan Cazenove as its joint broker. Sir Roy happened to be chief executive of the UK energy supplier at the time.

In the same year, Roger Carr, who was chairman of Centrica, had his own clash with Goldman Sachs.

Mr Carr was also chairman of Mitchells & Butlers when Goldman made an indicative £4.6bn debt-and-equity offer for the pub group, on behalf of a consortium in which it was one of the largest participants.

Mr Carr described the offer as "hostile and inappropriate", the bank withdrew from the consortium, and the bid evaporated. Mr Carr's anger struck a chord with Goldman – the bank acted as corporate broker to both Centrica and Cadbury, where Mr Carr was also a board member.

Goldman's private equity fund had also been involved in unsolicited approaches to ITV and

BAA. Those episodes prompted Hank Paulson, Goldman's then chairman and chief executive, to warn its bankers not to use its principal investment funds in hostile situations.

The potential for conflicts of interest for banks has intensified in recent years in tandem with the rapid development of new financial products. Full-service banks incorporating private equity funds, advisers, traders and asset managers under one roof are likely to run more risks than single-discipline boutiques.

Banks have so-called Chinese Walls, which are supposed to limit the flow of information between different businesses, such as proprietary trading and investment banking.

In reality, these walls are only as sound as the integrity of the banks that erect them.

Source: Financial Times, 5 March 2010, p. 21

Exhibit 4.7 Goldman looking at an own goal

Fixed income, currencies and commodities trading (FICC)

The FICC operations of an investment bank concentrate on sales and trading (e.g. market making) of highly liquid debt securities, swaps (see Chapters 15 and 19), currencies and commodities on behalf of client firms, rather than on their own account. The top 14 banks generate a combined revenue (income) of around $150 billion from FICC, which accounted for more than one-half of all revenues in 2009 and 2010 (admittedly this was a particularly good period for FICC as bid–offer spreads remained high in historical terms following the crisis). The big players in this market are Goldman Sachs, Bank of America, JPMorgan, Deutsche Bank, Citigroup and Barclays (following its acquisition of Lehman's New York operations).

The fixed income section of a bank specialises in deals in interest rate securities. This includes:

- high-grade (low-risk) corporate bonds: **domestic bonds** (under the laws and regulations of the country where they are issued where the issuer is a local firm), **foreign bonds** (the issuer comes from abroad but the bond is under the jurisdiction of the country of issue) and **international bonds** (or **Eurobonds**), where the bond is issued outside the jurisdiction of the country in whose currency it is denominated (see Chapters 10 and 11 for a description of bonds);

- **sovereign bonds** issued by governments (see Chapter 10);

- credit derivatives such as credit default swaps that allow investors to buy a kind of insurance against the possibility of a bond failing to pay the agreed interest and/or principal amounts (more in Chapters 15 and 19);

- high-yield securities such as high-yield bonds (see Chapter 11);

- bank loans – yes, there is a secondary market in bank loans;

- local authority/municipal debt;

- emerging market debt – bonds, etc. issued by governments or corporations in developing markets (some might be economically developed but under-developed with regard to financial markets);

- distressed debt – borrowers are not meeting their obligations under a debt agreement;

- mortgage-backed securities and other asset-backed securities – see securitisation later in the chapter and in Chapter 11;

- interest-rate derivatives such as interest rate futures – see Chapter 14;

- money market instruments – see Chapter 9.

There are other divisions that deal in currencies and currency derivatives (see Chapter 16). There is usually yet another division that specialises in commodities and commodity derivatives.

In all these FICC areas the bank often acts as a market maker in these products, creator of many of them, as an adviser and broker for clients and as a proprietary trader.

Equities

The equities section of an investment bank helps clients with their investing and trading strategies in shares and equity-linked investments. The more exotic instruments they deal in include:

▪ futures in shares and futures in market indices (e.g. the FTSE 100 index) – see Chapter 14;

▪ equity options giving the right but not the obligation to buy or sell shares at a pre-agreed price some time in the future– see Chapter 15;

▪ warrants on shares (similar to options but issued by the company rather than financial institutions);

▪ preference shares – see Chapter 12.

Again the bank will often act as market maker in these products, creator of many of them, as a broker for clients and as a proprietary trader.

Derivatives

Investment banks not only act as market makers or brokers in the derivative markets but also create derivatives (**originating**) and market them to clients. Much of the commodity market trading by investment banks is via derivatives such as futures, whereby the buyer enters into a contract to buy or to sell the underlying commodity at a fixed priced at a point in the future, say three months hence. They may assist firms trying to hedge in these markets, for example, an airline trying to fix the future price of its aviation fuel, or they may conduct proprietary trades to make a profit for the bank. Of course, the investment banks will also assist with non-derivative commodity trading by helping a client buy for immediate use some quantity of a commodity – **spot trading**.

It has been known for investment bankers to get too enamoured of the fancy derivative strategies they devised for companies and governments. They can be very complex and it can be almost impossible for the client to understand the full implications of the risks they are exposed to. Whether the lack of understanding is to be blamed on the clients or on the lack of effort on the part of the bankers to explain themselves is a moot point. Many Italian local authorities are fuming at the bankers for getting them into a mess with interest rate derivatives. Goldman Sachs has been heavily criticised in China for selling oil derivatives to state companies – see Exhibit 4.8.

Goldman stung by backlash in China

By Jamil Anderlini in Beijing

Public criticism of Goldman Sachs has come to China, where the bank has been attacked in the state-controlled media.

Parts of the media, apparently emboldened by congressional inquiries and public anger in the west, have openly slated Goldman, arguably the most successful foreign investment bank in China.

"Many people believe Goldman, which goes around the Chinese market slurping gold and sucking silver, may have, using all kinds of deals, created even bigger losses for Chinese companies and investors than it did with its fraudulent actions in the US," read the opening lines of an article in the China Youth Daily, a state-owned daily newspaper, last week.

The reports were critical of Goldman for designing and selling oil hedging contracts to state-owned Chinese companies that then lost billions of dollars when oil prices plunged, contrary to Goldman analysts' predictions, in 2008 and 2009.

Probably the most telling assertion is the complaint that Goldman has been too successful in China, that it has made too much money from underwriting initial public offerings, arranging deals and making its own private equity investments.

Goldman saw a 2007 investment in a pharmaceuticals export company of less than $5m rise to nearly $1bn at the company's IPO.

Source: *Financial Times*, 7 June 2010, p. 19

Exhibit 4.8   Goldman stung by backlash in China

Securitisation (and other structured products)

During the 15 years to the end of 2008 banks (particularly US banks) built an enormous business in re-bundling debt. So, say a bank has recently enticed 1,000 households to borrow money from it for a house mortgage. It now has the right under the law to receive monthly interest and principal from the households. The traditional thing to do is to hold on to those bank assets until the mortgagees pay off the loan. Banks increasingly thought it better to do something else: 'originate and distribute' debt. Thus once they have the right to the interest, etc., the 1,000 rights on the mortgages are put into a **special purpose vehicle (SPV)** – a separate company – that issues bonds to other investors. The cash raised from selling the bonds goes to the bank so that it can originate another 1,000 mortgages. The investors in the SPV receive regular interest on the long-term bonds that they bought, which is paid for out of the receipts of monthly mortgage payments by 1,000 households.

In theory, the bank makes a nice profit because it gets more for selling the rights than it lent out in the first place. As banks became greedier and keener to originate mortgages and play this game they found they did not have enough of their own money to lend in high volume. They thus turned to the wholesale money markets to raise money. Many of these wholesale loans were only short-term – they had to be repaid within days, weeks or months. This was fine if the banks could quickly securitise the newly originated mortgages. But what if everyone suddenly stopped buying securitised bonds? What if you as a bank had borrowed money for 30 days and then lent it out to mortgage holders for 25 years on the expectation of completing the securitisation (or simply expected to take out another 30-day loan when the first expired to tide you through to a securitisation the next month) and then everyone stopped buying securitised bonds or lending to banks wanting to do securitisations because of fears over the bank's solvency? Answer: financial system disaster.

As well as playing a major part in originating their own mortgage loans to people followed by securitisation, investment banks assisted other organisations to carry out securitisation, and they traded in the securitised financial instruments and their derivatives. A major driving motive for the rise in securitisation was to get around the prudential regulations for banks to hold high reserves. The more loans a bank has granted in addition to others that are still residing on the balance sheet, the more it has to hold in capital reserves. As we saw in Chapter 3, high capital reserves can lower the return on equity capital. Thus to raise returns banks took the mortgages off their balance sheets by selling them.

The structured finance departments of investment banks have gone beyond simple securitisation. They have developed some weird – and not so wonderful – instruments such as collateralised debt obligations (CDOs) – these are discussed further when we consider the financial crisis in Chapter 19.

Asset management

Many investment banks have fund management arms that manage assets on behalf of pension funds, charities or companies. They try to generate high returns relative to risk by selecting investments for the funds. The investments selected vary widely from shares and bonds to property and hedge funds.

They also manage the savings of private individuals through the unit trusts, OEICS, mutual funds and investment trusts that they set up and market. As managers they will receive a fee and, possibly, a bonus for exceptional performance.

Investment advice

Many investment banks have teams of investment analysts examining the accounts and other data relating to companies quoted on stock markets, so that they can make recommendations on whether or not their shares, bonds or other securities are good value for potential investors. Alongside the analysts there might be **private-client representatives** talking to individual investors and an **institutional sales force** assisting professional managed funds to find good investments and manage risk. As well as analysing companies they will provide analyses of industries, markets, macroeconomics and currencies worldwide.

Wealth management and private banking

Wealth management and **private banking** (terms that are used interchange- ably) are undertaken by a number of banks, some of which are investment banks. It involves services and advice to improve the management of the finan- cial affairs of high-net-worth individuals, including their investments, current deposit accounts (possibly in numerous currencies and jurisdictions), obtaining of loans and tax issues. The definition of a high-net-worth individual varies, but usually means they have over $1 million in net wealth besides the main home. There are some old and venerable names in this business such as C. Hoare and Co., and Pictet & Cie, but most of the universal banks also have private banking arms for their wealthier customers.

Prime brokerage for hedge funds

Some investment banks have **prime brokerage** arms that provide services for hedge funds (discussed in Chapter 17) such as acting as a broker buying and sell- ing blocks of shares (**trade execution**), derivatives, etc. for the fund, clearing and settlement of trades, risk management, back-office accounting services, cash management and custodial services. The main source of income for the bank from prime brokerage usually comes in the form of interest charged for lending to the hedge fund, fees for arranging debt supplied by others and income from stock (share) lending to enable the hedge fund to **sell securities short** (i.e. sell without first buying – the buying comes later, hopefully at a lower price than they were sold for). Another role for prime brokers is in helping their hedge fund clients find investors – call a **cap-intro** (**capital introduction**) service.

Investment banks are often in contact with wealthy family investment offices, private banking offices and institutional investors (**end-investors**) and so can point them in the direction of those hedge funds for which they are prime brokers. A few investment banks also supply fast electronic trading systems to hedge funds so that they can tap into the markets directly and create automated buy and sell strategies.

Private equity (venture capital) investment

This is finance for new and growing companies that have not gained a quotation on a stock exchange. It can consist of a mixture of debt and equity, and can be an investment for the bank itself or on behalf of clients of the bank. There is more on private equity in Chapter 17.

Websites

www.bankofengland.co.uk	Bank of England
www.bis.org	Bank for International Settlements
www.bba.org.uk	British Bankers' Association
www.ecb.int	European Central Bank
www.fsa.gov.uk	Financial Services Authority
www.ft.com	Financial Times
www.icmagroup.org	International Capital Markets Association
www.sifma.org	Securities Industry and Financial Markets Association

5

Other types of banking

The increased liberalisation of financial systems has led to banking being glo-balised, with foreign banks becoming increasingly important in domestic systems; we thus look at international banking. Then, alongside banks set up as shareholder-owned companies we have other types of organisations conduct-ing banking-type activities. For example there are a number of mutually-owned (owned by their customers) entities that invite deposits, make loans and partici-pate in the payment system. These include building societies, savings and loans and cooperative banks.

When people or businesses obtain an asset through hire purchase or leasing the obligations under the agreement are in many ways similar to a bank loan. These are certainly considered alternative ways of borrowing money and so can be included under banking. Indeed most of the large finance houses that operate in these areas are, in fact, subsidiaries of the major banks. Finally, this chapter high-lights the differences between conventional banking and Islamic banking.

International banking

International banking means banking business conducted across national bor-ders and/or with foreign currencies. This can be retail or wholesale banking, personal or corporate banking, as well as investment banking. Fifteenth-century Florentine bankers set up subsidiaries in other European countries to help their clients with trade finance and to lend large volumes. The clients were some-times Italian but there were many non-Italians who recognised their need to obtain finance and other banking services beyond the confines of their own nation. Nineteenth-century colonialism and globalisation led to a rapid expan-sion in banking, as British, Dutch and French banks established branches in places as far-flung as Australia and India, while building a strong presence in the Americas. Towards the end of the nineteenth century banks from many other countries (e.g. Canada and Japan) also developed international activities. The Americans were relatively slow in getting started because they were restrained by law from establishing branches abroad. The rules were relaxed but the US banks did not respond in any significant way until after the Second World War. Even as late as 1960 only eight US banks had overseas branches. But once they got going they grew rapidly, so that now over 50 US banks have branches abroad and some of these institutions have grown so they have become the dominant banks in many of the financial centres around the globe.

We need to be clear what we are talking about when we use the term international banking. There are many different levels and different types of services (see Exhibit 5.1). **Eurocurrency banking** is very big business – billions every day. This is money deliberately held outside the control of the regulators and governments of the currency. Thus, for example, there is a vast quantity of US dollars held in Eurocurrency accounts in London and other places outside the US which is lent out at Eurocurrency interest rates. There are also Euroyen (outside the control of the Japanese), EuroSwiss Francs, etc. This market in international money beyond government control was established long before the creation of the European currency, the euro. It is important to note that the Eurocurrencies are not confined to European countries; much of the trading takes place in Singapore, the Bahamas and the Cayman Islands. There is more on Eurocurrencies in Chapter 9.

As large companies established themselves in a number of countries they expected that their home country bank would expand with them and provide services when they operated abroad. So, a French company operating in the US may need banking services from the US-based branch of its French bank. It might need a loan in dollars to build a factory in Chicago, for instance. Or, when goods are sold in dollars it needs its bank to exchange them for euros. Of course, the French manufacturer could use a US bank, but companies often prefer to work with their home bank with which they have a long-term relationship, with mutual understanding of customs, culture and practices.

London is the largest cross-border lending financial centre with an almost 20 per cent share of worldwide activity. It established this position in the days of the Empire. As well as being at the centre of the English-speaking trading network it pulled in European bankers. The main attraction for the foreign banks coming to London before 1914 was that it allowed them to participate in the London money markets. Here they could invest surplus cash holdings in interest-bearing instruments that were highly liquid. They could not do this on the same scale in their home financial centres. In the 1960s and 1970s there was a rapid growth of foreign banks in London due to the take-off of the Euromarkets. US bankers tended to lead here. By the mid-1980s there were over 400 foreign banks. Since then there have been amalgamations and departures of smaller banks

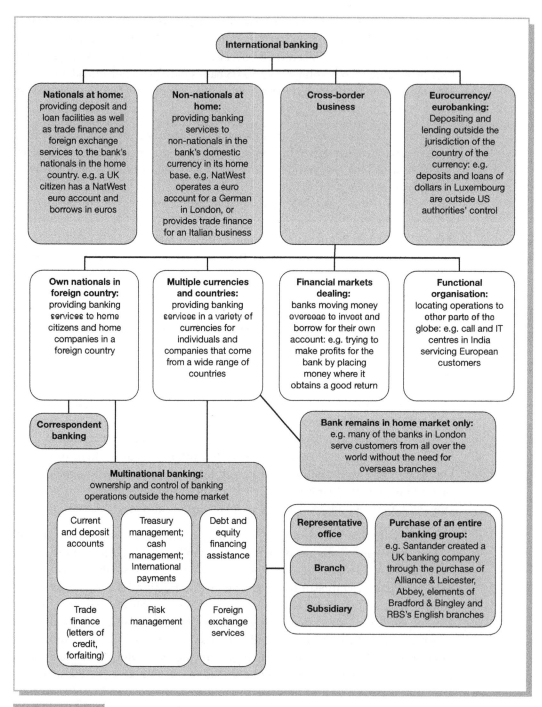

Exhibit 5.1   Different types of international banking

so that figure stands at around 250. Having a major presence in London seems to be seen as a requirement to be taken seriously as a player in the banking world. London is at the centre of the world time zones, has great depth and breadth of banking skills and support services (lawyers, accountants, etc.), and is the main Eurocurrency, international bond and foreign exchange trading location.

There are a number of different ways in which overseas banking can be organised. A very simple method that does not require the establishment of an office overseas is to employ the services of a **correspondent bank**. Here, a well-established bank in the country is asked to undertake tasks for clients of the foreign bank such as payment transactions, current accounts, custody services and investing funds in financial markets. They may also introduce banking clients to local businesspeople. Correspondent banks are paid a fee by the foreign bank.

An operation that requires slightly more commitment to a foreign banking environment is to open a **representative office**. These are often small, rudimentary affairs that assist the parent bank's customers in that country. They might provide information on the country to clients and help them form banking and business relationships in the country. However, they cannot provide core overseas banking business to clients, i.e. no deposits or loans in the overseas country can be made through the office. Representative offices are also used to entice potential foreign customers, acting as marketing offices for the parent.

An **agency office** is a greater commitment than a representative office. They are usually prohibited from accepting deposits from host country residents, but can be used to transfer other funds and make loans. They are not subject to the same full regulatory requirements as the host country banks, such as having insurance for deposits (so depositors can get money back from a government-run body if the bank goes bust – see Chapter 18).

A **branch** of the parent bank bears its name and legally acts as part of the overall bank. Creditors to the branch have a claim on the organisation as a whole, including the parent's assets. They often provide as full a range of banking services as the banking regulators in the host country allow. Branches are a very common way for banks to expand, but following the 2008 financial crisis and the problems caused by branches not maintaining capital reserves in the host country (e.g. money could be taken back to the parent, and, if the parent then fails, the depositors (or depositor insurer) may not recover their money) the regulators are pushing for less branch banking and more subsidiary banking.

A **subsidiary**, set up as a separate legal entity in the host country, will be subject to the same regulations as the host country banks. It has its own capital reserves kept within the country and has to follow the same regulatory procedures as the host country banks. If it runs into trouble then the host country authorities would expect the parent to pump in more capital, but, given the separate company status, the parent may not be obliged to do this and so a subsidiary structure may be safer for the parent. Subsidiaries may be grown from scratch or be formed as a result of an acquisition of a bank(s), as in the case of Santander in the UK, which bought a number of banks.

The mutuals

There are thousands of financial institutions that perform many bank-type functions but which are member-owned rather than owned by shareholders. These are mutually owned, the members usually being depositors (or depositors plus borrowers together). Profits are either distributed to members or they are ploughed back into the business. They are called by a number of different names, including mutuals, thrifts, building societies, cooperative banks, savings and loans, savings banks, people's banks, community banks and credit unions. Even with different labels they generally do much the same type of banking, but there are subtle differences in constitution, target members, borrowing purpose and legal structure from one country to another.

The big advantage they have compared with the corporate banks is that they do not have to pay returns to shareholders which, at least in theory, allows them to offer better rates to savers and borrowers. They also tend to develop a culture of cautious risk taking because they do not have to maximise profits by buying into the latest financial whizz-bang instruments or stretch their capital bases to conduct high levels of lending: thus they are better positioned to survive a financial crisis. However, while most prize conservative banking practices, some have been tempted to take higher risks through overseas expansions, venturing into investment banking and plunging into exotic instruments pools, such as US sub-prime mortgage-based instruments.

A general drawback with many mutuals is that they are vulnerable to going through a poor patch (e.g. a few borrowers failing to repay) because they do not have shareholders to turn to for fresh capital in a crisis, which can result in insolvency. They have to rely on an accumulation of profits and attracting new deposits to rebuild capital, and this can be too slow. Take the years 2008–10, when European shareholder-owned banks raised over €100 billion to buttress their capital by selling new shares. The mutuals, on the other hand, had limited options. Their main response was to increase the interest rate on deposits which resulted in a profits squeeze because they could not raise lending rates to the same extent. This happened at the same time that the regulators were ratcheting up the amount of capital reserves they had to hold. As a result many were forced into selling themselves or to combine with other mutuals or accept venture capital money.

There are 4,500 mutuals in Europe alone, and, with 50 million members, the mutually-owned financial institutions account for a very substantial share of all the customer deposits in many countries. In France, for example, over 40 per cent of depositors' money goes to cooperatives and the like. In Finland, Austria and The Netherlands the figure is around one-third, and in Germany and the UK it is over 15 per cent. Almost one in five Europeans is a member of a mutual. In Germany alone there are 30 million customers holding over €1,000 billion.

Origins of the mutuals

People are often vulnerable to the predator-like behaviour of local moneylenders. Early in the nineteenth century philanthropic Scots, English and Americans recognised the need for institutions that allowed the poor to save in a secure place and to borrow at reasonable interest rates as the need arose. These institutions were designed to avoid dominance by rapacious owners by making them mutually owned. Many Germans set up similar organisations later in the century to be followed by dozens of others in countries around the world. Mutuals were principally seen as a good way for thrifty, hard-working families to save up to buy a home or build their business.

We do not have the space to look at the mutuals in every country, so we will examine merely some of the leading economies.

Germany

In Germany each county or federal state seems to have its own Sparkasse or Landesbank (there are over 430 Sparkassen and a handful of Landesbanken). In the strictest sense these are often not mutuals because local governments own and control them, but they are established to help the people of a region rather than being run for shareholder benefit. The **Sparkasse** were founded by local and regional governments to raise finance for infrastructure projects and make loans to the poor, attracting deposits from households and firms. They opened up the possibility for ordinary people to create long-term, secure and interest-bearing reserves to cope with the adversities of life (illness, age, etc.). They lend over a fifth of all loans to German households and domestic companies.

Sparkassen are much smaller than the **Landesbanken**, which were originally established to act as 'central banks' to the savings banks, providing payment clearing and other services to them and helping them survive rough patches. They carry out some of the international, financial market-orientated banking activities on behalf of the savings banks which are too small to do this.

The Landesbanken are controlled by regional governments (with savings banks having a stake), but depend on funding from markets rather than customer deposits. Unfortunately, commercial sense often takes second place behind regional politicians' priorities in terms of local jobs, power and prestige. As a result German bank profitability is one of the lowest in Europe, dragged down by the frequent losses of the Landesbanken. The Landesbanken offer a full range of banking services, including international banking – they are universal banks. They are now much larger than most shareholder-owned banks, for example, WestLB has over €250 billion in assets, and BayernLB has over €340 billion. All told they make up about a sixth of German banking assets and lend about a quarter of corporate loans.

Until 2005 the Landesbanken benefited from state guarantees (creditors to the bank were reassured they would be repaid) which allowed them to borrow cheaply. This they did in abundance and then used the money raised to buy a lot of duff assets, such as US sub-prime mortgage-backed bonds and foreign property. They were prone to over-ambition, poor governance as well as excessive risk taking. Their adventurousness was to lead to the undoing of many of them in 2009. BayernLB and WestLB, for example, lost billions of euros and had to be bailed out by government. They still receive state aid. Many commentators see them as market-distorting competitors to the conventional banks due to their special privileges, as well as being unstable. Further, they call for their winding-down or privatisation. The EU Commission is furious at the way these inefficient giants are revived time and again by German politicians, thus putting pressure on the rivals not favoured by the government. Thus, Germany only has one world-class bank, Deutsche Bank.

There are also over 1,100 German credit cooperative banks that are owned by members of a profession or trade. The German coops account for about 13 per cent of lending to households and German companies and 18 per cent of mortgage lending. **Bausparkassen** accept deposits and provide finance for people wanting to buy a house. They also provide finance to build houses.

Spain

In Spain there are 17 **cajas** (more properly: **cajas de ahoro**, and often have Caixa in their titles) which account for 40 per cent of the retail assets held by the banking system and more than one-half of mortgage lending. These local savings banks have their roots in the Catholic church's attempts at providing

microfinance (very small deposits and loans) for the poor. But they were described as quasi-mutual because despite some control being in the hands of depositors and employees, they were heavily influenced by regional politicians and their cronies. During the decade up to 2007 the cajas raised vast amounts of money from the bond markets (mostly by using their rights to receive money from mortgagees as collateral – securitised bonds) and then lent heavily to property developers, other business organisations and to politically-motivated public works projects. The crash in the Spanish property market has been particularly painful, creating an enormous quantity of bad loans. The global financial crisis then exacerbated the problem. Before the crisis there were 45 cajas, but the weakest were forced to seek protection by merging with stronger ones as the government insisted that they reduce their cost bases, particularly by closing surplus branches. Other post-crisis innovations are the right to sell equity to investors (up to half the caja's equity) and the restricting of the number of elected politicians and public officials on their management and supervisory boards, with the intention of professionalising the management.

United States of America

In the US three types of organisation are collectively referred to as 'thrifts': savings and loan associations, savings banks and credit unions. **Savings and loan associations (savings associations)** are primarily focused on lending for real estate and house purchase by families. They have been around for over 180 years, and they grew rapidly until the crisis of the early 1980s caused by imprudent lending and the restriction of being tied to lending fixed rate while borrowing floating rate (on deposits) at a time of rising inflation and interest rates. Today 80 per cent or more of the finance they raise comes from savings accounts (most of the rest from the wholesale financial markets), while over 90 per cent of their assets are secured by real estate. There are over 1,000 S&Ls with over $1.5 trillion of assets.

US savings banks were established in the nineteenth century by philanthropists to encourage the poor to save. While they do lend for house purchase they are not as heavily concentrated on mortgages as the S&Ls. They are permitted to invest in a greater range of assets, so they hold large amounts of government bonds, money market instruments and corporate bonds. There are over 300 savings banks concentrated in the northeast of the US (S&Ls are located throughout the country).

Credit unions were established on both sides of the Atlantic in the early nineteenth century to help poor people by providing a safe place for their money and allowing them to borrow at reasonable interest rates. They are set up when people have some other association, e.g. church membership or workplace – a 'common bond membership'. The CU member regularly saves money into an account and can then borrow a multiple of the amount as small, fixed-term personal loans (rather than long-term mortgages). CUs are granted tax privileges to encourage the poor to save. Also employers often help with office space and items like free electricity. They offer checking (cheque) accounts, savings accounts, credit cards, certificates of deposit and online banking.

Typical loans sizes are $10,000–$15,000 with over one-third going for car purchase and one-third for house purchase. Most CUs have remained local but a few are national or international (e.g. Navy Federal Credit Union – $41 billion in assets and 3.4 million members). Multinational corporations often encourage workplace CUs (e.g. Boeing employees). The US has about 8,000 CUs with about 87 million members, accounting for around 10 per cent of consumer deposits and 15 per cent of consumer loans.

United Kingdom

Building societies go back as far as the eighteenth century. They had a very simple function within a town or small region: households (members) saved into them, and when they had saved enough they could borrow to purchase a house (if there was a good prospect of them being able to repay). They are not profit maximisers, but try to balance the interests of borrowers seeking low interest rates and savers wanting high interest rates.

They dominated the mortgage market until the 1980s but deregulation led to many new entrants, especially banks. In the last two decades of the twentieth century there was much deregulation so that building societies could offer cheque accounts, unsecured loans, ATMs and lend against commercial assets. In addition, today an increasing proportion of their funding has come from the wholesale markets rather than retail members, although this rarely exceeds one-third of liabilities. In 1900 there were over 1,700 building societies, but this has since dwindled as a result of building societies combining into larger groups and many larger groups converting themselves into limited companies with shareholders (**demutualisation**) and floating on the London Stock Exchange. Others were bought by banking groups. The reasons for converting to companies include: the ability to tap shareholders for funds to support the growth or survival of the business; to allow expansion into new areas such as life insurance and corporate lending; pressure from members to receive a windfall by selling their shares; and empire building by directors.

Of the remaining 49, Nationwide is the largest building society with £191 billion of assets. These organisations still account for about one-sixth of UK mortgage lending. The old building societies now converted to banks generally continued to focus on house lending and so we refer to them as **mortgage banks**. Most of these were bought by universal banks once they floated on the stock market. Thus, Halifax is part of Lloyds (previously part of Halifax Bank of Scotland which was bought by Lloyds in the 2008 crisis), as is Cheltenham & Gloucester. Abbey and Alliance & Leicester are part of Santander.

The UK also has over 400 credit unions with over 750,000 members with a common bond.[1] They have a history going back to the Industrial Revolution. Some of the larger ones offer current accounts, debit cards and cash withdrawals from ATMs. Life insurance is often included in membership. The affiliations range from taxi drivers to the Toxteth Community. According to the Association of British Credit Unions over £400 million is saved in UK CUs, and there is a similar volume of loans.

There is only one UK cooperative bank with 2 per cent of UK bank deposits and 300 branches (including Britannia (a building society) which merged with the Coop in 2009). It offers current accounts, savings accounts, credit cards and loans. The Co-operative Insurance offers a variety of insurance products and the Co-operative Investments offers products including unit trusts, investment bonds and pensions.

France, The Netherlands and Asia

In France the savings banks, **Caisses d'Epargne**, have powers to enter into a wide range of banking activities for retail depositors but not to lend commercial loans. France's biggest retail bank, Crédit Agricole, is a cooperative. It is majority owned by 39 French cooperative retail banks, *Caisses Régionales de Crédit Agricole Mutuel*. Other mutual/cooperative French banks to have large shares of the deposit market are Crédit Mutuel and Banque Populaire.

In the Netherlands over 40 per cent of all banking deposits are in cooperatives. Rabobank Nederland is an organisation that acts for 143 independent agricultural cooperatives, called **Rabobanks**. Collectively they form the second biggest banking institution in Holland.

There are tens of thousands of cooperatives in India and in China. Also, Japan has a thriving coop sector.

---

[1] Worldwide there are 40,000 CUs in 79 countries serving 114 million members.

Finance houses

A **finance house** is an institution that advances credit, usually through factoring, a hire purchase agreement or a lease. Strictly, these organisations are classified as 'non-bank institutions' but they provide debt finance and are often owned by the major banks, so are included in this chapter. Typically they do not take deposits but obtain their funds from the money and bond markets. Some of the largest finance houses are owned by commercial organisations such as General Motors, Ford or General Electric rather than banks.

Factoring

Factoring (or **invoice finance**) companies provide three services to firms with outstanding **debtors** (also called **trade receivables** – amounts not yet paid by customers), the most important of which is the immediate transfer of cash. This is provided by the factor on the understanding that when invoices are paid by customers the proceeds will go to them. Factoring is increasingly used by companies of all sizes as a way of meeting cash flow needs induced by rising sales and debtor balances. In the UK about 80 per cent of factoring turnover is handled by the clearing bank subsidiaries (e.g. HSBC Invoice Finance, Lloyds and Royal Bank of Scotland Corporate Banking). However, there are dozens of smaller factoring companies.

The provision of finance

At any one time a typical business can have a fifth or more of its annual turnover outstanding in trade debts: a firm with an annual turnover of £5 million may have a debtor balance of £1 million. These large sums create cash-flow difficulties which can pressurise an otherwise healthy business. Factors step in to provide the cash needed to support stock levels, to pay suppliers and generally aid more profitable trading and growth. The factor will provide an advanced payment on the security of outstanding invoices. Normally about 80 per cent of the invoice value can be made available to a firm immediately (with some factors this can be as much as 90 per cent). The remaining 20 per cent is transferred from the factor when the customer finally pays up. Naturally the factor will charge a fee and interest on the money advanced. The cost will vary between clients depending on sales volume, the type of industry and the average value of the invoices. The charge for finance is comparable with overdraft rates (1.5–3 per cent over base rate). As on an overdraft the interest is calculated on the daily outstanding balance of the funds that the borrowing firm has transferred to its business account. Added to this is a service charge that varies between 0.2 per cent and 3 per cent of invoiced sales. This is set at the higher end if there are many small invoices or a lot of customer accounts or the risk is high.

Sales ledger administration

Companies, particularly young and fast-growing ones, often do not want the trouble and expense of setting up a sophisticated system for dealing with the collection of outstanding debts. For a fee (0.75–2.5 per cent of turnover) factors will take over the functions of recording credit sales, checking customers' creditworthiness, sending invoices, chasing late payers and ensuring that debts are paid. Factors are experienced professional payment chasers who know all the tricks of the trade (such as 'the cheque is in the post' excuse) and so can obtain payment earlier. With factoring, sales ledger administration and debt collection generally come as part of the package offered by the finance house, unlike with invoice discounting (see below).

Credit insurance

The third service available from a factor is the provision of insurance against the possibility that a customer does not pay the amount owed. The charge for this service is generally between 0.3 per cent and 0.5 per cent of the value of the invoices.

Invoice discounting

Firms with an annual turnover under £10 million typically use factoring (with sales ledger administration), whereas larger firms tend to use **invoice discounting**. Here invoices are pledged to the finance house in return for an immediate payment of up to 90 per cent of the face value. The supplying company guarantees to pay the amount represented on the invoices and is responsible for collecting the debt. The customers are generally totally unaware that the invoices have been discounted. When the due date is reached it is to be hoped that the customer has paid in full. Regardless of whether the customer has paid, the supplying firm is committed to handing over the total invoice amount to the finance house and in return receives the remaining 10 per cent less service fees and interest. Note that even invoice discounting is subject to the specific circumstances of the client agreement and is sometimes made on a non-recourse basis (the selling company does not have to recompense the factoring company if the customer fails to pay).

The finance provider usually only advances money under invoice discounting if the supplier's business is well-established and profitable. There must be an effective and professional credit control and sales ledger administration system.

Charges are usually lower than for factoring because the sales ledger administration is the responsibility of the supplying company.

Hire purchase

With **hire purchase** the finance company buys the equipment that the borrowing firm needs. The equipment (plant, machinery, vehicles, etc.) belongs to the hire purchase (HP) company. However, the finance house allows the 'hirer' firm to use the equipment in return for a series of regular payments. These payments are sufficient to cover interest and contribute to paying off the principal. While the monthly instalments are still being made the HP company has the satisfaction and security of being the legal owner and so can take repossession if the hirer defaults on the payments. After all payments have been made the hirer becomes the owner, either automatically or on payment of a modest option-to-purchase fee. Nowadays, consumers buying electrical goods or vehicles have become familiar with the attempts of sales assistants to sell an HP agreement so that the customer pays over an extended period. Sometimes the finance is provided by the same organisation, but more often by a separate finance house.

There are clearly some significant advantages to this form of finance, given the fact that hire purchase together with leasing has overtaken bank loans as a source of finance for UK business purchases up to £100,000. The main advantages are as follows:

- *Small initial outlay*. The firm does not have to find the full purchase price at the outset. A deposit followed by a series of instalments can be less of a cash flow strain. The funds that the company retains by handing over merely a small deposit can be used elsewhere in the business for productive investment. Set against this are the relatively high interest charges (high relative to those at which a large firm can borrow, but can be relatively low for a small firm) and the additional costs of maintenance and insurance.

- *Easy and quick to arrange*. Usually at point of sale allowing immediate use of the asset.

- *Certainty*. This is a medium-term source of finance which cannot be withdrawn provided contractual payments are made, unlike an overdraft. On the other hand the commitment is made for a number of years and it could be costly to terminate the agreement. There are also budgeting advantages to the certainty of a regular cash outflow.

- *HP is often available when other sources of finance are not*. For some firms the equity markets are unavailable and banks will no longer lend to them, but

HP companies will still provide funds as they have the security of the asset to reassure them.

▪ *Fixed-rate finance*. In most cases the payments are fixed throughout the HP period. While the interest charged will not vary with the general interest rate throughout the life of the agreement the hirer has to beware that the HP company may quote an interest rate which is significantly different from the true annual percentage rate.

Leasing

Leasing is similar to HP in that an equipment owner (the **lessor**) conveys the right to use the equipment in return for regular rental payments by the equipment user (the lessee) over an agreed period of time. The essential difference is that the **lessee** does not become the owner – the leasing company retains legal title.[2] It is important to distinguish between operating leases and finance leases.

Operating lease

Operating leases commit the lessee to only a short-term contract or one that can be terminated at short notice. These are certainly not expected to last for the entire useful life of the asset and so the finance house has the responsibility of finding an alternative use for the asset when the lessee no longer requires it. Perhaps the asset will be sold in the second-hand market, or it might be leased to another client. Either way the finance house bears the risk of ownership. If the equipment turns out to have become obsolete more quickly than was originally anticipated it is the lessor that loses out. If the equipment is less reliable than expected the owner (the finance house) will have to pay for repairs. Usually, with an operating lease, the lessor retains the obligation for repairs, maintenance and insurance. It is clear why equipment which is subject to rapid obsolescence and frequent breakdown is often leased out on an operating lease. Photocopiers, for example, used by a university department are far better leased so that if they break down the university staff do not have to deal with the problem. In addition the latest model can be quickly installed in the place of an outdated one. The most common form of operating lease is contract hire. These leases are often used for a fleet of vehicles. The leasing company takes some responsibility for the management and maintenance of the vehicles and for disposal of the vehicles at the end of the contract hire period (after 12 to 48 months).

---

[2] However, with many finance leases, after the asset has been leased for the great majority of its useful life (majority of its value), the lessee may have the option to purchase it.

Operating leases are also useful if the business involves a short-term project requiring the use of an asset for a limited period. For example, building firms often use equipment supplied under an operating lease (sometimes called **plant hire**). Operating leases are not confined to small items of equipment. There is a growing market in leasing aircraft and ships for periods less than the economic life of the asset, thus making these deals operating leases. Many of Boeing's and Airbus's aircraft go to leasing firms.

Finance lease

Under a **finance lease** (also called a **capital lease** or a **full payout lease**) the finance provider expects to recover the full cost (or almost the full cost) of the equipment, plus interest, over the period of the lease. With this type of lease the lessee usually has no right of cancellation or termination. Despite the absence of legal ownership the lessee will have to bear the risks and rewards that normally go with ownership: the lessee will usually be responsible for maintenance, insurance and repairs and suffer the frustrations of demand being below expectations or the equipment becoming obsolete more rapidly than anticipated. Most finance leases contain a primary and a secondary period. It is during the primary period that the lessor receives the capital sum plus interest. In the secondary period the lessee pays a very small 'nominal', rental payment. If the company does not want to continue using the equipment in the secondary period it may be sold second-hand to an unrelated company.

Advantages of leasing

For companies that become lessees the advantages listed for hire purchase also apply: small initial outlay, certainty, available when other finance sources are not, fixed-rate finance and tax relief. There is an additional advantage of operating leases: the transfer of obsolescence risk to the finance provider.

Islamic banking

Under Islamic Sharia law the payment of *riba*[3] (interest) is prohibited and the receiver of finance must not bear all the risk of failure. Also investment in alcohol, tobacco, pornography or gambling is not allowed. However, Islam does encourage entrepreneurial activity and the sharing of risk through equity shares. Thus a bank can create profit-sharing products to offer customers. Depositors

---

[3] A strict interpretation of the word riba is usary or excessive interest.

can be offered a percentage of the bank's profits rather than a set interest rate. Borrowers repay the bank an amount that is related to the profit produced by the project for which the loan was made. Here are some examples.

- *Musharakah*. A joint enterprise is established by the bank and borrower. Both contribute capital plus management and labour (although some parties, e.g. banks, contribute little other than capital). Profit (loss) is shared in pre-agreed proportions – there is a prohibition against a fixed lump sum for any party. All partners have unlimited liability. Thus for a house purchase the property is purchased by the bank and clients (who contribute perhaps 10 per cent of the purchase price). The customer purchases the bank's share gradually, until he is made sole owner after a specified period, usually 25 years. Over the financing period, the bank's share is rented to the customer.

- *Ijara*. Example: a house (or aircraft, say) is bought by the bank and rented to the 'mortgage holder'. The house title may or may not be transferred when the contract ends.

- *Murabaha*. Example: a bank buys a house (car, or other property) and sells it to the customer at a fixed price – more than the bank paid – permitting the customer to pay in monthly instalments. When the final instalment is paid the house is transferred to the customer.

Over 600 banks and financial institutions offer services according to Sharia law. They are heavily concentrated in the Arabian Gulf countries, Malaysia, Pakistan and Iran. But, many conventional banks also offer Sharia products, e.g. HSBC and Lloyds have Islamic mortgages available. Growth has been driven by the rising consciousness of Islamic principles over the last 40 years and the rising wealth of Muslim oil states. What is regarded as compliant with Sharia in one part of the world may not be considered by Islamic scholars to be acceptable in another. Malaysia, for example, tends to be more liberal than Saudi Arabia. The UK has introduced tax,[4] legislative and regulatory changes to encourage Islamic financial services in the City. This has been successful, attracting over US$10 billion of funds to London, making it one of the top 10 centres. Despite its growth the volume of Islamic finance is still only around 1 per cent of the size of the conventional finance industry. Increasingly Islamic products are being used by non-Muslims, sometimes due to religious conviction (e.g. Quakers) or because that form of finance has qualities they are looking for.

---

[4] For example, stamp duty on a house sale is not paid twice (when the bank buys and when the customer buys from the bank).

Websites

www.abfa.org.uk	Asset Based Finance Association
www.abcul.org	Association of British Credit Unions
www.bankofengland.co.uk	Bank of England
www.bis.org	Bank for International Settlements
www.eurocoopbanks.coop	European Association of Cooperative Banks
www.bba.org.uk	British Bankers' Association
www.bsa.org.uk	Building Societies Association
www.ecb.int	European Central Bank
www.fla.org.uk	Finance and Leasing Association
www.fsa.gov.uk	Financial Services Authority
www.ft.com	Financial Times

6

Central banking

Between 2008 and 2011 many countries leaned heavily on the expertise and power of their central banks to bail them out of deep economic difficulties. Their banks were in crisis as the financial markets lost faith in the ability of them or their governments to repay money borrowed through bonds. Central banks slashed interest rates to historic lows, and in so doing probably saved us from a 1930s-style depression. This was still not enough to restore the banking system to health and so a raft of additional measures was implemented by the central banks, including raising the limit on the amount of money in each bank account that they guaranteed to refund if the bank went bust. They also acted as lender of last resort to a number of banks, so banks had somewhere to turn to raise finance. We have also seen massive quantitative easing programmes to lower long-term interest rates and boost bank reserves to encourage lending. While these emergency measures were effective in keeping the patient alive, thought was also given to the long-term health of the financial system. Thus we had the tightening of the capital and liquidity reserve ratios.

For most people the technical-sounding tools used by central bankers seem arcane and boring when talked about on the evening news. And yet if it wasn't for the vigilance and forward planning of these organisations we would have suffered a much worse fate as a result of the financial crisis. The financial world would have become a wasteland as bank after bank fell, and many important functions such as the mobilisation of savings for productive use would have taken decades to recover. It is vital that we continue to develop ways of strengthening the financial system through better regulation, rules on reserves and controlling the power of over-mighty universal banks.

Note that this chapter describes the wide variety of responsibilities that a nation *may* choose to allocate to the purview of the central bank. However, many countries decide to establish alternative organisations to undertake some of the tasks described here while leaving the central bank to concentrate on a few of them.

Monetary policy

If interest rates are held at a level that is too low then inflation will start to take off. This can be disruptive to businesses in addition to destroying the savings of people. It is especially problematic if inflation is high and fluctuating. Then, unpredictability makes planning very difficult. On the other hand, if interest rates are set at an excessively high level this will inhibit business activity, cause people to put off buying houses and reduce spending in the shops, leading to a recession with massive job losses. Clearly a society needs an organisation whose task it is to select the appropriate interest rate for the economic conditions it faces: neither too high nor too low. Central banks are given the task of managing the amount of money in an economy and the interest rates in that economy. That is, they conduct **monetary policy**.

To understand how a central bank controls money supply and interest rates you need to appreciate that it acts as banker to the banks (including other depository institutions, e.g. building societies). As well as accepting deposits from them it has special powers because it can insist that each bank leaves a certain proportion of the amount it has received as deposits from its customers (households, small businesses, etc.) at the central bank. If a bank's reserves at the central bank fall below the minimum required then they have to top this up. Furthermore, banks and other depository institutions like to maintain an additional buffer beyond the required reserves[1] at the central bank. This extra safety margin of money is called excess reserves. This is an amount that makes the bank feel comfortable about the prospect of a sudden outflow of cash – say dozens of large depositors withdraw billions over a period of a week (there is more on the need for reserves in Chapter 3). The target amount of the excess reserves may, in fact, be largely dictated by the banking regulator (which is usually the central bank) and may be strongly influenced by international agreements on the appropriate amounts (e.g. Basel III) – see 'Bank supervision' later in this chapter.

Thus the central bank has a liability – it accepted deposits from banks. Another liability of a central bank is what you see written on notes (or coins) that you have in your wallet or purse. The central bank 'promises to pay the bearer on demand the sum of...' or some similarly worded promise.[2] Thus a typical

---

[1] Called banks' operational deposits with the Bank of England in the UK.
[2] A long time ago you might have been able to take along your currency notes to the central bank and receive gold or silver in exchange. Today if you took along, say, a £20 note you will only receive other notes in return, say four £5 notes. Because these notes (and coins) are generally accepted as a medium of exchange and store of value they can function as money.

commercial bank will hold some of its assets in the form of reserves either at the central bank or in the form of vault cash in hand. As well as the money held in the banks an economy will have **currency in circulation**, that is outside of banks. The combination of the two is the monetary base:

Monetary base = Currency in circulation + Reserves

Reserves = Required reserves + Vault cash (excess reserves)

It is changes in these accounts that determine the size of a nation's money supply (everything else being held constant). If there is an increase either in the currency in circulation or reserves there will be an increase in the money supply. An increase in reserves, either cash deposited by a bank at the central bank or vault cash, leads to an increase in the level of deposits and thus contributes to the money supply. Central banks conduct monetary policy by changing the country's monetary base.

Typically, a central bank might insist that, say, 10 per cent of the amount deposited by customers be held as the **required reserve ratio** (reserves as a percentage of deposits). The reserve accounts held by banks at the central bank are used to settle accounts between depository institutions when cheques and electronic payments are cleared. A bank may also hold, say, another 5–10 per cent of the amount deposited by customers as excess reserves. It is important to note that the sole supplier of reserves – notes and coins and balances at the central bank as liabilities of the central bank – is the central bank.

The monetary base described above is often referred to as M0, which is a very extreme form of **narrow money**, i.e. defining what money is in a very narrow way. Banks can use this base to create **broad money**, which is a multiple of the monetary base. The definitions of broad money vary from country to country, but generally include money that is held in the form of a current (checking) account or deposit account, and some money market instruments. These broad money aggregates often have names such as M3 or M4. You can see why it is difficult to define money because banks can 'create money'. This is illustrated by Exhibit 6.1.

Remember: the creator of the monetary base is the central bank because it has a monopoly on the issuance of currency. If it has control over this then it can strongly influence the broader money supply (including deposits at banks) through the reserves requirements. So, once the system has settled down from the injection of a new deposit then it will be fairly stable – little money creation or removal.

Assume that all banks in a monetary system are required to keep 20% of deposits as reserves. Bank A has $100m of deposits from customers. Because it is sticking to the reserve requirement (both required by the central bank and its own prudential reserves policy) it lends out only $80m and keeps $20m as cash or in its account with the central bank (assume no vault cash for simplicity).

Bank A's opening balance sheet

Assets		Liabilities	
Reserves	$20m	Deposits	$100m
Loans	$80m		

If now deposits in Bank A are increased by $5m the position changes. Deposits rise to $105m and reserves rise to $25m as the additional $5m is initially held as reserves at the central bank

Bank A: an increase in deposits – intermediate period

Assets		Liabilities	
Reserves	$25m	Deposits	$105m
Loans	$80m		

This means that the reserve ratio has risen to $25m ÷ $105m = 23.8%. The bank earns no or little interest from reserves, so it will wish to reduce it back to 20% by lending out the extra. The next balance sheet shows the amount of lending that leaves a 20% reserve ratio, $84m.

Bank A: lending out just enough to attain minimum reserve ratio

Assets		Liabilities	
Reserves	$21m	Deposits	$105m
Loans	$84m		

▶

Exhibit 6.1   Money creation – the credit multiplier

Now let us bring in more banks. In lending an additional $4m Bank A will have an impact on the rest of the banking system. If the $4m is lent to a company and, initially at least, that company deposits the money in Bank B, then at the central bank, Bank A's account will be debited (reserves go down) and Bank B's account will be credited (reserves increase). Bank B will lend out 80% of the amount, or $3.2m, keeping $800,000 in reserves to maintain its 20% ratio of reserves to deposits. The $3.2m lent finds its way to Bank C which, again, holds 20% as reserves and lends the rest... and so on. At each stage 80% of the deposit is lent out, increasing the deposits of other banks, encouraging them to lend.

The effect on the banking system of an injection of $5m of money, under a reserve ratio of 20%

	Change in deposits, $m	Change in loans, $m	Change in reserves, $m
Bank A	5.00	4.00	1.00
Bank B	4.00	3.20	0.80
Bank C	3.20	2.56	0.64
Bank D	2.56	2.05	0.51
Bank E	2.05	1.64	0.41
Bank F	....	....	....
Bank G	....	....	....
Total of all banks	25	20	5

The credit multiplier is a reciprocal of the reserve ratio, which in this case = 1 ÷ 0.20 = 5. Following an injection of $5m into the financial system the whole process ends when an additional $25m of deposits have been created; equilibrium has been reached again. (The model is a simplification for illustrative purposes. In reality, there might be leakages from the system due to money flowing abroad, or people hold cash or buy government bonds rather than placing it in bank deposits.)

Exhibit 6.1   Continued

Let us think about where the initial deposit put into Bank A might have come from. If it came from a customer who withdrew it from another bank then the example is null and void because while Bank A benefits from the $5 million deposit the other bank, Bank X, sees a reduction in its reserves at the central bank by an equal amount. It can now lend less than it could before because it has to rebuild its reserves. Thus the stimulus effect of Bank A's deposit is exactly offset by the removal of money from the system by Bank X. If, however, the $5 million came from the central bank purchasing Treasury bills from an investor who then put the newly-created cash received into his account with Bank A then we have new money coming into the system and we can expect something like the credit multiplier effect shown above. The central bank is the only player here which can create money out of thin air and pump it into the system if the system is at equilibrium.

Thus, despite commercial banks' ability to create money on the way to equilibrium, there is a limit to the amount that the system as a whole can go up to, because for every dollar, pound, euro, etc. created there has to be a fraction held as a cash reserve. It is the central bank that controls the total volume of monetary base (reserves at the central bank plus cash in circulation and at deposit-taking institutions) and so the broader aggregates of money have an upper limit. Small changes in the monetary base can have a large impact on the amount of broad money in the system and so we often refer to the monetary base as **high-powered money**. It is the monetary base that central banks target to influence money supply, interest rates, inflation and economic output.

Central banks have three major tools they use to increase or decrease the money supply and interest rates:

- open market operations
- discount rate changes
- reserve requirement ratio changes.

Open market operations

This is the most important tool of monetary policy in most countries today. **Open market operations** means the buying and selling of government securities (Treasury bills and bonds) in the normal trading markets on a day-to-day basis. In purchasing government securities the central bank creates money to hand it over to those selling. It issues currency notes or it writes a cheque in the name of the owner. When the cheque is drawn on, the central bank just creates an amount of credit for itself to satisfy the buyer – money from thin air. When the central bank sells government securities the purchasers draw on their money in the banking system which leads to a lowering of reserves.

To illustrate the creation of money by a central bank we can take Bank A's balance sheet from Exhibit 6.1. The starting position is:

Bank A: Lending out just enough to attain minimum reserve ratio

Assets		Liabilities	
Reserves	$21m	Deposits	$105m
Loans	$84m		

The central bank wants to inject money into the financial system and lower interest rates. It offers to buy billions of dollars of government securities. One of the customers of Bank A sells $6 million of securities to the central bank. The central bank sends money to the customer of Bank A who deposits the newly-created money (an electronic record rather than cash) in Bank A.[3] Bank A adds this $6 million to its reserve account at the central bank. Now Bank A's balance sheet looks like this:

Bank A: Balance sheet after an injection of $6 million

Assets		Liabilities	
Reserves	$27m	Deposits	$111m
Loans	$84m		

Bank A has a very high reserve level relative to its deposits, $27 million ÷ $111 million = 24.3 per cent. The managers will want to employ the surplus money above that needed to maintain the target reserve ratio (20 per cent) to earn higher interest by lending it, thus new money flows into the financial system.

If the central bank wanted to drain money from the system through open market operations it would sell government securities to investors, which reduces the amount held by banks in their reserve accounts at the central bank or reduces vault cash. This would curb lending and raise interest rates.

Central banks tend to use Treasury securities to conduct open-market operations because the secondary market in these securities is very liquid and there is a large volume of these securities held by dealers and investors, meaning that the market can absorb a large number of buy and sell transactions without

---

[3] In many financial systems there is a select group of security dealers (often a wing of the major commercial and investment banks) with whom the central bank buys and sells government securities. It is these security dealers' deposit accounts that are credited and debited.

significantly moving the price. The main method used is a repurchase agreement – a repo – in which the central bank purchases securities with a prior agreement to sell them back to the counterparty after, say, 24 hours, 7 days or 14 days. The difference between the buying and selling price provides the effective interest rate. If the central bank wanted to drain money it would engage in a reverse repo, selling securities with a simultaneous agreement to buy them back for cash at a later date at a higher price (there is more on repos in Chapter 9).

Repos and reverse repos are, by their nature, temporary interventions because the opposite transaction takes place on maturity, a few days after the first buy or sell. There are times when the central bank wants to effect a more permanent change in the money supply. Then it can go for an outright transaction, a purchase or a sale that is not destined to be reversed in a few days.

What you need to bear in mind is that every day banks trade surplus reserves with each other. Banks always have an incentive to lend – even if only for 24 hours – if they find themselves with too many reserves. Each day there will be dozens of other banks that find themselves temporarily below the reserve level they need, and so they willingly borrow in the interbank market.

The main target for central banks is usually the overnight (24-hour) interest rate on loans of reserves from one bank to another. In the US this is the federal funds rate, in the eurozone it is the overnight repo rate in euros, and in the UK it is the overnight sterling repo rate. Switzerland opts for the Swiss franc LIBOR target rate.

When the central bank wants to change short-term interest rates it can often do so merely by announcing its new target rate and threatening to undertake open-market operations to achieve it rather than actually intervening. The money-market participants know that if they do not immediately move to the new rate they will find difficulties. For example, if the central bank shifts to target an interest rate lower than previously (i.e. it will lend on the repo market at a new lower rate) then anyone wanting to borrow will be foolish to borrow at a higher rate. Conversely, if the central bank announces a new higher target rate anyone wanting to lend will be foolish to accept a lower rate than the central bank's target, because it stands ready to trade at its stated rate.

Discount rate changes

There is an option for banks to borrow additional reserves from the central bank – this is **discount window borrowing**.[4] So, if Bank A is temporarily short of

---

[4] The European Central Bank offers loans at the **marginal lending rate** rather than the discount rate, in its **marginal lending facility**. In the UK the discount window is often referred to as **standing facilities**.

reserves it could ask the central bank to simply create additional reserves and add them to its account at the central bank. There is thus an increase in reserves in the financial system and an increase in the money supply. Furthermore, Bank A could borrow from the central bank's discount window even if it was not short of reserves. It can then lend the money to businesses and individuals or lend the additional reserves to other banks in the money markets (e.g. repo).

Discount loans have to be repaid. When they are, the total amount of reserves, the monetary base and the money supply will fall.

So, why are banks not continually borrowing from the discount window? Well, there's a catch. The central bank tends to charge an interest rate on discount window borrowing that is significantly higher (usually around 100 basis points) than banks can borrow in the money markets. If this interest premium falls then an increasing number of banks will borrow at the discount rate. If the premium rises then few banks will borrow this way. Thus banks rein in their lending to customers for fear of having to borrow themselves at punitive interest rates. The discount rate acts as a back-stop for the open-market target interest rate. The money-market (repo) rate will not rise above the discount rate, so long as the central bank remains willing to supply unlimited funds at the discount rate.

A few decades ago adjusting the discount rate was the main way in which many central banks effected monetary policy, but the problem with this approach became increasingly apparent. It is difficult to predict the quantity of discount rate borrowing that will occur if the discount rate is raised or lowered, and so it is difficult to accurately change the money supply. Today changes in the discount rate are used to signal to the market that the central bank would like to see higher or lower interest rates: a raising indicates that tighter monetary conditions are required with higher interest rates throughout; lowering it indicates that looser, more expansionary, monetary conditions are seen as necessary. Discount-rate borrowing is used by generally sound banks in normal market conditions on a short-term basis, typically overnight, at a rate above the normal, open-market, target rate. But, given the higher interest rate it is used sparingly. Companies in real trouble, unable to borrow in the money markets and experiencing severe liquidity problems, may have to pay an even higher interest rate than the discount rate to borrow from the central bank.

Reserve requirement ratio changes

The power to change the reserve requirement ratio is a further tool used by central banks to control a nation's money supply. A decrease in the reserve requirement ratio means that banks do not need to hold as much money at the central bank or in vault cash, and so they are able to lend out a greater percentage of their deposits, thus increasing the supply of money. The new loans result in consumption or investment in the economy, which raises inflows into other banks in the financial system and the credit multiplier effect takes hold, as illustrated in Exhibit 6.1. The process of borrowing and depositing in the banking system continues until deposits have grown sufficiently such that the new reserve amounts permit just the right amount of deposits – the target reserve ratio is reached.

The main drawback to using changes in the reserve ratio is that it is difficult to make many frequent small adjustments because to do so would be disruptive to the banking system (a sudden rise can cause liquidity problems for banks with low excess reserves). Open market operations, on the other hand, can be used every day to cope with fluctuations in monetary conditions.

Averaging reserves

The leading central banks usually do not require that reserves are a fixed percentage of deposits every day. Instead they insist on the average reserve ratio over a month being above a particular level. Thus, banks are permitted to go below the designated ratio for a number of days in the month, but will have to make up for this on other days. This allows a bank more flexibility because there are bound to be days when there is a large outflow (e.g. when millions of people pay their tax bills) which can be followed by a gradual rebuilding of reserves by borrowing from other financial institutions (or the central bank) over the following week or so.

How monetary policy affects the economy

The actions of the central bank are designed to have significant impact on the key economic variables. These relationships are shown in Exhibit 6.2. If the central bank believes that the economy needs to expand at a faster rate (while not unleashing high inflation) then it can follow the lightly-tinted route (selecting the most appropriate monetary tool). Lower interest rates encourage consumers to borrow and businesses to invest. If, however, it looks as though it is already expanding too fast to achieve the required inflation rate then the central bank can rein it in by following the darker-tinted route in which interest rates rise, money supply falls and people and businesses spend less.

Some central banks have a specific goal for inflation. For example, the European Central Bank (ECB) has a stated aim of a rate below, but close to, 2 per cent over

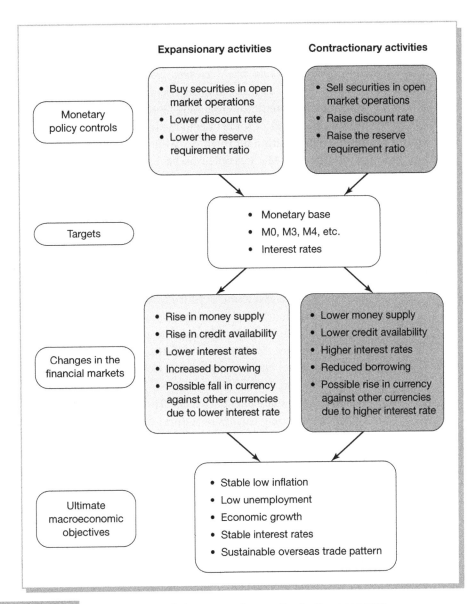

Exhibit 6.2   The flow-through from monetary policy to the economy

the medium term, whereas the Bank of England (BoE) is required to achieve 2 per cent, but anything within the 1–3 per cent range is regarded as acceptable in the short run, so long as there is a plan to move to nearer 2 per cent. Those central banks that have a specific target as well as those that do not, other than 'low and stable inflation', also take into account the impact of their actions on the other major macroeconomic variables. There are a number of further elements they consider:

- *High employment and steady economic growth.* Not only does unemployment often cause pain to those families affected by it, but the economy wastes resources in idleness, lowering long-term well-being. Having said that, it makes sense to allow some unemployment as people are happily searching for the right position for them. So, while they are searching they are classified as unemployed. Many people who have taken time out to attend college, raise a family or go travelling may re-enter the jobs market but not find an appropriate job quickly and so they are classified as unemployed. Matching people to suitable posts does not happen instantaneously, thus there will always be some amount of **frictional unemployment**. Another type is **structural unemployment**. This is where the skills people have do not match what the market needs or the location of people does not match the needs of employers. For example, in the 1980s tens of thousands of coal miners were made redundant and found it difficult to obtain new positions when their skill-set and location of their family homes were not suited to the newer industries. If the central bank tries to stimulate the economy through lower interest rates to such an extent that frictional and structural unemployment is reduced below its natural rate then inflation is likely to rise as output fails to keep up with the new quantities of money flooding the economy. Thus, we tolerate, even welcome, some unemployment. The best that policymakers can hope for is that the economy reaches its **natural rate of unemployment**, i.e. a level of **non-accelerating inflation rate of unemployment (NAIRU)**. To achieve long-run reductions in unemployment below the current NAIRU policymakers need to work on the supply-side efficiency of the economy, for example, raise skill levels, create a more pro-business, pro-innovation environment and culture, lower labour market rigidities inhibiting corporations from hiring and people from moving, and lower taxes to encourage investment by firms. The difficulty for our economic leaders is estimating the level of NAIRU. Is it at 4 per cent unemployment or 6 per cent? If a better job-finding service were launched would NAIRU decline significantly? It is around these issues that economists, central bankers and politicians debate.

- *Interest rate stability.* People and businesses are harmed by volatility in interest rates because of the additional uncertainty it introduces to their decision making, resulting in forward-planning problems, leading to lower economic output.

- *Stability of the financial system.* We discussed the main roles of the financial system players in Chapter 2, particularly the channelling of savings into productive use. These mechanisms can be disrupted if financial crises are permitted to occur. Just ask the Icelanders, Greeks and Irish if they value stability of the financial system. Instability can cause economic output drops, high unemployment, asset price crashes (e.g. houses) and austerity measures, cutting wages and pensions. While monetary policy is one tool to promote stability, there are many more measures that the central bank (or other designated regulators) can take. These are discussed later in this chapter.

▪ *Stability in the foreign exchange markets.* The economies of the nation states are increasingly integrated into the world economy with ever larger volumes of imports, exports and overseas investment. The value of a currency relative to others can have profound effects on the producers in that economy. For example, a rise in the currency may make exporting more difficult. Also, fluctuations in the currency make planning difficult. Thus central banks are cognisant of the impact of interest rate changes on the level and stability of the exchange rate.

Over a run of years the goal of price stability does not conflict with the other goals. For example, higher inflation does not produce lower unemployment so there is no long-term trade-off between these two goals. There might be a trade-off in the short run. So, lowering interest rates may encourage consumer spending, house purchase and corporate investment, and the taking on of more workers. But once the economy has reached its productive capacity limit, additional demand from the lower rates is likely to push up wages and prices, rather than output. The alarmed authorities then need to take firm action (e.g. much higher interest rates) to squeeze demand out of the economy, causing painfully higher levels of unemployment. All in all, it is better if price stability at a low inflation rate is pursued from year to year, rather than having to make corrections after explosions or slumps in demand. Stability promotes economic growth.

Having said this, it is important to avoid focusing excessively on inflation in the short term and thereby forcing economic growth to fluctuate too much. For example, for a number of months in 2010 and 2011 UK inflation was above the 3 per cent limit. Mervyn King, the Governor of the BoE, explained that it would be wrong to raise interest rates to counteract this, because he believed that the high inflation rate was merely temporary, and to raise rates while the UK economy was in recession could be very damaging. He, thus, temporarily prioritised growth over immediate inflation, while keeping a watchful stance on anticipated inflation a year or so down the line.

The independence of central banks

An important question for a government to decide is the degree of freedom they give their central bank to conduct monetary policy. Is it to be conducted by the central bank's own experts or should elected politicians have the ultimate say on whether interest rates should rise or fall?

There are two types of independence:

1 **Instrument independence**. The central bank can decide when and how to use monetary policy instruments without political interference.

2 **Goal independence**. The central bank decides the goals of monetary policy, for example inflation of 2 per cent or less.

Instrument independence is common, but goal independence is rare. The US central bank, the Federal Reserve (Fed), has both types of independence – politicians do not control the Board of Governors or the purse strings of the Fed (although they can influence the appointment of some board members). The European Central Bank has an extraordinary degree of independence. The member country governments of the Eurosystem are not permitted to instruct the ECB. The Maastricht Treaty, which established the monetary union, states that the long-term goal of the ECB is price stability, but did not specify what that meant, leaving it up to the Executive Board members to decide the target inflation rate. And, of course, the ECB has control over the tools it uses. Furthermore, whereas the US system can be changed by new legislation (if the politicians change the law they can establish control over the Fed), this is more difficult in the eurozone, because the Eurosystem's charter can only be altered by a revision of the Maastricht Treaty, which requires consent of *all* the signatory countries. In 1997 the Bank of England was given a high degree of instrument independence to decide when and how to raise or lower interest rates (prior to that the Chancellor of the Exchequer had ultimate control). However, the government can, in extreme economic circumstances, overrule the Bank for a limited period. The inflation goal is still established by the Chancellor.

The advantages of independence

■ *Political control can lead to higher inflation*. It is argued that politicians often have a short-term perspective driven by the need to impress voters before the next election. This may mean sacrificing a stable price level to achieve immediate improvements in unemployment, growth or house mortgage rates. The populace, also often short-sighted, sees the immediate improvement, but does not grasp the long-term damage wrought when inflation takes off in the low interest-rate environment.

▪ *Reduced temptation to support government spending.* The central bank regularly buys and sells bonds and Treasury bills previously issued by the government to influence the interest rates banks are charging each other when borrowing to top up their reserves. It is another step to start buying government instruments direct when the government wishes to expand its spending. In buying them the central bank will create new money which the government will put into the economy when it, say, buys new bridges or pays out more in social security. This can be dangerously inflationary. It is what Zimbabwe did in the 2000s – resulting in inflation of millions of per cent per year.

▪ *Politicians lack expertise.* Central bank employees have much more skill in this area than the average politician, or even the above average politician.

The disadvantages of independence

▪ *Undemocratic.* The central bank makes important decisions that affect everyone and yet it is in the control of people who are not accountable at the ballot box.

▪ *Central banks fail from time to time.* In the early 1930s central banks failed to put money into the financial system at crucial moments. They also failed to analyse and act upon the build-up to the 2008 crisis. Are these failures of independence? Were there wiser political voices outside the central bank anticipating problems and calling for robust countervailing action? I can't speak of the 1930s' politicians, but my memory of 2006 and 2007 is not peppered with smart politicians' warnings of doom.

Some academic research has investigated the correlation between independence and inflation performance and concluded that more independence leads to lower inflation without lower real economic performance (unemployment or output).

Quantitative easing

In extreme circumstances a central bank may find that short-term interest rates have been reduced to the lowest level they could go, and yet still economic activity does not pick up. People are so shocked by the crisis – increased chance of unemployment, lower house prices, lower business profits – that they cut down their consumption and investment regardless of being able to borrow at very low interest rates. This happened in 2009 and 2010. Annualised short-term interest rates in eurozone countries were less than 1 per cent, in the UK they were 0.5 per cent and in the US they were between 0 and 0.25 per cent. Clearly low short-term interest rates were not enough to get the economy moving, even with the additional boost of government deficit spending to the extent that up to one-eighth of all spending was from government borrowing.

In response another policy tool was devised: **quantitative easing**. This involves the central bank electronically creating money ('printing money') which is then used to buy assets from investors in the market. Thus pension funds, insurance companies, non-financial firms, etc. can sell assets, mostly long-term government bonds (but can include mortgage-backed securities and corporate bonds), and their bank accounts are credited with newly created money. This raises bank reserves, allowing more lending in the economy. Furthermore, the increased demand for government bonds raises their prices and lowers interest rates. In the UK the BoE bought £200 billion of such assets during 2009 and 2010. The Fed bought $1,750 billion bonds (mostly mortgage-backed and government), and then ran a second round (called QE2) in 2010–11 of $600 billion.

Safety and soundness of the financial system

The collapse of many banks into insolvency in 2008 is a reminder of the vulnerability of these institutions. The mere fear of a bank collapse can lead to recession/depression as a damaging wave of lowered confidence in financial institutions sweeps through economies. A hundred years ago banks would fail on a regular basis, but today we have a number of mechanisms to reassure people and businesses that their money is safe within the banking system. Some of these mechanisms were found wanting in the recent financial crisis and so policymakers are currently looking for fixes for these, but nevertheless the modern system is generally far safer than it was a hundred years ago.

Depositor insurance

Bank runs occur when depositors fear that because a bank holds in cash or near-cash only a fraction of the total deposits, that if, say, 20 per cent of depositors want to take their money in cash, the bank would not be able to pay and could be declared bust. Most of the time people are sanguine about this problem because they know that on a typical day the amount of net withdrawals (i.e. money taken from the bank minus money put into accounts at that bank) is a minuscule proportion of total deposits. This all relies on psychology: people have to have a great deal of confidence that the bank will be able to pay out when they want their money back. The trouble arises when something disturbs that confidence. In 2007, when news spread that Northern Rock, a building society turned bank, might be unable to repay depositors, panicked depositors queued around the blocks of towns and cities up and down the country to take out their money.

Losing one bank to a run, caused either by rational or irrational fear and rumour, is bad enough, but the problem stretches further than that because the bank subject to a run is likely to have lent other banks money or have other interbank transactions outstanding, e.g. it might be due to pay large sums on a number of derivatives deals. Once it feels under pressure from its depositors it might withdraw money it holds with other banks to raise some cash, causing one or two of them to have liquidity problems. They might then collapse, leading to yet more banks (which have lent to these banks or hold deposits from these banks) coming under pressure. And so a domino effect might flow through the banking system.

One way to reduce the risk of bank runs (and to make the system fairer for the innocent depositors) is for the government or some regulatory body to step in and say they will guarantee that depositors will be repaid even if the bank cannot do so. In the case of Northern Rock the UK government had to step in and guarantee all deposits without a limit on how much they would pay out to any one depositor. This was an extreme situation; normally a limit is set. Thus in the European scheme the limit is €100,000 per depositor. It is thought that people with large deposits are sophisticated enough to look after themselves, to be able to assess the bank's true financial status, and so should avoid high-risk banks, or at least demand a premium return for the additional risk. This policy does have a drawback though. In the autumn of 2010 corporations transferred billions of euros from their deposits in Irish banks because they were afraid the whole system was about to collapse and they saw the €100,000 of insurance as peanuts by comparison with their deposits. To some extent this fear became self-fulfilling as Irish banks lost cash and could not replace it other than by borrowing more from the ECB (see 'Lender of last resort' function below). Eventually the Irish financial system had to be rescued by the International Monetary Fund, European countries and the ECB.

In the US the insurer of deposits is not the Fed, but the **Federal Deposit and Insurance Corporation (FDIC)**, which pays out up to $250,000 per depositor. In the UK, until the Northern Rock crisis the **Financial Services Compensation Scheme** (outside of BoE) paid £30,000 in full and 90 per cent of the next £20,000. Because many depositors held more than £30,000 they knew that they were not fully covered and so rushed to withdraw their money from Northern Rock. Today the Scheme pays out full compensation up to the maximum of £85,000, which covers the vast majority of depositors.

Lender of last resort

Another safety net for banks and their depositors is the **lender of last resort** function of the central bank: to prevent a bank failure leading on to other bank failures the central bank will step in to provide reserves when no one else will lend to the banks. Following the September 11 2001 World Trade Center attack many cheques were stuck on grounded aircraft and so a number of banks missed an inflow of money for a few days, thus their reserves declined. Furthermore bank customers increased their demand for cash. The Federal Reserve kept the banking system going by adding $38 billion through repurchase agreements to the banks that needed money to restore their reserve levels. It also increased its discount window lending by 200-fold to $45 billion. The terrorists did not bring down the financial system.

In 2008 the sub-prime crisis produced a fear amongst the banks. They did not know the extent of another bank's exposure to the sub-prime mortgage instrument risk. In response they held onto cash and refused to lend it to other banks. The ECB and the Fed therefore provided very large volumes of short-term funds to the banks so that they could maintain reserve levels and not run out of cash.

Note that the lender of last resort function is not there all the time – it is for when the central bank governors judge there to be an emergency. Also, not every bank will be bailed out   many will be left to fail depending on the route they took to get to a poor liquidity or solvency position (was it fecklessness or bad luck? for example) or whether the bank's failure will cause a systemic collapse of the banking industry.

It is necessary to have both the lender of last resort role and deposit insurance schemes because insurance tends to cover only about 1 per cent of the outstanding deposits and liabilities – there are many financial deals, usually between banks, which dwarf retail deposits. These financial and corporate institutions need reassurance that the central bank will not permit a failure due to a bank running short of reserves – a liquidity crisis.

An extreme form of support for a bank is for the government to nationalise it, as happened with Northern Rock in 2008 and Anglo Irish Bank in 2009. While not fully nationalised, 83 per cent of Royal Bank of Scotland's shares and 41 per cent of Lloyds Bank shares are now owned by the UK taxpayer.

Too big to fail

The danger with having a lender of last resort facility available to banks is that it might encourage banks to take high risk. If their bets are successful then the managers and their shareholders reap the reward. If they fail they are bailed out by the central bank or government. This is a moral hazard problem, that is, encouraging bad behaviour. The problem for the rest of society is not too great when it comes to small banks, whose failure would not cause knock-on failures of other banks or financial institutions. The authorities often let these go bust and impose pain on the managers (lose jobs), shareholders (lose all value in their shares) and bondholders (bonds become worthless), to encourage other banks to believe that they will not be saved regardless of incompetence or recklessness. The problem arises with the large banks, which have numerous interbank and other borrowings and derivative transactions, that could pose a threat to the entire system should they fail; because if they go then many of their counterparties might lose so much in the fallout (liquidity-wise or solvency-wise) that they fail too. These are the banks that pose a **systemic risk**.

Rather than size being the criterion we should really focus on degree of importance and significance of the bank dubbed 'too important to fail'. The phrase 'too big to fail' has stuck with the media, but increasingly policymakers are using **'Sifi, systemically important financial institutions'**.

The regulators frequently face a difficult decision. For example, in 2008 Bear Stearns was saved because it was seen as necessary to step in and save the bank. Then along comes the failing Lehman Brothers asking for help. Rightly or wrongly the authorities felt that Lehman could be allowed to go without money from the central bank or government being pumped in to save it. Many now believe that this was an error, that Lehman posed a very high systemic risk which went unrecognised until it was too late (more on this story in Chapter 19).

Currently, governments and regulators are grappling with the problem presented of having so many banks that are too big to fail. Should we break them up into smaller units so that each individual unit can go bust without any systemic/domino effect? Should we tax them more because of the costs they impose on society? Should we impose very high capital reserve ratios and liquidity reserve ratios (and make them even higher for the most risky activities) to reduce the likelihood of liquidation? Should we introduce **living wills**, whereby banks have to report regularly to the authorities on how they would put into effect an orderly winding down of the business as well as how they would plan for recovery in a crisis?[5]

Bank supervision

It is important that an authority investigates and approves the appointment of those who operate banks and continues monitoring and surveillance to ensure they are operated well. This is **bank supervision** or **prudential supervision**. Banks can be powerful money-grabbing tools in the hands of crooks. They can

---

[5] A resolution regime would need to be established and authority to control a bank's demise be given to a resolution agency. This might involve forcing holders of bank bonds to accept losses alongside shareholders.

also be a temptation to over-ambitious entrepreneurs who may see a large pot of (depositors') money that could be used to invest in speculative ventures. Thus, the authorities (often central banks) license or charter all banks (and other deposit-taking institutions) to ensure that they are run by fit and proper persons. In this way any proposal for a new bank is scrutinised, as are the controllers of the bank. The regulator then requires regular reports and makes regular visits to the banks to ensure that there is compliance with the safety rules. This usually includes aspects shown in Exhibit 6.3.

The central bank may also consider whether consumers are sufficiently well-protected against unfair selling, bad advice, poor-quality products, as well as discrimination (e.g. racial). They may also look at whether the bank's electronic systems are safe against cyber attack (e.g. criminals hacking into accounts and stealing money). If, on examination, a bank performs badly on any of the CAMELS factors the regulator will order it to correct its behaviour. In extreme cases the bank will be closed.

It is not always the case that the central bank acts as the main supervisor of banks. In the UK the Financial Services Authority (FSA) is the primary bank supervisor until 2013 when responsibility will be handed over to the BoE, apart from consumer protection aspects (which will be handled by the Financial Conduct Authority – see Chapter 18).

Capital and liquidity adequacy

Banks know that they would be foolish to lend out all the money they take as deposits. It makes sense to have self-imposed rules on what proportion to keep in cash and what proportion to keep in short-term securities (e.g. money market instruments) that could fairly quickly be turned into cash. However, banks are foolish from time to time, and are tempted away from the rational path and therefore need externally imposed rules to prevent them from stepping over the line that takes them into imprudent territory. Holding cash and short-term lending is usually less profitable than long-term lending and so ambitious bankers, looking to boost profits, sometimes transfer more of their resources to long-term lending, leaving only a small buffer of cash or near-cash to meet immediate extraordinary cash outflows should, say, large numbers of depositors insist on a return of their money. In other words, they take excessively-high liquidity risk.

The other major risk is solvency risk. This is less to do with running out of cash in the immediate future and more to do with allowing the capital base of the bank to diminish to such an extent that the assets of the bank (loans to customers, etc.) are barely greater than the liabilities (e.g. deposits). In such a situation it would

	Examples of questions considered
C Capital adequacy	Does it have sufficient equity capital for the amount of lending it's doing? Are management prepared to obtain additional capital?
A Asset quality	Are the assets held too risky? Is there good diversification? Are there sound processes/systems for controlling risk (e.g. staff are abiding by prudent policies and have limits relating to the risk exposure that can be created)? Is there sufficient provision for bad debts (the bank examiner can force a write-off)?
M Management	Is the quality of its management good? Honest and competent at identifying, measuring, monitoring and controlling risk? Are there adequate controls and internal information flows? Good controls to prevent fraud?
E Earnings	Are earnings stable at a reasonably high level? Is the source of earnings high quality?
L Liquidity	Does the bank hold sufficient reserves? Are there plenty of assets that can be converted to cash quickly without serious loss of value? Does the bank have good access to money market loans?
S Sensitivity to market risk	Are management processes good for coping with interest rate risk, exchange rate risk, equity market risk and commodity risk? Is the bank particularly sensitive to these risks?

Exhibit 6.3   The CAMELS method of bank inspection

not take too many bad debt write-offs as customers go bust, for example, for the bank to find that it cannot repay all its depositors and other creditors. Other events that could reduce assets below liabilities include a collapse in value of the bank's complex securities holdings, fraud or the failure of a subsidiary.

Thus, it is possible for a bank to look good on a liquidity perspective – plenty of cash in the vault – but nevertheless its liabilities exceed its assets. Conversely, a bank could have plenty of capital, as assets greatly exceed liabilities, but run out of cash in the short term due to a large outflow over a matter of days. Obviously lowering both liquidity risk and solvency risk is important to the well-being of the financial system.

A safe reserve level

The questions regulators have grappled with for many decades are: what is a safe level for capital reserves? And, what is a safe level for liquidity reserves? If we look at capital reserves first we can start our thinking by recognising that some assets held by a bank have little or no risk of default. Obviously, as cash has no risk of default there is no need to keep a capital buffer for this asset. Some types of loans made by banks, for example lending to the German, UK or US governments, have some degree of risk of default but this is very small. On the other hand, lending to a manufacturer usually has a fairly high level of default. It is clear that we need different amounts of capital depending on the asset category. Thus, the total of all unsecured corporate loans a bank holds might need to be backed up with, say, 8 per cent of their balance sheet value composed of capital, whereas the loans to local government lending needs to be backed up with only, say, 1.6 per cent of their value in the form of capital.

This line of thought is leading us to the concept of **risk-weighted assets**. Thus if the 'normal' capital proportion put aside is 8 per cent for loans such as unsecured corporate debt this is given a weighting of 100 per cent, i.e. it is not reduced from the full 8 per cent. So a £10 million loan needs the bank to have £800,000 of capital – of course, the bank will also source money from depositors, etc. to lend the £10 million. A total of £10 billion of loans needs £800 million. The weight for mortgages might only be 50 per cent, which means that if the bank holds £5 billion of mortgages it has to back that with capital of £200 million ($0.08 \times 0.50 \times £5$ billion). The holding of government bills issued by a developing country as bank assets might require only 20 per cent of the full capital safety reserve – the risk-weighting is 20 per cent. Thus, a collection of £3 billion of bills will require £3 billion $\times 0.20 \times 0.08 = £48$ million.

Another way of looking at this is to first reduce the asset values by their risk-weighting and then take 8 per cent of the risk-weighted value – see Exhibit 6.4.

Assets	Full balance sheet value (£m)	Risk-weighting (%)	Risk-weighted value (£m)
Cash	100	0	0
Treasury bills	3,000	20	600
Mortgages	5,000	50	2,500
Unsecured loans	10,000	100	10,000
Total	**18,100**		**13,100**

Exhibit 6.4   A bank's capital risk-weighting

Total capital required: £13,100 million × 0.08 = £1,048 million. Thus, bank assets must exceed bank liabilities by £1,048 million to withstand the possibility of a substantial proportion becoming bad loans.

Basel I

Capital reserve levels are not just national affairs, because banking is international. The 'banker to the central banks' is the **Bank for International Settlements** based in Basel, Switzerland. The central bankers gathered together in the 1980s to discuss setting minimum solvency standards applicable to any bank from a member country of the Basel committee. Now the 'Basel rules' have been adopted in more than 100 countries.

To understand the Basel rules you need to first deal with a point of difficulty I have so far skipped over: defining what we mean by capital. The Basel I committee included a number of forms of finance (e.g. preference shares) as well as money raised from ordinary shareholders or the previous year's profit retained in the business.

Basel II

In the late 1990s regulators and bankers concluded that the Basel I rules were too simplistic because they took broad categories of loan and insisted that the same risk-weight apply to each. Thus, when any bank from an OECD (Organisation for Economic Cooperation and Development) country borrowed the lending was to be regarded as having the same risk-weighting (i.e. 20 per cent) as for all other OECD banks, regardless of whether it was a US bank or from a more risky country. The risk-weighting for this type of loan was much lower than lending to multinational corporations whose loans were often given a 100 per cent weight, and yet most observers would agree that many multinationals are safer borrowers than some banks in some OECD countries. Another bone of contention was that Basel I did not properly differentiate between a loan to a company with an AAA credit rating and one to a company with a much lower rating – they all carried the same weight. This led to a form of **regulatory arbitrage** in which, within a category (same risk-weight), banks mostly lent to the riskiest clients because this paid the highest interest without requiring any more capital than a low-risk, low-interest-rate loan.

Basel II was launched in the mid-2000s and made much greater use of credit ratings of both government debt and corporate debt to decide weightings. Thus, AAA or AA debt would get a zero weighting, whereas grades of B– or less would get a 150 per cent weighting. They went further, and recognised that a high proportion of bank assets did not have credit ratings and so banks were permitted to use 'internal ratings' devised from their own models to risk-weight assets (subject to monitoring by their national central banks). Also Basel II took account of market risk (the risk that financial market assets, such as securitised bonds, can decrease in price on the markets) and operational risk (the way the bank is run can lead to calamity, e.g. a rogue trader destroys the bank, or there are other operational dangers, e.g. another 9/11 attack could damage a bank's access to finance). Banks were also required to disclose some other risks, such as concentration risk (too many eggs in one basket) and liquidity risk.

Also, there are a number of off-balance sheet assets (and liabilities) for which capital needs to be assigned. Thus, the holding of positions in derivatives, or positions in the foreign exchange market or commodity market, of commercial letters of credit and bank guarantees creates the possibility of loss and so could erode capital. Under Basel II these items were risk-weighted and added to the on-balance sheet assets.

Unfortunately Basel II was not a success. Surprise, surprise, once the banks were able to use their own valuation and risk models to influence the regulatory capital level the amount they held fell. Well, you see, bankers were so smart that they had diversified away much of the risk, or they had bought insurance so that if a loan went bad the insurer paid up. Lower risk, therefore lower risk-weighting. Perfect. Except they forgot to account for the possibilities of asset returns all going down together (so much for diversification) or for the insurers/derivative counterparties going bust and not paying out.

Basel III

Basel II was rapidly overtaken by events: the financial crisis revealed that many banks had not been cautious enough in setting their capital and liquidity reserves. The regulatory framework simply did not work. The rules were complicated, carefully calculated from detailed formulae, but as with so much in finance, the answers were precisely wrong rather than roughly right. Only five days before Lehman went bust it had a safe-sounding capital ratio of 11 per cent. There was far too much optimism, far too much faith in the reported market value of assets, and far too little recognition of the possibility that the new-fangled financial instruments can lose value overnight and that, when they do so, many banks experience knock-on effects and they all collapse together in an enmeshed mass. Banks had moved so far away from simple deposit taking and lending into weird and dangerous securities that it was difficult for the regulators to keep up. Banks would deliberately structure an obligation so that it could be granted a low risk-weighting, even though the bankers knew that the real exposure was high. For example, if you took a group of mortgages that had a risk-weighting of 50 per cent and converted them into securitised bonds with an AAA rating you could sell them to other investors, taking them off the balance sheet. You could then replace the asset by buying other banks' AAA-rated mortgage-backed bonds and you no longer need to hold much capital reserve for them. Risk just seemed to disappear from the system.

Currently, Basel III is being designed and rolled out, and is much tougher. Firstly, the definition of what can be called capital has been narrowed down to exclude virtually everything other than money put in by bank shareholders or kept in the bank on behalf of shareholders from retained earnings. This is called '**core tier 1**' and leaves out preference shares, unsecured bonds, etc.

Secondly, core tier 1 is being effectively raised to 7 per cent, from the previous typical level of 2 per cent. The picture is a little more complicated than that however – as shown in Exhibit 6.5.

Those undertaking risky activities, especially trading financial instruments, such as securitised bonds in the market, face much higher capital requirements under Basel III. The capital reserve levels shown in Exhibit 6.5 are to be required in normal times. In a financial crisis regulators expect the buffer to be partially used up – thus it might fall to the minimum 4.5 per cent level.

These new rules are to be phased in over the period until the end of 2018. For the years 2013–15 the minimum (simply to operate as a bank) is to be gradually

'Minimum'

4.5%

Simply to operate as a bank this is required (up from 2% under Basel II)

'Conservation buffer'

2.5%

Any bank that wants to pay a dividend or bonuses to staff must have 4.5% plus 2.5%

'Countercyclical buffer'

0–2.5%

National regulators may impose this extra requirement in boom
times to counter the effects of a bubble

'Systemic groups' buffer'

1–2%

(estimated, still in discussion)

The systemically important financial institutions
that pose a global risk have to hold more

Exhibit 6.5   Basel III core tier 1 capital to be held by banks as a percentage of
risk-weighted assets

raised to 4.5 per cent of risk-weighted assets. In the four years after 2015 the
conservation buffer will be phased in on top of the minimum until the full 7 per
cent is reached. This seems a leisurely timetable, but many central banks have
already signalled that they expect their banks to achieve the targets much faster
than this. Some countries have already been explicit in stating that they will
go further than the Basel committee recommendations. Switzerland is insisting
that UBS and Credit Suisse expand the conservation buffer from 2.5 per cent to
8.5 per cent. However, three percentage points of that may be in the form of a
new type of capital called **contingent convertible (CoCos) instruments**. These
behave like bonds, paying a coupon, but convert to equity if a bank's capital
ratio falls below a predetermined level. The Swiss are also insisting on a 6 per
cent systemic groups' buffer, rather than 1–2 per cent. That is a total of 19 per
cent of risk-weighted assets as a capital buffer! At least it does not intend to add

a counter-cyclical buffer as well.[6] UK regulators have signalled that UK banks will also be subject to higher capital ratios than under Basel III – the current expectation is that 10 per cent will be the minimum core tier 1 ratio.

Basel III on liquidity risk

Basel III also deals with liquidity – the ability to pay out cash on deposit withdrawals and other outflows of cash while satisfying loan commitments and other obligations. Liquidity management consists of two parts:

1 **Asset management**. Making sure there is enough cash and near-cash available at any one time.

2 **Liability management**. Obtaining liquid resources quickly and avoiding excessive outflows of cash to repay creditors in the near-term. For example, the bank maintains access to the money markets and obtains additional funds for liquidity by borrowing there if required – it only needs to offer a slightly higher interest rate than others to obtain billions almost instantly. That is the theory at least, but we now have less faith in this method than bankers did before 2008 because all of a sudden no one was lending in these markets. The other aspect of liability management is not to have a high proportion of liabilities maturing in the next few months or years. Thus, long-term bond issues are to be favoured with a spread of maturities over many years.

The Basel III rules insist that banks maintain a high **liquidity coverage ratio**, that is enough cash and near-cash to survive a 30-day market crisis on the same scale as the Lehman-induced crisis – that is a complete freeze in the money markets so the bank cannot access borrowed cash. However, because many banks lobbied their governments hard saying that they could not reach this level of liquidity quickly without significantly reducing lending the implementation of this new rule has been delayed until 2015. Until then it is 'observational', regulators speak for monitoring as banks work their way up to the standard to see if there are serious unintended consequences. No politician wanted to take the slightest chance of reduced lending at a time when we were trying to recover from recession.

The other liquidity risk-reducing measure is known as the **net stable funding rule**. It seeks to reduce banks' dependence on short-term funding. The new rule will not apply until 2018 because of the current weakness of the banks in some countries.

---

[6] Switzerland, as a small country, has to be very careful, because the assets of its banks are many times annual GDP. A slip by them could bankrupt the entire nation, as happened to Iceland.

The current direction of travel is much more focused on **macro-prudential regulation** than previously. That is, trying to reduce systemic risks rather than assuming that a sound system can be built by focusing only on supervising individual banks (**micro-prudential regulation**). One aspect of this is to prevent bubbles building up in the financial system (e.g. irrational optimism about the increasing value of a group of assets, e.g. houses). Hence the extra capital added in boom times (a **counter-cyclical regulatory capital** regime). Another aspect is to prevent contagion across the system: measures here include high capital ratios for all banks at all times and inspections to ensure limited exposure to any one counterparty bank going bust. However, central banks will have a difficult time explaining to lenders, borrowers and politicians that we should have greater constraints on bank lending when times are good. Politicians are likely to ask why the central bank is slowing things down when clearly we are not in a bubble (they never see them beforehand), merely booming as a result of their brilliant and beneficent policies that have led us to a new era of faster growth.

Other activities of central banks

Banker to the government and national debt management

Central banks usually act as their government's banker. They hold the government's bank account and provide services such as deposit holding. As taxes go in the account balance rises, but as the government pays private contractors its account at the central bank will be debited, while the commercial banker to the contractor will see an uplift in its central bank account. The central bank may also administer the national debt, raising money by selling Treasury bills and bonds. Increasingly this task is undertaken by a separate organisation; in the UK by the Debt Management Office. **National debt** is the cumulative outstanding borrowings of a government. This can amount to a very large sum of money. For the UK the figure is over 80 per cent of the size of annual national output, Italy and Belgium are already over 100 per cent.

Currency issue

Central banks control the issue of bank notes and often control the issue of coins.[7] Notes are issued to commercial banks as they demand them, but in return their reserves at the central bank are surrendered. It is important that the central bank has a monopoly over deciding the size of the issue because excess amounts can result in high inflation, while too little can inhibit the economy. In the past, if the economy grew in nominal terms by 6 per cent the central

---

[7] In the UK, for example, coins are produced by another organisation, The Royal Mint.

bank would generally issue a further 6 per cent of notes to keep up with the needs of commerce. However, in recent times this relationship has become more complicated as we increasingly use electronic funds transfer rather than cash. In addition to increasing the volume of notes the central bank stands ready to replace banknotes that are wearing out.

Smooth functioning of the payments system

A central bank may run some or all of the payment systems in an economy, such as cheque clearing and for electronic transactions. Those systems it does not run it may oversee as a regulator.

Currency reserve control

Countries find it prudent to hold a reserve of gold and foreign currencies at their central banks. This can be useful as rainy-day money and for intervening in the foreign exchange markets, for example, using the foreign currency to buy the home currency, thereby increasing demand for it and raising its exchange rate. Even countries that permit a floating exchange rate (see Chapter 16) may want to smooth out sharp day-to-day fluctuations.

Coordination with other central banks and international bodies

We have already discussed one form of international cooperation (on solvency and liquidity rules) under the auspices of the BIS at Basel. The BIS also acts as a kind of banker to the central banks. It helps in the transfer of money from one central bank to another and keeps a proportion of the central banks' reserves. Central banks also work with the International Monetary Fund. For example, they worked together on the bail-out of the Irish government in 2010–11. Another international economic and financial point of discussion and coordination is the regular G20 meetings – gatherings of finance ministers, presidents and prime ministers of the 20 leading economies. Central bankers have a significant input in terms of preparing for the meetings and then may help with the process of implementing agreements.

Bank of England

The Bank of England is over 300 years old. Despite its name it is the central bank for the whole of the UK. It was originally mainly used as the government's bank that raised borrowed money for its master. In Victorian times it was granted a monopoly on the issue of new banknotes and was used to rescue individual banks and the banking system. It also managed the nation's foreign currency and gold reserves.

It is managed by the Court of Directors, which consists of a governor, two deputy governors and nine non-executive directors, responsible for the overall stability of the banking system as a whole:

- stability of the monetary system: setting interest rates and dealing with day-to-day fluctuations in liquidity;

- payment systems oversight and strengthening to reduce systemic risk;

- macro-prudential regulation of the financial system as a whole;

- authorisation and micro-prudential supervision of banks and other deposit-taking institutions (from 2013);

- note issuance;

- lender of last resort in selected instances – some banks will be allowed to fail;

- managing the UK's gold and currency reserves and intervening in the foreign exchange markets.

Monetary policy is decided by the **Monetary Policy Committee (MPC)** that consists of the Governor, his two deputies, the Bank's chief economist and director for markets and four outside experts. These experts are drawn from the academic community as well as the world of business (particularly banks). Also, they can and have been non-UK citizens, with expertise being the over-riding consideration. The MPC meets each month to decide on the short-term interest rate target. The BoE staff then engage in open market operations in the money market to move the market rates to the desired target. If the inflation rate falls below 1 per cent or rises above 3 per cent then the Governor has to write a letter to the Chancellor of the Exchequer explaining why.

European Central Bank

The European Central Bank (ECB), given responsibility for monetary policy in 1999, is part of the **European System of Central Banks, ESCB (Eurosystem).** The National Central Banks (NCBs) were not discarded but remain important parts of the regulatory system. The ECB and the ESCB control monetary policy for those countries that are members of the **European Monetary Union**, the eurozone. The governors of each of the 17 NCBs have a vote on the Governing Council that makes decisions on monetary policy. Each of the NCBs became independent of both the European Commission and the governments of the individual states when the ESCB was established, if they were not already independent.

The ECB, based in Frankfurt, has an executive board consisting of the president, the vice-president and four other members, who are appointed by a committee of heads of state for eight years. These six people are also voting members of the Governing Council. The Governing Council of 23 meets each month to decide monetary policy and announces the target short-term interest (repo) rate (the **target financing rate**).

Monetary operations are not centralised at the ECB, but are conducted by the individual national central banks. In open market operations (called **main refinancing operations (MRO)**), banks and other credit institutions submit bids to borrow and the central banks decide which bids to accept – the unattractively-priced offers will not be accepted. This is usually in the repo market or secured loans market. For discount lending (marginal lending facility) the national central banks will lend, against collateral, overnight loans at, say, 75 or 100 basis points over the target financing rate, thus providing a ceiling rate in the markets. Banks may also deposit money with the ECB and receive interest, say 75 or 100 basis below the target financing rate (**deposit facility**).

The ECB insists that banks hold a sum equivalent to 2 per cent of the amount held in cheque accounts and other short-term deposits in reserve accounts at the national central bank (interest is paid on this money at a low rate, currently 0.25 per cent).

As well as monetary policy, including the issuance of banknotes, the ECB is responsible for the conduct of foreign exchange operations and holds and manages the official reserves (gold and currency) of the eurozone countries. It also promotes the smooth working of payment systems. Prudential supervision of financial institutions is a responsibility of the NCBs, as are payment mechanisms and the stability of their national financial systems.

The US Federal Reserve

The Americans have a heightened fear of centralised power, and as a consequence emphasise the need for checks and balances in society. One manifestation of their mistrust was the failure of the nineteenth century experiments with establishing central banks because the public mistrusted such a nationwide system, especially if it could be manipulated by Wall Street money men. Thus for much of the nineteenth and the early part of the twentieth century there was no central bank to act as lender of last resort should banks' reserves get uncomfortably low. As a result there were regular runs on banks and hundreds of bank collapses. The 1907 crisis brought so many bank failures and massive losses to depositors that a consensus was finally reached to create a central bank, which was established in 1913.

However, the Federal Reserve is unlike other central banks because it was structured in such a way as to disperse power to the regions of the country and to disperse power amongst a number of individuals so that neither Wall Street nor politicians could manipulate it. There are 12 Federal Reserve banks, one for each region of the country. These are overseen by directors who are mostly drawn from the private sector banks and corporates in that region, so that they reflect the US citizenry. These regional Federal Reserve banks supervise the financial institutions in their area. (The New York one is the busiest on this score, with so many universal banks to watch over.) They also make discount rate loans to banks in their area; issue new currency; clear cheques; supervise the safety and soundness of banks in their area with regard to an application for a bank to expand or merge; and investigate and report on local business conditions.

In addition to the 12 regional Federal Reserve banks there is a Board of Governors of the Federal Reserve System based in Washington which has seven members called governors (usually economists), including the chairman, currently Ben Bernanke. These are appointed by the US President and confirmed by the Senate, but for terms much longer than those of the President or members of congress, at 14 years, to reduce the chance of political control of a governor.

Monetary policy through the use of open market operations is decided by the **Federal Open Market Committee (FOMC)** whose voting members include the seven governors of the Federal Reserve Board plus the presidents of the New York Fed and four other regional Feds.[8] Thus, there is input from the regions. Note that the Board has the majority of the votes. The FOMC meets about every six weeks to decide the general stance on open market operations (setting the target federal funds rate, which is the interest rate banks charge each other to lend their balances at the Federal Reserve overnight), but the actual day-to-day interventions in the money markets are conducted by the trading desk at the Federal Reserve Bank of New York. The manager of this desk reports back to the FOMC members daily.

The Board sets reserve requirements and shares the responsibility with the regional Reserve banks for discount rate policy. The Fed now pays interest on

---

[8] The 12 presidents of the regional Feds rotate as voting members. All 12 presidents attend the meetings; it is just that 7 of them participate in discussions but do not have a vote.

reserves. The Board plays a key role in assuring the smooth functioning and continued development of the nation's payments system. The Board approves bank mergers and applications for new activities, and regulates the permissible activities of domestic and foreign banks in the US. However, the safety and soundness of the US financial system is entrusted to a number of different government agencies alongside the Fed.

The chairman and his team have some other duties:

■ advising the nation's president on economic policy; and

■ representing the country in international negotiations on economic matters.

Websites

www.bankofengland.co.uk	Bank of England
www.bis.org	Bank for International Settlements
www.banque-france.fr	Banque de France (France's central bank)
www.nbb.be	Banque Nationale de Belgique (Belgium's central bank)
www.centralbank.ie	Central Bank of Ireland
www.nationalbanken.dk	Danmarks Nationalbank (Denmark's central bank)
www.dnb.nl	De Nederlandsche Bank (Netherland's central bank)
www.bundesbank.de	Deutsche Bundesbank (Germany's central bank)
www.ecb.int	European Central Bank
www.federalreserve.gov	Federal Reserve Bank
www.norges-bank.no	Norges Bank, Norway's Central Bank
www.bof.fi	Suomen Pankki (Finland's central bank)
www.riksbank.com	Sveriges Riksbank (Sweden's central bank)

7

Pooled investment funds

If you could not rely on soundly-run pension funds imagine how fearful you might be as you grew older, not knowing where your income was going to come from? Saving under the mattress is one way to reduce the fear. But wouldn't it be far better to save into a fund that invested that money in industries around the world or in government bonds, producing a nice steady accumulation of wealth? Wouldn't it be better to have the discipline of being a member of a scheme that every month deducts contributions from your salary – that you would barely notice – and places it at arm's length from you, under professional management, and you were forbidden to touch it until you were ready to retire? And even after retirement, you could only take a portion of it each year – imposing another discipline to avoid you over-optimistically spending, or investing in get-rich-quick schemes. Clearly, pension managers, trustees and consultants provide an important service.

Another group of organisations that allocates funds to the purchase of securities is the pooled or collective investment funds. These go under various names from mutual funds and unit trusts to investment trusts and sovereign wealth funds. They help investors to spread their savings across a range of securities under professional management.

Pensions

While many countries provide a basic state pension, this usually needs topping up by means of a supplementary pension to give a reasonable quality of life. There are many types of pension available, but usually the person wishing to have a pension in the future has to begin the process of putting money aside to fund it. This money is put into an organisation that invests it to provide the pensions when required. The total amount invested in these type of schemes is huge. IFSL[1] estimates that global pension assets totalled $31.1 trillion at the end of 2010. Figures for 2009 give a total amount for pension assets of $28.8 trillion.

---

[1] International Financial Services London, which has now changed its name to theCityUK.

The UK's share of the market is $2.5 trillion, the second largest after the US, whose 63 per cent share dominates the market, see Exhibit 7.1.

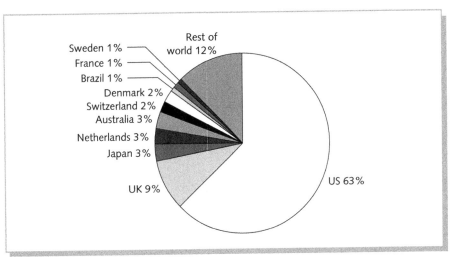

Exhibit 7.1   **Global pension assets 2009**
Source: www.thecityUK.com

In the future, pensions look like being a major problem for many governments. Populations in general are aging as a result of improved health care, disease control and healthier lifestyles. According to figures produced by the United Nations (UN) the percentage of people over 65 compared to the working population (aged 15–64) is set to rise considerably, see Exhibit 7.2. Without action, this is going to cause great difficulties for governments. Many countries are raising the retirement age, with an equivalent delay in pension provision to try to reduce the burden.

Unfunded schemes

In the UK three million workers (such as teachers and civil servants) are members of public **unfunded pension schemes**; these are termed **pay-as-you-go (PAYG)** schemes where the money put aside each month by employees and employers pays the pensions of current pensioners. This means that there is not a pot of accumulated money to pay pensions. If there is a shortfall, it is met by the UK Government Treasury. Already, there is about £1,000 billion in unfunded future pension payments for UK public sector workers. Looking around the world we see that the majority of state-funded pensions so far have been PAYG

	2010	2050
Japan	35	74
Italy	31	62
Germany	31	59
France	26	47
UK	25	38
Spain	25	59
Poland	19	52
US	19	35
China	11	38
India	8	20

Exhibit 7.2   Population aged over 65 as a percentage of working age population (15–64)

Source: UN World Population Prospects: The 2008 Revision

schemes, but many countries are in the process of reforming their pension provisions as these schemes have begun to prove unsustainable with the increasing age of the population and its increasing dependency on the State.

Funded schemes

Funded pension funds are designed so that the insured, and/or their employers, make regular payments to a pension fund, which will (hopefully) grow and provide future pension income. Many companies and other organisations such as universities already run such schemes for their staff. In the UK six million employees are currently paying into a workplace pension scheme. However, that still leaves 14 million salaried employees not saving into a workplace scheme, and the UK government is keen on ensuring that a much higher proportion of employees are members of a funded scheme. Thus, under the Pension Act 2008, UK employers, if they do not currently run a funded pension scheme, will be expected to put the equivalent of a minimum of 1–3 per cent[2] of the employee's salary to a new national pensions savings scheme – known as **Nest, the National Employment**

---

[2] Until October 2016 this is 1 per cent, between October 2016 and October 2017 the employer pays 2 per cent, thereafter the contribution is 3 per cent.

Savings Trust. The employee will be automatically enrolled, but can opt out, and is required to contribute 1–4[3] of salary, and an additional 1 per cent comes from the government in the form of tax relief. Nest is designed as a low-cost scheme so that even very small companies can contribute to it without having to establish their own schemes.

Increasing longevity and the sharp fall in return on pension fund assets over the past 20 years (especially returns from equities) have caused **pension deficits** in a considerable number of companies providing a kind of funded pension called defined benefit pensions – see below. The deficit arises when the actual amount of assets expected to be in the pension pot at retirement (with added investment income) is not sufficient to pay out the pensions required. Companies in the FTSE 100 (the largest companies on the London Stock Exchange) have deficits totalling about £90 billion in their employee pension funds.

Defined benefit

A **defined benefit (DB) pension** pays out a fixed amount based upon the number of years worked and the level of final salary or the average level of salary. So, for example, you might be a member of a final salary one-eightieth scheme, which means that the number of years you have been making contributions to the fund is multiplied by $\frac{1}{80}$ and the result is multiplied by your final year's salary (or some average over a number of years). So if you have worked and contributed for 40 years and your final salary is £30,000 you will, under a final salary scheme, be entitled to $\frac{40}{80} \times £30,000 = £15,000$ per year in retirement, and may receive three times that as a lump sum on retiring. Despite the scheme being set up as a separate organisation the sponsoring employer usually remains responsible for final provision of the pension. To reduce their risk they usually insist on significant contributions from the employee during their working life, 7.5 per cent of salary in the case of members of the Universities Superannuation Scheme with employing universities putting in another 16 per cent of salary each month.

Employers are finding that DB pensions are becoming too costly. Some companies (e.g. BT, BBC, Network Rail, IBM, Barclays and BP amongst many) are attempting to reduce their DB liabilities by closing the scheme to new employees, by taking out insurance (prohibitively expensive), transferring beneficiaries to a different scheme run by a financial institution, or by agreeing that the scheme be taken over by a financial institution.

---

[3] Until October 2016 this is 1 per cent, between October 2016 and October 2017 it is 3 per cent and after that the employee will technically pay 5 per cent, with 1 per cent of that being tax relief.

Defined Contribution

The **defined contribution (DC)** type of pension is becoming increasingly prevalent because it offers lower risk of unexpected liability to employers. The DC pension is a pension where the contributions (from employee and employer) are fixed, but the actual pension paid out is linked to the return on the assets of the pension fund and the rate at which the final pension fund is annuitised; at retirement age, an annuity is generally purchased with the accumulated funds to provide the pension.[4] As investment performance before retirement and annuity rates fluctuate with economic and financial volatility, it is entirely possible for the pension to be less (or more) than expected. There is no obligation for the employer to guarantee a level of pension under DC. If the fund underperforms while the employee is still working and saving in the scheme, or administrative costs rise, there will simply be a lower pension. In other words, the risk of poorly performing investments is transferred to the prospective pensioners.

Personal/private pensions

Personal or **private pensions** are not provided by the State. They put the onus of funding a pension solely on the recipient, who pays a regular amount, usually every month, or a lump sum to the pension provider who will invest it on their behalf. These funds are usually run by financial organisations such as insurance companies, building societies or banks. Personal pensions are often the optimal choice for people wishing to organise their own pension, people who are self-employed or whose company does not provide a suitable pension.

Personal pensions are a very tax-efficient way of providing for the long-term future in the UK:

- The contributions made qualify for full tax relief. This means that if say £2,880 is contributed from taxed earnings the government then adds back tax (at 20 per cent) to the fund amounting to £720, meaning that £3,600 is added to your pension pot. Higher-rate taxpayers are able to get additional tax relief.

- Once the money is in the fund it can grow without tax being levied on interest income, or on capital gains (however, dividend income is taxed).

- At retirement age, 25 per cent of the fund may be taken in cash, tax-free.

---

[4] Although the UK government is increasingly allowing continued investment rather than forcing pensioners to take out an annuity (which may produce as little as £5,000 per year (until death) for a lump sum of £100,000 drawn from the DC pension pot).

A pension may be taken whilst still in employment. There is a wide range of type of funds, each specialising in a different type of investment – UK or over-seas shares, passive tracker or actively-managed funds, corporate bonds and gilts, and cash.

Self invested personal pensions (SIPPs)

Self invested personal pensions are pension plans that allow the contributor to control the type and amount of investments made and have the same tax advantages as personal pension schemes. SIPPs were originally aimed at people with large pension funds (over £200,000) but are now available to anyone with a contribution of £3,600 or more per year. People with multiple pension schemes can bring them all under one SIPP wrapper, resulting in easier management. The downside of SIPPs is that there are likely to be more charges than for a standard personal pension; a set-up fee followed by fixed annual fees, plus charges for each deal. Online SIPP providers can offer a more cost-effective way of managing the plan.

SIPP plans can invest in a wide variety of investments: domestic or international shares, gilts, corporate bonds, unit trusts, OEICs, investment trusts, insurance company funds, exchange-traded derivatives, gold bullion, loans and deposit accounts or even commercial property.

Public pensions

Nearly all countries in the developed world provide some sort of state-funded, i.e. **public pension**, for their people. Sometimes these pensions are means-tested (people's incomes and assets are examined to ensure they are poor enough to qualify), and the State will top up the income of the really poor if the pension is insufficient. These pensions are funded by public money, taxes and revenues. Governments around the world are encouraging people to contribute to private or personal pensions, thus relieving them of an onerous responsibility.

In the UK a non-earnings related pension is paid by the State, based on the National Insurance contributions a person has put in over the course of their working life. The UK government, in line with other countries, has plans to increase the pension age to 66 (women 65) in the near future, with a further increase to 70 under discussion as a way of lowering the amount that has to be raised in taxes to pay these pensions.

Pension fund trustees, consultants and managers

Pension funds create large pools of assets and the task of the controllers of pension funds is to manage the assets well and generate sufficient income to pay out pension liabilities. Those in charge of the funds are in an incredibly influential position. Indeed pension funds are now the largest category of investor, they invest in both domestic and international financial markets and can have a huge influence on countries' wealth, development and industries.

Because this large 'float' (pension contributions paid in but not yet paid out as pensions) is available, there have been various scandals in the past, where pension fund cash has been used for other purposes (e.g. the Mirror pension fund plundered by Robert Maxwell, who was able to persuade the trustees of the Mirror fund to lend to or invest in other companies controlled by Maxwell, which then failed), or the company has gone bankrupt and thereby left the pensioners with nothing, or the money has been badly invested, leaving insufficient in the pot to pay out pensions. In many cases, if a pension fund collapses, the employee has no redress, unless fraud or criminal activity can be proved.

Avoiding misappropriation of the money in pension funds is therefore one of the most important tasks for **trustees**, who control the fund and hire managers to invest the money. Trustees are required to know and understand the various laws relating to pensions and trusts, their funding and the investment of their assets. Their overall objective is to set up their fund as a secure source of funds for retirement benefits, and oversee its management.

Consultants are asked to give their professional advice to trustees on the type and amount of investments to be made. They have access to a plethora of historic data from which they can advise on the best investment path to take and which investment managers are likely to out-perform the stock market, say. They may also help with the calculations for figuring out the amount needed to be put into the fund each year. These calculations take into account a number of estimates; the estimated return on assets, projected future wage growth (for DB schemes) and future inflation (if the pensions are index-linked, that is rise as inflation goes up).

Managers are tasked with investing and ensuring that the fund returns are satisfactory, but they can sometimes be too cautious or too rash with disastrous results for the pensioners. As pension funds increased in size, it became apparent that in most cases a single manager could not cope with the volume of investment. This started a trend towards decentralisation – employing multiple managers, each specialising in a particular asset class of investing. Some funds are run only by one or a number of in-house investment fund managers working directly for the fund. Others outsource their investment manager functions – this is where the consultants can help in selection. Still others have a mixture, with some of the money managed in-house and some by professional fund managers.

Pension fund asset holdings

Pension funds are major purchasers of long-term investments, which suit their liabilities well; they need to be able to generate sufficient to be in a position to pay out pension liabilities decades in the future. Until the recent financial crisis, many pension funds held a large proportion of their funds in equities; since then, equities have been reduced in favour of long-term bonds and fixed-rate instruments, which are thought to give a more secure return, see Exhibit 7.3. The important factor is to look at the long-term future stability of the fund, and invest where this can be best guaranteed.

	Equities %	Bonds %	Other %
United Kingdom	54	36	10
United States	58	35	7
Japan	36	47	17
Australia	42	19	39
Netherlands	28	47	25

Exhibit 7.3   2009 pension fund asset allocation

Source: UBS Pension Fund Indicators (TheCityUK Pensions Report 2011)

Figures from annual reports of the BT Pension Scheme (BTPS), the largest pension fund in the UK, with assets totalling £34,112 million, show just how wide-ranging their investments are. Exhibit 7.4 shows how the allocation of their investment assets changes over the years from 2001 to 2009. ('Inflation-linked' means government bonds whose returns go up with higher inflation; 'Other alternatives' includes investments in private equity.)

Following the financial crisis of 2008, BTPS policy has been to move out of higher risk UK equities (down to 10 per cent from 29 per cent in 2005), and into 'safer' fixed-rate securities, such as government bonds (part of 'fixed interest'). It is interesting to see the increase in investment in hedge funds, which were once regarded as highly speculative.

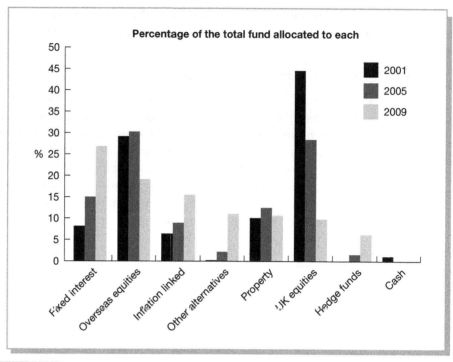

Exhibit 7.4   BT Pension Scheme investment assets 31 December 2001, 2005 and 2009

Source: BTPS Annual Report

BTPS is administered by a Board of 11 trustee directors who are jointly responsible for the administration of the scheme. Many of the investment decisions are taken by in-house managers but a large proportion of the money is placed with outside managers who charge a fee (say 0.5 per cent of funds under management per year) to invest, e.g. Legal and General Investment Management (LGIM), M&G Asset Management and Blackrock. The managers are answerable to the trustees.

BTPS had a deficit of £7.598 million at the end of 2009, and BT, the operating company, is planning to pay additional contributions over the next few years into the scheme to reduce the deficit. The fact that it has a deficit already is going to be compounded by the way in which the number of pension recipients has grown much larger than the number of contributing members still in work – see Exhibit 7.5. The drawbacks of a DB scheme which failed to collect enough from its workers or the company in decades gone by are clearly shown, as it may not be possible for current contributions to satisfy historic liabilities.

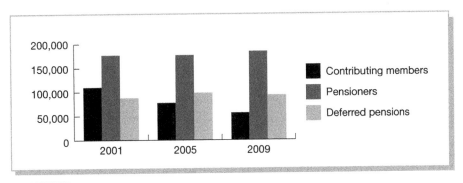

Exhibit 7.5 **BTPS pension membership 2001, 2005 and 2009**
Source: BTPS Annual Reports

BTPS have adjusted their investments to try and improve their asset return. Exhibit 7.6 shows some of their largest investments held directly by the scheme at the end of 2009 expressed as a percentage of the total investment assets of the scheme.

Investment	Asset class	Market value (£m)	% of total investment assets
LGIM UK Equity Index	Pooled investment vehicles	2,506	7.4
LGIM Europe Large Cap Equity Index	Pooled investment vehicles	1,358	4.0
LGIM North America Equity Index	Pooled investment vehicles	1,297	3.8
LGIM Japan Equity Index	Pooled investment vehicles	981	2.9
UK Treasury 2.5% Index Linked 2020	Index linked	658	1.9
LGIM Asia Pacific Equity Index	Pooled investment vehicles	575	1.7
Milton Keynes Shopping Centre	Property	264	0.8

Exhibit 7.6 **Some of BTPS's largest investments (2009)**
Source: BTPS Annual Report 2009

Regulations

In the UK, the **Pensions Regulator** is empowered by the government to regulate work-based pension schemes, and has wide-ranging powers to enforce its decisions. Its aim is to protect members' benefits and encourage high standards in running pension schemes. It has powers to compel companies to inject additional money into their pension schemes and to remove trustees should a conflict of interest get in the way of them acting solely for the pension fund members. The regulator also tries to limit the claims made by failed schemes on the Pension Protection Fund.

In the UK the **Pension Protection Fund (PPF)** was established in 2005 to compensate members of defined benefit pension funds should their company fail and be liquidated, leaving insufficient assets in the pension scheme to cover its pension liabilities. The PPF pays out up to 90 per cent of what has been promised, up to a maximum of £29,897.42 a year. The cash to finance the PPF comes from a levy imposed on all eligible pension funds.

Defined contribution pension scheme members lose out if fraud or theft occurs, and may then be eligible for compensation from the PPF, but they cannot claim compensation for shortfalls in the fund (unlike defined contribution members). Their contributions are invested with the hope that they will provide an adequate pension, so although the eventual pension will vary according to the ability (and luck!) of the pension fund managers, their individual fund cannot be in deficit other than through fraud or theft.

Collective investment

The idea of **collective investment (pooled funds)** has been around since around 1800. Its concept is simple; money from a group of people is gathered together and put into a range of investments. This reduces the risk of total loss for all contributors by enabling them to invest in a far wider range of investments than they could individually. Worldwide, collective investments are responsible for vast amounts of funds (see Exhibit 7.7), an astonishing $24 trillion administered by 65,735 funds. About half of these assets and funds are in the US. The UK contains over 2,000 funds responsible for £449,500 million.

Collective investment offers some significant advantages to the investor:

■ First, a more diverse portfolio can be created. Investors with a relatively small sum to invest, say £3,000, would find it difficult to obtain a broad spread of investments without incurring high transaction costs. If, however, 10,000 people each put £3,000 into a fund there would be £30 million available to

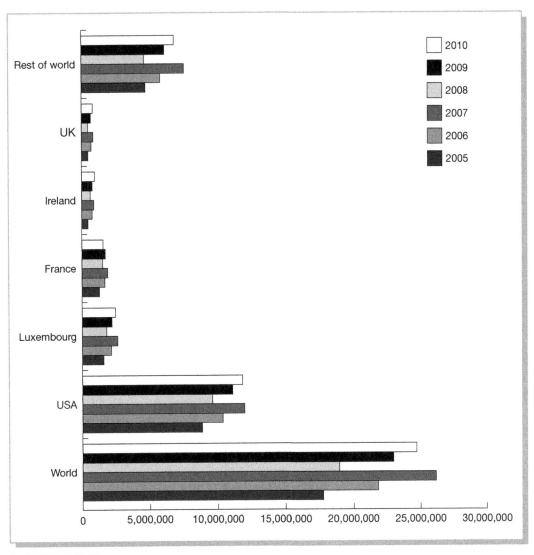

Exhibit 7.7   **Worldwide mutual (collective) fund assets in millions of dollars**

Source: Investment Company Institute, www.ici.org

invest in a wide range of securities. A large fund like this can buy in large quantities, say £100,000 at a time, reducing dealing and administrative costs per pound invested.

- Second, even very small investors can take part in the stock markets and other financial markets. It is possible to gain exposure to the equity, bond or other markets by collective investing for a small amount (e.g. £30 per month).

■ Third, professional management removes the demanding tasks of analysing and selecting shares and other securities, going into the market place to buy, collecting dividends, etc., by handing the whole process over to professional fund managers.

■ Finally, investment can be made into exotic and far-flung markets, South American companies, US hi-tech, Chinese technology, etc. without the risk and the complexities of buying shares direct. Collective funds run by managers familiar with the relevant country or sector can be a good alternative to going it alone.

These advantages are considerable but they can often be outweighed by the disadvantages of pooled funds, which include high fund management costs and possible underperformance compared with the market index. Also collective investors lose any rights that accompany direct share investment, including the right to attend the company's AGM or receive shareholder perks, and lose the fun of selecting their own shares with the attendant emotional highs and lows, triumphs and lessons in humility.

Open-ended investment vehicles (OEIVs)

OEIVs are a type of collective fund that does not have restrictions on the amount of shares (or 'units') the fund will issue. If demand is high enough, the fund will continue to issue shares no matter how many investors there are; the size of the fund is dictated by the amount of investment in it. The value of each share is dictated by the net asset value (NAV) divided by the number of existing shares. The NAV is defined as the total value of assets at current market value less any liabilities. Open-ended funds must buy back shares when investors wish to sell. The most common types of OEIVs are unit trusts, open-ended investment companies (OEICs), exchange traded funds (ETFs) and mutual funds.

Unit trusts

Unit trusts are issued in Australia, Ireland, the Isle of Man, Jersey, New Zealand, South Africa, Singapore, and the UK, and sold in units not shares. The first to be issued was in 1931 by M&G. According to the Investment Management Association (IMA) in 2011 there were 737 funds in the UK managing £220.8 billion: see Exhibit 7.8 for the 10 largest funds. They are administered by a trustee (usually a bank or insurance company rather than a single person) who is

		£ billion
1	Fidelity Investments	22.40
2	Threadneedle Investments	12.53
3	Scottish Widows Unit Trusts Managers	11.98
4	Invesco Perpetual	11.70
5	Legal & General Unit Trust Managers Ltd	10.89
6	M&G Group	9.29
7	Schroder Investments Ltd	9.25
8	Halifax Investment Fund Managers Ltd	8.44
9	Gartmore Investment Management Plc	6.61
10	SLTM	6.00

Exhibit 7.8   **The managed assets of the 10 largest fund providers in the UK**

Source: www.incademy.com

the legal owner of the trust's assets and runs the trust on behalf of its investors, appointing managers and making sure that the trust is run responsibly.

The value of the units is determined by the market valuation of the securities owned by the fund. So if, for example, the fund collected together £1 million from hundreds of small investors and issued 1 million units in return, each unit would be worth £1. If the fund managers over the next year invest the pooled fund in shares which increase in value to £1.5 million the value of each unit rises to £1.50.

Unit holders sell units back to the managers of the unit trust if they want to liquidate their holding. The manager would then either sell the units to other investors or, if that is not possible because of low demand, sell some of the underlying investments to raise cash to redeem the units. Thus the number of units can change daily, or at least every few days. There is no secondary market trading in unit trusts as all transactions are carried out through the trust managers.

Pricing

The pricing of unit trusts is divided into two parts, the bid price and the offer price. The offer price, the price a new investor has to pay, is calculated by valuing the investments underlying the fund once a day.[5] The bid price, the price a seller receives, is usually set 5–6 per cent below the offer price (for funds invested in shares). The difference between the bid and offer prices is called the spread and pays for two things; firstly, fund administration, management of the investments, marketing, as well as commission for selling the units; secondly, the market makers' spreads and brokers' commissions payable by the fund when it buys and sells shares.[6]

Most unit trusts are now priced on a forward basis, which means that the price paid by a buyer of units will be fixed at a future time (often 12.00 noon this day or the next day) so a buyer may not know the exact price at the time that they send a buy order. Some funds still charge the *historic* price, taking the value from the last daily valuation.[7]

Charges

There are three charges:

1   Initial charge ('sales' or 'front-end' charge). This is included in the spread between the bid and offer prices. So if the fund has a spread of 6 per cent it might allocate 5 per cent as an initial charge. Some unit trusts have dropped initial charges to zero – particularly those investing in interest-bearing securities (bonds, etc.) and **tracker funds** (those that do not try to spot shares that will outperform the market, but merely invest in a broad range representative of a stock market index – also called **passive funds**).

2   Annual charges. The annual management fee is typically 1.00–1.8 per cent. A further charge of about 0.2 per cent covers legal, custody, audit and other administration costs. Over time the annual fees have a larger effect in reducing the value of the investment than the initial charge.

3   Exit charges. Some funds make an exit charge instead of an initial charge if the units are sold within, say, the first five years.

---

[5] The current market price of the investments currently held plus dealing costs, management expenses and other charges is divided by the number of units in issue to give the maximum offer price that the trust can charge.
[6] Recently unit trusts have been given the option of single pricing, with charges shown separately. Most still have a bid–offer spread.
[7] Some use a mix of historic and forward pricing.

Reading the *Financial Times*

The *Financial Times* publishes unit trust bid and offer prices every day. An example is shown in Exhibit 7.9. The list for Schroders displays both unit trusts and OEICs (discussed below). OEICs have a single price.

Who looks after the unit holders' interests?

There are four levels of protection for the unit holder:

1 *The trustee.* These organisations, usually banks or insurance companies, keep an eye on the fund managers to make sure they abide by the terms of the trust deed – for example, sticking to the stated investment objectives (e.g. investing in Japanese shares). Importantly, the trustee holds all the assets of the fund in their name on the unit holder's behalf, so if anything untoward happens to the fund manager the funds are safeguarded. The trustee also oversees the unit price calculation and ensures that the regulations are obeyed.

2 *The Financial Services Authority (Financial Conduct Authority from 2013).* Only funds authorised by the FSA/FCA are allowed to advertise in the UK. Unauthorised unit trusts, most of which are established offshore (outside the jurisdiction of the FSA/FCA) are available, but they may carry more risk by virtue of their unregulated status.

3 *The Ombudsman.* Complaints that have not been satisfactorily settled by the management company can be referred to the Financial Ombudsman – see Chapter 18.

4 *The Financial Services Compensation Scheme.* Up to £50,000 is available for a valid claim – for example, when an FSA/FCA-authorised fund becomes insolvent or suffers from poor investment management (see Chapter 18 for more on this).

Types of trust available

Unit trusts in the UK offer a wide range of investment choice. UK All Companies funds invest at least 80 per cent of their assets in UK shares. Some funds focus investment in shares paying high dividends (UK Equity Income), others split the funds between equity and bonds (UK Equity and Bond Income), while some invest mostly in government bonds or corporate bonds. Some place the bulk of their money in smaller companies, some in Far East shares. A few trusts invest in commercial property. The possibilities are endless – see **www.investmentfunds.org** for a definition of dozens of classes of funds.

Schroders

Schroders (UK)
31 Gresham Street, London EC2V 7QA
Investor Services 0800 718777   Dealing 0800 718788
www.schroder.co.uk
www.ft.com/funds/schroders

Management company details

Initial charge expressed as a percentage of the amount put into units. 'C' indicates a periodic management charge deducted from capital. 'E' denotes that an exit charge may be made when investor sells

	Init Notes Chnge	Selling Price	Buying Price	+ or −	Yield
Authorised Inv Fun					
Absolute Return Bond Fund A Inc ♦ $3\frac{1}{4}$ C		44.2	45.68	−0.03	5.9
Absolute Return Bond Fund A Acc ♦ .. $3\frac{1}{4}$ C		93.77	96.92	−0.07	5.9
All Maturities Corporate Bond A Inc ♦ 0		54.94xd		−0.22	5.7
All Maturities Corporate Bond A Acc ♦ ... 0		60.57xd		−0.25	5.7
All Maturities Corp Bond I Acc (Gross) ♦ 0 C		183.7xd		−0.7	5.7
Asian Alpha Plus A Inc ♦ . 0		71.33		+0.33	0.4
Asian Alpha Plus A Acc ♦ 0		72.47		+0.34	0.4
Asian Income A Inc ♦ $5\frac{1}{4}$		196.5	208.6	+0.6	4.3
Asian Income A Acc ♦ .. $5\frac{1}{4}$		244.6	259.6	+0.8	4.2
Asian Income Maximiser A Inc ♦ .. 0		54.15		+0.15	7.0
Asian Income Maximiser A Acc ♦ . 0		57.4		+0.15	7.0
Corporate Bond A Inc ♦ $3\frac{1}{4}$		41.67xd	43.52	−0.14	6.1
Corporate Bond A Acc ♦ . $3\frac{1}{4}$		76.82xd	80.23	−0.26	6.1
Diversified Target Return A Inc ♦ .. 0		54.42xd		−0.08	0.1
Diversified Target Return A Acc ♦ . 0		54.64xd		−0.09	0.1
Diversified Target Return D1 Inc ♦ 0		56.45xd		−0.09	0.6
Diversified Target Return D1 Acc ♦ .. 0		57.09xd		−0.08	0.6
European A Inc ♦ .... $5\frac{1}{4}$		56.46		+0.45	0.0
European A Acc ♦ ... $5\frac{1}{4}$		56.46		+0.45	0.0
Euro Alpha Plus A Inc ♦ $5\frac{1}{4}$		114.5	120.9	+0.7	0.7
Euro Alpha Plus A Acc ♦ . $5\frac{1}{4}$		121.1	127.9	+0.9	0.7
Euro Smaller Cos A Inc ♦ $5\frac{1}{4}$		359.3xd	381.7	+1.1	0.3
Euro Smaller Cos A Acc ♦ .. $5\frac{1}{4}$		378.5xd	402.2	+1.3	0.3
Gilt & Fixed Interest A Inc ♦ .. $5\frac{1}{4}$ C		57.82	60.92	−0.25	4.1
Gilt & Fixed Interest A Acc ♦ . $5\frac{1}{4}$		165.9	174.8	−0.8	4.1
Global Alpha Plus A Inc ♦ 0		52.78		+0.56	0.0
Global Alpha Plus A Acc ♦ .. 0		52.77		+0.57	0.0
Global Climate Change A Inc ♦ . 0		56.75		+0.32	0.0
Global Climate Change A Acc ♦ 0		56.87		+0.32	0.0
Global Emerg Mkts A Inc ♦ $5\frac{1}{4}$		134.6	142.6	+0.8	0.4
Global Emerg Mkts A Acc ♦ .. $5\frac{1}{4}$		141.5	149.6	+1	0.4
Global Equity Income A Inc ♦ 0		42.5		+0.33	3.9
Global Equity Income A Acc ♦ 0		49.75		+0.39	3.9

Source: *Financial Times*, 29 June 2011

Selling (bid) and buying (offer) prices expressed in pence. 'xd' means ex dividend (a purchaser now would not receive the last announced dividend)

Single price – the buying and selling prices for shares in an OEIC are the same. The price is based on a mid-market valuation of the underlying investments. Managers'/operators' initial charges are shown separately

Price change on previously quoted figure (not all funds update prices daily)

Yield is the income paid by the unit trust in the last 12 months as a percentage of the offer price (after tax for shares, gross for bonds). The yield figures allow for buying expenses

Information about the timing of prices quotes/valuation
♦ 11.01–14.00
▲ 14.01–17.00
17.01–midnight
✠ 00.01–11.00

Exhibit 7.9   Unit trust prices in the *Financial Times*

Returns

The return on a unit trust consists of two elements; first, income is gained on the underlying investments in the form of interest or dividends; second, the prices of the securities held could rise over time. Some unit trusts pay out all income, after deducting management charges, etc., on set dates (usually twice a year)[8] in cash. On the other hand, accumulation units reinvest the income on behalf of the unit holders, and as a result the price of accumulation units tends to rise more rapidly than income units. The *Financial Times* shows listings for prices of income ('Inc') units (also called distribution units) and accumulation ('Acc') units.

Open-ended investment companies (OEICs)

OEICs (pronounced 'oiks') have been around since May 1997 and were introduced as a more flexible and simpler alternative to existing unit trusts. Many unit trusts have turned themselves into OEICs. An OEIC is a company which can be listed on the stock exchange and it issues shares whereas a trust issues units. OEICs are regulated in a similar way to unit trusts, so investor protection is much the same. Investment in OEICs may be made on a regular basis, or as a lump sum.

OEICs have an **Authorised Corporate Director (ACD)** managing the fund and a depositary (usually a large bank) supervising activities to safeguard their assets. The ACD's remit is to invest shareholders' funds in accordance with the fund's objectives. In 2011, there were 1,672 OEICs in the UK. Compared to unit trusts, OEICs have a simpler pricing system because there is one price for both buyers and sellers. Charges and dealing commissions are shown separately, which makes them more transparent than unit trusts. Some OEICs charge an exit fee. When OEICs are bought or sold, the share price is the value of all the underlying investments (NAV) divided by the number of shares in issue. The price is not based on the supply and demand for shares (as with investment trusts – see later) and is calculated daily, usually at 12 noon in London.

As an open-ended instrument the fund gets bigger and more shares are created as more people invest. The fund shrinks and shares are cancelled as people withdraw their money.

The OEIC may be a stand-alone fund or may have an 'umbrella' structure, which means that it contains a number of sub-funds each with a different investment objective, e.g. focusing on differing equities, US shares, UK shares, etc. Each sub-fund could have different investors and asset pools.

---

[8] Some trusts pay out quarterly or monthly.

Exchange-traded funds (ETFs)

First introduced in the US in 1990 **exchange-traded funds** (ETFs) take the idea of tracking a stock market index or sector a stage further. ETFs are set up as companies issuing shares, and the money raised is used to buy a range of securities such as a collection of shares in a particular stock market index or sector, say the FTSE 100, or pharmaceutical shares. Thus if BP comprises 8 per cent of the total value of the FTSE 100 and the ETF has £100 million to invest it will buy £8 million of BP shares; if Whitbread is 0.15 per cent of the FTSE the ETF buys £150,000 of Whitbread shares. (Alternatively, many ETFs do not buy the actual shares, but gain exposure to the share returns by the purchase of derivatives of the shares.)

They are open-ended funds – the ETF shares are created and cancelled as demand rises or falls. However, they differ from unit trusts and OEICs in that the pricing of ETF shares is left up to the market place. ETFs are quoted companies and you can buy and sell their shares at prices subject to change throughout the day (unlike unit trusts and OEICs, where prices are set by a formula once a day). Globally, there are over 2,000 different ETFs listed on over 40 exchanges with a total value over $1,200 billion. In the US alone over 800 ETFs are traded on the stock markets. They have become so significant there that around 30 per cent of New York Stock Exchange trading is in ETFs.

Despite an ETF's price being set by trading in the stock market they tend to trade at, or near to, the underlying net asset value (NAV) – the value of the shares in the FTSE 100, for instance. This is different from investment trusts, which frequently trade significantly below net asset value.

With traditional (physically-backed rather than derivatives-based) ETFs newly created ETF shares ('creation units') are delivered to market makers[9] ('authorised participants') in exchange for an entire portfolio of shares matching the index (not for cash). The underlying shares are held by the fund manager, while the new ETF shares are traded by the market maker in the secondary market. To redeem ETF shares the ETF manager delivers underlying shares to the market maker in exchange for ETF shares. ETF managers only create new ETF shares for market makers with at least £1 million to invest, so private investors are excluded at this level. However, private investors can trade in existing ETF shares in the secondary market.

If the price of an ETF share rises above the value of the underlying shares, there will be an arbitrage opportunity for the market maker. Arbitrage means the possibility of simultaneously buying and selling the same or similar securities in two

---

[9] As well as market makers other institutions receive them.

markets and making a risk-free gain, for example buying bananas for £1 in one market and selling them for £1.05 (after costs) in another. In this case the ETF share representing, say, the top 100 UK shares is trading above the price of the 100 shares when sold separately. Market makers, spotting this opportunity, will swap the underlying basket of shares for a **creation unit of ETF shares**, thus realising a profit by then selling the ETF shares into the market. Then the new supply of ETF shares will satisfy the excess demand and ETF prices should fall until they are in line with the underlying NAV.

If the ETF share price falls below the underlying shares' value the market maker will exploit this by having the ETF share redeemed by the ETF manager. The market maker ends up with the more valuable underlying shares and the supply of ETFs in the market place has fallen, bringing the price back up to the NAV. The advantage arising from market makers and ETF managers not handing over cash, but instead swapping ETF shares and underlying shares, is that there are no brokerage costs for buying and selling shares. This makes transactions cheap.

Spreads – the difference between market makers' buying and selling prices of ETFs – are generally around 0.05–0.3 per cent (although spreads can widen to 10 per cent or more at times of extreme volatility, for example, after 11 September 2001). While there is no initial charge with ETFs, annual management charges range between 0.2 and 0.75 per cent but are typically between 0.3 per cent and 0.5 per cent (these are deducted from dividends). All in all, ETFs are a cheaper way of benefiting from a rising market than unit or investment trusts.

Private investors can purchase ETFs from brokers. Their minimum charge is between £10 and £40 per trade. Prices are shown in the Managed Funds section in the *Financial Times* – see Exhibit 7.10. The *Financial Times* shows ETFs that track the US market (e.g. MSCI USA index), European shares (e.g. DJEurSTX 50), the UK market (e.g. FTSE 100) and dozens of other markets, from Japanese shares to government bonds. ETFs pay dividends in line with the underlying constituent shares or other income such as interest on bonds, quarterly or semi-annually. This is reflected in the yield (yld) column. Useful websites for ETF investors are iShares (http://uk.ishares.com) and Trustnet (www.trustnet.com/etf).

We have moved a long way from the simple traditional equity ETFs of the 1990s. Nowadays the ETF manager may not purchase all the shares in the index but merely a sample. This is useful for ETFs invested in say Chinese or Vietnamese shares where government restrictions may prevent purchasing all the shares in an index. The exchange-traded concept has been extended beyond equities and bonds to foreign exchange rates, commodities and commodity indices (**exchange traded commodities, ETCs**). Instead of the provider holding the

Exchange Traded Funds

Notes	Price	Chng	52 week High	52 week Low	Yld	Vol '000s
DJEurSTX50A€	£25.38	+0.49	£27.19	£20.99	3.4	9
DJEurSTX50I€	£24950.64	+142.50	£27209.97	£21058.44	3.5	–
FTSE 100St	£56.58	+0.74	£59.84	£46.85	2.6	0
MSCI Can A C$	£21.33	+0.51	£23.46	£17.94	1.5	1
MSCI Can IC$	£21148.47	+48.22	£23267.71	£18109.45	1.7	–
MSCI EMU €	£80.26	+1.23	£85.92	£65.18	2.9	4
MSCI EMU I€	£80380.54	+459.07	£85232.84	£67478.16	2.9	–
MSCI EMU VA€	£31.97	+0.18	£34.38	£26.53	3.4	–
MSCI Eurp A€	£42.02	+0.38	£44.34	£34.91	2.5	2
MSCI Eurp I€	£43959.79	+251.06	£44080.76	£35336.45	2.5	–
MSCI Japan St	£20.02	+0.15	£22.59	£17.68	1.3	1
MSCI Japan I¥	£19917.95	+25.85	£22508.83	£1797151	1.6	–
MSCI PexJp$	£27.39	+0.36	£30.01	£22.10	2.9	10
MSCI USA St	£77.54	+0.85	£80.30	£64.12	1.0	5
MSCI USA I$	£77504.22	+1231.02	£83083.91	£54578.05	1.0	0
MSCI World St	£82.14	+1.15	£85.43	£60	1.4	0
MSCI World I$	£80952.07	–	£84945.80	£68997.68	1.6	0

Source: *Financial Times*, 29 June 2011

Exhibit 7.10   Exchange traded funds

underlying instrument or commodity the investment is in swaps or other derivative instruments. The problem with derivative-based ETFs is that there is a risk that the counterparties providing the derivatives may not be able to meet their obligations and then the ETF holder may not have anything tangible backing up the ETF shares. Also if the ETF provider does not buy the underlying securities, but instead relies on derivatives, and then goes bust, it could be more complicated for an investor to retrieve their investment.

The use of derivatives for many ETFs – 'synthetic replication' of an index – has stimulated a debate in the ETF world as to whether ETFs consisting solely of derivatives are truly ETFs at all. But, regardless of some misgivings, it looks as though volume of synthetic ETFs will overtake that of the traditional physical ETFs – see Exhibit 7.11.

ETFs 'risk causing confusion'

By Chris Flood

Europe's exchange traded funds industry risks creating "confusion, disappointment and disillusion" among investors, according to Deborah Fuhr, global head of ETF research at BlackRock, who said the sector had reached "an important crossroads" after a decade of rapid growth.

Warning that "products which are not even funds are being called ETFs", Ms Fuhr said the industry was at risk of moving away from the traditional virtues of transparency and ease of understanding that had attracted retail and institutional investors.

With ETF assets in Europe forecast to increase by 30 per cent this year, BlackRock said it expected more hedge fund managers to create ETFs by using their own funds as the underlying exposure.

"Hedge funds are noticing the growth and appeal of ETFs which are simple and easy to understand but have powerful distribution networks," said Ms Fuhr.

Although ETFs could provide wider access to hedge funds as

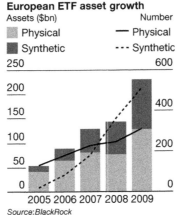

European ETF asset growth

Source: BlackRock

an asset class, Ms Fuhr cautioned that these new products would also be more challenging for investors to understand.

As developers work to include hedge funds, structured products and active funds within ETF wrappers, BlackRock argued this had led to the emergence of funds that did not provide transparency on their underlying portfolios, did not have real time estimates for their net asset value and did not

offer daily creation and redemption of their underlying units.

The comments come as the industry this month marks the 10th anniversary of the first ETF launch in Europe, the iShares DJ Stoxx 50, which was listed on the Deutsche Börse.

As of January, assets under management across Europe's ETF industry had risen to $217.9bn across 896 funds, although retail investors only account for 10 to 15 per cent of this market, compared to 40 to 50 per cent in the US.

The emergence of swap-based ETFs since 2005 has been one of the most important developments for European investors, when the advent of Ucits III regulations allowed for wider use of derivatives. BlackRock estimated there were 515 swap-based ETFs with assets of $101.9bn at the end of 2009, compared to 314 physically based ETFs with $125bn of assets.

Source: *Financial Times*, 12 April 2010, p.2

Exhibit 7.11   ETFs 'risk causing confusion'

Mutual funds

Sometimes the term **mutual fund** is used as a generic term for collective or pooled investments. However in the US and Canada the term has a specific meaning in terms of the organisation and legal structure. Mutual funds began in the US in Boston in 1924 and have become the major part of the US investment market. Around half the households in the US have shares in mutual funds with, in 2010, over 7,600 mutual funds managing assets totalling over $10.7 trillion.

They are administered by a group of directors appointed by the shareholders, who rely on them to run the fund correctly. The vast majority are open-ended funds, but there are some that are closed-ended. Securities belonging to the fund must be placed with a custodian (usually one of the major banks) for safekeeping. The value of each mutual share is dependent on the net asset value (NAV), which in the US is calculated daily at 4pm New York time. Mutual shares are sold to investors, and the manager of the fund, called the **portfolio manager**, buys investments according to the objective of the fund as set out in the prospectus. As with unit trusts and OEICs, investors can invest a relatively small amount of money, and be part of a professionally managed and diversified portfolio. There are various types of funds, including stock (equity) funds, bond funds, sector funds, money market funds and balanced funds (investing in a mixture of asset types).

Undertakings for collective investments in transferable securities (UCITS)

For anyone wishing to invest in funds outside their own country, problems occurred because there were no common regulations governing investment funds, and, in many cases, it was difficult to have any degree of trust in foreign investment companies. There was also a lack of a safety net (e.g. compensation scheme from the industry or government) if the fund turned out to be fraudulently or incompetently run. To counter these problems, the 1985 **UCITS directive** established **Undertakings for Collective Investments in Transferable Securities**, introducing European Union-wide rules governing collective investments that could be sold across the EU subject to local tax and marketing laws, so an investor could with confidence invest in French, German, Spanish, etc. funds, safe in the knowledge that the funds were subject to statutory regulations.

A subsequent directive in 2002 broadened the range of assets that harmonised funds can invest in and introduced new rules for the supervision of UCITS and a required simplified prospectus, to which firms may add extra information if they wish. The simplified prospectus is designed to be used as a universal marketing tool for UCITS throughout the EU, providing clear information about charges, costs and fund performance that can be easily understood by an average investor.

UCITS III further increased the flexibility of cross-border funds. They can now do many of the things that hedge funds can do, for example, such as use derivatives. The type of funds that choose to go down this route are called **Newcits**. Any eligible collective fund (e.g. UK unit trusts or OEICs, but not investment trusts) may apply for UCITS status enabling them to market their fund throughout the EU.

Closed-ended investment vehicles

These are collective investment vehicles (e.g. investment trusts) that do not create or redeem shares on a daily basis in response to increases and decreases in demand (in contrast to OEIVs, unit trusts and OEICs, etc.). They are publicly-traded companies that have raised their initial capital through an initial public offering (IPO) and have a fixed number of shares for lengthy periods, as with any other company that issues shares. They are actively managed and often concentrate on a particular sector or industry. The value of their shares fluctuates according to market forces.

Investment trusts (investment companies)

Investment trusts were first launched in London in 1868 to invest in foreign government bonds or fixed interest stocks. Investment trusts (companies) place the money they raise in assets such as shares, government bonds, corporate bonds and property. Unlike unit trusts, they are set up as companies (they are not trusts at all!) and are subject to company law. If you wish to place your money with an investment trust you do so by buying its shares. Investment trusts have their shares quoted on the London Stock Exchange where there is an active secondary market.

An investment trust has a constitution[10] that specifies that its purpose is to invest in specific types of assets. It cannot deviate from this. So it may have been set up to invest in Korean large company shares, US biotechnology shares, or whatever, and it is forbidden from switching to a different category of investment. This reassures the investor that money placed with a particular trust to invest in, say, UK large companies won't end up in, say, Russian oil shares. Of course, if you want to take the risk (and possible reward) of investing in Russian oil shares you can probably find an investment trust that specialises in these – there are, after all, over 400 investment trusts quoted in London, with total assets of £80 billion, to choose from.

As a company an investment trust will have a board of directors answerable to shareholders for the trust's actions and performance. With investment trusts being closed-end funds the amount of money under the directors' control is fixed, which enables them to plan ahead with confidence unconcerned that tomorrow investors may want to withdraw money from the fund. Investors cannot oblige

---

[10] Comprising its memorandum, articles of association and the prospectus on flotation.

the trust to buy the shares should they want to sell (in contrast to unit trusts and OEICs). They have to sell to another investor at a price determined by the forces of supply and demand in the secondary market. Purchases and sales are made through stockbrokers in the same way as for any other company share.

The selection of investments for the trust and the general management of the fund may be undertaken by an in-house team of investment managers who are employees of the trust (a **'self-managed'** trust) or the investment management task may be handed over to **external managers**. Most are externally managed.

Discounts and premiums

The biggest factor influencing the share price of an investment trust is the value of the underlying assets owned by the trust. This is expressed as a net asset value (NAV) per share. In theory the trust's share price should be pretty close to the value of the assets held, but in practice they frequently sell at a large discount to NAV – only a few sell at a premium to NAV. Discounts of 10–20 per cent are not uncommon; they have even reached 68 per cent. The main factor that drags the price below NAV is the lack of demand for the shares. Here is a typical example.

Example

In year X there is great interest in, say, eastern European smaller companies so an investment trust is set up and offers its shares (say, 50 million) for sale at £1 each. With the money raised, £50 million of eastern European company shares are bought by the trust. For the next year the underlying assets (all those shares in Polish companies, etc.) do no more than maintain their value of £1 per investment trust share, and so NAV is constant. Nothing in the fundamentals changes, but the enthusiasm for investing in these up-and-coming nations grows amongst the UK investing public. Investment trust shareholders who want to sell find that they can do so in the London Stock Exchange secondary market at above NAV. New buyers are willing to pay £1.08 per share – an 8 per cent premium to the NAV.

However, in the following year a worldwide recession strikes and investors head for safe havens; they pile into bonds and familiar shares at home. The NAV of the trust's shares falls to 60p as prices plummet on the eastern European stock exchanges. What is worse for the investment trust shareholders is that sentiment has become so pessimistic about eastern European companies that they can only sell their shares for 50p. They trade at a discount of 16.67 per cent to NAV (10p/60p).

Discounts may seem to present an excellent opportunity; you can buy assets worth 60p for 50p, but they can be bad for the investor if the discount increases during the time you hold the shares. As you can see from the last column in Exhibit 7.12, the discounts can be much larger than the example above. The *Financial Times* publishes the share prices and NAVs of investment trusts (companies) daily.

Investment Companies

Notes	Price	Chng	52 week High	52 week Low	Yld	NAV	Dis or Pm(−)

Conventional (Ex Private Equity)

Notes	Price	Chng	High	Low	Yld	NAV	Pm(−)
3i Infra	120.40xd	+1.40	1.25.30	108.20	4.3	117.5	−2.5
Abf Gd Inc	109.63	−1.38	115	95.50	3.6	113.3	3.3
AbnAsianIn †	172.50	+2.63	175	120	3.6	167.7	−2.8
Wts	46.75	–	52	28.50	–	–	–
AbnAllAsia	290	+0.50	326.25	205.10	1.1	347.2	16.5
AbnAsian	636.25	+4.75	670	327	1.3	673.7	5.6
AbnLatAmin	107.25	−0.13	150.50	102	1.7	107.7	0.4
Sub	14	−0.25	22.25	10.25	–	–	–
AbnNewDn	838.25	+2.50	940	708	1.2	919.5	88
AbnNewThai	264xd	–	288.50	207.50	3.0	305	13.5
Sub	66.75	−0.50	87.25	31.50	–	–	–
Abf Sml	672.50	+3	716	502	2.8	768.4	12.5
AbnSmlCo	133.25	−0.25	138.50	101	4.5	160.2	16.8
AbsoluteRet	117.50	+0.13	120.25	110	–	134.8	12.8
AcenciADbt	92	+1	92.25	70.25	1.9	101.9	9.7
ActiveCap	18	−0.50	22.50	13.37	–	20.7	13.2
AdvDvpMk	481	+0.25	515.50	388	–	530.5	9.3
Albany	268.50xd	–	290	241	3.8	323.9	17.1
Alliance †	376.40xd	+2.60	386.30	258.22	2.2	439.2	14.3
AltAstsOps	54.50	–	60.50	44.50	–	78.7	30.8
AltInvStrat	111.25	–	114.39	99.50	–	128.6	13.5
Altin $	£34.49	−0.37	£36.59	£28.77	–	£43.3	20.4
Art Alpha	304.50	+5.50	339.50	225	0.9	319.2	4.6
Sub	73.50	–	89	50	–	–	–
AshmoreG	776.75	−0.25	845.50	690	–	993.5	21.8
EUR €	7.67	–	–	–	–	–	–
USD $	7.87	−0.13	–	–	–	–	–
Athelney Tr	137.50	–	142	112	3.6	138.3	0.6
Atls Japan	80.50	–	86.25	33.04	–	85.2	5.5
Aurora	216.50	–	261.50	158	1.6	257.1	15.8
BSRT	103.13	−0.25	110.50	77	–	112.4	8.3

Price change compared to last trading day

Highest and lowest price in the last 52 weeks

Yield is the dividend in the last 12 months as a percentage of the share price. Dividends are normally paid twice yearly

Net asset value (NAV) in pence per share. The theoretical value of the underlying securities if liquidated immediately

Discount or premium (-); the share price discount or premium from NAV expressed as a percentage of NAV

Source: *Financial Times*, 29 June 2011
Note: the Monday edition of the FT displays the change in price over the week, the actual dividend in pence per share, when dividends are paid, market capitalisation and the date when a shareholder last qualified for the receipt of a dividend (the ex-dividend date).

Exhibit 7.12 Investment trust prices in the *Financial Times*

While much of the discount on a typical investment trust is due to negative sentiment there are some rational reasons for shares selling below NAV:

- Investors may think trust managers are incompetent and likely to lose more value in the future.

- NAV is calculated after deducting the nominal (stated book) value of the debt and preference shares. In reality, the trust may have to pay back more on the debt and preference shares than this.

- Liquidating the fund incurs costs (e.g. contract cancellations, advisers' fees, stockbrokers' fees) so NAV is not achieved.

Costs

When buying (or selling) investment trust shares, commission will be payable to the stockbroker[11] as usual when buying shares (usually £20–£40 for purchases of a few thousand pounds). The trust managers' costs for managing the investments and for administration are charged to the fund, either against annual income or against capital. A typical **total expense ratio**, **TER**, including the costs of investment management and administration, directors' fees, audit fees and share registration expenses, is between 1.5 and 1.8 per cent of the fund's value (but this excludes performance fees that managers often take).

Borrowing

Investment trusts have the freedom to borrow (unlike unit trusts or OEICs). Borrowing to buy assets is fine if the return on assets over time exceeds the interest charged. However, it is a doubled-edged sword. The risk associated with gearing up returns becomes all too apparent when asset values fall. Take the case of our trust investing in eastern Europe. If it had sold 50 million shares at £1 each and also borrowed £50 million to buy £100 million of eastern European shares the NAV would still start at £1 per share (£100 million of assets minus £50 million debt owed, for 50 million shares). If underlying asset values fall by 40 per cent because of the fall in the Warsaw Stock Exchange, the *net* asset value per share falls dramatically from £1 to 20p – an 80 per cent fall – because the assets fall to £60 million, but the debt remains at £50 million:

---

[11] Investment trusts are also sold through financial advisers. The trust may have a savings scheme allowing the investor to buy a few shares each month (starting from as little as £30 per month) or make a lump sum purchase.

Value of eastern European shares	£60m
Less debt	–£50m
	£10m

Net asset value per share: £10m/50m = 20p

You can see why trusts that borrow a lot can be very volatile.

Sovereign wealth funds (SWFs)

Sovereign wealth funds are collective funds set up and managed by governments. Thus a country that has a large flow of income, due to say oil, may establish a fund on behalf of its people so that they can gain a future income from the investment fund after the oil has gone. Given that they now control $3,000 billion to $4,000 billion of investments around the world their decisions on where to place money can have significant effects on finance and economics. They used to be buy-and-hold type investors looking for long-term returns. However following the financial crisis many were used as sources of finance to support their domestic economies; this kind of political interference may grow. The biggest sovereign wealth funds are from Abu Dhabi ($627 billion), Norway ($471 billion) and Saudi Arabia ($415 billion).

Custodians

Custodians are guardians or safe-keepers of securities. The term often refers to custodian banks, whose legal remit is to look after the various assets of investment companies, especially pension funds (and mutual funds in the US), in return for a fee. They safeguard the securities or other assets that the funds own, and check on and distribute dividend payments, capital gains and general information relating to the diverse range of assets. One of HSBC's custodianship tasks is to safeguard gold bullion bars (worth £33 billion in 2010) backing a gold investment fund.

Custodians provide a very necessary protection for investors against any illegal or fraudulent activities of any fund manager, who could be tempted into dishonest behaviour simply by the enormity of the amounts involved. The idea is to keep the assets at arm's length from the individuals running the fund. In the UK HM Revenue & Customs keeps a list of approved custodians. Domestic custodians look after domestic assets; global custodians oversee assets held in the rest of the world.

Institutional Shareholder Committee

The **Institutional Shareholder Committee**, founded in 1991, sets out the principles of behaviour for institutional shareholders (such as managers of pension and insurance funds, investment trusts, etc.). It also set standards of behaviour it expects from corporations in which its members hold shares and other securities. The members of the committee are **The Association of British Insurers** (the trade association for the 300 or so British Insurance Companies), the **Association of Investment Companies** (the trade association for the closed-ended investment company industry), the **Investment Management Association** (representing the UK investment management industry) and the **National Association of Pension Funds** (represents the interests of occupational pension schemes). In the case of pension funds, it advises that institutional shareholders' primary duty is to the beneficiaries of a pension scheme. It regularly updates its code and encourages fund managers to behave more like owners and to take an intelligent interest in their investments. If fund managers think that companies such as BP or Shell are not being run properly, they have a duty to intervene, rather than sitting quietly and watching as a crisis happens, a duty particularly relevant after the financial recession and company failures of 2008–09.

The four trade associations listed above keep an eye on corporate management and make recommendations on how institutional investors should vote on say the size of directors' pay. These tend to be widely supported by institutions and often result in the target company changing its decision.

Websites

www.theaic.co.uk	Association of Investment Companies
www.bestinvest.co.uk	Bestinvest, independent financial adviser
www.citywire.co.uk	Citywire, financial news and advice
www.cofunds.co.uk	Cofunds, investment advice
www.direct.gov.uk	HM Government Public Services
www.dwp.gov.uk	Department for Work and Pensions
www.fsa.gov.uk	Financial Services Authority
www.ft.com	Financial Times

www.ftse.com	Financial Times Stock Exchange
www.fundsdirect.co.uk	FundsDirect, fund supermarket
www.hemscott.com	Hemscott, Share Prices, Stocks, Investing & Company Information
www.ici.org	Investment Company Institute
www.iii.co.uk	Interactive Investor
www.incademy.com	Incademy investor adducation
http://uk.ishares.com	iShares
www.investegate.co.uk	UK quoted company announcements
www.investmentfunds.org.uk	Investment Management Association
www.lipperweb.com	Lipper (Reuters)
www.londonstockexchange.com	London Stock Exchange
www.moneyextra.com	Moneyextra
www.morningstar.co.uk	Morningstar
www.napf.co.uk	National Association of Pension Funds
www.oecd.org	OECD
www.pensionsadvisoryservice.org.uk	Independent pensions advice
www.standardandpoors.com	Standard & Poor's financial services company
www.thecityuk.com	TheCityUK (includes IFSL)
www.thepensionsregulator.gov.uk	Pensions regulator
www.trustnet.com	Trustnet, financial analysis

8

Insurance

Imagine life without insurance. Would you dare to drive a car? What if you had an accident and were required to replace someone else's car; or worse, you injure someone so badly that you have to pay out £1 million in compensation? Surely, the absence of car insurance alone would cause a reduction in economic output and in the quality of life because we would rarely take the risk of driving. The same logic applies to shipping goods around the world or constructing a building. Ship owners, airlines and builders cannot take the risk of hurting someone, or the risk of a fire or of loss of property from theft or accident, and so would generally refuse to take part in productive activity. We would all be poorer as a result. So clearly workers in the insurance industry help the rest of society go about pleasurable and business activity.

Insurance companies play important roles in the financial system, not only by reducing and transferring risk and in helping us save for our old age, but also as substantial holders of financial securities. Because they control enormous funds their investment decisions can have profound effects on the equity markets, the bond markets and the other places where they apply their money, such as property, private equity and hedge funds.

Size of the industry

According to Swiss Re, a leading global reinsurer,[1] in 2010 $4,339 billion of insurance premiums were paid.[2] This equates to roughly $600 for every single human being in the world. It is a vast industry, nearly doubling the amount of premiums paid in the past 10 years, and impinges on everybody's life. It is an important source of overseas income to the countries which provide it. In 2010 the UK had a 7 per cent share of the insurance market, third behind the US and Japan, see Exhibit 8.1.

---

[1] Reinsurance is when insurers buy insurance for their risks – see later.
[2] http://media.swissre.com/documents/sigma2_2010_stat_appendix_2.pdf

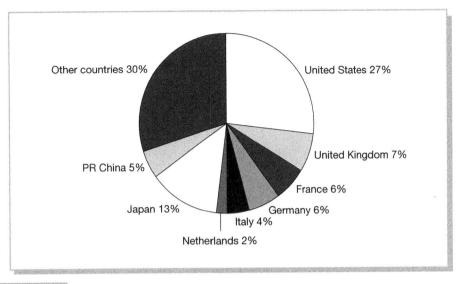

Global premium volume received 2010

Source: Swiss Re, *sigma* No 2/2011

There are also offshore tax haven countries which specialise in insurance. The largest of these is Bermuda, a self-governing British overseas territory, where company taxes are significantly lower than in most countries. Thanks to its position as a financial centre where most of the world's large insurance companies have a base, Bermuda has one of the highest per capita GDPs in the world, and is the biggest centre for reinsurance, a specialised form of insurance, where insurance companies insure their insurance business against loss. Bermuda, along with New York and London, make up the three main centres of reinsurance.

History of insurance

Insurance in some form has been in existence since ancient times, when traders faced the risk of financial ruin if their cargoes met with disaster. Traders might contribute to a fund from which those who suffered loss could claim some compensation. As trading developed and increased, rich businessmen would agree to pay for part of any losses in return for a sum of money, and would sign a contract to this effect, *writing* their name *under* the wording of the contract; this is where the term underwriting originates.

The first modern-day insurance companies were fire insurance companies formed after the Great Fire of London in 1666: Hand in Hand (1696), Sun Fire

Office (1710) and the Royal Exchange Assurance (1753). At the same period in London, a certain Edward Lloyd's coffee house became a centre for meetings of people with commercial interest in the rapidly expanding shipping industry.

Insurance firms

Insurance firms are either normal companies owned by shareholders or mutual organisations that are owned by their policyholders. The insurance firms' task is to make sure that they understand the risks involved, and that they receive more in premiums than they pay out in claims and running costs.[3] This has become more difficult with our increasingly litigious society, and the advent of new and expensive-to-replace technology, pollution and modern-day diseases such as AIDS and cancer. Insurance firms are regulated by domestic legislation, but where they establish offices abroad, these may be subject to less regulation, especially in tax-haven countries such as Bermuda. For the remainder of the chapter for brevity, insurance mutuals will be included in the term insurance company.

Insurance underwriting

Underwriting, assessing the risk involved and setting the terms and cost of the premium to be paid, is a complex job, and has to take into account any number of variables, while coming up with a premium that is both profitable to the insurance company and acceptable (competitive) to its customers. Because of the complexity involved, underwriters usually specialise in one particular type of insurance, such as motor, life, business, etc., so that they can build up their knowledge base and make sound decisions which will make money for their company but also attract custom. A lot of their decisions are based on historical statistics, which help them analyse the risk involved and the likelihood of a claim being made. The greater the amount of statistics available, the easier it is to predict risk. It is all a balancing act, and the underwriters' task is to ensure that the balance is weighted in favour of the company.

---

[3] Having said this, many insurance firms are not too worried if the claims or running costs are slightly greater than the premiums, if they have use of the float. The **float** is cash that accumulates because policyholders usually pay for insurance up front and there is a time lag before the claims roll in. This float can be invested to earn a return which can more than compensate for an operational loss.

Asymmetric information

There are various pitfalls which can trap the unwary underwriter or customer into making a bad decision. **Asymmetric information** is when one party in a negotiation or relationship is not in the same position as the other parties, being ignorant of, or unable to observe, some information which is essential to the contracting and decision-making process. Thus, while insurance companies ask prospective policyholders to provide a lot of information when trying to assess the level of risk exposure, the client will always know more than the insurer.

Adverse selection occurs when there is an opportunity or incentive for some firms/individuals to act to take advantage of their informational edge over others. Then the firms/individuals doing that activity will be disproportionately those taking advantage rather than being truly representative of the population as a whole, for example, the tendency for poorer-than-average risks to continue with insurance. This will raise the cost of insurance for the whole group, including those of less-than-average risk. Thus there is a proclivity among people in dangerous jobs or with high-risk lifestyles to buy insurance, knowing that insurance premiums are based on averages, and that they will therefore be at an advantage. Insurance companies and their underwriters try to cover this by limiting the insurance offered or by increasing premiums, but may then find that fewer people buy insurance cover.

Moral hazard recognises the danger that someone who is insured may be more likely to take more risk and be less careful because they are insured, so someone might not bother to lock their car 'because it's insured anyway'. Insurers try to minimise this problem by making the amount paid out in a claim less, for example, increasing the **excess** to be paid if the car is not locked (excess is the loss that the policyholder bears before the insurer pays out).

The insurance process

Insurance is sold in a variety of ways:

▪ direct from an insurer either at one of their offices, over the phone, or via the internet;

▪ through an agent who usually works for one insurer;

▪ through an insurance **broker** or independent intermediary who is not normally tied to any one particular insurer: brokers are paid commission on policy sales, and are able to search round and find the most suitable policy;

▪ through a bank, building society, solicitor, travel agent, mail order agent or accountant, who will receive commission on sales.

Wherever policies are obtained, the process is the same; a proposal form with relevant questions is completed and sent to the underwriter for assessment of the risk. If information given on proposals is incorrect, the insurance will be invalid.

Types of insurance

Insurance can be split into two types, life (or long-term insurance) and general (or non-life insurance). Both generate significant amounts of money in premiums (see Exhibit 8.2) with life policies taking the greater share, approximately 60 per cent compared with approximately 40 per cent for general insurance.

Year	General/non-life insurance $bn	Life/long-term insurance $bn	Totals $bn
2005	1,442	2,004	3,446
2006	1,549	2,126	3,675
2007	1,668	2,393	4,061
2008	1,781	2,439	4,220
2009	1,742	2,367	4,109
2010	1,819	2,520	4,339

Exhibit 8.2   **Global premium income (2005–09)**

Source: Swiss Re, sigma No 2/2011

Life/long-term insurance

Life insurance includes a variety of insurance policies which cover people in different ways for loss of life, usually their own.[4] Many life policies allow the insured to add money into the policy amount beyond what is needed for payouts on death, and so if the insured is still alive after, say, 10 years, a sum of money is received. Thus for many people it is a way of saving, and the insurance companies have to attract customers and compete against other forms of saving. There are several forms of life insurance:

---

[4] Long-term insurance also applies to permanent illness and disablement as well as death.

▪ **Term assurance,** in return for premiums, covers the policyholder for a set amount of time and will pay out if the policyholder dies within that set time. If the insured survives over the specified period, then no payout is made.

▪ **Whole of life** cover is more costly than term assurance because it is guaranteed to pay out when the insured dies as long as the premiums are up-to-date. The premiums tend to rise as the insured ages to cover the increased likelihood of mortality.

▪ **Endowment** policies are principally savings vehicles and pay out a set amount at a set future date (or on the earlier death of the insured) in return for premiums paid. They may be **without profits**, in which case they just pay out the amount set at the start of the policy, or **with profits** where the insured receives a bonus each year in the shape of a share of the fund's returns from investments made (if it makes a positive return) and at the maturity of the policy, these accrued profits are repaid to the insured. They are often linked to mortgages, where the insured pays only the interest on their mortgage, and the policy at maturity pays off the mortgage.

▪ **Annuities** provide a regular income until the death of the insured in return for a lump sum payment. The insurance company takes the lump sum and invests it in the financial markets and elsewhere to make a return.

▪ Insurance companies may also run **pension schemes** for individuals – see later in the chapter.

General/non-life insurance

This encompasses all other types of insurance. It is usually renewed annually, and the premium may be adjusted when required. There are broadly three categories:

1 **Property** insurance covers personal and business properties and contents against fire, theft, weather damage, and can also include flood, terrorism, earthquake, domestic appliances and other perils.

2 **Casualty** insurance includes aviation and marine insurance, car insurance, travel insurance, private medical insurance, pet insurance, accident, sickness or unemployment insurance, critical illness insurance and long-term care insurance.

3 **Liability** insurance protects the insured against third-party claims and includes employers' liability, public liability (e.g. a member of the public being hurt by falling masonry from a building site), product liability, commercial fleet liability (e.g. companies that use vehicles as part of their

business will have all their vehicles covered by one policy, so that if any of their fleet is involved in an accident, the vehicle and its driver are fully covered by insurance), pollution liability.

What do insurance companies do with the premiums?

All insurance companies take in premiums constantly, and they are therefore in possession of a substantial 'pool' or 'float' of ready cash which they are able to invest in various ways: see Exhibit 8.3 for UK insurance companies' investments.

Year Type of investment	2005 (£m)	2006 (£m)	2007 (£m)	2008 (£m)	2009 (£m)
UK public sector securities	205,121	210,238	212,219	195,673	198,580
Overseas public sector securities	50,925	48,077	57,280	80,596	88,283
UK ordinary stocks and shares	315,365	345,348	343,469	210,824	236,827
Other UK company stocks and shares	157,076	142,426	161,538	153,351	172,375
Overseas ordinary stocks and shares	172,092	186,429	226,939	205,949	244,414
Other overseas company securities	117,428	141,364	144,296	221,220	220,399
Unit trusts	144,615	172,763	199,867	177,029	202,790
Property	95,201	105,293	106,364	103,535	96,924
Cash and other investments	123,966	127,871	147,789	147,836	133,229
Total	1,381,789	1,479,808	1,599,762	1,496,012	1,593,820

Exhibit 8.3   **UK insurance companies' investment holdings**

Source: ABI

The distinction between the different types of insurance is important, as the type of business carried out influences the treatment of the premium income. General insurance companies must keep enough in cash or very liquid assets such as money market instruments to be able to pay out on claims whenever they occur. Usually, the amount needed to satisfy claims can be predicted, but in the case of a natural disaster, or in the case of an unusual run of claims, the insurance companies need to be able to pay out large sums of money very quickly. If their underwriters do their job efficiently, their float will grow steadily and if invested wisely can be a great source of revenue, as well as being a buffer against an excessive number of claims being made.

Life insurance companies on the other hand are able to predict to a far greater extent when they will need to pay out any claims. Their underwriters use sophisticated statistical analysis to work out when claims are likely to need to be met.[5] Therefore they do not require their assets to be readily available and can invest in longer-term investments such as bonds and company shares.

Exhibit 8.4 shows the assets under the control of insurance companies in six of the countries pre-eminent in insurance: $15,394 billion for these six countries. The investments they make are crucial to the viability of their companies.

	Life $ billion	Non-life $ billion	Totals $ billion
US	4,896	1,224	6,120
UK	2,347	229	2,576
Japan	2,171	384	2,555
Germany	842	850	1,692
France	1,719	288	2,007
Netherlands	387	57	444
Totals	12,363	3,031	15,394

Exhibit 8.4   Invested assets of insurance companies 2008

Source: IFSL (www.thecityUK.com)

---

[5] Having said this, they have been stunned in the past decade by increasing longevity – people are living far longer than was predicted in the models of the 1990s.

If insurance companies fail to underwrite or invest their assets competently, they run the risk of not being able to pay out on claims. But even if they are run efficiently, they could still suffer from a run of bad luck and run out of funds. Insurance companies need several years of profits to make up for a bad year on claims, and each year a number of companies fail when their capital has diminished to the point where it is likely that they will be unable to meet their insurance liabilities. Between 1969 and 1998 in the US insurance companies alone suffered over 640 insolvencies. Governments worldwide have increased regulations on insurance companies to ensure that they have sufficient financial funding and are run efficiently. In the UK since 2001 the Financial Services Authority (Financial Conduct Authority from 2013) has overseen all insurance companies including Lloyds. In the EU, a new directive in 2012, **Solvency II**, aims to implement solvency requirements (keeping a good reserve of capital) that better reflect the risks that companies face and deliver a supervisory system that is consistent across all member states.

Reinsurance

Reinsurance has evolved as an effective means of coping with the growing number and increasingly complex nature of risks. It is the process by which insurance companies lessen their exposure to risk by transferring the risk to a reinsurer. By transferring all or part of the risk, the insurance company is able to accept more or larger risks from a client. Insurers should only underwrite risk in proportion to the amount of capital they possess, so reinsurance is a way to expand their business without the need to raise further capital.

Reinsurance can be **proportional** or **non-proportional**:

- Proportional reinsurance is taken out for part of one particular risk, or part of all risks, and protects the original insurer against legitimate but unforeseeable or extraordinary losses. If a reinsurer takes on 45 per cent of a risk, they receive 45 per cent of the premium and in the event of a claim will pay out 45 per cent of the claim. An insurance company might ask a reinsurer to take on a percentage of all its business, say 20 per cent, and the reinsurer, in return for 20 per cent of all premiums, would assume responsibility for paying out 20 per cent of every claim. The original insurer receives a **ceding commission** as a thank you for providing business to the reinsurer.

- Non-proportional reinsurance is taken out to cover loss *over* a certain amount. For example, if an insurance company insures a shipping company against a loss of $5 million, it could choose to reinsure any loss in excess of, say, $1 million or $4 million.

Reinsurance is often split between a number of reinsurance companies to spread the risk, so that in the event of a large claim being made, no single company stands the whole amount. The five largest reinsurance companies are shown in Exhibit 8.5. They all have offices worldwide, and skilful underwriters to undertake this complex task.

	Country	Gross premiums ($ billion)
Munich Reinsurance Company	Germany	34.3
Swiss Reinsurance Company Limited	Switzerland	27.6
Hanover Rueckversicherung AG	Germany	14.7
Lloyd's of London	UK	12.7
Berkshire Hathaway Inc.	US	12.0

Exhibit 8.5 Largest global reinsurers 2009

Source: AM Best, *Best's Special Report*, 6 September 2010

The purchase of reinsurance by reinsurance companies is known as **retrocession**. It is entirely possible for a reinsurance company to unknowingly reinsure itself by taking on part of a risk that it has distributed among other reinsurance companies, which in turn redistribute the risk; this is known as **spiralling**.

The London market

The London market is a separate part of the UK insurance and reinsurance business centred in the City of London, and comprises **Lloyd's** and **Lloyd's syndicates, Protection and Indemnity (P&I) Clubs** and members of the **IUA (the International Underwriting Association of London)**. Together they provide international general insurance and reinsurance for complex large commercial risks. It is the only market in which all of the world's 20 largest reinsurance groups are represented. The amount of expertise available from these insurers means that brokers are able to underwrite just about any type of risk, and business is facilitated by their geographical proximity, with every kind of ancillary service providers, such as lawyers and IT, close at hand. The close community of specialist insurers and support service providers means that information spread is rapid and deals can be made quickly.

Exhibit 8.6 shows the size of the London market over the five years from 2005 to 2009, and how it has expanded to generate some £31,910 million in premiums.

	Share of London market				Type of insurance business		
Year	Lloyd's £m	Insurance companies – IUA members £m	P&I Clubs £m	Totals £m	Marine, Aviation and Transport (MAT) £m	Non-MAT business home and foreign £m	Non-marine reinsurance £m
2005	12,102	13,013	1,537	26,652	6,948	8,117	11,587
2006	13,827	8,944	1,535	24,306	7,610	8,280	8,416
2007	13,794	6,722	1,238	21,754	7,546	9,001	5,207
2008	15,689	8,055	907	24,651	8,478	10,306	5,867
2009	19,515	11,519	876	31910	n/a	n/a	n/a

Exhibit 8.6   **The London market premium income**

Source: ABI

International Underwriting Association (IUA)

The **IUA** is the world's largest organisation for international and wholesale insurance and reinsurance companies. It was formed in 1998 by the merger of two separate bodies which previously represented marine and non-marine insurance.

P&I Clubs

Protection and Indemnity (P&I) Clubs (often called Marine P&I Clubs) have been in existence for over 140 years and offer protection and indemnity (insurance) in respect of third-party liabilities and expenses arising from owning or operating ships. They do not cover the actual ships or their cargoes, but do cover third-party risks such as collision, pollution, injury to or loss of life of passengers or crew members, and a long list of other third-party liabilities. They are run on a mutual basis (owned by members and not run for profit), although there has recently been a trend towards demutualisation and the provision of insurance cover with fixed premiums.

Lloyd's

Edward Lloyd is believed to have opened his coffee house in Tower Street, London during 1688, and it soon became a meeting place for people with interests in shipping. In 1769 a group of underwriters and brokers moved to other premises, naming them 'New Lloyd's Coffee House'. When these premises became too small, the group of 79 each put in £100, leased and became joint owners of what was henceforth called 'Lloyd's of London' or just 'Lloyd's'. Business, and the expertise of the underwriters and brokers, grew, and in 1871 an Act of Parliament gave Lloyd's authority to acquire property and enact by-laws. Lloyd's had become an established business institution not only in British society but throughout the trading world.

The proficiency and experience of Lloyd's underwriters preserves its position at the forefront of the property and casualty insurance business, and their ability and willingness to undertake unusual risks keeps them in the public eye. Lloyd's is a meeting place where brokers and underwriters meet face to face and discuss requirements. Exhibit 8.7 gives the percentage breakdown of the insurance cover that they underwrote in 2010. Over one-half of the business is with North or South Americans; only 20% of their business is with UK individuals and organisations. Lloyd's members write insurance in over 75 jurisdictions and write reinsurance in over 200 countries and territories.

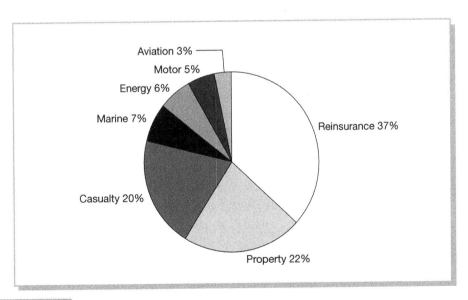

Exhibit 8.7   **Lloyd's: percentage of underwriting (2010)**

Source: Lloyd's Annual Report 2010

Among the more interesting risks that Lloyd's syndicates have underwritten are Father Christmas' beard; the 1981 Derby winner Shergar, which was owned by a syndicate of individuals when it was kidnapped in 1983 (payments were made to horse syndicate members who were insured for theft, but not to those who insured for loss of life); the legs of Betty Grable ($1 million each leg) and Michael Flatley ($47 million!); Ken Dodd's teeth; accidental injury to any of the Beatles; Bruce Springsteen's voice ($6 million); the taste buds of Egon Ronay; the risk that Queen Victoria's first born would be twins; and death from excessive laughter (this cover was taken out in the 1920s when the early comedic films were shown for the first time, and had a dramatic effect on their audience).

The structure of Lloyd's

Lloyd's is not an insurance company, it is a society of members. That is, a group of members who trade in insurance via brokers, in an environment run by the **Corporation of Lloyd's**, which is overseen by the **Council of Lloyd's**.

For a long time, it was made up of individuals (**Names**) who joined together in syndicates to underwrite an ever-larger range of risks. Syndicates ran (and still run) for one year only, then closed, and other syndicates would be formed, sometimes identical in membership to the one just closed, sometimes with some or all different members. Because claims take time to become apparent, three years after opening the syndicates accounts are closed, profit taken, and any liabilities taken into consideration. However, instead of putting aside reserves of cash to pay for these liabilities, it became common practice to reinsure them, usually with the same syndicate. In this way, it was possible for losses to accumulate year after year, and it was possible for new members to be liable for losses from years ago. This resulted in meltdown in the late 1980s and 1990s, following a string of natural disasters – the explosion of the Piper Alpha oil rig, the Exxon Valdez oil spill, an earthquake in San Francisco and Hurricane Hugo – combined with US courts awarding huge damages for asbestosis, pollution and health hazards. Some of the claims involved all-liability policies, and dated back tens of years. For over 300 years, individual underwriting members had accepted unlimited personal liability for the policies they signed and now they were faced with paying out huge claims dating back decades.

Lloyd's had gone through a profitable time and a huge expansion in the number of Names since the 1950s, when there were just over 3,000 members, to a high of over 32,000 in 1988. Faced with financial ruin, many Names refused to pay out, and sued Lloyd's for accepting their membership but not fully revealing the historic liabilities. From 1988 to 1992 Lloyd's suffered continual losses totalling nearly £8 billion, and the resignation of thousands of Names.

This brought about a complete reorganisation of Lloyd's; a separate insurance company called **Equitas** funded by a levy on members was formed in 1996 to take over all pre-1992 liabilities (Equitas was taken over by Warren Buffett's Berkshire Hathaway in 2006); for the first time, limited liability companies and institutions were allowed to be members and no *new* unlimited liability members were admitted, resulting in the steady decline of individual unlimited liability Names. This has had a dramatic effect on Lloyd's membership (see Exhibit 8.8). The Central Fund was established, by a levy on all premiums, to be used if members are unable to meet claims (now with over £2 billion); underwriting and risk management were improved; and syndicates had to produce a business plan which met with the approval of the Corporation of Lloyd's.

Year	1995	2000	2007	2009	2010
Individual	14,573	3,270	1,106	765	692
Corporate	140	854	1,020	1,241	1,445
Total active members forming	14,713	4,124	2,126	2,006	2,137
Syndicates	170	124	72	85	87

Exhibit 8.8   Lloyd's membership 1995–2010

Source: Lloyd's

Individuals or businesses wishing to invest in Lloyd's must have £350,000 in assets in reserve and about £200,000 in cash that they can place in Lloyd's as back-up for underwriting losses, should they occur. They are then able to buy the right to be a syndicate member and take a share in the syndicate's profit.

Exhibit 8.9 shows where Lloyd's syndicates get their capital from. Clearly, most of it now comes from the global insurance industry rather than from individuals.

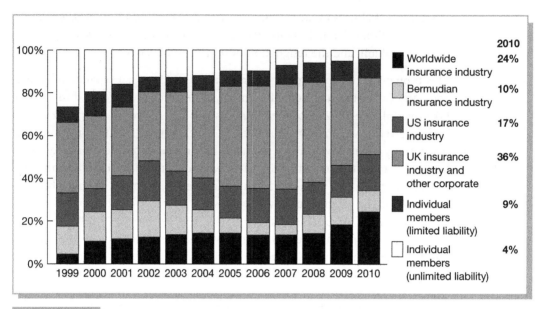

Exhibit 8.9   Source of capital for Lloyd's

Source: Lloyd's Annual Report 2010

At the centre of the Lloyd's system are the 85 or so syndicates that accept the insurance risk. Brokers working for the clients needing insurance shop around and negotiate a deal with one or more syndicates. Managing agents are responsible for managing a syndicate and the whole system is supervised by the Corporation of Lloyd's (see Exhibit 8.10).

Exhibit 8.11 describes the stages a new Name has to go through to underwrite insurance risk.

Money has to be kept in reserve and invested in safe and easily liquidated financial assets to meet the claims of policyholders. Lloyd's tries to be ultra-safe by having three pots of money. The first comes from premiums paid, the second from money supplied by Members and the third from a central fund which is topped up by Members each year (see Exhibit 8.12).

The article in Exhibit 8.13 shows where the money held in each of these three funds was invested, and discusses the current debate about the temptation to invest in less liquid and more risky securities to obtain higher returns.

Members of Lloyd's

These are the capital providers that accept the insurance risk via syndicates.
Included are major insurance groups, companies (some listed on stock markets), individuals and limited partnerships. Private members typically support a number of syndicates. Corporate members usually underwrite through a single syndicate.
Members choose which syndicate(s) to participate in for the following year (most stick with the same for many years)

Members' agents

Advisory and administration services to members.
Help set up limited liability partnerships for non-corporate members (i.e. individuals).
Arrange investment in a syndicate

Clients seeking insurance

Brokers

Working on behalf of clients

Face-to-face negotiation in the Underwriting Room, One Lime Street

Syndicates

(85 syndicates in 2010)
One or more Lloyd's Members that join together as a group to accept insurance risks.
The specialist underwriters within each syndicate price, underwrite and handle any subsequent claims.
Members receive profits or bear losses in proportion to their share in the syndicate for each underwriting year of account.
Some syndicates specialise in underwriting a certain class of insurance, e.g. aviation.
Many syndicates are now managed and funded by a single corporate group (member)

Corporation of Lloyd's

• Oversees market
• Establishes standards
• Sets the level of capital Members must provide to support their proposed underwriting
• Provides services to support market activities

Managing agent

(52 in 2010)
A company set up to manage one or more syndicates on behalf of members. Oversight of underwriting, employing the underwriter, handling day-to-day running of the syndicate's infrastructure and operations.
Managing agents are also located around the world, e.g. there are six firms in Brazil

Exhibit 8.10   The players at Lloyd's

High-net-worth investors keen to sign up as Names

By Ellen Kelleher

Scores of high-net-worth investors are already expressing an interest in signing up as Lloyd's Names to profit from next year's underwriting cycle for the London insurance market.

The way to follow suit is to join one of the three Lloyd's members' agents, Alpha, Argenta or Hampden. These groups set up limited liability underwriting vehicles and represent clients seeking to invest in particular syndicates at Lloyd's capacity auctions, held in September.

Members tend to support a variety of syndicates and spread their risk by underwriting different classes of insurance and reinsurance.

The costs of investing in the Lloyd's market remain high, as investors must have at least £350,000 in assets, which is used as collateral, and about £200,000 in cash, which is used to buy the rights to participate in the profits of syndicates.

Another £7,000 to £10,000 is required to start a limited liability partnership (LLP), which must be set up by the end of August to participate in the auctions for the 2010 account.

Prospective members can also purchase an existing LLP.

Members who have set up a limited liability underwriting vehicle must then deposit funds at Lloyd's in November to support their underwriting capacity for the following year.

To write a premium income limit of £1m for the 2010 year, for example, an account would require a £400,000 deposit, in the form of cash, shares, or bank guarantees.

Funds deposited are geared by about 2.5 times.

Syndicate capacity bought by members in a particular year is a tradeable asset which can gain or lose capital value and also pay yearly dividends in the form of underwriting profit...

....High-net-worth investors are attracted to the market for several reasons.

Losses are now capped, as investors can now only underwrite a group of syndicates through a LLP, which means that the maximum loss they face will be restricted to the capital pledged upfront.

A second benefit is that assets invested in Lloyd's can be used twice to achieve returns. For example, an investor could put up, say, a buy-to-let property or a share portfolio as collateral.

This allows investors to earn a double return on their assets. Also, any losses can be offset against income tax.

Source: *Financial Times*, 19 January 2009, p. 18

Exhibit 8.11   High-net-worth investors keen to sign up as Names

First: syndicate-level assets ('premium trust fund')	Premiums on policies received by a syndicate are held in its trust fund ready to pay out on claims (over £37 billion in 2010)
Second: members' funds at Lloyd's	Each member provides capital to support underwriting in case claims exceed premiums. This capital is held in trust as readily saleable assets to meet any Lloyd's insurance liabilities of that member, but not the liabilities of other members (over £13 billion in 2010)
Third: central assets	A further back-up is the Corporation's central assets to meet valid claims that cannot be met by the member. Members have to pay an annual contribution to maintain it (over £2 billion in 2010)

Exhibit 8.12   The three sources of capital to back up insurance promises at Lloyd's

Lloyd's considers riskier investments

By Steve Johnson

Not many investors managed to sail serenely through the financial crisis with scarcely a care in the world, but Lloyd's of London, the 322-year-old insurance market, was among this select band.

The insurance market's conservative investment strategy, heavy in government and corporate bonds, saw it chalk up annual returns of 5.6 per cent in 2007,

2.5 per cent in 2008 and 4 per cent in 2009.

In spite of this, there are signs that the 52 managing agents, the underwriters that manage the 84 syndicates and hold £46bn ($70bn, €52bn) of investable assets, are starting to embrace a little more risk.

The change is being driven by the increasingly paltry returns

available on short duration investment-grade debt and the fact that the notoriously cyclical underwriting market appears to be softening, putting pressure on agents to generate returns from the asset side of their balance sheet.

Others see a similar trend. David Osborne, senior consultant at Meridian, the largest consul-

▶

Exhibit 8.13   Lloyd's considers riskier investments

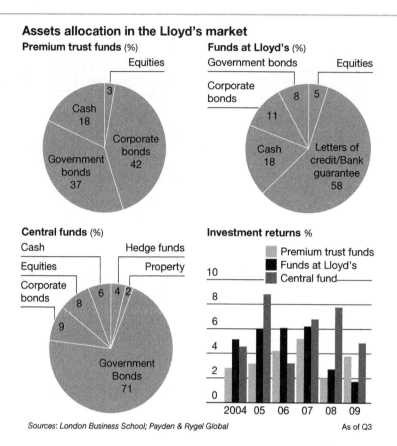

Assets allocation in the Lloyd's market

Sources: London Business School; Payden & Rygel Global   As of Q3

tancy in the Lloyd's market, says: "People are having to re-think their attitude to risk. If they take all the risk off the table and put the money in cash deposits they earn nothing in practice. It's a more difficult set of problems than the insurance market has ever faced before."

Russell Büsst, head of institutional fixed income at Amundi, which manages £2.6bn on behalf of 15 managing agents and 20 syndicates, adds: "The last underwriting cycle was pretty weak and people are trying to make their reserves work harder."

Managing agents have traditionally been highly conservative investors, with the bulk of their assets held in short duration government bonds and investment-grade credit.

These assets, alongside letters of credit provided by banks, still dominate the three layers of capital; members' trust funds, which hold premium income; members' funds at Lloyd's, which holds the capital each syndicate must put up to support its underwriting activity; and the central fund, a mutual fund that provides a backstop for large claims.

However, Robin Creswell, managing principal of Payden & Rygel Global, which manages $5bn for insurance organisations, says some of the larger Lloyd's players had dipped their toes into equities, high yield bonds and hedge funds over the past five years, a lead he expected others to follow...

...Hedge funds are more widely held still, despite their relative lack of liquidity...

...some agents have ventured into property funds in the past six months. However, emerging market debt remains unpopular – many syndicates write political

Exhibit 8.13   Continued

insurance risk, which is closely correlated to the sovereign risk embedded in this asset class…

…Luke Savage, finance director of Lloyd's, which manages the central fund, says just 2 per cent of agents' assets are invested in equities, compared to equity exposure of 10–15 per cent for continental European insurers. "We feel very comfortable having slightly less sparkling performance in return for not putting our members at risk," he says.

Source: *Financial Times*, 5 April 2010, p. 3

Exhibit 8.13 Continued

Websites

www.abi.org.uk	Association of British Insurers
www.fsa.gov.uk	Financial Services Authority
www.ft.com	Financial Times
www.igpandi.org	Protection and Indemnity Clubs
www.iua.co.uk	International Underwriting Association of London
www.lloyds.com	Lloyd's
www.swissre.com	Swiss Re
www.thecityuk.com	TheCityUK (includes IFSL)

Money markets

Governments, corporations and banks need to keep control of their finances, making sure that if they do spend or lend more than their income they have a way of tapping into sources of funds by borrowing for short periods. On the other hand, there are times when these organisations have surplus funds, for merely a day, a week or the next three months. They need to be able to lend these temporary surpluses to gain some return – to make their money work for them. Leaving the money in a bank current account is one option, but this provides relatively low interest. The money markets are a much better alternative in many circumstances. They provide higher rates of return for those with surplus cash, with a wide variety of instruments to suit the preferences of the lender. On the borrowing side they are cheaper and involve less hassle than organising a bank loan.

While individuals borrow or deposit savings in relatively small amounts, governments and corporations borrow or lend in millions or billions; they use the money markets as **wholesale markets** rather than **retail markets**. We thus define the money markets as wholesale financial markets in which lending and borrowing on a short-term basis takes place – that is, usually for less than one year.[1]

Interest from discount pricing

In a literal sense money is not actually traded in these markets. When governments or corporations find themselves in need of short-term funds they sell an **instrument** or **security** which carries the promise to pay, say, £10 million in 30 days from now. The purchaser of that promise will not pay the full £10 million because they want to receive an effective interest rate for lending. So they might pay, say, £9.9 million. Thus the security is sold for less than **face value (par or nominal value)**. The **discount** is the difference between face value and purchase

---

[1] However, a few money market instruments have maturities greater than one year.

price. The **yield**, the rate of interest gained by the holder, occurs when the instrument reaches maturity and the face value is paid by the issuer to the holder.

Having said this, not all money market securities are issued at a discount to face value. Certificates of deposit and interbank deposits (both described later) are issued at their face value, and redeemed at a higher value.

Secondary market

Many money market instruments are **negotiable**, i.e. they can be resold on the secondary market. So, staying with the example, after 20 days the original purchaser could sell this promise to pay £10 million in a further 10 days for, say, £9.96 million. Thus a profit can be made by trading on the secondary market before the redemption date – in this case £60,000.

However, it must be noted that a loss may be incurred. If the original purchaser (lender) can only attract buyers at a price of £9.87 million then it makes a £30,000 loss. This low price may occur if interest rates on similar financial instruments with 10 days to maturity are now yielding a higher rate of return because investors have become more wary and demand higher rates of return to compensate for higher risk – a lot can change in the financial markets in 20 days. Any potential secondary market purchaser would be silly to pay a price higher (receive a lower yield) than the going market rate for this particular issue – i.e. the potential buyer has an opportunity cost (the return on the best alternative use of their investment money) and so the best the original purchaser can get, if it has to sell, is £9.87 million. If it can avoid selling for another 10 days then it will receive the full £10 million from the borrower.

The secondary markets in money market instruments are generally very **liquid**; that is, the securities can be turned into cash quickly without the need to reduce the price significantly and transaction costs are low.

Yield

The discount and rate of return (yield) earned is dependent on the risk level and the **maturity** of the instrument. The maturity is the length of time between issue of the instrument (start of borrowing) and the time it is redeemed (money due is paid), or the length of time between when a security is priced or purchased in the secondary market and the date of redemption. The maturity length can vary from overnight (borrowing for just 24 hours) to three months to one year (or even more, occasionally). Interest is measured in percentage points, which are further divided into **basis points (bps)**. One basis point equals 1/100 of a percentage point.

The markets in short-term money

Money markets exist all over the world as a means of facilitating business. **Domestic money market** means that the funds are borrowed and lent in the country's home currency and under the authority of that country's regulators. There are also money markets outside the jurisdiction of the authorities of the currency they are denominated in – these are the **international** or **Euro money markets**. This is nothing to do with the currency in Europe: they were termed 'Euro markets' long before the euro was dreamt up.

Money markets are used by governments, corporations and institutions for both borrowing and lending. Pension funds and insurance companies also maintain a proportion of their investment funds (they lend on the money markets) in a liquid, low-risk form to meet unpredictable cash outflows (e.g. following a hurricane). These markets are also used by central banks to influence interest rates charged throughout the economy (see Chapter 6).

Money market instruments, often in very large amounts, are traded over the telephone and then completed electronically by brokers and traders operating from the trading rooms of the big banks and specialist trading houses. These **market makers** maintain an inventory of securities and advertise prices at which they will sell and prices (slightly lower) at which they will buy. By providing these middleman services they assist the players in the market to quickly find a counterparty willing to trade, thus enhancing liquidity. They are said to be traders in **short-term interest rate (STIR) products**.

Some of the trades are simply private deals with legal obligations to be enforced by each side, but some are conducted through a central clearing house with each party responsible for reporting the deal to the clearing house, which settles the deal by debiting the account of the buyer and crediting the account of the seller. The clearing house then holds the security on behalf of the buyer. The risk of a counterparty reneging on the deal (**counterparty risk**) is reduced by trading through a clearing house.

VODAFONE

You can get some idea of the importance of money markets to companies from the table below showing figures taken from Vodafone's annual report. Vodafone keeps a large amount of cash and cash equivalents in reserve: £4 billion in 2010. **Cash equivalents** are not quite cash but they are so liquid that they are **near-cash (near-money** or **quasi-money)**. They are financial assets that can easily be sold to raise cash, or which are due to pay back their capital value in a few days, with low risk regarding the amount of cash they will release. These are mostly money market instruments.

Vodafone keeps this large quantity of money available in this highly-liquid and low-risk form so that it can supply its various business units with the cash they need for day-to-day operations or for regular investment projects. Also it is useful to have readily-accessible money to be able to take advantage of investment opportunities as they fleetingly appear (e.g. the purchase of a company). Alternatively, the cash and near-cash is there because the company has recently had a major inflow – perhaps it sold a division or has had bumper profits – and it has not yet allocated the money to its final uses, such as paying billions in dividends to shareholders, launching a new product, buying another company or paying a tax bill. In the meantime that money might as well be earning Vodafone some interest; so the money that is surplus to the immediate needs of the various business units of Vodafone is gathered together and temporarily lent to other organisations in the money markets.

Vodafone's money market holdings

Cash and cash equivalents

	2010 £m	2009 £m	2008 £m
Cash at bank and in hand	745	811	451
Money market funds	3,678	3,419	477
Repurchase agreements	–	648	478
Commercial paper	–	–	293
Cash and cash equivalents as presented in the balance sheet	4,423	4,878	1,699

Money market funds

Private individuals with small amounts to invest can participate in money market transactions by investing in **money market funds**. These are administered by financial institutions that benefit from economies of scale by investing in a portfolio of money market securities. The process is that they buy *shares* in the money market fund. Investors earn a return, technically a dividend, but in effect an interest rate. Corporations may also deposit surplus cash in money market funds to obtain good rates of interest through professional management of the fund. They can also gain access to their money by withdrawing it from the fund on a 'same-day' access basis. It is also possible to put in place a **sweep facility** so that money exceeding a certain balance is automatically transferred at the end of each day from a bank account to a money market account (paying more interest), and vice versa.

Money markets in crisis

Money markets went through a crisis in 2008. A money market fund called Reserve Primary Fund had invested a substantial proportion of its funds in Lehman Brothers short-term debt. When Lehman went bust the fund was unable to return to investors the amount they had paid into it. This **'breaking of the buck'** is a great sin in the money market world, which is supposed to be incredibly safe. Subsequently credit markets froze up: investors in funds could not withdraw their money at short notice as per their agreement. The market became illiquid because the money market funds could not sell their securities to raise cash to pay out to investors clamouring to withdraw their money.

In response the industry bodies in the US and Europe tightened rules to make sure that there was much more easily accessible cash in the funds – see Exhibit 9.1 for the European response. Note that while the European market is very large at over $600 billion, the US market is far larger, at around $3,800 billion. **Triple-A** means that they have independently been assessed as having a very low risk of defaulting. **Overnight securities** are those where the lender receives back capital and interest one day after lending. An **enhanced fund** is one that takes more risk (or invests in lower liquidity securities) to try to generate a higher return. **Natural liquidity** means holding securities that pay back their capital in a matter of hours or days rather than the holder relying on being able to sell their securities to other investors in the secondary market.

New rules for money funds

By Steve Johnson

Europe's €430bn (£388bn, $630bn) triple-A money market fund industry will have to abide by higher standards of maturity, credit quality, liquidity and disclosure under new guidelines due to be unveiled today.

The move follows a series of problems in the supposedly low risk asset class during the credit crisis. A number of "enhanced" European money market funds suffered double-digit losses and the US Treasury felt compelled to prop up its domestic industry after one vehicle, the Reserve Primary Fund, "broke the buck", losing money for investors.

Although triple-A rated European funds avoided these problems the industry body, the Institutional Money Market Funds

Assets in triple - A rated Immfa money market funds
By currency type (bn)

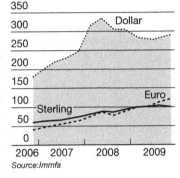

Source:Immfa

Association, has still decided to tighten its guidelines, which are mandatory for members…

…Funds will now have to manage liquidity by ensuring at least 5 per cent of assets are held in overnight securities and 20 per cent in securities maturing within one week. This is designed to ensure that funds, which all provide daily liquidity to investors, can meet redemption requests even if the secondary market seizes up.

"If liquidity disappears in the marketplace you cannot sell your assets. The only thing you can rely on is natural liquidity," said Nathan Douglas, secretary general of Immfa.

Immfa has also moved to tighten up credit quality by stipulating that the weighted average final maturity of a fund's assets must be no more than 120 days.

Source: *Financial Times*, 14 December 2009, p. 2

Exhibit 9.1   New rules for money funds

The interbank market

Originally, the **interbank market** was defined as the market where banks lend to each other, in both the domestic and international markets. This is a rather strict (old-fashioned) definition, and increasingly, as well as banks being lenders, this group includes large industrial and commercial companies, other financial institutions and international organisations. Thus, the interbank markets exist so that a bank or other large institution that has no immediate demand for its surplus cash can place the money in the interbank market and earn interest on it. In the opposite scenario, if a (highly respectable/safe) bank needs to supply a loan to a customer but does not have the necessary cash to hand, it can borrow what it needs on the interbank market.

There is no secondary trading in the interbank market; the loans are 'non-negotiable' – thus a lender for, say, three months cannot sell the right to receive interest and capital from the borrower to another organisation after, say, 15 days. The lender has to wait until the end of the agreed loan period to recover money. If a bank needs its funds, it simply ceases to deposit money with other banks.

The loans in this market are not secured with collateral. However, the rate of interest is still relatively low because those accepting deposits (borrowers) are respectable and safe banks. This interest rate creates the **benchmark** (reference) interest rate known as LIBOR – explained in the next section. Banks with lower respectability and safety will have to pay more than the benchmark rates set by the safest institutions.

Interest rates

In the financial pages of serious newspapers you will find a bewildering variety of interest rates quoted from all over the world. Following is an explanation of some of the terms in common use.

LIBOR

LIBOR or **Libor**, the **London Interbank Offered Rate**, is the most commonly used benchmark rate, in particular the three-month LIBOR rate, which is the interest rate for one bank lending to another (very safe) bank for a fixed three-month period.

Obviously these lending deals are private arrangements between the two banks concerned, but we can get a feel for the rates being charged by surveying the leading banks involved in these markets. This is done every trading day. The official LIBOR rates are calculated by the **British Banking Association (BBA)** by asking a panel of about 16 UK and international banks at what rates they could borrow money for unsecured loans of various maturities.[2] Contributor banks are asked to base their LIBOR submissions on the following question: '*At what rate could you borrow funds, were you to do so by asking for and then accepting inter-bank offers in a reasonable market size just prior to 11 am.*'[3] The rates from the 16 banks

---

[2] The size of the panel can vary from 8 to 20 banks, but it is usually 16. In February 2011, for instance, the number of contributing banks for US dollar LIBOR increased from 16 to 20.

[3] From the British Bankers Association: http://www.bbalibor.com/bbalibor-explained/the-basics. LIBOR is defined as: 'The rate at which an individual Contributor Panel bank could borrow funds, were it to do so by asking for and then accepting inter-bank offers in reasonable market size, just prior to 11.00 London time.'

are ranked in order from the highest to the lowest and the arithmetic mean of only the middle two quartiles is taken, i.e. if there are 16 reporting banks, the BBA removes the top four and bottom four rates quoted each day and averages the middle eight rates to calculate LIBOR.

The loans between banks are not just in sterling. London is the leading international financial centre of the world and lending takes place in a variety of currencies. Thus each day the BBA produces LIBOR interest rates for borrowing in 10 currencies with a range of 15 maturities from overnight to 12 months quoted for each currency, producing 150 rates each business day: see Exhibit 9.2 for the LIBOR rates produced on 31 December 2010.

Euro LIBOR		Japanese yen LIBOR		Australian dollar LIBOR		Swedish krona LIBOR	
	%		%		%		%
Overnight	0.60625	Spot/next	0.10000	Spot/next	4.84500	Spot/next	1.46250
1 week	0.53625	1 week	0.10600	1 week	4.84500	1 week	1.49250
2 weeks	0.58500	2 weeks	0.11500	2 weeks	4.85000	2 weeks	1.53550
1 month	0.71000	1 month	0.12625	1 month	4.85000	1 month	1.54500
2 months	0.81750	2 months	0.15375	2 months	4.89125	2 months	1.78250
3 months	0.93875	3 months	0.18813	3 months	4.95000	3 months	1.91250
4 months	1.00875	4 months	0.24413	4 months	5.00500	4 months	1.94750
5 months	1.09313	5 months	0.30125	5 months	5.05625	5 months	1.97750
6 months	1.18313	6 months	0.34750	6 months	5.13250	6 months	2.01500
7 months	1.23188	7 months	0.39750	7 months	5.19750	7 months	2.06250
8 months	1.28563	8 months	0.44313	8 months	5.28875	8 months	2.11000
9 months	1.33438	9 months	0.48750	9 months	5.37750	9 months	2.17500
10 months	1.38563	10 months	0.51313	10 months	5.47750	10 months	2.22250
11 months	1.42938	11 months	0.53750	11 months	5.57750	11 months	2.26000
12 months	1.47250	12 months	0.56625	12 months	5.67750	12 months	2.31000

Exhibit 9.2 **LIBOR rates for 31 December 2010**

Source: www.bbalibor.com

US dollar LIBOR	%
Overnight	0.25188
1 week	0.25438
2 weeks	0.25656
1 month	0.26063
2 months	0.28250
3 months	0.30281
4 months	0.34750
5 months	0.40250
6 months	0.45594
7 months	0.50813
8 months	0.55938
9 months	0.61250
10 months	0.66625
11 months	0.72063
12 months	0.78094

Swiss franc LIBOR	%
Spot/next	0.10333
1 week	0.11000
2 weeks	0.12667
1 month	0.14250
2 months	0.15833
3 months	0.17000
4 months	0.18750
5 months	0.21167
6 months	0.23833
7 months	0.27750
8 months	0.31917
9 months	0.36750
10 months	0.41833
11 months	0.46833
12 months	0.51667

Danish kroner LIBOR	%
Spot/next	0.82500
1 week	0.80750
2 weeks	0.83425
1 month	0.89350
2 months	1.02725
3 months	1.12125
4 months	1.22450
5 months	1.37450
6 months	1.46425
7 months	1.52100
8 months	1.55750
9 months	1.63000
10 months	1.67250
11 months	1.71250
12 months	1.75250

UK pound LIBOR	%
Overnight	0.56500
1 week	0.57250
2 weeks	0.57750
1 month	0.59250
2 months	0.64688
3 months	0.75750
4 months	0.84000
5 months	0.94438
6 months	1.05000
7 months	1.12750
8 months	1.21125
9 months	1.29188
10 months	1.37250
11 months	1.44125
12 months	1.50938

Canadian dollar LIBOR	%
Overnight	0.89500
1 week	0.98500
2 weeks	1.05000
1 month	1.10000
2 months	1.15000
3 months	1.23167
4 months	1.30000
5 months	1.36667
6 months	1.44333
7 months	1.51333
8 months	1.58333
9 months	1.65000
10 months	1.72500
11 months	1.80667
12 months	1.89833

New Zealand dollar LIBOR	%
Spot/next	3.14000
1 week	3.16750
2 weeks	3.18750
1 month	3.22250
2 months	3.27000
3 months	3.32500
4 months	3.35750
5 months	3.40750
6 months	3.45500
7 months	3.54500
8 months	3.61250
9 months	3.70250
10 months	3.81250
11 months	3.90250
12 months	4.00000

Note: The percentage rates shown in this table are all expressed as equivalent annual percentages, although the loans can vary from one night to one year.

Exhibit 9.2   Continued

Only the most creditworthy borrowers can borrow at LIBOR; less highly-rated borrowers will be able to borrow at LIBOR plus a number of basis points (e.g. LIBOR + 9); so if the three-month LIBOR in US dollars is currently 0.30281 per cent, the borrower will pay 9/100 of a percentage point more than this, i.e. 0.39281 per cent for three-month borrowing starting today and repayable in three months. These rates are expressed at an annual rate even though the loans may only be for a few days or weeks.

The three-month LIBOR rate has an effect on the other rates set on a variety of loans to individuals and companies. Because the LIBOR rate is calculated in different currencies, its influence is worldwide, and is particularly used in dollar lending outside of the US. LIBOR is used to price around $350,000 billion financial products worldwide – compare that figure with the output of all UK citizens in a year (GDP) of £1500 billion, or $15,000 billion for Americans. Exhibit 9.3 describes how the interest rates in the LIBOR markets declined dramatically during 2008 to leave rates at extraordinarily low levels during 2009 and 2010.

Little room for Libor to fall further

By David Oakley and Ralph Atkins

The year-long decline in money market rates appears to be over.

London Interbank Offered Rates, or Libor, are at record lows for dollars, euro and sterling, leading many pundits to say that they cannot fall much further. Three-month Libor rates have fallen almost to the levels of base rates in the US and the UK – and below base rates in the eurozone.

The question now is: at what point will they start rising again?

The reason rates have fallen so far so fast is that the extraordinary measures taken by the world's central banks since the collapse of Lehman Brothers have left the financial sector awash with liquidity.

It is also a clear sign that confidence has returned to the banking system, with institutions willing to lend to each other.

This is because fears over counter-party risk, which came close to breaking the financial system in the days following Lehman, have receded sharply.

The renewed confidence has even enabled some of the stronger banks to borrow well below Libor, which is fixed every day by the British Bankers Association through a survey of London-based banks.

However, bankers warn that Libor rates could start to rise again, undoing some of the efforts of the central banks, should the

global economy show any signs of faltering.

In particular, they say, the failure of banks to increase lending to businesses and consumers, which is critical for economic recovery, could put the money markets under strain.

In short, the money market – the first link in the borrowing chain – may appear to be repaired but, without circulation of funds to consumers and businesses, confidence could start to erode, sending Libor higher

Since the start of the month, the cost for banks to lend to each other over three months has stuck at about 0.28 per cent for dollars, compared with a

▶

Exhibit 9.3   Little room for Libor to fall further

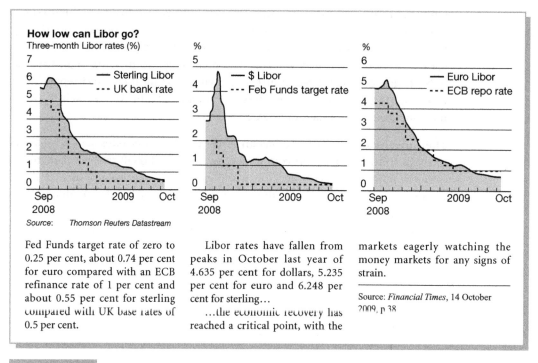

How low can Libor go?
Three-month Libor rates (%)

Source: *Thomson Reuters Datastream*

Fed Funds target rate of zero to 0.25 per cent, about 0.74 per cent for euro compared with an ECB refinance rate of 1 per cent and about 0.55 per cent for sterling compared with UK base rates of 0.5 per cent.

Libor rates have fallen from peaks in October last year of 4.635 per cent for dollars, 5.235 per cent for euro and 6.248 per cent for sterling…

…the economic recovery has reached a critical point, with the

markets eagerly watching the money markets for any signs of strain.

Source: *Financial Times*, 14 October 2009, p 38

Exhibit 9.3   Continued

EURIBOR and some other BORs

A rate similar to LIBOR is **EURIBOR (Euro Interbank Offered Rate)**, the rate at which euro interbank term deposits are offered between prime banks within the eurozone (not London) for periods of one week to one year. It does not cover overnight lending – see EONIA below for that. EURIBOR is calculated as a weighted average of unsecured lending transactions undertaken within the euro area by eurozone banks.

Many other countries have markets setting rates for lending between domestic banks. **TIBOR (Tokyo Interbank Offered Rate)** is the rate at which Japanese banks lend to each other in Japan. In Singapore we have **SIBOR** and in Hong Kong we have **HIBOR**.

Federal Funds Rate and prime rate

In the US, the equivalent to very short-term LIBOR is the **Federal Funds Rate (fed funds)**. This is the rate at which domestic financial institutions lend to each other overnight. It is strongly influenced by the US central bank, the Federal

Reserve. Banks often need to borrow from other banks to maintain a minimum level of reserves at the Federal Reserve.[4] This borrowing is usually unsecured (without collateral) and so is only available to the most creditworthy. The Federal Reserve can influence the fed funds rate by increasing or lowering the level of reserves in the system.

The fed funds interest rate (borrowing in the US) and the overnight US dollar LIBOR rate (borrowing in the UK) are usually very close to each other. If they were not close then a bank could make a nice profit borrowing in one overnight market and depositing the money in the other. If the US dollar LIBOR rate is higher, banks needing to borrow will tend to do so in the fed funds market; the increased demand will push up interest rates in the UK, while the absence of demand will encourage lower rates in the US dollar LIBOR market.

The US **prime rate** is the interest rate US banks charge the best corporate customers. It is also used as a benchmark for other loans, for example, consumer credit loan interest rates are often set as so many basis points above the prime rate.

EONIA

EONIA (Euro Overnight Index Average) is the effective overnight rate for the euro. It is calculated with the help of the **European Central Bank (ECB)** as a weighted average of overnight unsecured lending transactions undertaken within the euro area by eurozone banks.

EURONIA

EURONIA (Euro Overnight Index Average) is the UK equivalent of EONIA, a weighted average of euro interest rates on unsecured overnight euro deposits arranged by eight money brokers in London.

SONIA

SONIA (Sterling Overnight Interbank Average) tracks the actual sterling overnight rates experienced by market participants.

---

[4] If they get desperate then they could borrow from the Federal Reserve itself, but the **discount rate** charged is significantly higher than that payable to other banks overnight in the fed funds market.

Eurocurrency

The terms **Eurocurrency, Eurodollar, Euroyen, Euroswissfrancs**, etc. have nothing to do with the actual euro currency. Their name simply means that the currency is deposited and lent outside the jurisdiction of the country that issued the currency. For example, a Japanese firm might make a deposit in yen in a German bank; this would be a Euroyen deposit. An American corporation might pay an Australian corporation in dollars; these dollars are deposited in an Australian bank, and are Eurodollars.

Today it is not unusual to find an individual or corporation holding a dollar account at a UK bank – a **Eurodeposit account** – which pays interest in dollars linked to general dollar rates. This money can be lent to firms wishing to borrow in Eurodollars prepared to pay interest and capital repayments in dollars. The point is that both the Euroyen deposit and the Eurodollars are outside the control of their country of origin – the regulators have little influence on this market.[5]

Eurocurrency markets came about during the 1950s and 1960s, when substantial amounts of US dollars were deposited in Europe (mainly in London). Countries outside the US were wary about depositing their dollars in US banks, where they would be subject to stringent US regulations. 'Iron Curtain' countries were worried that their dollars could be seized or frozen for political reasons. They looked for banks outside the US where they could deposit their US dollars and earn market rates of interest. Also US corporations began to expand into Europe, and wanted their funds outside the control of the US authorities. So the Eurocurrency market was born, although strictly speaking, the term should be **international market**.

The title 'Euro' came about because the modern market was started when the former Soviet Union transferred dollars from New York to a Russian-owned bank in Paris at the height of the cold war in 1957. The cable address happened to be EUROBANK. This was long before the currency called the euro was conceived. Nowadays, daily **Eurosecurities** business is transacted in all of the major financial centres. To add a little precision: **Eurocurrency** is short-term (less than one year) deposits and loans outside the jurisdiction of the country in whose currency the deposit/loan is denominated. **Eurocredit** is used for the market in medium- and long-term loans in the Euromarkets, with lending rates usually linked to (a few basis points above) the LIBOR rates. Longer-term loans (usually

[5] Just to confuse everybody, traders in this market often refer to all types of Eurocurrency, from Eurosterling to Euroyen, as Eurodollars, and do not reserve the term for US dollars.

greater than six months) normally have interest rates that are reset every three or six months depending on the current LIBOR rate for, say, three-month lending; thus this interest rate is **floating** rather than **fixed**.

There are significant advantages for companies large enough to use the Eurosecurities markets:

▪ This finance can have lower transaction costs and better rates of return.

▪ There are fewer rules and regulations leading to speed, innovation and lower costs.

▪ It is possible to hedge foreign currency movements; a firm with assets denominated in a foreign currency may be able to reduce the adverse impact of exchange rate movements if it has liabilities in that same currency (see Chapter 16).

▪ The borrowing needs of some firms are simply too large for their domestic markets to fulfil.

The Eurodollar market has become so deep and broad that it now sets interest rates back in the US. For a very large proportion of US domestic financial instruments the interest rates are set at a certain number of basis points above US dollar LIBOR rates determined by banks operating out of London.

The Eurocurrency market allows countries and corporations to lend and borrow funds worldwide, picking the financial institution which is the most suitable regardless of geographic position. While the world economy is thriving, this works well. However, there have been some spectacular problems, with worldwide repercussions. In 2008, among others, Iceland's financial institutions were in trouble after they found themselves unable to renew loans in the international debt markets.

Treasury bills

Government agencies issue **Treasury bills (T-bills or Treasury notes)**.[6] They are negotiable securities, easily traded in the secondary market (liquidated) to release cash. Securities issued by reputable governments are regarded as risk-free investing because these institutions are able to raise income from taxes or by creating

---

[6] In Germany and Austria, a Treasury bill is called a Schatzwechsel; in Russia a Gosudarstvennoe Kratkosrochnoe Obyazatelstvo (GKO); and in France and Canada, a Bon de Trésor.

money, and there is minimal likelihood of default. This only applies if the country has a reputation for good financial management – Greece had a troublesome 2010 and 2011 when investors doubted the soundness of its government finances and pushed up the interest rates the government had to pay. If a government is short of money because tax revenues are slow to come in, it can issue T-bills to increase its funds. T-bills form by far the largest part of the money markets, and are generally sold by auction through a national government agency.

UK Treasury bills

UK Treasury bills are issued at weekly tenders by the **Debt Management Office (DMO)** with a **face value** or **par value** of £100 and are sold at a **discount to par** with a maturity date of 1 month (28 days), 3 months (91 days), 6 months (182 days) or 12 months.[7] They are sold by competitive tender to a small group of banks, which can sell them on in turn to other investors. Most holders of Treasury bills are financial institutions. Individuals may hold them, but the minimum purchase amount is £500,000.

Banks wishing to purchase in the weekly tender place bids defined by the yield they will accept. The bids are gathered and different yield prices accepted: the DMO determines what is the highest accepted yield and allocates bills to purchasers bidding below this yield. Purchasers bidding at or above the accepted yield may not receive the amount they bid for.

The buyer purchases a bill at a discount, and may redeem it at maturity or trade the bill in an active secondary market. The T-bill markets are both deep (many buyers and sellers) and liquid, so there is little risk that a holder cannot sell when necessary, with low transaction costs. During the time he has held the bill, he has made a **yield** or **investment return**, the difference between the price paid and the maturity value (or sale price in the secondary market), and this yield is calculated as an annual percentage (even when only held for a few days) which can then be compared with other types of investment. The **bond equivalent yield (bey)** (also known as **coupon equivalent rate** or **equivalent bond yield**) is the yield that is quoted in newspapers and it allows comparison between different types of securities by working out the **annualised** return on the price paid for an investment – see the Example opposite.

Exhibit 9.4 shows the results from the four sales of Treasury bills that took place weekly during February 2011, on the 4th, 11th, 18th and 25th. Note that the issues occurred at weekly intervals as the UK government borrowed more money

---

[7] In theory 12-month bills can be issued, but to date none has yet been offered for sale.

> **Example**
>
> ### BOND EQUIVALENT YIELD (bey) on a six-month bill
>
> $$\frac{(\text{Face value} - \text{Purchase price})}{\text{Purchase value}} \times 100$$
>
> $$\frac{100 - 98.50}{98.50} \times 100 = 1.522843\%$$
>
> **But** this does not represent the true annual discount rate, because the maturity of the bill is only 6 months, so the annual discount rate is calculated by multiplying by 365/182 days, i.e. around 2, for each half year.
>
> To calculate the bey on the Treasury bill sold for £98.50, a discount of £1.50:
>
> $$\frac{\text{Face value} - \text{Purchase price}}{\text{Purchase price}} \times \frac{\text{Days in year}}{\text{Days to maturity}} \times 100$$
>
> $$\frac{100 - 98.50}{98.50} \times \frac{365}{182} \times 100 = 3.054053\%$$

or simply replaced maturing debt. The tender date is Friday. The bills must be settled (paid for) by and then issued on the following Monday (issue date). The redemption date is the day when the face value of the bill (£100) will be paid to the holder. The nominal amount is the total amount of the face value of the bills offered at the tender (not what was actually paid for them).

The **bid to cover ratio** is the ratio of the amount that was actually bid and the amount of T-bills offered; if the number is greater than one it shows that there were more bids than the amount on offer. Although extremely rare it is not unknown for an offer to be undersubscribed,[8] and it is a sign of lack of confidence in the government's financial situation and/or indigestion in a market faced with an exceptionally high volume of government borrowing. The average yield is expressed as an annual rate (bond equivalent yield). In this month, Treasury bills yielded a rate as low as 0.4419 per cent per annum, or around 0.0368 per cent per month. The average price is the price paid by purchasers for bills which will pay the holders of the bills £100 in one month, three months or six months.

---

[8] This has only happened twice for UK Treasury bills, both times in 2008, with a six-month bill offered for sale in October and a three-month bill offered for sale in May.

TREASURY BILL TENDER RESULTS, 1–28 February 2011

Tender date	Issue date	Redemption date	Nominal amount (£ million)	Bid to cover ratio	Average yield (%)	Average price (£)
1 month						
4-Feb-15	7-Feb-15	7-Mar-11	500	3.35	0.447936	99.965650
11-Feb-15	14-Feb-15	14-Mar-11	500	4.29	0.448549	99.965603
18-Feb-15	21-Feb-15	21-Mar-11	500	3.54	0.441919	99.966111
25-Feb-15	28-Feb-15	28-Mar-11	1,000	2.32	0.462185	99.964557
3 months						
4-Feb-15	7-Feb-15	9-May-11	1,000	3.30	0.545785	99.864112
11-Feb-15	14-Feb-15	16-May-11	1,000	3.24	0.531117	99.867760
18-Feb-15	21-Feb-15	23 May 11	1,000	3.19	0.501527	99.807058
25-Feb-15	28-Feb-15	31-May-11	1,000	4.51	0.539746	99.864139
6 months						
4-Feb-15	7-Feb-15	8-Aug-11	1,500	4.54	0.685725	99.659242
11-Feb-15	14-Feb-15	15-Aug-11	1,500	4.04	0.687697	99.658265
18-Feb-15	21-Feb-15	22-Aug-11	1,500	4.06	0.694841	99.654728
25-Feb-15	28-Feb-15	30-Aug-11	1,500	6.25	0.695687	99.652416

Exhibit 9.4   DMO Treasury bill tender results, February 2011

Source: www.dmo.gov.uk

Take the three-month Treasury bill sold at tender on 18 February at a discount price of £99.867658. The results for the tender of this bill are in Exhibit 9.5. From this it can be noted that the actual bids from buyers varied from a yield of 0.51 per cent to a high of 0.548 per cent, with an average of 0.531527 per cent. The bill was over-tendered by a factor of 3.19, i.e. the amount on offer was £1 billion (at face value), and there were actual bids offered totalling £3.1905 billion.

During the life of the bill, its value fluctuates daily as it is traded between investors – see Exhibit 9.6, which gives the daily figures from 22 February to 14 March 2011 for this particular bill.

Three-month Treasury bill ISIN code GB00B3K20F10 maturing on 23-May-2011	
Lowest accepted yield	0.510000
Average yield	0.531527
Highest accepted yield	0.548000 (about 6.05% allotted)
Average rate of discount (%)	0.530824
Average price per £100 nominal (£)	99.867658
Amount tendered for (£)	3,190,500,000.00
Amount on offer (£)	1,000,000,000.00
Bid to cover ratio	3.19
Amount allocated (£)	999,991,500.00

Exhibit 9.5   Results of tender on three-month T-bill

Source: www.dmo.gov.uk

Redemption date	Close of business date	Price (£)	Yield (%)
23-May-2011	22-Feb-2011	99.857277	0.586
23-May-2011	23-Feb-2011	99.860408	0.580
23-May-2011	24-Feb-2011	99.861963	0.580
23-May-2011	25-Feb-2011	99.868675	0.571
23-May-2011	28-Feb-2011	99.872271	0.562
23-May-2011	01-Mar-2011	99.874686	0.559
23-May-2011	02-Mar-2011	99.876369	0.558
23-May-2011	03-Mar-2011	99.876466	0.564
23-May-2011	04-Mar-2011	99.879374	0.572
23-May-2011	07-Mar-2011	99.881184	0.571
23-May-2011	08-Mar-2011	99.882155	0.574
23-May-2011	09-Mar-2011	99.884076	0.572
23-May-2011	10-Mar-2011	99.886078	0.570
23-May-2011	11-Mar-2011	99.892274	0.562
23-May-2011	14-Mar-2011	99.895392	0.554

Exhibit 9.6   Data for Treasury bill (named GB00B3K20F10) 22 February to
14 March 2011

Source: www.dmo.gov.uk

The price is what a purchaser would pay for the bill on a particular day. The price increases as the days to maturity decrease, and on redemption day, in this case 23 May 2011, the holder will receive the face value of £100. The yield is the (annual) return (bey) a purchaser in the secondary market will achieve between purchase date and maturity date.

Emerging-market Treasury bills

Many emerging-market[9] economies are now able to issue Treasury bills in their own currencies, while some concentrate issuance in one of the major currencies of the world, especially the US dollar. By borrowing in the US dollar the lenders can borrow at lower interest rates because international lenders are less fearful of a decline in the local currency, but this means that when the country has to redeem the T-bills it faces the risk that the dollar has risen against the local currency and so more local currency than initially thought needs to be paid out to lenders. This problem has caused financial crises in a number of countries over the years, for example, Mexico in 1995, Russia in 1998 and Brazil in 1999.

US Treasury bills

US Treasury bills are sold by Treasury Direct, part of the US Department of the Treasury. They range in maturity from a few days to 52 weeks. They are sold at a discount to par value by auction every week, except for the 52-week bills which are auctioned every four weeks. Bidders bid for the bills in two ways (they have to choose one route or the other at the outset):

1 **Competitive.** Potential buyers specify the discount rate they are willing to accept. These bids may be:

   ■ accepted in full if the discount rate they specified is less than the discount rate set by the auction;
   ■ accepted only partially if their bid is the same as the cut-off level that sells the amount of bills the government is trying to sell in that auction;
   ■ rejected if the bidder stated a level of discount that is higher than that set at the auction.

   Competitive bids are accepted in ascending order until the quantity reaches the amount offered.

2 **Non-competitive.** The buyer agrees to accept the yield which was set at the auction (in other words, the price set by other investors). With a non-competitive bid the buyer is guaranteed to receive their full amount.

---

[9] Not yet fully-developed economies or financial systems.

All bidders, competitive and non-competitive, receive the same discount rate and so pay the same amount for their bills. Individuals may bid and the minimum purchase is $100.

Exhibit 9.7 gives the results of US T-bill auctions held during February 2011.

The 26-week T-bill issued on 24 February, initially sold at $99.921639, carries an annualised rate of interest of 0.157 per cent if held until the maturity date of 25 August. The return for the 26 weeks is about half this quoted rate because the US government is only borrowing for half of the year. The discount rate of interest, being a percentage of the par value of $100 rather than $99.921639, is less than this at 0.155 per cent.

Security term	Auction date	Issue date	Maturity date	Discount rate per cent	Investment rate per cent	Price per $100
4-WEEK	02-01-2011	02-03-2011	03-03-2011	0.160	0.162	99.987556
13-WEEK	02-07-2011	02-10-2011	05-12-2011	0.150	0.152	99.962083
26-WEEK	02-07-2011	02-10-2011	08-11-2011	0.175	0.178	99.911528
4-WEEK	02-08-2011	02-10-2011	03-10-2011	0.135	0.137	99.989500
52-WEEK	02-08-2011	02-10-2011	02-09-2012	0.305	0.310	99.691611
13-WEEK	02-14-2011	02-17-2011	05-19-2011	0.130	0.132	99.967139
26-WEEK	02-14-2011	02-17-2011	08-18-2011	0.165	0.167	99.916583
4-WEEK	02-15-2011	02-17-2011	03-17-2011	0.100	0.101	99.992222
13-WEEK	02-22-2011	02-24-2011	05-26-2011	0.110	0.112	99.972194
26-WEEK	02-22-2011	02-24-2011	08-25-2011	0.155	0.157	99.921639
49-DAY	02-23-2011	02-25-2011	04-15-2011	0.125	0.127	99.982986
4-WEEK	02-23-2011	02-24-2011	03-24-2011	0.120	0.122	99.990667
13-WEEK	02-28-2011	03-03-2011	06-02-2011	0.145	0.147	99.963347
26-WEEK	02-28-2011	03-03-2011	09-01-2011	0.170	0.173	99.914056

Exhibit 9.7   US Treasury bills auctioned February 2011

Source: www.treasurydirect.gov

The inverse relation between bill prices and interest rates

An investor buying a money market instrument with a maturity of six months expects the security to offer the same rate of return as other instruments with similar risk and time to maturity. If two weeks later interest rates on five and one-half month instruments being issued at that time suddenly shoot up, now there are securities being issued that offer any buyer a much higher rate of return to maturity. In the secondary market potential buyers are unwilling to pay the price they did only a few days ago because the high price equals a low effective interest rate. Because there are alternative investments offering much higher interest rates, the discount on the bill will grow larger as the price people are willing to pay falls, until the rate of return is the same as other instruments in the market. Thus we see the inverse relation between prices of money market securities in the secondary market and the effective interest rate to maturity: a rise in bill prices means interest rates fall, a fall in bill prices equals interest rate rises.

Commercial paper

Commercial paper (CP) is an unsecured short-term instrument of debt, issued primarily by corporations to help with financing their accounts receivable (debtors), inventories (stock) and meeting short-term cash needs, but can also be issued by banks and municipalities. The issue and purchase of commercial paper is one means by which the largest commercial organisations can avoid paying a bank intermediary a middleman fee for linking borrower and lender; corporations can avoid borrowing through loans from a bank and go direct to the financial market lenders.

Commercial paper promises to the holder a sum of money to be paid in a set number of days (it is a **promissory note**). The lender buys these short-term IOUs (I owe you's) and effectively lends money to the issuer.[10] The buyers include other corporations, insurance companies, pension funds, governments and banks. The investors in commercial paper buy it mostly from dealers, which are usually banks.

CP has a normal maturity of 30 to 90 days but can be up to 270 days, and it is usually issued at a discount.[11] The discount is higher than for Treasury bills, giving a higher rate of return for the lender, because there is more risk of default

---

[10] Originally the promise was written on paper, but today they are more often written electronically (they have been **dematerialised**).

[11] A small amount of commercial paper is issued with interest payments, but this is rare.

> **Example** **COMMERCIAL PAPER**
>
> If a corporation wishes to borrow £100 million for 2 months, it may issue commercial paper with a face value of £101 million, payable in 60 days' time. A purchaser is prepared to accept the promise of the company to pay out in 60 days and so buys some of the commercial paper, paying a total of £25 million for one-quarter of the total issue at a discount to the face value. In 60 days' time, the purchaser collects £25.25 million from the corporation, earning £250,000 in return for lending the corporation £25 million.

---

involved (the borrower may not repay), and because there is less liquidity in the secondary market.

Large corporations with a temporary surplus of money can lend it to other corporations at a higher rate of effective interest than a bank would pay. CP is issued with no **collateral**.

The main buyers, such as money market funds, are often restricted to having the bulk of their portfolios invested in issues with the highest credit rating. Demand is limited for lower-rated issues. In some countries using credit rating agencies to rate CP is rare, with the investors buying paper on the basis of the strength of the name of the organisation issuing it – only the largest, most well-known and trusted can issue in these places.

Some companies, such as General Electric, are such frequent issuers of CP that they employ in-house teams to do the selling. Other issuers use dealers. The secondary market in commercial paper is weak or non-existent. It is not easy to complete such deals and can be costly.[12]

Although any one issue of commercial paper is short-term it is possible to use this market as a medium-term source of finance by '**rolling over**' issues, launching another issue as one matures. In a **commercial paper programme (a revolving underwriting facility)**, a bank (or a syndicate of banks) underwrites a maximum sum for a period of five to seven years. The borrower then draws on

---

[12] One way of investing in commercial paper while obtaining liquidity is to invest via a money market fund: the fund buys a range of CP issues (and other instruments) and so, while it is committed to hold each CP to maturity, because it is well-diversified, with many securities maturing every day, it is able to pay out to money market fund investors when they demand it.

this by the issue of commercial paper to other lenders. If there are no bids for the paper the underwriting banks buy it at a specified price. A **multi-currency programme** can be arranged making use of different currencies.

Extendable commercial paper has a target date for redemption. This can be extended but only up to a total of 270 days. **Eurocommercial paper (Euro-CP)** is issued and placed outside the jurisdiction of the country in whose currency it is denominated.

CP is best used to finance operating expenses or current assets. It would be dangerous to use it to finance long-term company assets because it has to be paid back in a matter of days. While roll-over is often possible, it is by no means guaranteed and many companies have been caught out by relying too much on expecting to roll over.

US commercial paper (USCP)

The largest commercial paper market in the world is the US, distantly followed by Japan, Canada, France, the UK and other developed economies. Reuters reports that the commercial paper market in the US peaked in August 2007 to a total of $2.2 trillion billion when the credit crisis happened. By early 2011, the total had dropped to just over $1 trillion, of which over $300 billion was **asset-backed commercial paper (ABCP)**, commercial paper secured on the collateral of receivable assets such as monthly interest from mortgage payers, credit card holders, vehicle loans or some other regular income.[13]

Because its maturity is less than 270 days, US commercial paper is not subject to the time-consuming and costly registration process required by the Securities and Exchange Commission (SEC), the main US financial regulator.

The commercial paper market can be very influential in corporate life. For example, in 2005, Standard & Poor's downgraded the commercial paper of Ford and General Motors, making their commercial paper unattractive to investors, thus increasing the cost of financing to these companies, and reducing global

---

[13] The issuers of ABCP are usually special entities/companies set up by a bank. These SPVs (special purpose vehicles) buy the assets (rights to mortgage interest, etc.) after raising money from issuing commercial paper. Thus they are 'bankruptcy remote' from the parent company that supplied the assets – if they go bust the parent bank can still survive. Also they are perceived as less risky for the investors because of the security of the assigned assets, so if the parent goes bust the lenders still have the collateral in the SPV. (At least that was the theory, but in 2008 many SPVs and their parent banks disappeared or nearly blew up when they could not roll over the ABCP that they were accustomed to doing.) An SPV might be of a special type known as a structured investment vehicle, an SIV – see Chapter 19.

confidence in both the companies and their products. This contributed to their financial crisis in 2009, and General Motors was forced into bankruptcy.

Exhibit 9.8 describes how badly the CP market was hit by the loss of confidence in financial institutions in 2008.

Life returns to short-term lending market

By Paul J Davies

Commercial paper is a crucial source of short-term funding for companies, banks and other borrowers as they manage their weekly or monthly operations and cash flows.

The market was hit hard first in 2007 by fears over the subprime mortgage exposures of mainly bank-run off-balance sheet vehicles...

But following the collapse of Lehman Brothers in September, the rush by investors to pull cash out of any money market funds that did not invest solely in US Treasuries led to a more widespread collapse in commercial paper.

One of the most encouraging aspects of the short-term debt markets came from the details about how much commercial paper the Fed was buying through its support programmes to help ensure borrowers get the funding they need.

The asset-backed CP market.... expanded by $46.3bn but at the same time the Fed's holdings in its ABCP liquidity facility dropped by almost $1bn to $22.9bn. Its holdings peaked at $145.8bn in mid-October.

Source: *Financial Times*, 10 January 2009, p. 25

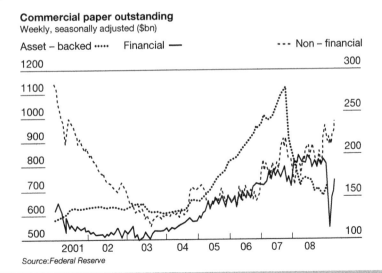

Commercial paper outstanding
Weekly, seasonally adjusted ($bn)

Asset – backed ····· Financial — --- Non – financial

Source: Federal Reserve

Exhibit 9.8   Life returns to short-term lending market

Credit ratings

Firms often pay to have their borrowing instruments rated by specialist **credit rating** organisations, such as Standard & Poor's, Moody's and Fitch Ratings, see Exhibit 9.9. The rating given is an evaluation made by the rating agency of the firm's ability to repay its debt and affects the interest rate on its debt instruments.

We would expect that firms in stable industries and with conservative accounting and financing policies and a risk-averse business strategy would have a lower risk of default and therefore a higher credit rating than a firm with greatly fluctuating income and high borrowing.

The highest ratings (AAA for long-term bonds and P-1, A-1+ and F1+ for short-term borrowing) indicate that the capacity to repay the interest and principal is extremely strong; the lower ratings (B, Cs and Ds) indicate that there is an increased likelihood of default. The top part of the table shows the ratings regarded as **investment grade**. The difference in yield between the different grades in the investment grade group can be as little as 30 basis points, but this can rise at times of financial trauma.

Ratings can be carried out on the firm, or on an individual CP or bond. If a loan does not have a rating, it could simply be that the borrower has not paid for one rather than that it is suspect.

The rating and re-rating of instruments is followed with great interest by investors and can give rise to some heated argument. Credit ratings are important to the borrowing corporation because those with lower ratings have higher costs. Occasionally the ratings agencies disagree over the rating of a loan, in which case it is said to have a split rating.

During the run up to the financial crisis of 2008, it was suggested that the credit ratings agencies gave unduly high ratings to loans that were shaky. Investors relied on their ratings of public companies and securities to gauge risk and make investment decisions, yet too many of their highly-rated investments proved to be risky and speculative.

Repos

A **repo** is a way of borrowing for a few days using a **sale and repurchase agreement** whereby securities are sold for cash at an agreed price with a promise to buy back the securities at a specified (higher) price at a future date. The interest on the agreement is the difference between the initial sale price and the agreed

Moody's		Standard & Poors		Fitch Ratings			
Long term	Short term	Long term	Short term	Long term	Short term		
Aaa	P-1	AAA	A-1+	AAA	F1+	Prime	Investment grade securities
Aa1		AA+		AA+		High grade	
Aa2		AA		AA			
Aa3		AA-		AA-			
A1		A+	A-1	A+	F1	Upper medium grade	
A2		A		A			
A3	P-2	A-	A-2	A-	F2		
Baa1		BBB+		BBB+		Lower medium grade	
Baa2	P-3	BBB	A-3	BBB	F3		
Baa3		BBB-		BBB-			
Ba1	Not Prime	BB+	B	BB+	B	Somewhat speculative	Non-investment grade, high-yield or 'junk' securities
Ba2		BB		BB		Speculative	
Ba3		BB-		BB-			
B1		B+		B+		Highly speculative	
B2		B		B			
B3		B-		B-			
Caa		CCC+	C	CCC	C	Substantial risks	
Ca		CCC				Extremely speculative	
C		CCC-				May be in default with little prospect of recovering	
/		D	D	DDD	D	In default	
/				DD			
/				D			

Exhibit 9.9   **Credit rating systems**

buy-back price. Because the agreement provides for collateral back-up for the lender, usually provided by the transfer of safe government-issued securities such as Treasury bills (but other very safe securities might be used), the interest rate is lower than a typical unsecured loan from a bank. If the borrower defaults on its obligations to buy back on maturity, the lender can sell the securities they bought in the first leg of the repo.

Repos are used by banks and financial institutions to borrow money from each other. Companies do use the repo markets, but much less frequently than the banks. This market is also manipulated by central banks to manage their monetary policy – see Chapter 6. The term for repos is usually between 1 and 14 days, but can be up to a year and occasionally there is no end date, an **open repo**. The best way to understand the repo market is through an example.

Example   REPURCHASE AGREEMENT

A high street bank has the need to borrow £6 million for 14 days. It agrees to sell a portfolio of its financial assets, in this case government bonds, to a lender for £6 million. An agreement is drawn up (a repo) by which the bank agrees to repurchase the portfolio 14 days later for £6,001,219.73. The extra amount of £1,219.73 represents the interest on £6 million over 14 days at an annual rate of 0.53 per cent.

The calculation is:

$$\text{Interest} = \text{Selling price} \times \text{Interest rate} \times \frac{\text{Days to maturity}}{\text{Days in year}}$$

$$\text{Interest} = 6,000,000 \times \frac{0.53}{100} \times \frac{14}{365} = £1,219.73$$

A **reverse repo (RRP)** is the lender's side of the transaction; securities are *purchased* with a promise to *sell them back* at an agreed price at a future date. Traders may do this to gain interest – by selling at a higher price than the purchase cost. Alternatively, it could be to cover another market transaction. For example, a trading house may need to obtain some Treasury bills or bonds temporarily because it has shorted them – sold them before buying – and needs to find a supply to meet its obligations, and so it places a reverse repo in order to get the securities now. In a transaction, the terms 'repo' and 'reverse repo' are used according to which party initiated the transaction, i.e. if a seller initiates the transaction, it is a repo; if the transaction is initiated by a buyer, it is a reverse repo.

Exhibit 9.10 shows the repo rates recorded by the **British Banking Association** in February 2011.

GBP	22-Feb	23-Feb	24-Feb	25-Feb	28-Feb
Overnight	0.50167	0.49833	0.49500	0.50000	0.50167
1 week	0.52333	0.52167	0.52000	0.52000	0.52167
2 week	0.53167	0.53000	0.53000	0.53000	0.53333
3 week	0.54167	0.54167	0.53833	0.53833	0.54000
1 month	0.55333	0.55167	0.54833	0.54833	0.55000
2 month	0.59000	0.58500	0.58167	0.57833	0.58333
3 month	0.63333	0.62833	0.63000	0.62000	0.62000
6 month	0.78167	0.78667	0.77833	0.76500	0.76000
9 month	0.89833	0.91167	0.89833	0.86667	0.86667
1 year	1.02167	1.04167	1.00667	0.97167	0.97833

Exhibit 9.10 **Repo rates in February 2011**

Source: www.bbalibor.com

These are all annual rates even though the terms are often very short. Thus, the one-week rate on 28 February is 0.52167 per cent when expressed annually – naturally the borrower will only pay around 1/52 of this.

Haircuts

Although the securities bought and sold are considered safe collateral for the lender of the cash, there is always the danger that the price of the bills, etc. might fluctuate during the period of the agreement to the detriment of the buyer. Therefore it is common practice to impose a **haircut** on the collateral, where the seller receives the amount of cash secured on the collateral less a margin (the haircut). So, if we take the repurchase agreement Example opposite, even if the securities handed over are valued at £6 million the borrower may only receive £5.9 million, allowing the lender an extra degree of safety should the value of the securities decrease and the borrower fail to buy them back at the agreed price.

Exhibit 9.11 shows how the repo market has declined since the collapse of Lehman. It also points out how dependent the US market is on two banks, and how the collateral used in the run-up to the crisis deteriorated.

Run on banks left repo sector highly exposed

By Michael Mackenzie in New York

The sharp reduction in financial leverage since the collapse of Lehman Brothers is illustrated by the steep decline in the use of repurchase or repo transactions by Wall Street dealers.

In a repo, an investor can borrow cash for a short period from another party, using securities as collateral for the loan.

Federal Reserve data shows that financing volumes of mortgages, US Treasuries and corporate debt by primary dealers has dropped nearly 50 per cent from levels seen before Lehman's demise.

"Everybody now pays more attention to due diligence and looks at their counter party risk a lot more closely," says Scott Skyrm, senior vice-president at Newedge, a repo broker dealer.

At the centre of the US repo market sits the tri-party model, where a custodian bank, Bank of New York Mellon and JPMorgan, helps to administer a repo agreement between two parties. An investor places its money with the custodian bank, which in turn lends it to another institution, and then assets are pledged as collateral for the loan.

Such a model functions well when liquid assets such as Treasuries are being used, as this type of collateral can easily be sold.

During the credit boom, which peaked in the first half of 2007, the type of collateral being pledged for cash in repo transactions had steadily migrated away from Treasuries and towards other assets such as private label mortgages and corporate securities. This reflected the drive by investment banks and investors to boost their leverage and garner higher returns.

"The tri-party repo framework that worked so well for Treasuries was not as robust for less liquid securities," says Lou Crandall, economist at Wrightson Icap. "The system works if the clearing banks are confident that they can liquidate collateral quickly."

The near-failure of Bear Stearns six months before Lehman's demise alerted the Fed to the dangers associated with having two clearing banks supporting the financial system.

Tri-party was very popular with investment banks as it allowed them to finance their balance sheets with short-term funding.

However, as soon as market sentiment turned negative on lower quality or more complex assets, investors who had funded these repo agreements began to pull their money out. That sparked a run on the investment banks, potentially exposing the clearing banks. This has left regulators and the market with one big fear: if one clearing bank ran into trouble, could the other step forward and support the system? There is also a separate issue, which is that when investors become worried about a particular institution, any move by a clearing bank to tighten standards could spark a bigger run on the borrower in question that ultimately results in bankruptcy or rescue.

Says Joseph Abate, money markets strategist at Barclays Capital. "There were a lot of assets that should not have been used as collateral in the repo market to start with. Repo is not a one-size-fits-all market."

Source: *Financial Times,* 11 September 2009, p. 35

Exhibit 9.11   Run on banks left repo sector highly exposed

Local authority/municipal bills

These are short-term instruments used to finance capital expenditure and cash flow needs. They are not common in the UK, but widely used in the US, where they are issued by many states, cities and local governments. A big attraction in the US is that the interest (but not the capital gain) is generally free of federal (and sometimes state and local) income taxes. There is a strong market in local authority bills and bonds in many European countries, notably France and Germany, where individual federal states issue them regularly. There are also many bill issues by companies close to governments (e.g. the French railway, SNCF, or the German postal service, Deutsche Bundespost).

Certificates of deposit (CDs)

Certificates of deposit are issued by banks when funds are deposited with them by other banks, corporations, individuals or investment companies. The certificates state that a deposit has been made (a **time deposit**) and that at maturity the bank will pay a sum higher than that originally deposited. The maturities can be any length of time between a week and a year (typically one to four months),[14] and there is a penalty on withdrawal before the maturity date (they are **term securities**). CDs are normally issued in lots ranging from £50,000 to £500,000 in the UK, or $100,000 to $1,000,000 in the US, with similar size lots in the eurozone and elsewhere.

Non-negotiable CDs must be held by the depositor until the CD reaches maturity. Negotiable CDs, although they cannot be redeemed at the issuing bank without a penalty, can be traded in a secondary market. The purchaser in the secondary market gains the right to collect the sum that the bank has promised to pay in, say, 40 days, including added interest. The rate of interest paid on negotiable CDs is lower than a fixed deposit because the attraction of high liquidity encourages depositors to accept a small gap between the amount deposited and the amount received on maturity.

A company with surplus cash can invest in a negotiable CD knowing that it can sell the CD for cash if necessary. The tradable value of the CD rises according to the remaining length of its maturity. At the centre of the secondary market is a network of brokers and dealers in CDs, striking deals over the telephone.

CDs are quoted in the trading market on a yield to maturity basis. So, if a deposit of £75,000 is made and a CD handed over which states that after one-quarter of a year the holder will receive £75,900, the yield to maturity is £900

---

[14] CDS can be issued with a maturity date of two years or longer. The instruments dated for more than one year may pay a variable rate of interest, with the rate altered, say, each year, based on the rates on a benchmark rate, e.g. LIBOR. It is possible to find short-term CDs with variable interest rates, for example, the interest on a six-month CD changes every 30 days depending on the one-month LIBID rate.

divided by £75,000 which is 1.2 per cent. This is the percentage return over one-quarter of the year so this needs to be multiplied by four to annualise it. Thus the annual rate of interest is 4.8 per cent. Of course the initial depositor may, if the CD is negotiable, sell this right to receive £75,900 on a set future date to another investor at any time during the three-month life of the CD.

As well as domestic currency CDs there are **Eurocurrency (Eurodollar) certificates of deposit**, outside the jurisdiction of the authorities of the currency of denomination.

Bills of exchange/banker's acceptances

Bills of exchange and **banker's acceptances** oil the wheels of international commerce. They enable corporations to obtain credit or raise money, and also to trade with foreign corporations at low risk of financial inconvenience or loss.

Bills of exchange

Exporters frequently grant their customers a number of months in which to pay. The seller draws up a bill of exchange (called a **trade bill**). This is a legal document showing the indebtedness of the buyer. The bill of exchange is forwarded to and accepted by the customer, which means that the customer signs a promise to pay the stated amount and currency on the due date. The due date is usually 90 days later but could be 30, 60, 180 days or any date ahead. (However, note that some bills of exchange are **sight drafts**, payable on demand immediately.)

The bill is returned to the seller who can either hold it until maturity, or sell it at a discount. Many bills of exchange are traded in an active secondary market. The purchaser in this market pays a lower amount than the sum to be received at maturity from the customer. The difference represents the discounter's interest payment. For example the customer might have signed the bill promising to pay £300,000 in 90 days. The bill is sold immediately by the exporter to a discount house or bank for £297,000. After 90 days the discounter will realise a profit of £3,000 on a £297,000 asset. Through this arrangement the customer has the goods on 90-days credit terms, the supplier has made a sale and immediately receives cash from the discount house amounting to 99 per cent of the total due. The discounter, if it can borrow at less than 1 per cent over 90 days, turns a healthy profit. The sequence of events is shown in Exhibit 9.12.

Bills of exchange are normally only used for large transactions. The effective interest rate charged by the discounter is usually a competitive 150 to 400

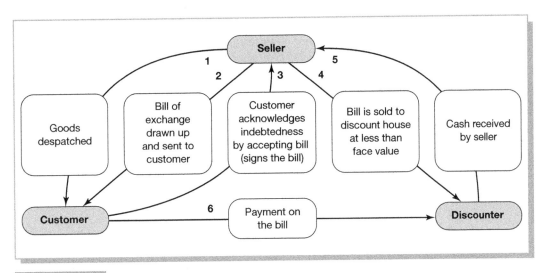

Exhibit 9.12   **Bill of exchange sequence**

Source: Global Financial Centres Report, sponsored by Qatar Financial Centre Authority and produced by Z/Yen Group

basis points over interbank lending rates (e.g. LIBOR). The holder of the bill has **recourse** to both of the commercial companies: if the customer does not pay then the seller will be called upon to make good the debt.

Banker's acceptances

A **banker's acceptance**, an **acceptance credit**, states that the signatory will pay a set amount at a future date: for example, an importer agrees to buy goods from an exporter and to pay in three months. The exporter sends a document saying that the money is due in three months to the importer's bank. This is 'accepted' by the importer's bank. Simultaneously the importer makes a commitment to pay to their bank the relevant sum at the bill's maturity. This commitment by a bank to pay the holder of the acceptance credit allows it to be traded in the money markets at relatively low effective interest rates because the bank is a more secure counterparty than the importer and therefore represents a lower credit risk to any subsequent holder of the instrument. When the maturity date is reached, the importer pays the issuing bank the value of the bill, and the bank pays the ultimate holder of the bill its face value.

Banker's acceptances are very useful for companies expanding into new markets where their name and creditworthiness are unknown, taking advantage of the superior creditworthiness of the bank signing the acceptance, which guarantees that payment will be made. When the banker's acceptance is issued, the company which requested it does not have to sell it immediately. The instrument can be used at any time up to its maturity to plug finance gaps.

Not all banker's acceptances relate to overseas trade. Many are simply a way of raising money for a firm. Here the bank signs the document proposing to pay in, say, 120 days. The client firm of the bank can then sell this acceptance in the discount market at any time it needs funds. Naturally, the bank will want reassurance that the client firm will pay it the sum under the agreement in 120 days.

There are two main costs involved:

1 The bank charges acceptance commission for adding its name to the acceptance.

2 The difference between the face value of the acceptance and the discount price, which is the effective interest rate. (Also, dealers take a small cut as they connect firms that want to sell with companies that wish to invest in banker's acceptances.)

These costs are relatively low compared with overdraft costs. However, this facility is only available in large amounts to the most creditworthy of companies. Exhibit 9.13 summarises the acceptance credit sequence:

1a Banker's acceptance drafted and sent by an exporter or its bank to importer's bank demanding payment for goods.

1b Importer makes arrangement with its bank to provide payment. Acceptance commission paid to the bank by importer.

2 Bank accepts the promise to pay a sum at a stated future date.

3 The banker's acceptance is sold at a discount.

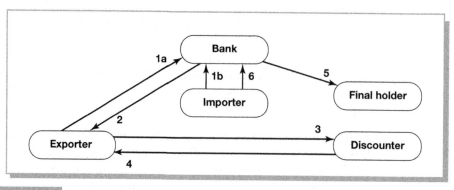

Exhibit 9.13   Banker's acceptance sequence – for an export deal

4 The discounter pays cash for the banker's acceptance.

5 The bank pays the final holder of the banker's acceptance the due sum.

6 The importer pays to the bank the banker's acceptance due sum.

The exporter is paid by banker's acceptance immediately the goods are despatched. It can also shield itself from the risk of exchange rates shifting over the next 60 days by discounting the acceptance immediately, and is not exposed to the credit risk of the importer because it has the guarantee from the importer's bank.

Money market interest rates in the *Financial Times*

The *Financial Times* publishes a table daily showing money market interest rates. See Exhibit 9.14 for a table showing rates for 28 June 2011. The *FT* shows a lot more information on **www.ft.com/bonds&rates**. The UK three-month Treasury bill rate of interest is not shown in this table, but on the front page of the *FT* every day, in a box at the bottom of the page, you will find the 'UK 3m' yield expressed as an annual rate.

Special Drawing Rights (SDRs) are a composite currency designed by the **International Monetary Fund (IMF)**. This currency basket is currently based on four key international currencies, consisting of the euro, Japanese yen, pound sterling and US dollar. The SDR rate of interest is the rate charged by the IMF on loans it makes to IMF members. It is an international reserve asset to supplement its member countries' official reserves should they not be deemed sufficient.

Ronia tracks actual repo overnight funding rates in sterling.

Comparative interest rates

Despite money market instruments having maturities of less than one year it can be seen from the *FT* table in Exhibit 9.14 that interest rates vary depending on the length of time to maturity. For example on 28 June 2011 a sterling interbank loan for one month cost 0.62875 per cent at an annualised rate, whereas a loan of similar default risk (i.e. very low), but lasting for one year, had an annualised interest rate more than double that, at 1.57625 per cent.

These yields to maturity also vary considerably over time – see Exhibits 9.15 and 9.16, which show comparative interest rates from the UK and the US over a 30-year period.

A number of observations can be made about the interest rates on different money market instruments:

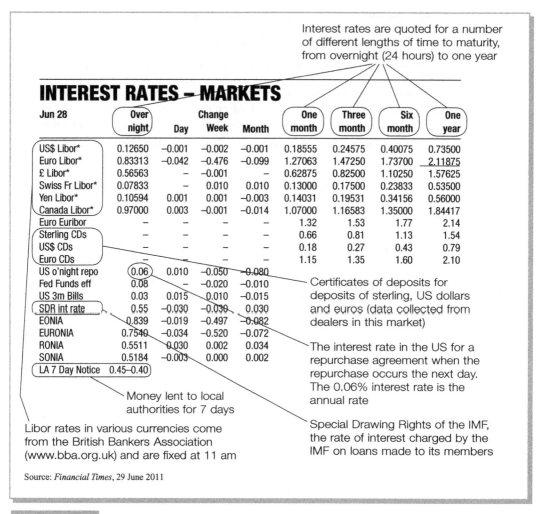

Interest rates are quoted for a number of different lengths of time to maturity, from overnight (24 hours) to one year

INTEREST RATES – MARKETS

Jun 28	Over night	Day	Change Week	Month	One month	Three month	Six month	One year
US$ Libor*	0.12650	–0.001	–0.002	–0.001	0.18555	0.24575	0.40075	0.73500
Euro Libor*	0.83313	–0.042	–0.476	–0.099	1.27063	1.47250	1.73700	2.11875
£ Libor*	0.56563	–	–0.001	–	0.62875	0.82500	1.10250	1.57625
Swiss Fr Libor*	0.07833	–	0.010	0.010	0.13000	0.17500	0.23833	0.53500
Yen Libor*	0.10594	0.001	0.001	–0.003	0.14031	0.19531	0.34156	0.56000
Canada Libor*	0.97000	0.003	–0.001	–0.014	1.07000	1.16583	1.35000	1.84417
Euro Euribor	–	–	–	–	1.32	1.53	1.77	2.14
Sterling CDs	–	–	–	–	0.66	0.81	1.13	1.54
US$ CDs	–	–	–	–	0.18	0.27	0.43	0.79
Euro CDs	–	–	–	–	1.15	1.35	1.60	2.10
US o'night repo	0.06	0.010	–0.050	–0.080				
Fed Funds eff	0.08	–	–0.020	–0.010				
US 3m Bills	0.03	0.015	0.010	–0.015				
SDR int rate	0.55	–0.030	–0.030	0.030				
EONIA	0.839	–0.019	–0.497	–0.082				
EURONIA	0.7540	–0.034	–0.520	–0.072				
RONIA	0.5511	0.030	0.002	0.034				
SONIA	0.5184	–0.003	0.000	0.002				
LA 7 Day Notice	0.45–0.40							

Certificates of deposits for deposits of sterling, US dollars and euros (data collected from dealers in this market)

The interest rate in the US for a repurchase agreement when the repurchase occurs the next day. The 0.06% interest rate is the annual rate

Money lent to local authorities for 7 days

Libor rates in various currencies come from the British Bankers Association (www.bba.org.uk) and are fixed at 11 am

Special Drawing Rights of the IMF, the rate of interest charged by the IMF on loans made to its members

Source: *Financial Times*, 29 June 2011

Exhibit 9.14   Interest rates – markets

- Generally, investors require extra return for longer lending periods, so overnight rates will normally be less than the rates on longer-term instruments (although this is not always the case). In Exhibit 9.16 US six-month T-bill rates are generally higher than those for three-month lending.

- The credit rating of the borrowing institution has a strong influence on the rate of interest charged. The rate offered by reputable national governments will usually be lower than the rate offered by a corporation wishing to raise cash by issuing commercial paper, or by a bank issuing certificates of deposit – see Exhibits 9.15 and 9.16. Instruments issued by some governments are deemed to be risk-free, whereas corporations, even with a high credit rating, are subject to financial fluctuations. However, some governments pay higher interest rates than many international corporates (e.g. Greece in 2011 paid more than HSBC).

▪ When expectations about future inflation rise, interest rates rise accordingly, leading to a decrease in the market price of money market instruments. Conversely when inflation expectations are lowered, interest rates fall, and the market price of the instruments rises. The high rates of interest offered in the 1980s largely reflect the high inflation of the time.

▪ Supply and demand: if banks need to borrow large sums of money quickly, they sell more short-term instruments. This increases the market supply of these instruments, and therefore pushes down their price, which in turn increases the rate of interest.

▪ Money market interest rates with similar terms to maturity move up or down with a high degree of correlation. They are all low-risk and short-term, thus there is a reasonable amount of substitutability between them for potential

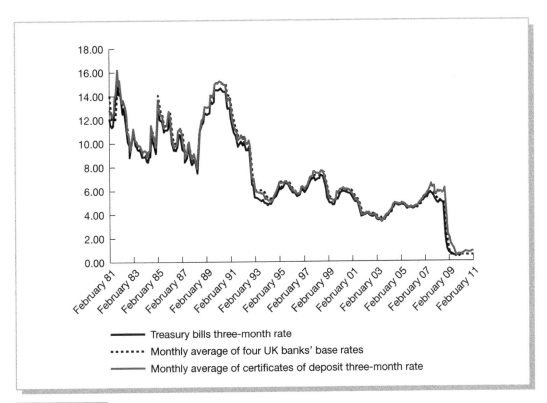

Exhibit 9.15   UK average interest rates 1981–2011 (per cent annualised rate)

Source: www.bankofengland.co.uk

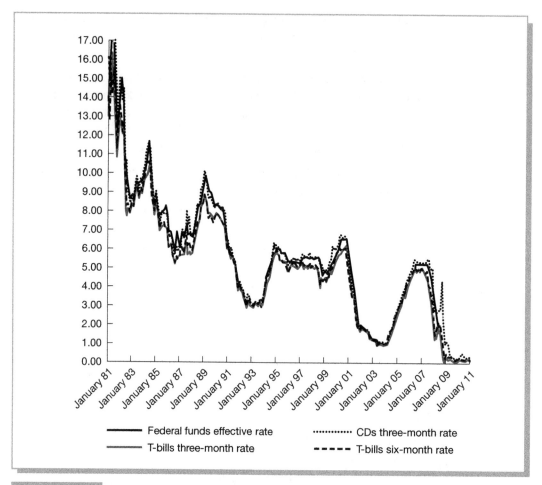

Exhibit 9.16   US average interest rates 1981–2011 (per cent annualised)

Source: www.federalreserve.gov

lenders. If interest rates in the CD market fell significantly below that in the commercial paper market, those banks needing to attract deposits might have difficulty doing so, as potential lenders put more money in the CP market. The banks will have to raise CD interest rates to attract deposits while the commercial paper borrowers will find they can offer lower rates – and so some convergence takes place.

■ Short-term interest rates can be lowered by central banks intervening in the markets when they judge that the economy is in need of a boost. You can see this in the years after the shock of the dot.com bust at the turn of the millennium and following the financial crisis of 2007–08.

A balance of objectives

Money markets have grown substantially over the past 30 years to trillions of dollars per year. Their growth has increased the opportunities for governments, corporations, banks and other organisations to lend and borrow, assisting the flow of funds in the economy and reducing the cost of obtaining money at short notice. They have also provided returns on surplus cash.

When making investments with surplus funds, corporations must recognise that they have to compromise between the three objectives of investment: security, liquidity and yield. Achieving more yield results in less security and/or liquidity. Low risk (high security) is usually the top priority for the temporary deployment of short-term surplus funds, because preservation of capital is necessary. If money is lost, raising alternative funds at short notice to run day-to-day operations can be expensive. If a firm has more than enough near-cash to cover any likely short-term requirements ('strategic cash'), then it could invest in longer-term, higher-yield instruments with reduced liquidity and/or higher risk.

Websites

www.bankofengland.co.uk	Bank of England
www.bba.org.uk	British Bankers' Association
www.bbalibor.com	British Bankers' Association LIBOR website
www.federalreserve.gov	US Federal Reserve in USA
www.ft.com/bonds&rates	Financial Times money market pages
www.fitchratings.com	Fitch
www.immfa.org	Institutional Money Market Funds Association
www.imf.org	International Monetary Fund
www.moodys.com	Moody's
www.standardandpoors.com	Standard & Poor's
www.treasurydirect.gov	US Treasury
www.wmba.org.uk	Wholesale Market Brokers' Association

10

Bond markets – governments and corporates

Governments and companies around the world have learned of the enormous power of the bond markets. James Carville, President Clinton's political adviser, once said:

> I used to think that if there was reincarnation, I wanted to come back as the president or the pope or as a .400 baseball hitter. But now I would like to come back as the bond market. You can intimidate everybody.

He had experienced the great difficulties politicians often have in going against the logic of bond investors. President Clinton tried to increase the gap between what the US government spends and what it raises in taxes. The administration expected to fill the gap by borrowing in the bond markets. But investors started to sell bonds raising the yields as they worried about all the additional borrowing and the risk of higher inflation in the economy. The President was forced to abandon the strategy and instead balance the government budget.

In 2011 many governments around the world were desperately dependent on the availability of money in the bond markets to allow them to spend one-third or more than they raised in taxes. If there was any hint of a government not being able to repay because it had over borrowed or that inflation was about to take off then investors refused to continue supplying new bond finance or pushed up the yields they required. This had a very sobering effect on the politicians from Ireland to the US, from Greece to the UK.

The bond markets also had a major role to play in the run up to the financial crisis in 2008, with securitised bonds and derivatives of securitised bonds at the heart of the matter. Then, in the recovery, companies queued up to sell new bonds to raise cash as they fought to survive the economic downturn. Without the bond markets being willing to supply those funds some of our leading companies would have met their demise; after all the banks were not willing/able to lend and equity investors were scared.

These are just a few examples that clearly demonstrate the value of developing an understanding of these markets and appreciation of the tremendous power of the collective will of the participants. This chapter and the next will provide a base for continued learning about the markets and their influences on all our lives.

The bond markets are concerned with loans for periods of more than one year in contrast to the money markets, where loans are for a few days, weeks or months. The concept of governments, companies and other institutions borrowing funds to invest in long-term capital projects and operations is a straightforward one, yet in the sophisticated capital markets of today with their wide variety of financial instruments and forms of debt, the borrowing and lending decision can be bewildering. Is the domestic bond market or the Eurobond market the better choice? If so, on what terms, fixed or floating rate interest, with collateral or unsecured? And what about high-yield bonds or convertibles? The variety of methods of providing long-term finance is infinite. Here we outline the major categories and illustrate some of the fundamental issues to be considered by a borrower and a lender.

Bonds

A bond is a long-term contract in which the bondholder lends money to a company, government or some other organisation. In return the company or government, etc. promises to make predetermined payments (usually regular) in the future which may consist of interest and a capital sum at the end of the bond's life. Basically, bonds may be regarded as merely IOUs with pages of legal clauses expressing the promises made. They are the most significant financial instruments in the world today with over $91,000,000,000,000 ($91 trillion) in issue. They come in all shapes and sizes, from UK government bonds to Chinese company bonds.

The time to maturity for bonds is generally between 5 and 30 years although a number of firms have issued bonds with a longer maturity date. IBM and Reliance of India have issued 100-year bonds as have Coca-Cola and Walt Disney (Disney's was known as the 'Sleeping Beauty bond'). There are even some 1,000-year bonds in existence; Canadian Pacific Corporation is paying a dividend of 4 per cent on a 1,000-year bond issued in 1883.

Bonds and equity compared

The advantage of placing your money with an organisation via a bond is that you are *promised* a return. Bond investors are exposed to less risk than share investors because the promise is backed up with a series of legal rights, for example, the right to receive the annual interest before the equityholders receive any dividend. So in a bad year (e.g. no profits) the bond investors are far more likely to receive a payout than the shareholders. This is usually bolstered with rights to seize company assets if the company reneges on its promise. There is a greater chance of saving the investor's investment if things go very badly for the firm if he or she is holding its bonds rather than its shares, because on liquidation the holders of debt-type financial securities are paid from the proceeds raised by selling off the assets first, before shareholders receive anything.

Offsetting these plus points are the facts that bondholders do not, (usually), share in the increase in value created by an extraordinarily successful business and there is an absence of any voting power over the management of the company.

Bonds are often referred to collectively as **fixed-interest securities**. While this is an accurate description for many bonds, others do not offer *regular* interest payments that are *fixed* amounts. Nevertheless they are all lumped together as fixed-interest to contrast these types of loan instrument with equities (shares) that do not carry a promise of a return.

The size of the bond markets

Bonds with up to five years left until they mature and pay their principal amount are generally known as **shorts**, but the boundary lines are often blurry; **medium-dated** bonds generally have maturities of between 5 and 15 years; **longs** are bonds with maturities of over 15 years. It should be noted that a bond is classified according to the time remaining to maturity, not the maturity when it was issued, so a 30-year bond which has only two years left until it matures is a short.

The volume of bonds issued throughout the world is vast, $91 trillion at the end of 2009 according to the Bank of International Settlements (BIS)[1] – see Exhibits 10.1 (a), (b) and (c). There were over $64 trillion in bonds outstanding (not yet

---

[1] The BIS figures include in the figures for domestic bonds a small fraction of money market instruments.

redeemed – the capital has not been paid off) in the domestic bond markets of countries.[2] In addition to these domestic bonds there were another $27 trillion of bonds issued outside the domestic markets on the international bond markets. To put these numbers in perspective the annual output (GDP) of the UK for one year is about £1.5 trillion.

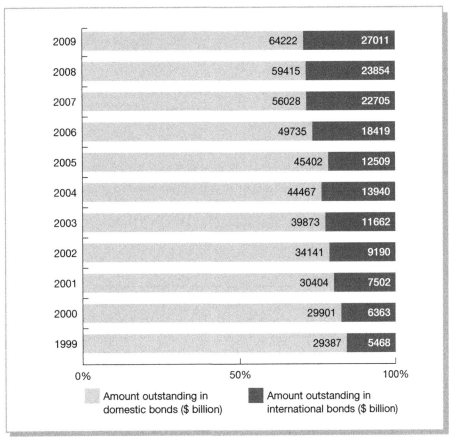

Exhibit 10.1a   World bond market, amounts outstanding (still owed) in billions of US dollars

Source: Bank for International Settlements

---

[2] This includes all currencies, even though they are summed in US dollars.

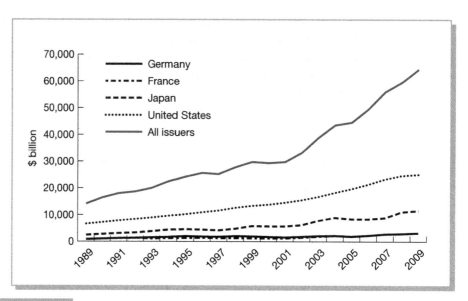

Exhibit 10.1b   The total of all issuers worldwide in the domestic markets, plus the four largest domestic markets, amounts outstanding

Source: Bank for International Settlements

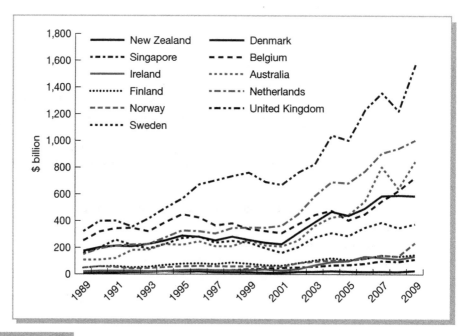

Exhibit 10.1c   Some of the other domestic bond markets

Source: Bank for International Settlements

Government bond markets

Most governments issue bonds to raise money when their tax receipts are less than their expenditure. We first look at the UK government bond market to get a feel for the workings of these markets, and then briefly consider the US, French, German, Japanese and Chinese government bond markets, known as **sovereign bond** markets. Sovereign bonds issued by reputable governments are the most secure in the world. National governments are aware of the need to maintain a high reputation for paying their debts on time. Furthermore, they are able to print more money or to raise taxes to ensure they have the means to pay (in most cases).

UK gilts

In most years the British government does not raise enough in taxes to cover its expenditure. It makes up a large part of the difference by selling bonds. These are called gilts because in the old days you would receive a very attractive certificate with gold-leaf edges (**gilt-edged securities**). Buying UK government bonds is one of the safest forms of lending in the world; the risk of the UK government failing to pay is very small – although a few doubts crept in following the high government spending during 2010.

While the risk of non-receipt of interest and capital is minute if you buy and hold gilts to the maturity date, you can lose money buying and selling gilts from year to year (or month to month) in the secondary market before they mature. There have been many occasions when, if you purchased at the start of the year and sold to another investor in the secondary market at the end of the year, even after receiving interest, you would have lost 5 per cent or more. On the other hand there were many years when you would have made large gains.

The UK government issues gilts via the UK **Debt Management Office (DMO)**. On 23 March 2011, the total amount of gilts in issue was £1,032.91 billion. This was rising at a rapid rate as the UK government spent around £160 billion more than it raised in taxes – approximately 12 per cent of gross national product, so one in every eight pounds spent was borrowed by the government!

Gilts are sold with a **nominal** (**face** or **par** or **maturity**) value of £100. This is not necessarily what you would pay. The nominal value signifies what the government will pay *you* (the bondholder) when the bond reaches its maturity or **redemption date** at the end of, say, 5, 10 or 25 years. You might pay £100, £99, £100.50, or some other sum for it, depending on the coupon offered and the general level of interest rates in the markets.

The **coupon** (sometimes called the **dividend**) is the stated annual rate of return on the nominal value of the bond. It is a percentage figure shown immediately after the name of each gilt. So, for example, the 'Treasury 4.5pc '42' pays out £4.50 each year for every £100 nominal. Then in the year 2042 the nominal value of £100 is paid to the holder when the gilt is redeemed. The coupons are paid twice yearly in two equal instalments (£2.25 each) on set dates.

The names assigned to gilts (also called **stocks**), such as Exchequer, Treasury or Funding, are useful for distinguishing one from another but have no particular significance beyond that. What is more important is whether they are dated, undated or conversion. **Dated** gilts have a fixed date(s) at which they will be redeemed. Some have a range of dates, for example, Exchequer 12pc, '13 – '17. This gilt will not be redeemed before the first date, 2013, and it must be redeemed before the second, 2017. Between these dates the government has the option of when to redeem at £100. Until it is redeemed £12 will be paid each year in coupons. A few **undated** gilts exist, such as War Loan 3½ pc, which may never be redeemed. They *can* be redeemed at the discretion of the government, but this is unlikely given the low coupon the government pays – it can go on paying £3.50 per year to the holder(s) of these bonds forever. **Conversion** gilts allow the investor to choose whether to convert a gilt to another more attractive one. Exhibit 10.2 discusses an unusually long-dated gilt. Note that even though the gilt pays 4 per cent per year on the nominal value, i.e. it pays £4 per year, it gives an interest rate of 4.569 per cent. Thus we conclude that it was sold for less than £100, providing a capital gain over the 50 years amounting to 0.569 per cent per year.

Prices and returns

The coupons showing on different gilts can have a wide range from 2.5 per cent to 12 per cent. These were (roughly) the rates of interest that the government had to offer at the time of issue. The wide variety reflects how interest rates have fluctuated during the past 80 or more years. These original percentages are not the rates of return offered on the gilt to a buyer in the secondary market today. So, if we take an undated gilt offering a coupon of 2.5 per cent on the nominal value we may find that investors are buying and selling this bond that offers £2.50 per year at a price of £50, not at its nominal value of £100. This gilt offers an investor today a yield of 5 per cent: £2.50/£50. Thus we see some bonds trading above and, as in this case, below the nominal value of £100 in the secondary market. By means of this variation in the price of the bond, investors are able to receive the current going rate of return for that type of investment.

Britain draws strong demand for 50-year gilt

By David Oakley

Britain drew strong demand for an ultra-long bond yesterday in a sign that new issuance of gilts has not been hit by the turbulence surrounding Greece and the peripheral eurozone economies.

The sale of £4.5bn of the UK's 4 per cent 2060 gilt was placed almost exclusively with domestic investors as pension funds and life insurance companies, needing these bonds to match their liabilities, bought the debt. Order books reached £7.5bn.

Bankers priced the bonds at the tight end of the range. However, the yield of 4.569 per cent was the highest ever for new 50-year debt, which was first launched in May 2005.

One syndicate banker said: "This shows that the UK has not been affected by worries about Greece and sovereign risk, although there is always strong structural demand from pension funds and insurance companies. This tends to give this part of the curve a strong bid."

The UK Debt Management Office said: "The domestic investor base provided the main support for the issue, taking around 97 per cent of the allocation. There was again strong direct interest from end investors, primarily fund managers, pension funds and insurance companies."

The sale brings the total Britain has raised via syndication this financial year to £30.5bn, slightly above its £30bn target. The UK has resorted to using syndications because the vast sums needed to fund its budget deficit have made selling bonds much harder. The UK is raising £225.1bn this financial year, a record. Syndications use banks to actively sell the debt to investors.

Barclays Capital, Deutsche Bank, Royal Bank of Canada and Royal Bank of Scotland managed the syndication.

Robert Stheeman, the head of the DMO, said: "The use of the syndication process, for the first time for a re-opening of an existing gilt, has enabled us to build up the UK's 50-year conventional benchmark issue to £11.5bn in size after only two transactions, something that would not have been possible by auctions alone."

Source: *Financial Times*, 24 February 2010, p. 32

Exhibit 10.2 Britain draws strong demand for 50-year gilt

Yield

There are two types of yields on dated gilts (and on other bonds with a fixed redemption date). The case of a Treasury 10 pc with 5 years to maturity currently selling in the secondary market at £120 will serve to illustrate the two different types. From the name of the gilt we glean that it pays a coupon of £10 per year (10 per cent of the nominal value of £100). For £120 investors can buy this gilt from other investors on the secondary market to receive a **current yield** (also known as the **flat yield, income yield, simple yield, interest yield, annual yield** and **running yield**) of 8.33 per cent.

$$\text{Current yield} = \frac{\text{Gross (before tax) interest coupon}}{\text{Market price}} \times 100$$

$$= \frac{£10}{£120} \times 100 = 8.33\%$$

This is not the true rate of return available to the investor because we have failed to take into account the capital loss over the next five years. The investor pays £120 but will receive only the nominal value of £100 at maturity. If this £20 loss is apportioned over the five years it works out at £4 per year. The capital loss as a percentage of what the investor pays (£120) is £4/£120 × 100 = 3.33 per cent per year. This loss to redemption has to be subtracted from the annual interest yield to give an approximation to the **yield to maturity, YTM,** or **redemption yield.** This is also called **gross redemption yield** ('gross' meaning that it ignores taxation on the bond: we do not know the bondholder's tax status and therefore cannot allow for tax deducted on the interest or capital received on the bond).

> Approximation to yield to maturity: 8.33% − 3.33% = 5%

While this example tries to convey the essence of YTM calculations, it over-simplifies and really we should carry out a compound interest-type calculation to get a precise figure (*Modern Financial Markets and Institutions* by Glen Arnold (2012, FT Prentice Hall) describes these).

The general rules are:

- If a dated gilt (or other dated bond) is trading at below £100 the purchaser will receive a capital gain between purchase and redemption and so the YTM is greater than the interest yield.
- If a dated gilt is selling at more than £100 a capital loss will be made if held to maturity and so the YTM is below the interest yield.

Of course, these capital gains and losses are based on the assumption that the investor buys the gilt and then holds it to maturity. In reality many investors sell a few days or months after purchase, in which case they may make capital gains or losses dependent not on what the government pays on maturity but on the present price another investor is prepared to offer. This, in turn, depends on general economic conditions; in particular projected general inflation over the life of the gilt. Investors will not buy a gilt offering a 5 per cent redemption yield over five years if future inflation is expected to be 7 per cent per year for that period. Interest rates (particularly for longer-term gilts) are thus strongly influenced by market perceptions of future inflation, which can shift significantly over a year or so.

Bond prices and redemption yields move in opposite directions. Take the case of our five-year gilt purchased for £120 offering a coupon of 10 per cent with a (approximate) redemption yield (YTM) of 5 per cent. If general interest rates rise to 6 per cent because of an increase in inflation expectations, investors will no longer be interested in buying this gilt for £120, because at this price it yields only 5 per cent. Demand will fall resulting in a price reduction until the bond yields 6 per cent. A rise in yield goes hand in hand with a fall in price.

Thus, if the investor has a time horizon of only a year or two, long-term bonds may be seen as risky investments – even if they have very low default risk, they have high **interest rate risk** – that is their prices in the secondary market can change significantly over periods of months or a year if general yields to maturity change. It is not uncommon for long-term bonds to lose 5 per cent of their value in a year, even if they are reputable government bonds – see Exhibit 10.3

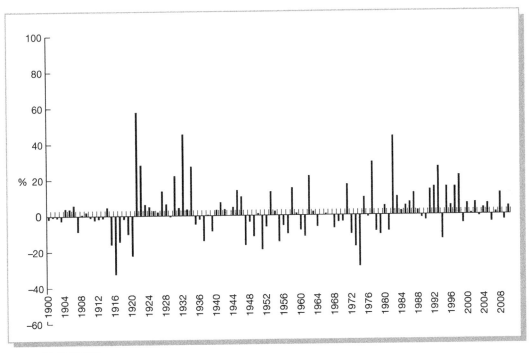

Exhibit 10.3   **Annual real gilt returns, 1900–2010 (%)**

Source: Barclays Capital, *Equity Gilt Study 2010*

Quotes

The gilts market is focused around **gilt-edged market makers (GEMMS)** who are prepared to buy from, or sell gilts to, investors. They quote two prices: the **bid** price is the price at which they will buy, the **offer** price is their selling price.

The difference between the bid price and offer price is known as the **dealer's spread**, i.e. their potential profit. The table shown in Exhibit 10.4 is from a Saturday edition of the *Financial Times*; the week-day editions are not so detailed. More information is available at www.ft.com/bonds&rates.

Note that the current redemption yield shown in the *FT* is relevant only if you are an investor on that particular day paying the price shown. However, if you bought your gilt years ago and expect to hold to maturity you will receive the yield that was obtainable at the time of purchase.

Redemption yields for gilts are quoted daily online by the Debt Management Office at www.dmo.gov.uk. Other sources of information on prices, and on the gilts market generally, include Bloomberg (www.bloomberg.com), Moody's (www.moodys.com), Standard & Poor's (www.standardandpoors.com), Fitch (www.fitch.com), JPMorgan (www.adr.com), and Bondscape (www.bondscape.net).

Cum-dividend and ex-dividend

Gilts usually pay coupons twice a year. Between payments the interest **accrues** on a daily basis. If you buy a gilt you are entitled to the accrued interest since the last coupon. You will receive this when the next coupon is paid. That is, you buy the gilt **cum-dividend**. Gilts (and other bonds) are quoted at **clean prices** – that is quoted without taking account of the accrued interest. However, the buyer will pay the clean price plus the accrued interest value (called the **dirty price** or **full price** or **invoice price**) and receives all of the next coupon. So, if you buy a gilt four months before the next coupon is due, you would pay the clean price, say £98, plus 60 days accrued interest.

If you bought just before the coupon is to be paid the situation is different. There would not be enough time to change the register to make sure that the coupon goes to the new owner. To allow for this problem a gilt switches from being quoted cum-dividend to being **ex-dividend (xd)** a few days before an interest payment. If you buy during the ex-dividend period the person you bought from would receive the accrued interest from the issuer – this would be reflected in the price you pay.

Index-linked gilts

There is a hidden danger with conventional gilts – inflation risk. Say, for example, that you, along with the rest of the gilt-buying community, think that inflation over the next 10 years will average 2.5 per cent p.a.. As a result you buy

Name of gilt and coupon (Treasury 3.25%)

Price – the mid-price between the market maker's bid and offer prices (the clean price without accrued interest) is shown for a nominal £100 of stock

Change in mid-price in previous day or week

The real rates of return on the basis of assumed inflation of 5% and 3%

Index-linked gilts – the interest and redemption value rise with the retail price index

GILTS – UK CASH MARKET

www.ft.com/gilts

Jul 1 Notes (Price £)	day's Chng	wk% Chng	Red Yield	52 Week High	Low
Shorts (Lives up to Five Years)					
Tr 3.25pc'11 .... 101.18	-0.02	-0.1	0.48	103.74	100.95
Cn 9pc Ln'11 .... 100.00	-0.26	-0.4	–	108.66	100.09
Tr 7.75pc'12-15 ⚘ 103.95	-0.02	-0.2	0.68	110.78	103.84
Tr 5pc'12 .... 102.97	-0.03	-0.2	0.59	107.27	102.85
Tr 5.25pc'12 .... 104.22	-0.03	-0.2	0.67	108.44	104.09
Tr 9pc'12 ⚘ 108.88	-0.06	-0.3	0.81	115.49	108.78
Tr 8pc'13 .... 115.51	-0.04		0.96	121.52	115.38
Tr 4.5pc'13 .... 106.12	-0.03	-0.3	0.82	109.36	105.68
Tr 2.25pc'14 .... 102.71	-0.06	-0.5	1.22	103.94	100.40
Tr 5pc'14 .... 110.96	-0.10	-0.7	1.46	114.35	109.05
Tr 2.75pc'15 .... 103.66	-0.10	-0.8	1.68	105.44	100.68
Tr 4.75pc'15 .... 111.54	-0.13	-0.9	1.87	115.02	108.49
Tr 8pc'15 .... 125.83	-0.16	-1.0	1.89	131.90	123.34
Tr 2pc'16 .... 99.62	-0.12	-1.0	2.09	100.74	95.68
Five to Ten Years					
Tr 4pc'16 .... 108.60	-0.16	-1.1	2.23	111.51	104.77
Tr 8.75pc'17 .... 135.62	-0.13	-1.3	2.47	142.66	132.55
Tr 5pc'18 .... 114.15	-0.08	-1.3	2.67	117.99	109.57
Tr 3.75pc'19 110.38	-0.08	-1.6	3.14	108.07	99.24
Tr 4.5pc'19 ⚘ 110.30	-0.05	-1.4	2.99	114.14	105.22
Tr 3.75pc'20 .... 102.84	-0.08	-1.9	3.39	107.49	98.01
Tr 4.75pc'20 .... 111.27	-0.12	-1.8	3.25	116.31	106.39
Tr 8pc'21 .... 139.32	-0.17	-2.0	3.32	147.53	133.53

Notes Price £	day's Chng	wk% Chng	Red Yield	52 Week High	Low
Ten to Fifteen Years					
Tr 3.75pc'21 .... 101.60	-0.03	-2.1	3.56	104.00	98.17
Tr 5pc'25 .... 111.48	-0.11	-2.1	(3.9)	118.90	107.23
Over Fifteen Years					
Tr 4.25pc'27 .... 101.74	-0.07	-2.1	4.10	109.11	97.65
Tr 6pc'28 .... 123.69	-0.08	-1.9	4.09	133.11	119.26
Tr 4.75pc'30 .... 107.30	-0.12	-1.8	4.20	116.53	102.70
Tr 4.5pc'32 .... 100.34	-0.10	-1.9	4.23	108.42	95.76
Tr 4.5pc'34 .... 103.30	-0.10	-1.8	4.27	111.90	98.36
Tr 4.25pc'36 .... 99.57	-0.07	-1.9	4.28	108.22	94.77
Tr 4.75pc'38 .... 107.93	-0.09	-1.9	4.26	117.38	103.64
Tr 4.25pc'40 .... 99.39	-0.10	-1.9	4.29	108.31	94.20
Tr 4.5pc'42 .... 104.08	-0.08	-1.9	4.26	113.59	58.63
Tr 4.25pc'46 .... 100.08	-0.07	-1.9	4.25	109.46	94.67
Tr 4.25pc'49 .... 100.10	-0.08	-2.0	4.25	110.05	94.85
Tr 4.35pc'55 .... 100.47	-0.08	-2.0	4.23	111.07	95.27
Tr 4pc'60 .... 95.50	-0.07	-2.0	4.22	105.53	90.13
Undated					
Cons 4pc ⚘ 80.12	-0.07	-2.3	4.99‡	89.71	75.82
War Ln 3.5pc 75.88	-0.07	-2.5	4.61‡	85.81	71.49
Cn 3.5pc'61 Aft ⚘ 74.11	-0.07	-2.4	4.72‡	83.56	69.92
Tr 3pc'66 Aft ⚘ 62.33	-0.06	-2.4	4.81‡	70.11	58.87
Cons 2.5pc ⚘ 53.28	-0.05	-2.4	4.69‡	60.12	50.25
Tr 2.5pc ⚘ 54.20	-0.05	-2.5	4.61‡	(61.29	51.06)

Index-linked Notes	Price £	day's Chng	wk% Chng	Yid (1)	Yid (2)	52 Week High	Low
2.5pc'11 .... (74.6)	307.22	-0.05	-0.1	–	–	-311.35	307.10
2.5pc'13 .... (89.2)	287.02	+0.05	0.0	–	–	-287.78	274.21
2.5pc'16 .... (81.6)	330.24	-0.27	-0.7	-0.93	-0.70	334.74	303.27
1.25pc'17 † (193.725)	110.54	-0.03	-1.0	-0.38	-0.38	112.36	106.43
2.5pc'20 .... (83.0)	334.67	-0.28	-1.2	† 0.08	0.21	341.84	302.61
1.875pc'22 † (205.65806)	115.12	+0.26	-1.8	0.51	0.51	118.14	107.98
2.5pc'24 .... (97.7)	293.03	+0.66	-1.6	0.52	0.61	299.76	260.36
1.25pc'27 † (194.06667)	108.73	+0.36	-1.4	0.69	0.69	115.52	99.39
4.125pc'30 .... (135.1)	280.36	+0.66	-0.9	–	–	-285.09	246.91
2pc'35 .... (173.6)	174.62	+0.42	-0.9	–	–	-177.46	150.03
1.25pc'32 † (217.13226)	111.48	+0.21	-1.3	–	–	-114.40	101.62
1.125pc'37 † (202.24286)	112.29	+0.17	-0.9	–	–	-114.54	102.03
0.625pc'40 † (216.52258)	100.22	+0.16	-0.9	–	–	-104.52	89.54
0.625pc'42 † (212.46452)	101.77	+0.26	-0.9	–	–	-103.50	90.35
0.75pc'47 † (207.7667)	107.73	+0.31	-0.8	–	–	-109.43	95.72
0.5pc'50 .... † (213.4000)	99.97	+0.30	-0.8	–	–	-101.57	88.02
1.25pc'55 † (192.2000)	130.92	+0.42	-0.6	–	–	-134.01	91.98

Prospective real redemption rate on projected inflation of (1) 5% and (2) 3%.
(b) Figures in parentheses show RPI base for indexing (ie 8 months prior to issue and, for gilts issued since September 2005, 3 months prior to issue) and have been adjusted to reflect rebasing of RPI to 100 in January 1987. Conversion factor 3.945. RPI for Sep 2009: 215.3 and for Apr 2009 211.5.
† For those bonds indicated, with a 3m lag, the 'clean' price shown has no inflation adjustment. The yield is calculated using no inflation assumption.
‡ Running yield.
Source: ThompsonReuters

All UK Gilts are Tax free to non-residents on application, xd Ex dividend. Closing mid-prices are shown in pounds per £100 nominal of stock. Weekly percentage changes are calculated on a Friday to Friday basis. Gilt benches and most liquid stocks, are shown in bold type. A full list of Gilts can be found daily on ft.com/bondprices.

Source: *Financial Times*, 2/3 July 2011

Redemption date (2019) – when repayment of the loan will take place

Highest and lowest price over the past year

Redemption yield (yield to maturity) in per cent per year (3.91%) based on the price in second column

Exhibit 10.4 Gilts – UK cash market

10-year gilts that have a redemption yield of 4.8 per cent giving a comfortable real income over and above cost-of-living rises. However two years later inflation starts to take off (oil prices quadruple, or the government goes on a spending spree, or whatever). Now investors reckon that inflation will average 6 per cent over the following eight years. As a result your gilt yield will fail to maintain your capital in real terms.

The UK government introduced a type of bond that ensures that you receive a return above the inflation rate throughout the entire life of the bond. These are called **index-linked stocks (gilts)**, where the coupon amount, and the nominal value as well, are adjusted or **uplifted** according to the **Retail Price Index (RPI)**.[3] The deal here is that the gilt initially offers to pay £100 at the end of its term, say 10 years away. It also offers to pay a low coupon, say 2 per cent. The key thing about index-linked bonds is that neither the capital sum on maturity nor the coupon stays at these levels unless inflation is zero over the next 10 years.

Say inflation is 4 per cent over the first year of the bond's life. The payout on maturity rises to £104. This inflation-linked up-lift happens every year. So, if over the 10 years the inflation measure has risen by 60 per cent the payout on the bond is £160. This means that you can buy just as many goods and services at the end with the capital sum as at the beginning of the bond's life (if you paid £100). (The situation is slightly more complicated than this in that the inflation figures used are those for the three months[4] preceding the relevant coupon dates, but this example illustrates the principle.) Furthermore, the coupon rate also rises through the years if inflation is positive. So after the first year the coupons go up by 4 per cent to 2 per cent × (1 + 0.04) = 2.08 per cent, so for every £100 bond, the coupon is £2.08.

Any future rises in inflation lead to further growth in the coupon, so that the last coupon will be 60 per cent larger than the one paid in the first year if inflation over the 10 years accumulates to 60 per cent, giving £3.20 per £100 nominal.

A final point on index-linked gilts: because most investors hold them to maturity secondary trading is thin and dealing spreads are wider than for conventional gilts.

---

[3] In 2011 there is a plan to issue index-linked gilts which are uplifted for the Consumer Price Index (CPI), a slightly different way of measuring general inflation than the Retail Price Index (RPI).
[4] For index-linked bonds issued before September 2005 the lag is eight months.

Government bonds around the world

Most countries in the world issue government bonds which are similar in format to UK gilts and are given a credit rating, see Exhibit 10.5. Some countries are regarded as very safe ('triple-A rated') and so can issue at a low real (after allowing for anticipated inflation) yield. Others, such as Ukraine are regarded as having more risk and so will have to pay a high risk premium to entice investors to buy their bonds. Credit ratings are discussed in Chapter 9 and later in this chapter.

As communications have become easy and electronic banking the norm, all bond markets worldwide are interconnected and interest rates have become linked, so, in general, bonds worldwide pay similar rates of interest if they carry the same risk (and inflation is anticipated to be the same). Exhibit 10.6 shows the interest rates for a few of the bonds of the leading government issuers.

US Treasury notes and bonds

Treasury notes are issued on behalf of the US government by Treasury Direct with a face value of $100 and a coupon payable every six months. They have a maturity of 2, 3, 5, 7 or 10 years, and are sold at monthly auctions, except for 10-year notes that are auctioned quarterly. The auctions are based on the yield amount and can be competitive or non-competitive. At the competitive auctions, only banks, brokers or dealers may bid, up to a maximum of 35 per cent of the total amount on offer, and they are allocated some or all of the requested amount. If they bid at a price higher than the rate that allows the government to sell all the notes they want to – the cut-off price (or yield) – they will receive all they bid for. For the non-competitive element individuals may also bid and they are guaranteed to receive the amount requested, but they will pay the price that is the outcome of the competitive bid auction. The notes may be traded at any time up to maturity, and their yield is quoted in financial publications.

Treasury bonds are auctioned quarterly, have a maturity date of 10 to 30 years and pay interest twice per year.

Treasury Inflation-Protected Securities (TIPS) are index-linked bonds whose principal value is adjusted according to changes in the **Consumer Price Index (CPI)**. They have maturities of 5, 10 or 30 years and interest is paid twice yearly at a fixed rate on the inflation-adjusted amount. The 5- and 30-year securities are auctioned once a year and the 10-year security is auctioned twice a year.

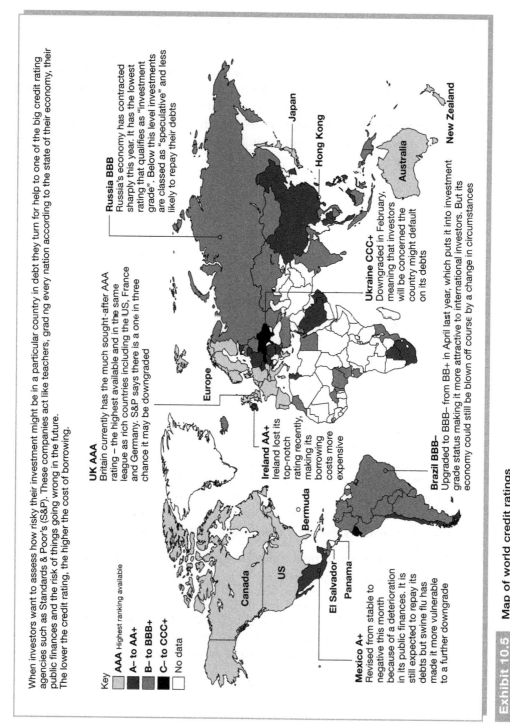

When investors want to assess how risky their investment might be in a particular country in debt they turn for help to one of the big credit rating agencies such as Standards & Poor's (S&P). These companies act like teachers, grading every nation according to the state of their economy, their public finances and the risk of things going wrong in the future. The lower the credit rating, the higher the cost of borrowing.

Key
- **AAA** Highest ranking available
- A– to AA+
- B– to BBB+
- C– to CCC+
- No data

UK AAA
Britain currently has the much sought-after AAA rating – the highest available and in the same league as rich countries including the US, France and Germany. S&P says there is a one in three chance it may be downgraded

Ireland AA+
Ireland lost its top-notch rating recently, making its borrowing costs more expensive

Europe

Canada

US

Bermuda

El Salvador

Panama

Mexico A+
Revised from stable to negative this month because of a deterioration in its public finances. It is still expected to repay its debts but swine flu has made it more vulnerable to a further downgrade

Russia BBB
Russia's economy has contracted sharply this year. It has the lowest rating that qualifies as "investment grade". Below this level investments are classed as "speculative" and less likely to repay their debts

Japan

Hong Kong

Australia

New Zealand

Ukraine CCC+
Downgraded in February, meaning that investors will be concerned the country might default on its debts

Brazil BBB–
Upgraded to BBB– from BB+ in April last year, which puts it into investment grade status making it more attractive to international investors. But its economy could still be blown off course by a change in circumstances

Exhibit 10.5 Map of world credit ratings

Source: http://image.guardian.co.uk/sys-files/Guardian/documents/2009/05/22/Credit-rating.pdf)

BONDS – BENCHMARK GOVERNMENT

Jun 28	Red Date	Coupon	Bid Price	Bid Yield	Day chg yield	Wk chg yield	Month yld	Year chg yld
Australia	12/13	5.50	101.85	4.69	0.05	−0.01	−0.17	0.13
	05/21	5.75	104.41	5.17	0.12	0.07	−0.07	−0.09
Austria	10/13	3.80	104.46	1.81	0.15	−0.02	−0.02	0.91
	09/21	3.50	100.21	3.47	0.11	–	0.05	0.33
Belgium	03/13	4.00	102.82	2.32	−0.08	0.06	0.07	1.23
	09/21	4.25	100.49	4.19	0.02	0.05	0.02	0.61
Canada	08/13	2.00	101.11	1.46	0.07	−0.07	−0.05	−0.09
	06/21	3.25	102.03	3.01	0.14	0.03	−0.06	−0.20
Denmark	11/13	5.00	107.61	1.70	0.10	−0.07	−0.13	0.77
	11/19	4.00	107.50	2.97	0.14	0.01	−0.03	0.24
Finland	09/12	4.25	103.28	1.49	0.10	−0.01	0.03	0.73
	04/21	3.50	101.65	3.30	0.12	–	0.01	0.41
France	01/13	3.75	103.31	1.56	0.11	−0.01	0.01	0.65
	02/16	2.25	98.66	2.56	0.14	0.01	0.01	0.69
	10/21	3.25	98.03	3.48	0.09	0.01	0.11	0.36
	04/41	4.50	105.83	4.15	0.13	0.07	0.20	0.35
Germany	06/13	1.75	100.50	1.49	0.15	−0.03	−0.08	0.91
	04/16	2.75	102.65	2.16	0.17	−0.01	−0.09	0.65
	07/21	3.25	102.50	2.96	0.13	0.00	−0.03	0.33
	07/40	4.75	118.52	3.70	0.14	0.07	0.17	0.33
Greece	05/14	4.50	55.83	29.13	0.18	−0.39	4.04	17.68
	06/20	6.25	53.50	16.55	−0.27	−0.88	−0.05	6.08
Ireland	04/16	4.60	69.64	13.61	−0.80	0.70	1.59	9.68
	10/20	5.00	61.84	12.03	−0.05	0.29	0.93	6.36
Italy	06/13	2.00	97.59	3.32	−0.01	0.24	0.30	1.27
	04/16	3.75	97.96	4.27	−0.01	0.20	0.29	0.93
	09/21	4.75	98.58	4.99	0.00	0.11	0.23	0.89
	09/40	5.00	90.30	5.76	−0.01	0.10	0.25	0.65
Japan	07/13	0.20	100.07	0.17	0.01	−0.01	−0.02	0.01
	06/16	0.40	100.05	0.39	−0.01	−0.02	−0.02	0.01
	06/21	1.20	100.98	1.09	−0.02	−0.03	−0.03	−0.06
	06/31	1.90	100.49	1.87	−0.02	−0.04	−0.03	−0.02
Netherlands	07/13	4.25	105.24	1.62	0.10	−0.03	−0.06	1.01
	07/21	3.25	99.72	3.28	0.09	−0.02	0.02	0.39
New Zealand	04/13	6.50	105.63	3.22	–	0.05	−0.03	−0.58
	05/21	6.00	107.83	4.99	−0.04	−0.05	−0.14	−0.52
Norway	05/15	5.00	108.60	2.63	−0.04	−0.09	0.01	0.01
	05/21	3.75	103.05	3.38	−0.01	−0.05	−0.01	0.15
Portugal	09/13	5.45	83.72	14.47	0.22	0.79	3.12	11.04
	04/21	3.85	55.77	11.65	0.11	0.32	1.80	5.87
Spain	04/13	2.30	97.61	3.67	−0.01	0.17	0.18	1.02
	04/21	5.50	98.81	5.66	−0.03	0.06	0.33	1.17
Sweden	05/14	6.75	112.33	2.23	−0.05	−0.09	−0.23	0.84
	06/22	3.50	106.21	2.83	−0.01	−0.03	−0.04	0.18
Switzerland	02/13	4.00	106.00	0.26	0.02	−0.05	−0.26	−0.11
	04/21	2.00	103.07	1.66	0.03	−0.02	−0.14	0.10
UK	03/12	5.00	103.02	0.61	0.06	0.02	−0.01	0.09
	09/15	4.75	112.08	1.75	0.11	−0.01	−0.22	−0.35
	09/20	3.75	103.88	3.26	0.12	0.04	−0.04	−0.13
	12/40	4.25	100.36	4.23	0.08	0.05	0.11	−0.01
US	06/13	0.38	99.77	0.49	0.15	0.11	0.01	−0.18
	05/16	1.75	100.73	1.59	0.21	0.06	−0.12	−0.32
	05/21	3.13	100.70	3.04	0.17	0.08	−0.03	−0.07
	05/41	4.38	100.69	4.33	0.19	0.13	0.09	0.26

London close.
Yields: Local market standard Annualised yield basis. Yields shown for Italy exclude withholding tax at 12.5 per cent payable by non residents.

Source: ThomsonReuters

Source: Financial Times, 29 June 2011

Redemption date May 2021

Coupon – the amount paid each year as a percentage of the nominal value of the bond, 5 per cent

Bid yield – the yield to redemption based on the market maker's bid price, 2.97 per cent

Bid price – the price at which a market maker will buy from an investor should they wish to sell. In the case of a UK government bond with the unit value of £100 the price is £103.02

Yield changes over one day, week, month or year. The yields to redemption change (almost) every day as the bond price moves with the shifts in demand and supply in the secondary market

Exhibit 10.6 Benchmark government bonds from the *FT*

US government notes and bonds are traded in an active secondary market (in an over-the-counter market rather than on a formal exchange), with dealers posting bid (buying) and ask (selling) prices, and trades conducted over the telephone or by electronic communication. Prices are quoted as a percentage of face value and on a clean basis.

French bonds

The French Treasury, Agence France Trésor (AFT), sells by auction **OATS** (Obligations assimilables du Trésor), which are 7–50-year bonds, mostly fixed rate, but some with floating or index-linked rates, and **BTANS** (Bons du Trésor à intérèts annuels), which are 2 to 5-year bonds with a fixed rate of interest.

German bonds

In Germany, the German Financial Agency, Bundesrepublik Deutschland Finanzagentur (BDF), issues at auction 2-, 5-, 10- and 30-year notes and bonds, some of which are index-linked and the minimum bid is €1 million. Two-year Federal Treasury Notes, Bundesschatzanweisungen (**Schätze**), 5-year Federal Notes, Bundesobligationen (**Bobls**), and 10- and 30-year Federal Bonds, Bundesanleihen (**Bunds**) are sold via pre-announced auctions by the Bundesbank, the German central bank, on behalf of the BDF.

The yield to maturity offered on German government bonds usually forms the reference or benchmark interest rate for other borrowings in the euro. In other words it is the lowest rate available with other interest rates described as so many basis points above, say, the 10-year bund rate.

Japanese bonds

The Japanese Ministry of Finance issues Treasury discount bills and bonds. Japanese government bonds (**JGBs**) with a maturity of 2, 5, 10 and 20 years are auctioned monthly, 30-year bonds are auctioned every other month, and 40-year bonds quarterly. Inflation-indexed linked JGBs are also issued for 10-year maturities. Retail purchasers must purchase a minimum ¥10,000; other purchasers must buy at least ¥50,000 worth of bonds. Many JGBs are traded in the over-the-counter secondary market. A few are traded on the Tokyo Stock Exchange and other exchanges.

Chinese bonds

In 2007 China began dealing in bonds and in 2009 they issued the first bonds denominated in the Chinese renminbi currency. These renminbi sovereign bonds were issued in Hong Kong, and available to foreign investors only. China is keen to expand the use of its currency worldwide, hoping to decrease its reliance on the US dollar (China is the largest holder of US Treasury bills, and so would be vulnerable if the dollar were to weaken).

Corporate bonds

Corporate bonds offer a higher rate of return than well-respected government bonds but, as you might expect, this comes with a greater degree of risk of failure to pay what was agreed (**default**). They can be a very useful way for companies to raise money without issuing equity or accepting the conditions of a bank loan.[5] Many corporate bonds are sufficiently negotiable (tradable) that they are **listed** on the London Stock Exchange and other exchanges in Europe, Asia or the Americas, but the majority of trading occurs in the **over-the-counter (OTC)** market directly between an investor and a bond dealer. Access to a secondary market means that the investor who originally provided the firm with money does not have to hold on to the bond until the maturity date. However, because so many investors buy and then hold to maturity rather than trade in and out, corporate bonds generally have very thin secondary markets compared with shares or money market instruments.

Corporate bonds have generally been the province of investing institutions, such as pension and insurance funds. Private investors tended not to hold them, mainly due to the large amounts of cash involved – occasionally £1,000 minimum, more often £50,000. The par value of one bond at, say, £50,000, €50,000 or $50,000 is said to have a 50,000 minimum 'lot' or 'piece'. However in 2010, the London Stock Exchange opened a secondary market trading facility for small investors, where lots are just £100 or £1,000 and the costs of trading are relatively low.

Infinite variation

Corporate bonds come in a variety of forms. The most common is the type with regular (usually semi-annual or annual) fixed coupons and a specified redemption date. These are known as **straight**, **plain vanilla** or **bullet** bonds. Other

---

[5] Some so-called 'corporate bonds' are in fact issued by business enterprises owned by the government and the biggest issuers are, in fact, banks rather than commercial corporations.

corporate bonds are a variation on this. Some pay coupons every three months, some do not pay a fixed coupon but one which varies depending on the level of short-term interest rates (**floating rate** or **variable-rate bonds**) and some have interest rates linked to the rate of inflation. In fact, the potential for variety and innovation is almost infinite. Bonds issued in the last few years have linked the interest rates paid or the principal payments to a wide variety of economic events, such as a rise in the price of silver, exchange rate movements, stock market indices, the price of oil, gold, copper – even to the occurrence of an earthquake. These bonds were generally designed to let companies adjust their interest payments to manageable levels in the event of the firm being adversely affected by the changing of some economic variable. For example, a copper mining company, with its interest payments linked to the price of copper, would pay lower interest on its finance if the copper price were to fall. Sampdoria, the Italian football club, issued a €3.5m bond that paid a higher rate of return if the club won promotion to the 'Serie A' division; 2.5 per cent if it stayed in Serie B, 7 per cent if it moved to Serie A, and if the club rose to the top four in Serie A the coupon would rise to 14 per cent.

Debentures and loan stocks

In the UK and a few other countries the most secure type of bond is called a **debenture**. Debentures are usually secured by either a fixed or a floating charge against the firm's assets. **A fixed charge** means that specific assets (e.g. buildings, machinery) are used as security, which, in the event of default, can be sold at the insistence of the debenture bondholders and the proceeds used to repay them. Debentures secured on property may be referred to as **mortgage debentures**. A **floating charge** means that the loan is secured by a general charge on all the assets of the corporation (or a class of the firm's assets such as inventory or debtors). In this case the company has a high degree of freedom to use its assets as it wishes, such as sell them or rent them out, until it commits a default which 'crystallises' the floating charge. If this happens a **receiver** will be appointed with powers to dispose of assets and to distribute the proceeds to the creditors. Even though floating-charge debenture holders can force a **liquidation**, fixed-charge debenture holders rank above floating-charge debenture holders in the payout after insolvency.

The terms bond, debenture and **loan stock** are often used interchangeably and the dividing line between debentures and loan stock is a fuzzy one. As a general rule debentures are secured (have the backing of collateral) and loan stock is unsecured but there are examples that do not fit this classification. If liquidation occurs the unsecured loan stockholders rank beneath the debenture holders and some other categories of creditors such as the tax authorities. In the US, Canada and some other countries the definitions are somewhat different and this can be confusing. In these places a debenture is a long-term unsecured bond and so the holders become general creditors who can only claim assets not otherwise pledged. In the US the secured form of bond is referred to as the **mortgage bond** and unsecured shorter-dated issues (less than 10 years) are called **notes**.

Trust deeds and covenants

Bond investors are willing to lower the interest they demand if they can be reassured that their money will not be exposed to a high risk. Reassurance is conveyed by placing risk-reducing restrictions on the firm. A **trust deed** (or **bond indenture**) sets out the terms of the contract between bondholders and the company. A **trustee** (if one is appointed) ensures compliance with the contract throughout the life of the bond and has the power to appoint a receiver (to liquidate the firm's assets). If a trustee is not appointed the usual practice is to give each holder an independently exercisable right to take legal action against a delinquent borrower.

The loan agreement will contain a number of affirmative covenants. These usually include the requirements to supply regular financial statements, interest and principal payments. The deed may also state the fees due to the lenders and details of what procedures should be followed in the event of a technical default, for example, non-payment of interest.

In addition to these basic covenants are the **negative (restrictive) covenants**. These restrict the actions and the rights of the borrower until the debt has been repaid in full. Some examples are:

■ *Limits on further debt issuance.* Lenders need to ensure that the loan does not become more risky due to the firm taking on a much greater debt burden relative to its equity base, so they limit the amount and type of further debt issues – particularly debt which has a higher (**senior**) ranking for interest payments or for a liquidation payment. **Subordinated debt (junior debt)** – with a low ranking on liquidation – is more likely to be acceptable.

■ *Dividend level.* An excessive withdrawal of shareholders' funds may unbalance the financial structure and weaken future cash flows.

■ *Limits on the disposal of assets.* The retention of certain assets, for example property and land, may be essential to reduce the lenders' risk.

■ *Financial ratios.* A typical covenant here concerns the interest cover, for example: 'The annual profit will remain four times as great as the overall annual interest charge.' Other restrictions might be placed on working capital ratio levels and the debt to net assets ratio.

While negative covenants cannot ensure completely risk-free lending they can influence the behaviour of the managerial team so as to reduce the risk of default. The lenders' risk can be further reduced by obtaining guarantees from third parties (e.g. **guaranteed loan stock**). The guarantor is typically the parent company of the issuer.

Repayments

The principal on many bonds is paid entirely at maturity. However there are bonds which can be repaid before the final redemption date. A common approach is for the company to issue bonds with a range of dates for redemption; so a bond dated 2018–2022 would allow a company the flexibility to repay the principal in over four years. Another way of redeeming bonds is for the issuing firm to buy the outstanding bonds by offering the holder a sum higher than or equal to the amount originally paid. A firm is also able to purchase bonds on the open market.

One way of paying for redemption is to set up a **sinking fund** that receives regular sums from the firm which will be sufficient, with added interest, to redeem the bonds (the firm may use this to pay off a portion of the bond each year). The sinking fund is overseen by a trustee. The bonds may either be purchased in the market at market prices or at face value. Alternatively bonds held by investors might be selected randomly and purchased. The bond with a sinking fund provision is less risky for the investor, because there is money being set aside; it carries a lower interest rate.

Some bonds are described as **irredeemable** (or **perpetual**) as they have no fixed redemption date. From the investor's viewpoint they may be irredeemable but the firm has the option to repurchase and can effectively redeem the bonds when they wish.

Deep discounted bonds and zero coupon bonds

Bonds which are sold at well below the par value are called **deep discounted bonds**, the most extreme form of which is the zero coupon bond. These are sold at a large discount to the nominal value. The investor makes a capital gain by holding the bond instead of receiving coupons. For example, a company may issue a bond at a price of £60 which is redeemable at £100 in eight years. These bonds are particularly useful for firms with low cash flows in the near term, for example firms engaged in a major property development that will not mature for many years.

Floating-rate notes (FRN) (also called variable-rate notes)

A major market has developed over the past two decades called the **floating-rate note (FRN)** market. Two factors have led to the rapid growth in FRN usage. First, the oscillating and unpredictable inflation of the 1970s and 1980s caused many investors to make large real-term losses on fixed-rate bonds as the interest rate fell below the inflation rate. As a result many lenders became reluctant to lend at fixed rates on a long-term basis. This reluctance led to FRNs being cheaper for the issuer because it does not need to offer an interest premium to compensate the investor for being locked into a fixed rate. Secondly, a number of corporations, especially financial institutions, hold assets which give a return that varies with the short-term interest rate level (e.g. bank loans and overdrafts) and so prefer to have a similar floating-rate liability. These instruments pay an interest rate that is linked to a benchmark rate – such as the LIBOR (London Inter-Bank Offered Rate – see Chapter 9). The issuer will pay, say, 70 basis points (0.7 of a percentage point) over LIBOR. The coupon might be set for the first six months at the time of issue, after which it is adjusted every six months, so if LIBOR was 3 per cent, the FRN would pay 3.7 per cent for that particular six months.

Credit rating

Firms often pay to have their bonds rated by specialist **credit-rating organisations** (see Chapter 9). The **debt rating** depends on the likelihood of payments of interest and/or capital not being paid (that is, **default**) and in some cases on the extent to which the lender is protected in the event of a default by the loan issuer (the **recoverability of debt**).[6] Government bonds from the leading economies have an insignificant risk of default whereas unsecured subordinated corporate loan stock has a much higher risk.

A top rating (AAA or triple A) indicates very high quality, where the capacity to repay interest and principal is extremely strong. Single A indicates a strong capacity to pay interest and capital but there is some degree of susceptibility to impairment as economic events unfold. BBB indicates adequate debt service capacity but vulnerability to adverse economic conditions or changing

---

[6] The rating agencies say that they do not in the strictest sense give an opinion on the likelihood of default, but merely evaluate relative creditworthiness or relative likelihood of default, and because rating scales are relative, default rates fluctuate over time. Thus, a group of middle-rated bonds are expected to be consistent in having a lower rate of default than a group of lower-rated bonds, but they will not, year- after year, have a default rate of say 2.5 per cent per year.

circumstances. B and C rated debt has predominantly speculative characteristics. The lowest is D which indicates the firm is in default. Ratings of BBB- (or Baa3 for Moody's) or above are regarded as **investment grade** – this is important because many institutional investors are permitted to invest only in investment grade bonds. Bonds rated below investment grade are called **high-yield (or junk) bonds.**

The agencies consider a wide range of quantitative and qualitative factors in determining the rating for a bond. The quantitative factors include the ratio of assets to liabilities of the company, cash flow generation and the amount of debt outstanding. The qualitative factors include the competitive position of the company, quality of management and vulnerability to the economic cycle.

The rating and re-rating of bonds is followed with great interest by borrowers and lenders and can give rise to some heated argument. Frequently borrowers complain that their ratings are not judged to be as high as they think they should be with the result that higher interest rates are payable on their bonds.

The same company can issue bonds with different ratings: one may be raised because it is **higher ranking** in the capital structure, meaning that if the firm runs into trouble and has difficulty paying its debts the holders of this bond will be paid before the holders of lower-ranking bonds (the **subordinated** debt). Another difference may be that one bond is secured on specific assets. The ranking order for bonds is:

- senior secured debt;
- senior unsecured debt;
- senior subordinated debt;
- subordinated debt.

The rating agencies also provide **issuer ratings** to firms and other organisations, which are assessments of the creditworthiness of the whole entity rather than a particular bond.

Bond credit ratings are available at www.standardandpoors.com, www.moodys. com, and www.fitchratings.com. The *Financial Times* shows credit ratings daily in the tables titled 'Bonds – Global Investment Guide' and 'Bonds – High Yield & Emerging Markets' together with yields to redemption and other details – see Exhibits 10.7 and 10.8 (more at www.ftcom/bonds&rates). These give the reader some idea of current market conditions and yield to maturity demanded for bonds of different maturities, currencies and riskiness. The ratings shown are for June 2011 and will not necessarily be applicable in future years because the

BONDS – GLOBAL INVESTMENT GUIDE

Jun 28	Red date	Coupon	Ratings S*	M*	F*	Bid price	Bid yield	Day's chge yield	Mth's chge yield	Spread vs Govts
US$										
Morgan Stanley	04/12	6.60	A	A2	A	105.51	1.43	–	–	1.19
Household Fin	05/12	7.00	A	A3	AA–	106.01	1.91	–	–	1.66
HBOS Treas UK	06/12	5.50	A+	Aa3	AA–	104.09	1.17	0.04	0.03	0.99
Verizon Global	09/12	7.38	A–	A3	A	109.36	1.05	–	–	0.36
Abu Dhabi Nt En	10/12	5.62	NR.	A3	–	104.37	2.23	0.10	–0.11	1.90
Bank of England	01/13	4.88	A	A2	A+	104.08	2.62	–	–	1.93
Goldman Sachs	07/13	4.75	A	A1	A+	104.75	2.66	–	–	1.97
Hutchison 03/33	01/14	6.25	A–	A3	A–	109.71	2.33	0.06	0.14	1.70
Misc Capital	07/14	6.13	A–	A3	–	108.16	3.52	–	–	2.31
BMP Paribas	06/15	4.80	AA–	Aa3	A+	103.31	3.90	0.19	0.66	2.37
GE Capital	01/16	5.00	AA+	Aa2	–	109.76	2.69	0.05	0.01	1.14
Erste Euro Lux	02/16	5.00	AA+	–	–	103.03	4.26	0.06	–0.26	2.69
Credit Suisse USA	03/16	5.38	A+	Aa1	AA–	111.10	2.82	0.05	–0.01	1.14
SPI E&G Aust	09/16	5.75	A–	A1	A–	113.59	2.91	0.03	–0.98	1.39
Abu Dhabi Nt En	10/17	6.17	NR	A3	–	107.72	4.73	–0.01	0.03	2.76
Swire Pacific	04/18	6.25	A–	A3	A	110.65	4.42	–0.03	0.08	2.25
ASNA	11/18	6.95	A	A3	A+	103.91	6.33	–	–	4.05
Codelco	01/19	7.50	A	A1	A+	122.10	4.07	–0.07	0.06	1.83
Goldman Sachs	02/33	6.13	A	A1	A+	101.91	5.97	–	–	1.48
Bell South	10/31	6.88	A–	A2	A	113.05	5.78	–	–	1.29
GE Capital	01/39	6.88	AA+	Aa2	–	112.64	5.94	0.19	0.28	1.67
Euro										
HSBC Fin	06/12	3.38	A	A3	AA–	100.83	2.47	0.12	0.21	1.23
Xstrata Fin CA	06/12	4.88	BBB+	Baa2	–	102.19	2.51	0.09	0.36	1.14
CCCI	10/12	6.13	A	A1	A	103.31	3.45	0.02	–0.01	2.26
Amer Honda Fin	07/13	6.25	A+	A1	–	107.37	2.50	0.04	–0.26	1.02
SNS Bank	02/14	4.63	A–	Baa1	BBB+	101.02	4.20	0.14	0.10	2.60
JPMorgan Chase	01/15	5.25	A+	Aa3	AA–	106.36	3.31	0.14	0.11	1.47
Hutchison Fin 06	09/16	4.63	A–	A3	A–	102.10	4.17	–0.11	–0.02	2.12
Hypo Alpe Bk	10/16	4.25	–	Aa3	–	98.52	4.56	0.09	0.26	2.39
GE Cap Euro Fdg	01/18	5.38	AA+	Aa2	–	107.37	4.07	0.14	0.01	1.57
Unicredit	01/20	4.38	A	Aa3	A	99.08	4.50	0.10	0.24	1.73
ENEL	05/24	5.25	A–	A2	A	101.77	5.06	0.18	0.18	1.84
Yen										
Amer Int	04/12	1.40	A–	Baa1	BBB	98.53	3.39	0.00	0.01	3.28
Citi Group 15	09/12	1.11	A	A3	A+	100.24	0.91	0.05	–0.01	0.78
ACOM 51	06/13	2.07	BB+	Ba3	A–	97.23	3.61	0.00	–0.07	3.45
Deutsche Bahn Fin	12/14	1.65	AA	Aa1	AA	103.78	0.53	0.02	0.01	0.28
Nomura Sec S 3	03/18	2.28	–	–	–	103.20	1.75	–0.02	–0.06	1.15
£ Sterling										
HSBC Fin	03/12	7.00	A	A3	AA–	103.55	2.08	0.04	0.16	1.47
Slough Estates	09/15	6.25	–	–	A–	108.22	4.05	0.06	–0.14	2.28
ASIF III	12/18	5.00	A+	A2	A	98.10	5.24	0.09	0.35	2.36

US$ denominated bonds NY close; all other London close. S* – Standard & Poor's. M* – Moody's. F* – Fitch.

Source: ThomsonReuters

Annotations:
- Gross (before deduction of tax) yield to maturity, 1.43%
- Redemption date, February 2016
- Coupon as a percentage of par value
- Bond price with par value set at 100
- Issuer
- Credit ratings
- Spread to the government bond interest rate (in this case Japanese). The extent to which the yield to maturity (bid yield) is greater than that on a government bond of the same length of time to maturity (in this case 1.15%)

Source: *Financial Times*, 29 June 2011

Exhibit 10.7 Bonds – global investment guide

BONDS – HIGH YIELD & EMERGING MARKETS

Jun 28	Red Date	Coupon	Ratings S*	M*	F*	Bid price	Bid yield	Day's chge yield	Mth's chge yield	Spread vs US
High Yield US$										
HSBK Europe	05/13	7.75	B+	Ba3	BB–	105.42	4.75	–	–0.07	4.36
Kazkommerts Int	04/14	7.88	B	B2	B–	97.60	8.86	–0.32	1.54	7.98
Berlin	10/16	10.25	NR	B1	–	110.19	7.84	0.23	0.20	6.18
High Yield Euro										
Royal Carib Crs	01/14	5.63	BB	Ba2	–	99.09	6.00	0.04	0.34	4.40
Kazkommerts Int	02/17	6.88	B	B2	B–	89.40	9.37	0.14	0.87	7.18
Emerging US$										
Bulgaria	01/15	8.25	BBB	Baa3	BBB–	116.25	3.34	0.17	0.24	2.60
Peru	02/15	9.88	BBB–	Baa3	BBB–	124.25	2.75	–0.01	0.01	1.99
Brazil	03/15	7.88	BBB–	Baa2	BBB	120.88	1.97	–0.02	–0.17	1.22
Mexico	09/16	11.38	BBB	Baa1	BBB	141.50	2.76	–0.03	–0.06	1.16
Argentina	01/17	11.38				36.50	41.18	0.02	0.31	39.66
Philippines	01/19	9.88	BB	Ba2	BB+	136.88	4.13	–0.01	4.13	1.81
Brazil	01/20	12.75	BBB–	Baa2	BBB	164.81	3.79	0.08	–0.24	0.75
Colombia	02/20	11.75	BBB–	Baa3	BBB–	154.13	4.22	0.04	–0.18	1.17
Russia	03/30	7.50	BBB	Baa1	BBB	117.56	4.46	–0.12	–0.06	2.86
Mexico	08/31	8.30	BBB	Baa1	BBB	137.25	5.27	–0.03	–0.13	0.94
Indonesia	02/37	6.63	BB+	Ba1	BB+	110.00	5.87	–0.07	0.00	1.53
Emerging Euro										
Brazil	02/15	7.38	BBB–	Baa2	BBB	113.80	3.24	–0.16	–0.23	1.38
Poland	02/16	3.63	A–	A2	A–	100.20	3.57	0.07	0.11	1.42
Turkey	03/16	5.00	BB	Ba2	BB+	102.25	4.45	–0.09	–0.07	2.32
Mexico	02/20	5.50	BBB	Baa1	BBB	106.45	4.57	0.08	–0.01	1.73

The change in the yield to maturity over the past day or month

US $ demoninated bonds NY close; all other London close. *S – Standard & Poor's, M – Moody's
F – Fitch.   Souce: ThomsonReuters

Source: *Financial Times*, 29 June 2011

Exhibit 10.8   Bonds – high yield and emerging markets

creditworthiness and the specific debt issue can change significantly in a short period. (In the table S* = Standard & Poor's, M* = Moody's and F* = Fitch.) A key measure in the bond markets is the '**spread**', which is the number of basis points a bond is yielding above a benchmark rate, usually the government bond yield to maturity for that currency and period to redemption.

The so-called 'emerging markets' are, to a large extent, now fully emerged, with many countries such as Brazil and Mexico having fully functioning corporate bond markets drawing on local savings to raise funds for businesses – see Exhibit 10.9.

Corporate bond issues go local to deliver capital lift

By David Oakley in London

Corporate bond issuance in emerging market currencies has surged to record levels this year, deepening the local sources of capital for companies.

Groups have tapped increasing demand for local currency bonds not only from foreign investors but also a growing number of domestic funds seeking exposure to corporate debt.

This has lowered the cost of borrowing and reduced the risk for companies that foreign fund managers might stop buying their debt in times of crisis.

Emerging market corporate bond issuance has jumped to $68bn so far this year, up 58 per cent on the same period last year, according to Dealogic.

Local currency corporate bond issuance has made up $49bn of this, a 29 per cent jump on the same period last year and a 308 per cent increase on the same period just three years ago, when these markets were smaller and more immature.

Companies that have tapped the market this year include multinationals such as Vale, the Brazilian iron ore producer,

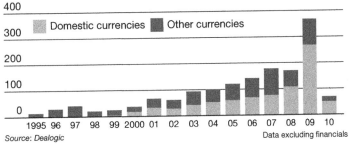

Corporate bond issuance in emerging market countries
Deal value, annual ($bn)

Domestic currencies Other currencies

Source: Dealogic

Data excluding financials

Pemex, the Mexican oil company, TNK-BP, the Russian arm of oil group BP....and CNPC, the Chinese energy group.

However, smaller companies are increasingly able to borrow in the local currency markets, helped by the development of pension fund industries in countries such as Mexico, Brazil, Chile and South Korea. This is because domestic pension funds want assets denominated in their own currencies.

For example, in Mexico, Alsea, the restaurant operator, and Infonavit, the government-backed mortgage lender, have issued bonds recently.

The local currency corporate bond markets have also been boosted by a lengthening of the

average maturity of emerging market government bonds.

This is enabling companies to issue longer-dated debt that gives them more stability as they can lock in fixed rates, often up to 10 years.

For example, the average maturity of government debt has risen above five years in Mexico, which is now longer than in the US with an average maturity of 4.8 years.

Brett Diment, head of emerging market debt at Aberdeen Asset Managers, said: "In effect, many emerging markets are becoming more like developed markets as they become more sophisticated."

Source: Financial Times, 24 March 2010, p. 17

Exhibit 10.9 Corporate bond issues go local to deliver capital lift

A lot of weight is placed on bond ratings by financial institutions and investors, who rely on them for investment actions and can feel aggrieved if the bond ratings fail to live up to expectation. The ratings agencies were criticised for not spotting the dangers in a number of bonds which gained their income from thousands of US mortgages, see Exhibit 10.10.

Rating agency model left largely intact

By Aline van Duyn and Joanna Chung

Big banks are not the only groups whose income is soaring on the back of commissions and fees from selling and trading the huge amounts of debt being sold by governments, banks and companies.

Credit rating agencies, the biggest of which are Moody's Investors Service and Standard & Poor's, have also seen a surge in revenue, as most debt that is issued – government-backed or not – comes with a credit rating for which the borrower pays a fee....

....The rating agencies remain central to the debt markets and their business models today remain largely intact, in spite of widespread claims that they exacerbated the credit crisis. The criticism centres on the fact that Moody's, S&P and Fitch gave triple A ratings to hundreds of billions of dollars of bonds backed by risky mortgages – but these securities have since been downgraded and are in many cases now worthless.

Ratings continue to be written into the official criteria used by many investors to define what debt they can and cannot buy. They are also still central to risk assessments by regulators. Ironically, some of the biggest

investors and borrowers are suing the rating agencies.

The largest pension fund in the US, the California Public Employees' Retirement System (Calpers), has filed a suit against the three leading rating agencies over potential losses of more than $1bn over what it says are "wildly inaccurate" triple A ratings. That is just one of many cases. S&P currently faces about 40 separate lawsuits from investors and institutions.

In the past, most lawsuits have failed because rating agencies are protected by the first amendment right to free speech. Their ratings are an "opinion" and therefore subject to free speech protections.

Whether this will continue to be the case is a key factor in the debate about the future of the industry.

This week's proposed legislation by the US Treasury to reform rating agencies is not widely regarded as fundamentally changing the business of ratings, even though it does put more controls in place.

Already, rating agencies have themselves undertaken reviews aimed at restoring confidence in their ratings, particularly on the structured finance part of the busi-

ness that includes bonds backed by loans such as mortgages and where most of the controversies have been. This week, a decision by S&P to upgrade bonds backed by commercial mortgages to triple A, just a week after severely cutting them from triple A, highlights the clout of ratings (and the scope to confuse investors).

It also highlights the potential for controversy in areas such as commercial real estate where further losses are looming. Without a triple A rating, those bonds would not be eligible for inclusion in government-backed funding programmes and their value would plunge.

Michael Barr, the Treasury's assistant secretary for financial institutions, portrayed the proposed legislation as an attempt to ensure that better information is put into the market and to encourage the right incentives for the issuance of ratings. Other models, including the investor-paid model, also have inherent conflicts of interest that would pose problems, Mr Barr said.

No matter what the reforms, "we are not going to be able to eliminate the need for investors to use their own judgment ... The

Exhibit 10.10   Rating agency model left largely intact

one thing we want to make clear ... no investor should take as a matter of blind faith what the ratings [agency's] judgment is," Mr Barr said this week.

The SEC, which has created a new group of examiners to oversee the sector, is looking for ways to reduce reliance on credit ratings. Mary Shapiro, chairman of the SEC, said at a Congressional hearing that new rules would be put forward later this summer.

She said one rule would require issuers to disclose preliminary ratings to get rid of "pernicious" ratings shopping (when a company solicits a preliminary rating from an agency but only pays for and discloses the highest rating it receives); disclose information underlying the ratings; look at sources of revenue disclosure and performance history of ratings over one, five and 10-year periods; and see how the SEC could get investors to do additional due diligence of its own.

"While the administration's proposals are well-intentioned, they are easily criticised as merely cosmetic," says Joseph Grundfest, a law professor at Stanford University. "If you really want change you have to recognise that the industry is dominated by two agencies and the SEC should create a new category of agencies owned by investors."

The status of rating agencies means they have access to information that is not made public, information they do not need to disclose, and this is one reason they are supposed to have better insights into companies and deals than ordinary investors might. It is this special status that some believe should be targeted. "When an opinion has regulatory power, which is what ratings have, it has to come with some accountability," says Arturo Cifuentes, principal with Atacama Partners, a financial advisory firm.

"It is not enough to say it is just an opinion, because it carries more weight than that in the financial system."

Source: Financial Times 22 July 2009

Exhibit 10.10 Continued

Bond default rates

Exhibit 10.11 shows the proportion of bonds that have defaulted 1, 2, 3, 4, 5 and 10 years after issue over the period 1990–2010. Notice the large differences in default rates between the ratings. After five years only 0.17 per cent of AA bonds defaulted, whereas 11.68 per cent of B bonds defaulted. When examining data on default rates it is important to appreciate that default is a wide-ranging term, and could refer to any number of events from a missed payment to bankruptcy. For some of these events all is lost from the investor's perspective. For other events a very high percentage, if not all, of the interest and principal is recovered. In the 1950s it was observed that defaulted publicly held and traded bonds tended to sell for 40 cents on the dollar. This average recovery rate rule-of-thumb seems to have held over time – in approximate terms – with senior secured bank loans returning over 60 per cent and subordinated bonds under 30 per cent.

Rating	1 year %	2 years %	3 years %	4 years %	5 years %	10 years %
'AAA'	0	0	0	0	0	0
'AA'	0	0	0	0.08	0.17	0.32
'A'	0.04	0.17	0.37	0.54	0.81	2.12
'BBB'	0.26	0.83	1.48	2.10	2.78	5.13
'BB'	1.12	2.74	4.15	5.23	6.04	12.33
'B'	3.10	7.72	9.93	10.55	11.68	15.21
'CCC to 'C	30.98	41.26	43.22	44.70	45.36	57.89
Investment grade	0.14	0.47	0.84	1.20	1.60	2.95
High yield	3.69	6.91	8.55	9.53	10.43	14.98
All Industrials	1.11	2.18	2.83	3.27	3.71	5.37

Source: Fitch Ratings Global Corporate Finance 2010 Transition and Default Study http://www. fitchratings.com/creditdesk/reports/report_frame.cfm?rpt_id=606665

Exhibit 10.11 Fitch Global Corporate Finance average cumulative default rates 1990–2010

Websites

www.treasurers.org	Association of Corporate Treasurers
www.bankofengland.co.uk	Bank of England
www.bis.org	Bank for International Settlements
www.bloomberg.com,	Bloomberg
www.bondscape.net	Bondscape
www.economist.com	Economist
www.ft.com/bonds&rates	Financial Times
www.fitchratings.com	Fitch
www.icma-group.co.uk	International Capital Market Association
www.BondMarketPrices.com	International Capital Markets Association – bond prices pages
www.investorschronicle.co.uk/bonds	Investor Chronicle bond prices, yield etc.
www.adr.com	JPMorgan
www.moodys.com	Moody's
www.standardandpoors.com	Standard & Poor's

11

Bond markets – the more exotic

Having introduced bonds in the last chapter we now need to look at some of the variations on the basic idea. Many of these markets have grown so much in the past two decades that they now rival the domestic corporate bond markets for scale and influence (e.g. the Eurobond market and securitised bond market). Others, such as the European high-yield bond, strips bond or Islamic bond (*sukuk*) markets, are still young with fast growth and huge potential. Convertible bonds are a very useful hybrid with debt-like features as well as equity-like features.

High-yield (junk) bonds

High-yield or junk bonds are debt instruments offering a high return with a high risk. They may be either unsecured or secured but rank behind senior loans and bonds, having credit ratings below BBB–. This type of debt generally offers interest rates 2–9 percentage points more than that on senior debt and frequently gives the lenders some right to a share in equity values should the firm perform well. It is a kind of hybrid finance, ranking for payment below straight debt but above equity – it is thus described alternatively as **subordinated, intermediate** or **low grade**. One of the major attractions of this form of finance for the investor is that it often comes with equity warrants or share options attached (see Chapter 15) which can be used to obtain shares in the firm – this is known as an '**equity kicker**'. These may be triggered by an event taking place such as the firm joining the stock market.

Bonds with high-risk and high-return characteristics may have started as apparently safe investments but have now become more risky ('**fallen angels**'), or they may be bonds issued specifically to provide higher-risk financial instruments for investors. This latter type began their rise to prominence in the US in the 1980s and are now a market with over $200 billion issued per year. The rise of the US junk bond market meant that no business was safe from the threat of takeover, however large – see the case study on Michael Milken.

> **Case study**   **THE JUNK BOND WIZARD: MICHAEL MILKEN**
>
> While studying at Wharton Business School in the 1970s Michael Milken
> came to the belief that the gap in interest rates between safe bonds and high-
> yield bonds was excessive, given the relative risks (rates of default and
> recovery of some of the money owed following default). This created an
> opportunity for financial institutions to make an acceptable return from junk
> bonds, given their risk level. At the investment banking firm Drexel Burnham
> Lambert, Milken was able to persuade a large body of institutional investors to
> supply finance to the junk bond market as well as provide a service to
> corporations wishing to grow through the use of junk bonds. Small firms were
> able to raise billions of dollars to take over large US corporations. Many of
> these issuers of junk bonds had debt ratios of 90 per cent and above – for
> every $1 of share capital $9 was borrowed. These gearing levels concerned
> many in the financial markets. It was thought that companies were pushing
> their luck too far and indeed many did collapse under the weight of their debt.
> The market was dealt a particularly severe blow when Michael Milken was
> convicted, sent to jail and ordered to pay $600 million in fines. Drexel was also
> convicted, paid $650 million in fines and filed for bankruptcy in 1990. The junk
> bond market was in a sorry state in the early 1990s, with high levels of default
> and few new issues. However, it did not take long for the market to recover.

Issuers of high-yield bonds

High-yield bond finance tends to be used when bank borrowing limits are
reached and the firm cannot or will not issue more equity. The finance it provides is cheaper (in terms of required return) than would be available on the
equity market and it allows the owners of a business to raise large sums of
money without sacrificing voting control. It is a form of finance that permits the
firm to move beyond what is normally considered acceptable debt:equity ratios
(financial gearing or leverage levels).

High-yield bonds have been employed by firms 'gearing themselves up' to
finance merger activity and also for **leveraged recapitalisations**. For instance,
a firm might have run into trouble, defaulted and its assets are now under the
control of a group of creditors, including bankers and bondholders. One way
to allow the business to continue would be to persuade the creditors to accept
alternative financial securities in place of their debt securities to bring the leverage (financial gearing) to a reasonable level. They might be prepared to accept a
mixture of shares and high-yield bonds. The bonds permit the holders to receive

high interest rates in recognition of the riskiness of the firm, and they open up the possibility of an exceptionally high return from warrants or share options should the firm get back to a growth path. The alternative for the lenders may be a return of only a few pence in the pound from the immediate liquidation of the firm's assets.

Junk bond borrowing usually leads to high debt levels resulting in a high fixed cost imposition on the firm. This can be a dangerous way of financing expansion and therefore the use of these types of finance has been criticised. On the other hand, some commentators have praised the way in which high gearing and large annual interest payments have focused the minds of managers and engendered extraordinary performance. Also, without this finance, many takeovers, buyouts and financial restructurings would not take place.

Fast-growing companies also make use of junk bonds. They have been particularly attractive sources for cable television companies, telecommunications and some media businesses which require large investments in the near term but also can offer a relatively stable profits flow in the long term.

Market price movements

Investment-grade bond prices and returns tend to move in line with government bond interest rates, influenced by perceptions of future inflation rather than the risk of default. Junk bond prices (and their yields), on the other hand, are much more related to the prospects for the company's trading fundamentals because the company needs to thrive if it is to cope with the high debt levels and raised interest, and cause the equity kicker to have some value. Thus the factors that affect equity valuation also impact on junk bond valuations. As a result high-yield bonds tend to be more volatile than investment-grade bonds, going up and down depending on expectations concerning the company's survival, strength and profitability.

Comparing US and European high-yield bond markets

The high-yield bond is much more popular in the US than in Europe because of European financial institutions' aversion (constrained by legislation) to such instruments and because of an attachment to bank borrowing as the main way to borrow. The European high-yield bond market is in its infancy. The first high-yield bonds denominated in European currencies were issued as recently as 1997 when Geberit, a Swiss/UK manufacturer, raised DM157.5 million by selling 10-year bonds offering an interest rate which was 423 basis points (4.23 per cent) higher than the interest rate on a 10-year German government bond (bund). Since then there have been hundreds of issues. However, the European high-yield market remains about one-quarter the size of the US's. Following a freeze in the high-yield market as risk aversion took hold after the 2008 crisis, the volume and price of bonds has risen (yield fallen) significantly – see Exhibit 11.1.

Junk bonds' new appeal shows little sign of fading

By Aline van Duyn, Nicole Bullock and Anousha Sakoui

Junk bonds will feature prominently in this year's accolades. A record amount of debt, more than $300bn in new bonds, has been sold by companies with credit ratings below "investment grade".

Junk bonds, rebranded by Wall Street as "high-yield bonds" after scandals in the 1980s, have also turned out to be one of the best investments of 2010. This year, US junk bonds have notched up returns of close to 15 per cent.

The stellar year in the US follows a chart-busting 2009, when issuance surged and junk bond indices made gains of more than 50 per cent, after sharp losses in 2008.

There has also been a notable boost in high yield issuance in Europe, until recently a niche market.

According to Credit Suisse, European companies have this year sold €51bn ($68.4bn) in junk bonds in all currencies, up 75 per cent from the previous record year in 2009. Bankers expected to see volumes rise further next year....

To judge the appeal of junk bonds, key for financing companies ranging from airlines, to casinos, to telecoms and

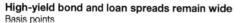

High-yield bond and loan spreads remain wide
Basis points

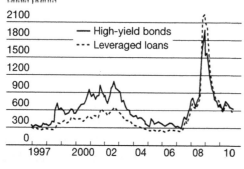

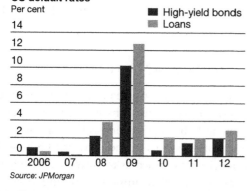

US default rates
Per cent

Source: JPMorgan

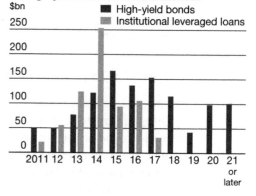

US high-yield bond and loan maturities
$bn

Exhibit 11.1   Junk bonds' new appeal shows little sign of fading

energy, investors look at the yields offered, but also how much higher the returns are relative to less risky bonds.

In terms of yields, junk bonds are offering some of the lowest returns ever.

According to a benchmark Bank of America Merrill Lynch index, the yield on US high-yield bonds is at around 7.9 per cent. The all-time low yield was 7.58 per cent, reached in February 2007, when banks were willing to lend almost limitless amounts of money to risky companies. In terms of the risk premium, known as the spread, there is quite a difference compared with the boom years.

A widely watched spread on the Bank of America Merrill Lynch index is trading at about 568 basis points over risk-free benchmark rates. The 2007 lows were about 241bp. "The spreads offer fair value," says Martin Fridson, global credit strategist at BNP Paribas Asset Management.

Source: *Financial Times*, 15 December 2010, p. 33

Exhibit 11.1   Continued

Local authority/municipal bonds

Local authority and municipal bonds are bonds issued by governments at a sub-national level, such as a county, city or state, which pay a fixed rate of interest and are repayable on a specific future date, similar in fact to Treasury bonds.[1] They are a means of raising money to finance developments, buildings or expansion by the local authority. They are riskier than sovereign bonds (the issuers cannot print their own money as governments might), as, from time to time, cities, etc. do go bust and fail to pay their debts. However, many issuers, particularly in Europe and the US, obtain **bond insurance**, from a private insurance group with a top credit rating, guaranteeing that the bond will be serviced on time. This reduces the interest rate they pay.

General-obligation bonds offer the bondholder a priority claim on the general (usually tax) revenue of the issuer in the event of a default, whereas a holder of a **revenue bond** receives interest and principal repayment from the revenues of a particular project (e.g. the income from a toll bridge).

In the UK they are out of favour at the moment, although Transport for London issued a 25-year bond in 2006 and there is talk of issuing a 'Brummie' bond (by Birmingham Council). In the US and some other countries they are big business – over $2,000 billion. US municipal bonds issued by state and local governments are usually tax exempt, which means that investors do not have to pay federal income tax on the interest they receive. Because of this concession they usually trade at lower yields to maturity than US government bonds. In Japan, over 30 prefectures and cities have issued bonds which total over ¥3.5 trillion. The German Länder (states) are also large issuers.

---

[1] They are sometimes called semi-sovereigns or sub-sovereigns.

Bonds are also issued by counties, school districts, airports, water systems and highways, with the aim of raising finance for specific targets. There are also quasi-state organisations issuing bonds in Europe. In France Electricité de France (EdF) and Societé Nationale des Chemins de Fer Français (SNCF, the French railway operator), and in Germany Deutsche Bahn (DB, the German railway company) are just some of the institutions which have issued bonds.

Convertible bonds

Convertible bonds (or **convertible loan stocks**) carry a rate of interest in the same way as ordinary bonds, but they also give the holder the **right to exchange** the bonds at some stage in the future into ordinary shares according to some pre-arranged formula.[2] The owner of these bonds is not obliged to exercise this right of conversion and so the bonds may continue until redemption as an interest-bearing instrument. Conversion of these bonds into shares may have the effect of diluting the value of individual shares – there is an increase in the number of shares as more are created, but not necessarily any increase in the profits/value of the company. Usually the **conversion price** is 10–30 per cent greater than the share price at the date of the bond issuance. So, if a £100 bond offered the right to convert to 40 ordinary shares the conversion price would be £2.50 (that is £100 ÷ 40) which, given the market price of the shares of, say, £2.20, would be a **conversion premium** of 30p divided by £2.20, which equals 13.6 per cent.

Venture Production, a North Sea oil explorer, issued convertible bonds in July 2005. The issue raised £29 million. The bonds were to be redeemed in 2010 if they had not been converted before this and were issued at a par value of £100. The coupon was set at 4.25 per cent and the conversion price was at 474p per share. From this information we can calculate the **conversion ratio**:

$$\text{Conversion ratio} = \frac{\text{Nominal (par) value of bond}}{\text{Conversion price}} = \frac{£100}{£4.74} = 21.1 \text{ shares}$$

Each bond carries the right to convert to 21.1 shares, which is equivalent to paying 474p for each share at the £100 par value of the bond.

Unusually, in this particular case, if the bonds were not converted or redeemed then the holder was to receive 110 per cent of par value rather than simply the

---

[2] Alternatively they may be convertible into preference shares.

par value in October 2010, to give a total yield to maturity of 5.904 per cent. The conversion price was set at a premium of 16 per cent over the ordinary share price at the time of pricing; this was 408p ((474 – 408)/408 = 16 per cent). At the time of the issue many investors may have looked at the low interest rate on the convertible and said to themselves that although this was greater than the dividend yield on shares (3 per cent) it was less than that on conventional bonds, but offsetting this was the prospect of capital gains made by converting the bonds into shares. If the shares rose to, say, £6, each £100 bond could be converted to 21.1 shares worth 21.1 × £6 = £126.6.

The value of a convertible bond (a type of **equity-linked bond**) rises as the value of ordinary shares increases, but at a lower percentage rate. The value could be analysed as a 'debt portion', which depends on the discounted value of the coupons, and an 'equity portion', where the right to convert is an equity option. If the share price rises above the conversion price investors may choose to exercise the option to convert if they anticipate that the share price will at least be maintained and the dividend yield is higher than the convertible bond yield. If the share price rise is seen to be temporary, the investor may wish to hold on to the bond. If the share price remains below the conversion price the value of the convertible will be the same as a straight bond at maturity.

Exhibit 11.2 describes some of the technical terms associated with convertibles.

Convertibles with large conversion premiums trade much like ordinary bonds because the option to convert is not a strong feature in their pricing. They offer higher yields and prices are not volatile. Those trading with a small conversion premium have lower yields and the prices are more volatile as they are more closely linked with the share price. The right to convert may specify a specific date or several specific dates over, say, a four-year period, or any time between two dates.

The advantages of convertibles

The advantages of convertible bonds to investors are:

■ Investors are able to wait and see how the share price moves before investing in equity.

■ In the near term there is greater security for their principal compared with equity investment, and the annual coupon is usually higher than the dividend yield.

Conversion ratio

This gives the number of ordinary shares into which a convertible bond may be converted:

$$\text{Conversion ratio} = \frac{\text{Nominal (par) value of bond}}{\text{Conversion price}}$$

Conversion price

This gives the price of each ordinary share obtainable by exchanging a convertible bond:

$$\text{Conversion price} = \frac{\text{Nominal (par) value of bond}}{\text{Number of shares into which bond may be converted}}$$

Conversion premium

This gives the difference between the conversion price and the market share price, expressed as a percentage:

$$\text{Conversion premium} = \frac{\text{Conversion price} - \text{Market share price}}{\text{Market share price}} \times 100$$

Conversion value

This is the value of a convertible bond if it were converted into ordinary shares at the current share price:

$$\text{Conversion value} = \text{Current share price} \times \text{Conversion ratio}$$

Exhibit 11.2   **Convertible bond technical jargon**

Raising money by selling convertible bonds has the following advantages to the issuing company:

- *Lower interest than on a similar debenture.* The firm can ask investors to accept a lower interest on these debt instruments because the investor values the conversion right. This was a valuable feature for many dot.com companies when starting out. Amazon and AOL could pay 5–6 per cent on convertibles – less than half what they would have paid on straight bonds.

- *The interest is tax deductible.* Because convertible bonds are a form of debt the coupon payment can be regarded as a cost of the business and can therefore be used to reduce taxable profit.

▦ *Self-liquidating.* When the share price reaches a level at which conversion is worthwhile the bonds will (normally) be exchanged for shares so the company does not have to find cash to pay off the loan principal – it simply issues more shares. This has obvious cash flow benefits. However, the disadvantage is that the other equity holders may experience a reduction in earnings per share and dilution of voting rights.

▦ *Fewer restrictive covenants.* The directors have greater operating and financial flexibility than they would with a secured debenture. Investors accept that a convertible is a hybrid between debt and equity finance and do not tend to ask for high-level security (they are unsecured and subordinated), impose strong operating restrictions on managerial action or insist on strict financial ratio boundaries. Many Silicon Valley companies with little more than a web-portal and a brand have used convertibles because of the absence of a need to provide collateral or stick to asset:borrowing ratios.

▦ *Underpriced shares.* A company which wishes to raise equity finance over the medium term but judges that the stock market is temporarily under-pricing its shares may turn to convertible bonds. If the firm does perform as the managers expect and the share price rises, the convertible will be exchanged for equity.

▦ *Cheap way to issue shares.* Managers favour convertibles as an inexpensive way to issue 'delayed' equity. Equity is raised at a later date without the high costs of rights issues, etc.

▦ *Available finance when straight debt and equity are not available.* Some firms locked out of the equity markets (e.g. because of poor recent performance) and the straight debt markets because of high levels of indebtedness may still be able to raise money in the convertible market. Firms use convertible debt to attract investors unsure about the riskiness of the company.

The bonds sold may give the right to conversion into shares not of the issuers but of another company held by the issuer – see the cases of Hutchison Whampoa, Telecom Italia and France Telecom in Exhibit 11.3. Note that the term 'exchangeable bond' is probably more appropriate in these cases.

Strip bonds

Strips/strip bonds are broken down into their individual cash flows. The dividends or coupons are separated from the bond and are then negotiable zero coupon instruments in their own right with a fixed maturity date and guaranteed payment at maturity. A bond with 7 years to run could be stripped into 15

Brakes applied to convertible bond market

By Rebecca Bream

In January Hong Kong conglomerate Hutchison Whampoa sold $2.65bn of bonds exchangeable into shares of Vodafone, the UK mobile phone operator. Hutchison had been gradually divesting its stake in the UK group since completing a $3bn exchangeable bond deal last September.

This was followed at the end of the month by Telecom Italia which sold €2bn of bonds exchangeable into shares of subsidiaries Telecom Italia Mobile and internet operator Seat.

In February France Telecom sold €3.3bn of bonds exchangeable into shares of Orange, completed at the same time as the mobile unit's IPO, and one of the biggest exchangeable bond deals ever sold in Europe.

Source: *Financial Times*, 6 April 2001, p. 35

Exhibit 11.3   Brakes applied to convertible bond market

separate zero coupon instruments, the 14 half-yearly dividend payments and the bond itself. As all parts of the bond are now zero coupon, they are traded at a discount to their nominal value.

The name 'strips' actually stands for **Separate Trading of Registered Interest and Principal of Securities**, but it is also a good name for its role of separating the coupon from the principal. The idea of stripping bonds and trading the coupons separately from the bond originated in the 1980s in North America, and involved the actual physical cutting of the coupon from its bond. The concept gained in popularity, partly because they can offer investing institutions the maturity profile they need and partly because there can be tax advantages in taking a capital gain rather than interest income. The UK started issuing gilt-edged strips in 1997 and by the mid-2000s most countries in the world of finance allowed stripping of government bonds, with Canada allowing stripping of all bonds, government, municipal and corporate.

To avoid the possibility of losing the actual coupon, which tended to be a small piece of paper, easy to mislay, the stripping is now done electronically and official records are kept. Not all bonds are strippable. In the UK the DMO lists all the separate parts of the bonds which are able to be stripped, the date on which the stripping commenced and which bonds have been reconstituted. In the US Treasury Direct gives the same information about US bonds. There are nearly 40 bonds which are strippable, resulting in some 7,000 individual strips. Reconstitution of a stripped bond is possible, where the bond is reassembled once more into a coupon-paying instrument.

Securitisation

In the strange world of modern finance you sometimes need to ask yourself who ends up with your money when you pay your monthly mortgage, or your credit card bill or the instalment payment on your car. In the old days you would have found that it was the organisation you originally borrowed from and whose name is at the top of the monthly statement. Today you cannot be so sure because there is now a thriving market in repackaged debt. In this market, a mortgage lender, for example, collects together a few thousand mortgage 'claims' it has (the right of the lender to receive regular interest and capital from the borrowers); it then sells those claims in a collective package to other institutions, or participants in the market generally. This permits the replacement of long-term assets with cash (improving liquidity and financial gearing) which can then be used to generate more mortgages. It may also allow a profit on the difference between the interest on the mortgages and the interest on the bonds. This can happen if the original mortgages pay, say, 6 per cent, and the bonds secured on the flow of payments from the mortgagees pay 5 per cent. The extra 1 per cent (less costs) can enable the originator to sell the bonds for a price in excess of the amount it lent to the mortgagees.

The borrower is often unaware that the mortgage is no longer owned by the original lender and everything appears as it did before, with the mortgage company acting as a collecting agent for the buyer of the mortgages. The mortgage company usually raises this cash by selling **asset-backed securities (ABS)** to other institutions (the 'assets' are the claim on interest and capital) and so this form of finance is often called **asset securitisation**. These asset-backed securities may be bonds sold into a market with many players. Usually a **special purpose vehicle (SPV)** or **special purpose entity (SPE)** is created separate from the originator of mortgages, etc. This new entity is then given the right to collect the cash flows from the mortgages. It has to pay the mortgage company for this. To make this payment it sells bonds sold secured against the assets of the SPV (e.g. mortgage claims). By creating an SPV there is a separation of the creditworthiness of the assets involved from the general credit of the mortgage company.

The sale of the financial claims can be either 'non-recourse', in which case the buyer of the securities from the mortgage firm, or the lender to the SPV (e.g. bondholder), bears the risk of non-payment by the borrowers, or with recourse to the mortgage lender (if the mortgagees fail to pay, then the original lender will make up the difference).

Securitisation has even reached the world of rock. Iron Maiden issued a long-dated $30 million asset-backed bond securitised on future earnings from royalties. It followed David Bowie's $55 million bond securitised on the income from his earlier albums and Rod Stewart's $15.4 million securitised loan from Nomura. Tussauds has securitised ticket and merchandise sales, Keele University has securitised the rental income from student accommodation and Arsenal has securitised £260 million future ticket sales at the Emirates Stadium. Loans to Hong Kong taxi drivers have been securitised, as have the cash flows from UK funeral fees.

Securitisation is regarded as beneficial to the financial system, because it permits banks and other financial institutions to focus on those aspects of the lending process where they have a competitive edge. Some, for example, have a greater competitive advantage in originating loans than in funding them, so they sell the loans they have created, raising cash to originate more loans. Other motives include the need to change the risk profile of the bank's assets (e.g. reduce its exposure to the housing market) or to reduce the need for reserve capital (if the loans are removed from the asset side of the bank's balance sheet it does not need to retain the same quantity of reserves) – the released reserve capital can then be used in more productive ways.

Securitisation was at the heart of the financial turmoil in 2007–08 when US sub-prime (poor quality) mortgage borrowers failed to repay in substantial numbers. Mortgage-backed bonds of SPVs plummeted in value, the asset-backed bond market froze and the businesses model of lending to households expecting to sell bonds backed with a bunch of mortgages (à la Northern Rock) became untenable as no one would buy the securitised bonds.

The really big players in the securitisation market are the US quasi-government bodies of 'Fannie Mae',[3] 'Ginnie Mae'[4] and 'Freddie Mac',[5] which buy collections of mortgages from banks and issue bonds backed by the security of these mortgages (mortgage bonds or mortgage-backed securities, MBSs). They also guarantee that investors will receive timely interest and principal regardless of whether the individual mortgage payers renege. This helps to keep down interest rates in the mortgage market. The US also has a large commercial mortgage-backed securities (CMBS) market where the flows of interest and principal payments come from companies paying off mortgages on commercial property (offices, factories, etc.). Spain (followed by Denmark) is the big player in the euro-denominated ABS market, issuing around one-half of them.

---

[3] A nickname for the Federal National Mortgage Association, FNMA, sponsored by the government.
[3] A nickname for the Government National Mortgage Association, GNMA, sponsored by the government.
[5] A nickname for the Federal Home Loan Mortgage Corporation, FHLMC. sponsored by the government.

UK securitisations are often different to those in the rest of the world because the assets backing the securitised bonds are usually changed over the life of the securitisation – see Exhibit 11.4.

Recent deals signal market's reopening in the same old style

By Jennifer Hughes

When Northern Rock decided to wind down its Granite master trust – now to be placed in the lender's "bad bank" rump – industry insiders predicted the death of a structure that had helped the UK dominate the European mortgage-backed market.

The Granite decision, in November 2008, put all bondholders in a queue for repayments that could take years, regardless of the maturity date of the paper they held.

Investors warned that they would demand far simpler structures before venturing near the sector again.

Less than a year later, however, two master-trust-backed deals in the last month have signalled the reopening of the market in the same old style.

They have reignited a debate about how best to structure an instrument considered crucial for boosting economic growth but which represents the very complexity that triggered the crisis.

Policymakers in Europe and the US have called for simpler, more transparent structures. The industry has responded with guidelines and templates for providing more data that many big issuers have agreed to follow.

But the UK, responsible for about half the total European market before the crisis, is a particular challenge because its biggest lenders use a different structure from the rest of the world.

Most mortgage-backed securitisations are based around stand-alone, ring-fenced bundles of loans.

Bonds are backed by the loans in deals known as "pass-throughs" because the mortgage repayments are passed to the bondholders almost as they happen.

This leaves investors with the risk of pre-payment – where the loans are repaid earlier than expected, meaning investors end up with extra cash they must reinvest – or of extension risk, where the bonds mature more slowly than expected.

In the UK, bankers have instead created master trusts – vast pools of mortgages which the lender would periodically top up with new loans and from which it would issue different bonds at different times.

The advantage was that this constant pool allowed the trust to issue the exact bonds investors wanted, such as ones with set maturity dates.

Investors were thereby freed from prepayment and extension risk and left only with credit risk, and the impact of any bad loans would be cushioned by the size of the whole giant mortgage pool.

Master trusts enabled the UK market to expand rapidly.

Investors liked the apparent relative simplicity of the deals. By buying bonds backed by a pool of

a known quality, they saved on the effort of analysing each deal in great depth.

But the upshot of the simple front was the complexity that lurked behind the master trust.

Because new loans are added to the existing collateral pool when new bonds are issued, the performance statistics of the older loans are diluted by the new loans.

Investors are unhappy at the way the structure leaves them at the mercy of the lender's treasury team, which can decide, under certain circumstances, not to repay the bonds until their legal maturity date.

This is further into the future than the set maturity date and reflects the long-term nature of mortgages.

In effect, this happened with Granite, where Northern Rock decided to no longer support the trust with new mortgages and where it will instead simply pay out on the existing bonds when the underlying mortgages are repaid.

"Everyone is comfortable with credit risk, but it's really also extension risk they've taken. It's not always at the issuer's discretion. They might have to extend if certain things happen."

Source: *Financial Times*, 29 October 2009, p. 37

Exhibit 11.4 Recent deals signal market's reopening in the same old style

Covered bonds

Covered bonds are similar to securitised asset-based bonds in that a specific group of assets (e.g. mortgage receivables) is used to back up the claims of the bondholders – they have the assets acting as collateral. However, there is one crucial difference compared with ABS which gives an extra layer of protection for investors. These assets and bonds are kept on the balance sheet of the issuing bank, which means that if the pool of assets runs into trouble (as many mortgages did in 2007–09) investors in the covered bonds can call on the originating bank to pay up or replace the bad assset – the risk is not transferred. If an underlying loan goes bad (e.g. the mortgagee stops paying) the originating bank has to replace that loan with another. Furthermore, if it is the originating bank that runs into trouble the investors in the covered bonds have the security of the ring-fenced assets separate from the parent. So long as the issuing institution remains solvent, the cash flows to the covered bondholders is independent of the performance of the assets. Because of their high level of backing, covered bonds are given high credit ratings (AAA), and are therefore a relatively low-cost way for financial institutions to raise money. Typical maturity ranges are 2–10 years. They are common in Europe, where they originated (in Prussia in the eighteenth century), now making up to one-third of bank debt securities. Germany has a particularly large covered bond (**Pfandbriefe**) market at around €1,000 billion outstanding. Spain and France have over €100 billion outstanding. The US market is only just getting going – see Exhibit 11.5.

Foreign bonds

A **foreign bond** is a bond denominated in the currency of the country where it is issued when the issuer is a non-resident.[6] For example, in Japan bonds issued by non-Japanese companies denominated in yen are foreign bonds. They are known as Samurai bonds and the interest and capital payments will be in yen. Other foreign bonds from around the world issued by non-domestic entities in the domestic market include Yankee bonds (US), Bulldog bonds (UK), Rembrandt bonds (The Netherlands), Matador bonds (Spain), Panda bonds (China), Kangaroo bonds (Australia) and Maple bonds (Canada).

Foreign bonds are regulated by the domestic authority of the country where the bond is issued. These rules can be demanding and an encumbrance to

---

[6] A bond denominated in the issuer's local currency and offered to local residents is a 'domestic bond'.

US bill raises fears for covered bonds

By Jennifer Hughes in London

US proposals for a covered bond market risk wrecking the products' centuries-old reputation for boring stability, an industry group has warned.

European banks are selling record amounts of the bonds, which have their roots in 18th-century Prussia and are backed by pools of loans that remain on a bank's books, unlike the toxic sub-prime securitisations the financial crisis made infamous.

The securities are considered ultra-safe because banks must replace dud loans and the pool is ring-fenced for the bondholders in bankruptcy.

A bill launched in the House of Representatives aims to give US products similar bankruptcy protection, considered vital for banks to get the low borrowing costs the bonds deliver in Europe. But the proposals allow for the US bonds to be backed by a far wider range of assets than is common in

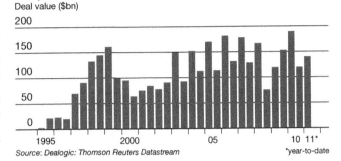

European covered bond issuance
Deal value ($bn)

Source: Dealogic; Thomson Reuters Datastream   *year-to-date

Europe, where up to four-fifths are based on high-quality mortgages.

Jens Tolckmitt, chief executive of the Association of German Pfandbrief Banks, said that using other assets, such as student or car loans, could damage the bonds' reputation if those backed by riskier assets attracted different investors who might not hold their nerve, as investors generally did in the crisis. "European-style covered bonds are bought by a very

stable investor base that likes seemingly boring products," Mr Tolckmitt said. "If you create something that appeals to hedge funds, those investors may not be there in a crisis."

No covered bond has reportedly defaulted, though 19th-century data are sketchy.

Source: *Financial Times*, 28 March 2011, p. 19

Exhibit 11.5   US bill raises fears for covered bonds

companies needing to act quickly and at low cost. The regulatory authorities have also been criticised for stifling innovation in the financial markets. The growth of the less restricted Eurobond market has put the once dominant foreign bond market in the shade.

Not all foreign bonds are issued by companies – the article in Exhibit 11.6 discusses the foreign bond issued by the Philippines government in Japan. Note the influence of LIBOR – even for deals as far away as Japan.

Philippines set to price $1bn of samurai bonds

By Lindsay Whipp in Tokyo and Roel Landing in Manila

The Philippine government is preparing to decide on pricing for up to $1bn of samurai bonds as early as next week as part of a plan to fund a budget deficit likely to reach a record this year.

The samurai bonds – yen-denominated bonds issued by overseas entities to Japanese institutional investors – will be partially guaranteed by the state-owned Japan Bank for International Cooperation, following its agreement last year to facilitate funding for some emerging economies.

JBIC has already provided such partial guarantees for samurai bonds issued last year by Indonesia, Colombia and Mexico. Indonesia has agreed with JBIC to issue $1.5bn of samurai bonds this year.

Guarantees from JBIC will help give Japanese institutional investors the confidence to invest in a country whose government's credit rating is below investment grade (Moody's rates the Philippines Ba3) and buy debt with a wider spread than the highest-rated names that tap the samurai market.

The 10-year bonds are likely to have a spread of 85-95 basis points over Libor, a banker said.

That compares with 10-year samurais sold last week by Rabobank of the Netherlands, which is rated triple A by Moody's and Standard & Poor's, sold with a spread of 35bp over Libor.

Source: Financial Times, 16 February 2010, p. 32

Exhibit 11.6   Philippines set to price $1bn of samurai bonds

Eurobonds (international bonds)

Let's get one misunderstanding out of the way: **Eurobonds** are unconnected with the eurozone currency! They were in existence decades before Europe thought of creating the euro; the first Eurobond issue was in 1963 on the Luxembourg stock exchange, with the $15 million issue by Autostrade, the Italian motorway company. The term 'Euro' in Eurobond does not even mean European.

So what are they then? External bonds is a simple way of describing them. More precisely, Eurobonds are bonds sold outside the jurisdiction of the country of the currency in which the bond is denominated. So, for example, the UK financial regulators have little influence over Eurobonds issued in Luxembourg and denominated in sterling (known as Eurosterling bonds), even though the transactions (e.g. interest and capital payments) are in sterling, and the Autostrade issue, although denominated in US dollars, was not subject to US regulations because it was issued outside the US. Bonds issued in US dollars (Eurodollar bonds) in Paris are outside the jurisdiction of the US authorities.

Eurobonds are medium- to long-term instruments with standard maturities of 3, 5, 7 and 10 years, but there are long maturities of 15 to 30 years driven by pension fund and insurance fund demand for long-dated assets. They are not subject to the rules and regulations which are imposed on foreign bonds, such as the requirement to issue a detailed prospectus.[7] More importantly they are not subject to an **interest-withholding tax**. In many countries the majority of domestic bonds are subject to a withholding tax by which basic rate income tax is deducted before the investor receives interest. Interest on Eurobonds is paid gross without any tax deducted – which has attractions to investors keen on delaying, avoiding or evading tax.

Moreover, Eurobonds are **bearer bonds**, which means that the holders do not have to disclose their identity – all that is required to receive interest and capital is for the holder to have possession of the bond. Eurobond holders are anonymous, making it possible for them to avoid paying tax in their own country. In contrast, domestic bonds are usually **registered**, which means that companies and governments are able to identify the owners. Despite the absence of official regulation, the **International Capital Market Association (ICMA)**, a self-regulatory body, imposes some restrictions, rules and standardised procedures on Eurobond issue and trading.

Eurobonds are distinct from euro bonds, which are bonds denominated in euros and issued in the eurozone countries. Increasingly people differentiate between the two by calling the old-style Eurobonds 'international bonds', leaving the title 'euro' for the currency introduced in 1999. Of course, there have been euro-denominated bonds issued outside the jurisdiction of the authorities in the euro area; these are Euroeurobonds.

The development of the Eurobond (international bond) market

In the 1960s many countries (e.g. the USSR), companies and individuals held surplus dollars outside of the US and were reluctant to hold these funds in American banks under US jurisdiction. Also stringent US tax laws were off-putting, as was the tough regulatory environment in the US domestic financial markets, making it more expensive for foreign institutions to borrow dollars in the US. These factors encouraged investors and borrowers alike to undertake transactions in dollars outside the US. London's strength as a financial centre, the UK authorities' more relaxed attitude to business, and its position in the global time zones made it a natural leader in the Euro markets.

---

[7] Although new EU rules mean that a prospectus is required if the bond is marketed at retail (non-professional) investors.

The market grew modestly through the 1970s and then at a rapid rate in the 1980s. By then the Eurodollar bonds had been joined by bonds denominated in a wide variety of currencies. The market was stimulated not only by the tax and anonymity benefits, which brought a lower cost of finance than for the domestic bonds, but also by the increasing demand from transnational companies and governments needing large sums in alternative currencies and with the potential for innovatory characteristics. It was further boosted by the recycling of dollars from the oil-exporting countries.

In 1979 less than $20 billion worth of bonds were issued in a variety of currencies. The rate of new issuance has grown 100-fold to around $2,000 billion a year, with a total amount outstanding (bonds issued but not yet repaid) of over $26,000 billion – see Exhibit 11.7. Corporations account for a relatively small proportion of the international bond market. The biggest issuers are the banks. Issues by governments ('sovereign issues') and state agencies in the public sector account for less than one-tenth of issues. Other issuers are international agencies such as the World Bank, the International Bank for Reconstruction and Development and the European Investment Bank. The two dominant currencies of issue are the US dollar and the euro, with the euro generally more popular than the dollar. Even though the majority of Eurobond trading takes place through London, sterling is not one of the main currencies, and what is more, it tends to be large US and other foreign banks located in London which dominate the market.

Types of Eurobonds

The Eurobond market has been extraordinarily innovative in producing bonds with all sorts of coupon payment and capital repayment arrangements (e.g. the currency of the coupon changes half-way through the life of the bond, or the interest rate switches from fixed to floating rate at some point). We cannot go into detail here on the rich variety but merely categorise the bonds into four broad types.

1 *Straight fixed-rate bond.* The coupon remains the same over the life of the bond. These are usually paid annually, in contrast to domestic bond semi-annual coupons. The redemption of these bonds is usually made with a 'bullet' repayment at the end of the bond's life.

2 *Equity related.* These take two forms:

   ■ *Bonds with warrants attached.* Warrants are options which give the holder the right but not the obligation to buy some other asset at a given price in the future. An equity warrant, for example, would give the right, but not the obligation, to purchase shares. There are also warrants for

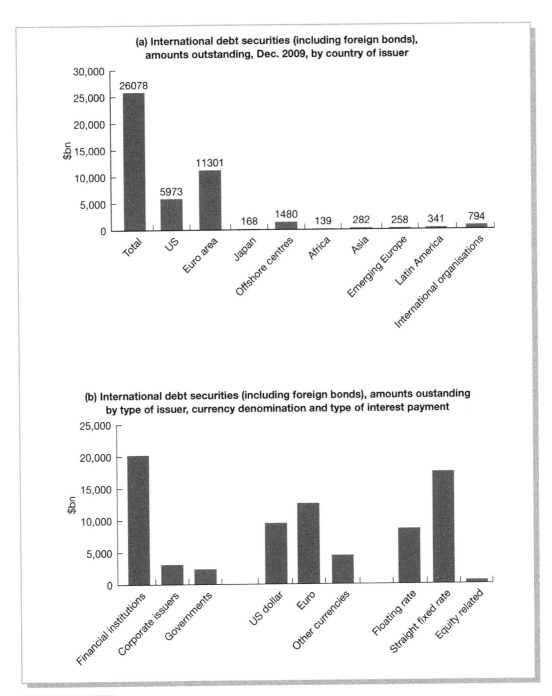

(a) International debt securities (including foreign bonds), amounts outstanding, Dec. 2009, by country of issuer

(b) International debt securities (including foreign bonds), amounts oustanding by type of issuer, currency denomination and type of interest payment

Exhibit 11.7   International bonds and notes outstanding and recent issues

Source: Bank for International Settlements, *Quarterly Review*, March 2010, www.bis.org

commodities such as gold or oil, and for the right to buy additional bonds from the same issuer at the same price and yield as the host bond. Warrants are detachable from the host bond and are securities in their own right, unlike convertibles.

- *Convertibles.* The bondholder has the right (but not the obligation) to convert the bond into ordinary shares at a preset price.

3 *Floating-rate notes (FRNs).* These have a variable coupon reset on a regular basis, usually every three or six months, in relation to a reference rate, such as LIBOR. The size of the spread over LIBOR reflects the perceived risk of the issuer. The typical term for an FRN is about 5 to 12 years.

4 *Zero coupon bonds.* These pay no interest but are sold at a discount to their face value, so that the holder receives his gain in a lump sum at maturity. This is of benefit in countries which have different tax regimes for income (interest payments) and capital gains (the difference between the purchase and selling price of a bond).

Within these broad categories all kinds of **bells and whistles** (features) can be attached to the bonds, for example: **reverse floaters** – the coupon declines as LIBOR rises; and **capped bonds** – the interest rate cannot rise above a certain level. Many bonds have **call-back features** under which the issuer has the right, but not the obligation, to buy the bond back after a period of time has elapsed, say five years, at a price specified when the bond was issued. This might be at the par value but is usually slightly higher. This is obviously not something bondholders favour, especially when the bond price has risen significantly above the par value. Because there are real disadvantages for investors, bonds with call features offer higher interest rates. Issuers like call features because a significant price rise for the bond implies that current market interest rates are considerably less than the coupon rate on the bond. They can buy back and issue new bonds at a lower yield. Also some bonds place tight covenant restrictions on the firm so it is useful to be able to buy them back and issue less restrictive bonds in their place. Finally, exercising the call may permit the corporate to adjust its financial leverage by reducing its debt. Call features are often not operative for the first seven years of a long-dated bond (e.g. 20 years).

A **put feature** gives the bondholder the right, but not the obligation, to sell the bond back to the issuer (usually at par value) on designated dates. It may be a valuable right if interest rates have risen, depressing the price of the bond in the market below what could be achieved by selling to the issuer. The mere existence of the right generally ensures that the price remains above par value. This extra advantage for the holder has to be paid for – usually achieved by the issuer offering a lower yield.

The majority of Eurobonds (more than 80 per cent) are rated AAA or AA although some are issued rated below BBB–. Denominations are usually $1,000, $5,000 or $50,000 (or similar large sums in the currency of issue – known as 1,000, 5,000 or 50,000 lots or pieces).

Issuing Eurobonds

With Eurobonds, and other large bond issues, a bank (**lead manager** or **book runner** or **lead underwriter**) or group of banks acting for the issuer invites a large number of other banks or other investors to buy some of the bonds. The managing group of banks may enlist a number of smaller institutions to use their extensive contacts to sell the bonds (the **selling group** or **syndicate**).[8] Eurobonds are traded on the secondary market through intermediaries acting as market makers. Most Eurobonds are listed on the London, Dublin or Luxembourg stock exchanges but the market is primarily an over-the-counter one, that is, most transactions take place outside a recognised exchange. Most deals are conducted using the telephone, computers, telex and fax, but there are a number of electronic platforms for trading Eurobonds. The extent to which electronic platforms will replace telephone dealing is as yet unclear. It is not possible to go to a central source for price information. Most issues rarely trade. Those that do are generally private transactions between investor and bond dealer and there is no obligation to inform the public about the deal. The prices and yields on some Eurobonds are shown in Exhibits 10.7 and 10.8.

Exhibit 11.8 presents the advantages and disadvantages of Eurobonds.

Euro medium-term notes and domestic medium-term notes

By issuing a note a company promises to pay the holders a certain sum on the maturity date, and in many cases a coupon interest in the meantime. These instruments are typically unsecured and may carry floating or fixed interest rates. **Medium-term notes (MTNs)** have been sold with a maturity of as little as 9 months and as great as 30 years, so the term is a little deceiving. They can be denominated in the domestic currency of the borrower (MTN) or in a foreign

---

[8] In some cases the issuer pays the investment bank(s) a fee to underwrite the bonds on a 'firm commitment' basis, which means that if any of the bonds are not bought by funds etc., then the underwriter will end up holding them. In other cases the bonds are underwritten on a 'best efforts' basis: the issuer accepts that they may receive less than they anticipated as the investment bank does not guarantee sales.

currency (**Euro MTN**). MTNs normally pay an interest rate, usually between 0.2 per cent and 3 per cent over LIBOR.

Advantage	*Drawback*
1 Large loans for long periods are available.	1 Only for the largest companies – minimum realistic issue size is about £50 million.
2 Often cheaper than domestic bonds. The finance provider receives the interest without tax deduction and retains anonymity and therefore supplies cheaper finance. Economies of scale also reduce costs.	2 Because interest and capital are paid in a foreign currency there is a risk that exchange rate movements mean more of the home currency is required to buy the foreign currency than was anticipated.
3 Ability to hedge interest rate and exchange rate risk, e.g. a Canadian corporation buying assets in Europe, such as a company, may finance the asset by taking on a Eurobond liability in euros, thus reducing variability in net value when expressed in Canadian dollars when the C$/€ exchange rate moves.	3 The secondary market can be illiquid.
4 The bonds are usually unsecured. The limitations placed on management are less than those for a secured bond.	
5 The lower level of regulation allows greater innovation and tailor-made financial instruments.	
6 Issuance procedures are simple and bonds can be issued with speed, allowing borrowers to take advantage of an opportunity (e.g. raising money for a corporate purchase) in a timely way.	
7 Being outside the control of governments they cannot be frozen in an international dispute.	

Exhibit 11.8   **Advantages and drawbacks of Eurobonds as a source of finance for corporations**

An **MTN programme** stretching over many years can be set up with one set of legal documents. Then, numerous notes can be issued under the programme in future years. A programme allows greater certainty that the firm will be able to issue an MTN when it needs the finance and allows issuers to bypass the costly and time-consuming documentation associated with each stand-alone note/ bond. The programme can allow for bonds of various qualities, maturities, currencies or type of interest (fixed or floating). Over the years the market can be tapped at short notice in the most suitable form at that time, e.g. US dollars rather than pounds, or redemption in three years rather than in two. It is possible to sell in small denominations (e.g. $5 million), and on a continuous basis, regularly dripping bonds into the market. The banks organising the MTN programme charge a **commitment fee** (around 10 to 15 basis points) for keeping open the option to borrow under an MTN programme, even if the company chooses not to do so in the end. Management fees will also be payable to the syndication of banks organising the MTN facility.

The success of an MTN programme depends on the efficiency of the lead manager and the flexibility of the issuer to match market appetite for lending in particular currencies or maturities with the issuer's demands for funds. The annual cost of running an MTN programme, excluding credit rating agency fees, can be around £100,000. The cost of setting up an MTN programme is high compared with the cost of a single bond issue (and more expensive than most bank debt, except for the very best AAA-, AA- and some A-rated companies). Many companies set one up because they believe that the initial expense is outweighed by the flexibility and cost savings that a programme can provide over time.

Islamic bonds (*sukuk*)

Sukuk (the plural form of the Arabic word Sakk from which the word cheque is derived) are bonds which conform to Shari'ah (Sharia) law, which forbids interest income, or *riba*. There was always a question mark over the ability of modern financing to comply with Islamic (Shari'ah) law which prohibits the charging or paying of interest, and insists that real assets underlie all financial transactions. Ways have been found to participate in the financial world while still keeping to Shari'ah law, although some Islamic scholars oppose some of the instruments created.

Whereas conventional bonds are promises to pay interest and principal, *sukuk* represent part *ownership* of tangible assets, businesses, or investments, so the returns are generated by some sort of share of the gain (or loss) made, and the risk is shared. Money alone should not create a profit and finance should serve the real economy, not just the financial one. They are administered through a **special purpose vehicle (SPV)** which issues *sukuk* certificates. These certificates entitle the holder to a rental income or a profit share from the certificate. *Sukuk* may be issued on existing as well as other specific assets that may become available at a future date.

From an inception in 1975, when the Islamic Development Bank and the Dubai Islamic Bank (the first commercial Islamic bank) were established to operate in strict accordance with Shari'ah law, Islamic banking has made significant progress worldwide, and it is estimated in 2011 that there is over $100 billion of *sukuk* outstanding (and over $1000 billion of Islamic finance, including bank sources).

Currently, there is some confusion over whether investors can always seize the underlying assets in the event of default on a *sukuk*, or whether the assets are merely placed in a *sukuk* structure to comply with Shari'ah law. Lawyers and bankers say that the latter is the case, with most *sukuk* being, in reality, unsecured instruments. They differentiate between 'asset-backed' and 'asset-based' *sukuk*:

- **Asset-backed.** There is a true sale between the originator and the SPV that issues the *sukuk,* and *sukuk* holders do not have recourse to the originator. The value of the assets owned by the SPV, and therefore the *sukuk* holders, may vary over time. The majority of *sukuk* issues are not asset backed.

- **Asset-based.** These are closer to conventional debt in that the *sukuk* holders have recourse to the originator if there is a payment shortfall.

Tesco and Toyota have both issued ringgit *sukuk* in Malaysia. In a further development in November 2009, General Electric (GE) became the first large Western corporation to expand its investor base into this arena with the issuance of its $500 million *sukuk*. The assets underlying these *sukuk* are interests in aircraft and rental payments from aircraft leasing.

The term structure of interest rates

It is not safe to assume that the yield to maturity on a bond remains the same regardless of the length of time of the loan. So, if the interest rate on a three-year bond is 7 per cent per year it may or may not be 7 per cent on a five-year bond of the same risk class. Lenders in the financial markets demand different interest rates on loans of differing lengths of time to maturity – that is, there is a **term structure of the interest rates**. Four of these relationships are shown in Exhibit

11.9 for lending to the UK, eurozone, Japanese and US governments.[9] Note that default (and liquidity) risk remains constant along one of the lines; the reason for the different rates is the time to maturity of the bonds. Thus, a 2-year US government bond has to offer about 1 per cent whereas a 10-year bond offered by the same borrower gives about 3.7 per cent. Note that the yield curve for the eurozone is only for the most creditworthy governments which have adopted the euro (e.g. Germany). Less safe governments had to pay a lot more in 2010 as investors worried whether they would default.

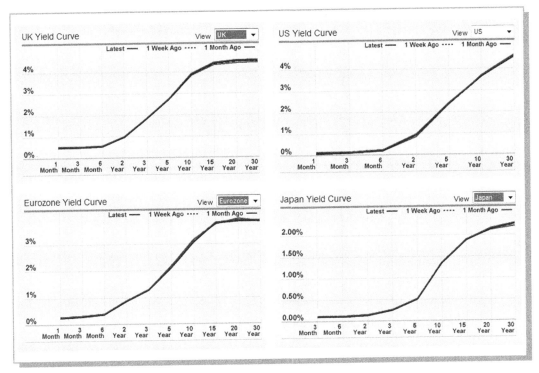

Exhibit 11.9   Yield curves for the UK, US, eurozone and Japanese government bills and bonds

Source: www.markets.ft.com/markets/bonds.asp, 23 March 2010

---

[9] Using the benchmark yield curves as examples of the term structure of interest rates may offend theoretical purity (because we should be using zero coupon bonds rather than those with coupons which have to be reinvested before the redemption date) but they are handy approximate measures and help illustrate this section.

An upward-sloping yield curve occurs in most years, but 2010 demonstrated an extreme upward slope because governments and central banks around the world forced down the short-term interest rates to try to reflate their economies. Occasionally we have a situation where short-term interest rates (lending for, say, one year) exceed those of long-term interest rates (say, a 20-year bond). A downward-sloping term structure (yield curve inversion) and a flat yield curve are shown in Exhibit 11.10.

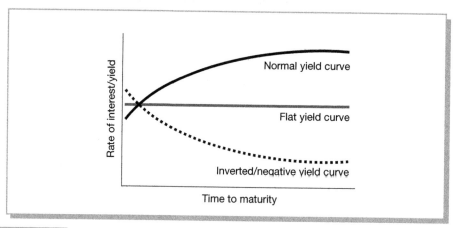

Exhibit 11.10   Upward-sloping, downward-sloping and flat yield curves

Three main hypotheses have been advanced to explain the shape of the yield curve (these are not mutually exclusive).

1 The expectations hypothesis

The **expectations hypothesis** focuses on the changes in interest rates over time. To understand the expectations hypothesis you need to know what is meant by a 'spot rate of interest'. The spot rate is an interest rate fixed today on a loan that is made today. So a corporation, Hype plc, might issue one-year bonds at a spot rate of, say, 8 per cent, two-year bonds at a spot rate of 8.995 per cent and three-year bonds at a spot rate of 9.5 per cent. This yield curve for Hype is shown in Exhibit 11.11. The interest rates payable by Hype are bound to be greater than for the UK government across the yield curve because of the additional default risk on these corporate bonds.

Spot rates change over time. The market may have allowed Hype to issue one-year bonds yielding 8 per cent at a point in time in 2010 but a year later (time 2011) the one-year spot rate may have changed to become 10 per cent. If

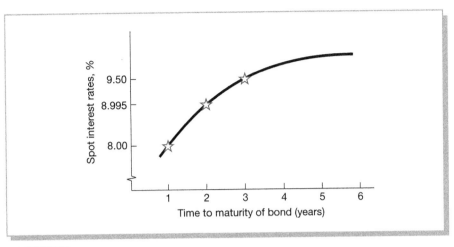

Exhibit 11.11 The term structure of interest rates for Hype plc at time 2010

investors expect that one-year spot rates will become 10 per cent at time 2011 they will have a theoretical limit on the yield that they require from a two-year bond when viewed from time 2010. Imagine that an investor (lender) wishes to lend £1,000 for a two-year period and is contemplating two alternative approaches:

1   Buy a one-year bond at a spot rate of 8 per cent; after one year has passed the bond will come to maturity. The released funds can then be invested in another one-year bond at a spot rate of 10 per cent, expected to be the going rate for bonds of this risk class at time 2011.

2   Buy a two-year bond at the spot rate at time 2010.

Under the first option the lender will have a sum of £1,188 at the end of two years. Given the anticipated change in one-year spot rates to 10 per cent the investor will only buy the two-year bond if it gives the same average annual yield over two years as the first option of a series of one-year bonds. The annual interest required will be 8.995 per cent (the maths for this is in Chapter 11 of Glen Arnold, *Corporate Financial Management*, FT Prentice Hall).

Thus, it is the expectation of spot interest rates changing which determines the shape of the yield curve according to the expectations hypothesis.

2 The liquidity-preference hypothesis

The expectations hypothesis does not adequately explain why the most common shape of the yield curve is upward sloping. The **liquidity-preference** hypothesis (**liquidity premium theory**) helps explain the upward slope by pointing out that investors require an extra return for lending on a long-term basis. Lenders demand a premium return on long-term bonds compared with short-term instruments because of greater interest rate risk and the risk of misjudging future interest rates. Putting your money into a 10-year bond on the anticipation of particular levels of interest rates exposes you to the possibility that rates will rise above the rate offered on the bond at some point in its long life. Thus, if five years later interest rates double, say because of a rise in inflation expectations, the market price of the bond will fall substantially, leaving the holder with a large capital loss. On the other hand, by investing in a series of one-year bonds, the investor can take advantage of rising interest rates as they occur. The 10-year bond locks in a fixed rate for the full 10 years if held to maturity. Investors prefer short-term bonds so that they can benefit from rising rates and so will accept a lower return on short-dated instruments. The liquidity-preference theory focuses on a different type of risk attaching to long-dated debt instruments other than default risk – a risk related to uncertainty over future interest rates. A suggested reinforcing factor to the upward slope is that borrowers usually prefer long-term debt because of the fear of having to repay short-term debt at inappropriate moments. Thus borrowers increase the supply of long-term debt instruments, adding to the tendency for long-term rates to be higher than short-term rates.

Note that the word liquidity in the title is incorrectly used – but it has stuck so we still use it. Liquidity refers to the speed and ease of the sale of an asset. In the case of long-term bonds (especially government bonds) sale in the secondary market is often as quick and easy as for short-term bonds. The premium for long-term bonds is compensation for the extra risk of capital loss; 'term premium' might be a better title for the hypothesis.

3 The market-segmentation hypothesis

The **market-segmentation hypothesis** argues that the debt market is not one homogeneous whole, that there are, in fact, a number of sub-markets defined by maturity range. The yield curve is therefore created (or at least influenced) by the supply and demand conditions in each of these sub-markets. For example, banks tend to be active in the short-term end of the market and pension funds to be buyers in the long-dated segment.

If banks need to borrow large quantities quickly they will sell some of their short-term instruments, increasing the supply on the market and pushing down the price and raising the yield. On the other hand, pension funds may be flush with cash and may buy large quantities of 20-year bonds, helping to temporarily move yields downward at the long end of the market. At other times banks, pension funds and the buying and selling pressures of a multitude of other financial institutions will influence the supply and demand position in the opposite direction. The point is that the players in the different parts of the yield curve tend to be different. This hypothesis helps to explain the often lumpy or humped yield curve.

A final thought on the term structure of interest rates

It is sometimes thought that in circumstances of a steeply rising yield curve it would be advantageous to borrow short term rather than long term. However, this can be a dangerous strategy because long-term debt may be trading at a higher rate of interest because of the expected rise in spot short-term rates and so when the borrower comes to refinance in, say, a year's time, the short-term interest rate is much higher than the long-term rate and this high rate has to be paid out of the second year's cash flows, which may not be convenient.

Websites

www.treasurers.org	Association of Corporate Treasurers
www.bankofengland.co.uk	Bank of England
www.bis.org	Bank for International Settlements
www.bloomberg.com,	Bloomberg
www.bondscape.net	Bondscape
www.economist.com	Economist
www.ft.com/bonds&rates	Financial Times
www.fitchratings.com	Fitch
www.icma-group.co.uk	International Capital Market Association
www.BondMarketPrices.com	International Capital Market Association – bond prices pages
www.investorschronicle.co.uk/bonds	Investors Chronicle bond prices, yield, etc.
www.adr.com	JPMorgan
www.moodys.com	Moody's
www.standardandpoors.com	Standard & Poor's

12

Equity markets

Equity markets are often portrayed as casinos. News reports show frantic traders speculating on where prices are going next, becoming euphoric if the shares have had a good run up, or thoroughly depressed if the market is down. Indeed, it is fair to say that there are many people who treat the equity markets as places to make a quick buck, who spend their lives and great deal of money trying to gain a short-term trading edge over others, not bothering to understand the underlying businesses behind the shares.

This image is unfortunate because alongside the speculators are millions of investors who genuinely try to understand the long-term prospects for a company, calculating a value for it and then deciding whether to allocate money to the firm to help it grow, to build that new factory, to make recently-invented medical instruments, or that latest mobile phone. Through the actions of these investors society gains new products, industries and wealth as money is taken from the dying sectors and reallocated to the new frontiers. It is not only society at large that benefits from the presence of equity markets. Anyone with savings in a pension scheme will want a portion of that money placed in shares with prospects of high rates of return over the next few decades.

To meet these societal needs stock markets have evolved through their history, never more so than in the past decade. Where before we had national stock markets in the financial centres of each country, today we have many markets combining to form international groups such as NYSE Euronext. To provide some competition for the national monopolies we have seen the growth of alternative trading platforms such as multilateral trading facilities and dark pools. At the same time technological innovation has changed the method of trading shares so that it is now very much built around sophisticated computer systems that can handle millions of transactions in a day, and can complete thousands of trades in less than the time it takes to blink. We have also seen the amazing growth of stock markets in Asia, to the point where they are a serious challenge to the old centres of equity finance in Europe and North America. Indeed, it is a fairly safe prediction to say that many Asian markets will come to be at least as great as London and New York in the next few years. This makes sense: every society needs equity investors to assist growth through the mobilisation of savings into productive use; and every investor would prefer to have the liquidity that is offered by stock markets than have the difficulty of finding a buyer should they need to sell.

The value of equity

Society needs people who are willing to take the risk of total failure of a business enterprise. Banks are not willing to accept that risk. They strike deals with companies whereby even if the profits are low or a loss is made they are still paid interest and capital. Also, they usually require collateral so that if the business plan turns out to be a dud the bank can recoup its money by selling off property or other assets (or, at least most of its money most of the time). Holders of other forms of debt capital, such as bonds, take similar low-risk/low-return deals.

Imagine if debt were the only form of capital available for businesses to grow. Very few would be established because it would be rare for managers to come across an investment project (e.g. new product-line factory) that offered the lenders the security they need. I can only think of one company that is virtually completely financed by debt. This is the water company for Wales. It can get away without many shares (equity) because there is so little uncertainty regarding its future income. It is regulated and the bills it charges to customers are highly predictable for years to come and so it can offer its lenders high security, not just from its cash flow but also from the land, reservoirs, etc. that it owns.

Now consider a company producing TV programmes. Could it finance itself entirely with debt? No, because if £100 million was put in by lenders to invest in 10 TV serials there is nothing for them to fall back on should one-half of shows be poorly received by viewers, or even if one-tenth is poorly received. They might be willing to lend, say, £40 million if the other £60 million came from investors who were willing to accept the risk of total loss. Then the lenders know that their money is likely to be reasonably safe (assuming that they have faith in the track record of the executives in charge and the historical statistics suggest that only two or three programmes are likely to be commercial flops). Naturally, the risk takers providing this £60 million of capital will want a high reward for putting their hard earned savings to such an exposure. They would also want some say over who the directors of the company are, and want the power to vote down major moves proposed by the managers. They will also require regular information on progress. These holders of shares in the success or failure of the enterprise act as shock-absorbers so that other parties contributing to a firm, from suppliers and creditors to bankers and leasing companies, do not have to bear the shock of a surprise recession, a loss of market share to competitors or a badly made TV series.

Another attractive feature of share capital for building businesses is that it does not have a date at which it will be redeemed by the company. Thus the managers (and creditors) know that the capital will be available for the very long term, that the shareholders cannot turn around one day and demand their money back.

Ordinary shares represent the equity capital of the firm and are a means of raising long-term finance to run the business. The holders of these securities share in the (hopefully) rising prosperity of a company. These investors, as owners of the firm, have the right to exercise some control over the company. They can vote at shareholder meetings to determine such crucial matters as the composition of the team of directors. They can also vote on major strategic and policy issues such as the type of activities that the firm might engage in, or the decision to merge with another firm. These ordinary shareholders have a claim to a share of the company's profits in the form of dividend payments, and in a worst-case scenario, a right to share in the proceeds of a liquidation sale of the firm's assets, albeit after all other creditors such as banks, tax authorities, trade creditors, etc. have been paid.

Annual, semi-annual or quarterly dividend payments are paid at the discretion of the directors, and individual shareholders are often effectively powerless to influence the income from a share – not only because of the risk attached to the trading profits which generate the resources for a dividend, but also because of the relative power of directors in a firm with a disparate or divided shareholder body. If a shareholder owns 100 shares of a company with millions of shares in issue, there is little likelihood of this person exerting any influence at all; institutional shareholders who often own very large amounts of shares are able to bring more pressure to bear.

Usually the lenders to the firm have no official control; they are unable to vote at general meetings and therefore cannot choose directors and determine major strategic issues. However, there are circumstances in which lenders have significant influence. For instance, they may insist that the company does not exceed certain liquidity or solvency ratio levels (not too much debt), or they may take a charge over a particular building as security for a loan, thus restricting the directors' freedom of action over the use and disposal of that building.

The attraction of holding shares is that if the company does well there are no limits to the size of the claim equity shareholders have on profit. There have been numerous instances of investors placing modest sums into the shares of young firms who find themselves millionaires. For example, if you had bought $1,000 worth of shares in Google in 1999, your holding would now be worth millions.

An attraction of share issuing for companies is that unlike a loan, share finance does not have to be repaid, which can be helpful if the company is short of cash. Offsetting this are some disadvantages; issuing shares is a costly business (share investors require higher rates of return and the transaction costs of the issue process can be high – see the next chapter on the costs of share issuance); issuing shares to external investors may mean loss of ultimate control of the company by the current dominant shareholders.

There is some lack of clarity as to the distinction between stocks and shares. Shares are equities in companies; stocks are financial instruments that pay interest (e.g. bonds). However, in the US shares are also called **common stocks** and the shareholders are usually referred to as the **stockholders**. So when some people use the term 'stocks' they could be referring to either bonds or shares.

Preference shares

Preference shares usually offer their owners a fixed rate of dividend each year. However if the firm has insufficient profits the amount paid may be reduced, sometimes to zero. Thus, there is no guarantee that an annual income will be received, unlike with debt capital. The dividend on preference shares is paid before anything is paid out to ordinary shareholders – indeed, after the preference dividend obligation has been met there may be nothing left for ordinary shareholders. Preference shares are attractive to some investors because they offer a regular income at a higher rate of return than that available on fixed interest securities (e.g. bonds). However this higher return also comes with higher risk, as the preference dividend ranks after bond interest, and upon liquidation preference holders are further back in the queue as recipients of the proceeds of asset sell-offs.

Preference shares are part of shareholders' funds but are not equity share capital. The holders are not usually able to benefit from any extraordinarily good performance of the firm – any profits above expectations go to the ordinary shareholders. Also preference shares usually carry no voting rights, except if the dividend is in arrears or in the case of liquidation. Many preference share prices and other data are listed in the financial pages of newspapers.

Advantages to the firm of preference share capital

These are the advantages:

- *Dividend 'optional'*. Preference dividends can be omitted for one or more years, giving more flexibility and a greater chance of surviving a downturn in trading.

- *Influence over management*. Preference shares are an additional source of capital which, because they do not have voting rights, do not dilute the influence of the ordinary shareholders. Thus it is possible to raise shareholder capital and retain voting control.

- *Extraordinary profits*. Preference shareholders receive a set return and do not share in extraordinary profits (unless the preference shares are 'participating' – see below).

- *Financial gearing considerations*. There are limits to safe levels of borrowing. If a firm is unable to raise finance by borrowing, preference shares are an alternative source of financing, if shareholders are unwilling to provide more equity risk capital. They can be an alternative, though less effective, shock-absorber in a year of poor profits to selling more ordinary shares.

Disadvantages to the firm of preference share capital

These are the disadvantages:

- *High cost of capital*. The higher risk attached to the annual returns and capital cause preference shareholders to demand a higher level of return than debtholders.

- *Dividends are not tax deductible*. Tax is payable on the firm's profit before the deduction of the preference dividend (as it is for ordinary share dividends). In contrast, interest has to be paid whether or not a profit is made. This cost is regarded as a legitimate expense reducing taxable profit – see Exhibit 12.1. Both firms have raised £1 million, but Company A sold bonds yielding 8 per cent, Company B sold preference shares offering a dividend yield of 8 per cent.

Types of preference shares

There are a number of variations on the theme of preference share. Here are some additional features:

- *Cumulative*. If dividends are missed in any year the right to receive a dividend is carried forward. These prior-year dividends have to be paid before any payout to ordinary shareholders.

	Company A Raised £1 million by selling bonds yielding 8%	Company B Raised £1 million by issuing preference shares with 8% yield
Profits before tax, dividends and interest	200,000	200,000
Interest payable on bonds	(80,000)	0
Taxable profit	120,000	200,000
Tax payable @ 30 per cent of taxable profit	(36,000)	(60,000)
Profit after tax	84,000	140,000
Preference dividend	(0)	(80,000)
Available for ordinary shareholders	84,000	60,000

Company A has a lower tax bill because its bond interest is used to reduce taxable profit, resulting in an extra £24,000 (£84,000 – £60,000) available for ordinary shareholders.

Exhibit 12.1 The effect of the tax deductibility of interest and the non-tax deductibility of preference share dividends

▪ *Participating.* As well as the fixed payment, the dividend may be increased if the company has high profits. (Usually the additional payment is a proportion of any ordinary dividend declared.)

▪ *Redeemable.* These have a finite life, at the end of which the initial capital investment will be repaid.

▪ *Irredeemables.* Have no fixed redemption date.

▪ *Convertibles.* These can be converted at the holder's request into ordinary shares at specific dates and on pre-set terms (e.g. one ordinary share for every two preference shares). These shares often carry a lower dividend yield since there is the attraction of a potentially large capital gain.

▪ *Variable rate.* A variable dividend is paid. The rate may be linked to general interest rates (e.g. LIBOR), or to some other variable factor.

Some unusual types of shares

In addition to ordinary shares and preference shares there are other, more unusual, types of shares.

Non-voting shares or reduced voting shares

These are sometimes issued by family-controlled firms which need additional equity finance but wish to avoid the diluting effects of an ordinary share issue. These shares are often called 'A' shares or 'B' shares (or N/V) and usually get the same dividends and the same share of assets in a liquidation as voting shares. The issue of non-voting or reduced voting shares is contentious, with many in the financial markets saying that everyone who puts equity into a company should have a vote on how that money is spent: the 'one share one vote' principle. On the other hand, investors can buy 'non-voters' for less than 'voters' and thereby gain a higher dividend yield. Also, without the possibility of issuing non-voting shares, many companies would simply prefer to forgo expansion. Around one-third of Europe's largest businesses fail to observe the one share one vote principle. And in America the Ford family own a mere 3.75 per cent of the shares; but when the motor company joined the NYSE in 1956 the family's shares were converted into a special class that guaranteed 40 per cent of the voting power, no matter how many ordinary shares are in issue. When Google floated in 2004 Larry Page and Sergey Brin, the founders, held 'B' shares each with 10 times as many votes per share as the 'A' shares issued to other investors. In the UK there are relatively few companies with reduced voting rights compared with continental Europe.

Deferred ordinary shares

These rank lower than ordinary shares for an agreed rate of dividend, so in a poor year the ordinary holders might get their payment while deferred ordinary holders receive nothing.

Golden shares

These are shares with extraordinary special powers, for example the right to block a takeover or to restrict the influence of minority shareholders. Governments hold golden shares in some of the biggest companies in the UK and Europe (Royal Mail Group, Rolls-Royce, National Air Traffic Control, BAE Systems, BAA and Eurostar in the UK, VW and Portugal Teleco). However European law states that golden shares are contrary to the EU principle of the free movement of capital and as such are illegal. Their numbers have dwindled.

Stock exchanges around the world

What is a stock market?

Stock markets are places where governments and industries can raise long-term capital and investors can buy and sell various types of financial instruments. Stock exchanges[1] grew in response to the demand for funds to finance investment and (especially in the early days) ventures in overseas trade. Until the Napoleonic Wars the Dutch capital markets were pre-eminent, raising funds for investment abroad and loans for governments and businesses, and developing a thriving secondary market in which investors could sell their financial securities to other investors.

Much early industrialisation was financed by individuals or partnerships, but as the capital requirements became larger it was clear that **joint-stock enterprises** were needed, in which the money of numerous investors was brought together to give joint ownership with the promise of a share of profits. Canal corporations, docks companies, manufacturing enterprises, railways, mining, brewing and insurance companies were added to the list of firms with shares and bonds traded on the stock exchanges of Europe, America and a few places in Asia in the nineteenth century.

Growth of stock markets

Since the nineteenth century stock markets have prospered and expanded globally. New markets have appeared in developing countries, to join and rival the traditional stock markets. Exhibit 12.2 details the relative sizes of the older and more established stock exchanges according to the total market capitalisation (number of shares multiplied by share price) of the companies traded on them.

The world has changed dramatically in the past 30 years. Liberalisation and the accelerating wave of privatisation pushed stock markets to the forefront of developing countries' tools of economic progress. The strong ideological opposition to capitalism has been replaced with stock markets in Moscow, Warsaw and Sofia. Even countries which still espouse communism, such as China and Vietnam, now have thriving and increasingly influential stock exchanges designed to facilitate the mobilisation of capital and its employment in productive endeavour, with – 'horror-of-horrors' to some hard-line communists – a return going to the capital providers.

---

[1] Stock exchange and stock market will be used interchangeably. Bourse is an alternative word used particularly in Continental Europe.

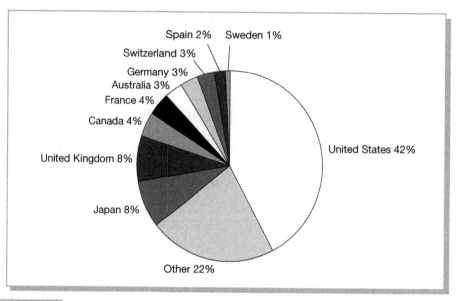

Exhibit 12.2   Relative sizes of global stock markets by market capitalisation

Source: © 2011 Elroy Dimson, Paul Marsh and Mike Staunton, *Credit Suisse Global Investment Returns Yearbook 2011*, Credit Suisse Research Institute. Elroy Dimson, Paul Marsh and Mike Staunton are authors of *Triumph of the Optimists: 101 Years of Global Investment Returns*, Princeton University Press, 2002.

China has two thriving stock exchanges, in Shanghai and Shenzhen, with over 2,000 companies listed. There are now tens of millions of Chinese investors who can only be properly described as 'capitalists' given that they put at risk their savings on the expectations of a reward on their capital. Exhibit 12.3 describes the rivalry between China's two main markets.

Today the important contribution of stock exchanges to economic well-being is recognised from Uzbekistan to Uruguay. There are now over 100 countries with exchanges and many of these countries have more than one exchange. Many markets have been amalgamated with larger ones; the London Stock Exchange, LSE, merged with the Borsa Italiana in 2007; the NYSE merged in 2006 with the Euronext group, itself a merger of the Paris, Amsterdam, Brussels and Lisbon exchanges, in 2008 with the American Stock Exchange, and in 2011 it is attempting to merge with Deutsche Börse; the US market NASDAQ merged in 2007 with OMX, the Scandinavian and Baltic group of exchanges (Stockholm, Helsinki, Copenhagen and Iceland, and Estonia, Latvia, Lithuania and Armenia) and also with the Boston and Philadelphia exchanges, with the result that NASDAQ OMX is the largest US electronic exchange, listing over 2,700

Shenzhen takes over as China's listing hub

By Robert Cookson in Hong Kong

For years, Shanghai has been the undisputed king of China's equity markets, vitalised by a steady stream of initial public offerings from the country's biggest and best state-owned enterprises.

But this year Shanghai has been outgunned by Shenzhen, its less glamorous rival in the south of China, because of an extraordinary boom there in IPOs by smaller, private companies.

The Shenzhen Stock Exchange has seen 246 companies raise a record $33.6bn by new listings this year, triple last year's total and much more than the $24.1bn raised in Shanghai...

Most of the companies listing in Shenzhen are small and medium-sized groups owned by private entrepreneurs, as opposed to the state-owned behemoths that typically gravitate to Shanghai.

"Chinese policymakers have seen the central importance to the country's future of allowing private companies greater access to private flows of equity capital," says Mr Fuhrman, chairman of China First Capital.

Shenzhen's IPO boom represents a substantial fresh source of capital for smaller private companies, which have typically been starved of funds by a state-owned banking system that has preferred to lend to other organs of the government.

The bourse is also an increasingly attractive place for private equity groups to make lucrative exits from their investments in China....

Shenzhen is still a relatively small part of China's financial system – the Rmb220bn ($33bn) raised by IPOs there this year is dwarfed by the Rmb6,000bn-plus in new loans that Chinese banks have extended during the same period.

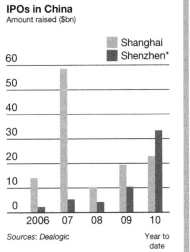

IPOs in China
Amount raised ($bn)

Shanghai
Shenzhen*

Sources: Dealogic   Year to date

But the IPO bonanza represents an important step in the evolution of China's financial markets.

Source: *Financial Times*, 19 October 2010

companies in the US and another 778 in Europe. In addition to actual mergers, many stock exchanges have holdings in other exchanges or have mutual trading agreements. For instance, the Tokyo Stock Exchange has a 4.9 per cent shareholding in the Singapore exchange.

Exhibit 12.4 focuses on the share trading aspect of 20 of these markets, but most markets usually also trade bonds and other securities. Note the size and importance now of markets outside Europe and North America.

End of 2010	Domestic equities market capitalisation* $ million	Total share trading in year $ million	Number of listed companies		
			Total	Domestic	Foreign
NYSE Euronext (US element only)	13,394,082	17,795,600	2,317	1,799	518
NASDAQ OMX (US element only)	3,889,370	12,659,198	2,778	2,480	298
Tokyo SE Group	3,827,774	3,787,952	2,293	2,281	12
London SE Group	3,613,064	2,741,325	2,966	2,362	604
NYSE Euronext (Europe)	2,930,072	2,018,077	1,135	983	152
Shanghai SE	2,716,470	4,496,194	894	894	NA
Hong Kong Exchanges	2,711,316	1,496,433	1,413	1,396	17
TSX (TMX) Group (Canada)	2,170,433	1,368,954	3,741	3,654	87
Bombay SE	1,631,830	258,696	5,034	5,034	NA
National Stock Exchange India	1,596,625	801,017	1,552	1,551	1
BM&FBOVESPA (Brazil)	1,545,566	868,813	381	373	8
Australian SE	1,454,491	1,062,650	1,999	1,913	86
Deutsche Börse	1,429,719	1,628,496	765	690	75
Shenzhen SE	1,311,370	3,572,529	1,169	1,169	0
SIX Swiss Exchange	1,229,357	788,361	296	246	50
BME Spanish Exchanges	1,171,625	1,360,910	3,345	3,310	35
Korea Exchange	1,091,911	1,607,247	1,798	1,781	17
NASDAQ OMX Nordic Exchange (European element)	1,042,154	750,279	778	752	26
MICEX (Russia)	949,149	408,078	250	249	1
Johannesburg SE	925,007	340,025	397	352	45

* The total value, at market prices, of all issued shares of companies quoted on the stock market.

Exhibit 12.4   The world's 20 largest stock exchanges at the end of 2010, ranked according to domestic market capitalisation of equities

Source: World Federation of Exchanges: www.worldexchanges.org.

A comparison of the major markets

Until quite recently the London Stock Exchange, LSE, was the leading stock exchange in the world for trading shares in overseas companies and one of the biggest for the trading of domestic company shares. However the electronic revolution and mergers have dramatically increased the market in foreign equity trading in the US, and NYSE Euronext and NASDAQ OMX now head the field in both foreign and domestic trading, see Exhibits 12.5 and 12.6. Looking only at domestic (home-grown companies) equity: China's domestic trading has shown a huge increase as it opens itself to capitalism.

More mergers and alliances between exchanges are bound to follow, not least because the major financial institutions that operate across the globe desire a seamless, less costly way of trading shares over borders. The ultimate ambition for some visionaries is a single highly liquid equity market allowing investors to trade and companies to raise capital, wherever it suits them, or at least to do so within a continent such as Europe. Ideally there would be no distortions in share price, costs of trading or regulation as investors cross from one country to another. Whether it is necessary to merge altogether Europe's disparate stock

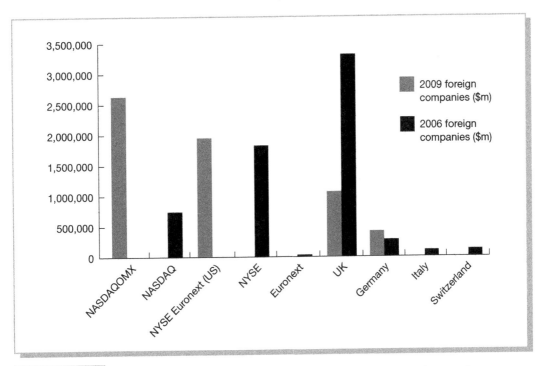

Exhibit 12.5   Value of equity trading in foreign companies on stock exchanges in year

Source: World Federation of Exchanges

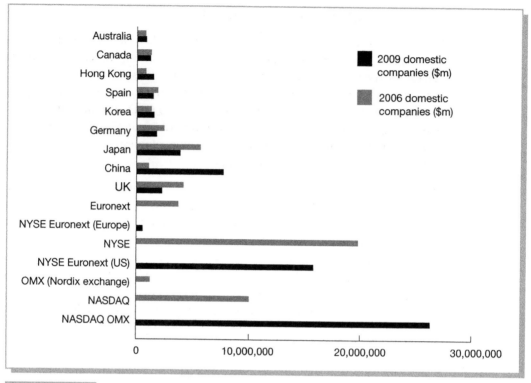

Exhibit 12.6   Value of equity trading in domestic companies on stock exchanges in year

Source: World Federation of Exchanges

exchanges to achieve frictionless pan-European trading is a matter that is currently hotly debated. Some argue that the absence of a single securities market damages the EU's competitive position *vis-à-vis* the huge, streamlined and highly liquid US capital markets. Furthermore, they say, it prevents European companies and investors enjoying the full benefits of the euro.

The importance of a well-run stock exchange

A well-run stock exchange has a number of characteristics. It is one where a **'fair game'** takes place; that is, where it is not possible for some investors and fund raisers to benefit at the expense of other participants – all players are on a level playing field. It is a market which is well regulated to avoid abuses, negligence and fraud in order to reassure investors who put their savings at risk. It is also one in which it is reasonably cheap to carry out transactions. In addition, a large number of buyers and sellers are likely to be needed for the efficient price setting of shares and to provide sufficient liquidity, allowing the investor to sell at any time without altering the market price. There are six main benefits of a well-run stock exchange.

1 Firms can find funds and grow

Because investors in financial securities with a stock market quotation are assured that they are, generally, able to sell their shares quickly, cheaply and with a reasonable degree of certainty about the price, they are willing to supply funds to firms at a lower cost than they would if selling was slow, or expensive, or the sale price was subject to much uncertainty.

2 Allocation of capital

One of the key economic problems for a nation is finding a mechanism for deciding what mixture of goods and services to produce. An extreme solution has been tried and shown to be lacking in sophistication – that of a **totalitarian directed economy** where bureaucratic diktat determines the exact quantity of each line of commodity produced. The alternative method favoured in most nations (for the majority of goods and services) is to let the market decide what will be produced and which firms will produce it.

An efficiently functioning stock market is able to assist this process through the flow of investment capital. If the stock market was poorly regulated and operated then the mis-pricing of shares and other financial securities could lead to society's scarce capital resources being put into sectors which are inappropriate given the objective of maximising economic well-being. If, for instance, the market priced the shares of a badly managed company in a declining industrial sector at a high level then that firm would find it relatively easy to sell shares and raise funds for further investment in its business or to take over other firms. This would deprive companies with better prospects and with a greater potential contribution to make to society of essential finance.

To take an extreme example: imagine the year is 1910 and on the stock market are some firms which manufacture horse-drawn carriages. There are also one or two young companies which have taken up the risky challenge of producing motor cars. Analysts will examine the prospects of the two types of enterprise before deciding which firms will get a warm reception when they ask for more capital in a sale of shares. The unfavoured firms will find their share prices falling as investors sell their shares, and will be unable to attract more savers' money. One way for the older firm to stay in business would be to shift resources within the firm to the production of those commodities for which consumer demand is on a rising trend. More recently there has been a dramatic shift in finance resources as markets supplied hundreds of billions to high-technology industries, such as mobile phone chip technology, for example, the Cambridge-based company, ARM plc, that designs and licenses 95 per cent of the world's chips for mobiles.

3 For shareholders

Shareholders benefit from the availability of a speedy, cheap secondary market if they want to sell. Not only do shareholders like to know that they can sell shares when they want to, they may simply want to know the market value of their holdings even if they have no intention of selling at present. By contrast, an unquoted firm's shareholders often find it very difficult to assess the value of their holding.

Founders of firms may be particularly keen to obtain a quotation for their firms. This will enable them to diversify their assets by selling a proportion of their holdings. Also, venture capital firms which fund unquoted firms during their rapid growth phase often press the management to aim for a quotation to permit the venture capitalist to have the option of realising the gains made on the original investment, or simply to boost the value of their holding by making it more liquid.

4 Status and publicity

The public profile of a firm can be enhanced by being quoted on an exchange. Banks and other financial institutions generally have more confidence in a quoted firm and therefore are more likely to provide funds at a lower cost. Their confidence is raised because the company's activities are now subject to detailed scrutiny. The publicity surrounding the process of gaining a quotation may have a positive impact on the image of the firm in the eyes of customers, suppliers and employees and so may lead to a beneficial effect on their day-to-day business.

5 Mergers

Mergers can be facilitated better by a quotation. This is especially true if the payments offered to the target firm's shareholders for their holdings are shares in the acquiring firm. A quoted share has a value defined by the market, whereas shares in unquoted firms are difficult to assess. The stock exchange also assists what is called 'the **market in managerial control**'. This is a mechanism in which teams of managers are seen as competing for control of corporate assets. Or, to put it more simply, mergers through the stock market permit the displacement of inefficient management with a more successful team. Thus, according to this line of reasoning, assets will be used more productively and society will be better off. This market in managerial control is not as effective as is sometimes claimed (it tends to be over-emphasised by acquiring managers).

6 Improves corporate behaviour

If a firm's shares are traded on an exchange, the directors may be encouraged to behave in a manner conducive to shareholders' interests. This is achieved through a number of pressure points. For example, to obtain a quotation on a reputable exchange, companies are required to disclose a far greater range and depth of information than is required by accounting standards or the Companies Acts. This information is then disseminated widely and can become the focus of much public and press comment. Before a company is admitted to an exchange the authorities insist on being assured that the management team is sufficiently competent and, if necessary, additional directors are appointed to supplement the board's range of knowledge and skills. In addition, investment analysts ask for regular briefings from senior managers and continuously monitor the performance of firms. For a quoted company, directors are required to consult shareholders on important decisions, such as mergers, when the firm is quoted. They also have to be very careful to release price-sensitive information in a timely and orderly fashion and they are strictly forbidden to use inside information to make a profit by buying or selling the firm's shares.

Tasks for stock exchanges

Traditionally, exchanges perform the following tasks in order to play their valuable role in a modern society:

- supervision of trading to ensure fairness and efficiency;

- the authorisation of market participants such as brokers and market makers;

- creation of an environment in which prices are formed efficiently and without distortion (**price discovery** or **price formation**): this requires not only regulation of a high order and low transaction cost but also a liquid market in which there are many buyers and sellers, permitting investors to enter or exit quickly without moving the price;

- organisation of the **settlement** of transactions (after the deal has been struck the buyer must pay for the shares and the shares must be transferred to the new owners);

- the regulation of the admission of companies to the exchange and the regulation of companies on the exchange;

- the dissemination of information (e.g. trading data, prices and company announcements): investors are more willing to trade if prompt and complete information about trades, companies and prices is available.

In recent years there has been a questioning of the need for stock exchanges to carry out all these activities. If we take the case of the LSE, the settlement of transactions was long ago handed over to CREST (discussed later in this chapter). Also the responsibility for authorising the listing of companies was transferred to the UK Listing Authority arm of the Financial Services Authority (the principal UK regulator). The LSE's **Regulatory News Service** (which distributes important company announcements and other price-sensitive news) now has to compete with other distribution platforms outside the LSE's control as listed companies are now able to choose between competing providers of news dissemination platforms.

New trading systems

Multilateral Trading Facilities (MTFs)

Traditional stock exchanges had virtual monopoly positions for the trading of shares and other securities in their home countries. They had little incentive to cut fees or to improve their trading technology. This resulted in the main users, institutional investment funds, banks, brokers and hedge funds becoming frustrated with the raw deal they were getting.

Starting in the US in the early 2000s they determined that the national stock exchanges could do with some competition, so they got together, chipped in a few million for start-up costs and created new trading platforms. These were equipped with nimbler technology and required far fewer staff than the traditional exchanges. They had narrower differences between the price to buy (bid) and the price to sell (offer) a share, lower execution (transaction) costs and the time between sending an order and the order being complete was much faster than the traditional exchanges. Not only did the institutions now have a cheaper way of trading shares but they could also use the presence of the new trading platforms to force the old exchanges to change their ways.

The Americans called these platforms **electronic communications networks, ECNs**. They are also known as **multilateral trading facilities, MTFs** (a term more favoured in Europe), and they have certainly had an effect. As recently as 2003 about 80 per cent of the trading volume in the shares listed on the NYSE was handled by the NYSE itself. Today less than one-quarter of the trades go through the NYSE; the rest are traded through a number of MTFs including BATS, Direct Edge and ArcaEx (and 'dark pools' – see later). NYSE is not alone; NASDAQ has lost a lot of trade to the new venues as well.

A major breakthrough in Europe occurred in November 2007, with the introduction of the EU's **Markets in Financial Instruments Directive (Mifid)** which has the aim of providing a 'harmonised regulatory regime for investment services across the 30 member states of the European Economic Area. The main objectives of the Directive are to increase competition and consumer protection in investment services'. Following this Directive, brokers acting on behalf of share (and other security) buyers and sellers must now demonstrate that they are achieving the keenest price and using the most efficient, cost-effective trading venues.[3] This encouraged the establishment of cheaper and faster electronic trading platforms to challenge the old ones. And, of course, European institutional investors were just as keen as their US counterparts to have alternatives to the national exchanges.

These traditional stock markets have lost a lot of trade to the new generation of European MTFs (such as BATS Europe, Chi-X and Turquoise). These trade the shares from companies quoted on a variety of national exchanges across Europe, and they are far less strictly regulated than stock markets. As recently as 2007 shares in the FTSE 100 index were traded largely through the LSE. Today there are 20 alternative trading platforms, five of which are MTFs (the others are 'dark pools' – discussed later). MTFs have taken around a one-third share of continental European share trading and about one-half of trading in large UK companies' shares, causing a drop in volume of trading at the LSE and other traditional stock exchanges. Japan has joined the movement. It now has five new competing trading venues outside the Tokyo Stock Exchange, but they are not (yet) taking much market share as the TSE's fees are not considered expensive and it offers a fast trading service.

The proliferation of trading venues means that prices are increasingly being set for shares in a number of different places. In 2007 Rolls-Royce's shares were publically traded in one place; now they are bought and sold on 14 platforms. This raises the difficulty of maintaining the quality of high transparency in trades required to promote trust in the market process. While the prices on the different platforms track one another only those traders with very sophisticated systems for seeing the trades going through each of the 14 venues can know what is going on, and whether there are opportunities to buy or sell quickly when discrepancies in prices make it worthwhile. This benefits linked-up traders who can act fast, but this is at the expense of ordinary investors. The splitting of trading between so many platforms has also led to concern that the important quality of liquidity is being lost. In response the EU and country regulators have listened to the voices calling for a **consolidated tape** which would list all

---

[3] 'Best execution' of a trade, a requirement of Mifid, means demonstrating that the broker obtained the best price, low cost of execution, speed and the likelihood of settlement of the trade going well.

the bid and offer prices from all venues, throughout Europe at least. The MTFs themselves have responded to the need for their customers to have access to a number of trading venues at the same time. They have introduced **smart order routing** that directs a trade to the platform that offers the best price, even if that is not on their facility.

Strong concerns have been raised by many about the lower level of regulation on MTFs. Regulators require the main national markets to employ a team of people to survey trades every day to ensure that the market is not being abused. MTFs are not required to do this. Xavier Rolet, CEO of the LSE, and other traditional stock exchange chiefs have complained of an uneven playing field because they have to bear the costly regulatory burden (according to Mr Rolet, the LSE has 150 regulatory staff compared with Chi-X's five and it pays about €5 million p.a. in regulatory fees compared with Chi-X's £125,000).

The main idea of introducing Mifid was to lower the cost of trading equities. But many professional asset managers are frustrated by the unintended consequences. While the cost of using platforms themselves has fallen between 20 per cent and 80 per cent (the old exchanges have lowered their charges significantly) there have been increases in complexity and in technology needed to access the new venues.

Trading speed

Nowadays most share dealing is done using linked computer systems in trading rooms set miles apart rather than telephone deals or face to face deals. Computer programs source the best buying and selling prices and execute the deals virtually instantaneously. Also, traders can link up to the markets without needing to ask a broker to execute a trade. Here are some benefits of electronic (e) trading:

- liquidity is increased (there are more buyers and sellers) because companies can trade with each other regardless of location;

- transparency can be increased; it is often much easier to find out security prices when the details are circulating the world electronically;

- competition is increased because e-trading removes barriers and encourages globalisation; traders can trade anywhere by just pressing a button – no need to go through brokers or exchanges;

- transaction costs are reduced to dealers and investors.

Electronic trading has gone further as some investors demand very fast dealing times. This has led to the development of **high-frequency trading** (HFT) which usually uses computer-programmed algorithms to buy or sell quickly. The blisteringly fast trading speed gives a milli-second advantage to the HF trader, enabling them to be the first to buy or sell shares, futures, options or other derivatives of shares. This is the key to the success of HFT, super-computers which can process massive volumes of information and make decisions based on that information. They respond when particular conditions occur, say, sell or buy when a certain share price hits a certain level, without the need for humans to punch in orders to keyboards. The drive for speed has led to traders placing their computer servers within exchanges' data centres so as to reduce the physical distance between systems – after all, a microsecond can make all the difference. The old exchanges have had to respond. For example, the LSE has installed what it describes as the quickest share trading system in the world on its Turquoise platform[4] which trades European equities in 124 microseconds, 2,000 times faster than the blink of a human eye. This is the time taken from the moment when a client inputs an order to the exchange and message comes back to the client that the deal is done.

HFT now accounts for more than half all equity trading in the US and one-third of Europe, and is causing concern in some quarters about the behaviour of the traders especially those who rely on computer-programmed responses. There is a worry that markets are becoming a playground for a few specialist traders rather than places that help economic activity by, say, raising capital for businesses. There is also the well-justified fear that the computer program might all send the same 'sell' signal at the same time causing a crash by automatically selling shares.

The trigger for a large market decline in the US on 6 May 2010 (a 'flash crash' when the market went down but rapidly rebounded 6 per cent in 20 minutes) was a trade put on by a conventional asset manager (using futures in a share market index), but the problem was greatly exaggerated by algorithmic-based HFT. The defenders of HFT counter the critics by saying that it benefits markets by providing liquidity and narrower bid-offer spreads because the HF traders arbitrage away price differences across multiple platforms.

Dark pools

If you are an institutional trader and you want to sell a large block of shares in a company, you have a problem. With the main exchanges you are usually required to advertise up-front the number of shares you wish to sell together

---

[4] A 51 per cent stake in Turquoise was purchased by the LSE in 2010. It offers trading in over 2,000 European shares.

with a price you are willing to accept. So, if the usual size of trade in your chosen share is between 1,000 and 10,000 and you suddenly come along and offer 200,000 shares, your inputting of that information on the exchange's dealing system is going to have an effect on the market price. Other traders instantly become aware that you are trying to shift an extraordinarily large volume and will lower the prices at which they are willing to buy to take advantage of your need. Similarly, there is a problem when you wish to buy a large block of shares in a company – the market moves against you.

The main solution to this problem is for you to break down the order into much smaller pieces. With modern computers you can instruct the exchange's system to display an order to sell, say, 5,000, and then as soon as that has been sold the system automatically posts another order for, say, 4,000, and then 6,000 when that has sold, and so on, until you have sold the full 200,000. You have not spooked the market and have hopefully obtained decent prices. Because electronic trading, with its greater ability to split large orders, has largely replaced older methods (pit trading and market maker-based trading – see later in the chapter, and in Chapter 4) the typical US order size of the 1990s has fallen from 1,400 shares or $40,000 to only 300 shares and $6,000 on NYSE or Nasdaq. In the UK average order sizes have fallen 90 per cent to around £8,000 on the LSE, and similar falls occurred in other markets such as Deutsche Börse and Hong Kong.

The solution of splitting large orders on the regulated exchanges has helped, but it does not work perfectly because experienced traders often recognise who is dealing and start to recognise that a pattern is emerging: they can see the displayed prices before the deal goes through, and they can see you adding orders regularly. To try and resolve this, since 2004, the large institutions such as banks have set up a number of new trading venues, called **dark pools**, where large orders can be placed anonymously without the need to advertise the price or size to the wider market *before* a trade is agreed. It is still a requirement that completed deals are announced to all market users but this is not as immediate as on the regulated exchanges (although regulators are calling for a speeding up). There are distinct advantages in not forewarning the mass of traders that a large body of shares is seeking a new home or someone is looking to bulk-buy shares. Even when a trade is published, there is no way of ascertaining whether it was a full or part trade that was executed, nor any way for investors to know what potential buyers and sellers are still around.

America now has over 40 dark pools in operation, with about half that number in Europe. A typical large order in a dark pool can be as large as 55,000 shares. Dark pools have taken about 8–10 per cent of share trading in the US, about 5 per cent of those in Europe and a growing proportion in Asia.

The **lit pools**, on the normal national exchanges, where prices, bid-offer spreads and offered sizes are visible to every member of the public contribute to transparency and the price discovery process – see later in this chapter. The problem with the proliferation of trading venues and dispersed order flow is the fragmentation of trading in a company's shares resulting in poorer liquidity on any one platform.

The London Stock Exchange

We will now concentrate on describing UK markets, but the principal features tend to be found in all stock exchanges.

A short history of the London Stock Exchange

The demand from investors in British companies to be able to buy and sell shares led to the creation of a market in London. At first this was very informal; holders of financial securities (e.g. shares) would meet at known places, especially coffee-houses in the ancient part of London known as the **City** (the Square Mile around which the Romans built a wall, just to the north-west of the Tower of London). Early in the nineteenth century the Stock Exchange developed a set of rules and procedures designed to enable investors to buy and sell shares with ease and to minimise the risk of fraud or unfairness.

The 'Big Bang'

Before the 'Big Bang' in 1986, brokers and other market service providers organised share and other security trading such that there was little competition, commission rates were kept high and trading was done on a face-to-face basis. It became clear in the 1970s and 1980s that the LSE was losing trade to overseas stock markets. For the LSE to remain competitive in the modern world, changes had to happen. '**Big Bang**' is the term used for a collection of reforms that resulted in fixed broker commissions disappearing, foreign competitors being allowed to own member firms (market makers or brokers), and the screen-based computer system of trading replacing floor-based face-to-face trading. The market makers and brokers quickly passed into the hands of large financial conglomerates.

Variety of securities traded

The LSE is a market place for many other types of financial securities besides shares – see Exhibit 12.7.

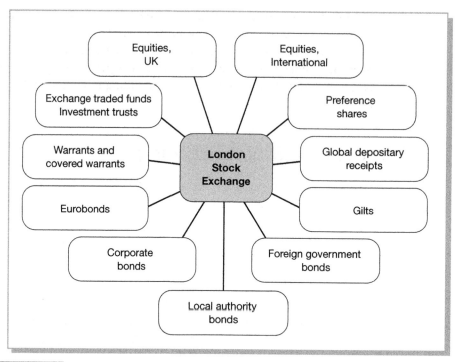

Exhibit 12.7   Variety of financial instruments sold on the London Stock Exchange

There are four types of **fixed-interest securities** traded in London: government bonds, local authority bonds, corporate bonds and Eurobonds. As well as long-term bonds the LSE also trades medium-term notes and specialised types of bond such as those that are convertible into shares. Specialist securities, such as **warrants** and **covered warrants**, are normally bought and traded by a few investors who are particularly knowledgeable in investment matters (warrants are discussed in Chapter 13).

Depositary receipts

There has been a rapid development of a market in **depositary receipts**. These are certificates that can be bought and sold, and represent evidence of ownership of a company's shares held by a depository. Their purpose is to allow investments in foreign companies without the rigmarole of going through all necessary checks and regulations. Thus, an Indian company's shares could be packaged in, say, groups of five by a depository (usually a bank) which then sells a certificate representing a bundle of shares. The depositary receipt can be denominated in a currency other than the corporation's domestic currency and dividends can be received in the currency of the depositary receipt (say, pounds) rather than the currency of the original shares (say, rupees). These are attractive securities for sophisticated international investors because they may be more liquid and more easily traded than the underlying shares.

The investment bank JPMorgan created the first **American Depositary Receipt (ADR)** in 1927 and today is the world's largest ADR depository. The non-American ones are usually referred to as **Global Depositary Receipts (GDRs)**. They may be used to avoid settlement (see later), foreign exchange and foreign ownership difficulties (government restrictions on investment by foreigners) which may exist in the company's home market. From the company's point of view depositary receipts are attractive because they allow a market in the company's shares (even though they are wrapped up in a depositary receipt) permitting fund raising and the other benefits of a quotation on a regulated global capital market without the company needing to jump the regulatory hurdles necessary to place its shares directly on an exchange for them to be traded.

DRs have been very useful as a means for companies in emerging countries (such as Kazakhstan, Brazil or India) to raise capital from the developed world's exchanges. However emerging nations have developed to such an extent that they now have wealthy investors looking to invest in the developed world, see Exhibit 12.8.

The London Stock Exchange primary market

Through its primary market in listed securities, the LSE has succeeded in encouraging large sums of money to flow annually to firms wanting to invest and grow. On its different markets, it has quoted over 2,600 companies with a total market value of over £4,000 billion. The vast majority of these companies raised funds by selling shares, bonds or other financial instruments through the LSE either when they first floated or by issuing further shares in subsequent years (e.g. through a rights issue – see Chapter 13). Some 1,178 companies are on the Exchange's market for smaller and younger companies, the Alternative Investment Market (AIM), which started in 1995. These companies, too, have raised precious funds to allow growth. The Main Market (Official List) includes 318 listings for companies registered outside the UK, and 86 listings for **TechMARK** companies which specialise in innovative technology and health care – see Exhibit 12.9. Within the Main Market there are additional small markets for **specialist funds (SFM)** – specialist investment funds such as hedge funds, private equity funds, and certain emerging market and specialist property funds, seeking admission to a public market in London, can use this market to

Emerging market bourses hunt western blue chips

By Steve Johnson

A swathe of emerging market stock exchanges are lining up to launch depositary receipt programmes, allowing local investors to access foreign companies without leaving their home market.

The move would also ease the way for western companies to raise capital from increasingly wealthy emerging market investors, mirroring a trend that has seen emerging market companies raise almost $200bn (£125bn, €151bn) by launching American and (European-listed) global depositary receipts since 2005.

In May, Standard Chartered, the UK-headquartered but emerging market-focused bank, blazed a trail by listing the first Indian depositary receipt – raising $500m in the process.

Telefónica, the Spanish telecoms company, and Dufry Group, a Swiss retailer, have listed Brazilian depositary receipts, while a number of Indian companies have launched DRs in Singapore.

Source: *Financial Times*, 9 August 2010, p. 1

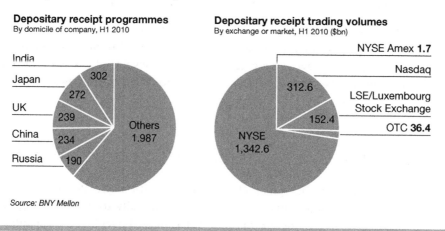

Depositary receipt programmes
By domicile of company, H1 2010

India 302
Japan 272
UK 239
China 234
Russia 190
Others 1.987

Depositary receipt trading volumes
By exchange or market, H1 2010 ($bn)

NYSE Amex **1.7**
Nasdaq
LSE/Luxembourg Stock Exchange
OTC **36.4**
312.6
152.4
NYSE 1,342.6

Source: BNY Mellon

Exhibit 12.8   Emerging market bourses hunt western blue chips

target institutional, professional and highly knowledgeable investors. There is also the **professional securities market (PSM)** – this is where depositary receipts are quoted and traded.

Newly listed UK firms on the LSE raised new capital by selling £6,998 million of shares in 2010. Another £12,360 million was raised by already listed firms selling shares through further issues of equity and by selling sterling bonds, convertibles and preference shares. In addition listed companies sold £184,465 million of Eurobonds to investors. Over on the more lightly regulated AIM market £3,550 million was raised – see Exhibit 12.10. At the same time as raising fresh capital companies transfer money the other way by, for example, redeeming

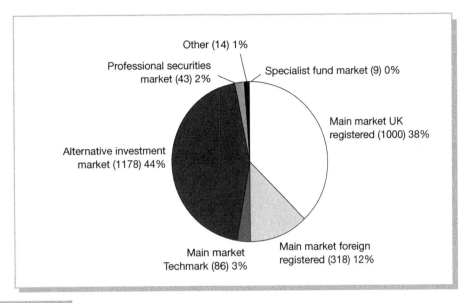

Other (14) 1%

Professional securities
market (43) 2%

Specialist fund market (9) 0%

Main market UK
registered (1000) 38%

Alternative investment
market (1178) 44%

Main market foreign
registered (318) 12%

Main market
Techmark (86) 3%

Exhibit 12.9 **All companies on the London Stock Exchange, 28 February 2011**

Source: London Stock Exchange

bonds, paying interest on debt or dividends on shares. Nevertheless, it is clear that large sums are raised for companies through the primary market. Each year there is great interest and excitement inside dozens of companies as they prepare for flotation. Since 1999, there have been over 900 new admissions on the Main Market and 2,750 on the AIM; these issues have raised billions for the companies involved.

Given the costs associated with gaining a listing (often much more than £500,000), it may be surprising to find that the market capitalisation of the majority of quoted companies is less than £250 million, see Exhibit 12.11. The average market capitalisation of AIM companies is under £25 million.

The secondary markets

There is a huge amount of shareholder-to-shareholder trading. In a typical month, over 12,000,000 bargains (trades between buyers and sellers) are struck between investors in shares on the LSE, worth over £200 billion. The size of bargains varies enormously, from £500 trades by private investors to hundreds of millions by the major funds.

The secondary market turnover exceeds the primary market sales. Indeed, the amount raised in the primary equity market in a *year* is about the same as the

	Main Market						AIM	
	New companies issuing shares		Other issues of shares and other securities		Eurobonds			
	No of co's	£m raised	No of issues	£m raised	No of issues	£m raised	No of new co's joining AIM	£m raised on AIM, incl. international & further issues
1999	106	5,353	893	9,917	1,022	85,515	102	1,076
2000	172	11,399	895	13,979	1,012	100,556	277	2,963
2001	113	6,922	866	14,824	935	83,342	177	1,600
2002	59	5,082	763	11,696	815	86,657	160	1,486
2003	32	2,445	618	4,920	1,096	118,755	162	2,443
2004	58	3,610	690	8,621	1,170	127,508	355	4,667
2005	86	6,078	772	8,099	1,099	148,309	519	8,791
2006	82	9,088	665	14,445	1,500	216,495	462	13,058
2007	73	7,613	477	8,995	2,025	165,925	284	10,116
2008	53	3,110	402	51,666	2,101	432,445	114	3,496
2009	17	458	378	73,907	1,858	254,571	36	2,988
2010	57	6,998	380	12,360	2096	184,465	102	3,550

Exhibit 12.10 Money raised by UK companies on the Main Market and money raised on the Alternative Investment Market (including international companies on AIM) 1999–2010

Source: London Stock Exchange factsheets

value of shares that trade hands *daily* in the secondary market. This high level of activity ensures a liquid market enabling shares to change ownership speedily, at low cost and without large movements in price – one of the main objectives of a well-run exchange.

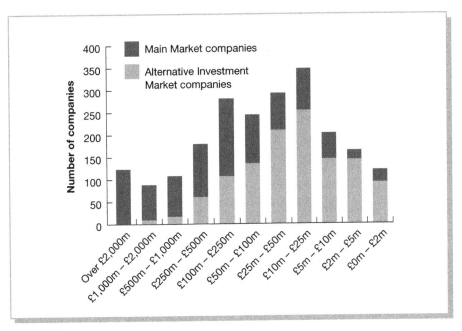

Exhibit 12.11 Distribution of UK companies by equity market value February 2011

Source: London Stock Exchange factsheets

How stock exchanges work

Types of trading

Traditionally shares were traded between two traders, face to face. A few stock exchanges around the world still have a place where buyers and sellers (or at least their representatives) meet to trade. For example, the New York Stock Exchange (NYSE) continues to make some use of a large trading floor with thousands of face-to-face deals taking place every working day (**open outcry trading**). This is the traditional image of a stock market, and if television reporters have a story about what is going on in the world's security markets, they often show an image of traders rushing around, talking quickly amid a flurry of small slips of paper on the NYSE trading floor. Most trading now however is done silently in front of banks of computers, with deals being completed in nano-seconds. The stress levels for those dealing remain as high, if not higher, than ever, as now a slight mistake with a finger on a keyboard can cause mayhem.

Quote-driven trading is how most stock exchanges were operated. With this type of approach, market makers give a price at which they would buy (lower price) or sell (higher price), and make their profits on the margins between buying and selling. Traditionally they operated in 'trading pits' and used an 'open outcry' system of trading, i.e. shouting and using hand signals to make trades, much like you might see bookmakers at a small horse race meeting. They were able to adjust their prices according to what other traders were doing. Although this type of trading does still take place, it has been superseded by electronic trading. Market makers input their prices ('bid' is the price at which they are willing to buy and 'offer' or 'ask' is the price at which they are willing to sell) to a computer system and dealing takes place electronically.

Criticism of trading systems based on market makers quoting bid and offer prices focused on the size of the middleman's (the market maker's) margin and led to the development of **order-driven trading**, where buyers trade with sellers at a single price so that there is no bid-offer spread. Most stock exchanges in the world now operate this type of system. These markets allow buy and sell orders to be entered on a central computer, and investors are automatically matched (they are sometimes called **matched-bargain systems** or **order book trading**). In 1997 the LSE introduced an order-driven service known as **SETS (Stock Exchange Electronic Trading System)** and an example will be used to explain how order-driven trading works.

SETS

SETS electronic order book uses powerful computer systems to execute millions of trades a day in milliseconds. Traders (via brokers) enter the prices at which they are willing to buy or sell as well as the quantity of shares they want to trade. They can then wait for the market to move to the price they set as their limit. Alternatively they can instruct brokers to transact immediately at the best price currently available on the order book system. Trades are then executed by the system if there is a match between a buy order price and a sell order price. These prices are displayed anonymously to the entire market. An example of prices and quantities is shown in the lower half of Exhibit 12.12 – a reproduction of a SETS screen as seen by brokers.

The buy orders are shown on the left and the sell orders on the right. So, we can observe for the Lloyd's shares someone (or more than one person) has entered that they are willing to buy 100,000 shares at a maximum price of 69.92p (bottom line on screen). Someone else has entered that they would like to sell 6,930 shares at a minimum price of 70.53p. Clearly the computer cannot match these two orders and neither of these two investors will be able to trade. They will either have to adjust their limit prices or wait until the market moves in their favour.

Trading Screen

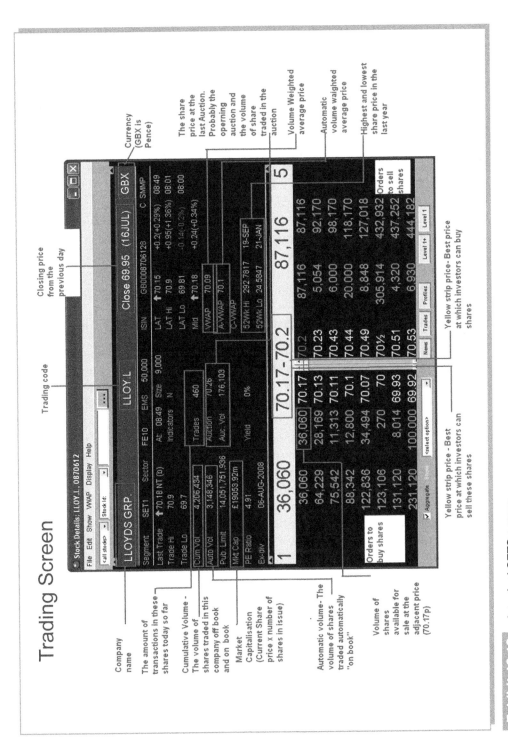

Exhibit 12.12 A typical SETS screen

Source: London Stock Exchange

As we travel up the screen we observe a closing of the gap between the prices buyers are willing to pay and the offering price of sellers. On the seventh line from the bottom we see that buyers want 36,060 shares at 70.17p whereas sellers are prepared to accept 70.2p for 87,116 shares. Now we are getting much closer to a match. Indeed if we look above the **yellow strip** we can see the price where buyers and sellers were last matched – the 'last traded price' is 70.18p. These screens are available to market participants at all times and so they are able to judge where to pitch their price limits. For example if I was a buyer of 5,000 shares entering the market I would not be inclined to offer more than 70.2p given the current state of supply and demand. On the other hand if I was a seller of 5,000 shares I would recognise that the price offered would not have to fall below 70.17p to attract buyers. If however I was a buyer of 110,000 shares rather than just 5,000 I have two options: I could set a maximum price of 70.2p in which case I would transact for 87,116 immediately but would leave the other 22,884 unfilled order in the market hoping for a general market price decline; alternatively, I could set my limit at 70.44p in which case I could transact with those investors prepared to sell at 70.2p, 70.23p, 70.43p and 70.44p. The unfilled orders of the sellers at 70.44 (120,000 – 118,170) are carried forward on SETS.

Supporters of the older quote-driven system say that a major problem with the order-driven system is that there may be few or no shares offered at prices close to a market clearing rate and so little trade can take place. In other words the market can be very illiquid. There may indeed be times when no sellers are posting sensible prices and other times when buyers are scarce. This is when the quote-driven system may be more liquid because market makers who make a book in a company's shares must continuously offer prices and are obliged to trade at the price shown. By way of counter-criticism, it is alleged there have been times when it has been difficult to contact market makers to trade at their displayed prices, even though in theory they are obliged to make themselves available to quote and trade at bid and offer prices throughout the trading day. To improve trading liquidity on SETS in 2007 the system was modified so that market makers can now post prices on it. Thus it offers a continuous order book with automatic execution, but also has market makers providing continuous bid and offer prices for many shares. It is thought that by having the two systems combined there will be tighter bid-offer spreads, greater transparency of trades and improved liquidity.

Clearing and settlement

When a trade has been completed and reported to the exchange it is necessary to **clear** the trade. That is, the exchange ensures that all reports of the trade are reconciled to make sure all parties are in agreement as to the number and the price of shares traded. The exchange also checks that the buyer and seller have the cash and securities to do the deal. The company registrar is notified of the change in ownership. Later, the transfer of ownership from seller to buyer has to take place; this is called **settlement**. These days clearing frequently does not just mean checking that a buyer and a seller agree on the deal; the clearing house also acts as a **central counterparty** that acts as a buyer to every seller and as a seller to every buyer. This eliminates the risk of failure to complete a deal by guaranteeing that shares will be delivered against payment and vice versa. **Clearing houses** and central counterparties (CCPs in Europe, Central Counterparty Clearing (CCCs) in the US) provide an invaluable service – they execute and guarantee every aspect of the transaction. Instead of having to wait for cheque clearance, or documents to be signed and arrive by post, traders set up accounts with clearing houses and CCPs so that transactions can be carried out immediately, with the CCP absorbing any loss should either default. With a CCP investors can also **'net' their trades**, so that if one part of the investing institution has bought 1 million shares while another has sold 1.5 million the trades are paired so that settlement is for only 500,000 shares.

To facilitate settlement a company called Euroclear UK & Ireland uses the technologically advanced **CREST** system and acts as a **Central Securities Depository (CSD)** for the UK and Ireland. CREST enables dematerialisation by keeping an electronic register of the shares, a record of shares traded on stock markets and provides an electronic means of settlement and registration. This system is cheaper and quicker than the old one which used paper – ownership is now transferred with a few strokes of a keyboard. The volume of this trading is huge, around 1.3 million transactions daily in over 16,000 securities, with a value in excess of £1.4 trillion. Under the CREST system shares are usually held in the name of a **nominee company** rather than in the name of the actual purchaser. Brokers and investment managers run these nominee accounts. Thus when an investor trades, their broker holds their shares electronically in their (the broker's) nominee account and arranges settlement through their membership of the CREST system. This increases the speed of transactions enormously. There might be dozens of investors with shares held by a particular nominee company. The nominee company appears as the registered owner of the shares as far as the company (say Sainsbury) is concerned. Despite this, the beneficial owners receive all dividends and any sale proceeds. Some investors oppose the CREST system because under such a system they do not automatically receive annual reports and other documentation, such as an invitation to the annual general meeting. They also potentially lose the right to vote (after all the company does not know who the beneficial owners are). Those investors who take their ownership of a part of a company seriously can insist on remaining outside of CREST. In this way they receive share certificates and are treated as the real owners of the business. This is more expensive when share dealing, but that is not a great concern for investors who trade infrequently.

There is a compromise position: personal membership of CREST. The investor is then both the legal owner and the beneficial owner of the shares, and also benefits from rapid (and cheap) electronic share settlement. The owner will be sent all company communications and retain voting rights. However, this is more expensive than the normal CREST accounts.

SETSqx

Trading on SETS is for companies whose trading is liquid, i.e. large companies with a high proportion of the shares held by a wide range of investors (a large **free float**) so there are plenty of shares traded each day. There are other means of trading for less frequently traded shares. **SETSqx (Stock Exchange Electronic Trading Service – quotes and crosses)** trades in Main Market and AIM shares which are less liquid and not traded on SETS. SETSqx combines order book technology (similar to the SETS method of trading) with the best of the LSE's quote-driven trading. On SETSqx a single market maker's quote can be displayed if a market maker is interested in quoting a price. (Ideally, the exchange would like many market makers' quoting prices so that competition encourages keener prices for share owners).

An investor wanting to trade with a market maker can do so in the normal way, but also can connect, usually via brokers, to the electronic system and put onto the system's screen display an order for shares stating a price at which they would like to trade, either to sell or to buy – particularly useful if there are no market makers in that share. If someone else on the system likes the displayed price they can phone the originator and a deal is done.

This may still leave some orders for trades unexecuted (i.e. no one phones up and trades at the advertised price). To cope with this, or to trade shares anonymously, throughout the day there are auctions in which investors make bids and the system matches up buyers and sellers. Now all Main Market shares either trade on SETS or SETSqx.

Quote-driven trading

The LSE's **Stock Exchange Automated Quotation (SEAQ)** system deals mainly in smaller, less liquid companies not on its Main Market. It is the LSE's quote-driven service that allows market makers to quote prices in AIM securities (those

AIM securities not traded on SETS or SETSqx) as well as a number of fixed interest securities. It lists over 800 companies on its electronic notice board where market makers display prices at which they are willing to buy or sell. The SEAQ computer gathers together the bid-offer quotes from all the market makers that make a market in that particular share. These competing quotations are then available to brokers and other financial institutions linked up to the SEAQ system.

Exhibit 12.13 goes through the stages in buying or selling on the LSE's SEAQ system. What happens when you, as an investor, telephone your broker to buy shares is this: when you mentioned the company name the broker immediately punched into their computer the company code. So within a second of your mentioning your interest in the company the broker has on their screen all the prices that different market makers are willing to pay as well as all the prices at which they are willing to sell the shares. It can be confusing and time consuming for the broker to look at all the prices to find the best current rates.

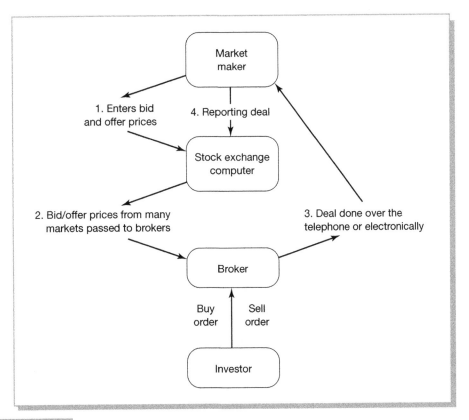

Exhibit 12.13 The SEAQ quote-driven system

Fortunately brokers do not have to do this as the screen displays a 'yellow strip' above the market makers' prices, which provides the identity of the market makers offering the best bid and offer prices (these are called **touch prices**). It is the price in the yellow strip that the broker will immediately report to you over the telephone. So, you might be told 105–109. If you were happy with 109p you would then instruct your broker to buy, say, 1,000 shares.

The market makers are obliged to deal (up to a certain number of shares) at the price quoted, but they have the freedom to adjust prices after deals are completed. Transactions may be completed by the broker speaking to the market maker on the telephone but an increasing number of trades are completed electronically. All trades are reported to the central electronic computer exchange and are disseminated to market participants (usually within three minutes) so that they are aware of the price at which recent trades were completed.

Share borrowing, lending and shorting

If a share price is expected to fall, some traders (usually large institutions) are in a position to borrow shares (paying commission to the lender) for say a month, sell them immediately at the market price and hope to buy the requisite amount of shares in a month's time at the expected lower price. This practice is known as **shorting**, or **going short**, selling shares before buying them. If the unexpected happens, and the share price rises, the trader will make a loss on his shorted shares. The opposite of going short is **going long**, where a dealer buys securities and holds on to them.

Brokers, often acting on behalf of institutions, lend some of the securities in their care to satisfy trading needs, taking commission from the deals. The lenders get equivalent securities back at the end of the loan term and the borrowers get a chance to trade without the injection of fresh capital.

The ownership of UK shares

The Office for National Statistics (ONS) provide figures for the ownership of UK shares from 1963 to 2008, and some dramatic changes can be seen, see Exhibit 12.14. The tax-favoured status of pension funds made them a very attractive vehicle for savings, resulting in billions of pounds being put into them each year. Most of this money used to be invested in equities, with pension funds becoming the most influential investing group on the stock market, taking nearly a third of the market in UK shares. However, more recently pension funds

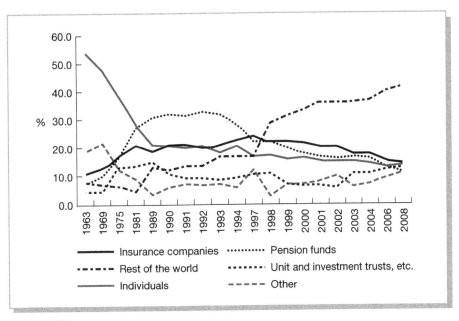

Percentage ownership of UK shares 1963–2008

Source: Office for National Statistics (ONS)

have been taking money out of quoted shares and placing it in other investments such as bonds and venture capital.

Insurance companies similarly rose in significance, increasing their share of
quoted equities from 10 per cent to about one-quarter by the 1990s, after which
they too moved their investments to bonds and overseas equities.

The group which shows the greatest decrease is ordinary individuals holding
shares directly. Small personal investors used to dominate the market, with 54
per cent of quoted shares in 1963. This sector has shown a continuous gradual
decline, falling to 13 per cent, but the reason for the decline is not that individual investors have become disinterested in the stock market, but that they have
shown a tendency to switch from direct investment to collective investment
vehicles, so probably the same number of people (if not more) are investing, but
in a different way. They gain benefits of diversification and skilled management
by putting their savings into unit and investment trusts or into endowment and
other savings schemes offered by the insurance companies.

The most remarkable trend has been the increasing share of equities held by
overseas investors: only 7 per cent in 1963, but over 40 per cent in 2008. This
increase partly reflects international mergers where the new company is listed

in the UK, and foreign companies sometimes floating their UK subsidiaries but holding on to a large shareholding. It also reflects an increasing tendency of investors to buy shares in overseas markets. The rising internationalisation of share ownership is not just manifest in the UK. For each of the following countries more than 30 per cent of the domestic company shares are owned by overseas organisations: Netherlands, Switzerland, Greece, Portugal, Poland, France, Norway, Sweden, Spain, Austria and Denmark.

Also note the rise in the 'other' category in Exhibit 12.14 over the last decade. This is largely due to the rising importance of hedge funds and venture capital companies.

Websites

www.advfn.com	ADVFN. Financial data
www.euroclear.com	Euroclear
www.fese.eu	Federation of European Securities Exchanges
www.fsa.gov.uk	Financial Services Authority
www.fsa.gov.uk/Pages/Doing/UKLA	United Kingdom Listing Authority
www.ft.com	Financial Times
www.ftse.com	FTSE Group. Stock market indices and information
www.hemscott.com	Hemscott – share prices and financial data
www.iii.co.uk	Interactive Investor
www.investegate.co.uk	Investegate – company information
www.investorschronicle.com	Investors Chronicle, weekly stock market analysis
www.lchclearnet.com	LCH.Clearnet – clearing house
www.liquidmetrix.com	Intelligent Financial Systems – information of trading in Europe's markets
www.londonstockexchange.com	London Stock Exchange
www.nyse.com	New York Stock Exchange
www.ons.gov.uk or www.statistics.gov.uk	Office for National Statistics
www.wsj.com	Wall Street Journal
http://uk.finance.yahoo.com	Yahoo! Finance. Financial data
www.world-exchanges.org	World Federation of Exchanges

13

Raising share capital

Raising money for a company by selling shares is a complicated business. There are so many factors to be properly coordinated. There are numerous legal issues, regulations to be observed, the marketing of the shares to potential investors and the underwriting process to organise, to name but a few.

Many institutions assist a company in floating its shares on a stock market for the first time, as well as help a company raising additional equity finance in the years following the initial public offering. This chapter describes their various roles, from investment bankers acting as sponsors to corporate brokers, registrars and lawyers. It also explains the regulations for stock market-quoted companies, such as the need to make public all price-sensitive information or the restrictions placed on directors.

It is important that a student of finance be able to read and interpret the data shown in the financial pages of newspapers, particularly the *Financial Times*. To help in this area the chapter has reproductions of the equity tables in the *FT*, together with explanations of what the entries mean.

Throughout this chapter there is focus on the UK, but the key principles are in place in all major financial centres.

Floating on the Main Market of the London Stock Exchange (LSE)

Once a company reaches a certain size, it has the possibility of floating on a stock market, **going public**, through a **new issue** of shares, also called an initial public offering (IPO). To become a listed company is a major step for a firm, and the substantial sums of money involved can lead to a new, accelerated phase of business growth. While this opens up fresh possibilities of investment finance from outside investors it also brings the disadvantage for current shareholders of giving away some influence and control as well as incurring some significant costs. Many, if not most, companies are content to grow without the aid of stock markets. For example JC Bamford (JCB), which manufactures earth-moving machines, has built a large, export award-winning company, without needing to bring in outside shareholders, and remains a private company.

The legal implications of obtaining a quotation as a listed company are enormous. Companies wishing to be listed on the Main Market have to sign a **listing agreement** that commits directors to certain standards of behaviour and levels of reporting to shareholders. The United Kingdom Listing Authority (UKLA), part of the Financial Services Authority (FSA) (the Financial Conduct Authority from 2013) rigorously enforces a set of demanding rules.

Joining the Main Market of the LSE involves two stages. The securities (usually shares) have to be: (a) admitted to the Official List by the UKLA (hence the term 'listed' company); and also, (b) admitted by the Exchange for trading.

Going public can wrack up huge costs, see Exhibit 13.1. The cost as a proportion of the amount raised varies but is usually at least 5 per cent and can be as high as one-third – many of the costs are fixed so if only a small number of new shares are issued the percentage costs are high.

	£
Financial advisers	200,000–400,000
Underwriters	400,000–1,000,000
Legal expenses	200,000–400,000
Accounting	100,000–300,000
Listing fees	< 20,000
Printing, public relations, etc.	< 100,000
Total costs	1,020,000–2,220,000

Exhibit 13.1   Typical floating costs for a company issuing £20 million of shares in an IPO on the Main Market of the London Stock Exchange

Many firms consider the stresses and the costs worthwhile because listing brings numerous advantages besides raising fresh finance, including providing shareholders with a dynamic, transparent and liquid secondary market for trading shares, a raising of the company's status and visibility, and the possibility of mergers with other firms.

All companies obtaining a full Main Market listing must ensure that at least 25 per cent of their share capital is in public hands,[1] to ensure that the shares are capable of being traded actively on the market. The UKLA usually insists that a company has a track record (in the form of accounting figures) stretching back at least three years. However, this requirement has been relaxed for scientific research-based companies and companies undertaking major capital projects. In the case of scientific research-based companies there is the requirement that they have been conducting their activity for three years even if no revenue was produced. Some major project companies, for example Eurotunnel, have been allowed to join the market despite an absence of a trading activity or a profit record. Companies can be admitted to the techMARK, part of the Official List, with only one year of accounts.

United Kingdom Listing Authority (UKLA)

The UKLA is responsible for approval of the prospectuses and admissions to the Official List (most of these companies are on the Main Market of the LSE, although PLUS markets – see later – may also admit Official List companies). The UKLA maintains details of all listed companies and updates its list daily with additions, cancellations, suspensions and restorations. It also rigorously enforces a set of demanding rules regarding the conduct of the company and its officials in the years following the listing.

The first step in floating a company is to apply to the UKLA to be put on the Official List. The listing fee is £225, plus an annual fee, based on the market capitalisation of the company, of at least £3,700 rising to over £1 million for capitalisations over £25,000 million.

---

[1] 'In public hands' means a free float, that is, the shares are not held by those closest to the company, such as directors, founding family or dominant shareholder, who may be unlikely to sell their shares. Occasionally a company is admitted with a free float of less than 25 per cent. For example, Eurasian Natural Resources had a free float of only 21.3 per cent when it joined the Main Market in 2008. The company successfully argued that it was large enough for its shares to have liquid trading in spite of the smaller free float.

Financial advisers

The sponsor

The key adviser in a flotation is the **sponsor**. This may be an investment bank, stockbroker or other professional adviser, but must be on the UKLA's approved list of sponsors. Directors, particularly of small companies, often first seek advice from their existing professional advisers, for example accountants and lawyers. Sponsors have to be chosen with care as the relationship is likely to be one which continues long after the flotation. For large or particularly complex issues investment banks are employed, although experienced stockbrokers have been used. The UKLA requires sponsors to certify that a company has complied with all the regulatory requirements and to ensure that all necessary documentation is filed on time.

The sponsor (sometimes called the **issuing house**) will first examine the company and the aspirations of the management team to assess whether flotation is an appropriate corporate objective by taking into account its structure, strategy and capital needs. The sponsor will also comment on the composition of the board and the calibre of the directors. The sponsor may even recommend supplementation with additional directors if the existing team does not come up to the quality expected. Sponsors can be quite forceful in this because they do not want to damage their reputation by bringing a poorly managed company to market. The sponsor will draw up a timetable, which can be lengthy – sometimes the planning period for a successful flotation may extend over two years. Another important function is to help draft the prospectus and provide input to the marketing strategy. Throughout the process of flotation there will be many other professional advisers involved and it is vital that their activities mesh into a coherent whole; this too is the sponsor's responsibility.

The corporate broker

When a **corporate broker** is employed as a sponsor the two roles can be combined. If the sponsor is, say, an investment bank the UKLA requires that a broker is also appointed. However, most investment banks also have corporate broking arms and so can take on both roles. Brokers play a vital role in advising on share market conditions and the likely demand from investors for the company's shares. They also represent the company to investors to try to generate interest. When debating issues such as the method of share issue to be employed, the marketing strategy, the size of the issue, the timing or the pricing of the shares the company may value the market knowledge the broker has to offer.

Underwriters

Shortly before the flotation the sponsor will have the task of advising on the best price to ask for the shares, and, at the time of flotation, the sponsor will usually underwrite the issue. Most new issues are underwritten, because the correct pricing of a new issue of shares is extremely difficult. If the price is set too high, demand will be less than supply and not all the shares will be taken up. The company is usually keen to have certainty that it will receive the expected money from the issue so that it can plan ahead. To make sure it sells the shares it buys a kind of insurance called **underwriting**. In return for a fee the underwriter guarantees to buy the proportion of the issue not taken up by the market. An investment bank sponsoring the issue will usually charge a fee of 2–4 per cent of the issue proceeds and then pays part of that fee, say 1.25–3.0 per cent of the issue proceeds, to sub-underwriters (usually large financial institutions such as pension funds and banks) who each agree to buy a certain number of shares if called on to do so. In most cases the underwriters do not have to purchase any shares because the general public are keen to take them up. However, occasionally they receive a shock and have to buy large quantities.

Legal expenses

All **legal requirements** in the flotation preparation and in the information displayed in the prospectus must be observed. Lawyers prepare the 'verification' questions which are used to confirm that every statement in the prospectus can be justified as fact. Directors bear the ultimate responsibility for the truthfulness of the documents. Examples of other legal issues are directors' contracts, changes to the articles of association, re-registering the company as a public limited company (rather than a limited company which is not able to offer its shares to the wider public), underwriting agreements and share option schemes.

Accounting

The **reporting accountant** in a flotation has to be different from the company's existing auditors, but can be a separate team in the same firm. The accountant will be asked by the sponsor to prepare a detailed report on the firm's financial controls, track record, financing and forecasts (the **long-form report**). Not all of this information will be included in the prospectus but it does serve to reassure the sponsor that the company is suitable for flotation. Accountants may also have a role in tax planning from both the company's viewpoint and that of its shareholders. They also investigate working capital requirements. The UKLA insists that companies show that they have enough working capital for current needs and for at least the next 12 months.

Registrars

The record on the ownership of shares is maintained by **registrars** as shares are bought and sold. Registrars keep the company's register and issue share certificates. There are about two dozen major registrars linked up to CREST through which they are required to electronically adjust their records of ownership of company shares within two hours of a trade taking place.

Listing fees

Listing fees are charged by stock markets for admission to listing, followed by annual charges, graduated according to the size of the company, see Exhibit 13.2 for LSE fees.

Main Market admission fees	**£**
Minimum (under £5m capitalisation)	6,708
Maximum (over £500m capitalisation)	388,173
Main Market annual fees	**UK**
Minimum (under £50m capitalisation)	4,410
Maximum (over £500m capitalisation)	43,470
	International
Minimum (under £25m capitalisation)	6,773
Maximum (over £1,025m capitalisation)	21,634
AIM admission fees	
Minimum (under £5m capitalisation)	6,720
Maximum (over £250m capitalisation)	75,810
AIM annual fee	5,350

Exhibit 13.2   **London Stock Exchange listing fees 2011**
Source: London Stock Exchange

Printing, advertising, public relations, etc.

Public relations and advertising companies are used to influence investors and persuade them to buy the shares. Although the shares are underwritten, and therefore there is a guarantee that they will all be sold, albeit maybe at a lower price than the offer price, it is a huge relief to all concerned if the public response is favourable and the shares are sold to investors. It demonstrates public confidence in the company and shows that the listing was justified, and the sponsors gauged investor appetite accurately.

Prospectus

To create a stable market and encourage investors to place their money with companies the UKLA tries to minimise the risk of investing by ensuring that the firms which obtain a quotation abide by high standards; this includes producing a well-crafted prospectus. The **prospectus (Listing Particulars)** is designed to inform potential shareholders about the company. This may contain far more information about the firm than it has previously dared to put into the public domain. The prospectus acts as a marketing tool as the firm attempts to persuade investors to apply for shares.

The content and accuracy of this vital document is the responsibility of the directors. Contained within it must be three years of audited accounts, details of indebtedness and a statement as to the adequacy of working capital. Statements by experts are often required: valuers may be needed to confirm the current value of property, engineers may be needed to state the viability of processes or machinery and accountants may be needed to comment on the profit figures. All major contracts entered into in the past two years will have to be detailed and a description of the risks facing the firm provided. Any persons with a shareholding of more than 3 per cent have to be named. A mass of operational data is also required, ranging from an analysis of sales by geographical area and type of activity, to information on research and development and significant investments in other companies.

Methods of issue

The sponsor will look at the motives for wanting a quotation, at the amount of money that is to be raised, at the history and reputation of the firm and will then advise on the best method of issuing the shares. There are various methods, ranging from a full-scale offer for sale to a relatively simple introduction. The final choice often rests on the costs of issue, which can vary considerably. Here are the main options:

▪ **Offer for sale.** The company sponsor offers shares to the public by inviting subscriptions from institutional and individual investors. Sometimes newspapers carry a notice and an application form. However, most investors will need to contact the sponsor or the broker to obtain an application form. Publications such as *Investors Chronicle* show the telephone numbers to call for each company floating. Also details of forthcoming flotations are available at www.londonstockexchange.com, and www.hemscott.com. Normally the shares are offered at a fixed price determined by the company's directors and their financial advisers. Occasionally, potential buyers name their price and, if it is sufficiently high, obtain shares – an **offer for sales by tender**.

- **Introductions** do not raise any new money for the company. If the company's shares are already quoted on another stock exchange or there is a wide spread of shareholders, with more than 25 per cent of the shares in public hands, the Exchange permits a company to be 'introduced' to the market. This method may allow companies trading on AIM to move up to the Main Market or foreign corporations to gain a London listing. This is the cheapest method of flotation since there are no underwriting costs and relatively small advertising expenditures.

- **Placing.** In a placing, shares are offered to the public but the term 'public' is narrowly defined. Instead of engaging in advertising to the population at large, the sponsor or broker handling the issue sells the shares to institutions it is in contact with, such as pension and insurance funds. The costs of this method are considerably lower than those of an offer for sale. There are lower publicity costs and legal costs. A drawback of this method is that the spread of shareholders is going to be more limited. To alleviate this problem the Stock Exchange does insist on a large number of placees holding shares after the new issue. A generation ago the most frequently used method of new issue was the offer for sale. This ensured a wide spread of share ownership and thus a more liquid secondary market. It also permitted all investors to participate in new issues. Placings were only permitted for small offerings (< £15 million) when the costs of an offer for sale would have been prohibitive. Today any size of new issue can be placed. As this method is much cheaper and easier than an offer for sale, companies have naturally switched to placings so there are now few offers for sale.

- **Intermediaries offer.** A method which is often combined with a placing is an intermediaries offer. Here the shares are offered for sale to financial institutions such as stockbrokers. Clients of these intermediaries can then apply to buy shares from them.

- **Reverse takeover.** Sometimes a larger unquoted company makes a deal with a smaller quoted company whereby the smaller company 'takes over' the larger firm by swapping newly created shares in itself for the shares in the unquoted firm currently held by its owners. Because the quoted firm creates and issues more new shares itself than it had to start with, the unquoted firm's shareholders end up with the majority of the shares in the newly merged entity. They therefore now control a quoted company. The only task remaining is to decide on a name for the company – frequently the name of the previously unquoted company is chosen. A reverse takeover is a way for a company to gain a listing/quotation without the hassle of an official new issue.

▪ **Book-building.** Selling new issues of shares through book-building is a popular technique in the US. It is starting to catch on in Europe. Under this method the financial advisers to an issue contact major institutional investors to get from them bids for the shares over a period of eight to ten working days. The investors' orders are sorted according to price, quantity and other factors such as 'firmness' of bid (e.g. a 'strike bid' means the investor will buy a given number of shares within the initial price range, leaving it to others to set the price, a 'limit bid' means the investor would buy a particular quantity at a particular price). These data may then be used to establish a price for the issue and the allocation of shares. The book-building approach is usually used for placings.

Post-listing obligations

The UKLA insists on certain **'continuing obligations'** designed to protect or enlighten shareholders. One of these is that all **price-sensitive information** is given to the market as soon as possible and that there is 'full and accurate disclosure' to all investors at the same time. Information is price sensitive if it might influence the share price or the trading in the shares. Investors need to be sure that they are not disadvantaged by market distortions caused by some participants having the benefit of superior information. Public announcements will be required in a number of instances, for example: the development of major new products; the signing of major contracts; details of an acquisition; a sale of large assets; a change in directors or a decision to pay a dividend. The website **www.investegate.co.uk** shows all major announcements made by companies going back many years. The FSA hands out fines to companies which do not comply with the rules, see Exhibit 13.3.

Listed companies are also required to provide detailed financial statements within six months of the year-end. Firms usually choose to make **preliminary profit announcements** based on unaudited results for the year a few weeks before the audited results are published. **Interim reports** for the first half of each accounting year are also required (within four months of the end of the half-year). The penalty for non-compliance is suspension from the Exchange.

Photo-Me fined £500,000 by FSA

By Brooke Masters, Chief Regulation Correspondent

Photo-Me International, the photo booth operator, has been fined £500,000 for failing to tell the market promptly that its effort to win a significant new contract had hit hurdles and that sales of minilabs were falling behind expectations.

The fine is the largest handed down by the Financial Services Authority for failure to disclose market-moving inside information quickly enough.

The City regulator said in its final notice that the failure created a false market in Photo-Me shares for 44 days in early 2007.

The fine is part of a string of enforcement actions carried out by a newly aggressive FSA, which also announced on Monday that it had fined Vantage Capital, the interdealer broker, a record £700,000 for allowing an unapproved person to perform a key leadership function for four years.

Margaret Cole, the FSA's enforcement director, said the Photo-Me action "demonstrates our commitment to enforcing the UK listing regime and ensuring clean, efficient and orderly markets".

Over the past two years, Woolworths, Wolfson Microelectronics and Entertainment Rights have all paid fines for failing to update the markets....

The FSA said it did not find that Photo-Me's directors had committed regulatory breaches. Its finance director at the time has died but the chief executive has returned to his position on an interim basis.

The FSA found that in late 2006, Photo-Me had led the market to believe it would win large sales contracts and "strong minilab sales". But the company then waited too long to announce it faced new competition for a contract with a US supermarket chain, and a director failed to open an e-mail with disappointing January sales information.

When Photo-Me finally issued a profit warning in March 2007, its shares dropped 24 per cent.

Source: Financial Times, 22 June 2010, p. 19

Exhibit 13.3   Photo-Me fined £500,000 by FSA

Share dealing by directors

There are strict rules concerning the buying and selling of the company's shares by its own directors once it is on the Stock Exchange. The Criminal Justice Act 1993 and the **Model Code for Director Dealings** have to be followed. Directors are prevented from dealing for a minimum period (normally two months) prior to an announcement of regularly recurring information such as annual results. They are also forbidden to deal before the announcement of matters of an exceptional nature involving unpublished information which is potentially price sensitive. These rules apply to any employee in possession of such information. When directors do buy or sell shares in their company they are required to disclose these dealings publicly. Most (free) financial websites (e.g. **www.advfn.com** or **www.iii.co.uk**) show all major announcements made by companies going back many years, including director purchases and sales.

UK Corporate Governance Code

There is a considerable range of legislation and other regulatory pressures designed to encourage directors to act in shareholders' interests. In the UK the Companies Act requires certain minimum standards of behaviour, as does the LSE. For example, directors are forbidden to use their position to profit at the expense of shareholders. There is the back-up of the financial industry regulator, the FSA and the Financial Reporting Council (FRC – an accounting body).

Following a number of financial scandals, guidelines of best practice in corporate governance were issued by the Cadbury, Greenbury, Hampel, Higgs and Smith committees, now consolidated in the **UK Corporate Governance Code**, which is backed by the FCA, LSE and FRC.[2]

The Alternative Investment Market (AIM)

There is a long-recognised need for equity capital by small, young companies which are unable to afford the costs of full listing. Many stock exchanges have **alternative equity markets** that set less stringent rules and regulations for joining or remaining quoted (often called **second-tier markets**).

Lightly-regulated markets have a continuing dilemma. If the regulation is too lax, scandals of fraud or incompetence will arise, damaging the image and credibility of the market, and thus reducing the flow of investor funds to companies. (This happened to the German market for small companies, **Neuer Markt**, which had to close in 2002 because of the loss of investor confidence.) On the other hand, if the market is too tightly regulated, with more company investigations, more information disclosure and a requirement for longer trading track records prior to flotation, the associated costs and inconvenience will deter many companies from seeking a quotation. In the UK there are many small young companies needing to raise equity capital but which are excluded from the Main Market because of the huge cost of obtaining and maintaining a listing. The Alternative Investment Market sets less stringent rules, regulations and costs for joining or remaining quoted.

The driving philosophy behind the AIM is to offer young and developing companies access to new sources of finance, while providing investors with the opportunity to buy and sell shares in a trading environment which is run,

[2] This is outlined in Chapter 1 of *Corporate Financial Management* by Glen Arnold. The latest version is available at www.frc.org.uk/CORPORATE/ukcgcode.cfm

regulated and marketed by the LSE. Efforts are made to keep the costs down and make the rules as simple as possible. In contrast to the Main Market, there is no requirement for AIM companies to have been in business for a minimum three-year period or for a set proportion of their shares to be in public hands – if they wish to sell only 1 per cent or 5 per cent of the shares to outsiders then that is OK. However, investors have some degree of reassurance about the quality of companies coming to the market. These firms have to appoint, and retain at all times, a **nominated adviser** and nominated broker. The nominated adviser, the **nomad**, is selected by the company from a Stock Exchange approved register, and must have demonstrated to the Exchange that they have sufficient experience and qualifications to act as a 'quality controller', confirming to the LSE that the company has complied with the rules. Unlike with Main Market companies there is no pre-vetting of admission documents by the UKLA or the Exchange, as a lot of weight is placed on the nomad's investigations and informed opinion about the company.

Nominated brokers have an important role to play in bringing buyers and sellers of shares together. Investors in the company are reassured that at least one broker is ready to help shareholders to trade. The adviser and broker are to be retained throughout the company's life on the AIM. They have high reputations and it is regarded as a very bad sign if either of them abruptly refuses further association with a firm. AIM companies are also expected to comply with strict rules regarding the publication of price-sensitive information and the quality of annual and interim reports. Upon flotation, an **AIM admission document** is required. This is similar to a prospectus required for companies floating on the Main Market, but is not as comprehensive and therefore lower cost. If we add the cost of financial advisers and of management time spent communicating with institutions and investors to the LSE fee, the annual cost of being quoted on AIM runs into tens of thousands of pounds. This can be a deterrent for many companies. The cost of an initial offering of shares when joining AIM is around £100,000–£200,000, but if additional money is raised by selling new shares the organisation and underwriting costs push this up over £500,000 in many cases. Nominated advisers argue that their policing role on behalf of the LSE means they have to incur much higher investigatory costs than was envisaged when AIM was first established, thus they have higher ongoing as well as initial costs.

However, there are cost savings compared with the Main Market. As well as the flotation prospectus being less detailed and therefore cheaper, the annual expense of managing a quotation is less. For example, AIM companies are not bound by the Listing Rules administered by the UKLA but instead are subject to the AIM rules, written and administered by the LSE. AIM companies do not have to disclose as much information as companies on the Official List. Price-sensitive information will have to be published, but normally this will require only an electronic message from the adviser to the Exchange rather than a circular to shareholders. Recently the LSE has tightened the rules on the quality assurance provided by nominated advisers, but this has raised costs for companies – see Exhibit 13.4.

Offsetting the cost advantages AIM has over the OL is the fact that the higher level of regulation and related enhanced image, prestige and security of OL companies means that equity capital can usually be raised at a lower required rate of return (the shares can be sold for more per unit of projected profit). However, as Exhibit 13.4 illustrates, AIM has pretty high standards of regulation anyway.

Tighter regime forces nomads to run from smaller companies

Aim groups are more of a risk to nominated advisers, who are charging more for their services, writes Brooke Masters

Fewer firms are serving as nominated advisers (nomads) to companies traded on London's junior market and many of those that remain are charging more for their services in the wake of last year's publication of the first-ever Aim rulebook and the first fines levied against a nomad.

The total number of nomads has fallen from 85 last February, when the rulebook was published, to 71. Some of the reduction is due to consolidation and tougher economic times, but the tighter rules helped drive away firms because they felt they could not make money while performing the record keeping and services required. Annual fees for ongoing nomad service to a £50m company now run between £50,000

and £75,000 a year, double the fees charged by some firms last year.

Andrew Monk, chief executive of nomad Blue Oar, says: "It is now more responsibility to look after an Aim company than a fully listed company and they're more likely to be riskier because they are a smaller company. You have to charge more."...

In a system invented by Aim, nomads serve as gatekeepers for London's junior market and are responsible for making sure the companies they advise adhere to the Stock Exchange's principles. The system is often lauded as more flexible and less costly for fledgling companies, but it has harsh critics who say it attracts companies with lower corporate governance standards.

While defending its approach, the London Stock Exchange has noticeably tightened up its rules and doubled the number of

people assigned to Aim's regulatory and enforcement staff. The rulebook also ratcheted up the pressure on nomads by spelling out specific actions they could, and should, take. That has forced some to do more and others to improve their record keeping.

Nick Bayley, LSE's head of trading services, says: "It's harder now for a nominated adviser to argue it acted with due skill and care, if it has failed without good reason to do the things expected under the new nomad rules."...

...Some nomads welcome the more explicit standards, arguing they will reassure investors.

"Liquidity is key to making the market a success and part of liquidity is getting investors to trust the advisers to regulate what is going on," says Nick Stagg, chief executive of Landsbanki Securities (UK).

Source: Financial Times, 18 June 2008, p. 21

Exhibit 13.4 Tighter regime forces nomads to run from smaller companies

The AIM is not just a stepping-stone for companies planning to graduate to the OL. It has many attractive features in its own right. Indeed, many OL companies have moved to AIM in recent years.

PLUS

PLUS is a stock exchange based in London, and is used by companies that do not want to pay the costs of a flotation on one of the markets run by the LSE. Companies quoted on PLUS provide a service to their shareholders, allowing them to buy and sell shares at reasonable cost. It also allows the company to gain access to capital, for example, by selling more shares in a rights issue, without submitting to the rigour and expense of a quotation on LSE. The downside is that trading in PLUS-quoted shares can be illiquid (not many buyers or sellers) and bid/offer spreads wide (30–50% is not uncommon).

PLUS is owned by PLUS-Markets group (**www.plusmarketsgroup.com**). Joining fees range from a minimum of £15,000 to £100,000 for the largest companies, and annual fees are between £5,665 and £51,500. In addition there are corporate advisers' fees of around £20,000, plus an annual retainer. If new money is to be raised there will be additional advisory and other costs. PLUS companies are generally small and often brand new, but there are also some long-established and well-known firms, such as Arsenal FC, Thwaites and Adnams.

Many companies gain a quotation on PLUS without raising fresh capital simply to allow a market price to be set and current shareholders to trade. If no money is raised, no formal admission document or prospectus is required, but the corporate adviser (to be retained by the company at all times) will insist that good accounting systems are in place with annual audited accounts and semi-annual accounts. The corporate adviser will also ensure that the company has at least one non-executive director, and adequate working capital. There are around 200 companies with a combined market capitalisation of around £2 billion quoted on the PLUS exchange. PLUS Market also provides a trading platform for all UK listed shares, plus some European shares and some unlisted shares.

Understanding the figures in the financial pages

The financial pages of the broadsheet newspapers, particularly the *Financial Times,* provide some important statistics on company share price performance and valuation ratios. Exhibit 13.5 shows extracts from two issues of the *Financial Times.* The information provided in the Monday edition is different from that provided on the other days of the week. (There is more discussion on these ratios in *The Financial Times Guide to Investing* by Glen Arnold).

The highest and lowest prices during the previous 52 weeks

Price/earnings ratio (PER) – share price divided by the company's earnings (profits after tax) per share in the latest 12-month period. A much examined and talked about measure

$$PER = \frac{Share\ price}{Earnings\ per\ share}$$

Market price – this is the mid-price (midway between the best buying and selling prices) quoted at 4.30 pm on the previous day

The dividend paid in the company's last full year – it is the cash payment in pence per share (after deduction of 10% tax for UK firms)

Dividend cover – profit after tax divided by the dividend payment, or earnings per share divided by dividend per share

$$Dividend\ cover = \frac{Earnings\ per\ share}{Dividend\ per\ share}$$

Share price change over the previous week

TUESDAY JULY 5 2011

Aerospace & Defence

Notes	Price	Chng	52 Week High	Low	Yld	P/E	Vol '000s
AvonRub...†	309.50	+1.50	340	105	0.8	15.5	13
BAE Sys....	319	+0.10	372.90	288.10	5.5	9.6	7,959
Chemring..†	638.50	+4	740	510.20	1.9	13.2	217
Cobham....	212.30	-1.50	248.80	188.60	2.8	15.8	2,419
Hampson..q	26.75	+0.50	61.75	18	–	3.3	8,561
Meggitt	385.50	+3.40	388.90	124	2.4	19	944
RollsRyc....	648	+0.50	664.19	314.06	2.2	22.7	5,719
Senior....	186	-1.60	193.60	108.80	1.7	16.4	752
UltraElc....	£17.09	+0.05	£19.03	£15.14	2	17.7	114
UMECO....q	379	+9	512.50	356.81	4.8	27.2	37

MONDAY JULY 4 2011

Aerospace & Defence

Notes	Price	Wks% Chg	Div	Div Cov	Mcap £m	Last xd
AvonRub †	308	-1.0	2.50	8.0	94.6	9.3
BAE Sys	318.90	+4.4	17.50	1.9	10,899.8	20.4
Chemring †	634.50	+3.7	12.40	3.9	1,233.0	23.3
Cobham	213.80	+3.1	6	2.2	2,410.4	4.5
Hampson q	26.25	-6.3	–	†	73.3	8.9
Meggitt	382.10	+6.5	9.20	2.2	2,964.8	9.3
RollsRyc	647.50	+6.3	14.40	2.0	12,122.4	27.10
Senior	187.60	+16.2	3.12	3.6	754.6	4.5
UltraElc	£17.04	+6.6	34.60	2.8	1,172.2	6.4
UMECO q	370	-2.6	18.25	0.8	178.1	12.4

Ex-dividend date is the last date on which the share went ex-dividend (new buyers of the shares will not receive the recently announced dividend after this date) 4 May in this case

Market capitalisation is calculated by multiplying the number of shares by their market price

Change in closing price on day before (Monday) compared with previous trading day

Dividend yield – the dividend divided by the current share price expressed as a percentage

$$\frac{Dividend\ per\ share}{Current\ share\ price} \times 100$$

Volume of trade in those shares on the previous day

Exhibit 13.5 London Share Service extracts: aerospace and defence companies

Indices

Information on individual companies in isolation is less useful than information set in the context of the firm's peer group, or in comparison with quoted companies generally. For example, if Tesco's shares fall by 1 per cent on a particular day, an investor might be keen to learn whether the market as a whole rose or fell on that day, and by how much. An **index** measures the relative value of a group of shares, and publishes the data for comparison purposes.

The oldest index is the **Dow Jones Industrial Average (DJIA)**, which began in 1896 with 12 stocks (only one of which, General Electric, is still on the index) valued at 40.74. The number of companies was increased to 30 in 1928 valued at 239, since when the number of stocks has remained the same, but the index is now valued at over 10,000, see Exhibit 13.6.

The companies on the Dow represent the largest and best-known US companies, and the DJIA is one of the few indices to be **weighted by the share price**, so higher priced shares are given more weight – they may be smaller companies in terms of market capitalisation than others in the index but their percentage share price changes have more effect on the index. In recent years the S&P500

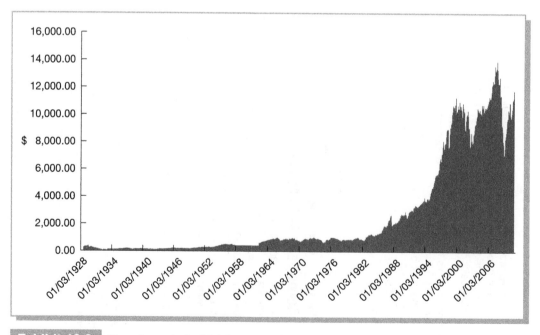

(Standard & Poor's 500) index has been given more attention than the DJIA because it more accurately represents the US market given that it contains 500 companies and is market capitalisation weighted. Most indices are **capitalisation weighted**. To calculate these indices each component share is weighted by the size of the company; by its market capitalisation (shares in issue × share price). Thus a 2 per cent movement in the share price of a large company has a greater effect on an index than a 2 per cent change in a small company's share price.

The oldest UK index is the **FTSE All Share index**, formed in 1962 with a base value of 100, comprising all companies on the London Stock Exchange above a certain size and liquidity. Since then the FTSE (a joint venture of the *Financial Times* and the London *Stock Exchange*) has produced an increasing number of indices, the most famous of which is the **FTSE 100, the 'Footsie'**, which began in 1984 with a base value of 1,000. It is an index of the 100 most highly capitalised UK-based **blue chip** companies, which generally have a market capitalisation over £2 billion (large and relatively safe companies are referred to as 'blue chips'). Twenty-one of the original companies are still on the list, and its performance is closely watched by investors throughout the world. It reflects the global economic climate, because the turnover of these London-quoted companies is largely derived from outside of the UK. It is calculated every 15 seconds so changes can be observed throughout the day. The FTSE 100 rose significantly in its first 16 years, but has done poorly since 2000 – it has not even matched inflation.

The FTSE manages thousands of different indices and has offices all over the world. Furthermore, there are many other agencies calculating indices, the most important of which are shown in Exhibit 13.7.

FTSE All-Share

This index is the most representative in that it reflects the average movements of over 600 shares comprising 98–99 per cent of the value of the London market. It is broken down into a number of industrial and commercial sectors, so that investors and companies can use sector-specific yardsticks, such as those for mining or chemicals – see Exhibit 13.8. Companies in the FTSE All-Share index have market capitalisations (roughly) above £40 million.

FTSE 250

This index is based on 250 firms which are in the next size range after the top 100. Capitalisations are generally between £300 million and £2 billion. (Also calculated with investment trusts removed.)

UK indices	Non-UK indices	
FTSE 100	NASDAQ Comp	US
FTSE 250	Dow Jones	US
FTSE 350	S&P500	US
FTSE All-Share	FTSE MIB	Italy
FTSE AIM All-Share	Xetra DAX	Germany
FTSE SmallCap	D J Eurostoxx 50	Eurozone
FTSE All-Small	CAC 40	France
FTSE Fledgling	AEX	Netherlands
	BEL20	Belgium
	PSI General	Portugal
	Nikkei 225	Tokyo
	Hang Seng	Hong Kong
	ASX All Ordinaries	Australia
	FTSEurofirst100	Europe
	FTSE All World	World

Exhibit 13.7   **Important stock market indices**

Source: London Stock Exchange

FTSE 350

This index is based on the largest 350 quoted companies. It combines the FTSE 100 and the FTSE 250. This cohort of shares is also split into two to give high and low dividend yield groups. A second 350 index excludes investment trusts.

FTSE SmallCap

This index covers companies (268 of them in July 2011) included in the FTSE All-Share but excluded from the FTSE 350, with a market capitalisation of about £40 million to £300 million.

FTSE Fledgling

This includes companies listed on the Main Market but too small to be in the FTSE All-Share Index.

FTSE AIM All-Share

Index of all AIM companies (except those with a low free float and low liquidity).

FTSE All-Small

Combines companies in FTSE SmallCap with those in the FTSE Fledgling (414 companies in July 2011).

These indices are shown daily in the *Financial Times* – see Exhibit 13.8.

Rights issues

In addition to, or as an alternative to, floating on a stock market, which usually involves raising finance by selling shares to a new group of shareholders, a company may raise finance by making a **rights issue**, in which existing shareholders are invited to pay for new shares in proportion to their present holdings. This is a very popular method of raising new funds, especially if the company does not want or is unable to finance through borrowing. It is easy and relatively cheap (compared with new issues). Directors are not required to seek the prior consent of shareholders, and the London Stock Exchange will only intervene in larger issues (to adjust the timing so that the market does not suffer from too many issues in one period).

Pre-emption rights

The UK has particularly strong traditions and laws concerning **pre-emption rights**. These require that a company raising new equity capital by selling shares must first offer those shares to the existing shareholders. The owners of the company are entitled to subscribe for the new shares in proportion to their existing holding, which enables them to maintain the influence of their existing percentage ownership of the company – the only difference is that each slice of the company cake is bigger because it is part of a larger financial asset. Rights issues are usually offered at a significantly discounted price from the market value of the current shares – typically 10–20 per cent. Shareholders can either buy these shares themselves or sell the 'right' to buy them to another investor. For further reassurance that the firm will raise the anticipated finance, rights issues are usually underwritten by financial institutions (the financial institution guarantees to buy any shares not sold).

FTSE ACTUARIES SHARE INDICES

UK SERIES

Produced in conjunction with the Institute and Faculty of Actuaries

www.ft.com/equities

	£ Stlg Jul 4	Day's chge%	Euro Index	£ Stlg Jul 1	£ Stlg Jun 30	Year ago	Div. yield%	Cover	P/E ratio	Xd adj	Total Return
FTSE 100 (100)	6017.5	+0.5	5193.5	5989.8	5945.7	4823.5	3.06	2.87	11.42	112.85	4006.40
FTSE 250 (250)	12102.3	+0.5	10445.0	12040.3	11934.0	9301.4	2.38	2.36	17.82	166.23	7451.41
FTSE 250 ex Inv Co (204)	12771.1	+0.6	11022.2	12695.1	12579.4	9717.5	2.52	2.46	16.16	184.18	7995.79
FTSE 350 (350)	3202.6	+0.5	2764.1	3187.6	3163.5	2553.1	2.96	2.81	12.01	57.88	4323.53
FTSE 350 ex Inv Co (304)	3187.3	+0.5	2750.8	3172.1	3148.1	2539.7	2.99	2.83	11.83	58.17	2213.17
FTSE 350 Higher Yield (111)	3170.1	+0.6	2736.0	3151.3	3133.4	2567.5	4.13	2.32	10.43	81.06	4166.49
FTSE 350 Lower Yield (239)	2933.6	+0.3	2531.9	2924.1	2895.7	2299.2	1.60	4.28	14.59	32.19	2813.12
FTSE SmallCap (268)	3311.4	+0.4	2857.92	3299.58	3272.86	2667.82	2.47	1.78	22.69	45.17	4041.62
FTSE SmallCap ex Inv Co (156)	2695.4	+0.4	2326.28	2684.36	2658.71	2193.44	2.94	2.06	16.49	45.26	3442.96
FTSE All-Share (618)	3134.9	+0.5	2705.64	3120.33	3096.72	2499.85	2.95	2.79	12.15	56.33	4285.93
FTSE All-Share ex Inv Co (460)	3111.3	+0.5	2685.27	3096.52	3073.02	2479.96	2.99	2.81	11.88	56.71	2197.48
FTSE All-Share ex Multinationals (551)	899.9	+0.3	643.71	896.83	890.09	741.80	2.99	2.44	13.72	16.25	1331.66
FTSE Fledgling (146)	5072.8	+0.3	4378.17	5056.04	5054.11	3935.67	3.37	‡	‡	66.14	8169.03
FTSE Fledgling ex Inv Co (93)	6114.6	+0.1	5277.25	6106.25	6121.16	4564.56	4.28	‡	‡	94.04	9641.23
FTSE All-Small (414)	2288.6	+0.4	1975.20	2280.49	2263.42	1837.10	2.54	1.43	27.44	31.06	3587.26
FTSE All-Small ex Inv Co (249)	2004.4	+0.4	1729.91	1996.61	1979.34	1618.00	3.04	1.57	20.93	33.35	3246.48
FTSE AIM All-Share (804)	870.6	+0.7	751.4	864.2	858.0	650.0	0.62	1.31	80.00†	3.37	895.75
FTSE Sector Indices											
Oil & Gas (25)	**9123.7**	**+0.8**	**7874.32**	**9054.10**	**9007.36**	**6639.53**	**2.61**	**4.16**	**9.22**	**145.80**	**6353.09**
Oil & Gas Producers (18)	8605.6	+0.7	7427.11	8542.85	8502.22	6283.03	2.66	4.16	9.02	138.77	6182.93
Oil Equipment Services (5)	26066.6	+1.6	22497.09	25646.00	25273.06	16900.01	1.22	3.99	20.53	322.22	16838.36
Basic Materials (35)	**8126.7**	**+0.4**	**7013.83**	**8095.80**	**8040.20**	**5616.13**	**1.41**	**8.01**	**8.85**	**74.63**	**6875.88**
Chemicals (7)	8368.5	+1.7	7222.54	8227.90	8123.16	5213.39	1.81	2.62	21.04	111.33	6522.62
Forestry & Paper (1)	7581.0	+0.9	6542.89	7510.51	7293.07	4320.60	2.61	3.20	11.97	172.84	6881.42
Industrial Metals & Mining (3)	8401.4	+0.4	7250.95	8364.34	8329.72	5677.79	0.41	14.98	16.44	16.84	6799.92
Mining (24)	25424.1	+0.3	21942.53	25343.96	25181.71	17685.12	1.39	8.41	8.58	226.66	11181.53
Industrials (113)	**3265.6**	**+0.5**	**2818.38**	**3250.39**	**3223.86**	**2519.83**	**2.45**	**2.30**	**17.72**	**45.09**	**2891.13**
Construction & Materials (10)	3997.4	+0.5	3450.04	3978.25	3929.29	3057.63	3.99	1.78	14.09	94.13	3466.19
Aerospace & Defence (11)	3508.6	+0.1	3028.10	3506.10	3490.15	3115.06	3.41	1.99	14.73	53.87	3275.85
General Industrials (6)	2683.0	+0.5	2315.57	2674.63	2633.55	1848.67	2.67	2.64	14.16	35.37	2504.59
Electronic & Electrical Equipment (12)	4212.2	+0.5	3635.34	4192.37	4120.50	2226.53	1.81	2.64	20.95	42.49	3362.15
Industrial Engineering (13)	8048.6	+1.3	6946.46	7943.58	7864.75	4798.64	2.06	2.74	17.67	112.06	8464.30
Industrial Transportation (8)	3416.9	+0.6	2949.00	3397.91	3379.34	3013.54	3.84	1.69	15.38	77.43	2436.51
Support Services (53)	4568.2	+0.5	3942.63	4546.68	4514.97	3664.64	1.96	2.44	20.92	57.15	4111.24
Consumer Goods (36)	**11365.0**	**+1.1**	**9808.67**	**11239.52**	**11167.41**	**9048.98**	**3.23**	**2.09**	**1483**	**199.62**	**6945.68**
Automobiles & Parts (2)	5583.6	+0.3	4818.94	5568.87	5520.04	2687.03	2.08	3.90	12.33	83.89	4577.26
Beverages (4)	10036.7	+1.1	8662.25	9925.66	9900.63	8066.89	2.65	1.82	20.66	67.32	6061.96
Food Producers (12)	5432.4	+1.3	4688.53	5363.11	5358.95	4612.08	3.32	3.29	9.15	98.38	3984.35
Household Goods & Home Construction (11)	5713.8	+0.9	4931.33	5645.81	5635.31	4770.22	2.70	2.56	14.48	86.09	3457.63
Leisure Goods (2)	3050.3	−4.0	2632.63	3178.57	3117.17	1927.87	3.25	1.79	17.13	36.71	2155.99
Personal Goods (3)	19938.4	+0.8	17208.05	19782.90	19528.97	10971.29	1.33	2.50	29.93	12.17	11575.44
Tobacco (2)	31870.5	+1.2	27506.15	31490.49	31108.99	25271.13	4.10	1.58	15.42	916.71	16106.70
Health Care (14)	**6882.8**	**+0.7**	**5940.26**	**6834.00**	**6816.09**	**5895.72**	**4.24**	**1.33**	**17.79**	**181.07**	**4170.91**
Health Care Equipment & Services (4)	3797.7	−0.4	3277.60	3812.48	3765.60	3250.36	1.49	4.32	15.55	31.13	2964.31
Pharmaceuticals & Biotechnology (10)	9550.1	+0.8	8242.34	9476.96	9456.98	8180.16	4.38	1.27	17.93	260.16	5106.31
Consumer Service (91)	**3417.2**	**+0.5**	**2949.25**	**3400.40**	**3386.05**	**2987.81**	**2.93**	**2.55**	**13.39**	**70.52**	**2709.41**
Food & Drug Retailers (6)	4855.9	+0.8	4190.97	4817.49	4826.92	4561.95	3.56	2.05	13.72	125.46	4754.31
General Retailers (25)	1660.9	−0.4	1433.43	1668.32	1661.59	1512.49	3.52	2.60	10.93	40.41	1610.33
Media (26)	4522.1	+0.7	3902.85	4492.78	4472.68	3605.19	2.45	2.40	16.97	74.05	2332.08

Source: Financial Times, 5 July 2011

Exhibit 13.8   FTSE Actuaries Share Indices

Example

Take the case of the imaginary listed company Swell plc with 100 million shares in issue. It wants to raise £25 million for expansion but does not want to borrow the money. Its existing shares are quoted on the stock market at 120p, so the new rights shares will have to be issued at a lower price to appeal to shareholders because there is a risk of the market price falling in the period between the announcement and the purchasing of new shares. The offer must remain open for shareholders to get their applications in for at least 2 weeks (10 working days).

Swell has decided to issue 25 million shares at 100p each, raising the required £25 million, thus the ratio of new shares to old is 25:100, a 'one-for-four' rights issue. Each shareholder will be offered one new share for every four already held. The discount on these new shares is 20p or 16.7 per cent. If the market price before the issue is 120p, valuing the entire company at £120 million, and another £25 million is pumped into the company by selling 25 million shares at £1, it logically follows that the market price after the rights issue cannot remain at 120p (assuming all else equal). A company that was previously valued at £120 million which then adds £25 million of value to itself (in the form of cash) should be worth £145 million. This company now has 125 million shares, therefore each share is worth £1.16 (i.e. £145 million divided by 125 million shares).

Shareholders have experienced a decline in the price of their old shares from 120p to 116p. A fall of this magnitude necessarily follows from the introduction of new shares at a discounted price. However, the loss is exactly offset by the gain in share value on the new rights issue shares, which were issued at 100p but have a market price of 116p.

This can be illustrated through the example of Sid, who owned 100 shares worth £120 prior to the rights announcement. Sid loses £4 on the old shares – their value is now £116. However, he makes a gain of £4 on the new shares:

Cost of rights shares (25 × £1)	£25
Ex-rights value (25 × £1.16)	£29
Gain	£4

When the press talks glibly of a rights offer being 'very attractively priced for shareholders', they are generally talking nonsense. Whatever the size of the discount, the same value will be removed from the old shares to leave the shareholder no worse or better off. Logically, value cannot be handed over to the shareholders from the size of the discount decision. Shareholders own all the company's shares before and after the rights issue – they can't hand value to themselves without also taking value from themselves. Of course, if the prospects for the company's profits rise because it can now make capital expenditures, leading to dominant market positions, then the value of shares will rise – for both the old and the new shares. But this is value creation that has nothing to do with the level of the discount.

What if a shareholder does not want to take up the rights?

As owners of the firm all shareholders must be treated in the same way. To make sure that shareholders do not lose out because they are unwilling or unable to buy more shares the law requires that shareholders have a third choice, other than to buy or not buy the new shares. This is to sell the rights on to someone else on the stock market (selling the rights nil paid). Indeed, so deeply enshrined are pre-emption rights that even if the shareholder does nothing the company will sell their rights to the new shares on their behalf and send the proceeds to them. Thus the shareholder is compensated for the fact that their shareholding has been diluted by the increased number of shares in issue.

Example

Take the case of the impoverished Sid, who is unable to find the necessary £25. He could sell the rights to subscribe for the shares to another investor and not have to go through the process of taking up any of the shares himself. Thus, Sid would benefit to the extent of 16p per share or a total of £4 (if the market price stays constant), which adequately compensates for the loss on the 100 shares he holds. But the extent of his control over the company has been reduced – his percentage share of the votes has decreased.

Ex-rights and cum-rights

Old shares bought in the stock market which are designated **cum-rights** carry with them to the new owner the right to subscribe for the new shares in the rights issue. After a cut-off date the shares go **ex-rights**, which means that any purchaser of old shares will not have the right to the new shares; that right remains with the former shareholder.

Placings, open offers and clawback

Some companies argue that the lengthy procedures and expense associated with rights issues (e.g. the time and trouble it takes to get a prospectus prepared and approved by the UKLA) frustrate directors' efforts to take advantage of opportunities in a timely fashion. Firms in the US have much more freedom to bypass pre-emption rights. They are able to sell blocks of shares to securities houses for distribution elsewhere in the market. This is fast and has low transaction costs. If this were permitted in the UK there would be a concern for existing shareholders: they could experience a dilution of their voting power and/or the shares could be sold at such a low price that a portion of the firm is handed over to new shareholders too cheaply. The UK authorities have produced a compromise, under which firms must obtain shareholders' approval through a **special resolution** (a majority of 75 per cent of those voting) at the company's annual general meeting, or at an extraordinary general meeting to waive the **pre-emption right**. Even then the shares must not be sold to outside investors at more than a 5 per cent or 10 per cent discount to the share price. While the maximum discount for Main Market companies under the listing rules is 10 per cent, the Association of British Insurers' guidelines are for a maximum of 5 per cent. This is an important condition. It does not make any difference to existing shareholders if new shares are offered at a deep discount to the market price as long as they are offered to them. If external investors get a discount there is a transfer of value from the current shareholders to the new.

In **placings**, new shares of companies already listed are sold directly to a narrow group of external investors. The institutions, as existing shareholders, have produced guidelines to prevent abuse, which normally allow a placing of only a small proportion of the company's capital (a maximum of 5 per cent in a single year, and no more than 7.5 per cent is to be added to the company's equity capital over a rolling three-year period)[3] in the absence of a **clawback**.

---

[3] Companies can ask to go beyond these limits if they give appropriate justification, but this is rare. Placings are usually structured so that a prospectus is not required, so this saves money. They can also be completed in a matter of days rather than weeks or months for rights issues.

Under a clawback existing shareholders have the right to reclaim the shares as though they were entitled to them under a rights issue. They can buy them at the price they were offered to the external investors. With a clawback the issue becomes an **open offer**. Under an open offer companies can increase their share capital by between 15 per cent and 18 per cent. Beyond that the investors (e.g. Association of British Insurers) prefer a rights issue. The major difference compared with a rights issue is that if shareholders do not exercise this clawback right they receive no compensation for any reduction in the price of their existing shares – there are no nil-paid rights to sell.

Vendor placing

If a company wishes to pay for an asset such as a subsidiary of another firm or an entire company with newly issued shares, but the vendor(s) does not want to hold the shares, the purchaser could arrange for the new shares to be bought by institutional investors for cash. In this way the buyer gets the asset, the vendors (e.g. shareholders in the target company in a merger or takeover) receive cash and the institutional investor makes an investment. There is usually a clawback arrangement for a vendor placing (if the issue is more than 10 per cent of market capitalisation of the acquirer). Again, the price discount can be no more than 5 per cent or 10 per cent of the current share price.

Bought deal

Instead of selling shares to investors, companies are sometimes able to make an arrangement with a securities house whereby it buys all the shares being offered for cash. The securities house then sells the shares on to investors included in its distribution network, hoping to make a profit on the deal. Securities houses often compete to buy a package of shares from the company, with the highest bidder winning. The securities houses take the risk of being unable to sell the shares for at least the amount that they paid. Bought deals are limited by the 5 per cent or 10 per cent pre-emption rules.

Warrants

Warrants give the holder the right to subscribe for a specified number of shares at a fixed price during or at the end of a specified time period. If a company has shares currently trading at £3 it might choose to sell warrants, each of which grants the holder the right to buy a share in the company at, say, £4 over the next five years. If by the fifth year the share price has risen to £6 the warrant holders could exercise their rights and then sell the shares immediately, gaining £2 per share, which is likely to be a considerable return on the original warrant price of a few pence. Warrants are frequently attached to bonds, and make the bond more attractive because the investor benefits from a relatively safe (but low) income on the bond if the firm performs in a mediocre fashion, but if the firm does very well and the share price rises significantly the investor will participate in some of the extra returns through the 'sweetener' or 'equity kicker' provided by the warrant.

There is no requirement for investors to hold warrants until exercised or they expire. There is an active secondary market on the LSE.

Websites

www.advfn.com	ADVFN. Financial data
www.aitegroup.com	Aite Group. Independent research and advice
www.economist.com	The Economist
www.euronext.com	Euronext
www.fese.eu	Federation of European Securities Exchanges
www.fsa.gov.uk	Financial Services Authority
www.ft.com	Financial Times
www.fsa.gov.uk/Pages/Doing/UKLA	UK Listing Authority
www.ftse.com	FTSE Group. Stock market indices and information
www.frc.org.uk/CORPORATE/ukcgcode.cfm	Financial Reporting Council, UK Corporate Governance Code
www.hemscott.com	Hemscott. Share prices and financial data
www.iii.co.uk	Interactive Investor
www.investegate.co.uk	Investegate. Company information
www.investorschronicle.com	Investors Chronicle, weekly stock market analysis
www.liquidmetrix.com	Intelligent Financial Systems
www.londonstockexchange.com	London Stock Exchange
www.nyse.com	New York Stock Exchange
www.plusmarketsgroup.com	PLUS exchange

14

Futures markets

From a small base in the 1970s derivatives have grown to be of enormous importance. Almost all medium and large industrial and commercial firms use derivatives, usually to manage risk, but occasionally to speculate and use arbitrage. Banks are usually at the centre of derivatives trading, dealing on behalf of clients, as market makers or trading on their own account. Other financial institutions are increasingly employing these instruments to lay off risk or to speculate. They can be used across the globe, and traded night and day.

Many fortunes have been lost by managers/traders mesmerised by the potential for riches in trading derivatives, while failing to take the time to fully understand the instruments they were buying. They jumped in, unaware of, or ignoring, the potential for enormous loss. This and the next two chapters describe the main types of derivative and show how they can be used for controlling risk (hedging) and for revving up returns (speculating).

What is a derivative?

A **derivative instrument** is an asset whose performance is based on (derived from) the behaviour of the value of an underlying asset (usually referred to simply as the 'underlying'). The most common **underlyings** include commodities (e.g. tea or pork bellies), shares, bonds, share indices, currencies and interest rates. Derivatives are contracts which give the right, and sometimes the obligation, to buy or sell a quantity of the underlying, or benefit in another way from a rise or fall in the value of the underlying. It is the legal *right* that becomes an asset, with its own value, and it is the right that is purchased or sold.

The derivatives markets have received an enormous amount of attention from the press in recent years. This is hardly surprising as spectacular losses have been made and a number of companies brought to the point of collapse through the employment of derivative instruments. Some examples of the unfortunate use of derivatives are:

■ Barings, Britain's oldest merchant bank, which lost over £800 million on the Nikkei Index (the Japanese share index) contracts on the Singapore and Osaka derivatives exchanges, leading to the bank's demise in 1995.

■ Long-Term Capital Management, which attempted to exploit the 'mispricing' of financial instruments. In 1998 the firm collapsed and the Federal Reserve Bank of New York cajoled 14 banks and brokerage houses to put up $3.6 billion to save LTCM and thereby prevent a financial system breakdown.

■ Financial institutions that were destroyed in 2008 because they bought derivatives whose values depended on US mortgage borrowers continuing to pay their mortgages. When a proportion could not pay their debts, the derivatives (of asset-backed bonds) became either very difficult or impossible to value. The uncertainty surrounding the value of these derivatives was a trigger for financial distress for hundreds of financial institutions that had no connection with the US mortgage market or the related derivatives.

■ Société Générale, which lost €4.9 billion in 2008 when a trader placed bets on the future movements of equity markets using derivatives (up to €50 billion was gambled at one time).

■ UBS lost over $2 billion in 2011 due to a rogue trader making bets on stock market movements through derivatives.

UBS lost over $2 billion in 2011 due to a rogue trader making bets on stock market movements through derivatives.

In many of the financial scandals derivatives have been used (or misused) to speculate rather than to reduce risk. This chapter examines both of these applications of derivatives but places particular emphasis on the hedging (risk-mitigating) facility they provide. These are powerful tools and managers can abuse that power either through ignorance or through deliberate acceptance of greater risk in the anticipation of greater reward. However, there is nothing inherently wrong with the tools themselves. If employed properly they can be remarkably effective at limiting risk.

A long history

Derivative instruments have been employed for more than 2,000 years. Olive growers in ancient Greece unwilling to accept the risk of a low price for their crop when harvested months later would enter into **forward agreements** whereby a price was agreed for delivery at a specific time. This reduced uncertainty for both the grower and the purchaser of the olives. In the Middle Ages forward contracts were traded in a kind of secondary market, particularly for wheat in Europe. In the seventeenth century a futures market was established in Osaka's rice market in Japan and tulip bulb options were traded in Amsterdam.

Commodity futures trading really began to take off in the nineteenth century with the Chicago Board of Trade regulating the trading of grains and other futures and options, and the London Metal Exchange dominating metal trading.

So derivatives are not new. What is different today is the size and importance of the derivatives markets. The last quarter of the twentieth century witnessed an explosive growth of volumes of trade, variety of derivatives products, and the number and range of users and uses. In the 30 years to 2011 the face value of outstanding derivatives contracts rose dramatically to stand at about $600 trillion ($600,000,000,000,000). Compare that with a UK annual GDP of around £1.5 trillion.

Forwards

Imagine you are responsible for purchasing potatoes to make crisps for your firm, a snack food producer. In the free market for potatoes the price rises or falls depending on the balance between buyers and sellers. These movements can be dramatic. Obviously, you would like to acquire potatoes at a price which was as low as possible, while the potato producer wishes to sell for a price that is as high as possible. However, both parties may have a similar interest in reducing the uncertainty of price. This will assist both to plan production and budget effectively. One way in which this could be done is to reach an agreement with the producer(s) to purchase a quantity of potatoes at a price agreed today to be delivered and paid for at a specified time in the future. Crisp producers buy up to 80 per cent of their potatoes up to two years forward. Once the forward agreements have been signed and sealed the crisp manufacturer may later be somewhat regretful if the spot price (price for immediate delivery) subsequently falls below the price agreed months earlier. Unlike option contracts, forwards commit both parties to complete the deal. However, the manufacturer is obviously content to live with this potential for regret in order to remove the risk associated with such an important raw material.

A **forward contract** is an agreement between two parties to undertake an exchange at an agreed future date at a price agreed now.

The party buying at the future date is said to be taking a **long position**. The counterparty which will deliver at the future date is said to be taking a **short position**.

There are forward markets in a wide range of commodities but the most important forward markets today are for foreign exchange, in which hundreds of billions of dollars worth of currency are traded every working day – this will be considered in Chapter 16.

Forward contracts are tailor-made to meet the requirements of the parties. This gives flexibility on the amounts and delivery dates. Forwards are not traded on an exchange but are **over-the-counter instruments** – private agreements outside the regulation of an exchange. This makes them different from futures, which are standardised contracts traded on exchanges. A forward agreement exposes the counterparties to the risk of default – the failure by the other to deliver on the agreement. The risk grows in proportion to the extent by which the spot price diverges from the forward price and the incentive to renege increases. A forward has the advantage over futures of being more available for long-term maturities, say arranging a purchase or sale three years from now, whereas most futures on regulated exchanges are limited to delivery dates within the next 12 months.

Forward contracts are difficult to cancel, as agreement from each counterparty is needed. Also to close the contract early may result in a penalty being charged. Despite these drawbacks forward markets continue to flourish – an example of which you can see in Exhibit 14.1.

Northern Foods passes price rises to customers

by Lucy Warwick-Ching and Ed Crooks

Customers will be hit by higher food prices as Northern Foods, maker of Fox's biscuits and Goodfellas's pizza, prepares to pass on £40m of rising commodity costs to customers, including the big supermarkets.

Stefan Barden, chief executive, said that in the last three months short supplies and high demand had pushed up the prices of cereals, dairy products, cocoa and fats. Poor harvests have also hit vegetables prices.

These cost increases are expected to add £32m–£40m to Northern Foods' £400m raw material bill, an increase of 8–10 per cent.

However, Mr Barden said that, thanks to long-term contracts, forward buying and hedging, the increase this year would only be between 4–5 per cent, resulting in an extra £16m–£20m.

Source: Financial Times,
10 October 2007, p. 25

Exhibit 14.1 Northern Foods passes price rises to customers

A simple futures deal

Futures contracts are in many ways similar to forward contracts. They are agreements between two parties to undertake a transaction at an agreed price on a specified future date. However, they differ from forwards in some important respects. Futures contracts are exchange-based instruments traded on a regulated exchange. The buyer and the seller of a contract do not transact with each other directly. The **clearing house** becomes the formal **counterparty** to every transaction. This reduces the risk of non-compliance with the contract significantly for the buyer or seller of a future, as it is highly unlikely that the clearing house will be unable to fulfil its obligation.

Example

Imagine a farmer wishes to lock in a price for his wheat, which will be harvested in six months. You agree to purchase the wheat from the farmer six months hence at a price of £60 per tonne. You are hoping that by the time the wheat is delivered the price has risen and you can sell at a profit. The farmer is worried that all he has from you is the promise to pay £60 per tonne in six months, and if the market price falls you will walk away from the deal. To reassure him you are asked to put money into what the farmer calls a **margin account**. He asks and you agree to deposit £6 for each tonne you have agreed to buy. If you fail to complete the bargain the farmer will be able to draw on the money from the margin account and then sell the wheat as it is harvested at the going rate for immediate ('spot') delivery. So, as far as the farmer is concerned, the price of wheat for delivery at harvest time could fall to £54 and he is still going to get £60 for each tonne: £6 from what you paid into the margin account and £54 from selling at the spot price.

But what if the price falls below £54? The farmer is exposed to risk – something he had tried to avoid by entering a futures deal. It is for this reason that the farmer asks you to top up your margin account on a daily basis so that there is always a buffer. He sets a **maintenance margin** level of £6 per tonne. This means you have to maintain at least £6 per tonne in the margin account. So, if the day after you buy the future, the harvest time price in the futures market falls to £57 you have only £3 per tonne left in the margin account as a buffer for the farmer. You agreed to buy at £60 but the going rate is only £57. To bring the margin account up to a £6 buffer you

▶

will be required to put in another £3 per tonne. If the price the next day falls to £50 you will be required to put up another £7 per tonne. You agreed to buy at £60, with the market price at £50 you have put a total of £6 + £3 + £7 = £16 into the margin account. By putting in top-ups as the price moves against you, you will always ensure there is a margin of at least £6 per tonne, providing security for the farmer. Even if you go bankrupt or simply renege on the deal he will receive at least £60 per tonne, either from the spot market or from a combination of a lower market price plus money from the margin account. As the price fell to £50 you have a £10 per tonne incentive to walk away from the deal except for the fact that you have put £16 into an account that the farmer can draw on should you be so stupid or unfortunate. If the price is £50 per tonne at expiry of the contract and you have put £16 in the margin account you are entitled to the spare £6 per tonne of margin.

It is in the margin account that we have the source of multiple losses in the futures markets. Say your life savings amount to £10 and you are convinced there will be a drought and shortage of wheat following the next harvest. In your view the price will rise to £95 per tonne. So, to cash in on your forecast you agree to buy a future for one tonne of wheat. You have agreed with the farmer that in six months you will pay £60 for the wheat, which you expect to then sell for £95. (The farmer is obviously less convinced than you that prices are destined to rise.)

To gain this right (and obligation) to buy at £60 you need only have £6 for the **initial margin**. The other £4 might be useful to meet day-to-day **margin calls** should the wheat price fall from £60 (temporarily in your view). If the price does rise to £95 you will make a £35 profit, having laid out only £6 (plus some other cash temporarily). This is a very high return of 583 per cent over six months. But what if the price at harvest time is £40? You have agreed to pay £60, therefore the loss of £20 wipes out your savings and you are made bankrupt. You lose over three times your initial margin. That is the downside to the gearing effect of futures.

The above example demonstrates the essential features of futures market trading, but in reality participants in the market do not transact directly with each other, but go through a regulated exchange. Your opposite number, called a **counterparty**, is not a farmer but an organisation that acts as counterparty to all futures traders, buyers or sellers, called the central counterparty at the **clearing house**. Also, in the example we have assumed that the maintenance margin level is set at the same level as the initial margin. In reality it is often set at 70 to 80 per cent of the initial margin level.

An exchange provides standardised legal agreements traded in highly liquid markets. The contracts cannot be tailor-made, for example, for 77 tonnes of wheat or coffee delivered in 37 days from now. The fact that the agreements are standardised allows a wide market appeal because buyers and sellers know what is being traded: the contracts are for a specific quality of the underlying, in specific amounts with specific delivery dates. For example, for sugar traded on NYSE Liffe one contract is for a specified grade of sugar and each contract is for a standard 50 tonnes with fixed delivery days in late August, October, December, March and May.

It is important to remember that it is the contracts themselves that are a form of security bought and sold in the market. Thus a December future priced at $282.5 per tonne is a derivative of sugar and is not the same thing as sugar. To buy this future is to enter into an agreement with rights and obligations. It is these that are being bought and sold and not the commodity. When exercise of the contract takes place then the physical amount of sugar is bought or sold.[1] However, as with most derivatives, usually futures positions are cancelled by an offsetting transaction before exercise.

Marking to market and margins

With the clearing house being the formal counterparty for every buyer or seller of a futures contract, an enormous potential for credit risk is imposed on the organisation given the volume of futures traded and the size of the underlying they represent. (NYSE Liffe, for example, has an average daily volume of around 5 million contracts worth hundreds of billions of pounds/dollars.) If only a small fraction of market participants fail to deliver this could run into hundreds of millions of pounds/dollars. Hence the clearing house operates a margining system. The amount of margin required depends on the futures market, the level of volatility of the underlying and the potential for default; however it is likely to be in the region of 0.1 per cent to 15 per cent of the value of the underlying. The initial margin is not a 'down payment' for the underlying: the funds do not flow to a buyer or seller of the underlying but stay with the clearing house. It is merely a way of guaranteeing that the buyer or seller will pay up should the

---

[1] Note that some futures contracts have cash delivery rather than physical delivery, see later.

price of the underlying move against them. It is refunded when the futures position is closed (if the market has not moved adversely).

The clearing house also operates a system of daily **marking to market**. At the end of every trading day the counterparty's profits or losses created as a result of that day's price change are calculated. Any counterparty that made a loss has his/her member's margin account debited. The following morning the losing counterparty must inject more cash to cover the loss if the amount in the account has fallen below a threshold level (the maintenance margin). An inability to pay a daily loss causes default and the contract is closed, thus protecting the clearing house from the possibility that the counterparty might accumulate further daily losses without providing cash to cover them. The margin account of the counterparty that makes a daily gain is credited. This may be withdrawn the next day. The daily credits and debits to members' margin accounts are known as the **variation margin**.

Example   MARGINS

Imagine a buyer and seller of a future on Monday with an underlying value of £50,000 are each required to provide an initial margin of 10 per cent, or £5,000. The buyer will make profits if the price rises while the seller will make profits if the price falls. In Exhibit 14.2 it is assumed that counterparties have to keep all of the initial margin permanently as a buffer.[2] (In reality this may be relaxed by an exchange.)

At the end of Tuesday the buyer of the contract has £1,000 debited from her member's account. This will have to be paid over the following day or the exchange will automatically close the member's position and crystallise the loss. If the buyer does provide the variation margin and the position is kept open until Friday the account will have an accumulated credit of £5,000. The buyer has the right to buy at £50,000 but can sell at £55,000. If the buyer and the seller closed their positions on Friday the buyer would be entitled to receive the initial margin plus the accumulated profit, £5,000 + £5,000 = £10,000, whereas the seller would receive nothing (£5,000 initial margin minus losses of £5,000).

---

[2] Initial margin is the same as maintenance margin in this case.

£		Day			
	Monday	Tuesday	Wednesday	Thursday	Friday
Value of future (based on daily closing price)	50,000	49,000	44,000	50,000	55,000
Buyers' position					
Initial margin	5,000				
Variation margin (+ credited) (– debited)	0	–1,000	–5,000	+6,000	+5,000
Accumulated profit (loss)	0	–1,000	–6,000	0	+5,000
Sellers' position					
Initial margin	5,000				
Variation margin (+ credited) (– debited)	0	+1,000	+5,000	–6,000	–5,000
Accumulated profit (loss)	0	+1,000	+6,000	0	–5,000

Exhibit 14.2   **Example of initial margin, variation margin and marking to market**

This example illustrates the effect of leverage in futures contracts. The initial margin payments are small relative to the value of the underlying. When the underlying changes by a small percentage the effect is magnified for the future, and large percentage gains and losses are made on the amount committed to the transaction:

Underlying change (Monday–Friday): $\frac{55,000 - 50,000}{50,000} \times 100 = 10\%$

Percentage return to buyer of future: $\frac{5,000}{5,000} \times 100 = 100\%$

Percentage return to seller of future: $\frac{-5,000}{5000} \times 100 = -100\%$

To lose all the money committed to a financial transaction may seem disappointing but it is as nothing compared with the losses that can be made on futures. It is possible to lose a multiple of the amount set down as an initial margin. For example, if the future rose to £70,000 the seller would have to provide a £20,000 variation margin – four times the amount committed in the first place. Clearly playing the futures market can seriously damage your wealth. This was proved with a vengeance by Nick Leeson of Barings Bank. He bought futures in the Nikkei 225 Index – the main Japanese share index – in both the Osaka and the Singapore derivative exchanges. He was betting that the market would rise as he committed the bank to buying the index at a particular price. When the index fell, margin payments had to be made. Leeson took a double or quits attitude, 'I mean a lot of futures traders when the market is against them will double up'.[3] He continued to buy futures. To generate some cash, to make variation margin payments, he wrote combinations of call and put options (**straddles**) for which counterparties paid premiums – see Chapter 15. This compounded the problem when the Nikkei 225 Index continued to fall in 1994: over £800 million was lost.

When markets are volatile the exchanges increase the size of the margins they require. In 2010 this, together with rising commodity prices, had a significant impact on farmers. As they tried to hedge the positions of their future crop sales in a market where prices moved up and down rapidly (but mostly up) the exchanges demanded more and more cash as margin. Farmers lose from price decreases in the cash market and so each year need to take a short position in the futures market, i.e. sell first and buy later to close their position. Then, if prices fall they make a profit on the futures, offsetting the loss on the actual crop when sold in the cash market. The main problem in 2010 was that the price of the futures of many commodities soared. The exchanges required more variation margin simply because both the futures position deteriorated for those with short futures positions and because the exchanges, increased the percentages for initial and maintenance margin because of the greater volatility, see Exhibit 14.3.

Settlement

Historically the futures markets developed on the basis of the *physical delivery* of the underlying. So if you had contracted to buy 40,000 lb of lean hogs

---

[3] Nick Leeson in an interview with David Frost reported in the *Financial Times*, 11 September 1995.

Farmers left short-changed by a margin call squeeze

By Gregory Meyer in New York and Jack Farchy in London

Times could not be better for US cotton farmers. Demand from mills is strong, this year's crop is a bumper one and prices are stratospheric.

But farmers belonging to Calcot, a cotton marketing co-operative in California, have not been reaping all the gains, at least not yet. The co-op this autumn told members final payments for their cotton would be delayed until next year because it is locked up as collateral for crop hedging deals.

Companies that own or produce physical commodities often sell futures contracts to protect their financial positions. When prices rise, however, the derivatives positions fall increasingly into the red, leading brokers to demand more collateral to ensure the companies' losses are not borne by the exchange.

With commodities markets experiencing sharp swings – prices have been soaring and plunging in the space of days or even hours in recent weeks – exchanges are demanding larger amounts of collateral from participants holding futures positions. Quite simply, the lengthy bull run in commodities means it is becoming ever more expensive to trade them.

Indeed, the so-called "margin calls" are eating into the cash flows of everyone trading futures contracts, from farming co-ops

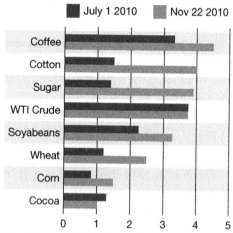

Futures contracts
Margin rates for hedgers ($'000 per contract)

■ July 1 2010   ■ Nov 22 2010

Source: Thomson Reuters Datastream: CME, ICE

such as Calcot to the world's biggest trading houses, banks and hedge funds. "The current futures market situation has put tremendous pressure on our financial resources to meet margin calls," the Calcot president has told members.

The effects of higher margin requirements have been particularly brutal in the agricultural sector, where prices for cotton, sugar, wheat and corn have all experienced violent swings. Cotton, for example, has doubled in price in just four months, before falling 22 per cent in less than two weeks.

"We've seen stress in cotton and in coffee and in sugar – just look at what prices have done in the last three to six months and you'll see where the stress is," says Michael Vellucci, with Brown Brothers Harriman, a privately held bank in New York.

Each significant move upwards means more margin for those who have taken short positions in the market. In ICE cotton, a market move of one cent requires an additional $500 in margin per 50,000-pound contract. Since July 1, cotton has risen more than 39 cents, meaning an additional $19,500 in margin per contract.

Exhibit 14.3   Farmers left short-changed by a margin call squeeze

The issue is not so much one of solvency since, barring an unexpected disaster such as crop failure, the trader or producer owns the underlying commodity as well as the short position on the futures market – the very nature of hedging price risk.

But for the duration of the hedge, the demands for margin can have a sizeable impact on a company's liquidity, or availab-lity of cash, especially for those whose exposure is not spread across commodities and global markets. Forced liquidation of short futures positions, moreo-ver, can give markets a further upward push.

As volatility rises, banks rate commodity trading as a riskier activity, requiring them to hold more capital or scale back the size of their positions. Likewise, as exchanges raise the "initial margin", or the amount of capital required to open a futures posi-tion, investors such as hedge funds who regularly take short-term bets are being forced to reconsider how they are allocating their funds to commodities.

Source: *Financial Times*, 23 November 2010, p. 35

Exhibit 14.3 Continued

you would receive the meat as settlement.[4] However in most futures markets today (including that for lean hogs) only a small proportion of contracts result in physical delivery. The majority are **closed out** before the expiry of the con-tract and all that changes hands is cash, either as a profit or as a loss. Speculators certainly do not want to end up with five tonnes of coffee or 15,000 pounds of orange juice and so will **reverse their trade** before the contract expires; for example, if they originally bought a future for 50 tonnes of white sugar they later sell a future for 50 tonnes of white sugar.

Hedgers, say confectionery manufacturers, may sometimes take delivery from the exchange but in most cases will have established purchasing channels for sugar, cocoa, etc. In these cases they may use the futures markets not as a way of obtaining goods but as a way of offsetting the risk of the prices of goods moving adversely. So a confectionery manufacturer may still plan to buy, say, sugar, at the spot price from its longstanding supplier in six months and simultaneously, to hedge the risk of the price rising, will buy six-month futures in sugar. This position will then be closed before expiry. If the price of the underlying has risen the manufacturer pays more to the supplier but has a compensating gain on the future. If the price falls the supplier is paid less and so a gain is made here, but, under a perfect hedge, the future has lost an equal value.

---

[4] If a seller of a future which is about to expire wishes to deliver the underlying (say cocoa, coffee or zinc) it gives the exchange notice of intention to deliver a few days before the expiry of the futures contract. Then the underlying is transported to a delivery point at the sellers' expense – the exchange usually maintains warehouses. The buyer who wishes to take physical delivery notifies the exchange when the contract expires. The exchange will decide which buyers may take away which warehoused underlying.

As the futures markets developed it became clear that most participants did not want the complications of physical delivery and this led to the development of futures contracts where only **cash settlement** takes place. This permitted a wider range of futures contracts to be created. Futures contracts based on intangible commodities such as a share index or a rate of interest are now extremely important financial instruments. With these, no physical delivery takes place and if the contract is held to the maturity date one party will hand over cash to the other (via the clearing house system).

Equity index futures

Equity index futures are an example of a cash settlement market. The underlyings here are collections of shares, for example 225 Japanese shares for the Nikkei 225. Hedgers and speculators do not want 225 different shares to be delivered say one month from now. They are quite content to receive or hand over the profit or loss made by buying and then selling (or the other way around) a future of the index.

The equity index futures table (Exhibit 14.4) from FT.com shows futures in indices from stock markets around the world for 27 October 2010. These are notional futures contracts. If not closed out before expiry (by the holder of a future doing the reverse transaction to their first – so if they bought the future first, selling will close the position) they are settled in cash based on the average level of the relevant index (say the FTSE 100) between stated times on the last day of the contract.

Exhibit 14.4 is very much a cut-down version of the futures available to traders. As well as the November and December delivery futures shown, NYSE Liffe also offers traders the possibility of buying or selling futures that 'deliver' in March, June and September. Delivery dates are the third Friday of the month.

The table shows the first price traded at the beginning of the current day (Open), the **settlement price** (usually the last traded price) used to mark margin accounts to market, the change from the previous day's settlement price, the highest and lowest prices during the day's settlement price, the number of contracts traded that day (Est. vol.) and the total number of open contracts (these are trading contracts opened over the last few months that have not yet been closed by an equal and opposite futures transaction).

Each point on the UK's FTSE 100 share index future is worth £10, by convention. So if the future rises from 5634.50 to 5684.50 and you bought a future at 5634.50 you have made $50 \times £10 = £500$ if you were to now sell at 5684.50.

EQUITY INDEX FUTURES

Oct 27		Open	Sett	Change	High	Low	Est. vol.	Open int.
DJIA	Dec	11049.00	11072.00	-52.00	1185.00	10970.00	1	5,787
DJ Euro Stoxx‡	Dec	2838.00	822.00	-26.00	2856.00	2811.00	1,249,363	2,021,455
S&P 500	Dec	1178.70	1178.80	-4.00	1178.90	1178.20	7	323,869
Mini S&P 500	Dec	1178.50	1178.75	-4.00	1179.00	1178.00	3,099	2,686,156
Nasdaq 100	Dec	-	2123.75	+7.75	-	2124.00	-	24,833
Mini Nasdaq	Dec	2123.50	2123.75	+7.75	2124.75	2123.50	53	452,922
CAC 40	Nov	3824.50	3796.50	-36.00	3850.50	3789.50	136,995	363,897
DAX	Dec	6613.00	6580.00	-53.00	6639.00	6562.50	145,073	179,479
AEX	Nov	339.20	336.95	-2.70	339.90	336.50	27,861	89,753
MIB 30	Dec	21200.00	21191.00	-99.00	21470.00	21130.00	18,590	41,712
IBEX 35	Nov	10660.00	10618.50	-100.00	10785.00	10605.00	12,388	37,044
SMI	Dec	6465.00	6482.00	-1.00	6520.00	6445.00	31,658	141,841
FTSE 100	Dec	5699.00	5634.50	-59.50	5699.50	5612.50	105,727	608,833
Hang Seng	Oct	23553.00	23109.00	-508.00	23711.00	23096.00	120,632	41,937
Nikkei 225†	Dec	9380.00	9410.00	+50.00	9400.00	9350.00	8,056	305,035
Topix	Dec	816.00	817.50	+1.50	818.00	815.50	372	389,021
KOSPI 200	Dec	248.20	246.50	-2.00	249.35	245.85	429,047	97,317

North American Latest. Contracts shown are among the 25 most traded based on estimates of average volumes in 2004. CBOT volume, high & low for pit & electronic trading at settlement.
Previous day's Open Interest. †Osaka contract. ‡Eurex contract

Source: Financial Times, www.ft.com. 27 October 2010

Exhibit 14.4   Equity index futures table from www.ft.com for close of trading on 27 October 2010

Example   HEDGING WITH A SHARE INDEX FUTURE

It is 27 October 2010 and the FT 100 is at 5646. A fund manager wishes to hedge a £13,000,000 fund against a decline in the market. A December FTSE 100 future is available at 5634.50 – see Exhibit 14.4. The investor retains the shares in the portfolio and *sells* 231 index futures contracts. Each futures contract is worth £56,345 (5634.5 points × £10). So 231 contracts are needed to cover £13,000,000: (£13,000,000 ÷ (£10 × 5634.5) = 231).[5]

---

[5] Technically 230.72 contracts are needed but we cannot deal in a fraction of a contract so we need to round up or down.

Outcome in December

For the sake of argument assume that the index falls by 10 per cent from 5646 to 5081, leaving the portfolio value at £11,700,000 (assuming the portfolio moves exactly in line with the FT 100 index). The closing of the futures position offsets this £1,300,000 loss by buying 231 futures at 5081 to close the position producing a profit[6] of:

Able to sell at 5634.5 × 231 × £10 =	£13,015,695
Able to buy at 5081 × 231 × £10 =	−£11,737,110
	£1,278,585

These contracts are cash settled so £1,278,585 will be paid. Furthermore, the investor receives back the margin laid down, less broker's fees.

Note that this was not a perfect hedge as more than £13 million was covered by the derivative (and the 10 per cent fall was from 5646 not 5634.50).

Over-the-counter (OTC) and exchange-traded derivatives

An OTC derivative is a tailor-made, individual arrangement between counterparties, usually a company and its bank. Standardised contracts (exchange-traded derivatives) are available on dozens of derivatives exchanges around the world, for example the CME Group (includes Chicago Board of Trade, CBOT, the old Chicago Mercantile Exchange and the New York Mercantile Exchange, NYMEX), NYSE Liffe, and the Eurex in Germany and Switzerland. Exhibit 14.5 compares OTC and exchange-traded derivatives.

There is intense competition between the 35 leading derivative exchanges around the world. They regularly design new types of futures to try to attract trade. Recent innovations include futures in house prices and in carbon dioxide. Exhibit 14.6 shows the largest derivatives exchanges.

---

[6] Assuming that the futures price is equal to the spot price of the FTSE 100. This would occur close to the expiry date of the future.

OTC derivative

Advantages

▪ Contracts can be tailor-made, which allows perfect hedging and permits hedges of more unusual underlyings. It also permits contracts of very long maturities.

▪ Companies with a longstanding relationship with a bank can often arrange derivative deals with it, without the need to find any specific margin or deposit. The bank is willing to accept the counterparty risk of its customer reneging on the deal because it regards this possibility as very low risk, given its long-standing knowledge of the firm.

Disadvantages

▪ It might be difficult to find a counterparty willing to take the opposite position for a very specific contract that suits you, for example, to buy 250 tonnes of orange juice exactly 290 days from now. Even if the counterparty can be found the deal might be at a disadvantageous price to you because of the limited choice of counterparties you have available.

▪ There is a risk that the counterparty will fail to honour the transaction, therefore close attention is paid to the creditworthiness of participants – those with less than high quality reputations may not be able to transact in OTC derivatives (unless secured by a great deal of collateral). Some OTC derivative markets now have a central organisation that is counterparty to both the long holder and the short holder, but central counterparties in the OTC markets are still the exception rather than the rule (although government and regulators are pressing for more involvement of central counterparties following the financial crisis during which many traders were left exposed when their counterparties disappeared through insolvency).

▪ Low level of market regulation with resultant loss of transparency (e.g. what deals have taken place?) and price dissemination (private deals are not usually made public).

▪ Often difficult to reverse a hedge once the agreement has been made. It is sometimes difficult to find a counterparty willing to do exactly the opposite transaction to your first position. Even if you found one, you then have two counterparty risks, and often the maturity dates of the two contracts do not exactly match, leaving some unhedged exposure.

▪ Higher transaction costs. Because they are tailor-made both sides need to scrutinise the deal (e.g. using expensive lawyers) and monitor counterparties subsequently. This extra cost is not worth it for small deals and so forward contracts are usually counted in millions of pounds, euros etc, whereas futures are usually in tens or hundreds of thousands.

▪ Transaction may not be settled promptly at the agreed time – whereas the clearing house or an exchange will insist on prompt settlement.

Exhibit 14.5   **OTC and exchange-traded derivatives**

Exchange-traded derivative

Advantages

- Counterparty risk is reduced because the clearing house is counterparty.
- High regulation encourages transparency and openness on the price of recent trades.
- Liquidity is usually much higher than for OTC – large orders can be cleared quickly due to high daily volume of trade.
- Positions can be reversed by closing quickly – an equal and opposite transaction is completed in minutes.

Disadvantages

- Standardisation may be restrictive (e.g. standardised terms for quality of underlying, quantity, delivery dates). Small companies, with say a £100,000 share portfolio to hedge or a €400,000 loan to hedge, find the standard quantities cumbersome. (Short-term interest rates can be hedged – see later. For euros this is in €1,000,000 multiples only.)
- The limited trading hours and margin requirements may be inconvenient.

Exhibit 14.5   Continued

Rank	Exchange	January to June 2010
1	Korea Exchange	1,781,536,153
2	CME Group in USA (includes CBOT and Nymex)	1,571,345,534
3	Eurex (includes ISE) in Europe	1,485,540,933
4	NYSE Euronext (includes EU (e.g. Liffe) & US markets)	1,210,532,100
5	National Stock Exchange of India	783,897,711
6	BM&FBovespa of Brazil	727,962,093
7	Chicago Board of Options Exchange	611,323,954

Source: http://www.futuresindustry.org/

Exhibit 14.6   The seven largest derivative exchanges – ranked by number of contracts traded and/or cleared

Buying and selling futures

A trader in futures must deal through a registered broker (a 'futures commission merchant'). NYSE Liffe provide a list of designated brokers (these follow rules and codes of conduct imposed by the regulators and the exchange). Gone are the days of open pit trading and those brightly coloured jackets in the UK. Trades are now conducted over a computer system on Liffe (LIFFE CONNECT™) or similar systems at other exchanges such as the Intercontinental Exchange (ICE) in the US. You can place a **price limit** for your trade – the maximum you are willing to pay if you are buying or a minimum if you are selling. Alternatively you can make an **at-the-market order**, to be executed immediately at the price determined by current supply and demand conditions. The buyer of a contract is said to be in a **long position** – he or she agrees to receive the underlying. The seller who agrees to deliver the underlying is said to be in a **short position**.

Demands to top up the maintenance margin may be made every day, so the trader cannot buy/sell a future and then go on holiday for a month (unless he or she leaves plenty of cash with the broker to meet margin calls). Prices are set by competing market makers on LIFFE CONNECT™. Real-time market prices are available on the internet, as well as historical prices (www.liffe-data.com). Trading costs include brokerage commissions, market maker's spread, taxes and fees imposed by the exchange.

Single stock futures

As well as being able to buy or sell futures on commodities or entire share indices, you can trade futures in a particular company's shares. You can agree to buy 100 or 1,000 shares (one future contract)[7] in, say, Royal Dutch Shell two or three months from now at a price that is agreed now (maximum of six months ahead). Exhibit 14.7 shows one of the stock futures traded on NYSE Liffe on 14 December 2010.

Suppose you want to speculate that Royal Dutch Shell will fall in price between 14 December 2010 (now) and the third Friday[8] in February 2011 (the delivery date for the February futures shown in Exhibit 14.7). You could sell, say, 1,000 contracts (100,000 shares for delivery in February) at a price of €24.289. (The ask price of €24.326 is what you can deal at with the market maker if you were going

---

[7] Usually euro denominated contracts are for a lot size of 100 whereas sterling-denominated companies have a lot size of 1,000.
[8] Many derivatives including many stock futures have delivery dates as the third Friday of the month, but some have the third Wednesday of the month or some other standard date.

ROYAL DUTCH SHELL PLC A SHARE EURO

[icon] Add to My Euronext

Codes and classification

| Code | RD | Market | NYSE Liffe London | Vol. | - | 14/12/10 |
| | | Currency € | | O.I. | 212 | 13/12/10 |

Underlying

Name	ROYAL DUTCH SHELLA	ISIN	GB00B03MLX29	Market	Euronext Amsterdam	
Currency	€	Best bid	24.58	14/12/10 16:14 Best ask	24.585	14/12/10 16:14
Time	CET	Last	24.58	14/12/10 16:14 Last change %	0.57	
Volume	3,664,714	High	24.605	Low	24.38	

Prices - 14/12/10

Delivery	Time (CET)	Last	Vol	Day volume	Bid	Ask	%+/-	Settl.
DEC 10	-	-	-	-	24.548	24.582	-	24.441
JAN 11	-	-	-	-	24.576	24.613	-	24.458
FEB 11	-	-	-	-	24.289	24.326	-	24.265
MAR 11	-	-	-	-	-	-	-	24.285

Note: Settlement price is for the trading day 13/12/2010

Vol – (Volume) is the number of contracts traded in the most recent transaction.

Day's Volume – Number of trades that have taken place so far in the trading day. This figure updates as the day progresses and more trades take place.

%+/– Percentage price of last trade compared to yesterday's settlement price.

Settl – The previous day's settlement price.

O.I. – (Open Interest) is the outstanding long and short positions of the previous trading day updated in the morning each day

Exhibit 14.7   Single stock (share) futures on NYSE Liffe – Royal Dutch Shell 'A' share priced in euros

Source: http://www.euronext.com/

long – buying. The market maker in these futures makes a spread profit of €24.326 – €24.289 if he fulfils both a buy and a sell order for one futures contract.) Imagine now that the February futures price falls to €20 in late February; you could close your position by buying 1,000 futures. Your profit would be:

Sold 100,000 shares at €24.289	€2,428,900
Bought 100,000 shares at €20	€2,000,000
	€428,900

You could have made this profit by putting down a margin of only about €150,000,[9] thus almost quadrupling your money in a few weeks.

On the other hand, if the February futures rose to €27 and you closed your position for fear of the price rising further, then the loss of €2,428,900 – €2,700,000 = –€271,100 would wipe out your initial margin, and you would be required to provide a further €121,100. If single stock futures are held to the delivery date then they are usually settled in cash rather than by the delivery of shares (i.e. if you have made a gain you receive it in cash). However, a few are settled with physically delivered shares. The *FT* no longer carries single stock futures data, but the Euronext (part of NYSE Liffe) website covers dozens of companies.

Short-term interest rate futures

Trillions of pounds, dollars and euros of trading takes place every year in the **short-term interest rate futures** markets. These are notional fixed-term deposits, usually for three-month periods starting at a specific time in the future. The buyer of one contract is buying the (theoretical) right to deposit money at a particular rate of interest for three months.

So if the current time is December you could arrange a futures contract for you to 'deposit' and 'receive interest' on, say £1,000,000, with the deposit starting next June and ending in September. The rate of interest you will 'receive' over the three summer months is agreed in December. (This is a notional receipt of interest, as these contracts are cash settled rather than actual deposits being made and interest received – see below for an example.) So you now own the right to deposit £1 million and receive x per cent interest for three months (at least in notional terms).

Short-term interest rate futures will be illustrated using the three-month sterling market, that is, deposits of pounds receiving notional interest for three months starting at some point in the future. Note, however, that there are many other three-month deposits you could make. For example, you could 'deposit' euros for three months, the interest rate on which is calculated with reference to 'Euribor 3m', which is the interest rate highly rated banks pay to other banks for three-month deposits of the currency of the eurozone countries, the euro. Other three-month deposits are often for money held outside the jurisdiction of the currency's country of origin (i.e. 'Euro' currencies, in the sense of being

---

[9] Initial margin varies depending on the volatility of the share, but it is generally in the range of 5–20 per cent of overall contract value.

international money and *not* the currency in the eurozone and include Swiss francs deposited in London (Euroswiss), Eurodollars and Euroyens – see Exhibit 14.8. (Eurocurrency is discussed in Chapter 9.)

INTEREST RATES – FUTURES

Dec 15	Open	Sett	Change	High	Low	Est. vol	Open int
Euribor 3m* FEB1	0.00	98.92	+0.02	0.00	0.00	–	1,541
Euribor 3m* MAY1	0.00	98.89	+0.01	0.00	0.00	–	–
Euribor 3m* SEP1	98.55	98.58	+0.02	98.59	98.54	84.866	344.932
Euribor 3m* DEC1	98.36	98.40	+0.02	98.41	98.35	93.157	348.739
Euroswiss 3m,* MAR1	99.80	99.79	–0.01	99.81	99.79	15.071	93.965
Euroswiss 3m*JUN1	99.72	99.71	–0.01	99.73	99.69	12.090	96.865
Euroswiss 3m* SEP1	99.61	99.61	–	99.62	99.57	10.122	61.921
Sterling 3m* JAN1	0.00	99.19	–	0.00	0.00	–	–
Sterling 3m* MAR1	99.15	99.15	–	99.16	99.13	49.997	280.688
Sterling 3m* JUN1	98.97	98.99	+0.01	99.00	98.95	58.162	238.445
Sterling 3m* SEP1	98.80	98.80	–	98.81	98.76	64.444	217.596
Eurodollar 3m† FEB1	99.625	99.63	–	99.625	99.595	2.671	15.390
Eurodollar 3m† MAY1	0.000	99.49	–	0.000	99.450	–	–
Eurodollar 3m† SEP1	99.270	99.29	–	99.305	99.245	207.871	904.643
Eurodollar 3m† DEC1	99.090	99.11	–	99.140	99.070	230.140	746.097
Fed Fnds 30d‡ Dec	0.000	99.83	–	0.000	0.000	–	98.298
Fed Fnds 30d‡ JAN1	0.000	99.83	–	0.000	0.000	–	64.748
Fed Fnds 30d‡ FEB1	0.000	99.82	–	0.000	0.000	–	56.037
Euroyen 3m‡‡ FEB1	0.000	99.665	–0.005	0.000	0.000	–	–
Euroyen 3m‡‡ JUN1	99.615	99.615	–	99.620	99.600	12.978	369.635
Euroyen 3m‡‡ SEP1	99.585	99.590	–	99.590	99.560	27.089	224.875
Euroyen 3m‡‡ DEC1	99.550	99.555	–0.010	99.560	99.525	15.011	162.893

Contracts are based on volumes traded in 2004   Sources: *NYSE LIFFE. †CME. ‡‡TIFFE

Source: *Financial Times*, 16 December 2010

Exhibit 14.8 Interest rates – futures

The unit of trading for a three-month sterling time deposit is £500,000. Cash delivery by closing out the futures position is the means of settlement, so the buyer would not actually require the seller of the future to accept the £500,000 on deposit for three months at the interest rate indicated by the futures price. Although the term 'delivery' no longer has significance for the underlying it does define the date and time of the expiry of the contract. This occurs in late September, December, March and June and the nearest two consecutive months (see www.euronext.com for precise definitions and delivery dates).

Short-term interest contracts are quoted on an index basis rather than on the basis of the interest rate itself. The price is defined as:

$$P = 100 - i$$

where:

P = price index;

i = the future interest rate in percentage terms.

Thus, on 15 December 2010 the settlement price for a June three-month sterling future was 98.99, which implies an interest rate of $100 - 98.99 = 1.01$ per cent for the period June to September – see Exhibit 14.8. Similarly the September quote would imply an interest rate of $100 - 98.80 = 1.20$ per cent for the three months September to December 2011.

In both cases the implied interest rate refers to a rate applicable for a notional deposit of £500,000 for three months on expiry of the contract – the June futures contract expires in June (i.e. the right to 'deposit' in June through to September expires in June) and the September future expires in September. The 1.01 per cent rate for three-month money starting from June 2011 is the *annual* rate of interest even though the deal is for a deposit of only one-quarter of a year.

The price of 98.99 is not a price in the usual sense – it does not mean £98.99. It is used to maintain the standard inverse relationship between prices and interest rates. For example, if traders in this market one week later, on 22 December 2010, adjusted supply and demand conditions because they expect generally raised inflation and raised interest rates by the middle of 2011, they would push up the interest rates for three-month deposits starting in June 2011 to, say, 2.0 per cent. Then the price of the future would fall to 98.00. Thus, a rise in interest rates for a three-month deposit of money results in a fall in the price of the contract – analogous to the inverse relationship between interest rates offered on long-term bonds and the price of those bonds.

In relation to short-term interest rate futures it is this inverse change in capital value when interest rates change that it is of crucial importance to grasp. Understanding this is more important than trying to envisage deposits of £500,000 being placed sometime in the future.

HEDGING THREE-MONTH DEPOSITS

An example of these derivatives in use may help with gaining an understanding of their hedging qualities. Imagine the treasurer of a large company anticipates the receipt of £100 million in late September 2011, slightly more than 10 months hence. She expects that the money will be needed for production purposes in January 2012 but for the three months following late September it can be placed on deposit. There is a risk that interest rates will fall between now (December 2010) and September 2011 from their present level of 1.20 per cent per annum for three-month deposits starting in late September. (The Sterling 3m September future in Exhibit 14.8 shows a price of 98.80, indicating an interest rate of 1.20 per cent.)

The treasurer does not want to take a passive approach and simply wait for the inflow of money and deposit it at whatever rate is then prevailing without taking some steps to ensure a good return.

To achieve certainty in September 2011 the treasurer buys, in December 2010, September 2011 expiry three-month sterling interest rate futures at a price of 98.80. Each future has a notional value of £500,000 and therefore she has to buy 200 to hedge the £100 million inflow.

Suppose in September 2011 that three-month interest rates have fallen to 0.95 per cent. Following the actual receipt of the £100 million the treasurer can place it on deposit and receive a return over the next three months of £100 million $\times 0.0095 \times \frac{3}{12}$ = £237,500. This is significantly less than if September 2011 three-month deposit interest rates had remained at 1.20 per cent throughout the 10-month waiting period.

Return at 1.20 per cent (£100m $\times 0.012 \times \frac{3}{12}$)   = £300.000

Return at 0.95 per cent (£100m $\times 0.0095 \times \frac{3}{12}$)   = £237,500

Loss   £62,500

However, the caution of the treasurer pays off because the futures have risen in value as interest rates have fallen.

The 200 futures contracts were bought at 98.80. With interest rates at 0.95 per cent for three-month deposits starting in September the futures in September have a value of 100 – 0.95 = 99.05. The treasurer in September can close the futures position by selling the futures for 99.05. Thus, a purchase was made in December 2010 at 98.80 and a sale in September 2011 at 99.05, therefore the gain that is made amounts to 99.05 – 98.80 = 0.25.

▶

This is where a **tick** needs to be introduced. A tick is the minimum price movement on a future. On a three-month sterling interest rate contract a tick is a movement of 0.01 per cent on a trading unit of £500,000.

One-hundredth of 1 per cent of £500,000 is equal to £50, but this is not the value of one tick. A further complication is that the price of a future is based on annual interest rates whereas the contract is for three months. Therefore £50/4 = £12.50 is the value of a tick movement in a three-month sterling interest rate futures contract. In this case we have a gain of 25 ticks with an overall value of 25 × £12.50 = £312.50 per contract, or £62,500 for 200 contracts. The profit on the futures exactly offsets the loss of anticipated interest when the £100m is put on deposit for three months in September.

Note that the deal struck in December was not to enter into a contract to actually deposit £100 million with the counterparty on the NYSE Liffe market. The £100 million is deposited in September with any one of hundreds of banks with no connection to the futures contract that the treasurer entered into. The actual deposit and the notional deposit (on NYSE Liffe) are two separate transactions. However, the transactions are cleverly arranged so that the value movements on these two exactly offset each other. All that is received from NYSE Liffe is the tick difference, based on the price change between buying and selling prices of the futures contracts – no interest is received.

Derivatives markets users

There are three types of derivatives users: hedgers, speculators and arbitrageurs.

Hedgers

To **hedge** is to enter into transactions which protect a business or assets against changes in some underlying. The instruments bought as a hedge tend to have the opposite-value movements to the underlying. Financial and commodity markets are used to transfer risk from an individual or corporation to another more willing and/or able to bear that risk.

Consider a firm which discovers a rich deposit of platinum in Kenya. The management are afraid to develop the site because they are uncertain about the revenues that will actually be realised. Some of the sources of uncertainty are that: (a) the price of platinum could fall, (b) the floating-rate loan taken out to develop the site could become expensive if interest rates rise and (c) the value of the currencies could move adversely. The senior managers have more or less decided that they will apply the firm's funds to a less risky venture. A recent graduate steps forward and suggests that this would be a pity, saying: 'The company is passing up a great opportunity, and Kenya and the world economy will be poorer as a result. Besides, the company does not have to bear all of these risks given the sophistication of modern financial markets. The risks can be hedged, to limit the downside. For example, the platinum could be sold on the forwards or the futures market, which will provide a firm price. The interest-rate risk can be reduced by using the interest futures markets or other derivatives. The currency risk can be controlled by using currency forwards or options [discussed in Chapter 16].' The board decide to press ahead with development of the mine and thus show that derivatives can be used to promote economic well-being by transferring risk.

Speculators

Speculators take a position in financial instruments and other assets with a view to obtaining a profit on changes in price. Speculators accept high risk in anticipation of high reward. The gearing effect of derivatives makes speculation in these instruments particularly profitable, or particularly ruinous. Speculators are also attracted to derivatives markets because they are often more liquid than the underlying markets. In addition the speculator is able to sell before buying (to 'short' the market) in order to profit from a fall. More complex trading strategies are also possible.

The term speculator in popular parlance is often used in a somewhat critical fashion. This is generally unwarranted. Speculators are needed by financial markets to help create trading liquidity. Many people argue that prices are more, not less, likely to be stable as a result of speculative activity. Usually speculators have dissimilar views regarding future market movements and this provides two-way liquidity which allows other market participants, such as hedgers, to carry out a transaction quickly without moving the price. Imagine if only hedgers with an underlying were permitted to buy or sell derivatives. Very few trades would take place each day. If a firm wished to make a large hedge this would be noticed in the market and the price of the derivative would be greatly affected. Speculators also provide a kind of insurance for hedgers – they accept risk in return for a premium.

Speculators are also quick to spot new opportunities and to shift capital to new areas of economic output. For example, if a speculator foresees a massive rise in the demand for cobalt because of its use in mobile phones they will start to buy futures in the commodity, pushing up the price. This will alert the mining companies to go in search of more cobalt deposits around the world and pump money into those countries that have it, such as Congo. The speculator has to examine the underlying economic messages emanating from the world economy and respond to them in a truthful manner – dumping the currency of a badly run country or selling bond derivatives in banks, for example. Those on the receiving end of those messages often resent having the truth revealed when they have tried to conceal it for so long and hoped to go on doing so.

Arbitrageurs

The act of **arbitrage** is to exploit price differences on the same instrument or similar assets. The arbitrageur buys at the lower price and immediately resells at the higher price. So, for example, Nick Leeson claimed that he was arbitraging Nikkei 225 Index futures. The same future is traded in both Osaka and Singapore. Theoretically the price should be identical on both markets, but in reality this is not always the case, and it is possible simultaneously to buy the future in one market and sell the future in the other and thereby make a risk-free profit. An arbitrageur waits for these opportunities to exploit a market inefficiency. The problem for Barings Bank was that Nick Leeson obtained funds to put down as margin payments on arbitrage trades but then bought futures in both markets – surreptitiously switching from an arbitrage activity to a highly risky, speculative activity. True arbitrageurs help to ensure pricing efficiency – their acts of buying or selling tend to reduce pricing anomalies.

Websites

www.money.cnn.com	CNN Financial News
www.nyxdata.com	Prices on Liffe
www.bloomberg.com	Bloomberg
www.cmegroup.com	CME group
www.reuters.com	Reuters
www.euronext.com	London International Financial Futures and Options Exchange (NYSE Liffe)
www.cboe.com	Chicago Board Options Exchange
www.theice.com	Intercontinental Exchange
www.eurexchange.com	Eurex. The European Derivative Exchange
www.isda.org	International Swaps and Derivatives Association
http://www.futuresindustry.org/	Futures Industry Association

15

Options and swaps

The problem with futures and forwards is that they do not allow you to benefit from a favourable movement in the underlying. Options, on the other hand, do. With an option you can choose at a later date whether or not you would like to proceed with the deal. If you let it lapse after a favourable movement in the underlying you can gain that benefit without suffering an equal loss on the derivative.

Swaps allow you to exchange a series of future cash payment obligations. For example, your company could have a loan agreement whereby it pays a series of interest amounts based on whatever six-month LIBOR is at the time, through a period of seven years. Obviously, the concern you have is that LIBOR might jump to a much higher level at some point in the seven years, which might jeopardise the firm. One solution is to agree with a counterparty to pay its fixed interest rate obligations if it agrees to pay you LIBOR every six months. This can reduce risk for both.

Credit default swaps, invented only in the 1990s, allow you to pass on the risk of a borrower defaulting on a debt deal to other participants in the financial markets, in return for a fee (premium). These are instruments that can be used to reduce risk or to speculate.

Options

An **option** is a contract giving one party the right, but not the obligation, to buy or sell a financial instrument, commodity or some other underlying asset at a given price, at or before a specified date. The purchaser of the option can either exercise the right or let it lapse – the choice is theirs.

A very simple option would be where a firm pays the owner of land a non-returnable **premium** (say £10,000) for an option to buy the land at an agreed price because the firm is considering the development of a retail park within the next five years. The property developer may pay a number of option premiums to owners of land in different parts of the country. If planning permission is eventually granted on a particular plot the option to purchase may be **exercised**. In other words the developer pays the price agreed with the owner at the time that the option contract was arranged, say £1,000,000, to purchase the land. Options on other plots may be **allowed to lapse** and will have no value. By using an option the property developer has 'kept the options open' with regard to which site to buy and develop and, indeed, whether to enter the retail park business at all.

Options can also be **traded**. Perhaps the option to buy could be sold to another company keener to develop a particular site than the original option purchaser. It may be sold for much more than the original £10,000 option premium, even before planning permission has been granted.

Once planning permission has been granted the greenfield site may be worth £1,500,000. If there is an option to buy at £1,000,000 the option right has an **intrinsic value** of £500,000, representing a 4,900 per cent return on £10,000. From this we can see the gearing effect of options: very large sums can be gained in a short period of time for a small initial cash outlay.

Share options

Share options have been traded for centuries but their use expanded dramatically with the creation of traded option markets in Chicago, Amsterdam and, in 1978, the London Traded Options Market. In 1992 this became part of the London International Financial Futures and Options Exchange, LIFFE. Euronext bought LIFFE in 2002, which later combined with the New York Stock Exchange, so LIFFE is now called NYSE Liffe.

A **share call option** gives the purchaser a right, but not the obligation, to *buy* a fixed number of shares at a specified price at some time in the future. In the case of traded options on NYSE Liffe, one option contract relates to a quantity of 1,000 shares. The seller of the option, who receives the premium, is referred to as the **writer**. The writer of a call option is obligated to sell the agreed quantity of shares at the agreed price sometime in the future. **American-style options** can be exercised by the buyer at any time up to the expiry date, whereas **European-style options** can only be exercised on a predetermined future date. Just to confuse everybody, the distinction has nothing to do with geography: most options traded in Europe are American-style options.

Call option holder (call option buyer)

Now let us examine the call options available on an underlying share – AstraZeneca on 17 December 2010. There are a number of different options available for this share, many of which are not reported in the table presented in the *Financial Times*.[1] A section of this table is reproduced as Exhibit 15.1. These are American-style options.

Call option prices (premiums) pence

Exercise price	December	January	February
2900p	41	94.5	101.5
3000p	–	41	52.5

Share price on 17 December 2010 = 2941p

Exhibit 15.1   Call options on AstraZeneca shares, 17 December 2010

Source: Financial Times. 18/19 December 2010. Reprinted with permission.

So, what do the figures mean? If you wished to obtain the right to buy 1,000 shares on or before late January 2011,[2] at an **exercise price** of 3000p, you would pay a premium of £410 (1,000 × 41p). If you wished to keep your option to purchase open for another month you could select the February call. But this right to insist that the writer sells the shares at the fixed price of 3000p on or before a date in late February will cost another £115 (the total premium payable on one option contract = £525). This extra £115 represents additional **time value**. Time value arises because of the potential for the market price of the underlying to change in a way that creates intrinsic value.

The intrinsic value of an option is the payoff that would be received if the underlying were at its current level when the option expires. In this case, there is currently (17 December 2010) no intrinsic value because the right to buy is at 3000p whereas the share price is 2941p. However, if you look at a call option with an exercise price of 2900p then the right to buy at 2900p has intrinsic value because if you purchased at 2900p by exercising the option, thereby obtaining

---

[1] The Saturday paper version presents a traded option table. For the other days of the week you need to go to www.ft.com, or the original source, www.euronext.com.
[2] The expiry date is the third Wednesday of the expiry month.

1,000 shares, you could immediately sell at 2941p in the share market: intrinsic value = 41p per share, or £410 for 1,000 shares. The longer the time over which the option is exercisable the greater the chance that the price will move to give intrinsic value – this explains the higher premiums on more distant expiry options. Time value is the amount by which the option premium exceeds the intrinsic value.

The two exercise price (also called **strike price**) levels presented in Exhibit 15.1 illustrate an **in-the-money option** (the 2900 call option) and an **out-of-the-money option** (the 3000 call option). The underlying share price is above the strike price of 2900 and so this call option has an intrinsic value of 41p and is therefore in-the-money. The right to buy at 3000p is out-of-the-money because the share price is below the option exercise price and therefore has no intrinsic value. The holder of a 3000p option would not exercise this right to buy at 3000p because the shares can be bought on the stock exchange for 2941p.

To emphasise the key points: the option premiums vary in proportion to the length of time over which the option is exercisable (e.g. they are higher for a February option than for a January option). Also, call options with lower exercise prices will have higher premiums.

An illustration

Suppose that you are confident that AstraZeneca shares are going to rise significantly over the next two months to 3200p and you purchase a February 2900 call at 101.5 pence.[3] The cost of this right to purchase 1,000 shares is £1015 (101.5p × 1,000 shares). If the share rises as expected then you could exercise the right to purchase the shares for a total of £29,000 and then sell these in the market for £32,000. A profit of £3,000 less £1,015 = £1,985 is made before transaction costs (the brokers' fees, etc. would be in the region of £20–£50). This represents a massive 196 per cent rise before costs (£1,985/£1,015).

However, the future is uncertain and the share price may not rise as expected. Let us consider two other possibilities. First, the share price may remain at 2941p throughout the life of the option. Secondly, the stock market may have a severe downturn and AstraZeneca shares may fall to 2700p. These possibilities are shown in Exhibit 15.2.

---

[3] For this exercise we will assume that the option is held to expiry and not traded before then. However in many cases this option will be sold on to another trader long before the expiry date approaches (at a profit or loss).

Assumed share prices in February at expiry date	*3200p*	*2941p*	*2700p*
Cost of purchasing shares by exercising the option	£29,000	£29,000	£29,000
Value of shares bought	£32,000	£29,410	£27,000
Profit from exercise of option and sale of shares in the market	£3,000	£410	Not exercised
Less option premium paid	£1015	£1015	£1015
Profit (loss) before transaction costs	£1,985	–£605	–£1015
Percentage return over 2 months	196%	–60%	–100%

Exhibit 15.2   **Profits and losses on the AstraZeneca February 2900 call following purchase on 17 December 2010**

In the case of a standstill in the share price the option gradually loses its time value over the three months until, at expiry, only the intrinsic value of 41p per share remains. The fall in the share price to 2700p illustrates one of the advantages of purchasing options over some other derivatives: the holder has a right to abandon the option and is not forced to buy the underlying share at the option exercise price – this saves £2,000. It would have added insult to injury to have to buy at £29,000 and sell at £27,000 after having already lost £1,015 on the premium for the purchase of the option.

A comparison of Exhibits 15.3 and 15.4 shows the extent to which the purchase of an option gears up the return from share price movements: a wider dispersion of returns is experienced. On 17 December 2010, 1,000 shares could be bought for £29,410. If the market value rose to £32,000, an 8.8 per cent return would be made, compared with a 196 per cent return if options are bought. We would all like the higher positive return on the option than the lower one available on the underlying – but would we all accept the downside risk associated with this option? Consider the following possibilities:

■ If the share price remains at 2941p:
  - return if shares are bought: 0%
  - return if one 2900 February call option is bought: –60% (paid £1,015 for the option which declines to its intrinsic value of only £410).[4]

---

[4] £410 is the intrinsic value at expiry (2941p – 2900p) × 1,000 = £410.

▪ If share price falls to 2700p:

- – return if shares are bought: –8.2%
- – return if one 2900 February call option is bought: –100% (the option is worth nothing).

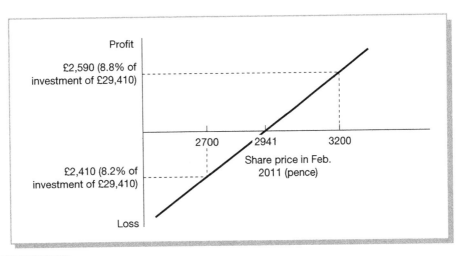

Exhibit 15.3 Profit and loss if 1,000 shares in AstraZeneca are bought on 17 December 2010 at £29.41

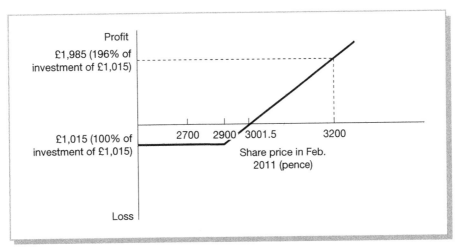

Exhibit 15.4 Profit and loss if one 2900 February call option contract (for 1,000 shares) in AstraZeneca is bought on 17 December 2010 and held to maturity

The holder of the call option will not exercise unless the share price is at least 2900p: at a lower price it will be cheaper to buy the 1,000 shares on the stock market. Break-even does not occur until a price of 3001.5p because of the need to cover the cost of the premium (2900p + 101.5p). However, at higher prices the option value increases, penny for penny, with the share price. Also the downside risk is limited to the size of the option premium.

Call option writers

The returns position for the writer of a call option in AstraZeneca can also be presented in a diagram (*see* Exhibit 15.5). With all these examples note that there is an assumption that the position is held to expiry. If the market price is less than the exercise price (2900p) in February the option will not be exercised and the call writer profits to the extent of the option premium (101.5p per share). A market price greater than the exercise price will result in the option being exercised and the writer will be forced to deliver 1,000 shares for a price of 2900p. This may mean buying shares on the stock market to supply to the option holder. As the share price rises this becomes increasingly onerous and losses mount.

Note that in the sophisticated traded option markets of today very few option positions are held to expiry. In most cases the option holder sells the option in the market to make a cash profit or loss. Option writers often cancel out their exposure before expiry – for example they could purchase an option to buy the same quantity of shares at the same price and expiry date.

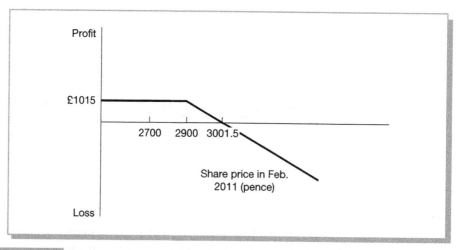

Exhibit 15.5   Profit and loss to a call option writer of one 2900 February call option contract (for 1,000 shares) in AstraZeneca on 17 December 2010

| Example | **AN OPTION-WRITING STRATEGY** |

Joe has a portfolio of shares worth £100,000 and is confident that while the market will go up steadily over time it will not rise over the next few months. He has a strategy of writing call options and pocketing premiums on a regular basis. Today (17 December 2010) Joe has written one option on February calls in AstraZeneca for an exercise price of 2900p (current share price 2941p). In other words, Joe is committed to delivering (selling) 1,000 shares at any time between 17 December 2010 and near the end of February 2011 for a price of £29, at the insistence of the person who bought the call. This could be very unpleasant for Joe if the market price rises to, say, £33. Then the optionholder will require Joe to sell shares worth £33,000 to them for only £29,000. However, Joe is prepared to take this risk for two reasons. First he receives the premium of 101.5p per share up front – this is 3.5 per cent of each share's value. This £1,015 will cushion any feeling of future regret at his actions. Secondly, Joe holds 1,000 AstraZeneca shares in his portfolio and so would not need to go into the market to buy the shares to then sell them to the optionholder if the price did rise significantly. Joe has written a **covered call option** – so called because he has backing in the form of the underlying shares. Joe only loses out if the share price on the day the option is exercised is greater than the strike price (£29) plus the premium (£1.015). He is prepared to risk losing some of the potential upside (above 2900p + 101.5p = 3001.5p) to gain the premium. He also reduces his loss on the downside: if the shares in his portfolio fall he has the premium as a cushion.

Some speculators engage in **uncovered (naked) option writing**. It is possible to lose a multiple of your current resources if you write many option contracts and the price moves against you. Imagine that Joe had only £20,000 in savings and entered the options market by writing 40 AstraZeneca February 2011 2900 calls receiving a premium of £1.015 × 40 × 1,000 = £40,600.[5] If the price moves to £33 Joe has to buy shares for £33 and then sell them to the optionholders for £29, a loss of £4 per share: £4 × 40 × 1,000 = £160,000. Despite receiving the premiums Joe has wiped out his savings.

---

[5] This is simplified. In reality Joe would have to provide margin of cash or shares to reassure the clearing house that he could pay up if the market moved against him. So it could be that all of the premium received would be tied up in margin held by the clearing house (the role of a clearing house is explained in Chapter 14).

Liffe share options

The *Financial Times* lists over 50 companies' shares in which options are traded – *see* Exhibit 15.6, which shows some option prices for 17 December 2010, including that of AstraZeneca. This table is a cut down version of the data available at www.euronext.com, where over 250 company options are traded through the day. Also a wider variety of strike prices are shown at www.euronext.com than the Financial Times can accommodate.

Put options

A **put option** gives the holder the right, but not the obligation, to sell a specific quantity of shares on or before a specified date at a fixed exercise price. Imagine you are pessimistic about the prospects for Sainsbury, the supermarket chain on 17 December 2010. You could purchase, for a premium of 12.75p per share (£127.5 in total), the right to sell 1,000 shares in or before late February 2011 at 370p (see Exhibit 15.6). If a fall in price subsequently takes place, to, say, 340p, you can insist on exercising the right to sell at 370p. The writer of the put option is obliged to purchase shares at 370p while being aware that the put optionholder is able to buy shares at 340p on the stock exchange. The optionholder makes a profit of 370 – 340 – 12.75 = 17.25p per share (£172.50), a 135 per cent return (before costs of £20 – £40).

For the put optionholder, if the market price exceeds the exercise price, it will not be wise to exercise as shares can be sold for a higher price on the Stock Exchange. Therefore the maximum loss, equal to the premium paid, is incurred. The option writer gains the premium if the share price remains above the exercise price, but may incur a large loss if the market price falls significantly.

Using share options to reduce risk: hedging

Hedging with options is especially attractive because they can give protection against unfavourable movements in the underlying while permitting the possibility of benefiting from favourable movements. Suppose you hold 1,000 shares in Sainsbury on 17 December 2010. Your shareholding is worth £3,721 (see price in brackets underneath 'Sainsbury' in Exhibit 15.6). There are rumours flying around the market that the company may become the target of a takeover bid. If this materialises the share price will rocket; if it does not the market will be disappointed and the price will fall dramatically. What are you to do? One way to avoid the downside risk is to sell the shares. The problem is that you may regret this action if the bid does subsequently occur and you have forgone the opportunity of a large profit. An alternative approach is to retain the shares and buy a

EQUITY OPTIONS

Option	Strike	Calls Dec	Calls Jan	Calls Feb	Puts Dec	Puts Jan	Puts Feb
AstraZeneca (*2941)	2900	41	94.5	101.5	–	48	135
	3000	–	41	52.5	59	97.5	203
Aviva (*385.900)	380	6	13.75	19	–	7.25	12.25
	390	–	8.25	13.5	4	12	17
BAE Systems (*325)	320	5	12.25	16	–	7	10.25
	330	–	7	10.5	5	11.75	14.5
Barclays (*259.75)	250	9.75	16	20.75	–	5.75	10.5
	260	–	10.25	15.25	0.25	10.25	15
BG Group (*1324.5)	1300	24.5	50.5	69	–	26.5	44
	1350	–	26	45	25.5	52	70
BHP Billiton (*2500)	2400	100	149	188.5	–	48	87.5
	2500	0.5	87.5	132.5	0.5	88.5	130
BP (*467.150)	460	7.25	16.75	22	–	9.25	16.25
	470	–	11.25	16.75	2.75	13.75	21.25
Br Airways (*270.200)	260	10.25	15.5	21.75	–	8.25	12.75
	270	0.25	11.75	15.75	–	10.75	16.75
BAT (*2455)	2400	55	81	104.5	–	26	46
	2500	–	28	49	45	72	92
BT Group (*182.400)	180	2.5	4.75	7.75	–	4.75	7.75
	185	–	2.75	5.5	2.5	7.75	10.25
Diageo (*1180)	1150	30	43	55	–	13	24
	1200	16	27.5	36	20	36	47
GlaxoSmKl (*1265.5)	1250	15.5	35	47	–	18.5	40
	1300	–	12	22	34.5	44.5	69
HSBC (*655.5)	640	15.5	24.75	32.5	–	9.25	16.5
	660	–	13.25	20.75	4.5	17.75	25.25
Kingfisher (*255.400)	250	5.5	10	13.5	–	4.5	7.75
	260	–	4.5	8	4.5	9	12.5

Option	Strike	Calls Dec	Calls Jan	Calls Feb	Puts Dec	Puts Jan	Puts Feb
Land Sec Gp (*657)	640	17	27.5	33.25	–	8.25	14
	660	–	15.25	21.25	3	16.5	22.25
Legal & Gen (*99.200)	98	1.25	4	5.5	–	2.5	4.5
	100	–	2.75	4.5	0.75	3.5	5.25
Lloyds Bg (*66.5)	64	2.5	4.25	5.5	–	2	2.75
	68	1.5	3	3.25	1.5	3.5	4.75
Man Group (*259.75)	290	4	13	17.75	–	8.5	13.5
	300	–	8	13	6	14.25	19
Marks & S (*375.400)	370	5.5	13.5	18	–	8.25	12
	380	–	8.75	12.5	4.5	13	16.75
Morrison (Wm) (*264.600)	260	4.5	8	10.5	–	3.5	5.5
	270	–	3	5.25	5.5	8.5	10
Rio Tinto (*4418)	4400	18	174.5	256.5	–	156	238.5
	4600	–	91	166.5	182	269	346
Royal Bk Scot (*37.820)	36	1.75	3.25	4	–	1.25	2
	38	–	2	2.75	0.25	2	2.75
Royal Dutch Shell 'B' (*2069.5)	2000	69.5	85	100	–	14.5	40.5
	2100	–	26	42.5	30.5	54.5	89.5
RSA Ins Gp (*124.100)	120	4	5.25	6.5	–	1	1.75
	125	–	3.25	3.25	3	3	4
Sainsbury (*372.100)	370	2	11.25	15.25	–	8.75	12.75
	380	–	7	11	8	14.5	18.5
Std Chartd (*1734)	1638	96	–	–	–	–	–
	1734	–	–	–	–	–	–
Tesco (*433.400)	430	3.5	10.75	15	–	7.25	11.25
	440	–	5.75	9.75	6.75	12.5	16.25
Vodafone (*170.050)	165	5	7	8.75	–	2	3.75
	170	–	3.75	5.75	8	3.75	5.75

Option	Strike	Calls			Puts		
Xstrata (*1449.5)	1400	Dec 49.5	Jan 91	Feb 122	–	41	70.5
	1450	–	62.5	94	0.5	62	93.5
3i Group (*328.5)	320	Dec 8.5	Mar 17.75	Jun 26	–	9.75	17
	330	–	–	–	1.5	–	–
Carnival (*2764)	2700	64	–	–	–	–	–
	2800	–	113	174	36	151.5	215
Compass (*579)	560	19	31	41	–	21	32.5
	580	–	–	–	1	–	–
Experian (*813.5)	800	13.5	37.75	53.5	–	29.5	43.25
	820	–	–	–	6.5	–	–
Impl Tobacco (*1941)	1900	41	71.5	98.5	–	75	107
	1950	–	–	–	9	–	–
IntCont Hotels (*1234)	1200	34	86.5	110	–	53	89
	1250	–	–	–	16	–	–
Intl Power (*435)	430	5	13.5	20.5	–	18.5	29
	440	–	–	–	5	–	–
ITV (*72.100)	68	4	5.25	7	–	5.25	6.75
	72	–	–	–	–	–	–
Lon Stk Exchg (*823)	820	3	32	49.75	–	47.75	60.75
	840	–	–	–	–	–	–
Natl Grid (*552)	540	12	25.25	–	–	12.5	–
	560	–	14	21.75	8	21.25	42.75
Next (*1985)	1950	35	97.5	137	–	110	180.5
	2000	–	–	–	15	–	–
Pearson (*1017)	1000	17	49	60.25	–	29.5	57.75
	1050	–	–	–	33	–	–
Reckitt Bnckisr Gp (*3577)	3500	77	118	168.5	–	180.5	235
	3600	–	–	–	23	–	–

Option	Strike	Calls Dec	Calls Mar	Calls Jun	Puts Dec	Puts Mar	Puts Jun
Reed Elsevier (*528)	520	8	25.5	32.5	–	16.75	33.25
	540	–	–	–	12	–	–
Rentokil Init (*97.850)	96	1.75	6.75	9	–	4.25	5.75
	100	–	4.75	7.25	2.25	6.25	8.25
Rolls-Royce (*630)	620	10	–	–	–	–	–
	640	–	26.25	35.75	10	34.25	50.5
SAB Miller (*2243.5)	2200	43.5	115	166.5	–	70.5	109
	2300	–	113.5	113.5	56.5	–	159
Sage (*275.800)	270	5.75	14.25	–	–	11.75	–
	280	–	9	13.25	4.25	17.5	23.75
Scot & Sthn Energy (*1185)	1150	35	52	–	–	31	–
	1200	–	24.5	40.5	15	58	73.5
Shire (*1530)	1500	30	86	117	–	56	84.5
	1550	–	–	–	20	–	–
Sm & Nephew (*655.5)	640	15.5	42.75	53.25	–	26	40.25
	660	–	–	–	4.5	–	–
Standard Life (*210)	205	5	–	–	–	–	–
	210	–	9.75	12.25	4.5	14	18.5
Unilever (*1972)	1950	22	–	–	–	–	–
	2000	–	55.5	84.5	28	99	138
Utd Utilities (*585.5)	580	5.5	23	–	–	16	–
	600	–	13.75	22.75	14.5	27	46.25
Whitbread (*1805)	1800	5	81.5	116.5	–	75.5	127.5
	1850	–	–	–	45	–	–
Wolseley (*1959)	1950	9	–	–	–	–	–
	2000	–	78.5	129.5	41	128.5	169.5
WPP (*783)	780	3	–	–	–	16	–
	800	–	29.25	47	17	44.25	66.75

*Underlying security price. Premiums shown are based on settlement prices. **Source: Euronext.Liffe** December 17
Total contracts. Equity and Index options: 1,417,589
Calls: 124,243 Puts: 116,159

Exhibit 15.6 Equity options table displayed in the *Financial Times* (or available at www.ft.com)

Source: Financial Times, 18/19 December 2010

put option. This will rise in value as the share price falls. If the share price rises you gain from your underlying shareholding.

Assume a 370 February put is purchased for a premium of £127.5 (see Exhibit 15.6). If the share price falls to 300p in late February you lose on your underlying shares by £721 ((372.1p – 300p) × 1,000). However, the put option will have an intrinsic value of £700 ((370p – 300p) × 1,000), thus reducing the loss and limiting the downside risk. Below 370p, for every 1p lost in a share price, 1p is gained on the put option, so the maximum loss is £148.5 (£21 intrinsic value + £127.5 option premium).

Thus hedging reduces the dispersion of possible outcomes. There is a floor below which losses cannot be increased, while on the upside the benefit from any rise in share price is reduced. If the share price stands still at 372.1p, however, you may feel that the premium you paid to insure against an adverse movement at 12.75p or 3.4 per cent of the share price was excessive. If you keep buying this type of 'insurance' through the year it can reduce your portfolio returns substantially.

Mexico wanted certainty over the amount it would gain by selling $13 billion of its oil on the international market in 2010, so it bought a put option – see Exhibit 15.7. Even though the cost was $1 billion the government thought it well worth it, especially after it gained so much on its put options in 2009.

Mexico buys $1bn insurance policy against falling oil prices

By Gregory Meyer in New York and Javier Blas in London

Mexico has taken out a $1bn insurance policy against oil prices falling next year, a clear signal that commodities producers remain wary about the threat of a double-dip recession.

The world's sixth largest oil producer said yesterday that it had hedged all its net oil exports for 2010, by buying protection against oil prices falling below $57 a barrel.

"We want this as an insurance policy," said Agustín Carstens, Mexico's finance minister. "If we don't collect any resources from this transaction, it's OK with us." That would mean the oil price had remained above $57 a barrel, he added.

Mr Carstens suggested he was not expecting prices to fall that low, but added: "More than any-

thing, it's a hedge against a really bad outcome."

The move follows a successful hedging strategy at $70 this year which netted Mexico more than $5bn on the back of low oil prices between January and June.

Although that figure is lower than expectations because of recent high oil prices, it still represents more than 7 per cent of

▶

Exhibit 15.7   Mexico buys $1bn insurance policy against falling oil prices

Mexican government revenues this year.

Barclays Capital, Deutsche Bank, Goldman Sachs and Morgan Stanley arranged this year's hedge. Bankers said Barclays Capital was leading next year's programme.

Mr Carstens, joined by senior executives from the banks, said Mexico's hedging showed that derivatives, "when used responsibly", could be "very useful". Mexico bought put options – contracts that give the holder the right to sell oil at a predetermined price.

His view contrasts sharply with recent comments made by senior Chinese officials, who criticised some of the same banks for selling derivatives products, including oil hedges, to state companies. Many suffered heavy losses this year.

Mexico has based its budget next year on an oil price of about $59 a barrel.

Olivier Jakob, of the Swiss-based consultancy Petromatrix, said there was potential for a drop in oil prices in 2010 unless demand recovered meaningfully. "The fundamental supply and demand picture looks weak, but the weakness of the US dollar and financial flows are supporting oil prices right now," he explained.

Source: *Financial Times*, 9 December 2009

Exhibit 15.7   Continued

Index options

Options on whole share indices can be purchased: for example, Standard & Poor's 500 (USA), FTSE 100 (UK), CAC 40 (France), XETRA Dax (Germany). Large investors usually have a varied portfolio of shares so, rather than hedging individual shareholdings with options, they may hedge through options on the entire index of shares. Also speculators can take a position on the future movement of the market as a whole.

A major difference between index options and share options is that the former are **cash settled** – so for the FTSE 100 option, there is no delivery of 100 different shares on the expiry day. Rather, a cash difference representing the price change changes hands.

Exhibit 15.8 shows the January expiry options for the FTSE 100 Index on 20 December 2010. The date of the download was 20 December and the FTSE 100 at that time was at 5,902. By convention (so everyone knows where they stand) the index is regarded as a price and each one-point movement on the index represents £10. So if you purchased one contract in January expiry 5,875 calls ('C') you would pay an option premium of 110 index points × £10 = £1,100.[6] The different calls and put strike prices are shown in the middle column of the table, with the call prices to the left and the put prices to the right.

---

[6] Notice that marketmakers have a bid/ask (offer) spread. So if you want to buy the 5,875 call option you would pay 110 points or £1,100 as a premium, but if you wanted to sell the option to the market maker you would receive 107 points or £1,070.

Codes and classification

Code	ESX	Market	NYSE Liffe London	Vol.	13,456	20/12/10
Exercise type	European	Currency £		O.I.	1,836,756	17/12/10

Underlying

Name	London FTSE 100	ISIN	GB0001383545	Market	LSE	
Currency	£					
Time	CET	Last	5,901.89	20/12/10 15:30 Last change %	0.51	
		High	5,913.83	Low	5,865.51	

January 2011 Prices - 20/12/10

		Calls									Puts							
Settl.	Day volume	Vol	Time (CET)	Last	Bid	Ask	AQ Bid	AQ Ask	Strike C	p	AQ Bid	AQ Ask	Bid	Ask	Last	Time (CET)	Vol	Day volume	Settl.
124.50	-	-	-	140.00	142.50	139.50	143.50	C 5,825	P	60.50	64.00	61.00	63.50	77.50	09:23	21	21	85.00
109.50	63	5	12:05	124.00	123.00	126.00	123.00	127.00	C 5,850	P	69.00	72.50	69.50	71.50	71.00	12:05	5	40	95.00
95.50	3	3	11:27	97.00	107.00	110.00	107.00	111.00	C 5,875	P	77.50	81.00	78.50	80.50	97.00	09:59	10	10	106.00
82.50	51	1	13:34	100.00	92.50	95.00	92.50	96.00	C 5,900	P	88.00	91.50	88.50	91.00	89.00	13:52	1	28	118.00
70.50	12	9	12:56	80.50	79.00	81.50	78.50	82.00	C 5,925	P	98.50	102.50	100.00	102.00	102.00	12:56	9	12	131.00

Note: Settlement price is for the trading day 17/12/2010

Vol – (Volume) is the number of contracts traded in the most recent transaction.

Day's Volume – Number of trades that have taken place so far in the trading day. This figure updates as the day progresses and more trades take place.

%+/– Percentage price of last trade compared to yesterday's settlement price.

Settl – The previous day's settlement price.

O.I. – (Open Interest) is the outstanding long and short positions of the previous trading day updated in the morning each day.

The columns titled 'Bid' and 'Ask' (without the 'AQ') show the actual prices of the bid–offer spreads quoted by dealers. The four columns titled either 'AQ Bid' or 'AQ Ask' show the AutoQuote bid–offer spreads for both types of option (Calls and Puts). The NYSE Liffe website provides a system ('AutoQuote', hence AQ) that **predicts** bid-offer spreads for those options. The AQ predicted bids and offers are frequently inaccurate. We need to concentrate on the Bid and Ask columns set by real market makers.

Exhibit 15.8   FTSE 100 index option for January delivery options, £10 per index point

Source: http://www.euronext.com/

Imagine that the following day, 21 December 2010, the FTSE 100 moved from its level on 20 December 2010 of 5,902 to 5,940 and the option price on the 5,875 January call moved to 150 index points (65 points of intrinsic value and 85 points of time value). To convert this into money you could sell the option at £10 per point per contract (150 × £10 = £1,500). In 24 hours your £1,100 has gone up to £1,500, a 36 per cent rise. Large gains can be made when the market moves in your favour. If it moves against you, large percentage losses will occur in just a few hours.

Note that there are many additional option expiry dates stretching months into the future other than the January one shown in Exhibit 15.8. In fact, there are eight months available: 'Nearest eight of March, June, September, December plus such additional months that the nearest four calendar months are always available for trading' (www.euronext.com).

Hedging against a decline in the market using index options

An investor with a £1,175,000 broadly spread portfolio of shares is concerned that the market may fall over the next two months. One strategy to lower risk is to purchase put options on the share index. If the market does fall, losses on the portfolio will be offset by gains on the value of the index put option.

First the investor has to calculate the number of option contracts needed to hedge the underlying. With the index at 5,902 on 20 December 2010 and each point of that index settled at £10, one contract has a value of 5,902 × £10 = £59,020. To cover a £1,175,000 portfolio (£1,175,000 ÷ £59,020 = 19.9) 20 contracts are needed (investors can trade in whole contracts only). The investor opts to buy 20 January 5,850 puts for 71.50 points per contract[7] – see Exhibit 15.8. The premium payable is:

71.50 points × £10 × 20 = £14,300

This amounts to a 1.2 per cent 'insurance premium' (£14,300/£1,175,000) against a downturn in the market.

---

[7] This is not a **perfect hedge** as there is an element of the underlying risk without offsetting derivative cover.

Consider what happens if the market does fall by a large amount, say, 15 per cent, between 20 December and the third Friday in January (when the option matures). The index falls from 5,902 to 5,016, and the loss on the portfolio is:

£1,175,000 × 0.15 = £176,250

If the portfolio is unhedged, the investor suffers from a market fall. However, in this case the put options gain in value as the index falls because they carry the right to sell at 5,850. If the investor closed the option position by buying at a level of 5,016, with the right to sell at 5,850, a 834-point difference, a gain is made:

Gain on options (5,850 − 5,016) × 20 × £10 =	£166,800
Less option premium paid	£ 14,300
	£152,500

A substantial proportion of the fall in portfolio value is compensated for through the use of the put derivative.

Swaps

A **swap** is an exchange of cash payment obligations. An **interest-rate swap** is where one company arranges with a counterparty to exchange interest-rate payments. For example, the first company may be paying fixed-rate interest but prefers to pay floating rates. The second company may be paying floating rates of interest, which go up and down with LIBOR, but would benefit from a switch to a fixed obligation. Imagine that firm S has a £200 million 10-year loan paying a fixed rate of interest of 8 per cent, and firm T has a £200 million 10-year loan on which interest is reset every six months with reference to LIBOR, at LIBOR plus 2 per cent. Under a swap arrangement S would agree to pay T's floating-rate interest on each due date over the next 10 years, and T would be obligated to pay S's 8 per cent interest.

One motive for entering into a swap arrangement is to reduce or eliminate exposure to rises in interest rates. Over the short run, futures and options could be used to hedge interest-rate exposure. However, for longer-term loans (more than two years) swaps are usually more suitable because they can run for the entire lifetime of the loan. So if a treasurer of a company with a large floating-rate loan forecasts that interest rates will rise over the next four years, they could arrange to swap interest payments with a fixed-rate interest payer for those four years.

Another reason for using swaps is to take advantage of market imperfections. Sometimes the interest-rate risk premium charged in the fixed-rate borrowing market differs from that in the floating-rate market for a particular borrower. See the following example.

Example | SWAPS

Take the two companies, Cat plc and Dog plc, both of which want to borrow £150 million for eight years. Cat would like to borrow on a fixed-rate basis because this would better match its asset position. Dog prefers to borrow at floating rates because of optimism about future interest-rate falls. The treasurers of each firm have obtained quotations from banks operating in the markets for both fixed- and floating-rate eight-year debt. Cat could obtain fixed-rate borrowing at 10 per cent and floating rate at LIBOR +2 per cent. Dog is able to borrow at 8 per cent fixed and LIBOR +1 per cent floating:

	Fixed	*Floating*
Cat can borrow at	10%	LIBOR +2%
Dog can borrow at	8%	LIBOR +1%

In the absence of a swap market Cat would probably borrow at 10 per cent and Dog would pay LIBOR +1 per cent. However, with a swap arrangement both firms can achieve lower interest rates.

Notice that because of Dog's higher credit rating it can borrow at a lower rate than Cat in both the fixed- and the floating-rate market – it has an absolute advantage in both. However the risk premium charged in the two markets is not consistent. Cat has to pay an extra 1 per cent in the floating-rate market, but an extra 2 per cent in the fixed-rate market. Cat has an absolute disadvantage for both, but has a comparative advantage in the floating-rate market.

To achieve lower interest rates each firm should borrow in the market where it has comparative advantage and then swap interest obligations. So Cat borrows floating-rate funds, paying LIBOR +2 per cent, and Dog borrows fixed-rate debt, paying 8 per cent.

Then they agree to swap interest payments at rates which lead to benefits for both firms in terms of: (a) achieving the most appropriate interest pattern (fixed or floating), and (b) the interest rate that is payable,

▶

which is lower than if Cat had borrowed at fixed and Dog had borrowed at floating rates. One way of achieving this is to arrange the swap on the following basis:

- Cat pays to Dog fixed interest of 9.5 per cent;

- Dog pays to Cat LIBOR +2 per cent.

This is illustrated as follows:

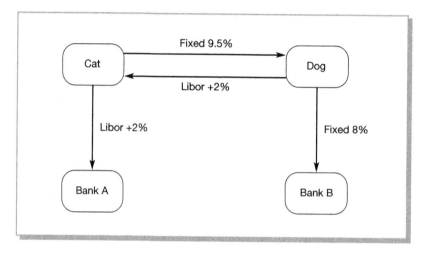

Now let us examine the position for each firm.

Cat pays LIBOR +2 per cent to a bank but also receives LIBOR +2 per cent from Dog and so these two cancel out. Cat also pays 9.5 per cent fixed to Dog. This is 50 basis points lower than if Cat had borrowed at fixed rate directly from the bank. On £150 million this is worth £750,000 per year.

Cat:

Pays	LIBOR +2%
Receives	LIBOR +2%
Pays	Fixed 9.5%
Net payment	Fixed 9.5%

Dog takes on the obligation of paying a bank fixed interest at 8 per cent while receiving 9.5 per cent fixed from Cat on the regular payment days. The net effect is 1.5 per cent receivable less the Libor +2 per cent payment to Cat – a floating-rate liability of Libor +0.5 per cent.

▶

Dog:

Pays	Fixed 8%
Receives	Fixed 9.5%
Pays	LIBOR +2%
Net payment	LIBOR +0.5%

Again there is a saving of 50 basis points or £750,000 per year.[8] The net annual £1.5 million saving is before transaction costs.

Prior to the widespread development of a highly liquid swap market each counterparty incurred considerable expense in making the contracts watertight. Even then, the risk of one of the counterparties failing to fulfil its obligations was a potential problem. Today intermediaries (e.g. banks) take counterparty positions in swaps and this reduces risk and avoids the necessity for one corporation to search for another with a corresponding swap preference. The intermediary generally finds an opposite counterparty for the swap at a later date. Furthermore, standardised contracts reduce the time and effort needed to arrange a swap and have permitted the development of a thriving secondary market, and this has assisted liquidity. This more developed approach, with a bank intermediary offering rates to swap fixed to floating, or floating to fixed is illustrated in the following example.

Example   **SWAPS WITH AN INTERMEDIARY BANK**

Paris Expori, a French property developer, has agreed to buy and develop a shopping centre in the heart of England. It will need to borrow £80 million to do this for a period of six years. The company treasurer has contacted a number of banks to enquire what they would charge if a term loan was granted by them. The quotes are for both floating rates and fixed rates. She has also looked into the possibilities of issuing a floating rate bond with the interest re-fixed to LIBOR at six-month intervals and the issuance of a fixed interest rate bond. She has concluded that all the fixed rates offered are excessively high – each quote is over 5.5 per cent. The best floating rate offer

▶

---

[8] Under a swap arrangement the principal amount (in this case £150 million) is usually never swapped and Cat retains the obligation to pay the principal to bank A. Neither of the banks is involved in the swap and may not be aware that it has taken place. The swap focuses entirely in the three-monthly or six-monthly interest payments.

is a reasonable LIBOR + 200 basis points, but the Board of Directors insist that, because the company already has too much exposure to a rise in interest rates, such a large loan should not add to the company's exposure.

The Treasurer's solution is to borrow £80 million at floating rate and then contact one of the banks offering swap rates to swap into a fixed rate. The date is 16 December 2010 and an idea of the swap rates available are shown in the *Financial Times* table displayed in Exhibit 15.9 – in reality you need to contact brokers and individual banks.

INTEREST RATES – SWAPS

Dec 16	Euro-€		£ Stlg		SwFr		US$		Yen	
	Bid	Ask	Bid	Ask	Bid	Ask	Bid	Ask	Bid	Ask
1 year	1.39	1.44	0.97	1.00	0.30	0.36	0.53	0.56	0.33	0.39
2 year	1.73	1.78	1.60	1.64	0.56	0.64	0.93	0.96	0.40	0.46
3 year	2.07	2.12	2.04	2.08	0.88	0.96	1.42	1.45	0.47	0.53
4 year	2.30	2.40	2.42	2.47	1.20	1.28	1.02	1.05	0.56	0.62
5 year	2.65	2.70	2.75	2.80	1.48	1.56	2.38	2.41	0.67	0.73
6 year	2.86	2.91	3.03	3.08	1.71	1.79	2.76	2.79	0.81	0.87
7 year	3.04	3.09	3.26	3.31	1.90	1.98	3.07	3.10	0.95	1.01
8 year	3.18	3.23	3.46	3.51	2.05	2.13	3.31	3.34	1.08	1.14
9 year	3.30	3.35	3.61	3.66	2.18	2.26	3.51	3.54	1.21	1.27
10 year	3.40	3.45	3.74	3.79	2.28	2.36	3.67	3.70	1.32	1.38
12 year	3.58	3.63	3.91	3.98	2.43	2.53	3.90	3.93	1.52	1.60
15 year	3.75	3.80	4.07	4.16	2.55	2.65	4.11	4.14	1.75	1.83
20 year	3.80	3.85	4.12	4.25	2.54	2.64	4.26	4.29	1.97	2.05
25 year	3.71	3.76	4.12	4.25	2.48	2.58	4.33	4.36	2.04	2.12
30 year	3.59	3.64	4.08	4.21	2.43	2.53	4.36	4.39	2.06	2.14

Bid and ask rates as of close of London Business. US$ is quoted annual money actual/360 basis against 3 month Libor. £ and Yen quoted on a semi-annual actual/365 basis against 6 month Libor. Euro/Swiss Franc quoted on annual bond 30/360 basis against 6 month Euribor/Libor with exception of the 1 year rate which is quoted against 3 month Euribor/Libor.

Source: ICAP plc.

Exhibit 15.9 Interest rates–swaps

Source: *Financial Times*, 17 December 2010

For this illustration we are most interested in the pound sterling columns (£ Stlg). Two prices are given for each contract period. The ask rate is the interest you would pay under the swap if you were to agree to pay fixed rate and receive the LIBOR rate set for each of the six months over the term of the agreement with the bank doing swap. The bid rate is the fixed rate you would receive from the bank in return for you paying LIBOR to it. The banks in these markets expect to conclude numerous deals both paying fixed and receiving fixed rates, and they make a few basis points of profit between the two.

Paris Expori must ensure that any deal it makes with a bank in the swap market matches the underlying floating rate loan transaction it has concluded with another bank – e.g. length of time to maturity, dates of resetting interest rates ('rollover dates'). The deal it wants to make in the swap market is to pay fixed rate and receive floating rate. Looking along the six-year row we see that the fixed rate payable is 3.08 per cent per annum if Paris Expori is a top ranking company. However it is not regarded as a counterparty as safe as one of these banks and so it will have to pay slightly more, say 3.15 per cent. This rate will be paid semi-annually – roughly one-half of 3.15 per cent for six months. In return Paris Expori will receive six-month LIBOR, which will be reset for each six-month period depending on market rates at the time.

Thus, on each of the six-monthly rollover dates the LIBOR rate of interest will be deducted from the agreed fixed rate of 3.15 and the difference paid by one party to the other. For example, if six months after the agreement starts LIBOR is set at 1.00 per cent (expressed as an annual rate) at the 11 a.m. London fixing, Paris Expori owes 3.15 per cent to the bank (which needs adjusting down for the six-month period) while the bank owes Paris Expori 1.00 per cent (half that for the six months). Rather than make two payments, only the difference changes hands, 2.15 per cent (half that for six months) – see Exhibit 15.10.

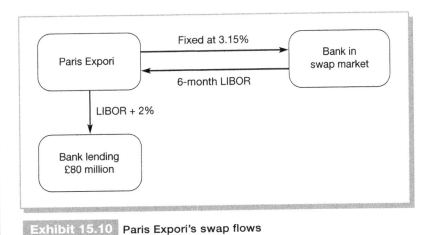

Exhibit 15.10 Paris Expori's swap flows

> Paris Expori is now receiving LIBOR to offset the payment of LIBOR it
> makes to the bank that lent it £80 million. However, it has to pay 200
> basis points more than this to the lending bank as well as the fixed rate
> of 3.15 per cent per annum: thus it has fixed its interest at 5.15 per cent
> for the six-year life of the loan. This is better than the 5.5 per cent offered
> as a direct fixed rate loan to the company.

There are many variations on the swaps theme. For example, a **swaption** is
an option to have a swap at a later date. In a **currency swap** the two parties
exchange interest obligations (or receipts) and (usually) the principal amount
for an agreed period, between two different currencies. On reaching the maturity date of the swap the principal amounts will be re-exchanged at a pre-agreed
exchange rate.

Credit default swap (CDS)

Until the early 1990s once a lender to a company had assumed the risk of loss
through default or a similar 'credit event' (failure of the borrower to abide by
the agreement) there was little that they could do except wait to see if the borrower paid all the interest and principal on time, as agreed at the outset. In other
words, the lender retained all the credit risk and could not pass any of it on to
others more willing to bear it. Today, however, we have an enormous market in
the selling and buying of protection against default (the total notional amount
outstanding on credit default swap contracts exceeds the total amount of debt in
the world!).

Under a **credit default swap (CDS)** the seller of protection receives a regular fee
(usually every three months over a period of years) from the buyer of protection, and in return promises to make a payoff should the underlying specified
reference entity (e.g. BP) default on its obligations with regard to a **reference
obligation**, i.e. a specific bond or loan. Thus the payment from the buyer of
credit protection is a regular amount but the payment the other way, from protection seller to buyer, is a contingent payment depending on whether there is a
credit event – see Exhibit 15.11.

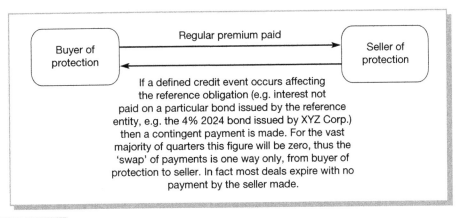

Regular premium paid

Buyer of protection → Seller of protection

If a defined credit event occurs affecting the reference obligation (e.g. interest not paid on a particular bond issued by the reference entity, e.g. the 4% 2024 bond issued by XYZ Corp.) then a contingent payment is made. For the vast majority of quarters this figure will be zero, thus the 'swap' of payments is one way only, from buyer of protection to seller. In fact most deals expire with no payment by the seller made.

Exhibit 15.11

Example   **CREDIT DEFAULT SWAP**

A pension fund manager has bought £20 million (nominal value) of bonds from a software company, Appsoft. He is concerned that at some point over the five-year life of the bonds the company will fail to meet its obligations – there will be a credit event. Even though this is unlikely the manager needs to make absolutely sure that he is protected on the downside. He thus consults one of the organisations that provide CDS prices (e.g. www.markit.com) to gain an idea of the amount he would have to pay for five years of protection. The prices on this website only give a general indication because they report only deals struck by one dealer some time the previous day. To obtain a more precise cost he will need to contact dealers.

The quote he is given is 160 basis points as the 'spread' expressed as a percentage of the notional principal per year. Thus for £20 million of cover he will pay an annual amount of £20m × 0.016 = £320,000. However, in this market it is normal for this payment to be split up into four quarterly amounts payable on 20 March, 20 June, 20 September and 20 December. Thus the quarterly payments will be approximately £80,000.

The cash flows between the pension fund and the CDS dealer (market maker) are shown on the left half of Exhibit 15.13. The pension fund manager makes quarterly payments and in return the CDS dealer pays an amount contingent on a credit event occurring. In most cases the CDS dealer never pays anything to the pension fund because the reference entity (Appsoft in this case) abides by its bond/loan agreements. Thus CDS arrangements are very similar to standard insurance and, in fact, many insurance companies have entered this market as protection sellers. The major difference between CDS protection and standard insurance is that with insurance you have to own the asset and suffer the loss to receive a payout.[9] With a CDS you can buy the 'protection' and receive a payout from the dealer regardless of whether you own the asset. So another fund may never own bonds in Appsoft, but can speculate in the CDS market; for example, make regular quarterly payments to the dealer in the hope that Appsoft commits a default and the dealer is forced to make a large payout.

The right side of Exhibit 15.12 shows the payments between the dealer and a hedge fund manager who will take on the credit event risk in return for a quarterly payment. Thus the dealer ends up both buying protection and selling protection. But notice that he has made a margin between the two. Protection is sold for 160 basis points and bought for 155 basis points.

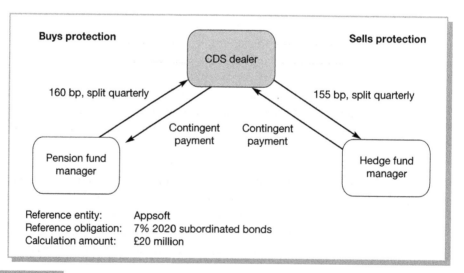

Exhibit 15.12 Credit default swap arrangement: five-year Appsoft with 155/160 bid/offer

[9] To take out insurance you have to have an insurable interest (the insured party can suffer a loss if the asset is damaged etc). This was introduced to prevent the phenomenon of people insuring an asset or another person and then destroying/murdering.

Settlement and credit events

Most CDSs are **physically settled** which means that when a credit event occurs the protection buyer will deliver debt assets of the reference entity to the protection seller. In return the protection seller pays their par value (£20 million in the case of Appsoft). The bonds or loans delivered do not have to be the specified reference obligation, but they cannot be subordinated (higher risk) to it – Appsoft might have issued some other bonds which the pension fund manager chooses to deliver instead of the bond acting as the reference obligation. Once the settlement process is triggered the CDS quarterly premiums paid by the protection buyer cease.

A minority of CDSs are **cash settled**, that is a credit event triggers a cash payment. To figure out how much is to be paid we first need to find the recovery value on the debt, that is the current market value of the instrument now that it has defaulted. A default does not usually result in the debt becoming completely worthless; a typical recovery rate on a defaulted bond is around 40 per cent of its par value, but this varies tremendously. For some defaulted bonds there may be an active secondary market which will fix the current price, for others it is necessary to conduct an auction process in which dealers submit prices at which they would buy and sell the reference entity's debt obligations. In the case of Lehman Brothers' October 2008 auction, the price was set at 8.625 through billions of dollars worth of actual trades, which means that dealers were still willing to pay 8.625 per cent of the par value of Lehman's bonds to hold them even though they were in default. The protection sellers therefore had to make up the remainder of the par value as a cash payment to the CDS holders, i.e. 91.375 per cent of the par value was paid out. When Metro-Goldwyn-Mayer defaulted in 2009 the bonds were valued at 58.5 per cent of par and so 41.5 per cent was paid out.

So far we have skipped over what we mean by a credit event. The following are the main categories:

- **Insolvency of the entity**.

- **Failure to pay**. Principal and/or interest not paid.

- **Debt restructuring**. When companies have difficulty paying their debt they negotiate with their lenders to vary the terms of their debt in their favour – for example, an extension of maturity, interest deferral, principal forgiveness, swapping debt for shares in the firm – resulting in a poorer deal for the lenders. These restructurings are often defined as defaults, but some CDS agreements specifically exclude this type of event due to the lack of clarity on whether a particular restructuring is really a default.

■ **Obligation acceleration.** At least one obligation under the debt deal has become payable before its normal maturity date – this may be due to the reference entity defaulting on another debt triggering an early payment.

■ **Repudiation/moratorium.** The borrower renounces its debt obligations and refuses to pay, for example, a government disclaims or disaffirms the validity of a debt claim.

We have focused on the use of CDS when you have an underlying credit exposure to hedge. However, most trades are 'naked CDS', i.e. the protection buyer or seller does not hold a debt in the reference entity. These naked positions have been criticised by politicians for exacerbating the financial crisis – the role of CDSs in the 2008 crisis is covered in Chapter 19.

Websites

www.advfn.com	ADVFN
www.money.cnn.com	CNN Financial News
www.nyxdata.com	Prices on LIFFE
www.bloomberg.com	Bloomberg
www.cmegroup.com	CME group
www.reuters.com	Reuters
www.wsj.com	Wall Street Journal
www.ft.com	Financial Times
www.fow.com	Futures and Options World
www.euronext.com	London International Financial Futures and Options Exchange (NYSE Liffe)
www.cboe.com	Chicago Board Options Exchange
www.theice.com	Intercontinental Exchange
www.eurexchange.com	Eurex, the European Derivative Exchange
www.isda.org	International Swaps and Derivatives Association
http://www.futuresindustry.org/	Futures Industry Association
www.markit.com	Markit Financial Information Services

16

Foreign exchange markets

This chapter looks at the foreign exchange (**forex** or **FX**) markets from a number of angles. Firstly, there is a description of the different types of FX markets, from simple spot 'immediate' delivery of one currency for another (immediate means within two days), to forwards which allow exchange of currency at a future date. Then we examine the way in which FX prices are quoted, with a particular emphasis on understanding the tables in the *Financial Times*. It has not always been the case that the main currencies have been allowed to float against each other determined by market forces. In the past rates of exchange were usually set by governments in a variety of interventionist regimes. We look at some of these alternatives to floating. Another important angle is the impact of shifts in FX rates on people and businesses. Significant sums can be lost and firms can go out of business if they fail to manage the risk. We discuss some of the techniques used, which helps to illustrate a number of the instruments available in the FX markets.

The currency markets

On the most basic level, foreign exchange markets are (hugely liquid) markets in which one currency is exchanged for another, at a rate usually determined by market supply and demand. For example, if there is a lot of demand from the UK for US dollars, then the buying actions of market players will lead to pressure for the price of each US dollar to rise and conversely the price of each UK pound will fall (less demand and greater supply).

FX trading takes place round the globe 24 hours a day. It is largely OTC (over the counter) trading where the trades are carried out between two parties directly without going through a regulated exchange. The huge amounts of trading make a significant impact on international flows of capital. Of the global total of $3.98 trillion estimated in 2010 (see Exhibit 16.1) over one-third is through London.

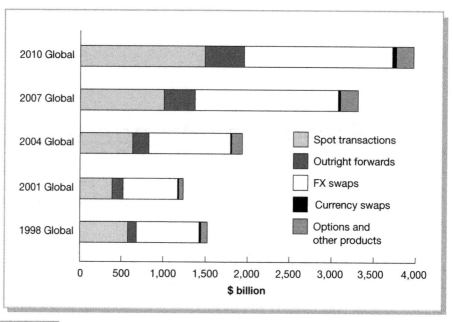

Exhibit 16.1   Global daily FX turnover in April, various years

Source: Triennial Central Bank Survey: Report on global foreign exchange market activity in 2010, Bank for International Settlements, www.bis.org

We can see from Exhibit 16.1 that there are many different FX markets. In other words, there are many different types of foreign exchange deals available:

■ **Spot transaction**: a single outright transaction involving the exchange of two currencies at a rate agreed on the date of the contract for value or delivery (cash settlement) within two business days.[1]

■ **Forward**: a transaction involving the exchange of two currencies at a rate agreed on the date of the contract for value or delivery (cash settlement) at some time in the future (more than two business days later). These contracts are negotiated and agreed between the two parties without going through a regulated exchange. Later in the chapter we look at the use of forward markets by corporations to fix the exchange rate for a transaction they will undertake months, or even years, from now. This brings a high degree of certainty about the rate of exchange at which they will be able to transact.

---

[1] Non-working days do not count, so a Friday deal is settled on the following Tuesday. There are also some exceptions, e.g. the US dollar/Canadian dollar deals are settled the next day.

▪ **Foreign exchange swap (FX swap)**: a single deal with two parts to it. Firstly, there is the actual exchange of two currencies on a specific date at a rate agreed at the time of the conclusion of the contract – this is usually a spot exchange but it can be a forward. Secondly, there is a reverse exchange of the same two currencies at a date further in the future at a rate agreed at the time of the contract. The rates of exchange are usually different in the two parts. These FX swaps take place all the time between professional players based in banks as they try to balance out their currency positions and reduce their risk exposure. They usually cover a period of no more than one week. As Exhibit 16.1 shows, these arrangements make up the largest element in the FX markets, but they are of little significance to non-bank players.

▪ **Currency swap**: a contract that commits two counterparties to exchange streams of interest payments in different currencies for an agreed period of time and usually to exchange principal amounts in different currencies at a pre-agreed exchange rate at maturity. These are the swaps discussed in Chapter 15 being linked to long-term loans with interest payments to be made – they should not be confused with FX swaps. A **currency swaption** is an option to enter into a currency swap contract.

▪ **Currency option**: an option contract that gives the right but not the obligation to buy or sell a currency with another currency at a specified exchange rate during a specified period.

▪ **Future**: foreign currency futures are exchange-traded transactions to exchange currency at a future date, with standard contract sizes and maturity dates – for example, £62,500 for next November at an agreed rate.

Although over one-third of all FX trading takes place in London (see Exhibit 16.2), with London carrying out twice as much trade as its nearest rival, the US, the actual currency that dominates is the US dollar, which acts as a counterparty in over 85 per cent of all trading on one side of the trade (see Exhibit 16.3). The currencies most commonly traded are USD, the US dollar ($), EUR, the euro (€), JPY, the Japanese yen (¥), GBP, the UK pound (£), AUD, the Australian dollar (A$), CAD, the Canadian dollar (C$) and CHF, the Swiss franc (SFr).

The US dollar has become the currency that is accepted and used worldwide. This is partly due to the legacy left from the Bretton Woods agreement (see later), but mostly to do with the size, strength and stability of the US economy.

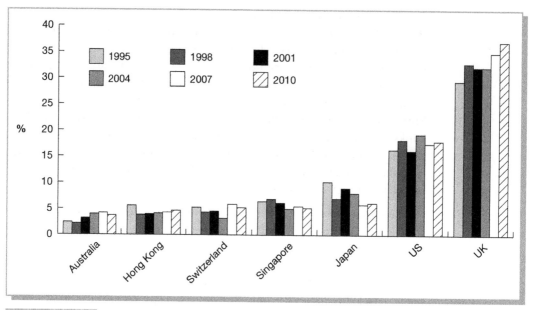

Exhibit 16.2   Percentages of global foreign exchange market turnover by country, daily averages in April 2010

Source: Triennial Central Bank Survey: Report on global foreign exchange market activity in 2010, Bank for International Settlements, www.bis.org

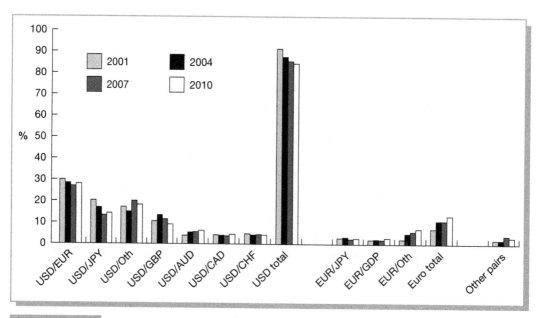

Exhibit 16.3   Percentages of global foreign exchange market turnover by currency pair, daily averages in April 2010

Source: Triennial Central Bank Survey: Report on global foreign exchange market activity in 2010, Bank for International Settlements, www.bis.org

FX trading

In contrast to equity trading, where most countries tend to have one major trading exchange (or, at most, a handful) and trading is tightly regulated, trading on the foreign exchange market does not have a focal position where all trading is supervised and data is collected and displayed. The trading is carried out in numerous locations, wherever a trader is and can access a computer screen or a mobile phone screen. Many trading platforms now offer an app for mobile phones and tablet computers, giving traders full access to all their facilities and data, enabling them to download data and carry out trading wherever they are. Individual investors can also take advantage of this new technology, giving them access to data that was once only available to professional traders.

Some of the trades are on regulated exchanges but most are not. Anyone with the requisite knowledge can take part in FX trading, and regulation is lax for the most part. Having said that, the vast majority of trading is done by major international banks and their subsidiaries, with reputations to lose, so there is a high degree of self-regulation.

Trading is constant, taking place on a 24-hour basis, with the high concentration of activity moving with the sun from one major financial centre to another. Most trading occurs when both the European and New York markets are open – this is when it is afternoon in Frankfurt, Zurich and London and morning on the east coast of the Americas. Later the bulk of the trade passes to San Francisco and Los Angeles, followed by Sydney, Tokyo, Hong Kong and Singapore. There are at least 40 other trading centres around the world in addition to these main ones.

Most banks carry out proprietary trading, i.e. they trade in the hope of making profits on behalf of the bank itself. The banks are in the process of concentrating their dealers in three or four regional hubs. These typically include London as well as New York and a site in Asia, where Tokyo, Hong Kong and Singapore are keen to establish their dominance. According to a survey by the magazine *Euromoney*, FX trading carried out by banks is highly concentrated, with over 77 per cent carried out by only 10 banks (see Exhibit 16.4), with Deutsche Bank having held top spot for the past six years.

When a non-bank organisation needs an FX deal they mostly trade with a bank, but there are exchanges for some types of dealing. The main difference between FX trading via banks and FX trading carried out on exchanges such as the Chicago Mercantile Exchange (CME) is that exchange trading tends to deal in standard amounts and maturities. The amounts and maturities of these contracts are fixed and inflexible, so they may be less suitable for company use, where the company might need to hedge specific amounts for a specific time, and

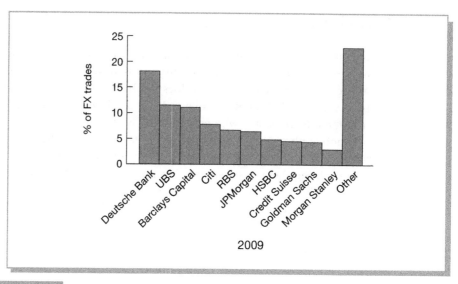

Exhibit 16.4 2009 FX trading by banks

Source: www.euromoney.com

would therefore be better served using the flexibility offered by a bank. Dealing through an exchange facilitates clearing and settlement, and exchange-traded currency instruments are liquid and tradable.

The buyers and sellers of foreign currencies are:

- commercial companies with export or import interests;
- international banks and commercial banks carrying out proprietary trading;
- dealers trading and acting as market makers in currency (usually the big banks);
- brokers buying and selling currencies on behalf of a client (e.g. a client bank or commercial firm);
- governments needing foreign currency for overseas trade or to pay for activities abroad;
- speculators or arbitrageurs taking advantage of perceived FX pricing anomalies;
- tourists or investors (e.g. in property or shares) needing to pay in foreign currency;
- fund managers investing abroad (pensions, insurance companies, etc.);
- central banks (smoothing out fluctuations or managing the rate to a desired level).

There are various ways in which deals are done. Firstly, there is the traditional approach of the two dealers talking on the telephone and agreeing to trade. One of the dealers here may be a non-bank customer such as a manufacturing firm. If the customer approaches the bank without going through an intermediary these are **customer direct trades**. However, a broker will frequently act on behalf of a customer to deal with banks in the FX markets – if conducted over the telephone these are **voice broker** trades. The trades between banks, referred to as **inter-dealer direct trades**, can be either via direct telephone communication or direct electronic dealing systems – these electronic deals are shown separately as the largest segment in Exhibit 16.5. Increasingly deals are conducted over electronic dealing systems. Banks are the main users of these systems, but there are special systems set up for customers. Some of these are run by a single bank as a **proprietary platform**. Others are managed by a group of banks – **multibank dealing systems**. Examples of multibank systems include FXAll, Currenex, FXConnect, Globalink and eSpeed.

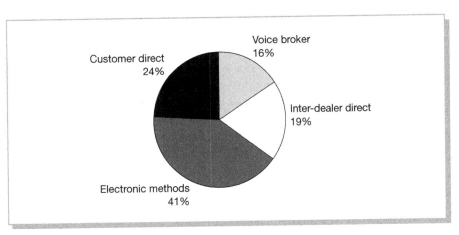

Exhibit 16.5 Foreign exchange market turnover by execution method, 2010

Source: *Triennial Central Bank Survey: Report on global foreign exchange market activity in 2010*, Bank for International Settlements, www.bis.org

The electronic platforms have allowed smaller banks to access the best prices and provide them with the opportunity to deal alongside the large banks on an even basis because of the transparency of the systems. Rapid price dissemination from electronic systems has, to a great extent, levelled the playing field, whereas in the old days only the large banks could 'see' the market prices through their telephone contacts.

Exchange rates

We now look more closely at exchange rates. We start with some terms used in FX markets. First, we provide a definition of an **exchange rate**:

An exchange rate is the price of one currency (**the base currency**) expressed in terms of another (**the secondary, counter or quote currency**).

Therefore if the exchange rate between the US dollar and the pound is US$1.60 = £1.00 this means that £1.00 will cost US$1.60. Taking the reciprocal, US$1.00 will cost 62.50 pence. The standardised forms of expression are:

US$/£ : 1.60   or   *US$1.60/£*   or   *USD1.60/£*

Exchange rates are expressed in terms of the number of units of the first currency per single unit of the second currency. Most currencies are quoted to four decimal places and the smallest variation used in trading is a **pip** which is one ten-thousandth of one unit of currency (e.g. $1), or 0.0001. So for the US$/£ exchange rate on 16 November 2010 the rate was quoted in the *Financial Times* as US$1.5988/£.

However, this is still not accurate enough because currency exchange rates are not generally expressed in terms of a single 'middle rate' as above, but are given as a rate at which you can buy the first currency (bid rate) and a rate at which you can sell the first currency (offer rate). This is called the spread and it enables market makers (traders) to make a profit on buying and selling currencies. In the case of the US$/£ exchange rate the market rates on 16 November 2010 were US$1.5988/£ 'middle rate':

	Bid rate	*Offer rate*
	↑	↓
US$/£	1.5986	1.5990
	↑	↑
	You can buy dollars from a bank or broker at this rate.	You can sell dollars to a bank or broker at this rate.

The difference (the spread) between bid and offer is 4 pips.

So if you wished to purchase US$1 million the cost would be:

$$\frac{\$1,000,000}{1.5986} = £625,547$$

However, if you wished to sell US$1 million you would receive:

$$\frac{\$1,000,000}{1.5990} = £625,391$$

The foreign exchange dealers are transacting with numerous buyers and sellers every day and they make a profit on the difference between the bid price and the offer price (the bid/offer spread). In the above example if a dealer sold US$1 million and bought US$1 million with a bid/offer spread of 0.04 of a cent, a profit of £625,547 – £625,391 = £156 is made.

Sources of information

Information on currency exchange rates is easily available in newspapers such as the *Financial Times*, or websites such as Reuters, Yahoo! Finance or any of the other numerous financial websites. Rates may vary very slightly between them all. Tuesday to Saturday the *Financial Times* reports the previous day's trading in over 50 of the most commonly-traded currencies in the FX market, giving their value relative to the dollar, euro and pound. The figures shown in Exhibit 16.6 relate to dealings on 12 November 2010. Of course by the time a newspaper reader receives the information in this table the rates may well have changed as the 24-hour markets execute their trades continuously. However, **www.ft.com** and other websites provide much more up-to-the-minute and detailed information.

The prices shown under the pound columns in Exhibit 16.6 are the middle price of the foreign currency in terms of £1 in London at 4 p.m. the previous afternoon. So, for instance, the mid-price of £1 for immediate delivery is 1.6338 Australian dollars. For the US dollar columns the prices for the pound and euro are the number of dollars per currency unit, either per pound or per euro. However, for other currencies the rate shown is the number of units of the other currency per US$1, for example, 1.0098 Canadian dollars per US dollar. For the euro columns the rate shown is the number of units of the other currency per euro – for example the spot mid-rate against the pound is 84.84 pence per euro.

On Mondays the *FT* publishes a much more comprehensive list of country exchange rates, again with their relative values against the dollar, euro and pound. While the most common currencies often have forward rates quoted, there are many currencies for which forward quotes are difficult to obtain. The so-called **exotic currencies** generally do not have forward rates quoted by dealers. These are currencies for which there is little trading demand to support international business, etc. On the other hand, spot markets exist for most of the world's currencies.

CURRENCY RATES

Nov 12	Currency	DOLLAR Closing Mid	DOLLAR Day's Change	EURO Closing Mid	EURO Day's Change	POUND Closing Mid	POUND Day's Change
Argentina	(Peso)	3.9613	0.00007	5.4280	0.0141	6.3981	0.0008
Australia	(A$)	1.0115	0.0091	1.3861	0.0158	1.6338	0.0145
Bahrain	(Dinar)	0.3771	–	0.5167	0.0013	0.6090	0.0000
Bolivia	(Boliviano)	7.0200	–	9.6192	0.0231	11.3384	-0.0007
Brazil	(R$)	1.7181	-0.0009	2.3542	0.0044	2.7750	-0.0016
Canada	(C$)	1.0098	0.0049	1.3836	0.0100	1.6309	0.0078
Chile	(Peso)	481.650	0.8000	659.981	2.6830	777.937	1.2440
China	(Yuan)	6.6370	0.0113	9.0944	0.0373	10.7198	0.0176
Colombia	(Peso)	1863.85	7.2000	2553.94	15.9923	3010.40	11.4427
Costa Rica	(Colon)	513.490	-3.6200	703.610	-3.2538	829.365	-5.8985
Czech Rep.	(Koruna)	17.9551	-0.0668	24.6030	-0.0320	29.0003	-0.1096
Denmark	(DKr)	5.4395	-0.0134	7.4534	-0.0004	8.7855	-0.0222
Egypt	(Egypt £)	5.7510	-0.0017	7.8803	0.0166	9.2888	-0.0034
Estonia	(Kroon)	11.4188	-0.0275	15.6466	–	18.4431	-0.0456
Hong Kong	(HK$)	7.7511	0.0006	10.6210	0.0263	12.5192	0.0001
Hungary	(Forint)	201.894	-0.4911	276.645	-0.0050	326.089	-0.8134
India	(Rs)	44.7425	0.4275	61.3084	0.7320	72.2659	0.6860
Indonesia	(Rupiah)	8924.50	26.5000	12228.8	65.6752	14414.4	41.9120
Iran	(Rial)	10405.0	–	14257.5	34.3365	16805.6	-1.0405
Israel	(Shk)	3.6745	0.0193	5.0350	0.0385	5.9349	0.0308
Japan	(Y)	82.3700	-0.1100	112.868	0.1214	133.040	-0.1859
One Month		82.3520	-0.0015	112.810	-0.0004	132.982	-0.0016
Three Month		82.2971	-0.0039	112.646	-0.0066	132.821	-0.0049
One Year		81.8845	-0.0045	111.650	0.0023	131.680	-0.0400
Kenya	(Shilling)	80.5000	0.1000	110.305	0.4023	130.020	0.1534
Kuwait	(Dinar)	0.2807	-0.0001	0.3846	0.0008	0.4534	-0.0002
Malaysia	(M$)	3.1145	0.0230	4.2677	0.0418	5.0304	0.0369
Mexico	(New Peso)	12.2557	-0.0242	16.7934	0.0074	19.7948	-0.0404
New Zealand	(NZ$)	1.2910	0.0079	1.7690	0.0150	2.0852	0.0126
Nigeria	(Naira)	150.700	0.1500	206.497	0.7024	243.403	0.2272
Norway	(NKr)	5.9486	0.0166	8.1511	0.0423	9.6079	0.0261
Pakistan	(Rupee)	85.6650	0.2700	117.383	0.6518	138.362	0.4275
Peru	(New Sol)	2.8025	0.0020	3.8401	0.0120	4.5265	0.0030
Phillippines	(Peso)	43.7200	-0.1550	59.9074	-0.0675	70.6144	-0.2548

	Currency	DOLLAR Closing Mid	DOLLAR Day's Change	EURO Closing Mid	EURO Day's Change	POUND Closing Mid	POUND Day's Change
Poland	(Zloty)	2.8656	-0.0101	3.9265	-0.0044	4.6283	-0.0166
Romania	(New Leu)	3.1343	-0.0011	4.2948	0.0088	5.0624	-0.0021
Russia	(Rouble)	30.7913	0.1698	42.1917	0.3337	49.7325	0.2712
Saudi Arabia	(SR)	3.7498	-0.0005	5.1381	0.0117	6.0565	-0.0011
Singapore	(S$)	1.2957	0.0065	1.7754	0.0132	2.0927	0.0104
South Africa	(R)	6.9363	0.0025	9.5044	0.0263	11.2031	0.0033
South Korea	(Won)	1127.85	20.1500	1545.44	31.2660	1821.65	32.4345
Sweden	(SKr)	6.8300	0.0042	9.3588	0.0282	11.0315	0.0060
Switzerland	(SFr)	0.9771	0.0040	1.3389	0.0086	1.5781	0.0062
Taiwan	(T$)	30.2105	0.1685	41.3960	0.3300	48.7945	0.2691
Thailand	(Bt)	29.7750	0.1500	40.7992	0.3033	48.0911	0.2393
Tunisia	(Dinar)	1.4188	-0.0015	1.9346	0.0027	2.2803	-0.0025
Turkey	(Lira)	1.4343	0.0012	1.9653	0.0064	2.3166	0.0018
U A E	(Dirham)	3.6727	0.0000	5.0325	0.0121	5.9320	-0.0004
UK (0.6191)*	(£)	1.6152	-0.0001	0.8484	0.0021	–	–
One Month		1.6148	0.0000	0.8483	0.0000	–	–
Three Month		1.6139	–	0.8481	–	–	–
One Year		1.6081	-0.0004	0.8479	0.0003	–	–
Ukraine	(Hryvnja)	7.9515	-0.0020	10.8956	0.0235	12.8429	-0.0040
Uruguay	(Peso)	19.8000	–	27.1310	0.0654	31.9800	-0.0020
USA	($)	–		1.3703	0.0033	1.6152	-0.0001
One Month		–		1.3699	0.0000	1.6148	0.0000
Three Month		–		1.3688	0.0000	1.6139	0.0000
One Year		–		1.3635	0.0001	1.6081	-0.0004
Venezuela †(Bolivar Fuerte)		4.2947	–	5.8848	0.0142	6.9365	-0.0004
Vietnam	(Dong)	19495.0	–	26713.0	64.3335	31487.4	-1.9495
Euro (0.7298)*	(Euro)	1.3703	0.0033	–		1.1787	-0.0030
One Month		1.3699	0.0000	–		1.1788	–
Three Month		1.3688	0.0000	–		1.1791	0.0000
One Year		1.3635	0.0001	–		1.1794	-0.0004
SDR		–		0.6398	-0.0007	0.8767	0.0012	1.0334	-0.0011

Rates are derived from WM/Reuters at 4pm (London time). * The closing mid-point rates for the Euro and £ against the $ are shown in brackets. The other figures in the dollar column of both the Euro and Sterling rows are in the reciprocal form in line with market convention. † New Venezuelan Bolivar Fuerte introduced on Jan 1st 2008. Currency redenominated by 1000. Some values are rounded by the F.T.
The exchange rates printed in this table are also available on the internet at http://www.FT.com/marketsdata
Euro Locking Rates: Austrian Schilling 13.7603, Belgium/Luxembourg Franc 40.3399, Cyprus 0.585274. Finnish Markka 5.94572. French Franc 6.55957, German Mark 1.95583, Greek Drachma 340.75, Irish Punt 0.787564, Italian Lira 1936.27, Malta 0.4293, Netherlands Guilder 2.20371, Portuguese Escudo 200.482, Slovenia Tolar 239.64, Spanish Peseta 166.386.

Exhibit 16.6   Currency rates from the *FT*

Source: Financial Times, 13/14 November 2010

The first forward price (middle price) is given as the 'one month' rate. Looking at the sterling and US$ rates you could commit yourself to the sale of a quantity of dollars for delivery in one month at a rate that is fixed at about US$1.6148 per pound. In this case you will need fewer US dollars to buy £1 in one month's time compared with the spot rate of exchange, therefore the dollar is at a **premium** on the one-month forward rate.

The forward rate for one month shows a different relationship with the spot rate for the euro against the pound. Here more euros are required (€1.1788) to purchase a pound in one month's time compared with an 'immediate' spot purchase (€1.1787), therefore the euro on one-month forward delivery is at a **discount** to the pound.

The *Financial Times* table lists quotations up to one year for the four strongest currencies, the dollar, euro, yen and pound, but, as this is an over-the-counter market, it is possible to go as far forward in time as required – provided a counterparty can be found. Use of forward exchange rates is widespread. For example, airline companies expecting to purchase planes many years hence may use the distant forward market to purchase the foreign currency they need to pay the manufacturer so that they know with certainty the quantity of their home currency they are required to find when the planes are delivered.

The table in Exhibit 16.6 displays standard periods of time for forward rates, one month, three months and one year. These are instantly available and are frequently traded. However, forward rates are not confined to these particular days in the future. It is possible to obtain rates for any day in the future, say, 74 or 36 days hence, for any amount of currency, but these would require a specific quotation from a bank.

Example | **COVERING IN THE FORWARD MARKET**

Suppose that on 12 November 2010 a UK exporter sells goods to a customer in France invoiced at €5,000,000. Payment is due three months later. With the spot rate of exchange at €1.1787/£ the exporter, in deciding to sell the goods, has in mind a sales price of:

$$\frac{€5,000,000}{1.1787} = £4,241,961$$

The UK firm bases its decision on the profitability of the deal on this amount expressed in pounds.

However, the rate of exchange may vary between November and February: the size and direction of the move are uncertain. If the pound strengthens against the euro and the rate is then €1.40/£, the UK exporter will make a currency loss by waiting three months and exchanging the euro received into sterling at spot rates in February. The exporter will receive only £3,571,429:

$$\frac{€5,000,000}{1.40} = £3,571,429$$

▶

causing a loss of

$$\begin{array}{r} £4,241,961 \\ -£3,571,429 \\ \hline £670,532 \end{array}$$

If sterling weakens to €1.10/£ a currency gain is made. The pounds received in February if euro are exchanged at this spot rate will be:

$$\frac{5,000,000}{1.10} = £4,545,455$$

and the currency gain will be

$$\begin{array}{r} £4,545,455 \\ -£4,241,961 \\ \hline £303,494 \end{array}$$

Rather than run the risk of a possible loss on the currency side of the deal the exporter may decide to cover in the forward market. Under this arrangement the exporter promises to sell €5,000,000 against the pound in three months (the agreement is made on 12 November for delivery of currency in February). The forward rate available (ignoring any market makers' spreads and transaction costs) on 12 November is €1.1791/£ (see Exhibit 16.6). This forward contract means that the exporter will receive £4,240,522 in February:

$$\frac{5,000,000}{1.1791} = £4,240,522$$

regardless of the way in which the spot exchange rate moves over the three months.

In February the following transactions take place:

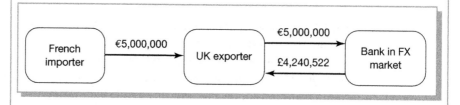

From the outset (in November) the exporter knew the amount to be received in February. It might, with hindsight, have been better not to use the forward market but to exchange the euro in February at a spot rate of, say, €1.1000/£. This would have resulted in a larger income for the firm. But in

November when the export took place there was uncertainty about what the spot rate would be in February. If the exporter had waited to exchange the currency until February and the spot rate in February had turned out to be €1.4000/£ the exporter would have made less.

Covering in the forward market is a form of insurance which leads to greater certainty – and certainty has a value. For many companies it is vital that they have this certainty about income and expenditure; they cannot afford to leave things and hope they will turn out satisfactorily.

Settlement

The vast sums of money traded every working day across the world mean that banks are exposed to the risk that they may irrevocably pay over currency to a counterparty before they receive another currency in return because settlement systems are operating in different time zones. A bank could fail after receiving one leg of its foreign exchange trades but before completing the other leg – this is called **Herstatt risk** after Bankhaus Herstatt, a German bank, which failed in 1974 with $620 million of unsettled trades. In this case the crisis was due to the time difference between Europe and the US; Bankhaus Herstatt received its dollar payments in Frankfurt, but ceased trading before the reciprocal payment could be made in New York. Its failure caused panic and gridlock in the FX markets, which took weeks to unravel.

Following this disaster, the major banks formed a new means of settlement, **Continuous Linked Settlement**, which began operating in 2002. The new entity, **CLS Bank**, is owned by banking members who trade in the FX markets. The whole point of CLS is **payment versus payment (P v P)**, simultaneous settlement of both legs of trading, thereby eliminating Herstatt risk, but also incurring charges (the charges are minuscule in relation to the sums involved, £0.07 for every £1 million of trading value). CLS claims to match payments within 38 minutes, and if a trade is not matched, it is returned to its originator, so there is no possibility of one party to the trade suffering loss due to the other party's failure to settle. Even though matching takes place in minutes, spot transactions will be settled (currency actually transferred) two days later. Settlement is offered in 17 currencies and nearly 10,000 banks, financial institutions and investment funds use the service, with up to a million trades settled daily.

Over 50 per cent of global FX trading uses multi-lateral netting, where the net value only of trades is settled. For example, if a bank sold $1 billion, but also bought $900 million, the settlement is for only $100 million. This reduces the forex risk element. CME in Chicago offers guaranteed clearing and settlement through its own clearing service, CME ClearPort, and claims never to have had any defaults in 100 years of trading.

Cross exchange rates

The major currencies of the world, US dollar, euro, pound and Swiss franc, are easily exchangeable directly into other currencies. Some currency pairs are traded much less frequently and so the market is thin and illiquid, which usually means costly. For example, the Philippines peso and the United Arab Emirates dirham would see little trade and so a company exporting from the Philippines to UAE receiving dirhams would have difficulty obtaining a quotation for a good rate of exchange. The traditional way of dealing with this was to exchange the dirhams into one of the major currencies, usually the US dollar, and then to exchange the dollars for pesos. Thus most currency rates are quoted in terms of the US dollar primarily, rather than against the 170 other currencies in the world – it simply becomes too cumbersome to quote all the possible two-currency rates and so the rate against the US dollar is set as the benchmark. Of course, today a single bank will be able to offer a service of quoting both the dirham:dollar and the peso:dollar rates, in which case it is not necessary to bother with the exchange to and from dollars, but merely to quote the rates and, if the client likes them, for the bank to transact dirhams for pesos.

> A **cross-rate** is the exchange rate of two currencies that are normally expressed in terms of a third currency, usually the US dollar.

Thus the Philippines peso and the UAE dirham are both cross currencies because they are normally quoted against the dollar. Tables of cross-rates are produced which show the exchange rate between these lesser used currencies. At first glance you see what appears to be a direct rate of exchange, say dirhams for pesos, but for most of these the rates are derived from prices against the US dollar. For example, if the exchange rates are four dirhams for one US dollar, and 60 pesos to one dollar, then the cross-rate of dirhams to pesos is as follows:

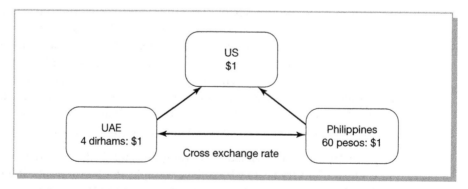

Four dirhams equal 60 pesos, therefore 1 dirham can be exchanged for 15 pesos.

Exchange rate regimes

Fixed FX regimes

Fixed exchange rates regimes require the participating countries to keep their currencies held at a constant rate or within a certain percentage of an agreed rate. Any deviation from the agreed percentage must be managed and brought back into line by the domestic central bank buying or selling its own currency. If there are significant changes to domestic economic circumstances, then a currency may be devalued or revalued, with the agreement of the participating countries.

Gold standard

Towards the end of the nineteenth century, trading countries adopted the **gold standard**, where their currency was fixed at a set price in gold. This encouraged stability in currencies relative to other currencies. It also prevented inflation, as economies could only grow their money supply in correlation to their supply of gold; it discouraged governments from overspending by issuing more banknotes than their reserves of gold warranted.

The gold standard enabled traders dealing overseas to exchange the income received in foreign currency for a set amount of gold and the amount of gold had a set value in their home currency, thus exchange rates were effectively fixed. People were entitled to exchange banknotes for actual gold, and banks issued banknotes based on the amount of gold held in their vaults.

The turmoil faced by the world as a result of World War I and then the economic crises of the 1920s and 1930s caused the gold standard to be discontinued. Governments needed to issue banknotes in excess of their gold reserves to stabilise their economies, having in many cases used much of their gold to finance warfare. A central bank's promise on its banknotes came to be based more on the country's credibility and economic standing rather than its actual physical holding of gold.

Various attempts were made to revive the gold standard, but it became increasingly difficult for any government to hold sufficient gold to guarantee all its banknotes in issue, while also altering money supply to make economic adjustments for its future stability and prosperity. A major drawback for reviving the gold standard is the limited supply of gold in the world and the physical impossibility of countries possessing gold reserves to cover their issue of currency, stifling any possibility of expansion. To give an idea of the numbers involved: the World Bank estimates that all countries' gold reserves in 2010 were 30 tonnes, valued at a little over £600 billion. In the UK alone, public spending in 2010 was a similar amount.

Bretton Woods

After the economic chaos following World War I the UK and US determined to try to prevent similar problems after World War II. To promote post-war economic and financial stability, delegates from all 44 allied countries gathered at the **Bretton Woods** conference (named after the New Hampshire town where it took place) in 1944. The negotiations resulted in an exchange rate system whereby the currencies were fixed to the US dollar, which in turn was fixed to the price of gold at $35 per ounce. At this time, the US was the major industrial nation in the world, and also held the most reserves of gold. This agreement kept the US at the forefront of the modern world and promoted the ever-present hegemony of the US dollar as the major world currency.

The participating countries had to keep within a **band** of 1 per cent of the fixed value and central banks would buy or sell the dollar against their own currency to keep within the limits. Leading the UK delegation was John Maynard Keynes, the world-renowned economist, who was instrumental in the planning of the other major achievements to come out of the conference, the World Bank and the International Monetary Fund, through which exchange rate stability was ensured.

The Bretton Woods agreement lasted for nearly 30 years until the 1970s when inflation, the cost of the Vietnam war and US welfare reforms forced the US to cancel the dollar's convertibility to gold. The US had started to export higher inflation to the rest of the world and there was an excess supply of US dollars in the world, more and more of which other countries tried to convert into gold at the agreed rate. Faced with drained gold reserves, in 1971 the US president Richard Nixon suspended the Bretton Woods agreement and allowed the US dollar to float against other currencies. Since then, most currencies have floated against other currencies, with central banks intervening when necessary to buy and sell their own currency to keep its value.

European Exchange Rate Mechanism

Following the collapse of the Bretton Woods agreement, some European countries made various attempts to establish fixed rates between their currencies to encourage trade.

The Maastricht Treaty in 1992 aimed to stabilise economic conditions and promote integration between European countries. It created the **Economic and Monetary Union (EMU)** which eventually led to the adoption of the euro in

1999 as the universal currency for most EU members. In the lead up to the EMU, the currencies of participating countries were subject to the **Exchange Rate Mechanism (ERM)** which kept each currency between strict limits.

Fixing exchange rates between European countries or adopting the euro had mixed blessings. While the stability of the currency helps in forward planning, the UK and Italy were forced out of the ERM in 1992 because the changing economic circumstances in their countries meant that the pound and the lira were set at an excessively high rate of exchange, stifling economic recovery.[2] In more recent years a common interest rate in the eurozone countries has meant an awkwardly low interest rate environment for Ireland, Greece and Spain which resulted in unsustainable property booms and wage rises followed by busts.

Pegs and bands

There are quite a few countries in the world which keep their **currency pegged** to the US dollar. They include Hong Kong, with its dollar pegged to the US dollar since 1998, and a number of emerging nations. While the HK$ is fixed to the US dollar it moves in line with that currency as it fluctuates against other currencies, so it is not fixed against other currencies. It is thought that the dollar is stable (relative to some developing countries, anyway), and so keeping pegged to the dollar helps to maintain a currency's own stability. It also helps to prevent the home currency rising against the dollar which may make exporting more difficult.

Floating FX regimes

Most major countries now adopt a **floating FX regime**, where the exchange rate for their currency is governed by supply and demand. This allows countries to keep control of their monetary policy, and it has been noted that floating rates are predisposed towards equilibrium, that is the supply and demand even each other out.

Some floating regimes do not have official limits for the movements of their currencies but nevertheless governments sometimes intervene to prevent their currency moving too far in a certain direction. These are known as **managed floats** or **dirty floats**. The low rate of the Chinese yuan against the US dollar has caused great frustration in many countries, despite it being managed to gradually appreciate (very slowly). Exporters from other countries argue that the Chinese government is keeping the yuan artificially low to boost its exporters.

---

[2] Technically the ERM allowed some floating of exchange rates, but within narrow bands.

FX volatility and its effects

You might wonder what is the significance of fluctuating FX rates. If you go on holiday to Europe, you might get more or less euro for your pound or dollar than last year – usually a fairly minor boost or inconvenience. But for companies trading millions, billions or trillions internationally, even small differences in exchange rates can have major consequences.

If a UK firm holds dollars or assets denominated in dollars and the value of the dollar rises against the pound, then the dollars and dollar assets are worth more in pounds and an FX profit is made. Conversely, should the pound rise relative to the dollar, dollars and dollar assets are worth less compared to the pound and an FX loss will be incurred. These potential gains or losses can be very large.

For example, as shown in Exhibit 16.7, between December 2007 and February 2009 the dollar appreciated by just over a third against the pound, so anyone who sold pounds for dollars in December 2007 and kept them would have made a 33 per cent profit on changing them back into pounds in 2009. If the money had also been put to work earning interest, more could have been realised.

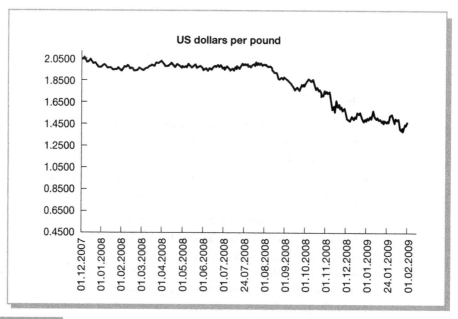

Exhibit 16.7   The exchange rates of the US dollar and GB pound

Source: www.oanda.com

Shifts in the value of foreign exchange can impact on various aspects of trading activities. Fluctuating FX rates may wipe out profits from a project, an export deal or a portfolio investment (e.g. a pension fund buying foreign shares). One of the problems caused by exchange rate fluctuations can be illustrated by an example.

Example **PROBLEMS CAUSED BY EXCHANGE RATE FLUCTUATIONS**

On 24 July 2008 two UK companies, GBX and GBA, each agreed to purchase $10,000 of goods from US company USY. GBX paid the $10,000 in July 2008 but GBA paid in January 2009, expecting to exchange pounds for dollars then.

At the time of purchase, the goods would have cost £5,012 if the pounds were exchanged at the prevailing spot rate. However, due to GBP/USD rates changing, when 24 January came, company GBA had to pay £7,283 to obtain $10,000, so GBA made a substantial FX loss compared with if it had obtained the dollars in July – 2008 see Exhibit 16.8.

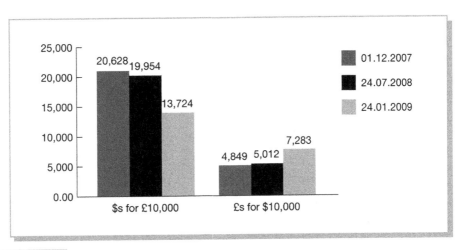

Exhibit 16.8 The relative value of 10,000 US dollars and GB pounds

Dealing with exchange rate risk

For firms which operate in international trade, there are a number of forms of exposure to risk. The following section illustrates a few strategies available to deal with some of the risks by focusing on the alternatives open to an exporter selling goods on credit. By going through these options we see the practical use of the financial markets for companies.

We will use the example of a UK company exporting £1 million of goods to a Canadian firm when the spot rate of exchange is C$1.60/£. The Canadian firm is given three months to pay, and naturally the spot rate in three months is unknown at the time of the shipment of goods. What can the firm do?

Forward market hedge

The first form of exchange rate risk management has already been mentioned. It is the most frequently employed method of hedging. A contract is agreed to exchange two currencies at a fixed time in the future at a predetermined rate. The risk of FX variation is removed for the company taking out the contract.

So if the three-month forward rate is C$1.65/£ the UK exporter could lock in the receipt of £969,697 in three months by selling forward C$1.6 million.

$$\frac{C\$1,600,000}{1.65} = £969,697$$

No foreign exchange-rate risk now exists because the dollars to be received from the importer are matched by the funds to be exchanged for sterling. There is still a risk of the importer not paying at all or on time, and the risk of the counter-party in the FX market not fulfilling its obligations.

Money market hedge

Money market hedging involves borrowing in the money markets. For example, the exporter could, at the time of the export, borrow in Canadian dollars on the money markets for a three-month period. The amount borrowed, plus three months' interest, will be equal to the amount to be received from the importer (C$1.6 million).

If the interest rate charged over three months is, 8 per cent annualised, 2 per cent for three months, then the appropriate size of the loan is:

$$C\$1.6 = C\$?(1 + 0.02) \qquad C\$? = \frac{C\$1,600,000}{1.02} = C\$1,568,627$$

Thus the exporter has created a liability (borrowed funds) which matches the asset (debt owed by the Canadian firm).

The borrowed dollars are then converted to sterling on the spot market for the exporter to receive £980,392 immediately:

$$\frac{C\$1,568,627}{1.6} = £980,392$$

The exporter has removed FX risk because it now holds cash in sterling three months before the debt was originally due, taking a small loss of £19,608, but this could be offset by three months' interest.

Three months later C\$1.6 million is received from the importer and this exactly matches the outstanding debt:

Amount borrowed + Interest = Debt owed at end of period

C\$1,568,627 + (C\$1,568,627 × 0.02) = C\$1.6 million

An importer could also use a money market hedge. A Swiss company importing Japanese cars for payment in yen in three months could borrow in Swiss francs now and convert the funds at the spot rate into yen. This money is deposited to earn interest, with the result that after three months the principal plus interest equals the invoice amount.

Currency option hedge

A **currency option** is a contract giving the buyer (that is, the holder) the right, but not the obligation, to buy or sell a specific amount of currency at a specific exchange rate (the strike price), on or before a specified future date.

A call option gives the right to buy a particular currency

A put option gives the right to sell a particular currency

The option writer (usually a bank) guarantees, if the option buyer chooses to exercise the right, to exchange the currency at the predetermined rate. Because the writer is accepting risk the buyer must pay a premium to the writer – normally within two business days of the option purchase. (For more details on options see Chapter 15.)

Exhibit 16.9 shows the currency options premiums for the currency rates between the pound GBP and the US dollar USD. This data is taken from the website of the Chicago Mercantile Exchange (CME) on 29 December 2010 as trading is taking place.

Type				
American Options ▼			Expiration	
			MAR 2011 ▼	
Strike Price	Type	Last	Change	Prior Settle
15200	CALL	0.0407 a	+0.0038	0.0369
15200	PUT	0.0180 b	−0.0028	0.0208
15300	CALL	0.0341 a	+0.0032	0.0309
15300	PUT	0.0215 b	−0.0033	0.0248
15400	CALL	0.0283 a	+0.0028	0.0255
15400	PUT	0.0257 b	−0.0037	0.0294
15500	CALL	0.0232 a	+0.0024	0.0208
15500	PUT	0.0305 b	−0.0042	0.0347
15600	CALL	0.0188 b	+0.0021	0.0167
15600	PUT	0.0360 b	−0.0046	0.0406

Exhibit 16.9   GBP/USD option for March 2011 as quoted in December 2010

Source: www.CME.com

Note: a and b refer to the price being at or below (a) or at or above (b) the previous price.

For the GBP/USD call options the purchaser has the right but not the obligation to purchase pounds for dollars. Potential call option buyers have a number of possible rates of exchange open to them. Exhibit 16.9 shows strike prices of $1.5200/£ to $1.5600/£ in the first column. The premiums payable, shown in the third column, are quoted as US dollars per pound. One contract is for £62,500, and only whole numbers of contracts on the exchange may be purchased. If you purchased a 15200 call option for expiry in March you would pay a premium of 4.07 US cents per UK pound (the total premium payable would be $0.0407 × 62,500 = $2,543.75), giving you the right to buy pounds with dollars in March at a rate of $1.52/£. Note that a less favourable exchange rate, for example 15600($1.56/£), commands a lower premium, only 1.88 cents per pound in the contract.

The purchase of a put option gives you the right but not the obligation to sell pounds and receive dollars. Again the quantity of a contract is £62,500.

The crucial advantage an option has over a forward is the absence of an obligation to buy or sell. It is the option buyer's decision whether to insist on exchange at the strike rate or to let the option lapse.

With forwards, if the exchange rate happens to move in your favour after you are committed to a forward contract you cannot take any advantage of that movement. We saw above that if the forward rate was C$1.65/£ the exporter would receive £969,697 in three months. If the spot exchange rate had moved to, say, C$1.5/£ over the three months the exporter would have liked to abandon the agreement to sell the dollars at C$1.65/£, but would be unable to do so because of the legal commitment. With an option there is always the possibility of abandoning the deal and exchanging at spot. When the Canadian firm pays, at the exchange rate of C$1.5/£ the exporter would receive an income of:

$$\frac{C\$1,600,000}{1.5} = £1,066,667$$

This is an extra £96,970.

An option permits:

▪ hedging against an unfavourable currency movement;

▪ profit from a favourable currency movement.

CURRENCY OPTION CONTRACT

Now, imagine that the UK exporting firm, when the goods are delivered to the Canadian firm, hedges by buying a three-month sterling call option giving the right but not the obligation to deliver Canadian dollars to a bank in exchange for pounds with a strike price of C$1.65/£. A premium will need to be paid up front. Assume this is 2 per cent of the amount covered, that is, a non-refundable 0.02 × C$1,600,000 = C$32,000 is payable two business days after the option deal is struck.

Three months later

The dollars are delivered by the importer on the due date. Should the option at C$1.65/£ be exercised? Let us consider two scenarios.

Scenario 1

The dollar has strengthened against the pound to C$1.5/£. If the company exercises the right to exchange at C$1.65/£ the UK firm will receive:

$$\frac{C\$1,600,000}{1.65} = £969,697$$

If the company lets the option lapse – 'abandons it' – and exchanges the dollars in the spot market, the amount received will be:

$$\frac{C\$1,600,000}{1.5} = £1,066,667$$

an extra £96,970.

Clearly in this case the best course of action would be to abandon the option, and exchange at the spot rate.

Scenario 2

Now assume that the dollar has weakened against sterling to C$1.8/£. If the treasurer contacts the bank (the option writer) to confirm that the exporter wishes to exercise the C$1.65/£ option the treasurer will arrange delivery of C$1,600,000 to the bank and will receive £969,697 in return:

$$\frac{C\$1,600,000}{1.65} = £969,697$$

If the option is abandoned and the C$1.6 million is sold in the spot FX market, the amount received will be:

▶

$$\frac{C\$1,600,000}{1.8} = £888,889$$

a loss of £80,808. This is unattractive and so the option will be exercised.

With the option, the worst that could happen is that the exporter receives £969,697 less the premium. However, the upside potential is unconstrained.

Option contracts are generally for sums greater than US$1,000,000 on the OTC (over-the-counter) market (direct deals with banks) whereas one contract on the CME is, for example, for £62,500. The drawback with exchange-based derivatives is the smaller range of currencies available and the inability to tailor make a hedging position.

Futures hedge

A **foreign currency futures** contract is an agreement to exchange a specific amount of a currency for another at a fixed future date for a predetermined price. Futures are similar to forwards in many ways. They are, however, standardised contracts traded on regulated exchanges. Forwards can be tailor-made in a wide range of currencies with variable amounts of currency and delivery dates, whereas futures are only available in a limited range of currencies and for a few specific forward time periods – see Chapter 14.

The vast majority of futures market trading in currencies is through the CME and ICE Futures US (formerly NYBOT), which is part of the Intercontinental Exchange (ICE) group. The CME, for example, deals in 49 futures and 32 options contracts on 20 currencies.

A single futures contract is for a fixed amount of currency. For example, the sterling contract is for £62,500. It is not possible to buy or sell a smaller amount than this, or to transact in quantities other than whole-number multiples of this. To buy a sterling futures contract is to make a commitment to deliver a quantity of US dollars and receive in return £62,500. One contract for euros is for €125,000.

On 3 December 2010 the CME and NYBOT (ICE Futures US) quoted contracts (shown at **www.ft.com**) for delivery in December 2010 and February and March 2011 – see Exhibit 16.10. For example, the March contract for euros and US$ was priced at 1.3369 at the end of the trading day (the 'Open' column indicates the rate at the start of trading on 3 December, the 'Sett' column indicates closing prices). This means that if you *buy* one contract you are committed to deliver US$1.3369 for every euro of the €125,000 you will receive in late March,[3] that is US$167,112.50. If you *sold* one contract at 1.3369 you would deliver €125,000 and receive US$167,112.50.

Dec 3		Open	Sett	Change	High	Low	Est. vol.	Open int.
£-Sterling*	DEC0	0.8485	0.8495	0.0021	0.8512	0.8484	7	4,220
£-Yen*	DEC0	110.6100	110.8850	0.0900	110.61	110.61	570	6,580
$-Can $ †	DEC0	0.9966	0.9954	−0.0008	0.9997	0.9918	97,966	94,410
$-Euro € †	DEC0	1.3213	1.3378	0.0176	1.3402	1.3192	381,834	186,909
$-Euro € †	MAR1	1.3206	1.3369	0.0175	1.3392	1.3185	16,376	16,868
$-Sw Franc †	DEC0	1.0075	1.0229	0.0167	1.0258	1.0050	52,251	41,331
$-Yen †	DEC0	1.1926	1.2061	0.0147	1.2118	1.1924	153,736	122,850
$-Yen †	MAR1	1.1943	1.2074	0.0147	1.2130	1.1940	5,987	5,379
$-Sterling †	MAR1	1.5588	1.5730	0.0163	1.5755	1.5572	5,166	3,084
$-Aust $ †	DEC0	0.9758	0.9897	0.0146	0.9911	0.9730	111,619	102,532
$-Mex Peso †	FEB1	–	80575	−275.00	–	–	–	1

Sources: * NYBOT; Sterling €100,000 and Yen: €100,000. †CME: Australian $: A$100,000, Canadian $: C$100,000, Euro: €125,000; Mexican Peso: 500,000, Swiss Franc: SFr125,000; Yen: ¥12,5m ($ per ¥100). Sterling: £62,500. CME volume, high & Low for pit & electronic trading at settlement. Contracts shown are based on the volumes traded in 2004.

Exhibit 16.10 Currency futures table

Source: *Financial Times*, 3 December 2010, www.ft.com

A firm hedging with currency futures will usually attempt to have a futures position that has an equal and opposite profit profile to the underlying transaction. Frequently the futures position will be closed before delivery is due, to give a cash profit or loss to offset the spot market profit or loss (for more details on futures see Chapter 14) – although physical delivery of the currency is possible.

To illustrate, if a US firm exports €125,000 worth of goods to a German firm on 3 December 2010 on four months' credit for payment in late March and the current spot exchange rate is US$1.3154/€, there is a foreign exchange risk. If the March future is trading at a price of US$1.3369 per euro, the exporter's position could be hedged by *selling* one euro futures contract on the CME.

---

[3] On the third Wednesday of the delivery month.

If in March the euro falls against the dollar to US$1.10/€ the calculation is:

Value of €125,000 received from customer when converted to dollars at spot in March (€125,000 × 1.10)	US$137,500
Amount if exchange rate was constant at US$1.3154/€	US$164,425
Forex loss	–US$26,925

However, an offsetting gain is made on the futures contract:

Sold at US$1.3369/€ (€125,000 × 1.3369)	US$167,112.50
Bought in March to close position at US$1.10/€ (€125,000 × 1.10)	US$137,500.00
Futures gain	+US$29,612.50

Alternatively the exporter could simply deliver the €125,000 received from the importer to the CME in return for US$167,112.50.

In the above example a perfect hedge was not achieved because the gain on the futures contract did not exactly equate to the loss on the underlying position (i.e. the euros to be received from the German customer). Perfect hedging is frequently unobtainable with futures because of their standardised nature which limits the amount (multiples of €125,000, for example) and timing (the underlying transaction takes place on a date where there is no future).

Websites

www.ukforex.co.uk	UK Forex Foreign Exchange Services
www.bis.org	Bank for International Settlements
www.FT.com	Financial Times
www.advfn.com	ADVFN. Provider of FX data
www.bankofengland.co.uk	Bank of England
www.currenex.com	Currenex
www.bgcpartners.com	eSpeed
www.ecb.int	European Central Bank
http://globalderivatives.nyx.com	LIFFE

www.euronext.com	Euronext
www.fxconnect.com	FXConnect
www.imf.org	International Monetary Fund
www.cmegroup.com	Chicago Mercantile Exchange
www.theice.com/futures	New York Board of Trade
www.fxall.com	FXAll
http://uk.finance.yahoo.com	Yahoo! Finance
www.ssgloballink.com	State Street Global Markets
uk.reuters.com	Reuters
www.oanda.com	OANDA. FX market maker and data provider
www.wto.org	World Trade Organisation
www.oecd.org	Organisation for Economic Co-operation and Development
www.cls-group.com	CLS group (Continuous Linked Settlement)

17

Hedge funds and private equity

Hedge funds and private equity have come in for more than their fair share of sensational headlines. However, the bulk of all their business consists of perfectly acceptable financial transactions. The problem is that they appear to be making more money for people who are wealthy already, and it is difficult for most of us to see the benefits they bring to the general public. The hedge fund manager, John Paulson, made over $4 billion for his fund by betting that mortgage lending in the US had reached unsustainable levels, and the value of securities linked to mortgages would have to fall. His predictions were right; mortgage lending was spiralling out of control and reaching bubble proportions, and millions of people suffered as the housing market contracted. The bubble had to burst, and we should welcome a view different to the complacent consensus. Perhaps we should pay more attention to the signals sent to the market by people like John Paulson that investors were generally being too optimistic about US mortgages. Should a fund manager be criticised because he made correct predictions? Is it right that such high bonuses should go to the managers of these funds?

Just as there will always be people with good business ideas, but not the means to put them into production, so there will always exist people with spare money looking for an interesting share investment outside the stock market and able to face the risk of a total loss of their investment. In a nutshell, that is private equity. Bear in mind that without private equity many companies that now thrive as household names would not have got off the ground. Companies like Google, Skype and Centerparks have brought great pleasure as well as wealth. These are usually high-risk ventures and we need skilful fund managers to continue to invest in these types of company, motivated by the drive to make profits for their investors and receive suitable recompense for their efforts and risk taking.

Both hedge funds and private equity aim to spot financial situations where there is a market inefficiency (irrational pricing) and use investment to gain advantage. Where they see things out of balance, hedge funds have the freedom to invest where normal investment managers cannot, notably by using short selling. Private equity comes to the rescue of many companies that would otherwise be unable to make progress through lack of funding. In both cases the motivation is not altruistic; hedge funds and private equity exist to make profit for investors (and for fund managers).

Over the past 30 years, there has been a huge growth in the amount of investment in hedge funds and private equity. Private investors and investment institutions (e.g. pension funds) seeking a profitable home for their funds have found that these two types of investment can offer good rates of returns. However, there are worries about the lack of information concerning the use to which their money is put. There are also worries that these types of funds can be very illiquid investments unsuitable for many investors (their money can be locked in for months or years), and that besides investment risk clients can suffer undue exposure to risks such as fraud.

Hedge funds

To the man in the street, there is a certain mystique about hedge funds. What are they? What do they do? How do they make money? The first half of this chapter seeks to demystify and explain them. Probably the one detail that everyone thinks they know about hedge funds is that they make money, lots of money, and indeed some of them do, see Exhibit 17.1.

Investing stars lead bumper year for hedge funds

By James Mackintosh, Investment Editor

To the outside world, hedge funds often look much like investment banks on speed: far bigger bonuses, far bigger risks and far bigger profits.

The latest figures seem to confirm that prejudice. In the second half of last year, the current top 100 funds made $70bn for their clients, and – assuming they took only the standard 20 per cent cut – fees for themselves of about $17.5bn.

The top 10 hedge funds, measured by all-time dollar returns, made profits for their investors of $28bn, equivalent to the profits of six of the largest banks. Paulson & Co, which employs about 120 people, made $5.8bn for clients in six months, more than the net income of Goldman Sachs, which employs about 32,500.

The data, calculated by LCH Investments, an investor in hedge funds managed by the Edmond de Rothschild group, may help to explain why Wall Street banks fought so hard to stop the Dodd-Frank rules banning them from hedge fund activity – a battle they ultimately lost.

The exit of the banks from proprietary trading, a kind of internal hedge fund, should help to boost hedge fund returns by reducing competition, many managers and investors believe. Indeed, the winding down of

Exhibit 17.1 Investing stars lead bumper year for hedge funds

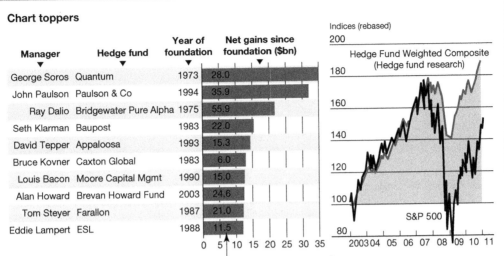

Chart toppers

Manager ▼	Hedge fund ▼	Year of foundation ▼	Net gains since foundation ($bn) ▼
George Soros	Quantum	1973	28.0
John Paulson	Paulson & Co	1994	35.9
Ray Dalio	Bridgewater Pure Alpha	1975	55.9
Seth Klarman	Baupost	1983	22.0
David Tepper	Appaloosa	1993	15.3
Bruce Kovner	Caxton Global	1983	6.0
Louis Bacon	Moore Capital Mgmt	1990	15.0
Alan Howard	Brevan Howard Fund	2003	24.6
Tom Steyer	Farallon	1987	21.0
Eddie Lampert	ESL	1988	11.5

(figures in bars) assets under management in strategy, $bn

Source: LCH Investments; Bloomberg: Thomson Reuters Datastream

many prop desks last year ahead of the rules, led by Goldman, may already have supported returns.

Nagi Kawkabani, chief executive of London- and Geneva-based Brevan Howard, the only non-US hedge fund to make the top 10 list, says: "It's a plus because there's less capital chasing the same trades we chase, but it may affect liquidity [in markets]."

But he cautions that the boost may be temporary. "It is not like the banks pulling out means their guys have suddenly gone off and started to paint. They will reappear somewhere else."

Future returns, then, will come down to the success of the traditional hedge fund pitch: skill and the ability to spend more on research and technology.

The best funds on the LCH rankings are those that manage to produce good returns even after expanding. The table is dominated by managers who have become investing stars and whose moves

are closely followed by would-be imitators.

George Soros, whose Quantum fund has made $35bn after fees for investors since it was set up in 1973, is ranked as the man who has done most for clients in dollar terms. He is closely followed by John Paulson, who entered history books by making the most money for investors – and himself – in a single year in 2007 with his bet against subprime. After that comes Bridgewater's Pure Alpha, run by Ray Dalio, whose research is some of the most sought-after on Wall Street. The words of Seth Klarman, founder of Baupost, next on the list, are widely sought after, with copies of his out-of-print book *Margin of Safety* selling for upwards of $1,000.

In the past six months only one fund – Steven Cohen's SAC Capital – fell out of the top 10, as the much larger San Francisco-based Farallon Capital Management pushed past it

with strong returns, continuing its recovery from a terrible time during the credit crunch. One widely respected fund, Renaissance Technologies' Medallion, is not included as no data are available since it took the decision to reject external clients a few years ago.

But not all of the all-time top 10 did well last year. Brevan told clients recently that all three of its big ideas had failed and it was basically flat on the year (an "aberration", says Mr Kawkabani).

The mass of smaller funds continued to underperform the leaders in the second half of last year. While the top 100 funds made $70bn on assets under management of $746bn, the 7,000 or so other funds, which run more than twice as much money, only managed to make $59bn for investors.

Source: *Financial Times*, 2 March 2011, p. 32

Exhibit 17.1 Continued

But there are many sceptical voices when it comes to whether the average hedge fund produces a high return – see Exhibit 17.2 for an interesting discussion of hedge fund performance.

Hedge funds struggle to justify star rating

By James Mackintosh

If it looks like a cow and moos like a cow, chances are the animal could make a tasty dish – but isn't venison. Investors should take note. Hedge funds, the most expensive item on the investment menu, have been producing returns almost identical to portfolios from the cheap burger joints of the advisory business, made up of 60 per cent equities and 40 per cent bonds.

No wonder hedge funds are worried. Bankers report increasing concern among these latter-day masters of the universe over how they will pay the fat bonuses their traders demand this year. Some high-profile managers have given up altogether.

"Absolute return", the ability to make money whatever the weather, is proving elusive. Hedge funds need to demonstrate to the pension funds and endowments that have become their biggest clients that they can earn returns that are independent of shares and bonds – the holy grail of institutional investors, who care about correlation more than returns.

Unfortunately for them, their similarity to the simple equity/bond portfolio seems to be increasing – undermining the industry even more than the insight a few years ago that hedge funds could be replicated with complex computer codes.

Furthermore, research shows that investors do far worse from hedge funds than standard measures suggest. Ilia Dichev at Emory University in Atlanta and Gwen

Yu at Harvard found that investors miss all the hedge fund outperformance by overtrading. Put simply, they buy funds that have already gone up and subsequently do less well, and sell funds that have gone down and subsequently recover. The pair conclude that actual investors in the "star" funds, which seem on paper to have the best returns, really earn 8-9 percentage points less.

Investors got another unwelcome reminder this month of the worst danger of investing in hedge funds: the risk that they cannot withdraw.

Hundreds of the largest investors in the sector were expecting final resolution of one of the most egregious uses of hedge funds' ability to restrict withdrawals.

Not surprisingly, some investors are unhappy with the situation. Hopefully they will learn the lesson: investments that make returns by investing in hard-to-sell assets are, well, hard to sell.

This links back into performance. During the boom years for hedge funds, huge numbers of funds boosted returns with private equity, over-the-counter derivatives and other hard-to-trade assets. Managers appeared smarter than they really were, because they were taking a risk they did not recognise.

Both absolute and uncorrelated returns, it turns out, are hard to earn without risk. And few managers want to take any sort of risk at the moment, leaving them making

returns more similar to the markets. Leverage is close to its lowest ever, after volatile trading repeatedly outfoxed managers. Simple strategies reliant on stockpicking skill have also been hurt by high levels of correlation between stocks.

Hedge funds still hold an allure, both for investors and, thanks to their secrecy, the media.

Put together the lack of uncorrelated returns, unjustifiably high fees, the past failure of investors to pick the funds that will perform in future and the danger of not being able to get one's money back, and hedge funds sound a lot less appealing.

As one big investor in the sector puts it: "If you can't generate alternative low or non-correlated returns, there is little point in the asset class."

Better, perhaps, to conclude that there is no asset class. Some hedge funds are truly uncorrelated, reliant on lawsuits, exotic derivatives, computer programs or the brilliance of their founders for returns. Others are little more than overpriced mutual funds. Investors need to accept that not everyone can get their money into the few hedge funds able to deliver what they want. Until then, investors are paying Cipriani prices for what too frequently turns out to be a cheeseburger and fries.

Source: Financial Times, 29 August 2010, p. 2

Exhibit 17.2   Hedge funds struggle to justify their star rating

What are hedge funds?

The origin of hedge funds goes back to 1949, when Alfred Winslow Jones, an investment manager from New York, came up with an innovative investment strategy; he took both short and long positions in shares. He sold shares he did not own by borrowing the shares (e.g. from a broker, for a fee) expecting them to fall in price so that he could buy them for less when he needed to return them to the broker and so make a profit (**short position**). At the same time, he bought shares he expected to rise in price (**long position**). If a share he expected to rise did actually rise in price he made money. If the share prices of those he had shorted did actually fall he made money on them also. Even if the entire market fell he would make money, so long as the shorted shares fell more than the long position shares. If the entire market rose he made money overall, so long as the long position shares rose more than the short position shares.[1]

The definition of Jones' hedge fund then is a fund that aims to achieve a good **absolute return,** to preserve the principal for investors, whether the market rises or falls. Standard conventional investment funds tend to be long only – buying assets such as shares in the hope that prices will rise. They seek to make a **relative return**, relative to the performance of a particular index or market. So, if their fund decreases in value by 20 per cent they receive a pat on the back if the market index against which they are measured went down by say 22 per cent over the same period. The type of fund Jones ran, by contrast, takes a **market neutral** strategy, aiming to make an acceptable return regardless of whether the market fluctuates up or down.

Jones' strategy was largely unknown until 1966, when *Fortune* magazine published an article describing his 'hedge fund' and how it had outperformed all other funds by a huge amount, even with the performance fee of 20 per cent taken into account (Jones charged clients 20 per cent of the profit he made for them). This led to the formation of numerous hedge funds and a massive expansion in the amount of hedge fund investment, with investors enthusiastically handing over their money to participate in the exceptional returns that hedge fund managers promised and sometimes delivered. Now hedge funds have grown so large that it is thought they account for well over 50 per cent of all trading on the London Stock Exchange and other world markets. There are nearly 9,500 hedge funds managing assets of over $1,900 billion (see Exhibit 17.3).

---

[1] Of course, this neat symmetry only works if the amount of short exposure to general market movements is the same as the long exposure, i.e. the position is 'market neutral' – see later in the chapter. If there is not a balance between the long exposure and the short exposure to overall market movements we have a 'relative value strategy'.

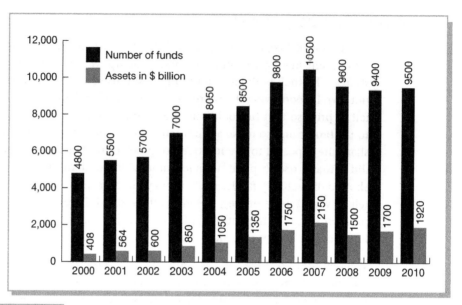

Exhibit 17.3 Number and assets of global hedge funds

Source: www.thecityuk.com

Who invests?

Most conventional fund managers are not only limited to a restricted list of investible assets, but they are subject to tough supervision by regulators. In comparison, hedge funds are for the most part lightly regulated and taxed, free to invest in a wide variety of markets and instruments. This freedom to range more widely than conventional funds was first fully appreciated by wealthy Americans, who, as individuals or through family trusts, placed large sums in the hands of hedge fund managers. Conventional investment funds are registered with the US regulator, the Securities and Exchange Commission (SEC), which imposes risk-reducing restrictions on the fund if it is to be allowed to accept money from ordinary savers. To prevent the need for registration and thus scrutiny and regulation by the SEC small US hedge funds keep the number of investors to 99 or less **accredited investors**. Accredited investors are those who are thought wealthy enough or professional enough not to need the protection of the SEC. They are supposed to be able to largely look after themselves in the financial jungle, to have sufficient knowledge and experience in financial and business matters that they are capable of evaluating the merits and risks of a hedge fund investment. As far as individual investors are concerned they are regarded as accredited investors and therefore hedge funds can accept their money if:

▪ They have individual net worth, or joint net worth with a spouse, that exceeds $1 million at the time of purchase, or income exceeding $200,000 in each of the two most recent years or a joint income with a spouse exceeding $300,000 for those years, and a reasonable expectation of the same income level in the current year.

An accredited investor may also be an institution such as a bank, insurance company or small business investment company. If the accredited investor is a trust or a charity (e.g. university endowment) then its assets must exceed $5 million.[2]

Most jurisdictions around the world have similar restrictions limiting access to hedge fund investment to only the professional and wealthy. However, hedge funds in Europe have developed new products recently that allow small investors to participate under the UCITS rules – see later in the chapter.

As you can see from Exhibit 17.4 the source of a large proportion of hedge fund money is still wealthy individuals and wealthy families, often investing through their endowments and foundations. Much of this money will be channelled through funds of funds which split the individual/family money between a number of hedge funds. Pension funds and corporations are also big contributors of money to be invested by hedge fund managers.

Lock-ups and gates

Money invested in hedge funds is often **locked up** for a period (which could be two years or more) during which time the funds are not available for withdrawal by the ultimate investors. Funds may also be **gated**; a limit is placed on the amount that can be withdrawn from the fund at any one time. A common gate is a 25 per cent limit in any one quarter. Gates and lock-ups are devices to prevent the manager having to liquidate funds at a time when prices are not favourable for redemption, and to prevent a run on funds. For example, if the manager has invested in a number of corporate bonds currently in a distressed state (e.g. coupon payments have been missed or covenants breached) because the issuing firms are struggling, he may be justified in refusing to repay hedge fund investors on demand. To do so would mean selling the distressed bonds before the benefits of the new arrangements (e.g. additional financial support) he is making with the distressed firms have worked through to make a profit.

---

[2] An alternative way of gaining SEC exemption is for the hedge fund to only obtain investment funds from qualified purchasers. This type of fund can have up to 499 investors. Qualified purchasers are:

- individuals with a net worth > $5 million;
- institutional investors with a net worth > $25 million.

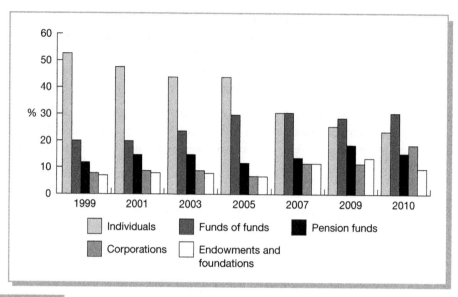

Exhibit 17.4   Global hedge funds, percentage share of source of capital

Source: www.thecityuk.com

Alternatively, the fund might have invested in very illiquid assets such as property loans that cannot be liquidated quickly to reimburse the fund's investors at short notice.

Side pocket

A **side pocket** enables a fund manager to separate a difficult-to-value or illiquid investment from all other investments. An investor who withdraws from the fund cannot redeem any investment which has been placed in a side pocket, until and unless the fund manager decides to liquidate it. This is because of the danger of putting a false value on these assets. If an investor could ask the manager to guess at the value and receive a payout based on that, this would be unfair to the remaining investors if the guess was over-optimistic and it turned out that the value when actually sold is much less. Side pockets restrictions were used a lot in 2008 when Lehman Brothers collapsed. Many hedge fund assets became impossible to sell and extremely difficult to value. It would have been unfair to allow some investors to withdraw holdings in hedge funds at that point based on theoretical or historical value. Naturally, any new investor's funds do not share in existing side pockets because it is impossible to judge the proportion of the asset they own relative to older investors.

Hedge fund registration

Mainly to reduce tax for investors, but also to lower the regulatory burden, 60 per cent of hedge funds are registered in offshore tax havens and the remainder in countries or states where regulations are not overly restrictive, such as Delaware in the US. Exhibit 17.5 shows the domicile of hedge funds. This explains part of the mystique; hedge funds are often not legally obliged to disclose their details for public consumption. Because of this lack of transparency, it is very difficult for an outsider to know the value of a hedge fund and its investments.

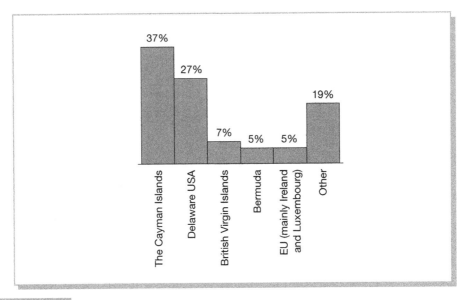

Exhibit 17.5 Domicile of hedge funds, 2010

Source: www.thecityuk.com

Fund managers

The quality of fund managers is crucially important to the success of a hedge fund. They usually have free rein to invest in whatever they choose, and most have a substantial personal investment in their fund. While being permitted to use idiosyncratic schemes for investing, prior to raising money from investors they usually state to investors the types of strategies they will be employing, for example, investing in shares both long and short, or investing in distressed debt.

There is much discussion about a fund manager's alpha. **Alpha** is the return achieved above the return expected given the risk class of investment that is engaged in – the 'risk-adjusted return'. The simplified way of estimating this is to judge the manager's performance by how many percentage points over the average benchmark return on an index such as the S&P 500 have been achieved. A manager who consistently produces good alpha is thought to possess good investing skill and is in great demand.

Hedge funds are managed by investment companies, which will generally be onshore companies registered and regulated by their domestic laws. For example, there are many managers based on the US East Coast in towns such as New York and the Gold Coast area of Connecticut, despite the funds themselves being registered in, say, the British Virgin Islands. They value being close to major financial centres from which they can draw talent. This also allows them to be close to their investors. These managers, either a single manager or a management team, perform the investment and administration of the funds. Sometimes they are part of large investment companies, sometimes they are run by a single manager.

Most UK hedge funds are incorporated in places like the Cayman Islands and so outside any UK regulations, however these funds are usually managed by UK-domiciled managers – usually with offices in Mayfair. The *managers* based in the UK are subject to Financial Service Authority regulations.

New York is the leading centre for hedge fund managers, with 41 per cent, followed by London with 19 per cent managing three-quarters of European hedge fund investments. These two locations, with their strong pools of professionals of every calling, are ideal providers of all professional, financial and managerial services to both hedge funds and other investment entities.

In return for their efforts, managers charge annual fees, generally between 1 and 2 per cent, but this can be up to 5 per cent, of the net asset value of the fund, plus a performance or incentive fee of generally 20 per cent, although this can be as much as 50 per cent, of any profits.[3] Commonly this is '2 and 20', that is a 2 per cent annual fee plus a 20 per cent performance fee. Taking, for example, JPMorgan, administering a fund of $50.4 billion (see Exhibit 17.6), even a 1 per cent management fee would be $504 million, plus a performance fee.

Performance fees are not paid in most other forms of investment, where it is usual to charge just an annual fee. Many other investment vehicles are banned from offering performance fees. The idea behind a performance fee is to encourage the managers to stretch themselves to make abnormal profits, but this can also encourage them to take undue risks, as there is no mechanism in place for them to share losses as well as profits, and even if losses are made they still earn

---

[3] Management fees are generally paid monthly or quarterly.

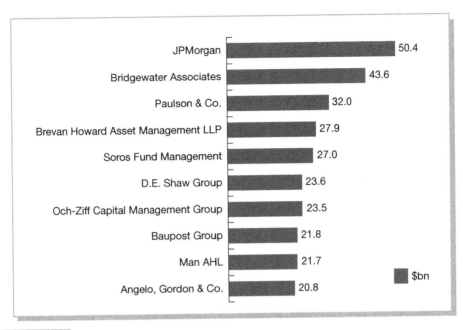

Exhibit 17.6   The 10 largest hedge funds, January 2010
Source: www.thecityuk.com, Hedgefund Intelligence

their management fee. Occasionally there may be a **clawback** scheme, where fees can be claimed back in the event of underperformance in years following good years with high fees paid to managers.

There are two commonly (but far from universally) used checks on performance fees:

1 **High water marks (loss carryforward provision).** Where a fund's performance has dropped, the manager does not receive a performance fee until the fund reaches its previous position. For example, if a fund is launched with $1 billion which rises to $1.2 billion in the first year due to good investment choices, the managers might take 20 per cent of the $200 million gain ($40 million) as a fee. If in the next year it drops to $1.1 billion the managers would not receive a performance fee. If in the third year the fund rises to $1.3 billion the performance fee only applies to the return above the previous high point ($1.2 billion) and so only 20 per cent of $100 million is paid, rather than the full return for that year of $1.3 billion – $1.1 billion.

2 **Hurdle rates** are set. Performance fees will only be triggered once the fund has achieved a minimum annualised performance. The hurdle might be set as the yield on a government treasury bill, LIBOR or a fixed percentage, say

5 per cent per year. When the hurdle rate is surpassed the manager may either be entitled to a performance fee as a percentage of the entire annualised return or just a share of the return above the hurdle rate.

Some funds charge investors for withdrawing money from a fund (redemption fee, withdrawal fee or surrender charge). This may apply only to the first year of the investment or to a specific proportion of the investment the investor made. This is to discourage disinvestment when the fund might be engaged in illiquid or complex investing strategies.

Hedge funds may restrict the flow of additional money to the fund to an amount that can be sensibly managed, and even close the funds to new investors. When these vehicles grow too large, the sheer volume of funds available can make it very difficult to place investments, and the scale of operations can result in loss of flexibility in selecting investment assets.

Fund of hedge funds

A **fund of hedge funds** is a fund that invests in other hedge funds, thereby spreading the risk, so if one hedge fund in the fund is doing badly, the others will compensate for this. A fund of hedge funds manager is expected to make a good, varied choice in hedge funds for investment, with the aim of producing far better than average returns. They are supposed to investigate the funds thoroughly to ensure that they are run with high integrity, efficiency and wisdom. This seems a good idea for investors, but the downside is that there are two lots of annual fees and performance fees to be paid out, usually on a 1 and 10 basis to the fund of hedge funds manager, plus 2 and 20 to the fund manager. Also, unfortunately, not all fund of hedge funds managers have been successful at boosting returns for investors despite their high fees.

Listed funds

While the majority of hedge funds are not listed and benefit from a lax regulatory regime, there are some which list on stock markets, and so make themselves available for the retail investor, who is normally priced out of the hedge fund market. Being listed means that the shares are liquid (investors can easily sell or buy the shares on the stock market) and dealings have to be transparent (holdings of the fund have to be detailed in the annual report). Traditional hedge funds are illiquid and opaque. The hedge fund run by Brevan Howard requires an initial investment of $20 million; however its BH Global Fund listed on the London Stock Exchange, offering investment in six of Brevan Howard's hedge funds, is available for £10.89 per share.

UCITS

The aim of the UCITS (Undertaking for Collective Investment in Transferable Securities) regulation, launched by the European Union in 1985, was to allow collective investment schemes to operate freely throughout the EU on the authority of a single member state. The regulating country supervises these funds closely, restricting what they can do, but once approved in that country a fund can advertise itself to investors in other EU countries. The investors may be individuals or institutions. A requirement is for UCITs funds to be highly liquid, permitting investors to be able to sell their investment at short notice; therefore the securities/assets held by the fund must be readily tradeable. They also have to be transparent (public disclosure of risks assumed and significant positions), and the portfolios must be well diversified. Also, the amount of leverage (borrowing, etc.) that can be used to gain exposure to underlying investments is constrained.

Historically, the UCITS structure was used merely for long only strategies, for example, for long-term equity investment by unit trusts. The UCITS III update of 2001 allowed UCITS compliant funds to use derivatives and opened the way for hedge fund strategies to be used. With proposed new legislation in the EU and the US threatening to curtail and regulate normal hedge funds, many of them have decided to register their funds as onshore UCITS compliant funds, which opens up for them the lucrative retail non-professional market. Hedge-fund-style vehicles available within the UCITS III framework have been dubbed '**newcits**'. Some of the hedge fund strategies are suitable for UCITS because they can be liquidated fairly quickly, such as equity long-short. But others, those that involve complex and illiquid strategies, are simply unsuitable.

In a 2011 survey conducted by Deutsche Bank, 55 per cent of hedge fund investors said they preferred to allocate money to onshore UCITS hedge fund vehicles rather than offshore funds. Indeed, over the 2011–12 period it is anticipated that more than $400 billion will flow into UCITS hedge funds, more than for traditional offshore hedge funds.

Another way for retail investors to dabble in hedge funds is to invest in a hedge fund exchange traded fund (ETF) (see Chapter 7). ETFs are normally a fairly cheap way of investing (typically 0.15–0.50 per cent of assets each year go as fees). However, hedge fund ETFs incur all the costly hedge fund fees, and do not always offer good returns.

Hedge fund indices

Some hedge funds have performed better than average, but many others are less than impressive, being broadly similar to any other investment returns. There is a problem in judging performance because of a general lack of reliable and independently verifiable information about hedge funds, making it difficult to track returns. Nevertheless there are a number of hedge fund indices. The compilers of these are faced with great difficulties, not least that the underlying investments are often obscure instruments that lack a daily price setting in a liquid market, and so until the investment is sold (which may be years away) we cannot judge the performance.

Also, there are dozens, if not hundreds of different strategies/types of assets bought and sold by hedge funds. This heterogeneity means that it is difficult to compare like with like – even within one asset class, say bonds, different fund managers will concentrate on bonds in different countries, credit-quality categories or issuer type. There is also the problem that each year hundreds of funds are launched and hundreds disappear, so it is difficult to figure out which fund performances to include in an index.

Fund participation (sending the information to an index creator) is voluntary which is likely to lead to self-selection bias because those that are doing well are more likely to volunteer to be included. There is also survivorship bias because those that have gone bust or folded through lack of interest due to poor performance may not be included in the index. End-of-life reporting bias occurs when a hedge fund is declining rapidly and stops reporting its performance to the index providers. Thus losses go unreported. Backfill bias occurs when a fund only starts reporting its performance when the strategy proves successful. The index compiler may then allow the successful managers to 'backfill' its historic data once the fund is ready (presumably after it has had a good run). This introduces a positive bias given that those that are never successful do not go into the index.

Some hedge fund index compilers are more rigorous than others. Hedge Fund Research, for example, insists that it eliminates survivorship bias by including all dead funds. Backfill bias is dealt with by only including performances after admission to the index.

Leverage

One major concern with hedge funds is the amount of leverage they use. Leverage gives the opportunity to invest greater sums than the amount of investors' capital. Leverage can be achieved by borrowing to invest or by entering into a financial transaction where the fund only has to come up with, say, 5 per cent or 10 per cent of the underlying exposure as a margin or deposit, usually through derivatives. It allows for greater profits, but if things go awry, it also gives the possibility of unlimited losses.

The problem with leverage was evidenced in a spectacular fashion in 1998, with the collapse of the hedge fund Long-Term Capital Management (LTCM). With two Nobel-prize winning economists in its team, LTCM used a strategy called fixed-income arbitrage, betting on minute differences in government bond prices and the expectation that these differences would converge. Because the differences were so small, it needed to use a huge amount of leverage to make a significant profit. Disaster struck when the Russian government defaulted on its bonds, causing bond prices in general to diverge considerably. LTCM had assets of $4 billion, but leverage of nearly $130 billion (a ratio of over 30 to 1). It owed vast sums to other financial institutions. If it failed to pay its debts they might become insolvent. With such enormous potential losses, which could damage the economy, the Fed persuaded a group of banks to bail LTCM out. A more normal leverage ratio is around 2.5, meaning that for every £1 obtained from investors the manager gains exposure to the price movements on £2.50 of assets. Note however that there are wide differences in leverage for the different strategies; so those that trade on pricing anomalies in fixed-income securities average leverage of around 6.5 while those engaged in equity long-short average 1.5, for example.

Hedge fund strategies

Jones' original strategy was revised, and a whole host of strategies emerged, all with one aim in mind, to make profit no matter what the state of world markets or economies, to make an absolute return. Some managers use analytical tools, some use financial modelling; all seek alpha. The range of hedge fund strategies changes over time as managers try to think up new schemes to exploit supposed superior information or analytical technique. The common themes linking them are that hedge funds are able to follow strategies that are often forbidden to traditional fund managers, managers are greatly incentivised by the fee structure, there is light regulation and a fundamental lack of transparency. Beyond that it is difficult to categorise the strategies as many of them overlap or comprise a mixture of strategies. Here we only have space to provide a brief description of *some* of the strategies.

Arbitrage

Arbitrage is taking advantage of small discrepancies in the prices of the same financial instrument or similar securities by simultaneously selling the overpriced security and buying the underpriced security. So, for example, identical shares could be selling in a number of different stock markets, and because of differences in local supply and demand are selling at, say, one-tenth of 1 per cent difference in two of them. An arbitrageur will buy shares in the lowest priced arena and simultaneously sell them in the higher priced market, making an immediate profit. These deals will help to close the gap because the increased buying demand in the low priced market will raise prices there, and the additional supply in the high priced market will lower prices there. Arbitrage goes hand in hand with leverage; the price disparity is usually very small and so leverage is needed for the financial gain to be worthwhile. For example, if the discrepancy is one-tenth of a per cent on an instrument priced at £2.35, then to make £2,350 an investment of £2.35 million must be made. If it is possible to borrow 90 per cent of a £235 million position, then the profit would be £235,000 if prices move according to plan, but huge losses can occur if price movements are unfavourable. If you borrow 90 per cent of the £235 million and the prices move the wrong way, you still owe £211.5 million!

Long/short

Long/short strategy (relative value) involves buying one type of financial instrument long and selling another instrument short to exploit pricing anomalies between related (but not identical) assets that are mispriced relative to each other. **Equity long/short** (Jones' original strategy) has been successful for some hedge funds. Managers may divide the funds with a bias one particular way, for example, 30 per cent of the fund can be exposed to short positions and 70 per cent long, or any particular ratio they choose. If leverage is used, a fund could be 30 per cent short and 100 per cent long, with the total of 130 per cent indicating leverage of 30 per cent. If the fund has a high exposure to short positions and a relative low exposure to longs (**dedicated short bias**) and then the market acts against their expectations, a great deal of money can be lost. Many funds apply long/short to two different stock market indices (and their derivatives) rather than individual shares. The long/short principle is also used for many other instruments, from bonds to derivatives.

Market neutral

Market neutral strategies are those that provide a return regardless of the overall market movement because the short position exposure is as great as the long position. The trader has no net exposure to broad market moves. They can be equity long/short, but are usually positions in other investments (often derivatives) where there is a price discrepancy to be exploited. The underlying strategy relies on the hope (not always fulfilled in the time that the hedge fund can maintain its position) that these prices will converge to a fair value.

Fixed income

Fixed-income relative value/fixed-income arbitrage evolved from classical arbitrage, but instead of identical securities the two securities bought and sold are merely similar. This is not the traditional 'riskless arbitrage' where you are bound to make a profit buying and selling the same security; in contrast this approach is based on a theory of a 'normal' price relationship between two assets that are somewhat substitutes for each other. Hedge fund managers become convinced that the difference in price between two similar assets (say, AAA-rated bonds issued by Tesco and Sainsbury) is unreasonably wide (perhaps much greater than the historical norm, or fundamental analysis indicates a mispricing) or narrow, and that they will revert to 'true relative value'. They sell short the relatively overpriced security and buy the underpriced security. Once prices have reverted to true value, the trade can be liquidated at a profit. However, these are risky strategies because the market can be perverse and push prices even further away from true value for many years. Another strategy is to benefit from small price differentials in fixed-income securities such as two issues of US government bonds, say a 30-year bond and one that has 29 years to run. Because of the resources needed in terms of capital, professional ability and technological infrastructure, fixed-income arbitrage tends to be used by larger hedge funds.

Convertible bond arbitrage

Convertible bond (or warrant) arbitrage. This is taking a long position in convertible bonds or warrants while hedging with a short position, typically by shorting shares in the same company. Convertible bonds and warrants are priced as a function of the share price; their value is derived from the price of the shares because they grant the right to convert to or purchase shares at a fixed price some time in the future. However, occasionally they are not priced efficiently due to illiquidity in the convertible and warrant markets, because of uncertainty over the rights on the convertible and because of analysts' neglect in these markets compared with the equity markets – the right to convert or purchase shares becomes underpriced. This is a form of risk 'arbitrage' and not the traditional risk-free arbitrage; the market can move prices even further away from the rational level for a long time.

Event driven

Event-driven strategies take advantage of special situations. For example, **distressed securities investing** is when hedge fund managers buy shares or debt belonging to companies that are experiencing serious financial problems and could be facing bankruptcy. They often believe that other investors have overreacted to the troubles and pushed market prices too low. Having investigated thoroughly, they think that a recovery of some value is possible. Other investors, particularly creditors, may lack the flexibility and patience of the hedge fund to hold on to distressed assets; for example, pension funds are often forbidden from holding sub-investment grade bonds or banks may be desperate to remove loans no longer paying interest from their balance sheets. The other creditors may not have the time or the special knowledge to assist a company through a reorganisation of its finances, which can take several years – they would rather sell now, even at a low price.

Merger artibrage

Merger arbitrage is another event-driven strategy. Often the shares of the target company will rise when the intention for one company to acquire the other is made public. Shares in the acquiring company often fall because of the tendency to over pay and reduce shareholder value. Despite the price movements the share price of the target typically remains below the acquisition price. This is usually because of doubts in the market that the merger will be completed – the potential acquirer could just walk away, the target managers put up a good defence or a monopolies inquiry is launched. Or it may be because the market is underestimating the potential for a second bid or rival offer for the target. So some funds take a long position in the target and a short position in the acquirer. If the acquirer has offered shares in itself in return for the shares in the target when the offer is accepted the hedge fund exchanges its shares in the target for shares in the acquirer. These shares offset the earlier short position in the acquirer. A risk of this strategy is the possibility of the merger failing to go ahead (e.g. the monopoly regulator prevents it) and therefore the target's shares fall significantly while the acquirer's might rise.

Activist strategy

The hedge fund buys a portion of the shares in a company and uses the ownership to press for improvement in returns to shareholders. The hedge fund manager engages with the company's board and management. They may rally other shareholders to insist on one or more management actions: divestment; breaking up the group and selling off divisions; share buy-backs; raised dividends; mergers with other firms; or even sale of the entire business or liquidation.

Global macro

Global macro funds profit (and lose) from bets taken against countries, currencies, global economic dislocations in interest rates and other macroeconomic variables. Using leverage, fund managers typically take concentrated positions in any type of financial instrument (equity, currency, commodity, interest rates, etc.), trying to ensure that the downside would not be catastrophic, but the upside has unlimited potential. They try to anticipate global macroeconomic events anywhere in the world. Returns can be spectacular, such as when George Soros' Quantum fund took a major position against the value of the UK pound, anticipating that the pound would devalue in 1992. Soros was proved right and governments were forced to devalue and withdraw from the European Exchange Rate Mechanism. He placed the equivalent of $10 billion in currencies other than sterling. When it devalued, his investments in those other currencies went up when translated back into sterling. Soros is thought to have made $1 billion from the dealings and became known as the man who broke the Bank of England. Soros saw a situation that was out of balance and that could not be maintained. **Global macro** positions may be 'directional' – betting on a rise in interest rates or a currency for example – or relative value – the pairing of two similar assets on a long and short position, looking for a current difference to change: for example, the interest rate on US 10-year Treasuries to move relative to the interest rate on German Bunds.

Fundamental growth

This involves investing in companies fund managers think have more earnings growth and capital appreciation potential than the average company.

Fundamental value

Fund managers invest in undervalued companies currently out of favour with the general body of investors.

Multi-strategy

These funds use the same pool of investment to invest in different strategies. The idea is that diversification makes for more consistent returns, but the downside is that it also prevents full exploitation of a successful strategy.

Private equity

We have looked at some of the details of raising money on the Stock Exchange in Chapters 12 and 13, but in the commercial world there are millions of companies that are not quoted on any stock exchange. We now consider a few of the ways in which equity capital is generated for these **unquoted firms**.

Private equity is medium to long-term finance invested in companies not quoted on any stock exchange to profit from their growth. It enables companies that are unable to access further funding from current shareholders or banks to obtain the required funding from other investors. It is not easy to distinguish between private equity and venture capital. Some use the term 'private equity' to define all unquoted company equity investment, others confine 'private equity' to investment in companies already well established, and apply '**venture capital**' to investment in companies at an early stage of development with high growth potential.

Private equity/venture capital in its modern form began in the US after World War II when a French immigrant, Georges Doriot, founded the American Research and Development Corporation (ARD) in 1946. ARD invested in and provided capital for new businesses, helping the economy regenerate. A gap was created because large, long-established and respectable companies listed on stock exchanges were more cautious in backing innovative projects that could, potentially, lead to large losses, and equity and bond investors tended to concentrate their money on stock exchange-quoted companies.

Private equity funds

Private equity usually takes the form of a fund that then invests in a group of companies. Many investments result in total loss and so private equity investment in a single company can be a huge risk. The diversity of private equity funds gives greater opportunities for good overall returns, even if a high proportion of the investee companies turn out bad performances.

The private equity managers that run these funds, looking for and evaluating investment opportunities in companies, are known as the **general partners (GPs)**. Other investors in the funds are called **limited partners (LPs)** and these can be institutions or individuals. The GPs select companies that are deemed suitable for investment using finance provided by their limited partners, and sometimes loans and bank borrowings. Both the GPs and the LPs can make spectacular returns. Take the case of 3i's investment in Hyva. The private equity fund bought the company for around €125 million and five years later in 2010 sold it for €525 million.

The GPs are paid management fees (usually 1–2.5 per cent) and a share (usually about 20 per cent) in the eventual capital gain, known as the **carried interest** (the carry). The fees cover all the management expenses of administering the private equity company or fund, and provide an income for GPs during lean times when the fund has not sold profitable investments. Limited partners may include pension or insurance funds, wealthy individuals or families, or sovereign wealth funds. Exhibit 17.7 shows the sources of funding for UK funds from 2007

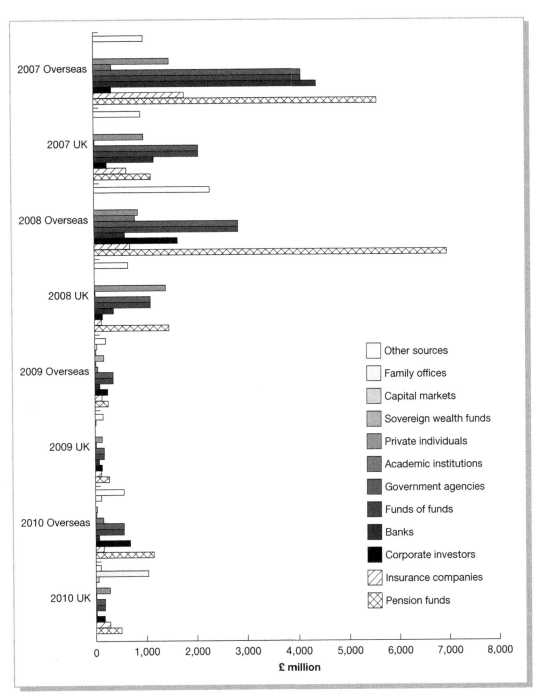

Exhibit 17.7   Source of funds for UK private equity funds, 2007 to 2010, either from UK investors or overseas investors

Source: bvca.co.uk

to 2010. It also shows the dramatic decrease in funding caused by the financial crisis of 2008–09. Limited partners allow their funds to be used by the GPs in return for a future capital gain, thus gaining a return that is taxed less heavily than salaried income. When the investee company is sold, or the private equity fund closed, the LPs share the remaining 80 per cent of the carried interest.

The size of the private equity and venture capital industry

In the UK, the British Private Equity & Venture Capital Association (BVCA), formed over 25 years ago, is the voice of the private equity and venture capital industry. It has more than 430 members managing over £230 billion of funds between them. In 2010, BVCA members invested a total of £20,447 million: £12,210 million overseas and £8,237 in the UK (see Exhibit 17.8).

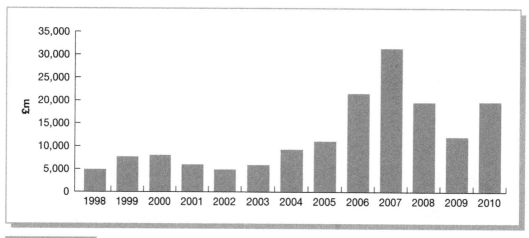

Exhibit 17.8   **Total amount invested globally by BVCA members**

Source: www.bvca.co.uk

The European Private Equity & Venture Capital Association (EVCA) has been performing a similar task in Europe for about the same length of time (see Exhibit 17.9).

In the US, the National Venture Capital Association (NVCA) represents the US venture capital industry. Their report, Exhibit 17.10, shows a decrease for 2009, but not as dramatic as the UK and European decreases. It is interesting to see on this chart the results of the dot.com bubble of the late 1990s and 2000, when venture capital poured into internet start-ups at every level. The internet craze seemed ever-expanding and ever-profitable, until 2000, when over $100 billion

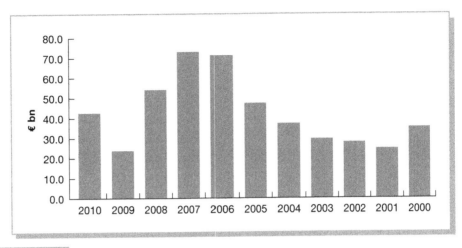

Exhibit 17.9   Annual European private equity investment

Source: www.evca.eu.

of venture capital was invested. In March 2000 the NASDAQ collapsed. This was the place that so many companies backed by private equity and venture capital had initial public offerings, turning themselves into stock market-quoted companies. Most of these plummeted in value in 2000, trillions of dollars of value were lost, and the venture capital industry shrank as investors became afraid of backing speculative ventures.

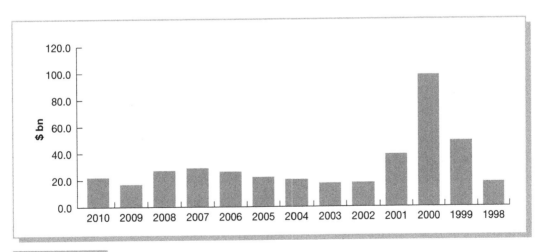

Exhibit 17.10   US venture capital investments

Source: www.nvca.org

The effect of the financial crisis is evident in Exhibit 17.11. In the years 2005 to 2009 private equity funds raised hundreds of billions more than they actually invested. Thus, today we have many funds with large stockpiles of cash looking for an investment home. The US has the biggest share of the private equity market with 36 per cent of investments, and the UK is the next largest with 13 per cent of all global investments (according to The CityUK).

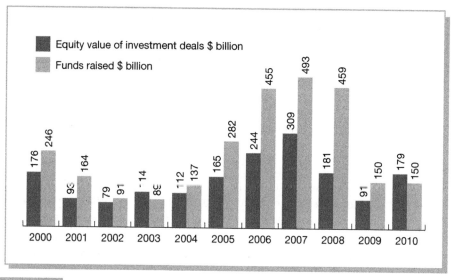

Exhibit 17.11 Global private equity market

Source: TheCityUK estimates based on PEREP_Analytics, Thomson Reuters, EVCA, PwC, AVCJ data

Why is private equity needed?

While more mature companies can turn to the stock market to raise debt or equity capital and small companies can usually rely on retained earnings, capital injections from the founder family and bank borrowing for growth, in between these lie **financing gaps** – intermediate businesses that are too large or too fast-growing to ask the individual shareholders (family and friends) for more funds or to obtain sufficient bank finance, but are not yet ready to launch on the stock market. Also there are many small start-up businesses with great ideas who simply lack wealthy family and friends able to put up the large amounts of equity capital needed to get going in the first place. Private equity may also provide funding for under-performing companies or those in financial difficulties that would prosper given adequate funds. Thus, for all these reasons, companies frustrated in their plans to exploit market opportunities due to a lack of available funds have welcomed the rapid development of the private equity industry over the past 40 years to fill these gaps in financing.

The costs and inconveniences of being listed on a stock market mean that many managers and shareholders prefer to obtain additional funds from private equity funds – even those that are perfectly capable of raising money on stock markets deliberately stay away from them. Private equity funds can be more long-term focused than stock market investors, allowing higher near-term investment in, say, research and development or marketing even at the expense of this year's or next year's earnings per share figures. The corporate managers also avoid the hassle of regular time-consuming meetings with institutional shareholders, so they are freer to get on with the job of creating long-term wealth for shareholders. They might also welcome the technical/managerial expertise and contacts that many private equity funds can draw on – many funds specialise in particular industries and develop a deep talent pool. Also, private equity shareholders are more likely to be in favour of granting directors and senior managers shares in the company if they perform well. This can make them very wealthy.

It is estimated by the BVCA that there are 10,000 UK companies with three million employees (one in six of the non-government workforce) financed by private equity money, so it is clear that private equity investment is crucial to the UK economy. Exhibit 17.12 provides a list of some well-known UK companies that are backed by private equity.

Business angels (informal venture capitalists)

Business angels are wealthy individuals who provide their own money to be used as capital in new business ventures. They generally have substantial business and entrepreneurial experience, and usually invest between £10,000 and £250,000 primarily in start-up, early stage or expanding firms. About three-quarters of business angel investments are for sums of less than £100,000 and the average investment is £25,000–£30,000. The majority of investments are in the form of equity finance but they do purchase debt instruments and preference shares. The companies they invest in will be years away from obtaining a quotation or being advanced enough for a sale to other companies or investors, so in becoming a business angel the investor accepts that it may be difficult to dispose of their shares, even if the company is progressing well. They also accept a high degree of risk of complete failure – which happens in about one in three cases. They usually do not have a **controlling shareholding** and they are willing to invest at an earlier stage than most formal venture capitalists. They often dislike the term 'business angel', preferring the title **informal venture capitalist**. They are generally looking for entrepreneurial companies that have high aspirations and potential for growth.

Agent Provocateur	New Look
Alliance Boots	Odeon & UCI Cinemas
Autonomy	Phones4U
Birds Eye Iglo	Pizza Express/Zizzi/Ask – Gondola Group
Cambridge Silicon Radio	Plastic Logic
CenterParcs	Poundland
Earls Court & Olympia	Pret A Manger
Findus Group (Foodvest)	The AA/Saga
Fitness First	Travelex
Jimmy Choo	Travelodge
Merlin Entertainments Group	Weetabix
Moto	West Cornwall Pasty Co
National Car Parks	

Exhibit 17.12   Well-known UK companies backed by private equity

Source: bvca.co.uk

A typical business angel makes one or two investments in a three-year period, often in an investment syndicate (with an **archangel**, an experienced angel investor, coordinating the group). They generally invest in companies within a reasonable travelling distance from their homes because most like to be 'hands-on' investors, playing a significant role in strategy and management – on average angels allocate 10 hours a week to their investments. Most angels take a seat on the board and are actively involved. On the other hand, there are many who have infrequent contact with their companies. Business angels are patient investors willing to hold their investment for at least a five-year period.

How business angels work

The main way in which firms and angels find each other is through friends and business associates, although there are a number of formal networks. See the British Venture Capital Association at **www.bvca.co.uk** for a list of networks. **Angel network** events are organised where entrepreneurs can make a pitch to potential investors, who, if they like what they hear in response to their questions, may put in tens of thousands of pounds. The popular *Dragons' Den* programme produced by the BBC is an example of business angels at work.

Entrepreneurs put forward their ideas to the 'Dragons', and if they are thought to be a good investment money from the Dragons will be invested. Prior to the event, the TV producers will arrange screening of the business opportunities to avoid time wasting by total no-hopers. Similar screening is generally carried out before an angel network event.

To be a member of a network, investors are expected either to earn at least £100,000 per year or to have a net worth of at least £250,000 (excluding main residence). If an investor has a specialist skill to offer, for example he or she is an experienced company director or chartered accountant, membership may be permitted despite a lower income or net worth.

Entrepreneurs need to be aware that obtaining money from informal venture capitalists is no easy task – the rejection rate runs at over 90 per cent; but if rejected the determined entrepreneur has many other angel networks to try. Returns on business angel investments are mostly negative. However, they can be spectacular; the angels who put €2 million into Skype multiplied their money by 350 times when the company was sold to eBay for €2.1 billion in 2005.

Venture capital

The business ideas backed by venture capitalists are usually new, innovative, often high-tech and usually very risky, brought to them by entrepreneurs. With little or no trading track record or financial history, new companies usually find obtaining finance for growth and expansion difficult, and this is where venture capital may be the solution. Venture capital is a medium- to long-term investment and can consist of a package of debt and equity finance. Many of the investments are into little more than a management team with a good idea – which may not have started selling a product or even developed a prototype. It is believed, as a rule of thumb in the venture capital industry, that out of 10 investments two will fail completely, two will perform excellently and the remaining six will range from poor to very good.

Venture capital funds

Venture capital funds are intermediaries who channel money from institutions or individuals into investment in private companies. Their aim is to help a number of companies grow in the expectation that in the future a company can be sold or floated on a stock exchange for a considerable profit. As with private equity, venture capital fund managers are the general partners (GPs) who actively participate in and manage the venture capital investment fund. The limited partners (LPs), such as pension funds or individuals, provide the capital for the venture capitalist to invest.

High risk goes with high return. Venture capitalists therefore expect to get a return of between five and 10 times their initial equity investment in about five to seven years. This means that the firms receiving equity finance are expected to produce annual returns of at least 26 per cent. Alongside the usual drawbacks of equity capital from the investors' viewpoint (last in the queue for income and on liquidation, etc.), investors in small unquoted companies also suffer from a lack of liquidity because the shares are not quoted on a public exchange.

Types of support

Private equity and venture capital offer support to a wide range of companies at varying stages in their development.

- **Seedcorn**. A form of venture capital providing financing to allow the development of a business concept. Development may also involve expenditure on the production of prototypes and additional research. Usually involves angel-investor funding rather than venture funds.

- **Start-up**. Also referred to as venture capital, a product or idea is further developed and/or initial marketing is carried out. The companies involved are very young and have not yet sold their product commercially. Usually involves angel-investor funding rather than venture funds.

- **Other early-stage**. Again, often referred to as venture capital, funds are provided for initial commercial manufacturing and sales. Many companies at this stage will remain unprofitable. Usually involves angel-investor funding rather than venture funds.

- **Expansion (development or growth)**. Companies at this stage are on to a fast-growth track and need extra financial support to fund increased production capacity, working capital and for the further development of the product or market. The company may be large enough to accept substantial investment from venture funds – if not then angel investment is more likely.

- **Management buyout (MBO)**. The acquisition of a company or part of a company by an existing management team. A team of managers buys a whole business, a subsidiary or a section from their employers, so that they own and run it for themselves. Companies are often willing to sell to these teams, if the business is under-performing or does not fit with the strategic core business. The MBO team has limited funds and so calls on private equity to provide the bulk of the finance.

- **Management buy-in (MBI)**. The acquisition of a company or part of a company by a new management team from outside the company. The new team of managers usually has insufficient finance to complete the deal and so partners with a private equity fund that usually buys the majority of the shares.

■ **Leveraged buyout (LBO).** The buyout of an existing company, with the capital raised (and therefore the capital structure for the company afterwards) being between 60 and 90 per cent debt finance. One advantage of this is that interest on debt is tax deductible, and therefore less company tax is paid. The major disadvantage is the risk of insolvency with so much debt to be serviced. Private equity groups usually provide the bulk of the equity and perhaps some of the debt or preference share capital with the rest coming from banks or the financial markets.

■ **Secondary purchase.** A private equity-backed company is sold to another private equity fund. This is one of the exit strategies, where the first private equity fund can make a capital gain by selling its equity in the company to another private equity fund.

■ **Public-to-private (PTP).** The management of a company currently quoted on a stock exchange may return it to unquoted status with the assistance of private equity finance to buy the shares, giving it the advantage of lower costs, less regulation and official and public scrutiny.

Private equity firms are less keen on financing seedcorn, start-ups and other early-stage companies than expansions, MBOs, MBIs and PTPs. This is largely due to the very high risk associated with early-stage ventures and the dispro-portionate time and costs of financing smaller deals. To make it worthwhile for a private equity or venture capital organisation to consider a company, the investment must be at least £250,000 – the average investment is about £5 mil-lion – and it is difficult to find funding for investments of less than £2 million. Business angels are the solution for lesser funding requirements.

Because of the greater risks associated with the youngest companies, the pri-vate equity or venture capital funds may require returns of the order of 50–80 per cent per annum. For well-established companies with a proven product and battle-hardened and respected management the returns required may drop to the high 20s. These returns may seem exorbitant, especially to the managers set the task of achieving them, but they have to be viewed in the light of the fact that many private equity or venture capital investments will turn out to be fail-ures and so, taken overall, the performance of the funds is significantly less than these figures suggest. In fact the BVCA, which represents 'every major source of venture capital in the UK', reports that returns on funds are not excessively high – see Exhibit 17.13.

Internal rates of return (IRR) to investors since inception of the fund from 1996 to December 2010, net of costs and fees. 470 UK-managed funds are included.

	Per cent per annum
Venture capital funds	−0.3
Small management buyouts	17.9
Mid management buyouts	13.2
Large management buyouts	17.8
Total	15.2
Comparators' returns over 10 years to Dec. 2010	
UK listed shares (FT All-share)	3.7
Overseas equity	4.2
UK bonds	5.5
Overseas bonds	7.2
Property	6.5

(Note: Excluding private equity investment trusts and Venture Capital Trusts)

Exhibit 17.13 Returns on UK private equity funds

Source: 2010 BVCA Private Equity and Venture Capital Performance Measurement Survey, BVCA, PricewaterhouseCoopers and Capital Dynamics, www.bvca.co.uk/

Venture capital funds are rarely looking for a controlling shareholding in a company and are often content with a 20 or 30 per cent share. However, MBI/MBO/LBO funds usually take most of the shares of a company because the management team can only afford a small proportion of the shares. The fund may also provide money by purchasing convertible preference shares, which gives it rights to convert to ordinary shares – this will boost its equity holding and increase the return if the firm performs well. It may also insist, in an initial investment agreement, on some widespread powers. For instance, the company may need to gain the private equity/venture capitalist's approval for the issue of further securities, and there may be a veto over the acquisition of other companies.

Even though their equity holding is generally less than 50 per cent the venture capital funds frequently have special rights to appoint a number of directors. If specific negative events happen, such as a poor performance, they may have the right to appoint most of the board of directors and therefore take effective control. More than once the founding entrepreneur has been aggrieved to find him or herself removed from power. (Despite the loss of power, they often have a large shareholding in what has grown to be a multi-million pound company.) They are often sufficiently upset to refer to the fund that separated them from their creation as 'vulture capitalist'. But this is to focus on the dark side. When everything goes well, we have, as they say in the business jargon, 'a win–win–win situation': the company receives vital capital to grow fast, the venture capitalist receives a high return and society gains new products and economic progress.

Private equity categories

As share investment outside stock markets has grown it has become differentiated. The main categories are shown in Exhibit 17.14 with private equity as the umbrella term covering the various activities. In this more differentiated setting the term venture capital is generally confined to describing the building of companies from the ground floor, or at least from a very low base.

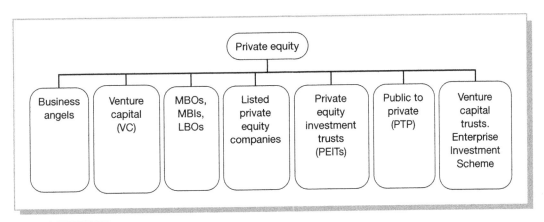

Exhibit 17.14 **Categories of private equity**

Management buyouts and buy-ins of established businesses (already off the ground floor) have become a specialist task, with a number of dedicated funds. Many of these funds are formed as private partnerships by wealthy individuals and a high proportion are American owned.

Small investors can buy shares in **listed private equity (LPEQ)** funds which are companies investing in unquoted companies but which have their own shares quoted on a stock exchange. There are about 80 investable listed private equity companies in Europe, with a total market capitalisation of €45 billion, of which €12 billion are London-listed companies (see **www.lpeq.com**). They come in two varieties; firstly, those that are straightforward listed companies and those that are listed as investment trusts. An example of the first type is Conversus Capital that is listed on Euronext-Amsterdam. It has $2.5 billion in assets under management, and a portfolio of over 1,800 unquoted companies in North America, Europe, and Asia.

Private equity investment trusts (PEITs) are the second type of LPEQs. They are stock market-quoted investment trusts with a focus on investing their shareholders' money in more risky, unquoted, developing companies. The disadvantage of listed private equity companies is the absence of special tax concessions compared with Venture Capital Trusts and Enterprise Investment Schemes – see below. However investors are able to exit their investments easily by dealing on the stock market.

Venture capital trusts

It is important to distinguish between venture capital funds and **venture capital trusts** (VCTs), which are investment vehicles with important tax breaks designed to encourage investment in small and fast-growing companies. VCTs are companies whose shares are traded on the London Stock Exchange. The tax breaks for investors putting money into VCTs include an immediate relief on their current year's income at 30 per cent (by putting £10,000 into a VCT an investor will pay £3,000 less tax on income, so the effective cost is only £7,000). Any returns (income and capital gains) on a VCT are exempt from tax. Investors can place up to £200,000 each per year into VCTs. These benefits are only available to investors buying new VCT shares who hold the investment for five years. The VCT managers can only invest in companies with gross assets of less than £15 million and the maximum amount a VCT is allowed to put into each unquoted company's shares is limited to £1 million per year. 'Unquoted' for VCT means not listed on the main list of the London Stock Exchange but can include AIM and PLUS companies. A maximum of 15 per cent of the VCT fund can be invested in any one company. Up to half of the fund's investment in qualifying companies can be in the form of loans. These trusts offer investors a way of investing in a broad spread of small firms with high potential, but with greater uncertainty, in a tax-efficient manner. But beware, many of the funds that have been in operation for a few years have shown low returns due to a combination of poor investment selection and high management charges.

Enterprise Investment Scheme

Another government initiative to encourage the flow of risk capital to smaller companies is the **Enterprise Investment Scheme (EIS)**. Income tax relief at 30 per cent is available for investments from £500 up to a maximum of £1,000,000 made directly (no need for a fund manager as with VCTs) into qualifying company shares. There is also capital gains tax relief, and losses within EISs are allowable against income tax. Investment under EIS means investing when the company issues shares, not the purchase of shares in the secondary market. The tax benefits are lost if the investments are held for less than three years. Investors are not allowed to hold more than 30 per cent of the shares in any EIS company. Certain trading activities are excluded, such as finance, property and agriculture (HMRC gives the definitive list of these exclusions). The company must have fewer than 250 full-time employees. It must not be quoted on LSE's Main Market and the most it can raise under the EIS in any one year is usually £10 million. The company must not have gross assets worth more than £15 million. Funds that invest in a range of EIS companies are springing up to help investors spread risk. EIS investors are unlikely to be able to regain their investment until the company is sold or floated on a stock market as there is usually no share trading for many years.

Private equity providers

There are a number of different types of private equity providers, although the boundaries are increasingly blurred as a number of funds now raise money from a variety of sources. The **independents** can be firms, funds or investment trusts, either quoted or private, which have raised their capital from more than one source. The main sources are pension and insurance funds, but banks, corporate investors, sovereign wealth funds and private individuals also put money into these private equity or venture capital funds. **Captives** are funds managed on behalf of a parent institution (banks, pension funds, etc.). **Semi-captives** invest funds on behalf of a parent and also manage independently raised funds.

How an independent private equity fund is established and managed

Many private equity funds are established as limited liability partnerships (LLPs),[4] raising capital from a group of investors. It is usually stated at the outset that it will be run down after 10 or 12 years and the value in the LLP will be distributed to members. The project is touted to potential investors (e.g. pension funds), often by the investor relations team or by using external placement

---

[4] A partnership in which some or all of the partners have limited liability. Thus each partner is protected from being liable for the misconduct or incompetence of other partners. In the absence of fraud or wrongful trading a partner cannot lose more than the amount invested. As a 'corporate body' it has a life independent of any individual member, and so does not have to be dissolved on the death or leaving of a partner.

agents. The investment strategy is set out, e.g. a focus on bio-technology or internet companies. The general partners will state a minimum to be raised to reach **first close**. When this is achieved the fund comes into existence. There may be a series of 'closes' beyond the minimum to create a much larger fund. The **final close** is the end of the capital-raising phase.

The investment phase now begins. The GPs are given discretion to invest the money and are usually given a period of up to five years to do so. They are likely to limit exposure to any one investment to under 10 per cent of the fund. They might arrange to borrow money to complete individual deals. For the larger investments, particularly MBOs and MBIs, the private equity fund may provide only a fraction of the total funds required. Thus, in a £50 million buyout the LLP might supply (individually or in a syndicate with other private equity funds), say, £15 million in the form of share capital (ordinary and preference shares). Another £20 million may come from a group of banks in the form of debt finance. The remainder may be supplied as mezzanine debt – high-return-high-risk debt that usually has some rights to share in equity values should the company perform.

Occasionally the LPs are given the opportunity to both participate in an investment via the private equity fund and to invest directly. This is called **co-investing**.

The fund usually holds on to the investments for three, five or more years to allow it to improve and grow. When the company is in a thriving state the private equity fund is likely to sell to realise a return on investment – an **exit**.

The performance-related return (carried interest) due to the GPs is generally based on the performance of the entire fund rather than on individual deals – although some do give deal-by-deal carried interest. In the first five years the managers are likely to be most dependent on the management fee of 1 to 2.5 per cent of funds under management rather than carried interest. In the period after five years they are likely to be most motivated by the carried interest on the maturing investments. The various stages are set out in Exhibit 17.15.

Exits

The exit is when private equity and venture capital investors reap their rewards; this is their goal towards which all efforts have been expended. Before the expiry of the fund (say after 10 years) moves will be made to sell the investments. Hopefully the companies within the fund will have prospered or been reorganised enough to make it an attractive proposition for resale or listing on a stock exchange.

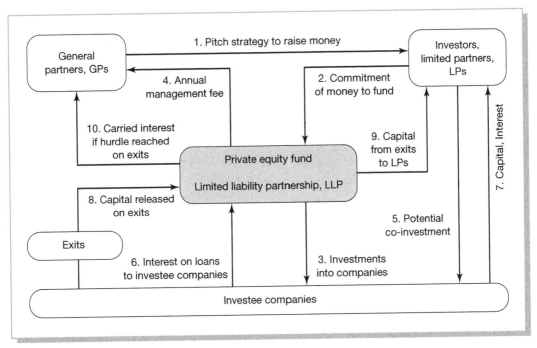

Exhibit 17.15 The operation of a private equity fund

Only when the investee company is sold do the private equity or venture capital partners receive any return on their investment, except for the GPs who receive annual fees.

The exit options are:

■ **Repurchase.** The company has prospered and the existing management is in a position to purchase the equity in the company, often accompanied by a general recapitalisation of the firm – more debt taken on.

■ **Secondary/tertiary/quaternary buyouts.** The equity is sold to another private equity group. This may then be sold on to a third buyer (tertiary buyout) and on occasions, a fourth (quaternary buyout).

■ **Trade sale.** The equity is sold to or merged with another company – usually one in the same industry – and a capital gain (loss) is realised for investors.

■ **Going public.** The equity is floated on a stock market and a capital gain is realised for investors.

■ **Liquidation.** The worst exit strategy – the company goes bust, and everyone makes a loss.

Websites

www.3i.com	3i (a leading UK private equity firm)
www.aima.org	Alternative Investment Management Association
www.angelinvestmentnetwork.co.uk	Angel Investment Network
www.bbaa.org.uk	The British Business Angels Association
www.beerandpartners.com	Beer and Partners
www.bis.gov.uk	The Department for Business, Innovation and Skills
www.bvca.co.uk	British Private Equity & Venture Capital Association
www.cmrworld.com	Cavendish Management Resources
www.dcxworld.com	The Development Capital Exchange
www.efama.org	European Fund and Asset Management Association
www.eif.org	European Investment Fund
www.equityventures.co.uk	Equity Ventures Ltd.
www.evca.eu	European Private Equity & Venture Capital Association
www.g2i.org	Gateway 2 investment
www.hedgefundintelligence.com	HedgeFund Intelligence – provider of hedge fund news and data
www.hennesseegroup.com	Hennessee Group – US hedge fund advice and statistics
www.hmrc.gov.uk	Her Majesty's Revenue and Customs (VCTs and Enterprise Investment Schemes)
www.hotbed.uk.com	Hotbed (unquoted investments)
www.thecityuk.com	TheCityUK
www.lpeq.com	Listed Private Equity (incorporates www.ipeit.com)
www.nvca.org	National Venture Capital Association
uk.finance.yahoo.com	Yahoo! Finance
www.venturegiant.com	Venture Giant

18

Regulation of the financial sector

It is a constant battle to maintain high levels of integrity and competence in the financial service sector. However, the financial service industry recognised long ago that it is in its own best interest to engage in that battle and establish minimum standards of behaviour. If the users of financial services fear that malpractice is prevalent they will not allow their funds to flow through the system and the financial sector will shrink. These minimum standards need some sort of enforcement mechanism beyond a gentleman's agreement that all participants will behave ethically. Crooks and incompetents would love to join an industry where the majority of providers act with probity, because they can free-ride on the industry's reputation. Thus we need regulation. This may be provided by the industry itself with the back-up of statutory laws or could be provided by the government in some form.

This chapter firstly explains why, despite its high cost, we have regulation, and then discusses the dangers that arise in a regulated system. The main tasks and activities required of regulators are outlined followed by an examination of one of the most sophisticated regulatory structures in the world, the UK's. We then look at the additional regulatory rules imposed at the European Union level and at the global level.

Regulation and supervision

Some people draw a distinction between regulation and supervision:

- **Regulation**: the process of rule making and legislation creating the supervisory system. The rules may come from the laws of the land or from the stipulations of the regulatory agency.

- **Supervision**: monitoring the position and behaviour of individual firms, and enforcing the regulations if required.

For our purposes we will assume that the word 'regulation' covers supervision as well.

Why do we need regulation?

Financial regulation is expensive. It costs hundreds of millions, even billions, to pay for regulators to carry out their tasks in a modern economy. There are further billions to be paid by the banks, insurance companies and other financial service firms in **compliance costs**, i.e. putting in place systems and training to ensure that staff behave according to the rules. These additional costs are likely to be passed on to clients. Then there are the potential losses because new organisations that are keen to provide a financial service are put off entering the industry by the costs and time of obtaining a licence from the regulator and the subsequent monitoring – perhaps society loses much innovatory and competitive fizz as a result. Exhibit 18.1 gives us some idea of the costs.

Oversight of banks costs US far more than EU

By Brooke Masters in London

The US spends more than six times as much to supervise banks and other credit institutions as the European Union, research has found.

The various federal and state agencies that supervise banks in the US spent $4.4bn on 18,000 frontline employees in 2009-10, while the 27 EU nations spent $2.2bn on 10,000 employees, according to analysis by the Oliver Wyman consultancy.

The US spends $1m per $1bn of banking revenue, compared with $150,000 in the EU.

The costs cover day-to-day supervision of the system for safety and soundness as well as consumer protection and conduct issues.

There are several reasons for the differences. The US has many more very small banks and spends correspondingly more on them. It also has about 10,500 institutions to safeguard, while the EU has 6,500. The two spend roughly the same per bank, at $150,000.

The US also has more overlap between its state and federal agencies.

Source: Financial Times, 24 January 2011, p. 8

Exhibit 18.1   Oversight of banks costs US far more than EU

So, given the costs, a fundamental question is: why do we bother with regulation? This section presents some ideas to answer that question.

Asymmetric information

Asymmetric information is one of the forms of market failure in financial services in which the market participants will drive the industry to a sub-optimal outcome if left to their own devices. The other two reasons for intervention, also forms of market failure – contagion and monopoly/oligopoly – are discussed later.

> **Asymmetric information** occurs when one party in a negotiation or relationship is not in the same position as other parties, being ignorant of, or unable to observe, some information which is essential to the contracting and decision-making process.

Managers and other employees of financial service companies have an information set that is often superior to that of the client's. This can lead to exploitation; for example, buyers of a financial product are unable to assess the true risk and return. Thus a large part of regulation is about ensuring that consumers receive relevant information about products in an understandable way.

Asymmetric information manifests itself in a number of ways:

- reducing safety and soundness for the consumer or a financial market counterparty;

- producing conflicts of interest within financial service firms which can be deleterious to the interests of consumers or counterparties;

- facilitating bad behaviour such as fraud;

- hiding and tolerating incompetence.

We will now look at each of these in turn.

Safety and soundness

Consumers are frequently unable to assess the safety and soundness of a financial institution or the products it provides. They simply do not have the time or the expertise to evaluate whether the organisation is taking too much risk with their money. An example here is the flood of money that went into Icelandic banks in the mid-2000s. Large numbers of savers from all over Europe were attracted by the high interest rates offered on deposit accounts. Little did they know that the accumulated bank deposits were lent out to high-risk ventures with only small amounts being retained as a safety buffer. The managers of these banks were tempted by the higher interest rates they could charge on the more risky lending, producing large, short-term (apparent) profits and therefore large bonuses. Regulators are supposed to conduct prudential bank regulation to protect consumers from unsound bank policies and actions. They clearly failed in the case of the Icelandic banks, so after their collapse the authorities (governments in this case) were forced to guarantee all deposits, which is an expensive way to protect depositors. They are now much keener on ensuring banks are managed for safety and soundness.

A large part of the bank regulator's role is to ensure that banks have enough capital buffer (surplus of assets over liabilities) to be able to cover their obligations, even allowing for a large potential diminution of asset value due to, say, loan defaults. They are also concerned that a bank keeps back a sizeable amount of cash and other liquid resources to be able to meet short-term liquidity outflows. Capital reserves and liquidity reserves were discussed in detail in Chapters 3 and 6 and so, despite this being a very important element in financial regulation, we will not discuss it any further here. Another element of safety and soundness for banks is that they do not have too many eggs in one (or a few) basket, say an excessive proportion of lending to one sector (e.g. property developers) – called **concentration risk**.

An example of asymmetric information outside of banking: buyers of insurance are usually unable to assess the likelihood of the insurance company becoming insolvent, and therefore unable to meet obligations to policyholders. The soundness of insurance firms is of great importance, not only to those with car and house insurance but also to the tens of millions of people who now save vast amounts through insurance products, from endowment mortgages and insurance bonds to personal pensions and retirement annuities.

Other questions in this area are: how sound is the stockbroker that holds your shares in one of its accounts? How safely managed is your company pension fund, or your investment trust or unit trust? Is your venture capital trust money being applied recklessly to absurdly risky ventures without adequate diversification?

Safety and soundness concerns arise not only in the relationship between financial service providers and consumers, they also arise in the trading that takes place between financial intermediaries; for example, interbank lending and borrowing, trading in the foreign exchange market or derivatives trading all involve a degree of counterparty risk.

Conflicts of interest

Conflicts of interest arise when a person or institution has a number of objectives (interests) and is free to choose which receives the most emphasis, when one of them might have the potential to corrupt the motivation to act. The choice made may not be one that would suit the consumer because it might be tainted by the self-interest of the financial service provider. But the consumer is unable to see the extent of the bias due to asymmetric information. Take, for example, an independent financial adviser who is supposed to advise a client on the best home for their savings, but who is tempted by the large commission paid by a unit trust company to push the client into their product.

Conflicts of interest can lead to the misuse of information, the providing of false information, the providing of biased or selective information, or the concealing of information.

- **Misuse.** An example of the misuse of information is **spinning** by an investment bank organising an initial public offering of a company's shares that it thinks will rise substantially. It allocates blocks of shares to a few select clients such as directors of companies that may give the bank a mandate to assist in raising capital (e.g. an IPO) in the future. These selected executives will make a killing in the week or two following the flotation. They will then repay the investment bank by directing their company to pay fat fees for a new bond or equity issue. This might be a lot more expensive for the company than if it shopped around for an arranger of funding. Thus the cost of capital raising is inflated and bankers take home large bonuses. Another example would be where an executive of a manufacturing firm is in possession of information that, when it is released to the market, will lead to a significant rise in the company's share price. In the meantime he buys shares in the firm expecting to profit from his insider knowledge.

- **False.** An example of false information dissemination can arise when auditing firms also supply a client company with management consulting services (e.g. advice on tax, management systems, strategy). The latter services can result in fees that are many times what they receive from the audit. Client companies may pressure auditors by threatening to move their consulting custom to another firm if they do not see things their way. In accounting much judgement is required about issues such as the value of a non-current asset or the likelihood of a customer debt being paid. There is therefore wriggle-room for putting a positive gloss on profits and balance sheet strength. This can easily tip over into false information in the sense of, while being within the letter of the accounting rules it breaks the spirit.

- **Biased**. An example of biased information arises in a badly organised investment bank which while issuing research reports and advising investors on good bond purchases also arranges a bond issue by a client company. A great deal of effort goes into understanding the company when arranging a bond issue, and the information generated may be useful to the research team supplying analysis to investors. However, the issuing firm would like to sell the bonds at as high a price as possible and so would like the researchers to be optimistic. If the fee received for organising the bond is sufficiently large then the investment bank may, if not properly controlled, select the information it releases to boost the potential sales level. These banks are supposed to have high 'Chinese walls' separating different departments to prevent these conflicts of interest, but it is surprising how positive many of them are about the equity or debt securities of their client companies (it is difficult to find negative comment).

A conflict was said to have occurred when credit rating agencies were accused of being too generous in rating the chance of default of bonds issued by many banks and special purpose vehicles set up to receive interest from US sub-prime mortgages in securitisation deals in the mid-2000s. The issuing company pays for the rating but the consumers of that information are the bond investors, hence the conflict of interest. The rating agencies were accused of trying to attract future rating mandates by being less than unbiased. They defended themselves vigorously saying that they cannot afford to be seen as anything other than impartial and objective if their ratings are to be taking seriously. They stand to lose their entire business franchise if they cannot be relied upon by bond buyers. Thus they have a high degree of self-policing. If bond-buyer faith in the rating agencies did ever seriously decline there would be a danger of a much reduced flow of funds to companies and therefore lower wealth in society.

- **Concealment.** An example of the concealment of information is when a bank has a loan outstanding to a company that it suspects is running into serious financial difficulties. Bank officers have access to this information but the bond issue department is nevertheless encouraged to sell bonds in the company without telling investors about the company's likelihood of distress. The loan is paid off and the bank earns a fee for selling the bonds.

Many conflicts of interest are not exploited even in the absence of regulation because the incentive to do so is not sufficiently high (and because of common decency). Also, financial firms often live and die by their reputations. Any conflict that became visible would be punished as other financial organisations and clients shunned the firm. Having said that, we still need regulation because these constraints may not work on particular individuals with immediate bonuses to puff up, or when the firm itself is excessively focused on short-term profits rather than long-term reputation.

Fraud

Financial markets present opportunities to make large profits over short periods of time; this is especially the case if a trusted professional lacks moral fibre. While the majority of people in the financial sector are honourable and of high integrity, such a honey pot is bound to attract greedy knaves who are clever enough to dream up a range of chicanery.

Incompetence

Consumers often receive poor service due to incompetence. This may be bad advice because of the inattention or ignorance of a financial adviser. For example, in 2011 Barclays had to pay a £7.7 million fine and £59 million in compensation for failing to provide adequate investment advice to more than 12,000 customers who were mis-sold investment funds.

There may be incompetence in managing a client's funds or their business interests. In financial services incompetence can continue undetected for years. For example, in the handling of pension fund money, the manager will render the service of investing to supply pensions decades after the savers have injected funds into the scheme. It may only be after retirement that it is revealed whether the scheme will meet the financial needs of the retirees.

Contagion

In some financial sectors, say banking, the failure of a company may lead to the failure of others leading to instability in the whole system. This is called **contagion risk**. As we have seen following the collapse of Lehman Brothers in 2008 contagion can have very serious consequences for the economic health of a nation as well as for consumers of financial products. If a domino effect takes hold, where one bank's failure (or perceived likely failure) to meet its obligations to other banks or clients leads to more bank collapses and further losses, it can ruin the entire system, possibly taking us down into a 1930s style depression.

The damage caused by spreading contagion is so bad that it is well worth the effort to ensure individual banks are unlikely to collapse by regulating the amount of capital and liquid assets they hold. It is also worth insisting that they write and continuously update 'living wills' so that they can be revived or closed down in an orderly way without fatally wounding other banks should they run into trouble. It is also advisable to insist that none is either too big to fail (i.e. the government cannot contemplate letting it go into bankruptcy) or 'too big to save', where no government can raise enough money to save it.

Monopoly/oligopoly

Many markets will, if left to their own devices, tend towards a structure where one or a few firms exert undue market power over product pricing. Consumers need protection against monopolistic/oligopolistic exploitation.

There are many forces encouraging movement towards monopoly in financial services apart from the desire to control prices. Economies of scale are such that it makes sense for many banks and other institutions to become very large. Banks with branches in every town and with capabilities to serve multinational firms in every country have an advantage in attracting customers. With stock exchanges, liquidity in share trading may be lowered if there is more than one national exchange. There are also network effects: a single payments system linking the major banks makes more sense than a number of competing systems, because each participant needs to make as many connections within the network as possible. Where natural monopoly makes sense there is even more need to regulate to avoid abuse by over-charging.

The drawbacks of extensive regulation

High compliance cost.

The cost to regulated firms of adhering to the rules will usually result in raised fees, lower return or some other penalty for consumers, because the institution is likely to pass the additional burden through to clients.

Moral hazard

The mere presence of regulation can cause **moral hazard**, which means that the presence of a safety net encourages adverse behaviour (e.g. carelessness). Thus regulation can be counterproductive, in that, if consumers believe that they will be bailed out by the government if things go wrong they will be tempted to take higher risk. Why not place your money in a deposit account offering an unrealistically high interest rate? The bank may go bust but your deposit is safe. Why not pay into a savings scheme offered by an insurance company offering a guarantee of doubling your money over four years? If the company fails you can insist on the government/regulatory fund making good on the promise. In this way irresponsible, badly managed and crooked banks and other financial institutions survive, drawing society's scarce resources away from more productive investment.

Agency capture

Agency capture occurs when those that are supposed to be regulated take some control of the regulatory process. Then the regulation is modified to suit the interests of the producers rather than the consumers. For example, under Basel II (see Chapter 6) the large banks managed to persuade the regulators that it would be sensible for capital requirements to be set in the mould of the banks' own internal risk models. Many people say that the banks were too influential in lowering capital limits, manipulating the rules on risk-weighting assets and in using their own models. This helped to precipitate the 2008 crisis as banks were found to have taken too much risk.

The regulated firms usually have far more financial interest in the activities of regulators than consumers; and so they apply themselves to persuading their overseers to relax their constraints. In many cases the people working in the regulatory organisation are paid significantly less than the financial service high flyers, and they can sometimes be intimidated or outsmarted. Furthermore, many of the more senior regulators have come from the industry they are now regulating and therefore share many of their attitudes and values. Also, they may expect to return to work in the industry following their stint as policemen, so may thus avoid offending potential future employers.

Stifling innovation and growth

The requirements to be licensed and the additional costs of subsequent compliance can impose such a bureaucratic load that few or no firms dare to enter the industry. Thus inefficient monopolies are sustained and oligopolies with implicit cartel-type arrangements persist in over-charging consumers because they are not challenged by new entrants.

Who should regulate?

A key question, once you have accepted the need for regulation, is: who should carry out the task? We have three possibilities: the industry itself, government, or a government agency.

The industry itself

Self-regulation has a number of advantages. The people within the industry have a clear need to preserve its high reputation. A further advantage of self-regulation is that the people most knowledgeable about the industry are those working in it. They know all the tricks currently being played and can quickly adapt the rules to deal with any new tricks. They also know the most efficient ways of running a decent industry and so can avoid regulatory overkill, such as unreasonably high safety standards or excessive compliance costs. In other words, self-regulation is usually 'lighter' than regulation by a government imposed body.

Even self-regulation requires the back-up of legislation to ensure, say, minimum standards to be able to join the industry and then to insist that participants abide by the rules. Without this insistence, free-riders will enter to enjoy the raised reputation of the industry with consumers, without having to pay the costs of compliance or suffer the constraints.

The arguments against self-regulation include the suspicion that the institutions will be continuously tempted to slacken the rules. Secondly, power to permit industry entry is put in the hands of the existing players, who might be tempted to put up barriers to discourage new firms from entering. A third problem is that it is difficult to regulate a firm that has activities in many different financial service industries. For example, conglomerate banks also offer investment products and insurance services, pension funds and investment advice. Unless the self-regulatory body's remit is very widely defined, misdemeanours, bad practice and fraud can seep in through the cracks between the regulators.

Self-regulatory organisations are usually dependent on funding from the industry itself to function, which could encourage it to be more favourably disposed towards the producer rather than the consumer.

The government

There are many cases where self-regulation is clearly not sufficient to maintain the integrity of the financial system and so governments are compelled to intervene by providing a regulatory structure. However, there is a danger here. Governments realise that they will be criticised if there is a financial scandal but will not receive much praise if a series of scandals are avoided. They can therefore have a tendency to err on the side of heavy regulation to reduce even small risks of failure. This will raise the cost to producers and consumers unreasonably. Also governments tend to be less agile than industry self-regulators in responding to new developments and tricks of the morally-challenged.

A government agency

This is designed to capture the best elements of the other two options. An organisation is established by the government, but the government does not control its day-to-day activities, nor intervene in its decisions. Instead of government bureaucrats the agency is run by a group of experts who have longstanding industry experience. The government establishes the guiding principles and goals but then stands back to avoid being tempted to meddle because of some political motivation. The government may, however, provide legislative back-up to ensure that the agency has strong powers, for example, the right to prosecute insider dealers in a criminal court or the right to fine firms caught disobeying the rules.

Using respected industry veterans to run the agency engenders greater practitioner respect for it than would be the case if government officers were in charge. This allows a lighter touch where the key focus is that the spirit of the rules be followed rather than the letter of the law. This approach requires subtlety that civil servants may lack. Also, poachers turned game-keepers are likely to be more alert and agile in keeping up with the latest tricks on the financial streets.

Even though ex-practitioners are in charge they have a statutory framework that prevents them from slackening the rules, or unreasonably restricting entry of new firms to a financial service. Also, the regulator can be given the powers to examine a full range of financial services and markets, and so can avoid the problem of some activities falling between the cracks of an industry by industry regulatory structure.

On the downside, the agency route can be a lot more expensive than self-regulation by the industry.

International competitiveness

Prior to the 2008 financial crisis there was much comment among those informed about financial matters concerning the problem of **competitive laxity** in regulation. That is, financial centres that try to impose strict rules find that financial institutions respond not by tightening their systems and raising probity, but by moving operations to a different jurisdiction, where the rules are looser. This sort of **regulatory arbitrage** is still very much on the minds of regulators and politicians today as they try to make the systems in their countries more robust. As soon as they announce that they will impose an extra rule to make things fairer and safer the cry goes up from the banks and others that they will lose out to overseas competitors who do not have to obey that rule. Furthermore, given that they will be at a competitive disadvantage they too might have to move abroad. The danger is that the regulators and politicians around the globe each back down in turn in the face of this pressure.

One solution is to stand up to the banks, etc. and say 'If you want to do very risky things or unfair things then we would prefer it if you did go somewhere else, so we are going to impose the rule ourselves even if no other country does the same' – this is termed the unilateral approach. Of course, the authorities would like to achieve international agreement (multilateral approach) so that all the financial centres impose the same rule to avoid regulatory arbitrage (as with Basel III), but this is difficult to attain.

The main features of a regulatory system

- *Licensing.* Is a person fit and proper to manage a provider of financial services? Only those who have met the standards required (integrity, honesty, capability) are allowed to provide a service in the industry. Training schemes and qualifications are encouraged by regulators to raise standards.

- *Mandatory information provisions and consumer education.* Customers should obtain the right information at the right time to help them make a decision. Financial products/services need to be clearly explained including risks, potential returns and costs such as charges. This must be presented in a consistent format to allow comparison. Regulators often accept a responsibility to educate and foster financial literacy. This is to reduce the need for more heavy-handed regulation.

- *Disclosure and monitoring.* Disclosure of information about the operations of the financial firm and on-going monitoring may reveal whether a conflict of interest exists, whether risk management procedures are sound, whether the managers are competent and the institution is run with integrity. This may involve off-site analysis of information provided and on-site inspections by the regulator.

- *Restricting activities.* Prohibiting certain firms from a line of business or prohibiting a particular combination of financial services within the same organisation or a ban on anyone from engaging in the activity, e.g. no mortgage lending without proof of borrower's income. Commercial companies are often not allowed to hold large equity stakes in a bank, and vice versa. Regulators may insist that financial service functions be separated. This may by splitting into in-house departments with Chinese Walls between them. Or insisting on separately capitalised group companies or splitting up the company. Anti-monopoly provisions restrict activity/prices.

- *Prudential limits.* For example: capital and liquidity requirements of banks and insurance firms; pension funds to have sufficient funds to meet commitments; and whether securities firms are in a sound financial condition.

- *Duty of care.* Prescribing appropriate financial institution behaviour to avoid harm to customers. No misrepresentation, fraud or mis-selling. Knowing the financial position, investment goals, knowledge and experience of the customer before providing advice or selling a service to ensure that it is suitable, for example, not selling a high-risk investment to someone needing a low-risk portfolio. Eliminating unfair terms in contracts. A firm must protect client assets while it holds them on behalf of the client – e.g. ringfencing them – see Exhibit 18.2.

FSA fines two City brokers for not ringfencing clients' money

By Alistair Gray

The City watchdog flexed its muscles again yesterday when it punished divisions of Astaire Group and Close Brothers for failing to segregate clients' money from their own.

The Financial Services Authority said Rowan Dartington and Close Investments put investors at risk in breaches during the financial crisis and fined them £511,000 and £98,000 respectively.

The penalties come days after the FSA fined JPMorgan's securities arm a record £33.3m for similar problems. They form part of a wider investigation into how banks and brokers protect client money.

Margaret Cole, the FSA's enforcement director, said: "Firms should be in no doubt that if they fail to get their house in order in this regard we will take action against them."

Shares in Astaire were suspended eight weeks ago after the City stockbroker said £1.4m went missing at Rowan Dartington, its wealth management arm.

The FSA said Rowan Dartington "could not rely on the accuracy of its internal books and records" after it failed to properly test and implement a new software system installed in May 2007.

Under FSA rules, banks, brokers and insurance companies are required to ringfence client money and keep it in separate accounts with trust status.

Of the £1.4m missing money, more than £1m remains unrecovered, Astaire added.

Meanwhile, Close Investments was fined for similarly failing to properly protect client money in the two years to January 2010.

No clients lost money as a result of the errors, both Close and Astaire said.

Source: *Financial Times*, 8 June 2010, p. 22

Exhibit 18.2   FSA fines two City brokers for not ringfencing clients' money

▪ *Fair trading on exchanges*. A fair treatment of traders, particularly retail investors. Prohibitions on insider dealing (using non-public information to trade financial securities) and market manipulation or abuse (e.g. spreading false rumours). Transparency of trading (e.g. open disclosure of price quotes by market makers). Best execution provisions (see Chapter 12). Prices of trades to be published. Issuers of securities to provide prospectus and financial statements (see Chapter 13).

▪ *Complaints handling and compensation*. Put systems in place to assist consumers pursuing a complaint against a firm and to secure recompense. Provide compensation if a firm is bust (e.g. bank deposit insurance).

▪ *Penalties*. In the event of non-compliance penalties may be imposed (e.g. fines, de-licensing, imprisonment, banning directors from the industry). For less serious offences a private warning or public censure may be sufficient.

Regulation of UK financial services

Now that we have covered the basic principles lying behind regulation we will look at the example of the UK to illustrate the range of responsibilities typically given to regulators.

Interestingly, the UK regulatory system is going through something of an upheaval at the time of writing. For over a decade the **Financial Services Authority (FSA)** has dominated the scene. It is a 'super-regulator' with oversight of an amazing range of financial sectors. This is in contrast to some systems (e.g. the US system) where there are a dozen or more regulators, each looking after one or a limited range of types of financial service.

In 2013 the FSA will split in two. The main body, the **Financial Conduct Authority (FCA)**, will still be a super-regulator covering a very wide range of financial services – see Exhibit 18.3. One important function, that of the individual regulation of the 2,200 biggest banks, insurers and brokers on the issue of safety and soundness (micro-prudential supervision) will be transferred to the new **Prudential Regulatory Authority (PRA)**, a subsidiary of the Bank of England. It will be responsible for granting permission for their activities and approving their senior management. It will have the powers to impose additional capital requirements, limit leverage and change the risk weighting of assets in order to reduce the risk of failure. It will be staffed by old FSA hands.

The Bank of England previously had the responsibility together with the FSA and the Treasury of ensuring the systemic safety of the banking system. That is, setting rules on capital and liquidity reserves for banks across the sector as a whole and imposing other rules to reduce contagion risk. Following the 2008 financial crisis it was thought wise to concentrate both this macro-prudential regulation in the hands of one regulator together with the micro-prudential regulation of individual banks (and other finance businesses), rather than have the 'tripartite' approach where people in the BoE, Treasury and the FSA are not quite clear which of them should be taking charge when a systemic threat arises – as was the case up to 2008. The additional consideration is that these systemically important institutions might need access to central bank funding in an emergency and so it is best if they are regulated by the Bank.

The Financial Conduct Authority will retain responsibility for protecting consumers and preserving market integrity, covering:

- investor protection, including that for bank customers;

- market supervision and regulation;

■ business conduct of banks and financial services, including approval of consumer-related managers and the supervision of investment managers and other firms whose failure would be non-systemic (they would not cause a contagion);

■ civil and criminal enforcement of market abuse rules;

■ UK Listing Authority – supervision of initial public offerings and subsequent monitoring of listed companies (see Chapter 13).

While most companies will only be answerable to one regulator, the PRA-supervised firms will be under the supervision of two regulators. The FCA will cover the good treatment of customers and general business conduct while the PRA will cover safety and soundness of the institution.

The Bank of England's **Financial Policy Committee (FPC)**, making decisions that apply to the entire sector to ensure system-wide financial stability including the avoidance of credit and asset bubbles, only meets four times per year to set rules. It might, for example, increase capital requirements above the Basel III minimum in normal times to ensure safety, and then lower them in a crisis so that the banks do not withdraw lending when the economy is already suffering. It may impose system-wide higher risk-weights against specific classes of bank assets in markets that appear too exuberant. It may insist that banks increase their forward-looking loss-provisioning when lending is growing fast. It might set nationwide borrowing limits such as maximum amount of a loan relative to the value of the property backing up that loan. The FPC has also been set the task of identifying emerging threats to the system from the 'shadow banking sector' – see later in the chapter. The PRA division does the hard work of day-to-day handling of individual institutions to ensure firm level stability and soundness. Of course, the Bank also has the Monetary Policy Committee to set interest rates and adjust the money supply – see Chapter 6.

The FSA/FCA can be described as semi-detached from government: it is financed by the industries it regulates, but its powers come from legislation; it often consults the financial services companies before deciding on principles, rules and codes of conduct, but it has basic principles approved by the government and it is answerable to the Treasury, which appoints its board, and through them Parliament.

The FSA/FCA tries to achieve the following:

■ maintain confidence in the financial system;

■ protect consumers;

■ reduce financial crime, such as money laundering, fraud and insider dealing;

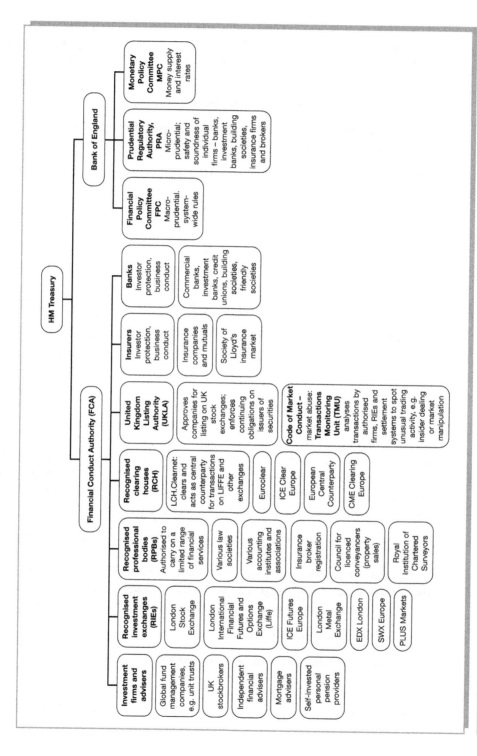

Exhibit 18.3   UK financial services industry regulation

▓ maintain financial stability – contributing to the protection and enhancement of stability in the UK financial system;

▓ help people to gain the knowledge, aptitude and skills to manage their financial affairs effectively by promoting public understanding of the financial system.

While pursuing these objectives the regulator makes it clear that it is not removing all risk for the investor. Investment risk is an inherent part of the system and those who take the benefits from an investment when everything goes right have to accept that from time to time investment losses will occur. Also, the complete absence of consequences for the client should a financial firm fail may encourage laziness in choosing a place for their money and other moral hazards, and so the FSA/FCA does not promise to rescue failed firms, nor guarantee all money deposited/invested with them (but see Financial Services Compensation Scheme later). The FSA/FCA also tries to maintain healthy competition by encouraging entry into the industry and trying to strike the right balance between the costs and benefits of tighter regulation.

The FSA/FCA also has powers over unregulated firms and persons regarding breaches of money laundering regulations and short selling. In addition, it has the power to prosecute unauthorised firms or persons carrying on regulated activities. Its market abuse powers are very strong – see Exhibit 18.4 for an example.

The FSA/FCA has a budget of over £450 million per year and employs over 3,000 well-paid staff. The amount each of the 29,000 regulated firms pays depends on its size and the type of business it undertakes. The minimum fee of £844 in 2011 was paid by 43 per cent of those businesses. The FSA/FCA also receives money from financial penalties imposed on errant firms (raising about 10–20 per cent of its budget).

The introduction of a single super-regulator for a country was unusual when in 2001 the FSA was given powers over several areas of financial services (it was set up in 1997 with a more limited remit). However, the advantages of a unified approach are well-recognised today, and many countries (e.g. Japan, Germany and Sweden) now have a super-regulator for their financial sectors. Increasingly, financial institutions provide a wide range of services and so a unified approach to regulation is needed. This allows greater insight into the firm's practices and avoidance of the problem of financial activities falling between the cracks of separate regulators' responsibilities. Also there are economies of scale in investigation and monitoring (having six different regulators visiting a firm and asking similar questions is clearly inefficient for the regulated and the regulator).

Broker fined for 'market abuse' in FSA crackdown

By Javier Blas, Commodities Correspondent

A commodities broker was fined for "market abuse" by the Financial Services Authority yesterday in the first such penalty and a sign that the City regulator is starting to crack down on price manipulation in the London-based raw materials markets.

The FSA said it had fined Andrew Kerr, a former broker at Sucden Financial, £100,000 and banned him from working in the financial industry. Mr Kerr has agreed to settle the case.

The regulator said Mr Kerr "deliberately manipulated" the Liffe robusta coffee futures and options markets on August 15 2007 on behalf of a client, which it did not identify. It is unclear whether the FSA will take action against the client, but coffee market participants said it was likely to do so.

Mr Kerr organised a series of trades during a key period of the day, which serves to price options, to boost artificially the price of coffee futures, the FSA said. Mr Kerr moved the market to $1,752 a tonne, up from about $1,145. The "small size of the coffee futures market meant that it was particularly vulnerable to price manipulation," the FSA said.

"Mr Kerr's financial benefit from the market manipulation was limited to his commission," the regulator said. But it added he was "doubtless motivated" by a desire to attract further business. Brokers estimated the commission at as low as $100 and no more than $500.

Source: Financial Times, 3 June 2010, p. 17

Exhibit 18.4   Broker fined for market abuse in FSA crackdown

Authorisation

All firms or individuals offering financial advice, products or services in the UK must be authorised by the FSA/FCA.[1] Engaging in a regulated activity without authorisation can result in a two-year prison sentence. The FSA insists on high standards when assessing for authorisation. These require competence, financial soundness and fair treatment of customers. Firms are authorised to carry out specific activities, for example, giving financial advice only, or managing a client's money in a fund, or stockbroking.

Monitoring

Even after initial approval, firms cannot relax as the FSA/FCA continues to monitor adequacy of management, financial resources and internal systems and controls. It also insists that any information provided to investors is clear, fair and not misleading. If there is a failure to meet these standards the firms can be

---

[1] Or have special exemption. A list of those registered as authorised by the FSA is at **www.fsa.gov.uk**.

fined or even stopped from doing business. The FSA/FCA also works closely with the criminal authorities and uses civil and criminal powers.

The FSA/FCA cannot look in detail at each of the 29,000 companies it regulates on a routine basis because this would impose an excessive cost burden on the industry, so it uses a 'risk-based approach'. It has a process for categorising firms into risk classes based on the likely impact that a firm would have on consumers or the market if it was to breach the rules (e.g. number of consumers likely to be affected and the systemic threat) and on the probability of that particular problem occurring. Firms that pose little risk of operating against the objectives of the FSA/FCA, labelled 'low-impact firms', are allowed to submit basic information in regulatory reports twice a year. They do not have regular visits. This 'light touch' regulation applies to over 90 per cent of the firms under supervision. This allows the regulator to concentrate resources on activities and institutions that appear to pose the greatest risk to customers and markets.

For medium and high-impact firms a regular (on a cycle of one to four years) risk assessment is made. This is used to determine a risk mitigation programme proportionate to the risks identified. More work is put in by the regulator in investigating a firm if the firm is large or particularly risky. High-impact firms will be subject to 'close and continuous' work, resulting in a schedule of regular visits to senior managers and a detailed examination of the control functions the firm has in place.

Of course, any firm that seems to be operating outside the spirit of the rules will receive a lot more attention, even if it is normally classified as low-impact. As a first step it may be required to complete a questionnaire. It may then receive a number of visits, and ultimately be punished (or individuals punished) through, for example, being fined, losing authorisation to operate or being subject to legal action.

The FSA/FCA emphasises broad principles rather than its rules. The problem with a regulator sticking strictly to rules is that they can result in inflexibility – just 'ticking boxes' – rather than concentrating the minds of the regulated on the spirit underlying the rules. Also a rule-based approach can be less flexible when it comes to permitting innovation from existing or new firms. A principles-based approach has less prescription and allows the regulator to meet new situations (e.g. new tricks by those smart people in the City) by using some degree of judgement rather than being hidebound by rules. Lawyers will forever be finding loopholes in rules; they find that more difficult if the rules are set in a framework of general principles, when the principles have greater weight.

Following the financial crisis the FSA became much less 'light-touch' and much more intrusive. There is a danger that London will lose the goodwill and openness that exists between the regulated and the regulator, and end up with a more antagonistic US-type of relationship where lawyers are to the fore.

Consumer complaints

There are three steps to be taken for a person with a grievance:

1 *Raise the issue with the financial service company*. All firms should have a formal complaints procedure, and the complainant is encouraged by the FSA/FCA to start here, giving the firm a chance to right the wrong. After all, the firm is best placed to check its records and see what happened. Most regulated firms have **compliance officers** whose job it is to ensure the FSA/FCA rules are being followed. Roughly three out of four complainants dissatisfied with the response of the company choose not to pursue it further, believing it would be futile to do so. However, there are further positive steps a complainant could take.

2 *Independent complaints scheme*. Most financial services firms belong to an independent complaints scheme – the FSA/FCA insists in most cases.[2] These are beneficial to the system because they increase the confidence of investors and other financial clients by responding to the fear of consumers that they lack knowledge (information asymmetry) to be able to stand up to the financial professionals. There are two types: arbitration schemes and ombudsman schemes. Under both the complaint will be investigated and, if found to be justified, the firm will be ordered to put matters right. Many of the schemes provide for a financial award, up to a maximum of £150,000. Under arbitration both the complainant and the firm agree in advance to accept the arbitrator's decision. Importantly, in accepting this the complainant gives up the right to take the case to court. The advantage is that it is much quicker and cheaper than going to court. Under the **Financial Ombudsman Scheme (FOS)** the independent and impartial ombudsman collects together the facts of the case and arrives at what seems to him or her a reasonable and fair settlement. The firm is then under an obligation to accept the decision,[3] but the complainant remains free to take the case to court. The service is free to consumers. The ombudsman's approach is less legalistic than arbitration and allows for more 'common-sense' factors of fairness. The FOS looks at complaints about most financial problems involving:

---

[2] The firm's literature should set out its regulatory body and scheme.
[3] Although they can appeal through the courts.

▪ banking;

▪ insurance;

▪ mortgages;

▪ credit cards and store cards;

▪ loans and credit;

▪ pensions;

▪ savings and investments;

▪ hire purchase and pawnbroking;

▪ money transfer;

▪ financial advice;

▪ stocks, shares, unit trusts and bonds.

If the FOS finds in the complainant's favour it can order a firm to pay compensation up to a maximum of £150,000. The FOS may even order the firm to pay compensation for distress and inconvenience on top of financial loss.

3 *Go to court.* Litigation is often expensive, time-consuming and frustrating, and so should only be contemplated as a last resort. A relatively fast and informal service is provided by the small claims track or the small claims court (maximum claim in England £5,000, Northern Ireland £2,000 and Scotland £3,000). The complainant does not need a solicitor, and court fees are low. The complainant may not even have to attend the court as judges can make judgements on the paper evidence.

Compensation

The complaint steps described in the last section are all well and good if the firm that has behaved badly is still in existence. But what if it is defunct? The **Financial Services Compensation Scheme (FSCS)** can compensate consumers (and small companies) if an *authorised* company is unable to pay money it owes. Note that if consumers do business with a firm not authorised by the FSA/FCA, e.g. an offshore company,[4] they are not covered by FSCS or the complaints procedure.

---

[4] One based and regulated outside the UK, such as in Bermuda or Jersey.

The FSCS service is free for the consumer and small business. It covers investments (e.g. bad advice, bad investment management), money deposited in accounts (at banks, building societies and credit unions), insurance products (e.g. car insurance, life insurance), mortgage advice, pensions and endowments. For investments and home finance (mortgages) the maximum payout is £50,000 per person. For deposit claims (e.g. bank accounts) the scheme pays £85,000 per person (per bank). For insurance the scheme pays 90 per cent of the loss.

In order to compensate victims of mis-selling or other malpractice the FSCS raises money from the financial service firms via a regular annual levy supplemented by additional levies in years of high compensation payouts, and this can be very costly for them.

Regulation of markets

Financial markets need high-quality regulation in order to induce investors to place their trust in them. There must be safeguards against unscrupulous and incompetent operators. There must be an orderly operation of the markets, fair dealing and integrity. However, the regulations should not be so restrictive as to stifle innovation and prevent the markets from being competitive internationally. London's financial markets have a unique blend of law, self-regulation and custom to regulate and supervise their members' activities.

The FSA/FCA supervises exchanges, clearing houses and settlement houses. It also conducts market surveillance and monitors transactions on seven **recognised investment exchanges (RIEs)** – see Exhibit 18.3. The RIEs work with the FSA/FCA to protect investors and maintain the integrity of markets. Much of the monitoring and enforcement is delegated to the RIEs. The London Stock Exchange, for example, vets new stockbrokers and tries to ensure compliance with LSE rules, aimed at making sure members (e.g. market makers and brokers) act with the highest standards of integrity, fairness, transparency and efficiency. It monitors market makers' quotations and the price of actual trades to ensure compliance with its dealing rules. It is constantly on the look-out for patterns of trading that deviate from the norm with the aim of catching those misusing information (e.g. insider dealing), creating a false or misleading impression to the disadvantage of other investors or some other market distorting action.

Regulation of companies

If you invest in a company by buying its shares or bonds, you have a right to receive information about that company, and to expect that there are laws and other pressures to discourage the management from going astray and acting against your interests.

There are various checks and balances in the corporate world, the most important being the requirements under the **Companies Acts**. The Department for Business, Innovation and Skills enforces the law and is able to intrude into a company's affairs. Accountants and **auditors** also function, to some extent, as regulators, helping to ensure companies do not misrepresent their position. The **Financial Reporting Council (FRC)** oversees corporate reporting. Furthermore, any member of the public may access the accounts of any company easily and cheaply at **Companies House** (www.companieshouse.gov.uk). The media keep a watchful stance – always ready to reveal stories of fraud, greed or incompetence. In the case of mergers of listed or other public limited companies, the **City Panel on Takeovers and Mergers** acts to ensure fairness for all shareholders. The **Office of Fair Trading** and the **Competition Commission** investigate, rule on and enforce remedies with regard to anti-competitive behaviour.

Fraud and money laundering

Fraud costs the UK economy an estimated £38 billion annually, equivalent to £765 for every adult member of the population.[5] The FSA/FCA is one of several UK organisations that investigates and responds to suspicions of fraud. The **City of London Police** is, however, the 'National Lead Force' for fraud with a remit to create a centre of excellence for fraud investigations and to use its expertise to help police forces across the UK.[6] It is particularly concerned with organised crime groups and securing major convictions. It manages hundreds of fraud investigations each year. In 2010, for example, it identified 124 organised criminal gangs and had 154 defendants charged and awaiting prosecution at court.

Exhibit 18.5 shows some examples of the frauds the City of London Police stopped.

The **National Fraud Authority (NFA)**, operating a website **Action Fraud**, is the UK's national fraud reporting centre providing a central point of contact for information about fraud. People who are scammed, ripped off or conned can report a fraud, find help and support. The National Fraud Authority is an umbrella government organisation that co-ordinates and oversees the fight against fraud.

Insurance companies club together to pay for the **Insurance Fraud Bureau (IFB)** to combat bogus insurance claims. If this was not tackled all our insurance premiums would rise to pay for payouts to criminals lying about damage, theft, etc.

---

[5] The National Fraud Authority figures for 2011.
[6] The City of London Police deal with other financial crimes and the threat of terrorism in the Square Mile as well as normal community policing.

In a boiler room investigation*, a Danish man was arrested by Spanish police and extradited to the UK in May 2009. This followed a joint investigation by the City of London and Dyfed-Powys Police. The fraudster was sentenced to nearly five years in prison after pleading guilty to running criminal operations that sold worthless or highly inflated shares to more than 500 investors, with a combined loss of more than £2 million.

Operation Soundwave led to a national and international investigation into a £25 million boiler room fraud. Over Christmas 2009, Northumbria and Greater Manchester Police assisted 20 City officers in making 12 arrests in the north of England. At the same time detectives travelled to Sweden to arrest the main suspect, and later had him extradited back to the UK.

A man who attempted to steal more than $170 million was sentenced to nine years after an international investigation. The 32-year-old Edinburgh man's complex fraud involved taking over corporate accounts before he was stopped by City of London Police officers.

*In a **boiler room scam** the fraudsters harass potential investors through regular telephone calls or over the internet, eventually persuading them that they should invest in a 'great opportunity'. Needless to say, they are selling something of little or no value. Millions of pounds each year are taken from savers – particularly old people.

Exhibit 18.5

Source: The City of London Police Annual Report 2009–10

The **Serious Fraud Office (SFO)** investigates and prosecutes serious or complex fraud and corruption exceeding £1 million in value. It is a part of the criminal justice system – but remains an independent government department (with a high degree of autonomy from political control). It builds cases and brings criminals to justice and so helps maintain confidence in the UK's business and financial institutions.

If a suspected fraud is likely to give rise to widespread public concern, be complex and thus require specialist knowledge to investigate, or be international in scope, then the SFO is usually the organisation that tackles it.

Money laundering is concealing the source of illegally obtained money. It is the process of changing money obtained from crimes, such as drug trafficking, into a form that appears to be legitimate. The process often involves multiple international transactions across currencies and financial institutions in order to obscure the source. To combat money laundering the UK regulators require that any bank, sharebroker or other financial firm being asked to open an account for a person or company has to verify the customer's identity. Even solicitors carrying out house conveyancing are required to see forms of identity such as passports, driving licence and utility bills of the purchasers. Financial firms are also required to look out for suspicious transactions and report them. The FSA/ FCA penalises firms that lack adequate systems and controls to detect and report money laundering. There are some people within the finance industry who help money launderers, using their contacts and knowledge about jurisdictions abroad where policing is lax. Criminal investigators are tasked with tracking them down. Suspected money laundering is reported to the **Serious Organised Crime Agency (SOCA)**, which is assisted by other investigating agencies such as the police. The City of London Police also have a major role here.

European Union regulation

As well as national financial service regulation we have another layer for the countries in the EU. We will concentrate on the basic principles that the EU legislators are applying, and look at a few examples of the pan-European rules that have already been introduced.

The fundamental objective of the EU is to promote movement towards a single market in financial services regardless of national boundaries. It is thought that movement towards such a goal will bring about improved welfare for consumers and faster economic growth. The **Financial Services Action Plan (FSAP)** is the process devised by the European Commission to provide momentum towards a single integrated market. It has three strategic objectives (not all are achieved):

1 *Establishing a single market in wholesale financial services*, including:

- the establishment of a common legal framework for securities and derivatives markets;

- providing the necessary legal certainty to underpin cross-border securities trading. This includes integrated securities settlement systems;

- the removal of the outstanding barriers to raising capital on an EU-wide basis. Many national rules hinder the offering of securities in other EU countries, making it costly. One action is to have common minimum rules on the contents of a prospectus when a company is raising money by selling securities (already, once a prospectus has been approved in one EU country it has a 'passport' to sell the securities in others);

- having a single set of rules for financial statements for listed companies. To a large extent this has been achieved because all EU countries have adopted International Financial Reporting Standards;

- rules on cross-border mergers of public limited companies, protecting minority shareholders.

2 *Making retail[7] markets more open and secure.* Creating a legal framework to allow financial institutions to offer their services throughout the EU by removing obstacles that hamper the cross-border purchasing or provision of these services. For example, single bank account or mortgage credit rules, reducing the charges on low-value transfers of money between EU countries by encouraging a more efficient, cheaper cross-border payments system (e.g. on credit card payments).

3 *Strengthening the rules on prudential supervision.* This covers areas such as capital and liquidity adequacy of banks and solvency margins for insurance companies.

There are two key elements for achieving these objectives:

1 *Mutual recognition.* If a financial firm has been authorised to offer a service by one EU member state it is then free to operate in other member states selling its service there without requiring further authorisation from the host countries.

2 *Application of minimum standards.* Agreeing minimum standards for financial services. This ensures that if a firm is authorised by its home regulator it abides by reasonably tough rules that would protect clients throughout the EU – there is not a 'race to the bottom' by countries deliberately offering a lax regulatory environment to attract financial service firms to set up in their countries or to promote the growth of their domestic firms by lowering their costs or allowing doubtful activity.

Note that there is no attempt to create either full harmonisation in which the rules are identical in each country ('one size fits all'), or a common regulatory structure with a large centralised bureaucracy or a single European regulator in Brussels. Politically, it is far easier for them to agree to adopt minimum standards and a 'passport' system, in which the granting of a licence in one EU country is sufficient for a financial firm to sell its services in all EU member states.

---

[7] Individuals rather than institutions.

Dozens of 'directives' have been published by the European Commission and then implemented by member countries. Examples are:

- *Capital Liberalisation Directive, 1988*. Money can be moved from one country to another without controls.

- *First Banking Directive, 1977*. Banks became free to open branches or establish subsidiaries in other member states. These were to operate under the supervisory rules of the host country. This limited the range of services to only those accepted by the host country's regulations. Thus a subsidiary of a French bank in Spain could only do what the Spanish regulators allowed local banks to do.

- *Second Banking Directive, 1989*. A single banking licence allowed operations throughout the EU. This allowed a bank licensed in one EU country to sell its services in other EU countries regardless of whether the host country normally allows these services to be provided by its domestic banks. The activities permitted under this rule are those on an approved list, and include securities business as well as banking services. As a safeguard the home and host country supervisors exchange information as they now have to share supervision. Home country regulators have the main responsibility, but host country regulators can impose monetary policy-related rules (e.g. liquidity reserves) and supervise consumer protection.

- *Market Abuse Directive, 2003*. A common EU legal framework for preventing and detecting market abuse and for ensuring a proper flow of information to the market. EU countries must reach the minimum standards in the directive. National regulators may pursue market abusers, including insider dealers, by either a civil case (requiring merely proof 'on the balance of probabilities') or a criminal case ('beyond reasonable doubt' – a much higher standard of proof). It also requires greater interchange of information between national regulators to better unearth wrong-doing.

- *Transparency Directive, 2004*. All issuers of publicly-traded securities must provide annual financial reports within four months of their year-ends. The directive also sets the minimum content of annual, half-yearly and interim management statements. In addition there are minimum notification requirements for both issuers and investors in relation to the acquisition and disposal of the major holdings in companies, for example, major shareholdings have to be publicly reported and any subsequent changes announced.

In addition to agreeing to abide by directives, occasionally the EU States agree that they will all impose common rules on the financial sector; for example, they did this with bankers' bonuses in 2010.

There is now a college of national supervisors – the **European System of Financial Supervisors**. Under this, three authorities, focused on different aspects of financial services, were created in 2011:

- **The European Banking Authority (EBA).** Headquartered in London, the EBA is concerned with ensuring EU-wide coordination on regulatory and supervisory standards with a focus on the stability of the financial system. It **stress-tests** European banks – examines and probes for weaknesses by imagining a set of adverse circumstances (e.g. a perfect storm combination of a rise in interest rates, high loan default rates and loss of bank access to money market funds). It will have much to say on the adoption of new capital and liquidity reserve standards over the next few years.

- **The European Insurance and Occupational Pensions Authority (EIOPA).** Based in Frankfurt, it focuses on EU coordination of rules for the protection of insurance policyholders, pension scheme members and beneficiaries. In the immediate future it will implement a new set of capital reserve rules for insurance companies (Solvency II), which result in more risk leading to more capital requirements.

- **The European Securities and Markets Authority (ESMA).** Located in Paris, it tries to improve the EU regulators' coordination on the functioning of markets and strengthen investor protection. It is charged with harmonising the regulation of issuance and trading of shares, bonds and other securities. It covers matters of corporate governance, auditing, financial reporting, take-over bids, clearing and settlement and derivative issues. It is currently working on a new directive on hedge funds and private equity and new rules on over-the-counter derivatives trading. It already has powers to fine credit rating agencies for breaching EU rules.

The committees of these three organisations, made up of the heads of national regulators, have the responsibility to try to achieve greater convergence of regulatory standards and practices across the EU. They will produce technical standards and plan for the adoption of EU regulatory law throughout the EU – some countries have been lax in adopting the EU-wide rules in the past, and so need a little chivvying along.

Despite past attempts to gain greater cooperation at the EU level, regulation remains mostly a national affair, embedded in domestic regulation. However, these new bodies will have the power to override national authorities in 'emergency situations'. Also, the political mood seems to be to grant more powers to pan-EU regulatory bodies, and it is thought that their powers to override national regulators will be extended into a greater range of products and markets than those listed above.

In addition to these three, a new EU body, the **European Systemic Risk Board (ESRB)**, was set up in 2011. It has whistle-blowing powers to prevent future crises. That is, it has powers to issue warnings and recommendations when it sees threats to economies or financial systems. The European Central Bank takes the lead role in the ESRB, but national central bankers dominate the board. We will have to wait and see if it is merely a talking shop fretting over, say, house prices in Spain and excess property lending in Ireland, but with no teeth to do anything about a wayward economy.

Many people, particularly in the City of London, think that too much control over financial services and markets is being granted to pan-European regulators, who may not fully understand the needs of a financial centre like the City, and who may have political agendas (e.g. to grab business from London).

Global regulation

Following the financial crisis in 2008 there is much more enthusiasm within the policy-making classes for supra-national regulation or, at least, coordination of regulatory rules. A good example of rules being set on a global scale (or at least for most of the world) is the Basel Committee's rules on bank capital reserves and liquidity rules – see Chapter 6.

To gain help from the **International Monetary Fund (IMF)** a country must open markets to overseas trade, flows of capital and liberate banks from stifling controls. The **Financial Stability Board (FSB)** is charged with the task of developing supervisory and other policies to promote financial stability. It also coordinates with the IMF in sounding alarm bells about vulnerabilities in the financial system. For example, it is currently working on the 'too big to fail' problem in banking.

There are a number of international organisations established by the relevant industry itself to promote higher standards of behaviour. For example, the **International Swap and Derivatives Association (ISDA)** is a global financial trade association for the world's major institutions that deal in privately negotiated derivatives.[8] Its purpose is to identify and reduce the sources of risk in the derivatives business. It sets standards for members, writes standardised contracts that members are encouraged to use, comments on netting and collateral arrangements, promotes sound risk management practices, and advances the understanding and treatment of derivatives and risk management.

---

[8] Its membership also includes many of the businesses, governmental entities and other end users that rely on over-the-counter derivatives.

Some gaps in the system?

One major problem is overcoming the political obstacles to effective international regulation. There is always a temptation for the country that would like to build up its financial service sector to race to the bottom, because footloose financial institutions are attracted by 'lightness of regulation', and will move. Thus regulatory arbitrage will always be with us, with some aspects of finance moving to the least regulated jurisdiction. Hence the need for robust international agreements on minimum standards. The problem is that each country examines a proposal for a tighter rule in the light of an assessment of the impact on its competitiveness. The intention of the national policymakers too often seems to be 'to find a regulatory regime that crimps competitors more than one's own companies'.[9] Hence the slowness in achieving worldwide (or G20) agreement on issues as diverse as bankers bonuses (the new US rules are more flexible than the EU ones) or banning investment banks from proprietary trading (the US is strict, other countries less so, leaving loopholes).

On the other hand, the widespread recognition that under-regulation contributed to the 2008 financial crisis has reinforced the view that policymakers do not serve their people well if they allow too much slack. The tension between the desire for an easy-going, light-touch, regulated financial centre – egged on by bankers, etc. threatening to leave for more accommodating environments – and the need to protect consumers will always be with us. It will be interesting to see how the politicians resolve the tension over the next few years. It does not help that such a high proportion of political party donations in the UK and US come from the finance sector. Buying political influence? You may think so, but I could not possibly comment.

Another major problem is that the regulators have paid little attention to the less obvious, but powerful, sectors within the financial system. I'm referring to the **'shadow banking system'**. This is the collection of non-bank entities that move money and risk around the global financial system, by-passing the banks. The usual candidates to be included in this group include:

- **Hedge funds.** Raising funds directly from wealthy individuals and institutional investors, they have a large and growing role in debt, equity and derivative markets. A failure of a large hedge fund could destabilise the markets and the banking system given that banks are often the counterparties in derivative and other deals, and they also lend to the funds.

---

[9] Joseph Stiglitz in the *Financial Times*, 10 February 2010, p. 13.

■ **Private equity funds**. Originally set up to raise funds from long-term investors to invest in unquoted companies, some have branched out into debt trading, and even have hedge fund arms. Failure of these ventures could pose a threat to banks and the wider system, as could a failure of a large leveraged buyout. Some funds have loan books larger than that of many banks. Much of that money was raised through bank borrowing, thus a failure to repay could imperil banks.

■ **Money market funds**. These by-pass the banks by taking short-term money from investors to buy commercial paper and other securities. It was their abrupt withdrawal from lending via commercial paper, etc. following some defaults, that caused corporates and banks to be unable to roll over their debt, leading many to failure in 2008. Many money market funds supplied cash for repayment over, say, 30 days. This was used to lend out on 25-year mortgages. Thus, non-banks (money market funds and special purpose vehicles issuing long-term bonds as securitised bonds) became conduits for maturity transformation, where short-term money is lent out into long-term securities. The expectation by those who borrowed from the money market funds was that they would always be there to supply more money, every 30 days. This was a silly assumption.

■ **Securitisation**. The securitisation of assets such as sub-prime mortgages greatly assisted the growth of the housing finance market. These securitised bonds were then repackaged (see Chapter 19) which created pockets of extreme risk in the financial system and as a result many banks failed.

■ **Commodity funds**. The banks are by-passed and money is placed at risk with large bets being taken on future movements of commodity prices using derivatives and borrowing. They might blow up resulting in huge losses, which might pose knock-on risks throughout the financial system, as banks might face bad debts.

■ **Clearing houses**. These processors of trading activity handle billions every day, asking for only a small margin in their role as central counterparties. They tend to have little capital in reserve, so in the event of a few defaults by traders the system might be in trouble. Contagious fear could spread if investors worry about the clearing house's promise to guarantee every deal. This could halt lending and other deals for a while.

■ **Inter-dealer broker**. If one of these organisations standing between traders and connecting them fails then billions could be lost.

Thus we face the problem that the regulators are busy constructing a strong Maginot Line,[10] such as raised Basel III capital and liquidity reserves, to protect banks, while the real danger may lie to the side. Risk can and has moved from the regulated and transparent elements in the system to the less-regulated opaque sector. The shadow banks have become enormous sources of credit and may well fuel the next bubble, as they assisted with the noughties one.

The Financial Stability Board has begun looking at shadow banking, and various governments and national regulators are starting to draw up lists of non-banks that might pose a systemic risk. But we are currently, in 2011, only at the talking stage. For those interested, Federal Reserve Board have put together a chart showing the players in shadow banking – see **www.ft.com/shadowbanks**.

Websites

www.actionfraud.org.uk	Action Fraud
www.bankofengland.co.uk	Bank of England
www.cepr.org	Centre for Economic Policy Research
www.cityoflondon.police.uk	City of London Police
www.companieshouse.gov.uk	Companies House
www.bis.gov.uk	Department for Business, Innovation and Skills
www.eba.europa.eu	European Banking Authority
www.ecb.int	European Central Bank
www.ec.europa.eu	European Commission
www.eiopa.europa.eu	European Insurance and Occupational Pensions Authority
www.esma.europa.eu	European Securities and Markets Authority
www.federalreserve.gov	Federal Reserve
www.financial-ombudsman.org.uk	Financial Ombudsman
www.financialstabilityboard.org	Financial Stability Board
www.fsa.gov.uk	Financial Services Authority
www.insurancefraudbureau.org	Insurance Fraud Bureau, IFB
www.icmb.ch	International Center for Monetary and Banking Studies
www.isda.org	International Swaps and Derivatives Association

[10] Defensive fortifications along the French–German border that Hitler avoided by going through Belgium in 1940.

www.nfib.police.uk	National Fraud Intelligence Bureau (NFIB)
www.imf.org	International Monetary Fund
www.sfo.gov.uk	Serious Fraud Office, SFO
www.soca.gov.uk	Serious Organised Crime Agency

19

The financial crisis

This is a difficult chapter to write. It would have been easy if all I had to do is give a run-down of the sequence of events that took place, or to lay blame at the door of 'greedy bankers', 'incompetent regulators' or 'inattentive governments'. But you already know about sub-prime mortgages, fancy derivatives and relaxed overseers. What I need to do is go behind the obvious and explore the underlying causes. These lie in the rather opaque and confused land of psychology, and in the area of the structure of organisations and systems.

While I will still provide the highlights of the crisis, so you will learn what happened to Lehman Brothers, Northern Rock, etc., they will be set in the much wider context of people factors. There are two aspects to this: (a) people behaving in irrational ways, and (b) people behaving in entirely rational ways from their perspective, given their incentives, but which resulted in a stupid/irrational outcome for the system as a whole.

The autistic mathematicians and the autistic financial economists[1]

The financial centres of the world hire thousands of people every year who are great at maths and mathematical economics. Some have degrees in engineering or physics, others in pure mathematics, economics or even rocket science. They are highly respected, usually have PhDs and can bamboozle you with their mastery of algebraic formulae and mental gymnastics. The pity is that they are

---

[1] In the following I am not implying that all mathematicians and economists are autistic in the medical sense of being unable to understand the emotions of others and have difficulty in social interaction; merely that they have a tendency to fail to properly include human emotions and other human traits such as cognitive and memory limitations in drawing conclusions about decision making and thus how financial markets work, while placing too much emphasis on cold, hard maths, assuming complete human rationality.

applying their skills to an area of intellectual endeavour, called finance, which is not fundamentally mathematical. As the great investors, such as Warren Buffett and Peter Lynch, both with decades of experience, tell us[2], all the mathematics you need was picked up at school by the time you were 14. They may be exaggerating to make a point, but what the mathophiles are failing to appreciate is that finance is a multifaceted discipline, in which the largest contribution is from the study of human psychology: humans acting in rational and irrational ways as individuals, and humans acting in groups in rational and irrational ways.

So, the mathematicians turn up at the financial centres on large salaries and they impress their bosses, the leaders of the banks and other institutions, who fail to fully take on board the assumptions behind the algebra. But, by golly, they know an impressive formula when they see one – or, at least they think they do. The self-confidence of the mathematician is further reinforced by the admiration and intellectual support of their closely related kin, the financial economists. These people have high algebraic skills too, and like to practise them as often as possible. There are many opportunities to converse in algebra with fellow autistic financial economists. There are regular seminars in the economics departments of universities the world over, where old and young economists start a presentation to fellow economists by making a number of assumptions about the world.

They simplify. They model, you see, so that the problem they are dealing with is tractable. In too many cases, in reality what they are doing is rushing to the bit that they really want to do (the bit they can cope with), where everything is neat and tidy, without too many messy human factors – that is, to use algebra to show an encapsulating view of the world. They love to show off modelling skill with algebra. So they spend one minute making assumptions about how humans behave. Usually these 'humans' are wonderfully rational, amazing calculating machines capable of absorbing infinite amounts of information and then ordering and processing it to make rational decisions – just as an economist would.

So, one minute for assumptions and then 49 minutes algebra, leaving 10 for questions. Ah great! Heaven. It does not matter that the assumptions might be a little unrealistic – look at the quality of the 'analysis'. The room is full of fellow blinkered followers of models, except for a few, who sit at the back and, if they are feeling brave, timidly suggest that perhaps the Emperor does not have many clothes on. The assumptions do not fit their everyday experience, it just does

---

[2] See either Arnold, G. (2009) *The Financial Times Guide to Value Investing*, Financial Times Prentice Hall, or Arnold, G. (2011) *The Great Investors: Lessons on Investing from the Master Traders*, Financial Times Prentice Hall.

not feel right. But those people are quickly silenced. Don't they understand that you have to model the world in a simplistic way, so that you can understand it? 'But', the brave soul might say 'if the assumptions and subsequent models leave out vital human factors, such as limited cognitive processing ability, the power of emotions to corrode rational decision making, and the all too apparent failings of individual and collective memory, will they reflect the way people actually behave in market places?' The rest of the room coughs and many have patronising thoughts about the inadequacy of the questioner's thinking. He or she will get it eventually – one day developing the ability to suspend disbelief.

What we have here is cognitive dissonance. The financial economists have a long-held view of the way people and the markets behave while many of the rest of us may see things differently. If we try to inject the thought of irrational actions into the economist's debate they suffer pain, anxiety, frustration as their deeply imbedded beliefs are challenged by clearly relevant facts. Many of the better ones have now taken on board the importance of human psychology and sociological studies, most have not. Furthermore, it is mathematical whizzes who tend to be hired in the financial centres.

Universities are not the only place for rational algebraic debate among financial economists. They have conferences all over the world where they gather, and then mutually reinforce their belief in the rightness of their methodological approaches. They have journals into which the most 'sophisticated' papers, in terms of mathematical prowess, have greater chance of inclusion. Those that focus on the 'soft' disciplines, with few formulae, are relegated to the low-ranking journals.

The products of the algebra-loving factories, products in terms of both ideas and trained disciples, are now powerfully positioned throughout the world. Not only were the disciples hired by banks, but these kind of thinkers were also recruited by the very best central banks, regulatory agencies, credit rating agencies and think tanks. The brightest of them gradually learn to moderate the stances they were taught at their prestigious *alma mater*, and increasingly become more multifaceted, multi-disciplinary. After all, they know from their own family life and simple observation on the street that people do not obey mathematical rules or the economist's model. Or, at least not consistently. Those trained as economists have a greater opportunity to become more disciplinary-inclusive than the mathematicians hired straight into the financial centres. These poor souls have less time than the economists to see the place of mathematics in a wider perspective.

Maths, it has to be acknowledged, is a useful tool, but only one tool among many. Charlie Munger, a great investor and a great thinker, says that we should beware of 'a man with a hammer' because such a man sees every problem as a nail. The rocket scientists hired by the banks and those that rely on them (supposedly overseeing them) should have more intellectual tools in the toolbox, ranging from the idea of the madness of crowds to the psychological effect of an incentive system.

Here I provide two brief examples of the over-reliance on simplistic models to make billion (or trillion) dollar decisions. You may detect a few more instances later in the chapter where models fail to capture the complexity of human-driven decision making as I run through the events of 2007 and 2008.

Example **MODELLING DEFAULT RATES ON SECURITISED LOANS AND BONDS**

David Li wrote a paper that was published in the Journal of Fixed Income in 2000.[3] This was very influential because it provided a neat model for pricing collateralised debt obligations (CDOs). These are explained in much more detail later, but for now you need to know that they are a kind of securitised bond (see Chapter 11), with the security being provided by debts owed, usually mortgage debt. Thus the holders of mortgage-based CDOs ultimately receive a return from the repayment of monthly mortgage amounts and borrowers redeeming their mortgages. I say 'ultimately' because CDOs were often (mostly) constructed from other securitised bonds, which get their income from mortgage payers.

The right to receive this flow of income needed to be valued, so that the holders, which were generally banks as well as some other financial institutions, could value their assets and estimate profits made over a period. The value of debt owed to you depends on the likelihood of the borrowers defaulting. David Li provided a formula useful for estimating CDO value without having to establish the likelihood of repayment from each of the thousands of mortgage payers. His short-cut was to use the market prices of credit default swaps (CDSs) (see Chapter 15) and the prices of bonds, that relate to that CDO. Now that investment bankers had a quick and easy way of valuing CDOs they could really go to town selling them and holding them on their balance sheets. From virtually nothing in 2000 the market grew to issue over $550 billion of CDOs per year by 2006, and had over $4,700 billion outstanding (for comparison,

[3] Li, D. X. (2000) 'On default correlation: A copula function approach', *Journal of Fixed Income*, March, Vol. 9, pp. 43–55.

UK annual GDP is around $2,000 billion and the total balance sheet capital of any nation's banks is far less). The CDS market was also boosted from under $1,000 billion of outstanding CDSs in 2000 to over $62,000 billion in 2007 (more than the output of goods and services for the entire world for one year).

It was not just the investment banks that adopted the formula; bond investors took comfort from it when deciding how much to invest, as did commercial banks from around the world who piled into US CDOs to obtain the high yield they were offering. Even more worrying, the rating agencies and the financial regulators used the model.

The limitations of the formula were available for scrutiny, but few bothered to look as they excitedly booked 'profits' (and bonuses) from creating, dealing and holding CDOs. The problem was that these reported profits were largely illusory because they failed to take account of the true risk. The inputs to the formula relied on obtaining numbers for default rates and the correlation between two or more credit risks, such as between two or more asset-backed securitised bonds held by a CDO. The mathematicians naturally measured these default rates and correlations over recent years and *assumed* that these were the relevant numbers for future-orientated estimations. They *assumed* that correlation was constant rather than volatile, ignoring the warnings of leading statisticians and experienced derivative dealers that asset prices can switch from low correlation to being very highly correlated when prices are falling across the board. The problem was that the early and mid-2000s were unusually benign for mortgage holders. Interest rates were down to very low levels and house prices were on a rising trend, and so very few defaulted. There was also low correlation between defaults – it was rare for all the different housing markets in America to be down at the same time, or so they thought.

You cannot blame the mathematicians, they are not trained to have the wider, longer-history perspective. They do formulas and calculations, not the soft stuff. Even if the mathematicians had qualms about the model's limitations, they had bosses who wanted to hold more and more CDOs, CDSs, etc. because they *seemed* so profitable. The problem is the bosses did not understand the maths and how the model worked – a single correlation number came out of the end of a black-box computer calculation and that was enough for them to punt a billion or two of the company's money. Thus we had a position where the balance sheet values of trillions of dollars worth of financial instruments were dependent on the assumption of a continuing benign housing market. When house prices stopped rising and defaults increased the value of CDOs fell.

Why did the credit rating agencies rate CDOs as low default risk, despite the obvious dangers in the assumptions? Well that is another story. One that will be addressed later in the chapter. (Hint: they made a lot of money from rating CDOs. They also employed a lot of algebra lovers.) For now here is a comment from Kai Gilkes, who worked for 10 years at rating agencies: 'Everyone was pinning their hopes on house prices continuing to rise. When they stopped rising, pretty much everyone was caught on the wrong side, because the sensitivity to house prices was huge... Why didn't rating agencies build in some cushion for this sensitivity to a house-price-depreciation scenario? Because if they had, they would have never rated a single mortgage-backed CDO.'[4]

To be fair to David Li, he did try to warn people that it was false reassurance to assume that correlations on default were always going to remain the same as they had been in the benign conditions of the late 1990s and early 2000s: 'Very few people understand the essence of the model... The most dangerous part is when people believe everything coming out of it'.[5] As so often with these models the originators provide plenty of warnings and provisos, but somehow the bankers and other followers tend to ignore them or fail to understand the subtleties.

Example | **MODELLING DAILY VALUE AT RISK**

Banks hold a very wide range of assets from corporate loans to complicated derivatives, and they bear a number of obligations. Senior managers of banks can lose track as to the extent to which the firm as a whole is exposed to risk. One division might be building up large holdings of bonds while another is selling credit default swaps, and yet another is packaging up mortgage bonds and selling CDOs. Perhaps what one division is doing will offset the risk that another is taking on. On the other hand, it might be that risk is merely compounded by the combination of

▶

---

[4] Li quoted in Salmon, F. (2009) 'Recipe for Disaster: The Formula that Killed Wall Street', *Wired Magazine*, 23 February 2009.
[5] Quoted in Salmon (2009).

positions. Each day the mix of assets and liabilities changes and therefore the risk exposure changes.

Back in the 1990s some bankers[6] thought it would be a good idea to produce a single number that encapsulated the overall risk profile of the bank each evening. The senior managers could look at that and be reassured that they were not taking excessive risk. If the number started to look dangerously high then they could instruct a reweighting of assets and obligations until a safety margin was restored. The measure that they came up with is called **value at risk**, or **VaR**, which asks 'if tomorrow is a bad day (e.g. a number of different asset classes such as shares and bonds, fall in market price significantly) what is the minimum that the bank will lose?' VaR is an estimate of the loss on a portfolio over a period of time (usually 24 hours is chosen) that will be *exceeded*[7] with a given frequency, e.g. a frequency of 1 day out of 100, or 5 days out of 100. Another way of looking at the frequency element is called the confidence level. Thus with a 99 per cent confidence level set the VaR might turn out to be $100 million. Therefore for 'one-day VaR' there is a 1 per cent chance that the portfolio could lose more than $100 million in 24 hours. A 95 per cent confidence level means that there is a 95 per cent chance that the loss will be less than the derived figure of, say, $16 million for a day, and a 5 per cent chance that it will be greater than $16 million.

So, how does a bank calculate VaR estimates? They need some numbers and some assumptions. One assumption often made is that returns on a security (share, derivative, bond, etc.) follow a particular distribution. The usual assumption is the normal distribution where there is a large clustering of probabilities of returns around the average expected return and then very small probabilities at the extremes ('thin tails'). Also, the distribution of possible outturns is symmetrical about the mean – there is the same chance of being, say, £3 million above the average expected return as being £3 million below it – see Exhibit 19.1 for a

---

[6] JPMorgan led on this.

[7] Many books and articles get this wrong and say the VaR is a measure of the *maximum* amount of money at risk rather than a level that will be exceeded. In reality the loss can go much higher than the VaR figure. The VaR figure is better seen as a minimum loss on a bad day. Obviously, this misunderstanding and misrepresentation would have been read by many bankers and therefore contributed to their failure to understand the extent of their bank's risk exposure.

normal distribution of probabilities, a bell-shaped symmetrical curve. The usual source of data, whether combined with a normal distribution assumption or not, is a long time series of an historical data set of daily return data for the securities – then the mathematicians assume that this represents the future distribution of returns. Another important source of information is the calculation of the extent to which asset returns moved together in the past. Then it is assumed that these correlations remain true for future estimations.

Exhibit 19.1 shows a possible output from using VaR. On the right-hand side the return numbers increase but the probability of earning those high returns decreases significantly the further we move away from the average expected return. The probabilities for returns below average are symmetrical with those above average, in this case, where we assume 'normality'. (If we used real past return data the distribution may not be quite normal and the maths for calculating the confidence level becomes more complicated, but it can still be handled. Skewed distributions just create more fun for the mathematicians.) You can read off the 99 per cent chance of not losing more than the amount marked by the 1 per cent line. If the 1 per cent line is at $100 million then one day out of 100 we would lose more than $100 million, in theory.

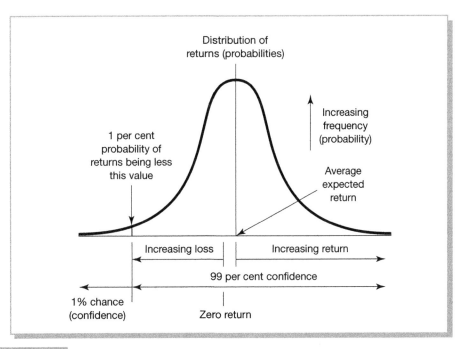

Exhibit 19.1   A VaR analysis assuming a normal distribution of the probabilities of return on an asset or collection of assets

A key assumption is that the past data have a very close bearing on the future probabilities. Even using the normality method you need past data to estimate the size of the various probabilities. So, you might gather data from the previous three or five years. If unusual/infrequent events are not present in that dataset you might be missing some extreme positive or negative possibilities. One of these events might have a massive impact on risk but might be missed if the data set is limited to a period of stability. Indeed it might be missed even if the dataset is extensive if the event is very rare. An influential writer on derivatives and market player, Nicholas Taleb,[8] was warning us long before the crisis that the mathematicians were not allowing for the possibility of extreme events (called black swans) – that the tails of the distribution are in fact much bigger, 'fatter', than generally supposed, because extreme things hit us more often then we anticipate. There are 'high-impact rare events', often caused by human reactions to apparently insignificant triggers; reactions such as exuberance, fear and panic. Asset returns and liabilities, which appeared to be uncorrelated, suddenly all move together to a much greater extent than short-memory players in financial markets expect. There are risks out there that we did not know existed, until it is too late. The more experienced old-hands know that unexpected and unimaginable events shape the markets, leaving them with question marks concerning the extent to which they can trust three year historical data to be the only guide.

VaR led many senior bankers into a false sense of security prior to the crisis. They were thus emboldened to double and triple their bets on securities such as mortgage CDOs because they appeared to produce high profits without raising VaR much. Many regulators insisted on the disclosure of VaR. Indeed, under the Basel capital rules for banks VaR could be used as an argument for lowering capital requirements. Banks jumped at the chance of lowering capital buffers so as to increase return on equity (see Chapters 3 and 6) – they leveraged themselves up. They particularly liked to stock up on 'high-quality' mortgage-based CDOs because the model told them that they had trivial VaR and so they were required to hold only trivial capital reserves. Yes, the regulators have much to answer for, too. They placed far too much faith in these mathematical models. They even allowed banks to do their own calculations of risk exposure, and more or less accepted that for setting capital limits.

Prior to the summer of 2007 banks tended to use historical evidence going back between one and five years to estimate VaR. By then a large part of their exposure was to the mortgage market. In the mid-2000s this had been as placid as the

[8] Taleb, N.N. (2001) *Fooled by Randomness: The hidden role of chance in life and in the markets*, Texere Publishing;. Taleb, N.N. (2007) *The Black Swan: The Impact of the Highly Improbable*, Random House.

sea was when the Titanic was crossing the Atlantic – no trouble encountered for day after day. It would seem that VaR gave little indication of real likely losses. For example, in the autumn of 2007 Bear Stearns reported an average VaR of $30 million[9] which is tiny for a bank with so many assets. It could withstand days and days of such losses and barely notice. So according to VaR it was hardly at risk at all. And yet within weeks it was bust, losing $8,000 million of value. As the complete failure of the bank approached, the VaR number did rise slightly to $60 million because it started to incorporate data for the more recent days when securities became more volatile as the market mayhem started – but it still had lots of older placid data pushing the number down. It turned out that 'highly unlikely events' such as a correlated fall in house prices all over the US, and the fall in market prices of derivatives and bonds can all happen at the same time. The average person on the street could have told them that, but these mathematicians and financial economists could not see past their complex algebra. The guys over at Merrill Lynch were perplexed: 'In the past these AAA CDO securities had never experienced a significant loss in value'.[10] But how long was that 'past' – if they could find a decade of data they would have been lucky, because these instruments were so young. As the crisis got under way most of the large banks experienced losses that should only happen once in 1,000 years (according to their models) day after day. In their language these were six-sigma (standard deviation) events, which were virtually impossible from their faithful-to-the-algebra perspective. Indeed, in August 2007 the market experienced several 25-sigma events – these should happen only once every 14 billion years, that is, since the Big Bang! How confusing for them – the model let them down when it really mattered. Triana (2009) likens VaR to buying a car with an air bag that protects you 99 per cent of the time, that is when conditions are moderate, but if you have a serious crash it fails.

Bear Stearns understood the problems with VaR. Take this statement from their filing with the Securities and Exchange Commission in February 29 2008:

> VaR has inherent limitations, including reliance on historical data, which may not accurately predict future market risk, and the quantitative risk information generated is limited by the parameters established in creating the models. There can be no assurance that actual losses occurring on any one day arising from changes in market conditions will not exceed the VaR amounts shown below or that such losses will not occur more than once in 20 trading days.

---

[9] Triana, P. (2009) *Lecturing Birds on Flying: Can mathematical theories destroy the financial markets?* John Wiley and Sons, Inc.
[10] Triana (2009).

> VaR is not likely to accurately predict exposures in markets that exhibit sudden fundamental changes or shifts in market conditions or established trading relationships. Many of the Company's hedging strategies are structured around likely established trading relationships and, consequently, those hedges may not be effective and VaR models may not accurately predict actual results. Furthermore, VaR calculated for a one-day horizon does not fully capture the market risk of positions that cannot be liquidated in a one-day period.'[11]

Despite this list of doubts they had used it because everyone else did (and the regulators allowed them to get away with it):

> However, the Company believes VaR models are an established methodology for the quantification of risk in the financial services industry despite these limitations. VaR is best used in conjunction with other financial disclosures in order to assess the Company's risk profile.[12]

Being 'established' is not the same as being best suited to the task. They are basically saying: 'If all the other fellas are using it to leverage up profits and bonuses, why can't we?' This is not very scientific, no matter how much algebra you use to bamboozle.

Once faith in VaR had evaporated those lending to banks became afraid that the risk metrics they publicly announced under-reported their real exposure. They took the action that you or I would take when told that borrowers might default on what they owe: stop lending any more and try to call in old loans. The problem is the entire banking system was a complex web of loans to each other and once confidence had gone the whole system collapsed. Notice the key words here are not quantifiable – 'afraid', 'confidence' – these fuzzy things are just as important to understand about finance as the maths, if not more so.

Reflexivity

George Soros is the most famous and the most respected of the hedge fund managers, who made a fortune for himself and the backers of his Quantum Fund. However, his first love and abiding passion is economic philosophy. Indeed it is

---

[11] http://www.sec.gov/Archives/edgar/data/777001/000091412108000345/be12550652-10q.txt
[12] Ibid.

his understanding of the importance of human thought on market prices that made him and his investors so much money. At the heart of his ideas is reflexivity in markets, in which the behaviour of market prices results from a two-way feedback mechanism with participants (e.g. investors) moving prices and fundamentals in response to their (faulty) perceptions, and their perceptions, in turn, formed by market movements and fundamentals. Knowledge of this human tendency can help identify bubbles and irrational downward spirals.

Early in life Soros developed his philosophy of how people in social structures operate as a group to occasionally lead the economic (or political or social) fundamentals away from a near-to-equilibrium state to a far-from-equilibrium state. His observations and anticipations of financial market movements are but a sub-set of manifestations of his theory of 'reflexivity'. The same philosophical base can be used to describe and analyse, for example, the movement of a society from an open, rule-of-law, democratic form to one increasingly closed and authoritarian. It can also be used to describe and explain individual human interactions such as love and hate, amongst a host of other applications.

In contrast to the 'rational man model' assumed by most economists Soros observed that decisions are based on people's perception or interpretation of the situation. Furthermore, their decisions can change the situation, alter the fundamentals (e.g. the price of houses in a country or the price of dot.com shares). Then changes in the fundamentals thus caused are liable to change the perceptions of individuals. And so on.

Soros was born in Hungary in 1930. Living under both Nazi and Communist regimes provided Soros with a healthy respect for the objective aspect of reality. His experiences of living in the far-from-equilibrium conditions of first the German and then the Russian occupation of his country provided insight which played an important role in preparing him for a successful career as a hedge fund manager. He, more than most, became aware that stability is a commodity that come and goes.

When admitted to the London School of Economics he chose to study economics but quickly found it a trial for two reasons: (a) he was poor at maths, and economics was increasingly becoming a mathematical discipline; and (b) he was more interested in addressing the foundations of economics, such as the assumptions of perfect knowledge, while his teachers preferred algebraic constructs built on such time-honoured assumptions.

The bright spots in his university experience were his encounters with Professor Karl Popper, who supplied inspiring ideas and engaged with Soros seriously.

> Karl Popper... maintained that reason is not capable of establishing the truth of generalisations beyond doubt. Even scientific laws cannot be verified because it is impossible to derive universally valid generalisations from individual observations, however numerous, by deductive logic. Scientific method works best by adopting an attitude of comprehensive scepticism: Scientific laws should be treated as hypotheses which are provisionally valid unless and until they are falsified... He asserted that scientific laws cannot be verified... One nonconforming instance may be sufficient to destroy the validity of the generalisation, but no amount of conforming instances are sufficient to verify a generalisation beyond any doubt.'[13]

The economists' need to maintain the assumption of perfect knowledge on the part of economic actors directly contradicted Popper's contention that understanding by humans is inherently imperfect. Yet economists kept trying to create a discipline with generalisations comparable with those of Isaac Newton in physics, resulting in a discipline increasingly convoluted and mathematical.

In rejecting the standard economists' model and influenced by Popper, Soros started developing a framework of human behaviour in which misconceptions and misinterpretations play a major role in shaping the course of history. Market participants do not base their decisions on knowledge alone because biased perceptions have a powerful impact not only on market prices but also the fundamentals that those prices are supposed to reflect. Note for now the two influences of biased perceptions – many readers of Soros' work only take on board the first and thus glibly conclude that he is not saying anything particularly original – the original bit is the second element:

- First element: influencing market prices.

- Second element: influencing the fundamentals those prices are supposed to reflect.

Classical economics

The Enlightenment view of the world is that reality lies there, passively waiting to be discovered. Reason acts as a searchlight to illuminate that reality. Thus, there is a separation between, on the one hand, people's thoughts and understanding of the world and, on the other, the object. The thinking agents cannot

[13] Soros, G. (2008) 'The crash of 2008 and what it means', *Public Affairs*, New York, pp. 35–6.

influence the underlying reality. Thus in natural science we can explain and pre-dict the course of events with reasonable certainty. Economic and other social areas of 'study' – Soros does not permit the use of the word 'science' with social disciplines – tried to imitate Newtonian physics and develop 'laws' to describe the fundamental processes. To make their models work in a 'scientific' manner economists would simplify reality by making assumptions, for example, that market participants base their decisions on perfect knowledge, or that supply and demand curves could be taken as independently given (with supply not influencing demand, and demand not influencing supply, except through the classical interaction on the economist's diagram).

For the physical scientists it is obvious that to gain knowledge there must be a separation between thoughts and their objective. The facts must be independent of the statements made about them. So, the Earth will move around the Sun in a fairly predictable pattern regardless of what the observer thinks about the move-ment. Many economists follow a sequence of logic analogous to the physics model in trying to describe economic outcomes – see Exhibit 19.2.

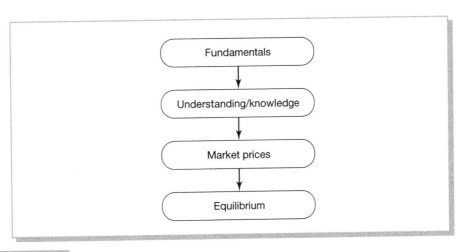

Exhibit 19.2 Classical economics

When we move away from the physical sciences we frequently encoun-ter a problem. In social phenomena it is often difficult to separate fact from thoughts. The decision maker in trying to make sense of the world attempts to be a detached observer, but can never fully overcome the fact that they are part of the situation they seek to comprehend. For example, people and human organisations, such as lending institutions, try to understand the underlying facts about the housing market, but in doing so – and in taking action – they influence the reality of the house supply, demand and prices. Under the classical economics paradigm demand and supply curves are supposed to determine the market price. But, it seems reasonable to suggest that in many cases these curves are themselves subject to market influences, in which case prices cease to be uniquely determined. We end up with fluctuating prices rather than equilibrium.

Another example: it is thought that the markets are on the look-out for a recession looming over the horizon, that they anticipate it. Soros takes a different viewpoint, believing that it is more correct to say that markets help to precipitate recessions. That:

- markets are always biased in one direction or another; and

- markets can influence the events they anticipate.

For example, it would be difficult to argue that the reaction of the financial markets to news coming out of the US residential mortgage market in 2008 did *not* influence events to take us into recession. Similarly the spread of investment pessimism in Europe in 2011 contributed to the downturn.

Soros' paradigm

So, the widely held paradigm that financial markets tend towards equilibrium is both false and misleading. Soros contends that, first, financial markets never reflect underlying reality accurately, and, second, that, occasionally, these distortions affect the fundamentals that market prices are supposed to reflect. These ideas provide profound insight into both the setting of prices and the movement of underlyings.

The economists' classic model does allow for deviations from the theoretical equilibrium, but only in a random manner, and the deviations will be corrected in a fairly short time frame. Soros says that market prices do not reach the theoretical equilibrium point; they are in a continual state of change relative to the theoretical equilibrium.

Participants in the financial markets have expectations about events. These expectations affect the shapes of both the supply and the demand curves. Decisions to buy or to sell an asset are based on expectations about future prices and future prices are, in turn, contingent on buy or sell decisions in the present.

The act of thinking by market participants has a dual role. On the one hand, they are trying to understand the situation; on the other, their understanding (or misunderstanding) produces actions that influence the course of events. The two roles interfere with each other. The participants' imperfect understanding leads to actions and the course of events bears the imprint of that imperfection.

The term 'reflexive' comes from a feature of the French language, where the subject and the object is the same. It also means reflection (not reflexes).

We are all taught to think in terms of events as a sequence of facts – one set of facts leads to another set of facts, and so on, in a never-ending chain. However, this is not how the part of the world affected by humans actually works. The facts are first subject to the participants' thinking, then the participants' thinking connects to the next set of facts. As can be seen in Exhibit 19.3 market participants look at the fundamentals through a fog of misconceptions, misunderstandings and misjudgments. They have biased perceptions. In trying to understand – 'the cognitive function' – they make mistakes. In their biased state they then take action – 'the manipulative function' – and this moves market prices.

So far, so conventional: standard economics allows for the less well-informed actors to make misinterpretations and poor decisions because markets are not perfect, and for them to do so as a herd. Soros' insight is that, rather than a return to theoretical equilibrium as the participants realise their errors (or the errors are merely part of a large set of off-setting random events), the distortions in market prices create distortions in the fundamentals – the 'prevailing trend' itself is altered – and simultaneously the perceptions of participants is altered in response to the fundamentals changing, resulting in an indeterminate outcome, as perceptions feed off the course of events and the course of events feeds off perceptions. We get indeterminacy in both the cognitive and manipulating functions because of the reflexive connection between them.

In most cases the reflexive interaction is relatively insignificant, because there are forces at play that bring thinking and reality together, such as people learning from experience or new evidence coming to light. These are termed 'near-equilibrium conditions' and the impact of reflexivity can be disregarded. In these cases classical economic theory applies, and the divergence between perceptions and reality can be ignored as mere noise.

Occasionally, however, the reflexive interaction can lead to massive market distortions, with no tendency for them to come together – 'far-from-equilibrium conditions' – leading to boom/bust sequences. In this case, the theories developed around the assumption of equilibrium become irrelevant. We are presented with a one-directional process in which changes in both perceptions and reality are irreversible (at least for a period). Just as mutation has a role in biology so misconceptions and mistakes play a role in human affairs.

When thinking about Exhibit 19.3 try to picture the stages presented following one another so quickly that the whole thing becomes a blur of concurrently occurring (and cross-impacting) cognitive function, manipulative function, market prices and fundamentals. People taking decisions make an impact on the situation (the manipulative function), which changes the situation, which is liable to change their perceptions (the cognitive function). 'The two functions operate concurrently, not sequentially. If the feedback were sequential, it would produce a uniquely determined sequence leading from facts to perceptions to new facts and then new perceptions, and so on. It is the fact that the two processes occur simultaneously that creates an indeterminacy in both the participants' perceptions and the actual course of events.'[14]

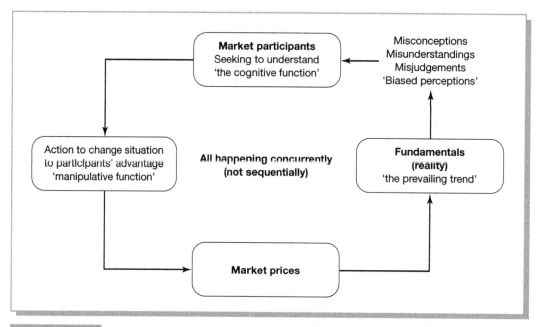

Exhibit 19.3   A two-way reflexive connection between perception and reality

If we take the stock market, for example, we observe that people trade shares in anticipation of future prices, but those prices are contingent on the investors' expectations. We cannot assume that expectations in the market is a form of knowledge in the same way that a physical scientist can predict the motions of the stars – the movement of the stars is truly independent of the expectations of the scientist. In the absence of knowledge, participants bring in an element of judgement or bias into their decision making. Thus, outcomes diverge from expectations.

Soros uses 'equilibrium' as a figure of speech. He does not see a stable equilibrium from which deviates the occasional boom/bust process. Equilibrium should

[14] Soros, G. (2008), p. 10.

be seen as a moving target because market prices get buffeted by the fundamentals they are supposed to reflect.

Bubbles

Soros sees bubbles as consisting of two components:

1 a trend based on reality;

2 a misconception or misinterpretation of that trend.

Usually financial markets correct misconceptions, but, occasionally misconceptions can lead to the inflation of a bubble. This happens when the misconception reinforces the prevailing trend. Then a two-way feedback might occur in which the prevailing trend, now puffed up by the initial misconception, then reinforces the misconception. Then the gap between reality and the market's interpretation of reality can grow and grow. In maintaining the growth in the gap the participants' bias needs a short circuit so that it can continue to affect the fundamentals. This is usually provided by some form of leveraged debt or equity.

At some point the size of the gap becomes so large that it is unsustainable. The misconception is recognised for what it is, and participants become disillusioned. The trend is reversed. As asset prices fall the value of collateral that supported much of the loans for the purchases melts away, causing margin calls and distress selling. Eventually, there is an overshoot in the other direction.

The boom/bust sequence is asymmetrical. It slowly inflates and accelerates, followed by a more rapid reversal. Soros says that there are eight stages to the boom/bust sequence. We will take the example where the underlying trend is earnings per share ('the prevailing trend') and the participants' perceptions (cognitive function) are reflected in share prices through the manipulative function, i.e. they buy or sell shares pushing the prices up or down. In turn, the change in share prices may affect both the participants' bias and the underlying trend.

Thus, share prices are determined by two factors:

1 the underlying trend – earnings per share (eps);

2 the prevailing bias.

Both (1) and (2) are influenced by share prices, hence a feedback loop.

In Exhibit 19.4 the divergence between the two curves is an indication of the underlying bias. Soros said that the true relationship is more complex than we are representing here because the earnings curve includes, as well as the underlying trend, the influence of share prices on that trend. Thus the prevailing bias is expressed only partially by the divergence between the two curves – it is also partially already reflected in those curves.

Stage 1 – no trend recognition

The underlying trend is gently sloping upwards, but is not yet recognised.

Stage 2 – recognising the trend and reinforcement

The trend is recognised by market participants. This changes perceptions about the underlying. The newly developing positive prevailing bias pushes shares along. At this stage the change in share prices may or may not affect the underlying trend, i.e. the level of earnings of companies. If it does not then the reflexive boom does not materialise – the correction in share prices leads to the loss of the underlying trend, i.e. eps do not continue to rise abnormally.

If the underlying trend is affected by the rise in share prices then we have the beginning of a self-reinforcing process, and we start to move into a far-from-equilibrium state. The underlying trend becomes increasingly dependent on the prevailing bias and the bias becomes increasingly exaggerated.

Stage 3 – testing

Both the prevailing bias and the trend are tested by external shocks – there may be several tests, but here we show only one. Prices suffer setbacks. If the test causes the bias and trend to fail to survive then the potential bubble dies.

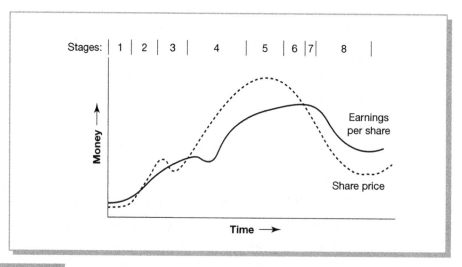

Exhibit 19.4   The boom/bust model

Stage 4 – period of acceleration

Survival through the tests makes both the bias and the trend stronger. The underlying trend (eps) becomes increasingly influenced by share prices. Also the rise in share prices becomes increasingly dependent on the prevailing bias. Both the bias and the trend become seemingly unshakable. Conviction is so strong that share price rises are no longer affected by setbacks in the earning trend. Now far-from-equilibrium conditions become firmly established – the normal rules no longer apply.

Stage 5 – unsustainability

Exaggerated expectations reach such a peak that reality can no longer sustain them. This is 'the moment of truth'.

Stage 6 – twilight period

Participants realise that their prevailing bias is high and they lower their expectations. The trend may be sustained by inertia, but is no longer reinforced by belief, so it rises at a lower rate. This is the twilight period or period of stagnation – people no longer believe in the game, but continue to play.

Stage 7 – tipping point

The loss of belief eventually causes a reversal in the trend that had become ever more dependent on an ever stronger bias. When the trend reverses we have the crossover or tipping point.

Stage 8 – catastrophic downward acceleration

A downward trend reinforces the now negative prevailing bias – the gap between share price, as a reflection of expectations, and the eps levels is now negative. A crash occurs. Eventually the pessimism goes too far and the market stabilises.

Reflexivity does not follow a predetermined pattern

Soros emphasises that this is only one possible path resulting from the interplay of a trend and a prevailing bias. Some far-from-equilibrium reflexive situations follow this pattern of initial self-reinforcement, unsustainability of the gap between thinking and reality, followed by collapse, creating an historically significant event. But there are also reflexive interactions that correct themselves before they reach boom proportions, and thus do not become historically significant. There is nothing determinate or compulsory about the boom/bust pattern. The process may be aborted at any time. Also, there are many other processes going on at the same time, for example, changes in other asset markets, changes in the regulatory environment, changes in the political or social environment. The various processes may interfere with one another leading to boom/bust sequences being hit by external shocks. There may be patterns that tend to repeat themselves in far-from-equilibrium situations, but the actual course of events is indeterminate and unique.

Applying reflexivity to the crisis[15]

The housing bubble of the 2000s is a sub-part of a much larger super-bubble that stretches back to the early 1980s.

Housing bubble

The US housing bubble followed the course described by Soros in his boom/bust model. Lax lending standards were supported by a prevailing misconception that the value of the collateral for the loans was not affected by the willingness to lend. Loans were packaged up into financial securities and sold on to unsuspecting investors around the world. Those securitised bonds issued in the early stages of the boom showed a low default rate on the underlying mortgages. Credit rating agencies based their estimates of future default rates on the recent benign past – another misconception. As house prices rose the rating agencies became even more relaxed as they rated CDOs. In trying to perceive future risks and returns all participants failed to recognise the impact that they, themselves, made.

While Wall Street was creating all these weird and obscure financial instruments mortgage originators became increasingly aggressive in encouraging ordinary people to take on the responsibilities of a mortgage. The value of a loan as a proportion of the value of a house got higher and higher. Towards the end of the boom people who had no job and nothing to put down as a deposit on a house were being granted mortgages. The attraction of fee income lies at the heart of this. The mortgage arrangers received a fee for arranging the mortgage regardless of what happened to the house owner thereafter; the banks received fees for arranging securitised bonds, and yet more fees for CDOs, and yet more fees for even more complex instruments.

But all of this was okay, if you believed that the value of homes and thus collateral for the loans was growing and would continue to grow. This belief, for a while, created its own fulfilment: faith in the housing market led to more loans; the additional demand for housing stimulated by the availability of cheap

[15] Other examples of reflexivity in action are described in Arnold, G. (2011) *Great Investors: Lessons on Investing from the Master Traders*, FT/Prentice Hall.

mortgages led to house prices rising, providing more collateral; confidence in the housing market rose due to the additional collateral and low rates of default on mortgages because home owners could easily refinance in a rising market to avoid default; more loans were forthcoming; and so on.

People became dependent on double-digit house price rises to finance their life-styles. As they withdrew housing 'equity' through remortgages the savings rate dropped below zero. When home owners became over extended and house prices stopped rising they had to cut back on remortgaging. There was a reduction in demand from both people moving and from people staying put and remortgaging. The moment of truth came in the spring of 2007 when New Century Financial Corp. went into bankruptcy. People started to ask questions: perhaps the value of the collateral for mortgages was not destined to rise forever and was artificially supported by the willingness of lenders to make fresh loans? If they stopped, per-haps much of the 'value' in houses would prove to be an illusion?

A twilight period followed when house prices were falling but participants continued to play the game – new mortgages were signed and securitisations created. In August 2007 there was a significant acceleration in downward price movements. Over the next year contagion spread from one segment of financial markets to another, until Lehman's collapse sparked a further downward lunge.

The super-bubble

The super-bubble also reached its tipping point in 2007–08. This reflexive proc-ess evolved over a period of a quarter of a century. The main prevailing trend was ever-more sophisticated methods of credit expansion, supported by the trend to globalisation and the trend towards the removal of regulations with increasing financial innovation.

The prevailing misconception was 'market fundamentalism', which promotes the notion that markets should be free to find their own level with very little intervention by regulators. Market fundamentalism became a guiding principle in the financial system in the early 1980s.

The long-term boom combined three major trends, each of which contained at least one defect:

■ *Trend 1 – Ever increasing credit expansion.* The long-term credit expansion was manifest in rising consumer loan to value of asset (house) ratios and the expansion of credit as a percentage of GDP. This trend has been helped by the authorities' response to any sign of economic downturn or threat to the banking system. Learning lessons from the Great Depression they were quick to stimulate the economy through counter-cyclical lower interest rates or loose fiscal policy, and if anything endangered the banks there would be bail-outs.

After a few years of intervention the participants started to think there was an asymmetry to the risk of credit expansion. If they expand credit (lower lending standards) and things go right, then the lenders are the winners. If they expand and things go wrong, then they will be bailed out by the authorities. This is an example of the moral hazard problem, in which the presence of a safety net encourages adverse behaviour.

High levels of leverage became normal. Indeed, banks, hedge funds and private equity firms thrived on it. Credit terms for car loans, credit card debt, commercial loans as well as mortgages all reached absurdly easy levels. Japan was another source of credit expansion. During its grindingly long recession it held interest rates near to zero. This encouraged the 'carry trade': international financial institutions borrow in yen and invest the borrowed funds elsewhere in the world at higher yields. The US was not alone. The love of leverage infected other economies from the UK to Spain.

■ *Trend 2 – Globalisation of financial markets.* The process of globalisation of financial markets accelerated with the petro-dollar recycling[16] in the 1970s, but it got a significant boost with Thatcherism and Reaganism in the 1980s. They saw globalisation of financial markets as a useful development because freeing up financial capital to move around the world makes it difficult for any state to intervene, to tax capital or to regulate it because it can evade such moves by transferring somewhere else. Financial capital was promoted to a privileged position. Governments often have to put the aspirations of their people in second place behind the requirements of international capital – we saw this in 2010–11 with the eurozone financial crisis as governments desperate to impress the financial markets with their stewardship of the economy cut budget deficits. The market fundamentalists, who dominated political and financial thinking in the quarter century until the 2007 crisis, thought that taking our lead from the markets was a good thing.

According to the market fundamentalists, globalisation was to bring about a level playing field. In reality the international financial system ended up in the hands of a consortium of financial authorities answerable to the developed countries. The whole system has favoured the US and the other developed countries at the centre of the financial system, while penalising the developing economies at the periphery. The 'Washington consensus' (IMF, World Bank, etc.) sought to impose strict market discipline on individual less-developed countries if they ran into difficulties. But when the Western financial system is threatened the rules are bent.

---

[16] The oil producing nations in OPEC put up the price of oil, producing massive inflows of cash which they then invested elsewhere in the world.

Furthermore the US has the benefit of the dollar being the main international reserve currency, accepted by central banks around the world – these organisations, such as the central bank of China, would often invest current account surpluses in US government and agency bonds. This permitted the US to intervene in markets to counter its downturns and financial crises – inflating credit – while other countries were forced to live within their means. Also, it was safer to hold assets at the centre, and thus the US sucked up the savings of the world as US consumers went on a spending spree. Perversely capital flowed from the less-developed world to the US.

▪ *Trend 3 – Progressive removal of financial regulations and the accelerating pace of financial innovation.* Between the end of World War II and the early 1980s banks and markets were strictly regulated. President Reagan, however, would refer to the 'magic of the marketplace' especially after market fundamentalism received a significant fillip from the manifest failures of communism and other forms of state intervention. An amazing array of new financial instruments was invented, and many were widely adopted. The more complicated the financial system became the less participants and regulators could understand what was going on.

Periodic financial crises over the quarter century (such as the Long-Term Capital Management crisis, the dot.com bubble crash, the 2001 terrorist attacks) served as tests of the prevailing trend and the prevailing misconception. When these tests were passed, the trend and the misconception were reinforced. Progressively, in an atmosphere of *laissez-faire*, the authorities lost control of the financial system and the super-bubble developed.

The US housing bubble brought the super-bubble to a point of unsustainability – both the trends and the misconceptions became unsustainable; then a tipping point was reached for both bubbles, with the sub-prime crisis acting merely as a trigger that released the unwinding of the super-bubble.

The flaw in the market fundamentalist view is that just because state intervention is subject to error does not mean that markets are perfect.

> The cardinal contention of the theory of reflexivity is that all human constructs are flawed. Financial markets do not necessarily tend towards equilibrium; left to their own devices they are liable to go to extremes of euphoria and despair. For that reason they are not left to their own devices; they have been put in the charge of financial authorities whose job it is to supervise them and regulate them… The belief that markets tend

towards equilibrium is directly responsible for the current turmoil; it encouraged the regulators to abandon their responsibility and rely on the market mechanism to correct its own excesses.[17]

Some of the more proximate causes of the crisis

The decade leading up to 2008 was unprecedented in terms of innovation in the financial markets. But alongside some good innovations there was an out-of-control complexity, combined with ignorance, reliance on a narrow range of mental models and misaligned incentives.

Low interest rates

The September 2001 attack on the World Trade Center led to a loss of confidence which compounded the cautiousness of consumers and investors following the dot.com bust of 2000. Recession and deflation was a possibility and so interest rates were lowered in the West. In the US, short-term rates stayed around 1 per cent between 2002 and 2004. Deflation did not occur and the rate of interest was frequently less than the inflation rate. Interest rates were further lowered by the huge amount of Chinese savings being invested in US government Treasury bills and bonds.

Low interest rates encouraged a boom in house prices, and in economic output. Low interest rates also led to a 'search for yield': investors and bankers discontented with low returns on deposits and safe investments became prepared to accept more risk to obtain higher rates of return.

Innovation in the mortgage market

In the US, two government-sponsored enterprises (GSEs), Fannie Mae and Freddie Mac, were at the centre of mortgage securitisation at the start of the 1990s. They bought bundles of mortgages from mortgage originators (e.g. banks) and then created and sold mortgage-backed securities (MBSs), a type of asset-backed security (ABS). The GSEs guaranteed the interest and principle on these MBSs. And given that the government was likely to rescue its creations if they ran into trouble a guarantee from the GSEs was taken to be as good as a guarantee from the US Treasury.

---

[17] Soros, G. (2008), pp. 94–104.

The GSEs would not take just any old mortgage. They usually insisted that the house owner owed no more than 80 per cent of the value of the house (loan-to-value ratio, LTV) and the maximum size of mortgage was $417,000. They also investigated the borrower's income, state of employment, history of bad debts (if any) and amounts of other assets. In other words, this system is pretty safe because only the most creditworthy enter it. It was for 'prime' mortgages only.

Now for some innovation: in the early 1990s new lenders emerged who were willing to lend to people who did not qualify as prime borrowers. They would often employ independent firms of mortgage brokers to persuade families to take out a mortgage. The brokers received a commission for each one sold. The number of sub-prime lenders grew significantly over the 12 years to 2005 and the proportion of mortgages that were sub-prime rose to over 20 per cent. The rise of this market attracted the interest of the big names on Wall Street (e.g. Goldman Sachs, Merrill Lynch, Lehman Brothers, Bear Stearns and Morgan Stanley) who bought up sub-prime lenders. These borrowers could be charged higher interest rates than prime borrowers. They could also be charged large fees for setting up the loan. The sub-prime market boomed. By 2005 the largest US mortgage provider was the sub-prime lender Countrywide Financial, which had grown fast from 1980s obscurity.

A key characteristic of the new lenders is that they lent at different interest rates to different groups of mortgagees classified on the basis of likelihood-of-default statistical models. These relied heavily on the borrower's **credit score**. These scores were calculated by examining a number of borrower characteristics, the most important of which became the absence (or low incidence) of missed or delayed payments on previous debts. The statisticians had discovered a high correlation between credit scores and defaults on mortgages in the 1990s and so it made sense to them to carry on with them in the 2000s. The problem is that the statisticians had not fully taken on board the extent to which mortgages in the 2000s were different to mortgages in the 1990s, particularly at the sub-prime end of the market.

Many of the 2000s mortgages required much less documentation than in the 1990s. People were often not even required to prove their level of income. They could just state their income. Nor was it necessary to pay for an independent valuation of the house, borrowers could just state the value of the house. Stated income loans were convenient for those without regular work, but anyone with common sense can see the potential temptation to overstating income to speculate on rising prices (they quickly became known as 'liar loans' on the street – a clue that the mathematicians could have picked up on if they had taken time to glance up from the algebra).

Another change was the help given with the deposit on the house. Whereas traditionally households would have to find 10 per cent or 20 per cent of the house value as a down-payment, in the new era brokers could offer a second mortgage (called a 'piggyback') which could be used as the deposit, so 100 per cent of the value of the house could be borrowed. Taking things a stage further, the UK's Northern Rock offered mortgages that were 125 per cent of the value of the house.

A further change was the increasing use of mortgages that had very low interest rates for the first two years ('teaser rates'), but after that they carried rates significantly higher than normal – 600 basis points above LIBOR was merely the average, many paid much more, i.e. well into double figures.

More rational players in this market allowed for the qualitative changes that had taken place in the housing markets in the noughties, rather than simplistically using a mathematical model developed in the 1990s for estimating default likelihood. Those wedded to quantified data in the statistical series had difficulties adjusting to the new reality.

Originato and hold to originate-and-distribute

Traditionally, if a bank grants a mortgage it keeps it on its books until it is repaid. This is called the **originate-and-hold model**. In this way banks have every incentive to ensure that the mortgagee can repay and can help those few who have temporary problems along the way. Fewer and fewer banks kept mortgages on the books in the 2000s. They preferred the **originate-and-distribute model**, selling them to other investors, usually through securitisations. Alongside this development was the movement of investment banks to use their own money to invest in securities rather than only provide (lower-risk) advice and other fee-based activities.

In the 1990s only around one-quarter of sub-prime mortgages were packaged up into securitisation vehicles and sold to bond investors. By the mid-2000s three-quarters were. In the good old days Freddie and Fannie dominated this market. In the boom of the mid-2000s the private firms overtook the GSEs and issued vast quantities of mortgage-based securities – over $1,000 billion per year, cumulating to $11,000 billion by 2007. The leaders of this pack included the Wall Street investment banks as well as Countrywide and Washington Mutual.

Pressure was applied to the mortgage brokers to generate more mortgages which could then be repackaged so that the investment banks could generate fees and other profits from the transaction. The mortgage brokers were only too happy to oblige, so they ran after people to sign up for mortgages to receive commission. No job, no deposit, on welfare benefits? Don't worry, we have just the mortgage for you!

Despite losing their lead the GSEs still participated. Apart from holding hundreds of billions of dollars worth of MBSs they had created, they also bought over $1,000 billion of MBSs issued by the private firms. They felt safe because they had put in place 'safeguards': first, if the loans were at more than 80 per cent of LTV they insisted on insurance being purchased from private insurance firms that paid out in the event of default. Second, the credit rating agencies had checked out the default likelihood on the private MBSs they bought and had concluded that they should be granted AAA status. What could go wrong?

Collateralised debt obligations (CDOs)

The financial markets were not only awash with freshly-minted plain vanilla securitised bonds, with mortgage income being paid into a trust (company or partnership), which then serviced the bond coupons. Something as simple as that was so 1990s. No, in the bright new era the innovators had to go one stage further, and then two and then three.

In straightforward securitisations (see Chapter 11) the bonds issued by the special purpose vehicle (SPV) are all the same. Each bondholder has an equal share in the returns generated on the underlying loans and will suffer an equal loss in the event of a proportion of the borrowers defaulting. But, thought the innovators, there are bond investors who are willing to take the high risk of, say, the first 5 per cent of borrowers defaulting. They will do this for a high interest rate, say 25 per cent per year. They will then hope that only, say, 4 per cent actually default over the next 10 years. Now that the first hit from defaulters has been accepted by the high-risk takers the other bonds that could be sold on that pool of loan obligations have a much lower chance of suffering a loss. If the underlying loans are mortgages then investors can see from the statistical data that it is rare that more than 4 per cent of mortgagees fail to repay. Thus if the first 5 per cent of defaults is to be absorbed by the holders of the high-risk bonds – often called the **equity tranche** (even though they are bonds) – then there is hardly any chance of the low-risk bondholder suffering any loss through defaults. That is the theory, anyway.

A **collateralised debt obligation** is a bond issued by an SPV set up by a deal structurer, usually an investment bank, where the SPV holds a pool of loans or a pool of debt securities.[18] The bonds are issued in a number of different classes or tranches, each with their own risk and return characteristics.

---

[18] The underlying assets could be commercial loans, credit card debt, property loans, corporate bonds or other debt.

Note that while the underlying securities might be mortgages, credit card debts, car loans debts, etc. from the first stage of securitisation, they can also be a collection of asset-backed securitised bonds. Thus, many (most in 2005–07) CDOs were actually securitisations of securitised bonds.

We will start with an example where the CDO holds a collection of mortgages, rather than ABSs. Imagine that Hubris and Grabbit (H&G), that well-known investment bank, has granted $1 billion of mortgages to families throughout America. These are all sub-prime and so have a relatively high chance of default, therefore it would be difficult to persuade bond investors, most of whom can only invest in AAA-rated bonds, to purchase securitised bonds in a plain vanilla asset-backed securitisation. If the overall rate of interest charged to mortgagees is 9 per cent then Hubris and Grabbit could create a CDO vehicle as shown in Exhibit 19.5. H&G sells the rights to the mortgage income and principal to the SPV that then issues CDO bonds.

If it is accepted by potential CDO bondholders that there is a 4 per cent default rate then an equity tranche (also known as the first-loss tranche or toxic waste) of CDOs could be created raising $100 million for the SPV by selling bonds in it.

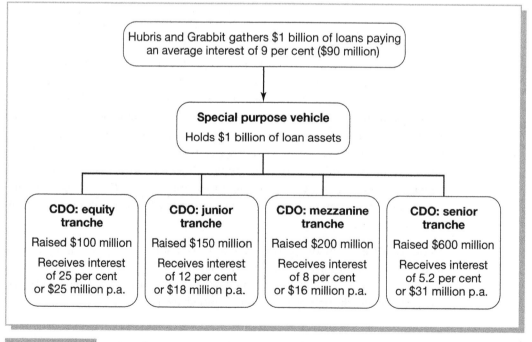

Exhibit 19.5   An example of a collateralised debt obligation

If the estimates of default prove over time to be spot on, then of the original $1 billion, $40 million will be lost. The only tranche-holders that will suffer will be the equity tranche, and they will still have $60 million left, plus the interest that has accumulated. To take this risk let us assume that these investors require 25 per cent per year interest. They might be lucky and only 2 per cent default in which case they accumulate a large sum. On the other hand, if, say, 13 per cent of the mortgagees default it will wipe out their investments, as well as impact on the returns for the next tranche.

This is the **junior tranche**. They have invested $150 million in a deal that gives them a fairly high rate of return at 12 per cent. But some of this will be forfeited if the default rate goes above 10 per cent. Because of the risk of experiencing a default these securitised bonds might be given a credit rating of around BBB– ('investment grade', but only just), and so could be bought by a range of financial institutions.

Tranche 3 is the **mezzanine tranche**, paying 8 per cent, and will only suffer losses if the defaults amount to more than $250 million (the amounts absorbed by the equity and junior tranche holders). It might gain a single A credit rating. If Tranche 3 raised $200 million then the final tranche, **senior tranche**, will comprise $600 million paying, say, 5.2 per cent per annum and will be granted an AAA rating.

Note that the interest rates charged by the CDO holders to the SPV, when measured on a weighted average basis, are lower than the 9 per cent charged to the house owners. This means that Hubris and Grabbit sell $1 billion of loans for a total of $1.05 billion, making a profit of $50 million.

If you think this is complicated enough, the innovators had hardly warmed up. Some CDOs were structured to have 17 or more different tranches. A **CDO squared (CDO²)** was made up of a package of other CDOs (which, in turn, might be made up of a variety of asset-backed bonds). Then there were **synthetic CDOs of ABS**: these take on credit risk using credit default swaps rather than holding ABSs or CDOs.

Banks were greatly encouraged to create CDOs by the capital reserve rules. If they held $1 billion of mortgages on their books they were required to hold, say, $40 million (4 per cent) of regulatory capital. If the bank sold 95 per cent of the loans in the form of CDOs, retaining 5 per cent in the form of the equity tranche, then it was required to hold much less equity capital.

Rating agencies

The credit rating agencies generally do not rate the equity tranche because of the high risk of loss. However, they play a pivotal role when it comes to the perception held by investors of the other tranches. We have already covered how these overseers of default risk became entranced by algebraic constructs such as David Li's (Gaussian copula) model with its emphasis on correlation between assets in a pool. On top of the default rates and correlations of defaults we need to add the difficulties for the rating agencies of first of all figuring out likely recovery rates should a mortgage or a mortgage-backed securitised bond default – will the organisers of the CDO be able to recover 70 per cent of what was lent to a mortgagee? Or will it be 40 per cent? This is difficult to judge, or is the correct word 'guess'? And secondly, the possibility of renegotiating or rescheduling the interest payments for a borrower that is running into difficulty. Being flexible with borrowers on conventional loans when they go through difficult times is relatively straightforward for the originate-and-hold lenders, but once the original mortgage has been through a couple of rounds of securitisation the connection with the mortgagee is greatly weakened and so specially tailored rescue reschedulings of payments become more difficult, which in itself increases the odds of total default. Thus, trying to measure the possible outcomes and likely future default rate/cash flow from owning a CDO is incredibly difficult.

Despite the difficulties and therefore the obvious need to err on the side of conservatism, the credit rating agencies are fully aware that they are in competition with each other. The customers for their services are the people trying to sell a bond or CDO. These customers only need a rating from one of the raters, thus they shop around. To start with Moody's developed a reputation for being fairly tough in granting investment grade status. The result was that Standard & Poor's picked up more fees from CDO issuers. Moody's later modified its cautious stance. Its mathematical models were altered and more asset-backed securities (ABSs) and CDOs could be accepted as investment grade. This resulted in a booming fee income. You may think that they were persuaded to stray from the path of rigour, but I could not possibly comment.

But consider this: when it comes to rating corporate bonds there are thousands of potential customers, from BP to Unilever. It is fairly easy to be forceful in turning down a fee if one bond issuer out of a thousand is being too pushy in wanting an excessively favourable rating. The raters' long-term reputation can be preserved so that ratings on the thousands of other bonds rated are better trusted by bondholders. When it came to CDOs and other new-fangled securities such as SIVs (see below) the rating agencies were faced with a small group of banks that dominates the market. With the banks threatening to take their large fees to another rating agency you may think it far more difficult to resist the pressure to look at an issue favourably. They, quite naturally, did not want to offend the banks, especially given that towards the end of the boom one-half of their fee income could be from this 'structured finance' sector. The rating agencies worked very closely with the issuers of CDOs to advise on the cut-off points for the various tranches; they would help them structure them in such a way that the top AAA-rated element was as large as possible to maximise profit from selling the CDOs. To do this they did not investigate the underlying individual mortgages but relied on statistical databases: 'We aren't loan officers. Our expertise is as statisticians on an aggregate basis. We want to know, of 1,000 individuals, based on historical performance, what percentage will pay their loans?'[19] They used these statistical databases even when 40–50 per cent of the mortgages going into a CDO SPV were 'stated income' loans for people with checkered credit histories. To have such a high proportion of loans to high-risk mortgagees was a relatively new phenomenon – so what *reliable* data on default could they use?

To demonstrate the academic rigour of their models the rating agencies showed investors exactly how they worked. They even published them on the internet. This had a side effect: it presented an opportunity for the bankers to tweak any new complex financial engineering scheme they were contemplating, so that they could exploit loopholes in the agencies' models, and achieve that all-important triple A rating (this game is called 'ratings arbitrage').

Structured investment vehicles (SIVs)

Here is an idea: mortgage-backed securities (MBS) composed of long-term debt obligations carry higher interest rates than can be obtained by borrowing short term through the money markets. So, thinks a bright banker, why not create billions and billions of dollars worth of MBS paying, say, 8 per cent per year and then put them into an SPV that is financed by commercial paper, paying, say, 7 per cent per year. The extra 1 per cent can come to us, the bankers, less a few expenses, of course. The more MBS we create, the more we can make on the difference between the short-term interest rate and the long-term interest rate. So what we need to do is put lots of pressure/incentive on mortgage brokers to generate more mortgages so that my bonus next year can be even greater than last year.[20]

In ancient financial history, that is the 1980s, when bankers were more cautious, these types of vehicles were known as **conduits**. In order for them to obtain the very high credit ratings needed to sell commercial paper they had to offer investors belt and braces security. The sponsoring organisation, usually an investment bank, would provide an equity buffer by placing money in the conduit, and would also guarantee a line of credit. In other words, if the pool of mortgages

---

[19] Claire Robinson, head of asset-backed finance for Moody's, quoted in Lowenstein, R. (2008) 'Triple–A Failure', *New York Times Magazine*, 27 April.

[20] They also invested in other long-term assets such as corporate bonds, Treasury bonds, ABSs and CDOs based on credit card receivables and student debt. In addition they raised money from medium-term notes as well as commercial paper.

ran into trouble and/or the commercial paper buyers refused to purchase paper for the next three-month period or whatever, the bank would step in and provide money to repay the maturing asset-backed commercial paper (ABCP) so that the legally-separate SPV did not have to sell its assets in a 'fire sale' to repay the short-term money market investors.

Over time, with statistical models saying that the 2000s were a much calmer and safer environment in which to lend on the security of mortgages and ABSs, the idea of the conduit grew into the **structured investment vehicle (SIV)**. These too needed high ratings to sell commercial paper, but this time the sponsoring bank's guarantee of a line of credit was smaller and outside investors (other than the bank) were brought in to take an equity stake in the SIV. The advantage of these changes was that the investment bank could keep SIVs off its balance sheets. So it had a nice profit earner without the need to hold much regulatory capital. This could lead to great improvements in bank return on equity. Under the Basel rules for capital requirements, because the SIVs raised a proportion of their money other than from the sponsoring bank, and because the credit lines offered were less than a year in duration, the bank did not have to hold capital reserves for the exposure. The amount of equity capital held within an SIV was typically only 5 per cent or 10 per cent of the assets. Thus they were 10 or 20 times geared.

Of course, you can see the flawed thinking: however many mathematical models you build to calculate past default rates on mortgages, etc., and however many databases you look at to estimate the likelihood of the commercial paper market drying up, you cannot exclude the possibility that the people making decisions will suddenly change behaviour *en masse*. In particular, you need to remember that money market investors are looking for very safe investments. If there is even a hint of trouble in the SIVs they will all pull their money at the same time; not just from that SIV, but from the entire sector. If dozens of SIVs are then forced to sell their assets to repay commercial paper as it falls due, then these assets (ABSs, CDOs, corporate bonds, Treasury bills, etc.) fall in value, further undermining the asset base of banks and other institutions. SIVs are required to regularly announce the value of their assets – that is to 'mark-to-market' – and so they could not hide and delay reporting losses, they were there for all to see.

One of the remarkable features of this period is the lack of understanding by regulators, governments, credit agencies and the financial press[21] of what the banks were doing. CDOs and SIVs were only explained to them and to us after the crash. They had grown very big in a very short period of time.

---

[21] With the exception of Gillian Tett at the *Financial Times* and a handful of others. Professor Nouriel Roubini of New York Stern School of Business was warning of the impending crisis in the mid-2000s. Practitioners ignored or dismissed his comments, and derogatorily called him 'Dr Doom'.

The internationalisation of risk

The activities discussed above were not confined to the US. London became the world's leading packager of SIVs, for example. Spanish mortgages were popular for CDO creation, and German banks bought vast quantities of AAA-rated US CDOs that offered a rate of return higher than on normal AAA-rated bonds (perhaps the high return should have raised some questions in their minds). Despite the doubt expressed by staff members, the Royal Bank of Scotland grew its CDO business very fast, holding large quantities. UBS of Switzerland had $50 billion of CDOs on its trading desk in 2007. 'We were just told by our risk people that these instruments are triple A, like Treasury bonds. People did not ask too many questions,' said Peter Kurer, a member of the board.[22] Ah, that all-too-human failing: trusting people who have complex models to show you, that you don't understand.

Charles Pardue, one of the team who helped create acceptance for CDOs and SIVs through the intellectual work at JPMorgan (which was taken to ridiculous extremes by others), made the comment:

> I don't think that we should kid ourselves that everything that is being sold is fair value. I have been to dealer events where bankers are selling this stuff and the simplicity of the explanation about how it works scares me... there are people investing in stuff they don't understand, who really seem to believe the models, and when the models change it will be a very scary thing.[23]

Credit default swaps (CDSs)

Credit default swaps (described in Chapter 15) were important contributors to the crisis because they could be used to speculate on defaults without the need to hold the underlying corporate bond, ABS, CDO or SIV. Thus a seller of a CDS could sell credit protection on, say, $10 million of bonds and receive a premium of, say, $150,000. If a default does not occur the seller makes a $150,000 profit. CDSs are bought and sold in a secondary market, with their prices rising if the default risk rises. It was not unusual to find that the amount of CDS outstanding for a given bond, CDO, etc. was a multiple of the underlying collateral value. Thus, there might be $500 million bonds in issue and $5 billion of CDS contracts outstanding on those bonds. If the bond defaults then the maximum loss is $500 million, but if the CDS sellers have to pay out they need to find

[22] Quoted in Tett, G. (2009) *Fool's Gold: How Unrestrained Greed Corrupted a Dream, Shattered Global Markets and Unleashed a Catastrophe*, Little, Brown, p. 163.
[23] Quoted in Tett, G. (2009), p. 118.

$5 billion. Thus, you can see how liability exposure was multiplied by the use of these derivatives, especially when you consider that by mid-2007 the total notional amount of CDSs outstanding was more than $45,000 billion (the US mortgage market was 'only' $7,100 billion).

A key contributor to the crisis was that the payout on default under a CDS is merely a promise. So it is only as good as the financial strength of the seller. There was no central counterparty to back up that promise as there is with exchange-traded derivatives. Once the financial strengths of numerous CDS sellers were demolished the insurance that purchasers of CDSs thought they had evaporated.

Monoline insurers

The story of the crisis would be incomplete without discussing the monoline insurers. Many investors in ABSs, MBSs, CDOs and SIVs were naturally concerned that these securities might be riskier than the promoter or the credit rating indicated. So, to provide extra reassurance the sellers of these instruments sought to take out insurance, similar to car insurance, with a premium up front and a payout if an event happened, such as non-payment of interest or principal. The **monoline insurance** firms started out as very low-risk organisations which offered insurance on bonds issued by US municipal authorities (states, towns, etc.). The buyers of the bonds would accept a lower yield (pay a higher price) if they came with an insurance guarantee. The sellers were willing to pay the insurance premium because they could then sell the bonds at a raised price (because they were now rated AAA) to more than compensate for the insurance premium.

Insurance is only as good as the soundness of the company providing the guarantee. So in the 1970s, 1980s and 1990s monoline insurers had very conservative balance sheets, allowing them to raise money by selling triple A-rated bonds in themselves. Insuring US municipalities (that raise taxes) results in a completely different order of risk than insuring the new securities backed by mortgages. However, in the noughties the monolines thought they could stretch their expertise to this arena. The mathematicians at the monolines followed the same models used by the banks, rating agencies and regulators, and so concluded that these complex instruments were low risk and therefore only a small insurance premium was required. They also became greedy, with some of them insuring 150 times the amount of their equity buffer. The slightest wobble in the sub-prime housing market and they would be insolvent as they paid out on defaults. They would not be able to raise more money in the event of a rise in mortgage delinquencies because the rating agencies would quickly reduce their ratings from AAA.

Many buyers of the fancy new instruments came to rely on the reassurance provided by the monolines. When they failed to meet their obligations this led to great losses for some organisations, and when those organisations could not meet their obligations it led to losses for their creditors.

The crash

From 2002 the foreclosure rate (that is, proportion of US mortgage holders with whom the bank has got fed up with missed payments and repossessed the house) actually *fell* to 1 per cent in the first quarter of 2005. Over the same period the proportion of loans that was delinquent (mortgagees had not stuck to the agreement, but not so badly as to qualify for repossession) *fell* to 4.31 per cent. This seemed odd, because there had been a large rise in the proportion of mortgages classified as sub-prime. Rising house prices had helped, because those with short-term money worries could remortgage (take out an extra loan on the security of the house) or sell the house for a profit; Americans did this in great volumes as the richest people in the world borrowed to sustain consumption at higher levels than income (there was a negative savings rate). Low interest rates and low unemployment also helped. However, this was the calm before the storm.

Some early rumblings

In the spring of 2005 the credit rating on the debt of General Motors was downgraded to junk status. This was not unusual; many issues of corporate debt are downgraded every month. The difference this time was that investors in credit default swaps and CDOs started to panic, causing their market prices to move wildly. So wildly that they were moving more than was assumed in the models. The market was (a) showing signs of nervousness, and (b) failing to behave according to the models.

US foreclosures and delinquencies rose in 2006 and 2007. In the first quarter of 2007 foreclosures rose to a record level of over 2 per cent of outstanding mortgages. In February 2007 HSBC announced that its US subsidiary focused on sub-prime lending, Household Finance, had experienced sharply rising default levels. New Century Financial (second largest sub-prime lender) made a similar announcement. Now the cost of buying default protection against BBB-rated bonds of CDOs through credit default swaps rose significantly, but at least the market was still operating and CDS protection could be bought. Many bankers retained their optimism and wanted to stay in the leveraged loan game. They could not afford to reduce the next quarter earnings by withdrawing from a large part of their business, even if they had qualms about the long-term safety of the transactions. Chuck Prince, the CEO of Citigroup, famously told the *FT* in the summer that the party would end at some point but there was so much liquidity that it would not be disrupted by turmoil in the US sub-prime market:

> When the music stops, in terms of liquidity, things will get complicated. But as long as the music is playing, you've got to get up and dance. We're still dancing... At some point, the disruptive event will be so significant that instead of liquidity filling in, the liquidity will go the other way. I don't think we're at that point.[24]

By the third quarter of 2007 foreclosures on sub-prime loans reached almost 7 per cent. Analysts were starting to believe studies that estimated that about 20 per cent of sub-prime mortgages would end in foreclosure. Whereas in the old days the lenders could have negotiated extra time to sell the house to raise more for both the bank and the family, or to let the borrower stay in the house making reduced payments, now, with securitisation, there was little opportunity for negotiation and rescheduling.

Bear Stearns had established two hedge funds and retained close financial links with them. The hedge funds had borrowed heavily to buy CDOs and other high-credit rated issues (on less than $1 billion of capital they had $15 billion of CDOs). For a while the cost of borrowing was less than the income from the CDOs, so they reported high profits (and paid large bonuses). In the summer of 2007 these sub-prime-focused funds reported difficulties – in one month alone the mark-to-market value of the CDOs, etc. fell by 19 per cent. They tried to sell some assets to repay the creditors now demanding their money back. If they were not repaid they were entitled to take possession of their collateral. Merrill Lynch, which was owed roughly $850 million, and JPMorgan, which was owed $500 million, took possession of their collateral. Disaster was averted by Bear Stearns taking on the responsibility of compensating many of the hedge funds' creditors. And so, although the market was shaken, it was not yet too frightened.

Deutsche Industriebank, IKB, a medium-sized German lender, had sought to make large profits by entering the SIV market. It sold its commercial paper to European pension funds and investment funds of US public sector bodies, which trusted the triple A or double A ratings, to invest in mortgage-linked CDOs. When in July 2007 Moody's and Standard & Poor's reduced the ratings on some sub-prime mortgage bonds, and after the collapse of Bear Stearns' funds, the

[24] Nakamoto, M. and Wighton, D. (2007) 'Bullish Citigroup is "still dancing" to the beat of the buy-out boom', *Financial Times*, 10 July.

investors in IKB's SIV knew they had made a mistake. They bargained for very low risk, and now the reassurance of high credit ratings was being removed. They lacked the skills or the data to value the securities that the SIV had invested in – they relied on credit ratings only. So, in their fear, they stopped buying fresh commercial paper. The offshoot SIVs of IKB had $20 billion of assets compared with the bank's liquid assets of $16 billion. The parent could not find the money to put into the SIVs to prevent the commercial paperholders insisting on a fire sale of assets to repay them within days. Such a fire sale was impossible anyway, given the lack of liquidity in the CDO markets. In the end, the German government forced a group of banks to lend enough to IKB for it to survive. Disaster averted.

Meanwhile, over in Paris, BNP Paribas stopped investors in three of its funds from being able to redeem their investments. It said that it was impossible to value the funds because of high exposure to the US sub-prime market. This disturbed investors.

Aware of a growing sense of foreboding among investors, some of the large banks, such as HSBC and Citibank, brought the assets and liabilities of their SIVs onto their balance sheets so that nervous outside investors could be paid off. Many banks started to realise that their assets were shrinking while they faced a market place where it was difficult to raise short-term money – confidence was slipping fast. Some managed to obtain infusions of capital from sovereign wealth funds through the selling of a number of new shares. Others could not persuade anybody to buy their shares to bolster their defences.

The MBS and CDO markets worsened to the point where it became difficult to sell even plain vanilla AAA MBSs. People realised that they just did not know what the fancy securities were worth in a falling housing market.

In August 2007 American Home Mortgage Investment Corporation filed for bankruptcy due to losses on mortgage-related assets and the inability to sell commercial paper. Countrywide, which had operated an almost conveyor belt machine approach to generating mortgages to sell on in a securitised form, said it was starting to stockpile mortgages because of a scarcity of investors. Tension was starting to spread and bankers decided to stop lending to any other financial institution that looked at all risky. They were starting to hoard cash. This was a rational response from the individual banks' perspective but the result was that the interbank loan market, commercial paper and other markets experienced rising interest rates and difficulties in funding. By this stage much of the world economy was dependent on the assumption of reasonably-priced-money-always-available. When it became apparent that this was a false assumption, fear increased. It increased further when the default rates on sub-prime mortgages were announced in the autumn, now at 16 per cent. This perplexed some because the economy was still growing and unemployment was low. The answer lay in very bad financial decisions: people had become overstretched after being seduced by the offer of a loan to buy a house that they could never have repaid given their low income. The chickens were coming home to roost.

A UK trigger

Northern Rock had built itself up from a small ex-building society into the fifth largest UK lender by taking advantage of the securitisation craze. By 2007 most of the funding for its mortgages came from a process of originate-and-distribute. It had nothing to do with US sub-prime, but had built up its own sub-prime operation and more damagingly it had come to rely on a quick selling-on of its loans to the wholesale financial markets to generate a flow of cash to cover mortgages it had already granted. When the psychology of fear swept over the markets, taking the place of enthusiasm for mortgage-related structured securities, suddenly the message went out around the world to stop investing in anything mortgage related. Northern Rock found itself with thousands of mortgages that it had to refinance within days or it would run out of cash. It could not find that cash in the frozen wholesale market and the possibility of attracting deposits from individual savers was a non-starter given the amount the bank now needed to fund. So it turned to the Bank of England to ask for emergency support.

Once word got out that Northern Rock was short of cash millions of savers panicked. They quickly withdrew money from their online accounts and they queued around the block outside its branches. For the first time since the nineteenth century the UK had a bank run. The government was forced into reassuring depositors by guaranteeing all deposits with the bank. The Bank of England provided funds to keep it operating. Northern Rock was so badly wounded that no private buyer would take it on. So in early 2008 it was nationalised.

The UK regulatory system was particularly badly prepared for overseeing the financial innovations of the noughties. Regulation was split between the Financial Services Authority, the Bank of England and the Treasury. The FSA was given responsibility for judging bank strategies. From its limited perspective, what it saw was that banks were complying with its rules and so it did not intervene. It did not have a system-wide focus and did not appreciate the threat from CDOs and SIVs. That was left up to the BoE, which did make noises about the worryingly fast growth of the banks' balance sheets, but without the backing of the FSA and the Treasury, it lacked the power to intervene.

Following the Northern Rock fiasco, in April 2008, the Bank of England introduced the Special Liquidity Scheme which enabled banks to swap their mortgage-backed securities and other assets for Treasury bills. These could then be sold in the market to raise cash.

A major US trigger – Bear Stearns

By the winter of 2007–08 analysts, particularly those at the rating agencies, were having considerable doubts about their model assumptions. For example, the recovery rate for foreclosed mortgages was assumed to be 70 per cent. But that was calculated before the massive rise of sub-prime and the growth of the worse forms of sub-prime. These were termed NINJAs which stands for No Income, No Job or Assets. They were granted on the assumption that house price rises would pay off the mortgage when the family moved. When they knew they were to be repossessed these households would leave their property in a much worse state than those in the 1990s. And, of course, house prices were falling. So now the analysts estimated that only 40 per cent of the loan amount would be recovered on a foreclosure. What made things even worse was that in some areas, as house prices fell and repossessions rose, the neighbourhood became blighted – nobody wanted to live there. This, together with growing negative equity (house worth less than mortgage), created a reflexive feedback loop, a self-fulfilling view on the future of house prices in that area. This psychological problem was not allowed for in the mathematical models on default levels. By now even the mathematicians were becoming frightened.

Citigroup had been one of the most enthusiastic creators of CDOs, particularly in 2006 and 2007. Many of these would be held on its balance sheet until buyers could be found. By the end of 2007 the amounts reached the staggering level of $55 billion. On top of that it had made promises to repay within days $25 billion of commercial paper secured by CDOs. It had to announce potential write-offs of up to $11 billion. It was not alone: Merrill Lynch wrote off $20.2 billion and UBS $15 billion. Bank shares fell dramatically.

Prior to the crisis the bankers had managed to persuade the regulators that the complex instruments they were creating would disperse risk to those most able to bear it – hinting that it would be borne by non-bank institutions and funds. In reality the CDOs, etc. seemed to be piling up on banks' balance sheets as they swapped assets between themselves and held inventories of them until they could be sold. They had concentrated risk rather than dispersed it.

For the next few months the write-offs announced by Citi, Merrill and UBS grew larger as banks found themselves at the centre of a downward spiral. The more losses that were revealed, the less confidence investors had. The less confidence, the more assets had to be sold (or marked-to-market) in a declining market, leading to lower confidence and thus reduced values.

Bear Stearns had become increasingly dependent on the repo market (see Chapter 9) to raise short-term funds. Using repos means that a substantial proportion of funding has to be rolled over on a daily basis. It used mortgage-backed bonds as collateral. Once confidence in these instruments declined Bear found difficulties in obtaining short-term loans. In March 2008 the regulators realised that Bear was in trouble and that if it defaulted on its current repos it would cause panic in the wholesale markets. To prevent that they negotiated for other financial institutions to buy it. Eventually JPMorgan agreed to do so, but at a price that left little value for the previous shareholders in Bear. The directors had destroyed shareholder value on a massive scale.

The rescue of Bear, with the regulators to the fore, and the subsequent slashing of US prime interest rates reassured the markets for a few months as they reasoned that the government and the Fed would not allow a major bank failure and a crash. But this sanguine view had to contend with some disturbing facts: (a) the assets of the SIVs had grown to be worth several trillion dollars – these needed regular refunding in a depressed market; (b) the shadow banks (SIVs, hedge funds, money market funds, etc. – see Chapter 18), which are regulated much less than the banks, now had a complex web of trading obligations with the banks, including $60,000 billion of CDSs. The system was so interconnected and so opaque that no one could figure how it could unravel if more confidence was lost.

The Lehman trigger

By 2008 the mortgages granted in 2005–06 at low teaser rates switched from the lower than normal rate to a much higher interest rate as the two-year grace period came to an end. The analysts were anticipating an accelerated default rate. This would reduce confidence in mortgage-related instruments further. Some analysts in spring 2008 estimated the loss in the prices of CDOs would turn out to total $400 billion. By September, with US houses 20 per cent down from their peak prices, things were so bad in the securitised market that the loss in value weakened Fannie Mae and Freddie Mac to the point where they were taken into conservatorship (nationalisation) by the Fed. They had both operated with relatively small capital bases on which was piled a great deal of debt. A number of writers of credit default swaps on Freddie and Fannie securities suffered losses, hitting sentiment hard.

Lehman Brothers, like Bear Stearns, had drawn a high proportion of its funding from the repo market and had an enormous exposure to residential mortgage bond instruments and commercial property. Once the other financial institutions suspected that Lehman was losing money to the point where it might default they simply stopped lending to it. It was on the point of collapse when the Fed assembled the heads of the major banks to cajole them into rescuing it. The government or the Fed could not rescue another irresponsible financial institution. They were already receiving criticism for rescuing Bear and the GSEs. If the regulators go on like this, it was said, they will create moral hazard in which financial institutions take outlandish risks knowing that the authorities will step in to prevent failure and the loss of those highly-paid jobs and all those bonuses for 'risk taking'.

'No more soft touch' was the message. An example had to be made to ram home the idea that financial organisations would suffer the consequences of their actions. Ideally Lehman's operations, asset and liabilities would be taken over by another bank(s) with its shareholders' value being wiped out and senior management removed. However, no other bank wanted to take on Lehman's positions and it was made bankrupt on 15 September. Not only did writers of CDSs on Lehman's debt have to take a hit but, on that day, it was counterparty to roughly $800 billion of CDSs. Because of the intertwined financial obligations institutions around the world had with Lehman's investors, the failure of Lehman to meet its obligations had a whole series of knock-on effects. They panicked. Some examples of the knock-on effects included:

▪ London-based hedge funds with money held by Lehman had their assets frozen, so they could not complete deals they had made.

▪ Managers and investors in money market funds had believed that the authorities would save Lehman and therefore their holdings of Lehman's debt was safe. Now the perception changed. They swallowed losses on Lehman and nervously looked around for who might be next. Fear and caution led to sharp reduction of short-term money availability, and spiralling interest rates. The Reserve Primary Fund, a money market fund, 'broke the buck' (the net asset value dropped below the amount put in by investors), causing even greater aversion to supplying finance to the commercial paper market – the market size fell by $500 billion in one week.

▪ The largest writer of credit default swaps, AIG, the world's largest insurance company, was headed towards losses of over $180 billion. It had nowhere near this amount of money to make good on its promises. Ben Bernanke of the Fed said that he was very angry that AIG, a stable insurance company, had developed hedge fund-type derivative positions (CDOs) that completely overshadowed its normal business.

▪ Stock markets fell, wiping away billions of paper wealth, helping to create a sense of doom.

■ Institutions refused to deal with one another as rumours flew around about which would be the next to collapse. Trust had evaporated. Those financial economists, mathematicians and heads of banks were made painfully aware that markets need human trust and confidence more than they need complex mathematics.

Now the dominoes fell fast:

■ In September 2008 AIG was granted an $85 billion loan from the Fed in exchange for a 79.9 per cent equity stake in the business (effectively nationalisation). It was too big and too interconnected to be allowed to fail.

■ In the same month Merrill Lynch was so desperate that it agreed to be taken over by Bank of America.

■ A few days later one of the largest UK banks, the ailing HBOS, was bought by Lloyds, and then Washington Mutual (sixth largest US bank) collapsed and was sold to JPMorgan for a fraction of its previous value.

■ Then the UK government was forced into nationalising Bradford and Bingley.

Government actions

Bank rescues

In days after the loss of Lehman the US Treasury and the Fed were shocked at the extent of the knock-on effects, and knew they had to do something. They proposed the creation of a fund of $700 billion to buy 'troubled assets' from the banks.[25] However, this was quickly changed to a plan to inject money directly into banks rather than merely purchase assets from them. The bank leaders were gathered together and told that they would have to accept the injection of government money for preferred share stakes or they would not be eligible for any future bail-out.

The government holding of shares in Citigroup was increased so that it was, in effect, nationalised. When Bank of America realised just how rotten the assets of Merrill Lynch were it needed a further government injection. The government also permitted Goldman Sachs and Morgan Stanley to change from being technically classified as brokers into banks, allowing them to benefit from government bail-outs including access to the Fed funds discount window (the US lender of last resort function – see Chapter 6). Goldman was forced to ask for an

---

[25] Called the Troubled Asset Relief Program (TARP).

infusion of cash by selling $5 billion of preferred stock offering a very high dividend to Berkshire Hathaway (chairman – Warren Buffett).

The US Treasury insured the $3,400 billion money market mutual fund industry (it would not allow shares in money market funds to fall below the $1 in value put in by savers) to encourage investors to retain their savings in the system. This was bailing out 30 million Americans and comprised one-half of all deposits at domestic US banks. If this had not been done US savers would have become very wary. The cascade of fear might have caused a Depression.

Over in London the government and the Bank of England were dead set against bank bail-outs, because they did not want to encourage moral hazard. However, once they realised the full extent of leverage in the system and that the banks faced not just a liquidity problem (as with Northern Rock) but a solvency problem (see Chapters 3 and 6) they decided to act. Mervyn King at the BoE was shocked:

> When we started this crisis there was a widespread view that banks were well capitalised. But now we realise that the problem was that assets sitting on their balance sheets which were supposed to be risk-free, carried a lot of risk. Perceptions of the value of those assets and the risks changed radically.[26]

The BoE set about injecting £200 billion of cash into the money markets. The government guaranteed £250 billion of bonds issued by banks and bought equity stakes in some leading banks. Royal Bank of Scotland received £20 billion in new equity and Lloyds, which had avoided the lure of structured finance and was strong before it bought the less disciplined HBOS, received £17 billion.

Dexia was rescued by the governments of Germany, Luxembourg and Belgium, while the Irish government stopped a run on its banks by guaranteeing all deposits (a move that was to later virtually bankrupt the government). Hypo Real Estate was saved by the German government and Fortis was nationalised by the Dutch. Iceland nationalised its banks which had liabilities many times the size of the economy of its 320,000 people, and was forced to seek financial help from the International Monetary Fund.

Economy rescues

Recession started in the US economy at the end of 2007 and grew worse through 2008 to become the worst since the 1930s. Similar downturns were experienced in Europe, and the leading developing countries suffered a slowing down

---

[26] Quoted in Tett, G. (2009), p. 283.

in growth. To combat lowered confidence in the economic future and rising unemployment, Western governments pumped up demand in the economy by dramatically increasing deficit spending – i.e. spending far more than is raised in taxes by borrowing the difference. The rapidly rising levels of government debts will have severe long-term consequences as we ask later generations to pay off the bill for this borrowing. They also have dramatic political consequences, with many governments being rejected by the electorate for not preventing, or failing to effectively deal with, the crisis.

Western central banks reduced interest rates to close to zero to encourage economic activity (see Chapter 6 for a discussion on monetary policy). Governments and central banks also purchased bonds from the private sector (usually banks) to lower interest rates at the medium and longer end of the yield curve as well as supplying money to the system. This quantitative easing is discussed in Chapter 6, as are a number of other regulatory responses such as living wills and tighter bank capital ratios (see also Chapter 18).

Concluding comments

Following each crisis there is always a feeling that, as we rush around tightening that regulation, banning that type of security or changing that incentive, we are merely preparing for the last war. Even now, so soon after the last bust, clever bankers with mastery of complex maths will be working on innovative securities that will be designed to get around this or that regulation (regulatory arbitrage); fool this or that credit rating agency; and bemuse and impress impressionable trustees of other people's money from pension funds to insurance funds and hedge funds. Hopefully there is a greater proportion of mathematical model sceptics, who while accepting that the models have their uses, realise that they need to be moderated, supplemented and even overridden by human decision makers, who take into account a wide range of factors beyond those immediately quantifiable.

Arnold's golden rules

1 If you cannot understand it, don't invest in it. Have an acute awareness of the perimeter of your circle of competence: do you know what you know, and know what you don't know? Don't trust others peddling complexity because you fear looking foolish when everyone else is saying what wonderful clothes the Emperor has. Complexity, particularly mathematical complexity, is not the same as sophistication. Modification for regulators: if you don't understand it, why are you allowing it?

2 If it looks too good to be true, it probably is. How did anyone believe
   that a CDO of ABSs could hold a credit rating of AAA, the same as for a
   highly-reputable corporation, and yet offer hundreds of basis points more
   in interest?

3 Be wary of the power of some innovations to grow a new market quickly and
   then destroy it. 'Successful innovation by its very nature initially outstrips
   our ability to regulate it,'[27] said Robert Merton. Paul Volcker, a former
   chairman of the Fed, has doubts about the value of increasing the complexity
   of financial instruments. As he reflected on the financial scene he put the
   complexity merchants in their place by saying that over the past 30 years the
   most useful innovation was the automatic teller machine: 'I wish somebody
   would give me some shred of neutral evidence about the relationship
   between financial innovation recently and the growth of the economy.'[28]

4 Beware of collective delusion. The pressure from the crowd to believe in a
   bad idea is powerful. Think independently. Even those supposedly great
   authorities, the regulators and the credit rating agencies, were proved to have
   hopelessly inadequate methods and a weakness for believing the prevailing
   wisdom, so you need to think for yourself.

5 High leverage is dangerous. Warren Buffett says that 'it's kind of like alcohol.
   One drink is fine, but 10 will get you in a lot of trouble. With leverage,
   people have a great propensity to use it because it's so much fun when it
   works. There should be some ways of controlling leverage'.[29] Bankers focus
   on return on equity in the short run. So, for a given return on assets, the
   greater the proportion of those assets financed by leverage, the higher the
   return on equity. They can become addicted to raising earnings per share
   each quarter or half year by increasing leverage. They can do this for many
   years before the risk becomes apparent. They need help in controlling their
   addiction, which is where the regulators come in.

6 Avoid situations of interdependence that result in confused entanglement,
   where no one knows who is really holding the risk.

---

[27] Speaking in 'Making the Financial Markets Safe: An Interview with Robert Merton'
(2009), interviewed by David Champion, *Harvard Business Review*, October.

[28] Quoted in Braithwaite, T. (2011) 'Greenspan hits at Dodd–Frank law', *Financial Times*,
30 March.

[29] Speaking in an interview with Guy Rolnik (2011) 'Warren Buffett: The US is
moving toward plutocracy', *TheMarker*, http://english.themarker.com/warren-buffett-
the-u-s-is-moving-toward-plutocracy-1.351236

7 Do not have incentive systems where it's heads I win, tails the other guy loses. Many of the bankers working in ABSs, CDOs, CDSs and SIVs took home large bonuses in the good times (over $1 million each year) regardless of the impact on those they were dealing with. Even when things turned sour many retained highly-paid positions.

8 When financial bubbles blow up, remember Cinderella, who knew it could not last but could not see clocks on the wall to tell her when it would all turn to pumpkins and mice, and besides which she was having so much fun. Everyone thinks they will be able to get out five minutes before midnight.[30]

9 Recognise that banks are not very good at self-regulation. As well as the authorities insisting on robust capital and liquidity reserves, they must implement some form of separation of the 'casino' activities of investment banking trading and derivatives activities from the retail banking operations. This must be structured so that the former can be allowed to go bust, taking shareholder and wholesale market creditor wealth with them, but the retail bank activities can carry on following a government bail-out, preserving the value to society of the deposit taking, business-lending and money-transmission functions. They should also insist on detailed and regularly updated plans for the orderly recovery or liquidation of a bank if it should at some point in the future run into trouble.

10 Remember that banks are full of smart people who will exploit a gap or loophole created because national authorities do not create regulatory structures that work across borders.

There will be another crisis, in fact there will be many. I don't know when or where or what form they will take, but I do know that structures created by humans are subject to emotional surges, cognitive failure, hubris born of neat modelling and the tendency to forget most of the golden rules and the lessons of history. The best that we can hope for is that it is not too soon.

---

[30] I'm grateful to Warren Buffett for this analogy.

Index

Comprehensive. Authoritative. Trusted

9780273723967   9780273727873   9780273723745

9780273745822   9780273722014   9780273729846   9780273712671   9780273724520

9780273729105   9780273727835   9780273763031   9780273729969   9780273736868   9780273761990

9780273756668   9780273735656   9780273745471   9780273738022   9780273742999   9780273734444

9780273756200   9780273750468   9780273743552   9780273730002   9780273751335   9780273746430

Change your business life today